Management Consulting:
A Guide for Students

David Biggs

SOUTH-WESTERN
CENGAGE Learning™

Australia • Brazil • Japan • Korea • Mexico • Singapore • Spain • United Kingdom • United States

SOUTH-WESTERN
CENGAGE Learning

**Management Consulting
A Guide for Students
David Biggs**

Publishing Director: Linden Harris

Publisher: Thomas Rennie

Development Editor: Jennifer Seth

Editorial Assistant: Charlotte Green

Content Project Editor: Alison Cooke

Head of Manufacturing: Jane Glendening

Senior Production Controller: Paul Herbert

Marketing Manager: Amanda Cheung

Typesetter: KnowledgeWorks Global, India

Cover design: Adam Renvoize

For product information and technology assistance, contact **emea.info@cengage.com**.
For permission to use material from this text or product, and for permission queries,
email **clsuk.permissions@cengage.com**.

The Author has asserted the right under the Copyright, Designs and Patents Act 1988 to be identified as Author of this Work.

British Library Cataloguing-in-Publication Data
A catalogue record for this book is available from the British Library.

ISBN: 978-1-4080-0791-4

Cengage Learning EMEA
Cheriton House, North Way, Andover, Hampshire, SP10 5BE, United Kingdom

Cengage Learning products are represented in Canada by Nelson Education Ltd.

For your lifelong learning solutions, visit
www.cengage.co.uk

Purchase your next print book, e-book or e-chapter at **www.CengageBrain.com**

Printed in Croatia
1 2 3 4 5 6 7 8 9 10 – 12 11 10

Brief Contents

Contents

Foreword

M anagement consultancy is such a fascinating yet misunderstood profession. And what a significant profession too: it's an industry barely a century old, yet is now as deeply embedded in the economy as other professional services such as accountancy or law.

Fascinating, as it touches every area of work. It seems to be indispensable in central and local government, the health service and education. Businesses in telecommunications, financial services, energy and transport are prodigious consumers of consultancy services. Whatever the business, from micro-lenders to multinational corporations, there are consultancy firms ready to provide advice.

Misunderstood. We've all heard the old joke about the definition of a consultant: someone who borrows your watch to tell you the time. Or the fear that the phrase 'The consultants are coming in' can create in the minds of employees — 'we'll all be losing our jobs'.

I've been recruiting for firms of management consultants for over 25 years. I've seen the changes in the profile of a typical recruit: from the scarred industry veteran bringing deep knowledge of a market or function, through the bright young technology-savvy undergraduate, to the assertive, ambitious MBA. And how the consulting firms themselves have responded to the needs of their clients: switching from colleges of experts to powerhouses of IT.

But the common thread has been the attractiveness of the work. Sure, there are times when analysing reams of data in a windowless office on an industrial park, or the midnight sessions grappling with complex spreadsheets in an anonymous hotel room off a motorway junction, might not seem fulfilling. The early morning flights to distant cities, the week after week of staying away from home, can take its toll. Yet the exposure consultancy offers to a variety of organizational problems, at a variety of organizations, working alongside people who come from a variety of professional backgrounds, is difficult to match elsewhere. There can be few other careers which pack so much learning into the working experience. It offers the opportunity to take that learning, if you wish, out of consulting and into the workplace in a more mainstream role. There are senior figures in government and business whose earlier years in consulting have given them a firm foundation for a subsequent successful career in their chosen field. And there is also the possibility of returning to consultancy at a much later stage in working life.

For those who progress through the ranks of a firm to become a Partner or Director, the financial rewards can be very attractive indeed. Equally, the path may lead you to hang out your own sign and practise as an independent consultant, working the hours and on the projects you select for yourself.

But back to the beginning. For those who are considering entry to consulting, or are just starting out on their careers in this industry, Dr Biggs's book is a valuable insight into the profession. It shows the reality of management consultancy and its power to deliver real and lasting results. Students who want to become practitioners will find much to help them decide whether consultancy will be their job for life, or a stepping stone on their journey to the commanding heights of industry. Whatever decision you make, you will find your time in consulting intellectually and financially satisfying. I wish you success.

Don Leslie, BLT

Preface

T his book has been developed for individuals interested in management consultancy either as a practice, a career or as an industry. It is useful for the student and consultant alike as it gives an unbiased account of criticisms and benefits of the practice and industry. The text is also designed to be practical, demonstrating how techniques in consultancy work and how students can develop consultancy skills. It has been created to support universities in their teaching of management consultancy at final year undergraduate and postgraduate levels.

So why the motivation to write such a guide on management consultancy? This concerns where I find myself today, as a former consultant and graduate recruiter turned back to postgraduate education.

When I was a consultant, many of the graduates we interviewed, either through traditional or case study interviews, weren't employable. The exceptional individuals, that did manage to get through the selection process, tended to need a lot of development and few survived to be long term. The reasons for this were clear. Typically, new consultants would not see the inside of a client's office for months. This meant frustration on both sides. The consultant would get frustrated as they completed tedious back office work that involved little client communication. The consultancy firm would also get frustrated as the fee revenue potential for graduates was limited. In some organizations this would lead to the consultancies encouraging graduates to leave or adopting an up or out policy.

Yet, the basics of consultancy are straightforward enough to understand with time, perseverance and strong character. Many graduates are not given this opportunity. In my own career, I was lucky to build up my skill level as an internal consultant to start with and then onto being an external consultant for a number of years. Indeed, several of those years were spent with mentors who typically had decades of consultancy experience. And many of their words of wisdom form the Thought Provoking points within the chapters.

So, when I finally left full-time consultancy and went into higher education, I embarked on changing our postgraduate programmes to produce employable and sought-after graduates. There were many texts available to our students on consultancy. Most of them though were not particularly suitable, either being too academic or too practitioner based. Thus, I decided to write my own text that would combine the best of the academic literature in terms of critical review along with the practitioner based literature saying how it should be done. This was combined with my own view of the industry, much of which — for instance using the Johari window to describe organizations from a consultancy perspective — is a unique contribution to the literature.

Nevertheless, I cannot say that I alone am responsible for this guide to the practice and industry of management consultancy. Many others, most of whom are practising consultants, have contributed to the guide. This has been done to ensure that the guide is up-to-date and relevant for practice and academic discipline built on years of experience and research within the industry.

David Biggs

Acknowledgements

This book would not have been possible without the following people: Don Leslie (BLT) for his support; Nick Wills (Computer Sciences Corporation) for his wit and insight into the industry; Neil Crumbie (Atkins Management Consultants) for his years of support; the Management Consultancies Association (especially Stephanie Mitchell but also Alan Leaman and Fiona Czerniawska); The Institute of Business Consulting; Association of Management Consulting Firms; International Council of Management Consultancy Institutes; Tony Restell and Bryan Hickson (top-consultant.com); Sarah Penrose and Eileen Whelan (Deloitte); Gavin Clayton and team (Innovative HR Solutions); Barbara Bridge (The Lamberhurst Corporation Consultancy Network); Jo Maddocks, Sarah Speers and John Cooper (JCA Ltd); Ethan Schutz and Gary Copeland (The Schutz Company, Inc); Scott Harvey (Scott Harvey Consultancy); Emily Hutchinson (EJH Consulting Ltd); Benedict Eccles (The Trust Partnership); Michael Markham (CPD Certification Service); Adrian Starkey (Accelerating Talent Ltd); Alan Bourne (Talent Q UK Ltd); Shane McGarrigle and Nigel Povah (A&DC Ltd); Dai Jones, Phil Tyson, Jermaine Ravalier, Steve Baker, Simon Toms, David Brookes and Julie Collins (Psychology, University of Gloucestershire); Jocelyne Fleming, David Dawson and Martin Wynn (Business School, University of Gloucestershire); John Hockey and Claire Shadwell (Education, University of Gloucestershire); Jan Merrigan and Lorna Meredith (University of Gloucestershire); eLiz Hartnett (Open University); Nick Oldnall (NHS); Alex Steele (improwise); James Cullup (SERCO); Adrian Banks (University of Surrey); all of the consultancies mentioned in the book and those that chose to remain anonymous but still contributed; the reviewers that slaved through my draft chapters and gave me kind advice; Thomas Rennie and Leandra Paoli at Cengage Learning for encouraging me with the text; Avril Gover for her hard work and assistance on the book; and last but not least, Evelyn and Rupert Farrow, who I dedicate this book to along with my two daughters Ciara and Niamh.

The publisher would like to thank the many copyright holders who have kindly granted us permission to reproduce material throughout this text. Every effort has been made to contact all rights holders but in the unlikely event that anything has been overlooked please contact the publisher directly and we will happily make the necessary arrangements at the earliest opportunity.

List of Reviewers

The publisher and author would also like to thank the following for kindly contributing case studies used throughout the text:

Benedict Eccles, Independent development and training consultant
Roger Gill, University of Strathclyde Business School
Scott Harvey, Scott Harvey Consultancy
Angela Mitchell and Merlin Gardner, Deloitte Touche Tohmatsu, UK
Terry Mughan, Anglia Ruskin University
Professor John McAuley, Sheffield Business School Sheffield Hallam University

We would also like to thank the following for providing feedback on the text at various stages:

Steve Brown, University of Exeter
Stephen Grinsell, Newcastle Business School
Gareth Jones, Cardiff School of Management
Christel Niedereichholz, Institute for International Management Consulting
Sami Saarenketo, Lappeenranta University of Technology

About the Author

David Biggs graduated in 1993 with a BSc Psychology with Computing (University of Ulster) and then with an MSc in Occupational Psychology (University of Nottingham). David worked as an occupational psychologist in management development and recruitment in 1994 and then in performance management in 1995. His experiences in performance management led David to start a part-time PhD in 1996 examining temporary workers. David then worked for a specialist training provider where he led a small team of trainers for two years and then moved to an International Management Consultancy. During this period (1998–2002), David led several consultancy and research projects and developed an appetite for research both in the UK and abroad. At the same time, David lectured on a part-time basis at several locations including: University of Swansea, Cambridge Marketing College and University College Northampton. David then worked for a niche Assessment Centre consultancy providing management development and assessment services. David joined Gloucestershire in September 2003 and lectures at undergraduate and postgraduate level. He developed the MSc in Business Psychology, developed the MSc in Occupational Psychology and delivers consultancy services.

Walk Through Tour

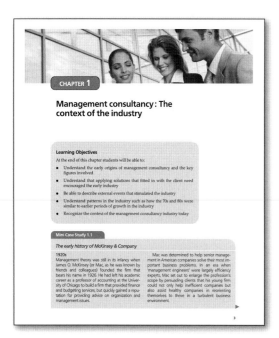

Learning objectives – bullet points at the start of each chapter focus on the main ideas that need to be understood in each chapter.

Introduction – outlines the kinds of principles and issues you will meet in the chapter.

Mini Case Studies – these appear at the start of each chapter to foreground the main concepts of the chapter in a real-world situation.

Industry Snapshots – appear throughout each chapter to show how issues are applied in real-life business situations.

Thought Provoking Points – provide interesting insights and observations about the key issues that are being discussed.

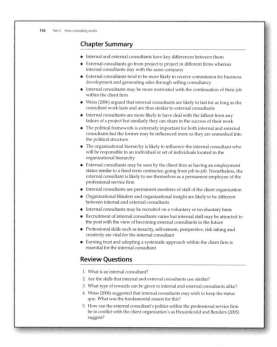

Summary – each chapter ends with a comprehensive summary that provides a thorough recap of the key issues in each chapter, helping you to assess your understanding and revise key content.

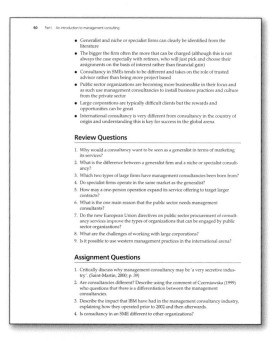

Review Questions and Assignment Questions – are provided at the end of each chapter to help reinforce and test your knowledge and understanding.

End of Chapter Cases – long cases discuss in depth the issues and principles encountered during the chapter.

About the Website

Visit the Management Consulting companion website at www.cengage.co.uk/biggs to find valuable teaching and learning material including:

FOR LECTURERS:

- Instructor's Manual
- PowerPoint Slides
- Extra Questions and Answers
- Additional Case Material

FOR STUDENTS

- Extensive Web Links

An introduction to management consulting

The first part of this book introduces the topic of management consultancy. Chapter 1 creates a context for the book giving a historical overview of the industry. This is useful in providing a background to the industry describing the factors that led to the rise or demise of consultancies over the years.

Chapter 2 takes the context further defining management consultancy as both an industry and practice. It initially concentrates on the concept put forward by the Management Consultancies Association of 'adding value'. Criticism of management consultancy is introduced here from both an academic and practitioner standpoint. Impression management, management rhetoric and related concepts are critically appraised using the latest research providing a critical understanding of consulting. The chapter then goes back to basics and asks the fundamental question, 'Why use consultants?' This question is answered using a well-known model in psychology, the Johari window, but applied to an organizational setting. The chapter then details research of what consultants and clients themselves have agreed on 'Why use consultants?'

The final chapter in this section examines the different types of consultancies in today's global economy. The issue of size is introduced, with the larger consultancies compared with more specialist organizations. Different fields of consultancy activity are detailed examining assignments for markets which include: SMEs, public sector, private sector and international.

CHAPTER 1

Management consultancy: The context of the industry

Learning Objectives

At the end of this chapter students will be able to:

- Understand the early origins of management consultancy and the key figures involved

- Understand that applying solutions that fitted in with the client need encouraged the early industry

- Be able to describe external events that stimulated the industry

- Understand patterns in the industry such as how the 70s and 80s were similar to earlier periods of growth in the industry

- Recognize the context of the management consultancy industry today

Mini Case Study 1.1

The early history of McKinsey & Company

1920s

Management theory was still in its infancy when James O. McKinsey (or Mac, as he was known by friends and colleagues) founded the firm that bears his name in 1926. He had left his academic career as a professor of accounting at the University of Chicago to build a firm that provided finance and budgeting services, but quickly gained a reputation for providing advice on organization and management issues.

Mac was determined to help senior management in American companies solve their most important business problems. In an era when 'management engineers' were largely efficiency experts, Mac set out to enlarge the profession's scope by persuading clients that his young firm could not only help inefficient companies but also assist healthy companies in reorienting themselves to thrive in a turbulent business environment.

1930s

In 1933, the arrival of Marvin Bower provided James O. McKinsey with a strong advocate and a fellow visionary. Bower held both a J.D. and an M.B.A. from Harvard University. He adamantly believed that management consulting should be held to the same high standards for professional conduct and performance as law and medicine.

Following Mac's early death, Bower began to carefully shape the firm into its present form by insisting on a few core principles:

- Client interests must be placed before those of the firm.
- Engagements should only be undertaken when the value to the client was expected to exceed the firm's fees.
- The firm's ownership should be restricted to active partners.

Firm members must be professionals trained and motivated to do outstanding work and make a permanent career with the firm. By the end of the 1930s, under Bower's stewardship, the term 'management consulting' began to replace 'management engineering,' and the professional management consultant was born. Bower, who later became managing director, served clients until the late 1980s and remained a valued friend and counsellor to the firm until his death in 2003.

1940s

World War II profoundly affected the American business landscape, and our work shifted to issues of national import as we helped several major companies convert their production facilities to support US troops.

As our client base continued to grow, we established new offices in Chicago, Los Angeles, and San Francisco. As we grew, so too did our commitment to our 'one firm' concept. We believed then (and now) that only by remaining a single organization, rather than a loose confederation of offices, could we simultaneously deliver the best possible client service and treat our own people with utmost fairness and integrity.

It's our belief in 'one firm' that allows us to view our consultants as a global talent pool – one we can draw on as needed to provide the best service to our clients, regardless of location.

Source: http://www.mckinsey.com/ Reproduced with permission of McKinsey & Company.

Introduction

As our opening case study demonstrates, the management consultancy industry has an extensive history that can be traced back even further than the 1930s to the nineteenth century (Ferguson, 2002). This chapter details the fascinating history of the management consultancy industry using academic sources and material from well-known consultancies. This involves examining how consultancies have thrived, survived or died in a notoriously demanding industry. In detailing this history, the text is able to describe the context of the industry, which then serves as a background for many of the following chapters.

The History of Management Consultancy

The early years

With the onset of the industrial revolution in late eighteenth century Britain, the sharing of 'management' knowledge and ways to encourage productivity were common practices. Employees trained in one technique of manufacturing might move to another employer and share what they had learnt (Evans, 2001; Ferguson, 2002). Internationally, this activity occurred also with less well developed countries observing how things were done abroad. In Britain a century later in 1849, Harding and Pullein founded a partnership later joined by Frederick Whinney that would be the British origins of Ernst & Young although the company has extensive American roots being formed as separate partnerships in Chicago and in Cleveland at the start of the twentieth century (Ernst & Young, 2009). So what was happening in the US that made the industry possible? McKenna (2006a) provides us with a good account of the early management consultancy industry.

McKenna (2006a) explained that in the US during the 1870s, the traditional patterns of employment were altered in what is described as a second industrial revolution. Researchers and scientists often had to commercialize their own patents externally and engineers started to sell their knowledge as consultants to the 'science based' industries (McKenna, 2006a). At the same time investments into these industries produced much profit and as such directors of firms such as Standard Oil, General Electric and AT&T employed freelance engineers as either short-term consultants or research staff thereby facilitating innovation within their industry (McKenna, 2006a).

In the 1880s, two firms were created that can today be recognized as the beginnings of the management consultancy industry in the US (McKenna, 2006a). During 1886 a Massachusetts Institute of Technology (MIT) professor Dr Arthur D. Little created the first management consultancy firm of his own name (Saint-Martin, 2000). The company emphasized science, engineering and invention in its original form. However in 2002, the company filed for bankruptcy although the brand name was bought out by a French consultancy Altran Technologies so still exists today (see http://www.adl.com/about-us.html for more details).

During the 1890s Frederick W. Taylor worked as a management consultant (Riordan, 2009) performing studies at the time that would be influential in his Scientific Management theories published in 1911 (Matthewman, Rose and Hetherington, 2009). McKenna (2006a) stated that many individuals, such as F.W. Taylor, worked at this time as consultants and many engineering based firms started around this period. Indeed, Taylor may be thought of as the first management consultant installing his systematic working practice for a fee (Kipping, 2002).

It would be a while for the first management consultancies to emerge in the US. Indeed, Arthur D. Little and other similar firms in the Boston region such as Stone & Webster weren't really the archetypal management consultancy and were instead 'general management know how' hired for a price (McKenna, 2006a). This was also the practice outside of the US although anecdotally some argue that due to managers not wanting to appear incompetent and asking for consultancy support the spread of management consultancy outside of the US was limited.

Nevertheless, just before and during the early part of the twentieth century notable firms emerged in the US. During 1898, the practice that would become Coopers & Lybrand and then PricewaterhouseCoopers was founded (Riordan, 2009). In 1914, Arthur Andersen and Clarence DeLany founded an accounting practice that would become Arthur Andersen LLP. In addition, Edwin Booz develops his own consultancy practice performing research for companies such as Goodyear, the Canadian Pacific Railroad and Photographers Association of the United States (Riordan, 2009). This company then becomes Booz and Company and is regarded as one of the earliest true management consultancies (McKenna, 2006a).

In Europe, at the beginning of the twentieth century, organizational consultancy became increasingly sort after by firms interested in what was happening in the US economy just as the actual process of manufacturing was adopted by the US from Europe. In Sweden, Oskar Sillacuteen a professor at the Stockholm School of Economics worked in both an academic role and also part-time as a consultant in the newly established Industrial Office (Engwall, Furusten and Wallerstedt, 2002). This meant that practical matters of business in the growing Swedish economy could be addressed through academic inquiry and expertise – a practice that still exists today (Wright, Clarysse, Lockett and Knockaert, 2008) and that is highlighted in Thought Provoking points 1.1 and 1.2 below.

Thought Provoking point 1.1

Academia in consultancy – Positives

The link between academia and consultancy thrives today, with academics often becoming employed as part-time consultants. Academics who offer their skills as a consultant are welcomed as they can provide a valuable academic rigor to consultancy practices.

Thought Provoking point 1.2

Academia in consultancy – Negatives

Although individual academics working as consultants are often applauded, some consultancies do not like it when universities in their own right as businesses bid for management consultancy work. This is because universities invariably do not have the same running costs of consultancies, e.g., the office space, support staff, IT, etc. Universities in this regard are already being paid for by student fees and taxpayers' money and don't have to rely on consultancy income. Thus, there is unfair competition between consultancies and universities if the two compete for management consultancy assignments.

During the early years of the twentieth century, well known promoters of the theories of scientific management rose to fame in the US, including influential figures such as Henry Gantt who in 1910 published *Work, Wages and Profits* (Riordan, 2009). Gantt was most famous for influencing the project management tradition with the chart that bears his name that marks time as a resource. However, many of the proponents of F.W. Taylor's theories, such as Gantt, Frank Gilbreth, Harlow Person, Morris Cooke, etc., worked as independent consultants (McKenna, 2006a). Companies in the US such as Bedaux, founded by a French immigrant in the US in 1916, went international to Europe and other regions from 1926 onwards (Kipping, 2002). Indeed, Bedaux went from strength to strength and in the 1920s onwards spawned several subsidiaries most notable of which was British Bedaux Ltd founded in the UK in 1926 (Ferguson, 2002).

In Europe, Berend Willem Berenschot joined an engineering practice in 1922 and strived to change the reputation of consultants who were seen as reorganizers and drivers of efficiency (Karsten and van Veen, 2002). In 1925, Berenschot actively supported the founding of an Institute for Efficiency which enhanced the role of consultants within the Netherlands (Karsten and van Veen, 2002). In Norway in 1928 Industrifondets Rasjonaliseringskontor (IRAS) was established as the first consulting firm which would later be merged into PA Consulting in 1989 (PA Consulting, 2009). Many of these early European roots of consultancy were still strongly wedded to the principles of scientific management, which came under increasing attack (Henry, 2002).

During the 1920s, America became increasingly disinterested with striving for efficiency. This resulted in many of the firms wedded to scientific management dying out during the 1930s (Henry, 2002). In Europe, Germany produced its own version of scientific management called industrial rationalization. This was perceived as a more humane version of scientific management which was subsequently adopted by other European countries (Ainamo and Tienari, 2002). The exceptional companies that didn't perish with the fall in popularity of scientific management tended to survive in the international market till the 1960s. These surviving companies altered themselves drastically to survive, delivering more services than those proposed by scientific management principles alone (Henry, 2002; McKenna, 2006a).

From the 1920s into the 1940s

In the early management consultancy industry it was the alliance between engineers and accountants that paved the way forward rather than the rigid principles of scientific management (McKenna, 2006a). In 1926, James McKinsey founded a consultancy with his own name (see Mini Case Study 1.1) and soon after formed a partnership with Andrew Thomas Kearney (Riordan, 2009). The firm described themselves at this point as 'consultants and engineers' but mainly completed auditing work for clients during this early period (Riordan, 2009). This union is the start of the two consultancies McKinsey & Company and A.T. Kearney both of which thrive in the twenty-first century.

Booz Allen Hamilton also forms a partnership in 1929 hiring its third employee, Jim Allen to form the core of the firm. Interestingly though, the initial formation of the company is listed as 1914 (see Industry snapshot 1.1 for more details), a time when Ed Booz allegedly shared an office with a man who sold bath towels (Riordan, 2009).

A summary of the history of Booz Allen Hamilton

In 1914, Edwin Booz had an idea. He believed that companies would be more successful if they could call on someone outside their own organizations for expert, impartial advice. In doing so, he created a new profession – management consulting – and the firm that would bear his name, Booz Allen Hamilton.

In our role as consultants, Booz Allen has been privileged to see, take part in, and catalyze many key events in the spheres of both business and government. We have been involved in the emergence of modern corporations in the 1920s and 1930s, the Allied mobilization in World War II, the beginning and end of the Cold War, the dawn of the Space Age, the evolution of the personal computer, the break-up of old telephone systems and the creation of new ones, early public-private sector work in the European Union, the emergence of strong economies in Asia and South America, the waves of deregulation in the 1980s, the movement of environmental protection, and the birth of the modern US National Football League.

In addition, we have been witness to or participant in the reunification of Germany, the Gulf Wars, the response to the terrorist attacks of 9/11, the rise and fall of business cycles, and dramatic shifts in the ways that commerce, war, and peace have been conducted.

Source: http://www.boozallen.com/about/history. Reproduced with permission from Booz Allen Hamilton.

In the US during the 1930s, regulatory change increased the impact of the management consultancy industry. In 1929, the stock market crashed heralding the beginning of the Great Depression (Djelic, 2004). McKenna argued that rather than being a slow progress of evolution that strengthened the industry, it was the formation of policies such as the Glass-Steagall Banking Act passed by the US Congress in 1933 that stimulated the industry (McKenna 2006a). This legislation prohibited commercial banks from collaborating with brokerage firms or participating in investment banking activities (Djelic, 2004). In essence, the act stopped the practice of auditing by the banks putting this activity into the grasp of the early management consultancy industry. At the same time, the US Securities and Exchange Commission prevented professionals such as lawyers, accountants, and engineers from acting as consultants (McKenna, 2006a). This served as a stimulus to the industry whereby the number of management consultancy firms grew from an average of 100 in 1930 to 400 in 1940 (ACME,[1] 1964). Nevertheless, management consultancies were still less common in the US and in Europe than other professionals such as accountants or engineers (McKenna, 1996).

However, by the end of the Second World War consultancies were increasingly being used by corporate America (McKenna, 1996). Indeed, the growth rate of management consultancies in the 1930s was about 15 per cent each year and this continued on at about 10 per cent each year during the 1940s (McKenna, 1996; 2006). During this time, new consulting firms such as PA Consulting, Akins, Proudfoot Consulting and Bossard Consultants were formed.

In 1939, James McKinsey died of pneumonia at the age of 48. This event caused the original firm to split as Marvin Bower and Andrew Tom Kearney differed on

---

[1]ACME served as the professional voice of the industry and still exists today rebranded as the Association of Management Consulting Firms (AMCF)

how the practice could grow. Kearney kept the Chicago office and renamed it A.T. Kearney. Bower encouraged the development of McKinsey & Company by bringing in fresh new talent. This talent, although lacking in business knowledge, applied analytical techniques learnt from the major business schools of the day that were directly relevant to industry (Riordan, 2009). Indeed, the practice of hiring MBA students from the top business schools still exists today. Bower also insisted on having the professional standards of a leading law firm, instigating three rules:

1. put the interests of the client ahead of revenues
2. tell the truth and don't be afraid to challenge a client's opinion, and
3. only agree to perform work that is necessary and something McKinsey can do well.

Cited from Riordan (2009)

Bower was adamant that creating the right impression was essential for the consultancy role. Consultants, Bower allegedly said, should wear hats and long socks although he later relaxed his ruling on wearing hats through his own actions (see Industry snapshot 1.2).

Other companies in the US were also emerging during the 1940s. Proudfoot Consulting, for instance, was founded by Alexander Proudfoot in 1946 who wanted to partner with clients ensuring positive change (Alexander Proudfoot, 2009). The company activity was implementing effective organizational change through using, specialist knowledge and concepts such as the 'Produfoot Concept of Lost Time' (Alexander Proudfoot, 2009). The company exists today rebrauded in 2009 back to their original name the Alexander Proudfoot Company, who form part of the Management consulting Group (Alexander Proudfoot, 2009)

Industry snapshot 1.2

Marvin Bower – the father of management consultancy

Marvin Bower has been called the father of the management consultancy industry (Byrne, 2003; Edersheim, 2004). Marvin was born on the 1st August 1903 raised in Cleveland. After high school, Bower attended Brown College (Edersheim, 2004). At Brown two professors caught the young Bower's attention. The first was, not surprisingly given Bower's business prowess, was an economics professor. The second was a psychology professor who demonstrated the importance of effective communication and competencies in dealing with people (Edersheim, 2004).

Indeed, Bower found using different techniques in dealing with people extremely useful in a summer job working for Thompson, Hine and Flory (TH&F). TH&F were given bad debts from firms that

supplied retailers but who had failed to recapture the debt. Bower found that by successfully engaging the retailers in person rather than by sending a 'dunning' letter that was more common in the 1920's that companies that owed money were much more likely to pay the debt (Edersheim, 2004).

Bower, with the finances received through various summer jobs was able to fund himself through law at the Harvard Law School (Edersheim, 2004). After graduating, he worked for a Cleveland law firm for a short while before returning back to University to strengthen the business side of his curriculum vitae (Edersheim, 2004). Bower then graduated with an MBA from the fledgling Harvard Business School and in 1930 worked for the corporate law practice at Jones, Day, Reavis & Pogue in Cleveland (Edersheim, 2004; Hindle, 2002).

Although, some have said that Bower's first choice of career was the legal profession (Hindle, 2002). Fortunately for us, Bower was still very much attracted to business. The business side of Bower was to be realised in 1933, when he caught the attention of James McKinsey. McKinsey liked Bower's ideas especially about 'the firm' being a professional management based practice (Martin, 2003). McKinsey consequently offered Bower a job in the New York branch of the Chicago based firm (Edersheim, 2004; Martin, 2003).

Following McKinsey's death in 1937, the two offices based in Chicago and New York split. The Chicago office was taken over by AT Kearney but in New York, Bower grew the business as McKinsey & Company (Martin, 2003). Bower was fierce about quality and professional standards and upheld these at all times (Edersheim, 2004).

Schleler, (2000) cites one example where Bower demonstrated that giving the client the correct advice meant much more than business revenue. In this example, the project results for an important project were being delivered to a major client. However, the presentation was being frequently interrupted by the autocratic head of the company, who was arguably the source of the company's losses. After many frequent interruptions, Bower stood up and said to the autocratic head, 'the main problem in this company is you'. This led to a stunned silence. Nevertheless, many of the people in the board meeting agreed with Bower. Nonetheless, the rest of the board did not usurp the head. This ultimately led to the consultancy team not being hired again. Nevertheless, an important principle was made that in detailing the truth, however unpalatable to the client, is in the long term interests of the client and the consultancy and should always take precedent over revenue (Martin, 2003).

Bower's professional approach was allied with the ability to use effective interpersonal communication with the client. This often meant simplifying concepts down so they made common sense

(Martin, 2003). Allied to this approach, Bower brought in the brightest graduates of Harvard Business School growing the McKinsey firm. Bower would turn down work that was not in the firm's interest to pursue. He concentrated the firm's practice not only on giving sound business advice but also becoming almost business partners in exchange (Schleler, 2000). This meant that as Bower once put it, 'If you looked after the client, the profits would look after themselves' (Hindle, 2008, p219).

Through his work at McKinsey, Bower took the fledgling industry and set its course towards the profession it has become. This included not only the types of management consultancy services that could be sold but also the professional standards it must uphold for it to be respected. Indeed, throughout his life Bower regarded himself more as a professional rather than as a businessman (Edersheim, 2004). Some suggest that this professionalism is a return of Bower's want of being a lawyer (Hindle, 2002). Conversely, it may be that Bower took great pride in developing a professional stance for 'the firm' an aspect that James McKinsey identified with back in 1933.

Bower served as managing director of McKinsey and Company from 1950 to 1967, remaining a key leadership figure as director and partner until 1992. Bower died aged 99 on the 22nd January 2003 in Florida and his legacy, through his firm and his influence on the industry, lives on.

References

Byrne, J.A. (2003), Goodbye to an ethicist. *BusinessWeek*; 2/10/2003, Issue 3819, p38

Edersheim, E.H. (2004), *McKinsey's Marvin Bower: Vision, Leadership, and the Creation of Management Consulting.* New Jersey:John Wiley and Sons Inc

Hindle, T. (2008), *Guide to Management Ideas & Gurus.* London:The Economist/Profile Books Ltd

Martin, D. (2003), . *The New York Times.* Retrieved from http://www.nytimes.com/2003/01/24/business/marvin-bower-99-built-mckinsey-co.html#

Schleler, C. (2000), Consulting Innovator Marvin Bower: Putting Customer Needs First Was A Key For Him. *Investor's Business Daily.* Retrieved from http://www.mckinsey.com/aboutus/mckinseynews/pressarchive/pdf/mckinsey IBDpt2.pdf

In the UK, the engineering firm WS Atkins & Partners was established in 1938 by Sir William Atkins. This company rapidly expanded to include specialist services such as engineering sciences, architecture and project management. Later the firm would be one of the largest engineering and multidisciplinary consultancies in the world with a sizeable management consultancy division. Also in the UK, PA Consultants was founded in 1943 by Ernest Butten, a former employee of Bedaux (Kipping, 2002). PA stands for 'Personnel Administration' and the company was initially formed aiding the recruitment and development processes of other organizations (PA Consulting, 2009). PA Consulting would become a sizeable multidisciplinary consultancy with over 3000 people reported in 2008 (Inside Careers, 2008). Ove Arup established offices in London and Dublin in 1946 founding what would become a global firm of designers, engineers, planners and business consultants which today has more than 9000 employees worldwide and an annual turnover exceeding £475 million (Arup, 2009).

Consultancy firms in France were created during and after the Nazi German occupation (Henry, 2002). In 1943 the Compagnie d'organization rationnele du travail, which later became CORT Consultants was probably the first to be formed (Henry, 2002). After the defeat of Nazi Germany by the Allies, Europe needed much in the way of rebuilding and restructuring. This profited engineering based consultancy firms such as Arup and Atkins. Furthermore in France, Yves Bossard formed an organization in 1946 and into the early 1950s that would become Bossard Consultants, a management consultancy with a distinct European accent (Henry, 2002; Riordan, 2009). Indeed, before its merger with CapGemini in 1996 Bossard Consultants had 800 consultants in total, 450 of which were based in France (Computergram, 1996).

In the Netherlands, there was a rapid programme of industrialization after the economy had been severely damaged during the Second World War (Karsten and van Veer, 2002). The Dutch government at this time embarked on massive training initiatives for all types of roles supported by unions and employers. Nevertheless, it lacked the facilities to deliver the training considered to be invaluable employability skills. And, just as in the US example with the Glass-Steagall Banking Act, consultancies developed to meet this urgent demand offering training services (Karsten and van Veer, 2002). Indeed, one of these Dutch companies, Berenschot (founded by Berend Willem Berenschot who helped initiate the Dutch consultancy industry in the 1920s) grew quickly and even began exporting consultancy and training services to the US in 1951 (Karsten and van Veer, 2002).

The 1950s and 1960s

McKenna argued that just as in the 1930s the adoption of specific legislation served as a boost to the industry (McKenna, 2006a). The same was also the case in the 1950s, where policies aimed to restrict collusive information between firms and to discourage monopolies served as a stimulant to the consultancy industry. Computing firms such as IBM were prohibited from offering computer consultancy advice and gave 'the emerging field of information technology consulting to the large accountancy firms' (McKenna, 2006a; p. 21).

Arthur Andersen and Company benefited greatly from providing this service into corporations encouraging the IT industry to evolve. Indeed, Andersen's were involved with the first installation of computer systems for General Electric specifically for business purposes (McKenna, 2006a). Due to the anti-monopoly laws that restricted IBM's activities, other computer based consultancies developed. Indeed, IBM fell into decline up until 1991 when the last remnants of the anti-trust legislation were lifted. Shortly after Lou Gerstner (a former McKinsey consultant) took over the leadership of the company reigniting the consulting aspect of the group (Gerstner, 2002; McKenna, 2006a). IBM's changes at this time are detailed in Chapter 3 where we examine large corporations in the industry. It must also be noted that IBM was listed in 2008 as having the highest number of employees for a firm with a substantial consultancy element (Inside Careers, 2008).

The need for management consultancy services also brought the need for expertise. In the 1950s, recruitment for management consultancy talent was fierce especially in terms of hiring MBAs from leading business schools as firms followed Bower's example in McKinsey & Company to recruit the best (Riordan, 2009). James Allen being the sole surviving founder of Booz, Allen & Hamilton, restructured the consultancy by hiring large numbers of graduates who had strong analytical skills. Booz, Allen & Hamilton became a leading management consulting firm by 1970 and is still strong today (see Industry snapshot 1.3).

Industry snapshot 1.3

Booz Allen's opening website greeting

Booz Allen Hamilton has been at the forefront of strategy and technology consulting for 95 years. Providing a broad range of services in strategy, operations, organization and change, information technology, systems engineering, and program management, Booz Allen is committed to delivering results that endure. Headquartered in McLean, Virginia, Booz Allen has 20,000 employees and generates annual revenue of over $4 billion.

Source: http://www.boozallen.com. Reproduced with permission from Booz Allen Hamilton.

During the 1950s most of the first generation consultancies diversified their activities from their original Taylorist inspired roots (Kipping, 2002). In the UK in 1956, the Management Consultants Association (MCA) was formed by the big four consultancies at the time which included: British Bedaux Ltd; Production Engineering; Urwick, Orr and Partners; and PA Consulting. However, with the possible exception of PA Consulting the market share of the big four declined from the 1960s and survived only through mergers or takeovers of other companies in the 1980s and 1990s.

Nevertheless, the management consultancy industry was not in decline – instead there was a new breed of consultants (Kipping, 2002). The second generation of consultancies emerged from the late 1950s from the US. Companies like Arthur D. Little and Booz, Allen & Hamilton thrived. The difference between these consultancies and the first generation was the focus on people rather than processes and organization. In a 1968 interview, James Allen stated that:

> The thing that gave management consulting its greatest impetus was the approach that Ed Booz took, that is: thinking in terms of people and the organization of them as being the key factors in successful management. This has been borne out by many individuals who founded great corporations.

Higdon, 1969; p. 129

McKinsey and Company had rapidly been taken over in terms of market share during the 1950s by companies such as Booz Allen. Nevertheless, by 1959 the organization had set up their first international office in London and by the end of the 1960s had a third of its revenue being generated by international business (Kipping, 2002).

Strategy also became an essential commodity of the management consultancy industry and the re-emergence of some of the early firms not wedded to Taylorist principles inspired other companies. Bruce Henderson started his career off in General Electric as a strategic planner moving swiftly into the Arthur D. Little consultancy practice. Then in 1963, Henderson set up the Boston Consulting Group, the first pure strategy based consultancy (Kipping, 2002).

Indeed, in the 1960s the management consultancy industry was starting to establish itself as a multi-billion-dollar industry (Saint-Martin, 2000). During this period, audit work had generally declined so many of the accountancy firms looked for new areas to exploit, joining the consultancy industry. The big eight firms then emerged at the end of the 1960s that had these accountancy roots bringing more professionalism into the industry seen as particularly important in countries outside the US (Saint-Martin, 2000). The big eight consisted of:

1. Arthur Andersen
2. Coopers & Lybrand
3. Ernst & Whinney
4. Arthur Young
5. KPMG Peat Marwick
6. Deloitte, Haskins & Sells
7. Touche Ross
8. PriceWaterhouse

Quoted from Saint-Martin, 2000; p. 44

Nevertheless, there were plenty of other consultancies around in 1969 with Higdon (1969) citing 54 major consultancies in total. Table 1.1 demonstrates the major consultancies listed in 1969 in rank of revenues based on Higdon's work. However, revenues cited in 1969 were converted to a comparable basis by multiplying by growth in the CPI which rose from 34.8 in 1968 to 160 in 1996. Interestingly, the consultancy ranked top in terms of revenue in Table 1.1, the Planning Research Corporation, no longer trades today although during the 1970s they were involved in project work as diverse as examining the effect of increased tax on cigarettes through to creating FORTRAN compilers in the US. Other companies listed as marked not applicable are where the revenues in 1996 were not available due to the firm's disappearance. Indeed, by 1996, 24 of the 54 companies listed had either stopped trading or had been merged into other companies, so only 15 had survived into the late 1990s.

The 1970s and 1980s

The 1970s was a period of slow economic growth for many companies, although consultancies such as the Boston Consulting Group (BCG), McKinsey & Company

Table 1.1   Top consulting firms ranked by revenues in 1968

Firm	No of consultants	Real revenues '68	Real revenues '96	Ave. growth rate	Revenue rank '68	Revenue rank '96
Planning Research Corporation	3000	236	#N/A	#N/A	1	NA
Booz Allen & Hamilton	1500	215	1100	15%	2	8
Peat, Marwick, Mitchell & Co.	700	129	990	24%	3	10
McKinsey	462	103	1500	48%	4	4
WOFAC Company	550	69	#N/A	#N/A	5	NA
Arthur D. Little	230	64	514	25%	6	15
Alexander Proudfoot PLC (UK)	300	64	165	6%	7	30
URS Corporation	400	53	#N/A	#N/A	8	NA
H. B. Maynard & Company	450	43	#N/A	#N/A	9	NA
Ernst & Ernst	400	43	1390	112%	10	5
Diebold Group	450	34	#N/A	#N/A	11	NA
Lybrand, Ross & Montgomery	318	32	1324	143%	12	6
Management Science America	300	32	#N/A	#N/A	13	NA
A. T. Kearney	255	30	346	38%	14	20
Kurt Salmon Associates	200	28	62	4%	15	38
Lester B. Knight & Associates	225	28	#N/A	#N/A	16	NA
Creasap, McCormick & Paget	160	26	#N/A	#N/A	17	NA
Operations Research	240	23	#N/A	#N/A	18	NA
Stone & Webster Consultants	275	21	#N/A	#N/A	19	NA
Arthur Andersen & Company	150	21	4220	699%	20	1
Touche, Ross, Bailey & Smart	150	21	1045	173%	21	9
Auerbach Corporation	190	21	#N/A	#N/A	22	NA
Price Waterhouse	125	21	1200	196%	23	7
Arthur Young & Co.	150	21	1390	228%	24	5
Worden & Risberg	150	17	#N/A	#N/A	25	NA
Haskins & Sells	180	16	1045	230%	26	9
EBS Management Consultants	100	13	#N/A	#N/A	27	NA
Harbridge House	60	13	#N/A	#N/A	28	>40
S. D. Leidesdorf & Co.	100	13	#N/A	#N/A	29	NA
Bonner & Moore Associates	100	13	#N/A	#N/A	30	NA
Glendinning Associates	100	13	#N/A	#N/A	31	NA
Fantus Company	100	11	#N/A	#N/A	32	NA
Case & Company	100	11	#N/A	#N/A	33	NA
Donahue, Groover & Associates	100	11	#N/A	#N/A	34	NA
Woods, Gordon & Co.	125	11	#N/A	#N/A	35	NA
George S. May	400	26	85	8%	36	36
Handley-Walker Company	60	9	#N/A	#N/A	37	NA
S. J. Capelin Associates	70	9	#N/A	#N/A	38	NA
R. Dixon Speas Associates	63	9	#N/A	#N/A	39	NA

Source: http://www.careers-in-business.com/consulting/crank68.htm. Reproduced with permission from careers-in-business.com.

and Booz Allen still remained successful. BCG, Booz Allen and other consultancies created symbiotic links with leading business schools such as Harvard based in Boston, Massachusetts. Organizational theories and techniques developed at leading business schools aided the creation of analytical tools and approaches. It was from this type of link that the new field of strategic management emerged, which set the groundwork for many consulting firms to follow (Riordan, 2009). Indeed, Boston in the early 70s became almost a Mecca for consultancies where one apparently could not walk the streets without bumping into a consultant (Riordan, 2009). Notable consultancies, such as formed by William W. Bain, developed during this period combining client relationship management with analytical techniques learnt from the business schools (Riordan, 2009).

During the 1970s, the IT industry filling the gap that IBM was forced out of by federal law expanded rapidly. In 1977 Nolan, Norton & Company was formed specializing in information technology management consulting. The company was subsequently bought out by KPMG and Richard Norton now works as an American business school professor (see http://drfd.hbs.edu/fit/public/facultyInfo.do?facInfo=bio&facEmId=rnolan for more details). Indeed, other organizations, such as Axent Technologies based in southern England that specialized in IT protection and firewalls emerged. This company had originated as an idea in a consultancy by individuals who thought computer systems of the future may be attacked from outside by unscrupulous individuals. The consultancy decided not to develop the idea; however, not disheartened the former consultants went it alone forming their own company that was eventually merged with the Symantec Corporation in 2000.

In the rest of Europe, similar expansion was also being made. The French company Sogeti acquired two large IT services companies, CAP and Gemini Computer Systems in 1975 eventually becoming Capgemini. During the later 70s and 80s, Capgemini became a European leader in consultancy expanding into the American market and in 1989 was positioned as being among the five leaders in its sector worldwide (see Industry snapshot 3.1). In the Dutch banking sector, AD Little and McKinsey & Company both contributed towards the raft of mergers and acquisitions that took place in the Netherlands (Arnoldus and Dankers, 2005).

In the UK, the Bank of England was reorganized in a high profile assignment that led McKinsey & Company to perform similar projects for the World Bank (McKenna, 2006a). BCG also examined the British motorcycle industry focusing on competitive strategy using theoretical business models from Japanese rather than American sources (McKenna, 2006a).

The management consultancy industry continued to grow during the 1980s and into the 1990s (Fincham and Clark, 2003). By the end of the 1980s, rather than there being just a handful of firms. The industry had significantly changed, becoming one of the fastest growing aspects of most advanced economies concerned with companies both big and small (Fincham and Clark, 2003).

The 1990s into the twenty-first century

The expansion of the industry during the 1990s continued at a double digit pace (McKenna, 2006a). In the UK, consultancy demonstrated consistent growth, with typical revenue returns increased by 19 per cent (Ferguson, 2002). Ferguson argued that there were two main streams in consultancy: strategy and operations or performance improvement. Ferguson also noted that during this period there was the development of e-business services and globalization of consultancy (Ferguson, 2002). E-business arrived due to the development of the Internet and this underpinned many of the developments associated with the spread of IT through organizations. This included B2B, business to business applications but also B2C, business to customer applications that was revolutionized by the Internet and associated products such as instant messaging (Bailey and Biggs, 2005).

However, as noted in this chapter this was not a young profession emerging from the 1980s (Ferguson, 2002; McKenna, 2006a). Interestingly during this period, academics became interested in the industry. Higdon (1969) was probably the earliest academic book written on the subject, but during the 1990s notable figures such as Robin Fincham, Timothy Clark, Matthias Kipping and Lars Engwall to name but a few arose in the literature. Some of these early accounts were quite scathing of the industry and will be examined in depth in later chapters, especially in the next chapter.

Ironically though, some of the more practical consultancy books written highlighting the services of consultancies benefited these firms. Saint-Martin (2000) stated that the consultancy that employed Hammer and Champy after their 1993 groundbreaking book on business process reengineering more than doubled its annual revenue from $70 million to $160 million the year after. Other books have also been published from consultancies such as Deloitte (Bishop and Hydoski, 2009), AT Kearney (Laudicina, 2004), BCG (Stern and Deimler, 2006) and McKinsey & Company (Friga, 2009; Rasiel & Figa, 1999; 2001). Most consultancies also contribute to leading business management publications such as the *Harvard Business Review* or even publish their own journals, a few of which are shown in Table 1.2.

Table 1.2	Consultancy	Journal	Website journal (or example journal) located
Journals produced by leading consultancy firms	Accenture	*Outlook*	http://www.accenture.com/Global/ Research_and_Insights/Outlook/default.htm
	AT Kearney	*Executive Agenda*	http://www.atkearney.com/index.php/ Publications/ea-volume-xi-number-2.html
	Booz Allen Hamilton	*Strategy & Business*	http://www.strategy-business.com
	Boston Consulting Group	*Pespectives*	http://www.bcg.com/impact_expertise/ publications/files/Perspective_411_Richer_ Sourcing_Sept04.pdf
	Deloitte	*Deloitte Research*	http://www.deloitte.com/dtt/section_node/ 0,2332,sid%253D15288,00.html
	McKinsey & Company	*McKinsey Quarterly*	http://www.mckinseyquarterly.com

> ### Thought Provoking point 1.3
>
> *Naming consultancies in case studies*
>
> Many books written often do not mention the consultancies that the case studies are from, presenting watered down versions of the original. Yet, consultancies have traditionally done well from advertising what they do. For instance, a Director interested in strategy will soon find the BCG book and guess what consultancy can help with strategy, BCG of course. So in this text the author has invariably sought publish case studies direct from the firms involved.

During the later 1980s and into the 1990s, Anglo-American consultancies started to emerge as the dominant players in the management consultancy industry (Saint-Martin, 2000). The 'Big six' accountancy firms in 1989 became the 'Big five' in 1999 and are now the 'Big four' in 2009 and comprise: PriceWaterhouseCoopers, Ernst & Young, KPMG, and Deloitte. Only Accenture is now not listed as they do not have anything to do with accountancy practice having had a rather problematic split with Arthur Andersen in 2000. The range and type of consultancies that exist today are highlighted to a greater degree in Chapter 3 that examines the extent of the industry. Nevertheless, before we can explore the industry in depth, a more critical examination of the industry and what it does is called for.

Conclusion

This chapter has presented a rather whistle stop tour of management consultancy aimed to give context to the industry. Interestingly, several events that occurred during the twentieth century really boosted the industry. And during its inception, the industry has tried hard to rid itself of the criticisms it faced and present a professional image (Higdon, 1969). The early years of the industry dominated by engineers and accountants still exists in part today, with the 'Big four' accountancy firms completing consultancy as do engineering firms like Atkins and Arup. One of the most recent developments was the rise of information technology based consultancy practices. Again, this will be examined more in Chapter 3, but in essence firms such as Capgemini, Hitachi Consulting and IBM without its historical restrictions have strengthened the management consultancy industry.

Chapter Summary

- Knowledge sharing of management and improving productivity has arguably been around since the industrial revolution started in the UK in the mid eighteenth century
- McKenna (2006a) argued that it was the second industrial revolution led by the US that heralded the origins of the management consultancy industry
- Ernst & Young trace their history back to a British partnership formed in 1849 but the firm also has strong American roots

- Arthur D. Little was formed by an MIT professor of the same name in 1886
- Consultancy served to stimulate the economies of countries such as Sweden around the turn of the twentieth century
- F.W. Taylor was arguably one of the first freelance management consultants at the turn of the twentieth century
- Taylor's ideas gave a short boost to the industry but by the 1930s most firms that did not go beyond his ideas failed
- Taylor's ideas did go international but again were most famous in Germany which produced its own industrial rationalization and then exported that to other European countries such as Finland
- In America, in 1929 ACME was founded and later rebranded to be the Association of Management Consulting Firms emphasizing the professional nature of the industry
- Regulatory change of the 1930s, especially the Glass-Steagall Banking Act 1933, stimulated the industry as banks could no longer conduct company audits
- Growth of the industry during the 1930s and 1940s was evident
- In the 1940s, leading consultancies hired top business school graduates as opposed to industry experts changing recruitment practices
- After the Second World War, consultancy grew in Europe
- In the UK, the American company Bedaux spawned several consultancies that founded the Management Consultancies Association in the 1950s to improve the professionalism of the industry
- During the 1950s anti-monopoly legislation restricted IBM's position and led to gaps in the market in consulting and IT that were rapidly filled by other companies
- During the 1960s accountancy firms increasingly received more revenue from their consultancy business
- The 1970s saw the economy slowing and more strategy based consultancies emerged
- IT firms started getting into the consultancy market during the 1990s and the anti-monopoly legislation was finally lifted from IBM in 1991
- Practitioner orientated books sold consultancy services and many of the top consultancies hired authors to write practical guides about their service provision
- Now in the early part of the twenty-first century, the industry is dominated by accounting practices, IT firms and engineers, all of whom have historical claims to the industry

Review Questions

1. When in the nineteenth century can the origins of Ernst & Young be traced to?
2. Although knowledge sharing was evident in the eighteenth century when does McKenna (2006a) trace the origins of the management consultancy industry to?

3. What are the positives and negatives of academia in consultancy?

4. Why did McKinsey and Company split in 1939?

5. What area of business management did Booz Allen and the Boston Consulting Group specialize in?

6. What are the three dominating influences in management consultancy today?

Assignment Questions

1. Did the ideas of F.W. Taylor influence the early management consultancy industry and did these ideas persist?

2. Critically discuss the differences between the European and US management consultancy industries before the 1940s.

3. Describe Marvin Bower's impact on the management consultancy industry.

4. Describe how the Big 8 in 1969 became the Big 5 in 1999 and then the Big 4 in 2009.

Case Study 1.1

Deloitte's one firm strategy

By Angela Mitchell, Merlin Gardner

The consultancy market has experienced unprecedented change through the 1990s and over the last decade. Strong growth over this period has been driven by waves of new ideas, not least the introduction of technology in all its forms: from enterprise resourcing planning systems during the boom years of the late 90s, through the inflation and bursting of the internet bubble, a trend towards offshoring, to today's market where cost reduction is the service in demand.

Throughout this time, the competitive landscape has been in flux. Of particular significance was the major restructure in the early 2000s as most of the 'big 5' professional services firms sold off their consultancy practices in response to market perceptions and regulatory pressures in the aftermath of Enron. Ernst & Young, KPMG and PricewaterhouseCoopers all sold their consulting businesses – to CapGemini, BearingPoint and IBM respectively. Deloitte, however, retained its consultancy business and embarked on a new 'One Firm'

strategy to maximize the opportunity from this unique positioning.

This case study outlines how the delivery of an end-to-end service, involving multiple service lines, can add exponential value to the client. It also sets out some of Deloitte's lessons learned in organizing and incentivizing the practice to achieve this.

Traditionally, professional services firms have gone to market and sold work by service line (for example: consulting, audit, tax, corporate finance). This model is not always conducive to offering the best client service. Firstly, staff working in one area may not understand the competencies and skills offered by other parts of the firm, and so will miss out on opportunities for these to provide more rounded and complete client advice. Secondly, and perhaps more seriously, the firm's recognition and reward structures may motivate staff to work in service silos, delivering as much as possible of an engagement from within their own team or division, when perhaps other teams have additional or more relevant skills. The result is rarely the best outcome for the client, who may receive very different service depending upon which part of the firm was originally engaged. It is important to remember that clients do not care which service line they are speaking to. They have a challenge – and they would like it solved. The best solution to this challenge will often come from a multi-disciplinary team, possessing a blend of different skills.

In 2000, Deloitte was perhaps best known as an audit and financial advisory firm, but consultancy was also a core and expanding part of the business. Having retained its consultancy capability, whilst other firms sold theirs, Deloitte had a valuable differentiator. In particular, the firm was well positioned to provide a broad and comprehensive service, supporting the client from the start of an issue or initiative, through to the implementation of a solution. Whilst many firms could compete on advisory services and many others could compete on implementation and operational services, few could offer such a full breadth of support through the lifecycle of the business.

For example, consider a company that has enjoyed success in its local market, but is now seeking to develop and grow its business. Typically, this will trigger a series of questions:

1. Which products and services should be developed? Where and how should they be taken to market?

2. What technology systems, processes and organizational structures will best support cost effective operations and the planned strategic changes and growth?

3. How should the company be organized and located to maximize investment incentives and to minimize its tax burden?

4. What structure will best meet the company's ongoing financing needs and how should these needs be secured?

5. How should the organization plan and deliver this significant business change?

Organizations in such a position need a broad consultancy advisor, and preferably one that can support them through the journey, from the initial strategy through to its execution and implementation.

Emphasizing the breadth and integration of our capability, we moved to a single brand, 'Deloitte' in 2003, and subsequently introduced the 'One Firm' strategy in 2004. Our overall strategy was to focus on the client, not the service organization, at a time when other organizations were looking internally at divesting and rebuilding their consulting businesses. Deloitte's approach was based on the following strategic choices:

1. Collaborate as *one Deloitte team*, going to market with a portfolio of businesses that can team effectively to serve clients with distinction.

2. Develop and maintain *four world-class* businesses (audit, tax, consulting and corporate finance).

3. Attract and retain the best people, becoming known as the place *where the best choose to be*.

4. Be a *client-centric organization* and deliver exceptional client service with an *unrelenting focus on quality*.

5. *Own the high ground*, leading the profession in restoring public trust in auditing and business advisory services.

We planned to drive incremental value for our clients by leveraging synergies across the different facets of our capability. The One Firm approach supported the delivery of more complex engagements. By offering co-ordinated support across a variety of different areas, clients received a more joined up and valuable service. Client relationships were strengthened and staff benefited from more challenging and rewarding work.

The 'One Firm' strategy started to break down internal barriers, with staff going to market as 'Deloitte' for all services, adopting an integrated approach to marketing supported by a high profile 'Have you asked Deloitte?' campaign. However, embedding this culture needed considerable effort and required incentives. Our lessons learned include:

- The approach requires staff (especially senior managers and above) to understand all the firm's service lines. This does not mean making a technology consultant an expert in tax, for example, but it does mean that the technology consultant needs to understand where we can help clients on tax issues and who to go to for advice on this internally.

- Firm-wide propositions are necessary so that clients can understand the value of having a broad and end-to-end service offering at their disposal. We invested in the development and marketing of propositions such as 'Business Critical Programmes', 'Enterprise Cost Reduction' and 'Finance Transformation'.

- It is key to focus on relationships within current and target clients. We established cross-firm client target lists, representing a balance of industries and organizational maturity. We targeted and approached these organizations in a co-ordinated manner, drawing on our full range of competencies.

- Forming multi-disciplinary client teams and account development teams gives huge benefits in cross-fertilization of ideas and skills and understanding of other areas of the business.

- It is important to formally recognize cross service line activity and referrals. Our assessments of partner and staff performance recognize sales for any service line as strongly as the originator's own service line.

- Communication of examples and rewarding of successes is important and needs to be constantly reinforced.

- The co-ordinated approach needs to be applied at all levels of the organization, not just partners, in order for it to be successful.

Deloitte's strategy has:

- differentiated the firm in the market place through unmatched breadth and depth of services;

- created an ability to deliver comprehensive solutions and become 'advisor of choice' for clients;

- introduced a more collaborative culture;

- facilitated the delivery of more challenging and interesting engagements;

- through the above, created a reputation that has helped the firm to attract and retain the best talent.

However the market and competitor landscape continues to evolve and as such so too does Deloitte's strategy and approach to maintain and further expand its position.

Questions

1. In what ways might a consultancy structure its workforce to maximize its success?

2. What advantages does a consultancy offer compared to a team of contractors?

3. What are the key advantages of a 'full service' consultancy compared with a more niche operator?

Further Reading

Ferguson, M. (2002), *The Rise of Management Consulting in Britain.* Aldershot: Ashgate

Fincham, R. and Clark, T. (2003), Management consultancy: Issues, perspectives, and agendas, *International Studies of Management & Organization*, 32(4), 3–18

Kipping, M. (2002), Trapped in their wave: The evolution of management consultancies, in Clark, T. and Fincham, R. Eds *Critical Consulting: New Perspectives on the Management Advice Industry.* Oxford: Blackwell Publishers Ltd

McKenna, C.D. (2006a), *The World's Newest Profession: Management Consulting in the Twentieth Century.* New York: Cambridge University Press

Riordan, W. (2009), A brief history of the management consulting profession. *Careers in Business* Retrieved from http://www.careers-in-business.com/consulting/hist.htm

Saint-Martin, D. (2000), *Building the New Managerialist State: Consultants and the Politics of Public Sector Reform in Comparative Perspective.* Oxford: Oxford University Press

CHAPTER **2**

Benefits and critiques of consultancy

Learning Objectives

At the end of this chapter students will be able to:

- Distinguish management consultancy both as a practice and an industry
- Be able to define management consultancy
- Appreciate the academic debate in terms of criticisms raised towards the industry and practice
- Be knowledgeable about impression management as a criticism of the industry
- Recognize that some aspects of the job of a management consultant can be quite temporary in nature although they are permanently employed
- Have an appreciation of the Johari model
- Apply the Johari model to organizations explaining the benefits of management consultancies
- Understand other benefits of management consultancy proposed by recent research with consultants and clients

---

Mini Case Study 2.1

HIV/AIDS epidemic strategic simulation

The global HIV/AIDS epidemic is at the inter-section of public health, political policy, and corporate interests, confronting all humanity with the greatest challenge of our age. In October 2003, Booz Allen focused firmwide expertise on this most complex issue, hosting a groundbreaking HIV/AIDS strategic simulation in India.

Working with the Global Business Coalition on HIV/AIDS and the Confederation of Indian Industry, Booz Allen brought together a diverse mix of more than 200 government, business, and nonprofit leaders to the three-day simulation event – a risk-free environment in which participants could test possible courses of action and see the potential economic, social, and political impacts of each. Conducted in New Delhi, the event was an unprecedented gathering of public and private leaders to explore how to address the growing HIV/AIDS epidemic in India through multisector partnerships.

The premise of the simulation was the need for public–private collaboration. Governments cannot and should not handle the burden of this epidemic alone. The scope of the challenge requires the resources and expertise of the business community and the nonprofit sector as well.

The setting of the simulation underscored the urgency of the situation. India now accounts for about four million HIV/AIDS cases, and the number could grow as much as ten-fold by 2025. With that kind of growth, India's HIV/AIDS population in 2025 would dwarf the current global burden. The growing crisis has the potential to reverse India's significant recent economic growth and disrupt political stability – an issue of equal concern to business and government stakeholders. The simulation showed that India still has an opportunity to act and alter the course of the epidemic.

Participants included national governments grappling with the implications of this growing pandemic, businesses attuned to the economic consequences, donors responsible for funding choices, and civil society leaders fighting every day to stop further spread of the disease and support those living with it.

'Booz Allen brought an approach to the issue of HIV/AIDS that has rarely been used', says Trevor Neilson, the executive director of the Global Business Coalition on HIV/AIDS.

> The simulation gave policy leaders a new way of collaborating that allowed them to understand the impact of their decision making, so

that those leaders were able to see they had an opportunity, and that decisive action on their part could lead to millions of lives saved.

Participants were divided into nine teams representing industry, government, and civil society stakeholders, with a mix of sector representatives assigned to each team. The simulated epidemic evolved as a result of actions taken by the teams. Ten years' time was simulated over a series of three moves, forcing participants to address real-world dilemmas and choices, and to manage the short- and long-term consequences of their actions.

Over the course of the simulation, teams experienced first hand the consequences of relying on broad prevention and education programmes as the disease spread rapidly to the middle class. They grappled with the challenges of funding constraints, as they rushed to develop programmes. The cumulative effects of all their actions were calculated in real time at the end of each 'move', enabling participants to see the impact of different courses of action, for instance, the number of infections and deaths avoided through disease prevention and treatment programmes and the impact of the disease on overall gross domestic product and the output of different market sectors.

Susan Penfield, a vice president in Booz Allen's McLean, Virginia office says:

> People came on Friday night and stayed the entire weekend because they felt compelled to be there . . . Some came from far away, and there was a large local Indian contingent as well. They were passionate about this cause, about figuring out ways to do things differently, for India. They want to change, want to own the challenges. Experiencing it, I myself felt changed coming back.

Ratan Tata, chairman of Tata Sons and chairman of the Indian Business Trust for HIV/AIDS, says:

> The simulation exercise was so creative that it has motivated the 200 participants, from across the world, but especially from India, to make a new level of commitment to the HIV/AIDS

issue ... I believe there is a crucial need for an explosion of new initiatives and new partnerships in India, which will make an enormous difference in addressing this issue in the future.

New partnerships

One such initiative that is already under way is Tata Steel's expansion of its well-established workplace and community activities to encourage effective HIV/AIDS prevention through mass awareness and education. In Jamshedpur, India, the company has 21 community clinics serving 140 000 people that can be scaled up to accommodate testing and treatment services for the community.

Neilson says:

The simulation led to new partnerships between government and business, and new corporate HIV/AIDS programmes being announced by Indian businesses ... Booz Allen had a catalytic effect on India on this issue at a time when India really needed it. We're planning next to do it in China, and we'd like to do it in as many places as possible.

Source: http://www.boozallen.com/about/article/9510078. Reproduced with permission from Booz Allen Hamilton.

Introduction

In the last chapter, the rise of the management consultancy industry was documented with leading authorities on the subject giving an in-depth view of the start and progression of the industry. This chapter follows on from this, examining why organizations, governments or countries (such as demonstrated in Mini Case Study 2.1) should need consultancy services, and discussing the benefits and criticisms of the industry.

What is Management Consultancy

A definition

Management consulting can be defined as both an industry and a practice. The practice and the industry aid organizations or larger concerns to improve their performance, by the analysis of existing issues and through the development of improvement plans. The professional body of management consultants in the UK, the Management Consultancies Association (MCA) define it as:

> Management consultancy is the creation of value for organizations, through the application of knowledge, techniques and assets, to improve performance. This is achieved through the rendering of objective advice and/or the implementation of business solutions.
> *Cited from Alan Leaman writing for Inside Careers, 2008; p. 15*

Adding value

From the MCA definition above the creation of value for organization is of the utmost concern for the management consultancy industry. Adding value is also often quoted in the literature generated by consultancies (Clark and Salaman,

1998a). For example, the Office of Government Commerce (2006) produced a guide with the MCA and Institute of Management Consultancy (now the Institute of Business Consulting) specifically for the public sector demonstrating how consultants can add value. In this guide, a simple framework is promoted for use with hiring consultants on public sector projects and for giving sound advice. The framework calls for civil servants to determine the capacity in which consultants are engaged and their role in project delivery (Office of Government Commerce, 2006).

However, some would argue that adding value to a client is not the chief aim of the management consultancy industry (Clark, 1995; Fincham, 1995). Their aim has more to do with impression management and convincing managers that they need consultants that are familiar with the latest management know-how (Fincham, 1995).

An understanding of the critical literature is needed to have a balanced view of the industry. The next section details the criticism raised at the industry primarily from an academic perspective. In other chapters, this critical review is also retained to ensure a balanced well-read view of the industry, especially in Chapter 16 where some of the more vocal critics are considered (e.g., Craig, 2005, 2006; McKenna, 2006a).

Criticism of the Industry

Most individuals have heard the joke that originated in the 1960s that 'a management consultant is someone who will borrow your watch to tell you the time' (Sturdy, Handley, Clark and Fincham, 2009). The early management consultancy literature examined the process of using consultants for the contracting manager (Bellman, 1971, 1972; Frankenhuis, 1977; Kelley, 1979) or the practice of being either an external or internal consultant (Bellman, 1973; Pinto and Noah, 1980; Robinson and Younglove, 1984; Schaffer, 1976; Scharf, 1987). However, by the mid 1990s, academics turned their attention critically on the management consultancy industry using a variety of perspectives ranging from the historical (McKenna, 1996) through to the more business orientated (Clark and Salaman, 1998a, 1998b; Fincham, 1995). These perspectives will now be examined in depth.

Management rhetoric

Clark (1995) was perhaps the first person to examine the industry in a critical light in his well-regarded book. He reported that the industry had grown approximately 200 per cent from 1985 to 1992 in contrast to the growth in manufacturing at 6 per cent and the service sector at 30 per cent. Clark (1995) stated there were two reasons for this increase in business. Organizations feel the need to react in response to their changing external environment. This means 'embarking on programmes of profound organizational change' (Clark, 1995; p. 2). Secondly due to the need for change, managers have to possess new values, skills and qualities necessary to lead the change or at least kick start the process. If managers do not have these skills, and Clark (1995) argued that management consultancies may convince managers that they do not, then this gives rise to the need to employ consultants.

Clark (1995) argued that through rhetoric and persuasion, management consultants convince their clients that they need their services. This is especially so during turbulent times. Nonetheless, Clark (1995) argued that there hasn't really been a time in economic history where the economy was stable and non-turbulent. Yet, it is the promotion of the need for change to managers, even in less turbulent times, that has led to the formation and phenomenal increase of the management consultancy industry according to Clark (1995).

Fincham (1995), another influential academic in the consultancy field, built upon the ideas put forward by Clark (1995). He concentrated on two aspects of consultancy practice, namely business process reengineering (BPR) and the commodification of managerial knowledge.

Fincham (1995) noted that consultants have their knowledge:

> packaged and honed, shaped to meet clients' needs, and transmitted via a range of sales media.
>
> *Cited from Fincham, 1995; p. 707*

BPR had been made popular by Hammer and Champy (1993) according to Fincham (1995). This book has undoubtedly been popular selling two million copies worldwide (Fincham, 1995; Saint-Martin, 2000). Other authors, such as Obolensky (1994), have also benefited from this need for BPR knowledge by the managerial community (Fincham, 1995). Fincham (1995) described BPR as a management fad but also as a change agent that succeeded previous fads such as 'excellence' and culture.

Fincham (1995) explicitly stated that he did not want to examine whether or not BPR works. Instead, he investigated why BPR had such a high market value in terms of management knowledge. Fincham (1995) believed that writing a bestselling book was by far the most effective way of reaching and influencing millions of managers. Indeed, in Chapter 1 it was noted that launching a practice-based consultancy book had a massive knock-on effect for the consultancy where in one instance it doubled the revenue received (Saint-Martin, 2000). Fincham (1995) further argued that once the consultancy technique was out there in the wider domain, managers would clamber to get hold of consultants who knew how to put the techniques, exemplified by the published book, into practice.

Fincham (1995) felt that most of the techniques, such as BPR, put forward were too simplistic for the real world. Boldly, he suggested that if managers bought into such techniques then they were rather naïve. Fincham (1995) explained that this was because most managerial fads stripped out the uncertainties associated with the real world. Later Fincham (1995) warned that BPR could mean job losses and lead to job insecurity rather than an empowered workforce as it allegedly claimed. Nevertheless, Hammer and Champy (2001) argued that BPR does not necessarily equate to jobs being lost. Instead, the practice involves business practices being improved through analysing them in a systematic fashion.

Undoubtedly, although BPR is still used today (Bevilacqua, Ciarapica and Giacchetta, 2009; Hammer and Champy, 2001; Lin, Fan and Newman, 2009) it still has a huge amount of hype surrounding the concept (Vergidis, Turner and Tiwari, 2008). Vergidis *et al.* (2008) contended that only by using the sophisticated theoretical developments in dealing with business processes can business benefits be realized. They argued that most marketable forms of BPR or business process management (BPM) were simplified, watered down versions of more complicated techniques since developed. A position that Clark (1995) and Fincham (1995) would argue was true with their main criticism being that these watered down techniques don't necessarily work well in the real world but are promoted by management consultancy hype. However, it is then only through employing management consultants that the more complicated techniques are used.

Industry snapshot 2.1 illustrates this point whereby the original request by the client to analyse its departments in terms of a particular model was amended in favour of more in-depth qualitative techniques. Critics may argue that this is an example of where a consultancy enhances their fees by expanding the original brief of the project in their favour due to the additional time taken to complete the project. Conversely, if the consultancy had not changed the project design and just delivered what the client had originally decided upon then this arguably would have been bad practice as it was foreseeable that using the technique suggested by the client would not have given them the detailed information on individual and team-working practices they required.

Industry snapshot 2.1

Changing the scope of a programme to improve the client service

A client commissioned a project investigating the different ways in which it could work with subcontractors who were essential for the client's core business. In concluding this project, a small one day conference was held. The client who occupied a geographically remote site had a number of experts flown in to present during the day. One of the presentations regarded team-working and relied heavily upon Belbin Team roles to explain team-working to the client.

The client was so impressed with the Belbin Team role model that they approached the consultant who gave the presentation for more information. From this discussion they decided to commission a number of projects examining team roles within the different departments at the site. The client was firmly wedded to the Belbin Team role concept; however, after further discussion it became apparent that the use of this model alone would not be enough to satisfy their needs. This was discussed directly with the client and then the subsequent proposal promoted in-depth qualitative research, which would investigate a wide variety of individual and team-working practices.

The project was very successful and was repeated in other departments after the analysis had been completed.

Thought Provoking point 2.1

Managers love the Myers Briggs Type Indicator

A very popular type based measure used by managers is the MBTI, based on the augmented ideas of Carl Jung. Nevertheless is the MBTI's popularity with management due to its strong theoretical underpinnings or the oversimplification of human relations and behaviour?

Clark and Salaman (1998a, 1998b) argued that not only convincing a client of the consultancy's worth was important but so was impression management. Indeed, Thought Provoking point 2.2 has probably been considered by most students reading this text, whereby impressions are important. Furthermore, in Chapter 1, McKenna (2006a) demonstrated how impression management worked in the early industry with Marvin Bower decreeing what consultants should wear.

Thought Provoking point 2.2

Don't wear character socks to an interview

Although I have spent a lot of time in my career reducing the biases of employing managers, one disagreement I lost was in a management consultancy. The senior recruitment director refused to take on someone due to wearing character socks. The candidate was fairly weak but I did worry that the socks did sway the recruitment decision.

Clark and Salaman (1998a) developed the idea of impression management building on the work of Clark (1995) using the concept of a dramaturgical metaphor. The idea behind this is that procurement managers employing the services of management consultants have an inability to determine the quality of the consultancy, they in effect, 'don't know what they are getting until they get it' (Clark and Salaman, 1998a; p. 35). In this respect, consultants have to create favourable impressions to their clients conveying somehow the value that they add to their business. In conclusion, they added:

> Management consultancies are therefore 'systems of persuasion' par excellence and impression management is not external to the core of their work but is at its core.
>
> *Clark and Salaman (1998a); p. 35.*

Igo and Skitmore (2006) researched the opinion of employees in management consultancies. They reported that according to those that work in the industry most consultancies tend to have a dominant market-oriented culture rather than a more developmental one. This would seem to support Clark and Salaman's (1998a) claim that impression management through marketing activities is at the core of the management consultancy industry. Conversely, marketing is at the heart of many organizations even in the public sector where government agencies have to advertise what they do for members of the general public (even the security agencies – as shown in Figure 2.1.)

Kieser (2002) also added to the critical view of the management consultancy industry using fashion theories. He defined a management concept as:

> A discourse that evolves around a buzzword like Scientific Management, Fordism, Lean Production, or Re-engineering.
>
> *Kieser (2002); p. 167*

This discourse, Kieser (2002) argued, may then become written text either through management books, as Fincham (1995) suggested, or in popular articles and consultancy marketing material and presentations. The idea of a management

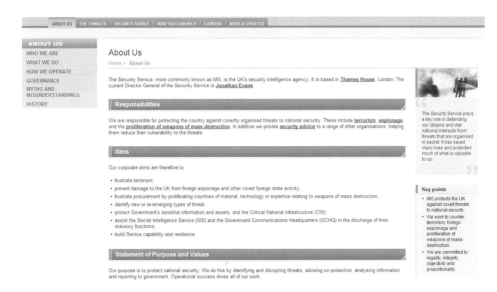

Figure 2.1

MI5 about us (retrieved from http://www.http://www.mi5.gov.uk/output/about-us.html). Crown copyright, 2009

concept is according to Kieser (2002) at best an extension of the original idea associated with the buzzword. Management concepts may be either deliberately or not vague, as 'what is meant by [the concept of] empowerment' (Kieser, 2002; p. 168). This vagueness instigates a discussion about the concept, which may be in printed form. It will at the very least encourage consultants, managers, and then business school professors to investigate the management concept and as such may even enter the academic arena.

A management fashion is when a management concept becomes fashionable (Kieser, 2002). The management concept may come first and then become fashionable, or conversely a management fashion may be discussed in various printed forms and then become a management concept. Kieser (2002) investigated different types of fashion theory applying it to the area of management consultancy. He suggested that out of the four major paradigms (trickle down theories, collective selection theories, marionette theories and ambivalence theories) that marionette theories were the most applicable. Marionette theories state that a producer in a capitalist economy invents a fashion which gives a fictitious advantage that can be achieved when a real benefit cannot be attained.

Entrepreneurs place an emphasis on greater elegance or prestige that an item or service has, which translates to adding value where basically there isn't any (Kieser, 2002). So this practice appeals to an individual's pride (Kieser, 2002). He further added that the same principle can be applied to management consultancy. Firms increasingly demand consultancy services so that their perceived value can be realized within their organization. The important aspect here is that it is just a perception of value rather than a real level of value added. Figure 2.2 demonstrates how this process works. Management fashions lead to a perceived loss of control by managers. Managers who then wish to have that control back employ consultancy services to achieve this.

Going even further, Kieser (2002) argued that consultants invoke fear in their clients and raise their hopes, encouraging greed. Thus, if a client doesn't take up the services of a consultancy, they face bankruptcy – the fear aspect. And if a client

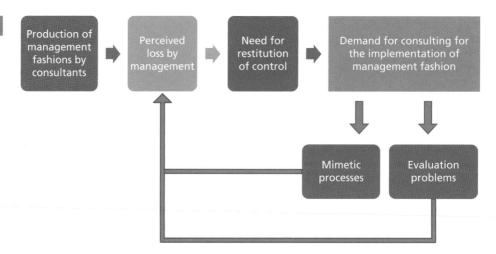

Figure 2.2

A model for explaining management consultancy growth. Adapted from Kieser (2002); p. 173

does take up the consultancy services they are likely to restitute their control within the business, sell more and increase success – the hope and greed aspect. This impression is created in four ways:

1. Offering instruments, such a the Boston Consulting Group (BCG) matrix to the client
2. Providing a more business orientated language socialising the manager so that they convey the illusion of control
3. Convincing the client that consultants can foresee threats of the future.
4. Basing the purveyed concepts from the consultancy on real management issues

Impression management is certainly a criticism of the industry. Nevertheless, it is an important concept in consultancy in creating a good client relationship, as explored further in Chapters 5 and 6. Without a doubt, the critics of the industry suggesting that consultants just seek to impress clients with management rhetoric, would find it difficult to justify the massive increase in the industry. Indeed, Fincham (1999) himself stated that consultancy work and consultancy strategies do add value and a critical understanding to the client. Furthermore, Marsh (2009) challenges the stereotypical images of the slick showman aiming to maximize his fees. Indeed, she suggested that throughout history individuals have given advice, from the Greeks through to the Renaissance and into the modern day; this is the value added to organizations that the MCA defining the industry and practice imply.

Outsourcing difficult decisions

Kieser (2002) argued that due to the lack of control that managers feel and the need to reassert this control, consultancies are employed. McKenna (2006a) indicated that one of the functions of management consultants is to support difficult operational decisions in the organization. Indeed, in Chapter 16 it is noted that McKenna (2006a) believed this is a future strand of the consultancy industry especially given the credit crunch in 2008 and subsequent economic crisis.

In this regard, the manager can almost outsource the rationale for unpopular decisions such as making people redundant to the consultancy (Ringland and Shaukat, 2004). This was a popular use of consultancies back in the late 1980s when most global economies were in recession and is likely, as McKenna suggested in his interview, to be prevalent in 2009 onwards (See Industry snapshot 16.1).

Nevertheless, Bäcklund and Werr (2008) examined the big four consultancies comprising of Accenture, BCG, KPMG and McKinsey & Co in terms of their marketing material and self presentations to clients. They argued that rather than superseding the client in terms of making an unpopular decision, consultancies act in a way that stands by their client supporting them rather than replacing them. The view that consultancies do aid companies to make difficult decisions therefore requires further research to fully explore this issue.

The consultant in the industry

The consultancy industry is notoriously a tough but rewarding environment to work in (Sadler, 2001). Yet again there is a paucity of research in this area. In Chapter 14, the eight consultancy competency framework was created from job analysis taken from two different consultancies. This demonstrates some of the difficult behaviours that need to be mastered by the consultant to perform well in the industry, such as tolerance for stress and uncertainty. Nevertheless, there has been other academic interest in the individual consultant in the industry.

Barley and Kunda (2004) investigated IT consultants though concentrated on fixed term contractors. They demonstrated how these contractors form their own identity and many especially the younger contractors:

> felt the pain of estrangement. Many wanted to be accepted as legitimate members of the community to which they were temporarily attached and saw the limits placed on their membership as a form of rejection.
>
> *Barley and Kunda, (2004); p. 215*

Thus, consultants often thought of themselves as outsiders even though they really wanted to display 100 per cent commitment to the company in a similar way to other temporary members of staff (Biggs and Swailes, 2006). Interestingly, consultants occupying both the commissioned based workers and consultants without commissions sections can be directly contrasted to contractors and other temporary staff as shown in Figure 2.3.

Figure 2.3 demonstrates that although there is a clear line between permanent and temporary jobs. There is, however, like in the concept of yin and yang, some temporary aspect in permanent jobs and some permanent aspect in temporary jobs. Individuals for whom the commission received from sales, or other work, forms the majority of their salary, such as commission only consultants, are the most temporary of all permanent workers. This is because if their sales or work declines they will have to tolerate a reduction in income. However, due to the risk involved with this, often these types of individuals do very well financially as long as they are actively employed. Recent research has indicated that although individuals may have much of their overall income removed if they do not reach their target sales figure, demonstrating the temporary nature of their work, they still insist that they are permanent workers (Biggs and Toms, In Prep.). This is in line with Figure 2.3 that clearly delineates between permanent and temporary workers, but shows how each may have both permanent and temporary aspects as in the Chinese principle of yin and yang.

Consultants who do not get a direct commission from their work still proceed from one assignment to another, like fixed term contractors or agency workers. In

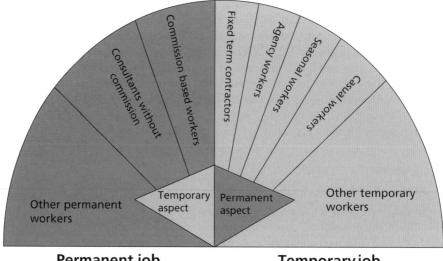

Figure 2.3

Yin and yang of
permanent and
temporary work

this regard, the old consultancy saying, that 'you are as good as your last project' comes into mind here, and while the consultant is protected, like every other permanent employee in legal terms (Biggs *et al.*, 2006) there is an aspect of being temporary as shown in Figure 2.3.

Thought Provoking point 2.3

I have not done the same job for the last 35 years

Being an occupational psychologist, I am always fascinated by what people do in their working careers. I was once quite taken aback when a Director of a consultancy said that he had worked there for over 35 years, which at the time had been longer than I was born. I asked him whether he had ever had got bored of the same job, to which he replied, 'this job has never been the same, it varies not so much day to day but definitely month to month and year to year – else I would have never have stuck with it!'

Costas and Fleming (2009) investigated the personal experience of an individual consultant within a leading multinational global consultancy. They used 16 semi-structured interviews with consultants and participant observation of 12 human resource based workshops. Interestingly, they found that there was an experience of 'self-alienation' reported primarily as what the consultancy required them to do was incongruent to their own self.

Sturdy (1998) commented that if employees are expected to behave in a manner in which they may not necessarily feel entirely comfortable as has been found in the management consultancy industry (Costas and Fleming, 2009), then often what will arise are attitudes of cynicism. Additionally, humour may provide relief as has been found in other occupations such as teaching (Hurren, 2006). In consultancy protecting the real self from the perceived environment may be achieved through remarks about:

1. Absent third parties, e.g., competitors
2. Consultants
3. Clients (although rarely made and often not directly critical).

The use of humour is important in protecting the individual who seeks to get the occasional break from the serious nature of the industry. This point is highlighted by Costas and Fleming (2009) who cite a consultant saying:

> I think there is a point in consultancy when your work person becomes more of who you are even outside of work and those original things . . . that made you as a person interesting, becomes secondary to who you are.
>
> *Costas and Fleming (2009); p. 370*

Developing an ability to laugh at aspects of the job thus may help protect against this self-alienation (Sturdy *et al.*, 2009). Humour is also essential to develop rapport with the client and to create a team based working environment where people get along with each other despite the fiercely competitive nature of the work that they face (Sturdy *et al.*, 2009).

Benefits of the Industry

Why use consultants? – Back to basics

Earlier on in the chapter, it was argued that the chief reason that consultants are employed is to add value to the organization that procured the consultancy. Throughout the text, this will be demonstrated further by providing detail on how and why consultancy operates. Nonetheless, before closing this chapter, it would be interesting to explore the basic reasons for employing consultants.

The Johari window

Luft and Ingram (1955) developed a system of assessing a person's individual and interpersonal awareness. They coined the phrase the Johari window using a combination of their first names, Joseph and Harry. Luft and Ingram (1955) had a list of 55 adjectives that a person and others that knew the person would concentrate on (see Table 2.1). From this list, the individual would use the adjectives to describe what they felt was known to others and then unknown to others. This formed the two quadrants of the arena or public self and the façade or the hidden self. The adjectives were then used by others that knew the individuals. Those adjectives that both the others and the individual had labelled as known to self, were in the public self quadrant. Anything else was known by others but not by the individual were listed as blind spots. A further quadrant was also revealed in that adjectives not selected by either the individual or the others were in the unknown or unconscious self (see Figure 2.4).

There are numerous variations of the Johari window as it is commonly modified for personal development. Its purpose is to reveal the four quadrants

Table 2.1		Adjectives used to create the Johari window				
able	accepting	adaptable	bold	brave	calm	caring
cheerful	clever	complex	confident	dependable	dignified	energetic
extroverted	friendly	giving	happy	helpful	idealistic	independent
ingenious	intelligent	introverted	kind	knowledgeable	logical	loving
mature	modest	nervous	observant	organized	patient	powerful
proud	quiet	reflective	relaxed	religious	responsive	searching
self-assertive	self-conscious	sensible	sentimental	shy	silly	spontaneous
sympathetic	tense	trustworthy	warm	wise	witty	

Source: Luft and Ingram (1955)

and then increase the public self. This is done by seeking feedback from others where an individual can reveal his or her blind spots. Nevertheless, often people will not give feedback voluntarily unless the individual reveals something personal about themselves from the hidden self quadrant, e.g., a person says I feel nervous in presenting to large groups, the person giving the feedback then states that they shouldn't feel nervous as they present well; nevertheless perhaps they should consider pausing more as sometimes it is as though they are rushing through their speech. The purpose of using the Johari window in personal development is to enlarge the public self and reduce the blind spots, the hidden self and also encroach upon the unconscious or unknown self.

The Johari window can also be applied to organizations, with the top management being the individual and the rest of the organization being the others (see Figure 2.5). How consultancies can add value in this circumstance is by reducing conflict between management and the rest of the organization. Blind spots are uncovered through staff engagement and surveys. Management can also be more open and honest about their strategies again encouraging staff to speak out. The consultancy, or an external body, can also reveal the hidden aspects of the organization that both the staff and management cannot see. This means getting into the 'unconscious' or unknown area of the business, which is where consultancy can provide the greatest value.

Figure 2.4

The Johari window. Adapted from Luft and Ingram (1955)

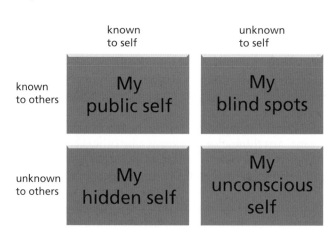

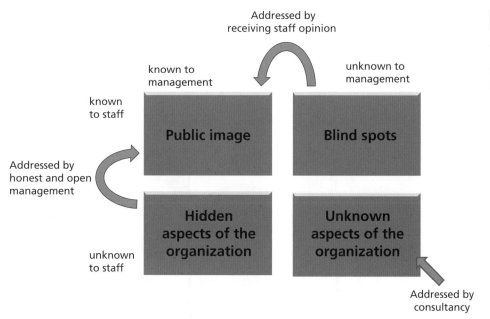

Figure 2.5

The Johari window applied to organizations

Thought Provoking point 2.4

A Birmingham rubber manufacturer at the point of collapse

The Managing Director of a Birmingham rubber manufacturing plant had put two mortgages on his home and accrued much in the way of debt to try and keep his company afloat. Yet, none of the staff were aware of the financial trouble the company was in and were putting in extensive claims for overtime to try and keep up the business. So using the concept of the Johari window model, the consultancy encouraged the MD to reveal the 'hidden aspects' of the firm, while we worked on revealing the unknown elements, such as strange processes, delays in engineering aspects and conflicts within the organization.

Ringland and Shaukat (2004) before they investigated the future of the industry with 120 consultants and industry clients, used global data from three professional bodies (MCA, IMC and AMCF) and research conducted by Capital Energy to ascertain the key reasons why management consultants are employed. These results are given in Figure 2.6. Five areas were revealed to be of importance consisting of: implementation, specialist knowledge, blame, independence/impartiality and finally validation/assurance.

Ringland and Shaukat (2004) demonstrated that consultancies were hired for a variety of reasons shown in Figure 2.6. These reasons ranged from providing their specialized expertise to giving temporary assistance during a finite project through implementation.

Ringland and Shaukat (2004) argued that because management consultancies are exposed to numerous issues and problems throughout the global economy. They develop their expertise and become aware of the industry's 'best practices' becoming experts (as one section of Figure 2.6 demonstrates).

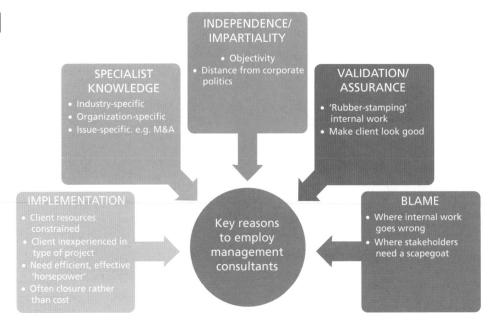

Figure 2.6

Key reasons to employ management consultants. Adapted from Ringland and Shaukat (2004)

Though the transferability of these best practices may be the subject of debate (Kieser, 2002; Sturdy *et al.*, 2009). It is likely that consultancies are able to add value to organizations that hire them. The remaining chapters within this text will critically examine both the practice and the industry of management consultancy.

Chapter Summary

- The MCA's definition of management consultancy clearly states that its concern is to create value for organizations
- Critics of the industry suggest adding value is not of primary concern but impression management is at the core
- Clark (1995) examined management rhetoric suggesting this had more to do with the increase of the industry rather than purely adding value to client organizations
- Fincham (1995) suggested that the creation of a fad was best achieved through writing a popular management book
- Critics argue that watered down techniques don't necessarily work well in the real world but are promoted by hype
- Management consultancies do have a dominant market-oriented culture
- Kieser (2002) applied marionette fashion theories to the industry stating that false benefits were promoted as real ones could not be realized
- Marsh (2009) challenged the impression management angle suggesting that the notion of a slick showman aiming to maximize his fees through suave methods was deceiving

- Recent research has revealed the tough nature of the consultancy lifestyle but more studies are needed in this area
- Humour is often used as a way for the individual to retain their sanity in a serious and demanding world (Sturdy, et al,. 2009)
- Luft and Ingram (1955) developed the Johari window model, which can be applied to individuals and individual organizations revealing where issues have failed
- Ringland and Shaukat (2004) summarized research that found management consultancies were employed in five key areas consisting of:

  - implementation
  - specialist knowledge
  - blame
  - independence/impartiality
  - validation/assurance.

Review Questions

1. What is the definition of management consultancy?
2. What does 'adding value' entail?
3. Describe briefly the concept of impression management.
4. What were the two reasons given by Clark (1995) for the 200 per cent increase in the management consultancy industry?
5. What according to Fincham (1995) is the best way of reaching and influencing millions of managers?
6. Define a management fashion.
7. What two opposing feelings did Kieser (2002) state that consultants may invoke in their clients to increase their sales prospects?
8. What is the Johari window?
9. What were the five areas where consultants were employed according to Ringland and Shaukat (2004)?

Assignment Questions

1. Management consultancy can be equally described as a practice and an industry. Critically evaluate this claim.
2. Ascertain whether Clark (1995) is correct in his claim that impression management is core to management consultancy, using examples where necessary.
3. Are management concepts and management fashions interrelated?
4. Critically evaluate whether the advice from management consultants is used to support or supersede unpopular business decisions.

Case Study 2.1

Applied Sonics Special Products (ASSP)

By Terry Mughan, Anglia Ruskin University

Applied Sonics Special Products (ASSP) is the Suffolk-based Acoustic Materials arm of Applied Sonics UK (ASUK). International markets play a key part in its future but progress so far in growing this business has been hampered by a lack of knowledge and skills in this area.

The company

ASSP converts foam into acoustic materials products for the marine and construction industries to suppress noise using advanced design and fitting techniques. It employs 50 people and has an annual turnover of approximately £4 million. It currently exports between 10–15 per cent of its total sales. The company was drawn into international activities by the shift of UK manufacturing activities to Eastern Europe but now see overseas markets as a core part of their future business. Phillip Morgan, Sales Director, enlisted the help of The Applied Business University to try to 'Europeanize' ASSP and improve knowledge of international markets. He sees exporting as a major element of future growth for the company.

Our company has been successful in the UK market but we are feeling the pinch of competition from overseas. We need people who understand overseas markets and clients so that we can get all possible benefits from overseas clients in terms not just of sales but also of product innovation.

The business issue

Phillip's sensitivity to the need to work better with foreign clients stems from the company's efforts to sell into the French market. ASSP made numerous approaches to the biggest player there but never seemed able to get their foot in the door. Although they are sure they have a better product to offer than the existing supplier the French company seemed remarkably complacent, even bureaucratic. Most importantly, the French client expected ASSP to speak and write French in all their prospecting communication. Applied Sonics had neither the language skills nor the knowledge of the French market to deal with this challenge. Although they had participated in UKTI's Passport to Export Success programme, which advises on the use of translators and interpreters, they were sure that they needed to find a more embedded solution.

Finding a solution

This experience prompted ASSP to act on two levels. Phillip approached his UKTI Advisor in Suffolk, Roger Baker, to look into ways of bringing the language resource into the company. Roger put Phillip in touch with The Applied Business University who had been working with UKTI for some time to try to set up a foreign language student placement scheme. Phillip decided to apply for a student under a funded scheme that had just been introduced in the East of England. The plan was to employ a languages graduate who would also develop a new European sales strategy. The application was successful and a French-speaking graduate was found and employed. Phillip signed up and Applied Sonics Special products suddenly had an impressive range of resources at its disposal.

Business impact

Applied Sonics UK was simultaneously going through large-scale review and internal restructuring. The three branches in the UK had traditionally operated more or less independently but changes in the market were making this costly and inefficient. ASSP's international sales strategy was therefore closely monitored with a view to informing the new strategy. A full study of prospective markets was carried out and it was decided to focus the strategy on the marine sector. Four European markets, France, Spain, Italy and Denmark were

▶

earmarked for fuller investigation and exploratory visits. European exhibitions were targeted as key sources of leads and a more comprehensive relationship management approach was developed. Immediate efforts were made to develop a better working relationship with the key French and Spanish clients as these were the language and culture sensitive markets. The Applied Business team led workshops designed to improve understanding of the French clients and ways of doing business, immediately prior to critical visits being undertaken. The result of these visits was much more positive than on earlier occasions and the SSP team now understand better how the British approach to business needs to be modified in many international markets.

The dual approach to international sales taken by ASSP demonstrates how complex the challenge can be for a company of this size. Immediate resource is needed to drive the sales that justify the investment but skills and knowledge development need to be built at the same time. Managing this process across three geographically remote sites adds an extra level of complexity to the challenge, particularly when international markets require frequent communication and presence by sales staff. Whilst it was the case that each site manufactured different products, there was a traditional view that the office in Wales was 'Head Office' and that set the agenda on a strategy level across all sites.

Phillip is sure that university-level skills make a difference to his kind of company.

> We started off thinking that language skills were the only thing we needed. Europeanizing turned out to be a fair bit more than that. We need to learn about our clients and markets and ways of prioritizing them. The Applied Business gave us the opportunity to do this at a manageable cost. This has delivered tangible results in European markets.

The company-wide strategic review incorporated an assessment of the exporting progress made by Phillip at ASSP. It also looked at issues of governance, efficiency and synergies across the three company locations and for Phillip's board colleagues these matters turned out to be far more important than export sales figures. The review resulted in a new over-arching strategy which sought to obtain cost-reductions and marketing synergies across all locations and products of ASUK. This required of Phillip and his team a more coordinated role in a top-down strategy which drained his department of time and resources needed to build the foreign market proximity that was the key to sustainable improvement in export sales. He also lost the budgetary authority needed to commission further work with The Applied Business team and extend the contract of the graduate administrator.

Phillip does not regret instigating this project but feels that some benefits have been won and others lost.

> We know a lot more about the markets that matter to us now and can always build on this knowledge. I feel we have lost some momentum and have talked this through with the Board who understand my concerns. The company as a whole is moving forward now and I am sure we can build on the work we have done when the time is right.

Questions

1. How can a company like ASSP, with limited resources, seek out consulting support for international expansion? Think of the range of advice and consulting services available in the private and public sectors.

2. What are the key tools and objectives you would work towards in helping a company internationalize? Think of the full range of market entry methods and how you would envisage short and long-term objectives.

3. Does it make sense to develop an export sales strategy as a unique project, independently of broader marketing strategy?

4. What are the factors to be aware of when negotiating a contract with ASSP as a company? Could this contract have been put together better to guarantee a lasting solution for the company?

Further Reading

Barley, S.R. and Kunda, G. (2004), *Gurus, Hired Guns and Warm Bodies*. Princeton: Princeton University Press

Clark, T. and Fincham, R. Eds (2002), *Critical Consulting: New Perspectives on the Management Advice Industry*. Oxford: Blackwell Publishers Ltd

Clark, T. and Salaman, G. (1998a), Creating the 'right' impression: Towards a dramaturgy of management consultancy, *Service Industries Journal*, 18(1), 18–38

Costas, J. and Fleming, P. (2009), Beyond dis-identification: A discursive approach to self-alienation in contemporary organizations, *Human Relations*, 62(3), 353–378

Karantinou, K.M. and Hogg, M.K. (2001), Exploring relationship management in professional services: A study of management consultancy. *Journal of Marketing Management*, 17(3–4), 263–286

Sturdy, A., Handley, K., Clark, T. and Fincham, R. (2009), *Management Consultancy Boundaries and Knowledge in Action*. Oxford: Oxford University Press

Vergidis, K., Turner, C.J. and Tiwari, A. (2008), Business process perspectives: Theoretical developments vs. real-world practice, *International Journal of Production Economics*, 114(1), 91–104

CHAPTER 3

Different types of consultancy

Learning Objectives

At the end of this chapter students will be able to:

- Determine the different types of consultancy activity

- Recognize the difference between consultancies in terms of their generalist or specialist nature

- Understand that the size of a consultancy may bring different advantages and disadvantages

- Know that size will influence the type of assignment that the consultancy may go for or the collaborations it may make

- Recognize the fields of consultancy activity in terms of SMEs, public sector organizations, large corporations and international work

Mini Case Study 3.1

Building structural advantage (Accenture)

Winning companies see beyond today and toward the future state of the business. They look around corners and position the business for the transformational opportunities of the future. These strategic initiatives can be more difficult to execute, but they can also be the key to high performance for the business. Structural advantage is driven by efficiently managing the assets of the business. There are four pillars of structural advantage:

- Capital structure
- Organizational structure
- Geographic presence
- Portfolio of businesses.

To gain structural advantage, companies should assess and rationalize their portfolio of assets. Based on that analysis, they should consider changing the structure of the business if appropriate for the organization. Actions might include financial restructuring to improve debt to equity ratios, organizational consolidation and restructuring to improve agility, reconfiguring physical assets based on a global resource and site location strategy and acquiring or divesting businesses to reshape the portfolio of businesses for the future. Structural initiatives are intended to reduce the cost and complexity of the business operating model, drive long-term profitable growth and demonstrate multiyear expectations to the market.

As an example, Accenture worked with a high-tech equipment manufacturer to identify a 30 per cent cost reduction in real estate costs. The savings were driven by developing a global resource and site location strategy, which included extensive use of flexible office space for an increasingly mobile workforce and the alignment and consolidation of the efforts of each corporate function to use shared services out of low-cost locations so as to eliminate duplication of effort and redundant locations.

Accenture collaborates with many clients to pursue structural advantage. For instance, offshoring takes non-strategic processes performed by headquarters or business units and moves them offshore for lower costs and greater economies of scale. In addition, it's no secret that a sound acquisition strategy during a downturn can result in purchasing strategic assets well below market value. Accenture teams with its clients to contribute valuable insights for the client when it is considering target markets and potential acquisitions.

Running an onshore/offshore strategy team, Accenture is helping a communications client execute its acquisition strategy as part of its broader overall growth plan. Just like operating advantage initiatives, savings from structural advantage initiatives can also be used to help fund those acquisitions and drive greater synergies for the business.

Back in the late 1990s a large retail client experienced a 50 per cent decline in earnings before interest and tax (EBIT) and share price, its competitors were considering a takeover and its focus was on survival. During this crucial time, the retailer teamed with Accenture on a number of initiatives aimed at optimizing key capabilities and continually improving business performance. The results were dramatic as same-store sales increased by more than 15 per cent and market capitalization more than doubled. Good for the customer – good for the bottom line.

By 2004, the retailer had become the leader in its market. For high-performance businesses, the drive to stay ahead of the pack is never ending. Not content to rest on its success, the retailer teamed again with Accenture to continue its transformation to an even more customer-focused enterprise whilst also achieving additional cost savings.

Initiatives included IT and business process outsourcing, supply chain optimization, improved analytics and reporting, enhanced functionality and performance of websites, and the support of international and new business model expansions. Many of these initiatives already have achieved intended cost savings and value.

This is one of many examples of our ability to deliver high performance for our clients. RSCM is a dual effort, with operating advantage and structural advantage mutually important in building the sustained value of the company. That dual approach is a part of what makes the Accenture difference.

Source: Accenture, 2009, The Winning Edge in Uncertain Times. http://www.accenture.com/NR/rdonlyres/81CA32EA-606B-4890-BF51-D981C934AE9A/0/339200812_SCO_PDF_v18 LowRes_M.pdf%20(page%207). Reproduced with permission.

Introduction

The management consultancy industry is very vibrant as clients demand more and more from their consultancies (Czerniawska, 2008). Offshoring, as described in our opening case study, seems to be increasingly popular at the moment although it is always difficult to predict what lies in store for any industry (Czerniawska, 2008). Indeed, it is always difficult to quantify any industry or practice although this is the aim of the current chapter.

Some have described the management consultancy industry as 'very secretive' (Saint-Martin, 2000; p. 39). Many of the case studies published on management consultancy sites demonstrate only their successes but sometimes recognizing their failures is equally as important. Literature on the darker side of management consultancy has emerged, for instance, O'Shea and Madigan (1997). However, due to litigation concerns many of the more critical views of consulting have perhaps not been aired or are perhaps difficult to reach.

Often in the industry it is well known that 'you are as good as your last project'. Thus, advertising consultancy projects that have gone wrong is unlikely to happen internally let alone externally. Nevertheless, learning the pitfalls of management consultancy is essential for survival. One of these pitfalls is joining the wrong consultancy.

A person needs to select the most appropriate consultancy to join. For instance, an individual may be more suited towards say strategy consultancy, like BCG, or they may be more in-tune with a niche consultancy like JCA Occupational Psychologists who work through deeper level of attitudes, feelings and motivations to deliver practical benefits in the workplace.

Thought Provoking point 3.1 illustrates this on a humorous level. In essence, the internal consultant (myself) preferred that he was more externally facing and the external consultant (my colleague) wanted to be in an internal environment. From this thought provoking point it is clear that neither individual was in a consultancy of their choice. However, a few years later both individuals had moved into the roles they preferred.

Thought Provoking point 3.1

'I want your job', 'No, I want your job'

A colleague and I once described our experiences of our first jobs post Masters degree, with McKinsey and MFI, which for both of us had some limitations. Indeed, we both agreed that if we had had each other's jobs, we would have been much happier! Both of us were only at these organizations for a year mainly to add the experience on to our respective cv's, which is sometimes very wise to do straight after a Masters degree.

Different Types of Consultancy

Are consultancies different?

This chapter investigates the different types of consultancy out there in the twenty-first century drawing upon practitioner and academic knowledge. Czerniawska (1999) questions whether there is a differentiation between the management consultancies that exist. She used the comments from the 1996 consultancy report of Ernst & Young, Accenture, Coopers & Lybrand (now PWC) and KPMG to explore this point by illustrating that there was little differentiation between the consultancies.

Twelve years on from that time, in 2009 the point is still valid, so from the following statements can you pick out the consultancy?

- A well-planned and well-executed strategy lies at the heart of high performance. [We] help organizations create and implement breakthrough operational and transformational solutions. Our innovative strategies and our unique integration of business and IT strategy solutions enable high performance.

- Our Management Consulting business is focused on becoming the premier provider of transformation and delivery services. We provide a comprehensive range of services to a diverse range of clients across a number of markets in the UK.

- Part of Europe's largest multidisciplinary consulting firm, we are a leading provider of business, technology and project/programme consultancy to clients in the public and private sectors.

- [We have] nearly 60 years of experience worldwide covering a wide range of areas of expertise. Our work across many industries allows us to bring the best practice from one industry and apply it to another.

Again, just like Czerniawska (1999) argued it is difficult to ascertain the differences between the consultancies (who in 2009 are: Accenture, Mouchel, Atkins and Alexander Proudfoot), nevertheless, differentiation is there to perhaps more of a degree than the consultancies back in 1996 (Czerniawska, 1999). For instance, the first consultancy (Accenture) is certainly more strategy, change and IT driven. The second consultancy (Mouchel) is more generalist providing a 'comprehensive range of services' although they clearly want to be the 'premier provider of transformation and delivery services'. The third consultancy highlights its multidisciplinary basis, but again is fairly general being 'a leading supplier of business, technology and project/programme consultancy'. The last consultancy (Alexander Proudfoot) is also fairly generalist, covering 'a wide range of areas of expertise'.

Czerniawska (1999) argued that differentiation between consultancies is essential so that clients don't see all management consultancies 'as part of an indistinguishable mass' (Czerniawska, 1999; p. 68). Nevertheless, on the marketing side, it is clear that consultancies also want to generate the greatest amount of interest in their services. As such consultancies do not want to exclude possible areas of business that they could deliver. Here is the dilemma that consultancies face, do they become generalist or do they seek more specialist markets?

Generalist Versus Specialist

The Inside Careers (2009) booklet on the management consultancy industry stated that the types of firm within the business vary enormously. However, it broadly defines them in range from the large generalist consultancies, who offer end-to-end solutions, through to the more niche firms that offer more specialist skills.

Company	No. of Employees
A.T. Kearney	2,700 (worldwide)
The Boston Consulting Group	4,500
Capgemini	90,000 (worldwide); 10,000 (UK and Ireland)
Deloitte	150,000 (worldwide)
Diamond Management & Technology Consultants	c. 600
Ernst & Young	135,000 (worldwide)
Hewitt	c. 2,000 (UK)
IMS Consulting	120
LECG	850 plus (worldwide); 80 (London)
L.E.K. Consulting	850 plus
McKinsey & Company	9,000 (consultants)
Mercer	Over 3,000
Monitor Group	1,500
OC&C Strategy Consultants	460 (worldwide)
Oliver Wyman	2,900 plus
PA Consulting	3,000
PricewaterhouseCoopers LLP	c. 15,00 (UK)
Roland Berger Strategy Consultants	2,000 (worldwide); 40 (UK)
Value Partners	400 (worldwide)

Table 3.1

Consultancy firms in the UK

Source: Reproduced from 'Management Consultancy: The official career guide to the profession' (2008). Published by Cambri Available online at www.insidecareers.co.uk

Generalist firms

Generalists are large consultancy firms that offer a wide range of services (Inside Careers, 2009). Table 3.1 demonstrates some of the large consultancies in the UK although it must be noted that not all the large consultancies are in this table, such as more engineering based practices like Atkins who have a total headcount of 17 270 with 11 650 individuals located in the UK (Atkins, 2008). In addition, many niche consultancies that are out in the market are also not represented in Table 3.1. Nevertheless, Table 3.1 shows the major players in the management consultancy industry. By far the largest consultancy is Deloitte with a total headcount of over 150,000 staff worldwide. This consultancy developed out of the large accountancy firms as mentioned in chapter one, e.g., Accenture. Other consultancies have grown out of the IT sector as with firms such as IBM and Cap Gemini (See Industry example 3.1). Other firms also have grown out of the large accountancy firms as mentioned in Chapter 1, e.g., Accenture.

IBM is also a fascinating case study of how a business can be transformed from an overweight giant into an efficient multinational corporation. Gerstner (2002) the former CEO of IBM described the firms transformation. A former management consultant with McKinsey & Company, Gerstner took dramatic action to stabilize IBM in the 1990s and remained as CEO until 2002. In his book, he details the approach he employed to orientate the business to be more customer focused,

Blazing a trail from Grenoble to Mumbai

Since the company's founding in 1967, Capgemini has established itself as one of the top five IT services and consulting companies worldwide. Over the past four decades, we have witnessed periods of success, challenge and reappraisal.

> Forty years on, our challenge is to maintain our momentum, while preserving our differences and the spark of innovation that enables us to work in an original way both together and with our clients.
>
> Paul Hermelin, CEO Capgemini

Our long-term growth and the accompanying expansion of our service offering have relied on internal evolutions, international acquisitions and organic expansion. The following timeline gives an overview of our journey:

The early years (1967–1975)
Capgemini traces its roots to the French city of Grenoble, where Serge Kampf founded Sogeti in 1967. By 1975, the acquisition of two large IT services companies, CAP and Gemini Computer Systems, had established the company as a European leader, present in 21 countries.

Time for expansion (1975–1989)
The company continued to grow and develop, shifting its focus from capital-intensive machine solutions to high-value intellectual services. By 1989, internal restructuring, European expansion and American market entry had positioned the company amongst the five leaders in its sector worldwide.

New strategies for growth (1990–1997)
Capgemini built a world-class management consulting practice through a series of strategic acquisitions including United Research (1990) and the Mac Group (1991) in the US and Gruber Titze and Partners (1993), and Bossard (1997) in Europe.

Building the future (1998–present)
As the global IT market evolved, we increased emphasis on two of our businesses: local professional services and outsourcing. We have also developed an approach we call Rightshore®. This approach relies on both offshore capabilities – including 12 000 people in India as of February 2007 with the acquisition of Kanbay, as well as offshore centres in Morocco and Argentina – and nearshore resources in countries including Poland and Spain.

Source: http://www.capgemini.com/about/capgemini/history overview. Reproduced with permission.

reduce waste and dramatically turn around the business. Much of the pressure on IBM was to, as in many large companies, split up the firm. However, Gerstner resisted believing that with size brought significant advantages of bringing together various skills and areas of knowledge. This cultural change at IBM could also be seen after Gerstner left in 2002, when IBM bought PricewaterhouseCoopers for an estimated purchase price of $3.5 billion in cash and stock (IBM Archives, 2009).

Management consultancies, like the relevant part of IBM, are generalist due to their size. This very size leads the organization to operate in a range of different areas and different markets and industries. This has great advantages when the consultancy bids on work as they can bring in experts ranging from archaeologists to zoologists depending on the assignment. This practice is extremely effective as larger consultancies can mix various specialists together.

Generalists can bring together different areas of expertise quickly as they operate within the same firm. And just as Gerstner (2003) described, this size brings about its own unique advantages. Specialist firms can perform in a similar manner if they go beyond their organizational boundaries and link up with other firms. Nevertheless, this is not as easy as combining specialist areas if you are not all working for the same firm.

Specialist firms

Specialist firms operate in a variety of different markets in a similar manner to the generalist management consultancies (See Chapter 10 for more details). Nevertheless, by their very nature these firms concentrate on particular areas of the market. Inside Careers (2008) in its review of the management consultancy industry stated that much of the growth in the UK over the last decade or so had been the result of consultants leaving the larger firms and setting up their own consultancy practice. Indeed, when a consultant leaves a larger firm they may set themselves up as a specialist and be a limited company or even sole trader. Figure 3.1 demonstrates this, whereby three types of consultancies listed range from the large firms, down with increased specialization to the one-person operations. Niche firms are the somewhat half way house and tend often to be partnerships or associations that have grown into small and medium enterprises.

Industry snapshots 3.2 and 3.3 are extracts from small firms that demonstrate the remit of this type of business. Both firms are quite small in size consisting of one person in snapshot 3.2 and the same for snapshot 3.3.

Interestingly, the first snapshot is registered as a limited company. Many organizations and management consultancies insist that associates are limited

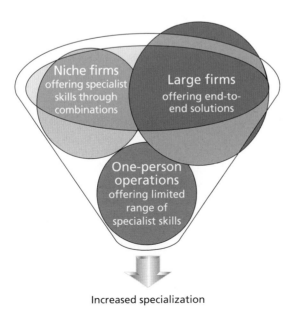

Figure 3.1

Broad range of consultancy practices

Niche firms
offering specialist skills through combinations

Large firms
offering end-to-end solutions

One-person operations
offering limited range of specialist skills

Increased specialization

companies, which is why Emily did this in the first snapshot. In contrast, the second company is a sole trader. This is because the level of associate work completed in this company is much less than the first snapshot. In addition, associate work tends to be conducted through personal contacts and working with previous employers so a sole trading practice is not a hindrance and saves having to pay for an accountant each year as self-assessment can be used for tax purposes. However, some of my previous employers do insist that the company should be limited and not a sole trader and thus this limits the amount of associate work that can completed.

Interestingly both the firms in the Industry snapshots 3.2 and 3.3 operate in the occupational/business psychology arena. But there are plenty of niche firms in

---

Industry snapshot 3.2

Extract from a niche firm's offering via their website

Emily Hutchinson is a Chartered Occupational Psychologist with over 12 years' experience of helping organizations. In January 2004 she was featured in the *Independent on Sunday* as one of Britain's ten Leading Occupational Psychologists.

- She combines a strong academic and research knowledge base with practicality and experience of organizational life.

- She is as comfortable with shop floor staff as with directors, and is also experienced at dealing with regulators and unions.

- She has an extensive network of carefully selected associates enabling flexibility of approach.

Source: http://www.ejhconsulting.co.uk/. Reproduced with permission.

Industry snapshot 3.3

An example of a small firm's website

Background – who are we?

Based in the heart of Cheltenham, Afresh is a niche consultancy that specializes in reducing worker conflict, improving employee relations, competency framework design, and assessment centre exercise design. With easy links to Birmingham, Oxford, Bristol and London, Afresh can aid your organization to fulfil its potential through its people.

Afresh is managed by Dr David Biggs who is a Chartered Occupational Psychologist licensed by the British Psychological Society and a Member of the Association for Business Psychologists. David has been delivering consultancy services in Business Psychology since 1994.

Throughout his career, David has worked in recruitment, training and organizational change with a diversity of organizations. David has made several radio and television appearances discussing his research (temporary working, applicant reactions, etc.) and is currently working on writing a management consultancy textbook.

Source: http://www.a-fresh.co.uk. Reproduced with permission.

other areas that management consultants operate in. In the first snapshot some indication is given on the use of 'carefully selected associates'. This is perhaps the next stage in the evolution of consultancies in terms of setting up niche companies. By using associate consultants, the offering a person can make is much greater. This means more work can be gained by the firm that forms temporary partnerships with other firms.

This combination of associates may indeed lead to a niche company. A niche company differs from the one-person operation as it will encompass more individuals working together. Many small consultancy firms in the UK are set up like this with individuals, perhaps previously employed by a larger consultancy, getting together and then forming their own firm. This could either be because individuals who work on their own decide that there are more benefits by working together with others, or it may be that the company is initially formed like this.

Using another Cheltenham based consultancy, JCA (Occupational Psychologists) Ltd, as a direct contrast to the other smaller based firms, Figure 3.2 illustrates the current website of JCA Ltd. This firm has more staff than the other firms, indeed, 16 staff in total. This gives this firm an advantage of being able to deploy more consultants that work in the same firm similar to the larger concerns. However, its disadvantage is that out of the area of occupational psychology, such as in strategy or BPR, it may not have the power or expertise that would be located

Figure 3.2

Website of a niche consultancy company (Source: www.jca.biz. Reproduced with permission)

in one of the larger management consultancies. This gets back to the point that Gerstner (2003) makes that with larger companies there are distinct advantages and offerings that can be made by combining the skills and competencies of many different professions.

Size does matter

Having worked in both small and large consultancies, I would argue that size does matter in terms of the types of assignments that you get placed on. The advantages with the smaller firms are that you can have quite an impact on the strategic direction of the business and promote aspects of the firm that you have an interest in developing. For instance, in one firm I worked for I promoted project management training and this part of the business flourished (even when I left) with the firm now offering PRINCE2 project management certification. The disadvantages with larger consultancies is that you may not have the same level of impact in terms of strategic direction as you would in the smaller concern until at managing consultant level or above.

Advantages of size: Bigger organization means bigger fees?

In examining the differences between smaller firms and larger consultancies it is noted that combinations of specialist firms may be able to complete the same work as the bigger organizations. Nevertheless, Czerniawska (1999) points out fee rates are often much less in the smaller consultancies than in the larger ones.

Two reasons may account for this fee differential. For the larger companies, size means that there can be a higher level of investment, much more of a global reach, a flexibility of resources and the ability to address the client's concerns from numerous directions and from different disciplines (Czerniawska, 1999).

More money may be invested in marketing for these larger companies developing advocates of the business that indeed may have even been former employees themselves. The second reason maybe that the smaller consultancy can pass on to the client the savings from reduced business expenses in comparison with the larger consultancies, e.g., no office to support, no support staff to pay, etc. Certainly at the moment, consultancies of different sizes exist fulfilling the different needs of the clients that employ both the large concerns and the niche players.

Fields of Consultancy Activity

So far the different sizes of firms have been considered. In Chapter 10, the types of projects that different firms complete are detailed but at this point it is worthwhile investigating the different fields of consultancy activity. This leads on further in the book to illustrate how different types of consultancy may operate in that field.

Small and medium enterprises

> Micro, small and medium-sized enterprises (SMEs) are the engine of the European economy. They are an essential source of jobs, create entrepreneurial spirit and innovation in the EU and are thus crucial for fostering competitiveness and employment.
>
> *Günter Verheugen (European Commission, 2009; p. 3)*

Small and medium-sized enterprises (SMEs) are a fascinating yet often under-appreciated type of business in the field of management consulting. The average business concern in the European economy employs less than six people (European Commission, 2009). Furthermore some 23 million SMEs provide around 75 million jobs and represent 99 per cent of all enterprises in the 25 countries that make up the enlarged European Union. Small and medium-sized enterprises are also important for other large economies such as the US; however, most business research is only conducted in larger organizations (Biggs and Crumbie, 2000; Mughan, Lloyd-Reason and Zimmerman, 2004).

Harris-Loxley and Page (2001) explicitly state that consultancy in SMEs is different to mainstream consultancy. And given the extent of SMEs in the global economy it is worth detailing their guidance. Harris-Loxley and Page (2001) argued that a fundamental difference between consulting for SMEs is that rather than being project based and a kind of one hit wonder as with larger firms, SMEs prefer sustained support, almost like having a trusted advisor on hand to discuss issues. However, this needs to be time effective for both the client and the consultant (so as not to eat too much of the clients profits).

Mistakes made consulting with SMEs according to Harris-Loxley and Page (2001) include:

- Assuming that experience gained from large firms is equally applicable to SMEs
- Not fully investigating the Owners/Managing Directors' impact on the company relating to its growth and what their plans are in the long term for the organization
- Recognizing the importance of understanding all the elements that affect the business
- Assuming that the directors are unprofessional and don't want to learn.
- Assuming that a report will answer the firm's development needs
- Recognizing that the most successful outcome will be based on becoming a 'learning partner' with the firm
- Cutting staff or applying financial controls without considering the consequence of people being made redundant or becoming unmotivated
- Ensuring that the consultants' personality and values fits with those of the client

Adapted from Harris-Loxley and Page (2001); pp. 363–364

Above all else Harris-Loxley and Page (2001) stated that the consultant needs to become a 'trusted friend and mentor' (Harris-Loxley and Page, 2001; p. 381). In this way, the consultancy in a SME is different to consultancy within larger firms. The owner of an SME is likely to feel quite alone at times, setting the strategy of the company themselves. So consultancy only works in this situation if the owner has a consultant who can provide services as a trusted advisor. In any consultancy project within an SME the owners or managing directors are in essence the judge, jury and executor so need to be brought on board with any assignment (Griffiths and Light, 2009).

In Taiwan, it was found that owners were in favour of consultants whereas managers who didn't own the business were much more resistant (Chen, Sun, Helms and Jih, 2008). This was mainly because with the owners the consultants were more 'friend-like', but the managers distrusted them as they thought they may be replaced by them or that the consultants just applied the latest management 'fad' to the business (Chen *et al.*, 2008). Indeed, the successful television series Gordon Ramsay's *Kitchen Nightmares* demonstrates this point, in that most of the restaurants' failing is due to issues such as staffing, bad food, poor service, poor atmosphere that needs to be corrected if the small business is to succeed. This is often very visible from the outside, in a Johari window sense, but often difficult to see from within the business as Gordon Ramsay's show demonstrated so clearly.

Figure 3.3

Chef Gordon Ramsay targets failing SME restaurants in Channel 4's hit series *US Kitchen Nightmares*. Source: © Oliver Knight / Alamy.

Public sector consultancy

The public sector is increasingly becoming more businesslike in its focus and as such consultancy can aid these government sponsored organizations (Roodhooft and Van Den Abbeele, 2006). Roodhooft and Van Den Abbeele (2006) argued that consultancies are used by the public sector due to the following reasons:

1. To reduce workload in the organization.
2. To provide increased knowledge or competence due to the lack of this expertise existing in the organization.
3. To provide a third party, independent perspective on an issue or problem.
4. To use consultants as 'change agents' bringing in public sector reform.

Adapted from Roodhooft and Van Den Abbeele (2006); p. 493

Nevertheless, the most critical literature on management consultancy has investigated its use within the public sector. David Craig, for instance, condemns the management consultancy industry in his 2006 book, *Plundering the Public Sector: How New Labour are Letting Consultants Run Off With £70 Billion of Our Money*. Craig (2006) argued that the amount of money being spent on consultants by public sector organizations has increased dramatically. Using the 2003 to 2004 period, Craig (2006) stated that spending on consultancy has risen by 460 per cent in local government, 340 per cent in the NHS, and 178 per cent in the Ministry of Defence.

Indeed, between 2005 and 2006, approximately £2.8 billion was spent on consultants, with central government accounting for £1.8 billion (House of Commons Committee of Public Accounts, 2007). Nevertheless, with larger ICT projects currently being undertaken such as NPFIT for the NHS, the current bill may be much larger, but it is difficult to discern how much is currently being spent by the public sector (Craig, 2006).

Nevertheless, many public sector organizations now outsource essential business functions, such as recruitment, to consultancies. Indeed, the public sector has been faced with many changes and consultancies can provide support on the strategic role of an organization as well as take on some of its functions, such as recruitment, training and organizational development (Jarrett, 2001). In this regard, it is difficult to claim that the public sector does not benefit from consultancy as Berry (2007) details in his article in *Personnel Today* reprinted as Industry snapshot 3.4.

Industry snapshot 3.4

Consultants strike back at House of Commons Committee of Public Accounts report

A House of Commons Committee of Public Accounts report claimed that millions of pounds were being wasted on the services of management consultants (Berry, 2007). The report into the public sectors use of consultants found that reliance on management consultancy had risen dramatically (Berry, 2007).

Many reasons were given in for the increased spending; however, the Chairman of the Committee Edward Leigh MP, concluded that more could be done to improve value for money. Specifically, it concluded that, 'Getting a better grip on the use of consultants would lead to efficiency gains of more than £500 million a year' (House of Commons Committee of Public Accounts, 2007; p.3).

However, the Management Consultancies Association (MCA) hit back at the report (Berry, 2007). The MCA's chief executive said that it is unlikely that the public sector are not getting full value from the work of management consultants (Berry, 2007). Indeed, there is no evidence that consultancies are delivering poor value for money. Conversely, there is evidence of inadequate control procedures highlighted in the government report (Berry, 2007).

Restell (2007) also detailed the lack of control procedures. He argued that if the government squanders public money then surely it should be them and not consultants who should be in the dock. Yet, headlines like the following clearly put the blame at the consultants:

Anger as government pays £63 a second to consultants (The Scotsman)

Labour blows £2 billion-a-year on army of Whitehall advisers (Evening Standard)

Restell (2007) further stated that although there are inevitably projects that fail to deliver suggesting that no benefits are received through spending taxpayers money on consultancy is farcical.

References

Berry, M. (2007) Management consultants hits back at Commons Public Accounts Committee report which claims departments waste millions of pounds on their services. *Personnel Today*, 26/6/2007 Downloaded from http://www.personneltoday.com/articles/2007/06/26/41236/management-consultants-hits-back-at-commons-public-accounts-committee-report-which-claims-department.html

Restell, T. (2007) Consultants in the dock again. *Top consultant* 19/6/2007 Downloaded from http://top-consultant.blogspot.com/2007/06/consultants-in-dock-again.html

House of Commons Committee of Public Accounts (2007) Central government's use of consultants: *Thirty-first Report of Session 2006–07* Retrieved from http://www.publications.parliament.uk/pa/cm200607/cmselect/cmpubacc/309/309.pdf at 30.3.09

Jarrett (2001) detailed the challenges for working in the public sector as a consultant. Many consultancies, have specialized in this type of work but Jarrett (2001) claims there are three main challenges:

1. The consultant's task not only concerns the project being undertaken but should be seen as part of a wider political and organizational system
2. The consultant should avoid prejudging the situation and acting out of anxiety or confusion in terms of answering the client as the 'expert'
3. The consultant should develop a wide repertoire of consulting styles and form a deep understanding of the psyche of the public sector organization

In essence, at the heart of public sector consulting is the need to understand the wider political environment in which the organization is placed. This also involves enabling the client to run projects or programmes. Indeed, a case study dealing with political issues within the public sector is given in Mini Case Study 3.2 below. This was an interesting case that involved the development of an expert system that the client could then use to give feedback to unsuccessful candidates that may fear they were being discriminated against on the basis of race (Biggs and Sagheb-Tehrani, 2008).

Mini Case Study 3.2

Promoting managers from ethnic minorities in a public sector firm

Improving the representation of individuals in managerial positions from minority groups has been made a priority in UK public sector organizations. The client with over 130 000 employees made this a priority and instigated a Personal Improvement Programme (PIP) aimed to develop employees in specific racial groups who were under-represented at managerial level. The client thus employed a consultancy well-known for their work in the field of assessment and development.

The scheme devised operated within UK legislation under the provision of the Race Relations Act 1976 and the Race Relations Amendment Act 2003 that allowed special access to training and development to individuals from an ethnic minority. The focus of the scheme was supported but self-initiated development and, as such, selection for the programme was based on the motivation of the individual to improve, learn and develop.

Selecting individuals who are keen to learn and develop is somewhat problematic especially when language and cultural barriers are taken into account (Hufton and Elliott, 2000; Fox, 2005). The consultancy worked closely with the client to ascertain how it was possible to select individuals. This involved meetings not only with the client but with a working group that they had created which specifically employed people from different races and cultural backgrounds.

Addressing the issue of selection, the client had already developed a competency framework that assessed a number of behaviours. This was used to assess those applying for the development programme in two stages, a competency based application form and then an assessment centre.

However, the client was not happy that those that were rejected in the first stage of assessment would receive no feedback on how well they did. This was difficult to remedy as the consultancy did not really want to write over a hundred feedback reports based on why the competency based application was unsuccessful. This would have been very costly for the client. Other problems were also apparent. The assessment team were predominantly white middle class individuals. The client wanted feedback to be culturally sensitive; yet, this was difficult for a predominantly white middle class consultancy.

Thus working with the client, it soon became apparent that some out of the box thinking was required. This was lubricated by the good level of working relationship that Caroline, the project manager, had formed with the client. In addition, one of the key consultants on the project had knowledge in devising expert systems specifically for writing feedback reports. This approach was then adopted by the client, favoured over traditional feedback methods on the basis of sensitivity, wording, time and cost. The project was a great success and repeated the following year, when the author was reemployed as an associate with his previous employer.

Questions

1. What were the political issues at work in this project?

2. Did forming a close working relationship with the client lead to the innovative solution of using an expert system?

Adapted from Biggs and Sagheb-Tehrani (2008)

Another way of examining the use of consultants within the public sector is examining the procurement process. Roodhooft and Van den Abbeele (2006) described the difference between procurement in the private and public sectors whereby the public sector seemed to be much less skilled in market management, using the competitive tendering process, providing specifications, negotiation regulation and monitoring of consultancies than their private sector counterparts. They provide a unique insight into the procurement process and conclude that the public sector (at least on the basis of the 26 organizations surveyed) need to develop better purchasing skills and utilize upper management to a greater extent in the procurement function.

Interestingly, some public sector organizations are biased against small firms in the procurement process although this is not reported in the literature (Roodhooft and Van den Abbeele, 2006). Nonetheless, in responding to tenders small companies cannot usually compete with the larger firms. Issues such as a low turnover or not having turnover for the last three years would discount many niche firms in applying for contracts. In addition, the government has often a pre-procurement scheme that would limit the companies that can apply to tender unless they have already been vetted through schemes such as S-Cat (See Industry snapshot 3.5 for more information) or other lists of preferred suppliers. However, it does tend to be the larger companies that can get on these lists of preferred suppliers and have the spare time and capacity to apply for such schemes, although they may not amount to work in the immediate future. All in all these types of issues tend to restrict the government's use of sole traders or limited companies that can offer cheaper and sometimes better more bespoke services in favour of the larger companies.

Industry snapshot 3.5

Fujitsu – explanation of S-Cat

S-Cat is a catalogue based procurement scheme established in 1997 to provide public sector organizations with a simplified means of procuring and contracting for a wide range of IT related consultancy and specialist services.

It is a sister catalogue to the GCat (the Government IT Catalogue) and GTC (telecommunications) catalogues and is managed under a framework agreement with pre-defined Terms and Conditions, by OGC buying solutions (The Office of Government Commerce).

Procuring IT and business consultancy services can be a time consuming and costly process both for purchasers and contractors. S-Cat reduces the time and costs associated with procurement by offering a pre-tendered call off facility. Fujitsu Services was the most successful of the suppliers to S-Cat in the year 2001–2002 transacting business through the catalogue with a value in excess of £25 000 000.

The scheme provides the following benefits:

- Compliance with EC procurement legislation
- Ability to call off urgent requirements quickly
- Ability to split large complex projects into more manageable chunks without having to go through a long procurement for each sub project
- Competitive fee rates
- Wide choice of skills and services across multiple categories
- Ease of ordering
- Sound contractual protection based on best practice
- e-commerce facilities
- Comprehensive management information.

▶

Fujitsu Services is an approved S-Cat supplier in 12 of the 13 categories:		Category 7	Consultancy and support services in respect of Computer and Communications Security, Systems auditing, Contingency Planning and Disaster Recovery
Category 1	IS Strategy Development	Category 9	Provision of Telecommunications Consultancy
Category 2	Programme and Project Management		
Category 3	IT Architecture Design (including Networking and Communications)	Category 10	Training services including technical and management
Category 4	Requirements Specification, Procurement, Evaluation Modelling, System Acceptance and Implementation	Category 11	Application Development, maintenance and testing
		Category 12	Business and Management Consultancy
Category 5	'Body Shop' Supply of IT Specialist and general Administration Personnel	Category 13	Advice and support services for Record, Data and Knowledge Management
Category 6	Consultancy and support services in respect of Electronic Commerce including EDI, Multimedia and Internet/Intranet Services		Source: http://www.fujitsu.com/uk/industries/localgovernment/cat/scat.html on 3 April 2009.

Roodhooft and Van den Abbeele (2006) argued that the new European Union directives in public sector procurement that come into force on 31 January 2006 should open up the market. They suggested that the following three different methods of procurement will make it easier for a variety of consultancy firms to apply being:

1. *Open procedure*: where all interested suppliers may submit a tender
2. *Restricted procedure*: whereby only invited suppliers may submit a tender (such as those on S-Cat or list of preferred suppliers)
3. *Negotiated procedure*: whereby in special circumstances specific suppliers may be invited to submit a tender and the contract notice doesn't need to be published

Adapted from Roodhooft and Van den Abbeele (2006); p. 495

Nevertheless, as with most organizations bound with rules and regulations there are often ways around the procedures for procurement set by the government or by other authorities. An example of this can be seen in Thought Provoking point 3.3, whereby the preferred supplier was given a rather large contract without public notice within the European Union.

Thought Provoking point 3.3

We're hiring you and don't want anyone else

A large public sector organization had a rule in which if a contract was less than £25 000 there was no need to publish a contract notice for this work. In essence, the organization wanted to hire a team to examine various parts of their organization in relation to their management structure and project management skills. Because the client had already selected the team to do this work, they decided that rather than publishing a large contract and having a competitive tendering process, it was better to split the work down into ten projects all of which had to come in below the £25 000 mark. Obviously, this process aids the client as they do not need to submit a formal contract notice. However, it may also disadvantage them as the team that won the work may have been overpriced and less skilled than alternatives that may have been available in that country.

Large corporations

Roodhooft and Van den Abbeele (2006) compared their public sector organizations with companies as their counterparts. These organizations based in Belgium were large corporations selected on the basis that they had a minimum turnover of €250 million and at least 250 employees in 2001. On average these companies were larger with an average turnover of €887 million and at least 2959 employees in 2001. These large corporations spent approximately €3.84 million on consultancy service, which is much less than what is reportedly spent by the public sector as noted in the last section.

Large corporations like SMEs and public sector organizations have their own set of challenges (Jeans and Page, 2001). However, unlike other organizations the opportunity in large corporations can be very enticing and although challenging can bring great reward (Jeans and Page, 2001). Many of the rewards, however, have their darker side and Table 3.2 demonstrates some of the common mistakes made in consulting with large corporations. Many of the mistakes reported in the table have been detailed in other chapters, such as the project management chapter, and are thus detailed in other parts of this text.

Jeans and Page (2001) detail that working with large corporations is different as often one person will not know the entire picture. This is often why it is essential (as shown in Table 3.2) to use more than one source of information within the organization when collecting facts. This ensures that a broad base of knowledge about the organization is developed. In addition, often rather than just informing a large corporation about the change they have to make, it is much more common that the consultants employed will be expected to have a much greater hands-on role (Jeans and Page, 2001).

International consultancy

Engwall and Kipping (2002) in their influential book on the management consultancy industry describe the role of management consultants in much detail using an international basis of comparison. Although at times, their views can be critical at other times it is positive describing consultancy firms as responsible for disseminating management ideas on the international front. Nevertheless, this is written from a largely western and European perspective. Eccles points out in Case Study 3.1, consulting on the international front is not the same as consultancy in the west. Indeed, my ex-management consultancy colleagues and I share many of the experiences that Eccles described, some of which, such as giving jobs to influential people to secure contracts, can be quite alarming from a western perspective.

Typical mistake	Consequence	Advice
Taking matters at face value	Solutions not thorough enough; purely based on what has been said	Be prepared to dig deeper and confirm what has been said to you via at least two sources of information
Misreading the politics and power structure	Recommendations not made to the people 'in charge'	Find out who are the decision-makers in reality
Disregarding personal agendas	Solutions presented may be blocked	Ensure that solutions at least in part recognize personal agendas
Becoming involved in the personal politics	Getting sucked up in the political aspects of the organization	Understand, recognize but don't become part of the politics of the situation
Scope/Project creep	The client asks can you look at this, etc.	Be clear about the boundaries of the project and what is and what is not permissible under the project scope
Overstaying your welcome	Clients get used to you but realize you are less effective than before	Make sure you have an exit strategy upfront with the client

Table 3.2

Typical mistakes made in consulting with large corporations

Source: Adapted from Jeans and Page (2001)

Hall (1999) also echoes the sentiments of Case Study 3.1 at the end of this chapter, in that it is not relevant for consultants to just parachute in and then not take into account local customs and ways of doing business. International consultancy brings its own rewards of international travel and represents an ideal way of being immersed into the culture of another society. Consultancy on a global level should not be about homogenizing business practices to a western way of thinking (Hall, 2001). Moreover, it should be about applying the proper techniques into organizations and recognizing their differences in terms of culture and politics. Later on in this text, power and politics are examined in much greater depth in Chapter 9 and in part in Chapter 15 where ethical considerations are detailed.

Chapter Summary

- Czerniawska (2008) states that the management consultancy industry is vibrant but always difficult to quantify
- Only the successes in management consultancy are often reported although in recent years (especially in the public sector) a more critical view of the consultancy industry has been developed
- Differentiation is difficult in an industry that wants to provide a comprehensive range of services

- Generalist and niche or specialist firms can clearly be identified from the literature
- The bigger the firm often the more that can be charged (although this is not always the case especially with retirees, who will just pick and choose their assignments on the basis of interest rather than financial gain)
- Consultancy in SMEs tends to be different and takes on the role of trusted advisor rather than being more project based
- Public sector organizations are becoming more businesslike in their focus and as such use management consultancies to install business practices and culture from the private sector
- Large corporations are typically difficult clients but the rewards and opportunities can be great
- International consultancy is very different from consultancy in the country of origin and understanding this is key for success in the global arena

Review Questions

1. Why would a consultancy want to be seen as a generalist in terms of marketing its services?
2. What is the difference between a generalist firm and a niche or specialist consultancy?
3. Which two types of large firms have management consultancies been born from?
4. Do specialist firms operate in the same market as the generalist?
5. How may a one-person operation expand its service offering to target larger contracts?
6. What is the one main reason that the public sector needs management consultants?
7. Do the new European Union directives on public sector procurement of consultancy services improve the types of organizations that can be engaged by public sector organizations?
8. What are the challenges of working with large corporations?
9. Is it possible to use western management practices in the international arena?

Assignment Questions

1. Critically discuss why management consultancy may be 'a very secretive industry'. (Saint-Martin, 2000; p. 39)
2. Are consultancies different? Describe using the comment of Czerniawska (1999) who questions that there is a differentiation between the management consultancies.
3. Describe the impact that IBM have had in the management consultancy industry, explaining how they operated prior to 2002 and then afterwards.
4. Is consultancy in an SME different to other organizations?

Culture-fit: Challenges of international consultancy

By Benedict Eccles an independent development and training consultant practising in the UK, Europe, Africa, the Middle East and Far East

Working abroad has demanded that I consistently need to check whether the work I am doing is culturally 'fit for purpose'. My work has related to the introduction of strategic planning processes, governance structures and leadership development in young and rapidly developing countries, through fledgling democracies, relatively wealthy Gulf States and large communist nations. Political, social, religious and other cultural imperatives have all influenced my work in some way – whether I have been conscious of it or not – in terms of organizational power, planning, leadership models, management style, motivation and other processes.

Power

Social status can be very important and have an 'invisible' impact on organizations. Therefore, managers and staff may be responding to wider considerations at work and as a consultant, I have sometimes been unaware of this; it has impacted on issues like project planning, management motivation and even winning contracts. In my experience, social status can have primacy over visible organizational roles.

Leadership

In Europe, the power of democratic leaders is influenced by regular national and regional elections; in Eastern Europe, these elections did not always synchronize in the early stages of democratization. Therefore, I might meet with several politicians during a project's duration and local continuity would be lost (or the consultants were the only continuity!).

In the UAE, power is mainly vested in tribal hierarchies. Many of the leaders who have commissioned external consultancies, have experienced 'western', as well as indigenous, educational systems. These extensively educated leaders are therefore in a unique position and understand issues in a different way to consultants, local

managers and the local staff charged with developing a project and this difference in understanding can impact upon effectiveness. For example, just because a leader may have been educated at Royal Military Academy Sandhurst, it doesn't mean that their national public service organizations will adapt to John Adair's Action-Centred Leadership Model. Specific local research is limited, but acknowledges cultural impact on leadership styles.

Planning

Developing strategies for emerging organizations abroad can implicitly challenge the basic reasoning behind linear planning models: where do we want to be in the future, where are we currently and what changes do we need to make in order to go from present to future states? This is largely because of resourcing – some wealthy organizations may be 'resource rich' and not want to streamline their operation strategically and other financially poor organizations may have major issues in the procurement of the required resources.

Furthermore, the dependence on planning models such as TQM and ISO 9000 amongst others are regularly used by external foreign consultants. These tools – many developed in the West – must be culturally appropriate if they are to be effective. Change is often a slow process and the primary aim of any first organizational strategic plan might be to become a planning organization – identifying targets, data capture and analysis and aligning resources.

Management styles

With possible differences in power, leadership, planning processes and motivational factors, management styles also reflect strong cultural influences. If you consider McGregor's X Y Theory, the adoption of such tools used effectively in a western 'individualistic' culture may be inappropriate for a Far Eastern 'collectivist' culture. 'Participative' approaches may be frowned upon initially as 'top down' decision-making is not only common, but also preferred by some. For example, a presidential select committee I worked with in Africa tasked with governance responsibility for a national project initially found decision-making very difficult – out of a sense of responsibility to make the right decision.

Recruitment, selection and promotion

Human resource processes are also driven by local culture and, personally, I have found this a provocative issue. If a project recommends importing a UK-developed recruitment and selection system abroad, it can fail to engage with the local client, alienate colleagues, select the wrong people and hinder strategic development. For example, what I have judged in past work as 'corrupt' processes in foreign countries from a values perspective might be called 'networking' in the UK; if projects ignore the personal influence of an applicant or a manager, it can restrict change opportunities; when I consider diversity issues, it is in context of my own culture and I have to check that perspective so as not to recommend what might be an ineffective or irrelevant criterion locally.

Some emerging countries commonly use external international consultants from countries such as France, Australia, Egypt and America. These consultants can all bring different approaches to projects and we must be careful to avoid 'organizational cultural imperialism' – 'this is how we do it at home, so it should be done this way here'. To be effective, it is essential that clients own their development. In my own practice, I need to facilitate the local leading of change processes as identified by that culture. I am not imposing anything. Just because the European Union and UK government commission or sponsor a project, it

does not guarantee success. Consultants must build trust, behave appropriately and focus on the client's needs.

All effective projects and strategies I have been involved with accommodate this through a localization sub-strategy – the replacing of external consultants with internal local staff as objectives are achieved.

Motivation

Whilst motivational factors can be universally common, the influence of single factors can appear to vary owing to culture. For example, for some individuals in an Arab Muslim country, spirituality and religious faith is a primary conscious motivator for public service – therefore it can be essential to correlate organizational goals with such important drivers with different colleagues. Theories such as David McClelland's Motivational Needs Theory and Frederick Hertzberg's Hygiene Factors – whilst influential – need to be tested for cultural suitability.

With culture informing our values, and values informing our behaviour, work is not immune from these powerful and often invisible factors. Whilst the world is a smaller and faster place, making local cultural mistakes has restricted effectiveness, been unethical, caused offence and lost contracts. Ultimately, if we impose inappropriate systems, we can create negative psychological effects and organizations fail. Making local cultural mistakes can also lose business contracts.

Questions

1. What contractual agreements should you seek prior to commencing such work and how would you approach these issues?

2. As a change agent working in a different national culture, what can consultants do to improve their effectiveness?

Further Reading

Czerniawska, F. (2008), The future of the industry. In Inside Careers (2008) *Management Consultancy – The Official Career Guide to the Profession*. London: Cambridge Market Intelligence Ltd

Gerstner, L.V. (2002), *Who Says Elephants Can't Dance?: Inside IBM's Historic Turnaround*. HarperBusiness

Harris-Loxley, R. and Page, T. (2001), Small and medium-sized firms, In, Sadler, P. (Ed) *Management Consultancy: A Handbook of Best Practice*. London: Kogan Page Ltd.

IBM (2009), *IBM Highlights 2000–2006*, downloaded from http://www-03.ibm.com/ibm/history/documents/pdf/2000-2006.pdf on 22 March 2009

Inside Careers (2009), *Management Consultancy – The official career guide to the profession.* London: Cambridge Market Intelligence Ltd. Retrieved from http://www.insidecareers.co.uk/__80257624003cca58.nsf/idlive/7wmlnncwis/$file/ICmancon0910.pdf

Mughan, T., Lloyd-Reason, L. and Zimmerman, C. (2004), Management consulting and international business support for SMEs: Need and obstacles. *Education & Training*, 46(8–9), Special issue: Critical perspectives of VET in a small business context, 424–432

Wood, P. (1996), Business services, the management of change and regional development in the UK: A corporate client perspective, *Transactions of the Institute of British Geographers*, 21(4), 649–665

How consulting works

The second part of this book critically explores how consulting works in practice. Chapter 4 initially investigates how consultancy may range from being methodo-logically driven to more laissez-faire or bespoke. However, it is argued that most assignments are not purely bespoke due to the costs involved in developing a new system for every project. The remainder of Chapter 4 thus details the tried and tested techniques that are used in consultancy assignments.

Chapter 5 establishes a crucial aspect of consultancy consisting of the client–consultant relationship. Models that describe this relationship are put forward and evaluated. This leads on to a critical appraisal of the steps in forming relations with a client.

Chapter 6 then extends this work further by describing client engagement. This describes contractual concerns and leads to more practical matters of managing client expectations and establishing their goals.

The section then finishes by investigating the differences between internal and external consultants. Commonalities between internal and external consulting are given and the advantages and disadvantages of both are described.

CHAPTER 4

Models, theories and approaches of consultancy

Learning Objectives

At the end of this chapter students will be able to:

- Understand the continuum between method driven or the more laissez-faire approaches in consultancy

- Be aware of the contribution that different disciplines can give to consultancy

- Understand why it is often necessary to have multidisciplinary teams in a consultancy assignment

- Be knowledgeable about matrix based models of consultancy such as the BCG Growth-Share Matrix

- Be knowledgeable about mnemonic based models of consultancy such as the McKinsey's 7 S model

- Have a critical appreciation of value chain analysis

- Be knowledgeable about financial based models equating cost with benefit

- Be aware of the contribution that ratio analysis can give to consultancy

Mini Case Study 4.1

Quest Worldwide with TMD Friction Group (MCA Management Awards Platinum Award 2008)

TMD Friction was a private-equity buyout gone wrong. Bound for bankruptcy, the automotive supplier was a 'distressed company with distressed management', as one observer saw it. To halt the slide, the chairman brought in a new CEO, Derek Whitworth, and a new financing structure. The price of the deal? A swift change in the firm's performance and its culture.

TMD needed to double profitability, improve customer service, introduce new products faster, reduce inventory and rationalize manufacturing. Problem was, TMD had been created by merging two friction material producers – firms that had not been properly integrated and continued to work independently. And manufacturing plants in the UK, Germany, Sweden, France, Spain, Italy, the US, Mexico, Brazil and China all had different histories, practices and attitudes. Global projects were hard to manage across country fiefdoms, and, back at head office, the 'three-piece suits' were perceived as distant, mistrustful and autocratic.

Though customers valued the products highly, they found the company slow, inconsistent and navel gazing. 'The cultural task was huge', admits Detlev Spanholz, TMD's senior vice-president for quality and customer satisfaction. 'Everything was different – not just systems and practices, but the underlying business philosophy of the original companies. We'd tried modern techniques like kaizen but they didn't stick.'

Quest Worldwide proposed a three-pronged attack: a top-down strategy and leadership drive; a bottom-up focus on people engagement, teamwork and rolling improvement; and a customers-in-process improvement.

The executive leadership team committed to a one page business plan. But instead of taking this down the line of functional teams, new executive teams were set up to focus on a customer or product segment. Then all 400 leaders, managers and supervisors spent an intense four days being trained in best management practices.

Nine step-jump improvements defined in the plan were converted into programmes. The 3300 staff who weren't managers received two-day performance improvement training delivered by their peers: the 15 coaches and 190 facilitators developed by Quest.

Resistance was inevitable. In Germany, the improvement methods clashed with traditional practices. But by collaborating with works councils, TMD and the unions agreed a radical change in work practices. In the US, pressured staff found it hard to find time for training. Careful prioritization and no little determination sorted that issue out, without affecting production.

Just 12 months on, TMD has motored to sales growth of 11 per cent in a market growing just 1.4 per cent. Set-up times and scrap rates are both down by more than half. New business wins are up from 40 per cent to 70 per cent, at significantly improved margins, and productivity has risen by 10 per cent.

Improvements are evident everywhere. A new product in Mexico was so well received that a second production line is being installed, securing growth. By proposing 70-plus improvements and hitting bottlenecks with problem-solving teams, packaging output in Essen increased from 400 to 850 units per person. Along the bottom line, profit has increased by 20 per cent and most of the targets set for 2009 have been met in just a year. TMD is no longer an automotive industry basketcase. Its market value has more than doubled.

Source: http://www.mca.org.uk/sites/default/files/2008%20 Management%20Winners.pdf. Reproduced with permission.

Introduction

The opening Mini Case Study describes how a consultancy, in this instance Quest Worldwide, rescued an organization from the brink of disaster. Whilst some commentators may argue this was done through instilling fear and greed into the client by the consultancy (Kieser, 2002), the increased profit margins, performance and market value of the organization is impressive, so much so that it won the esteemed MCA platinum award for 2008. So how on earth did the consultancy do this?

The Mini Case Study indicated that they used three main approaches focusing on the leadership, how the leadership acted downwards to the staff and also how the workers operated back up to the leadership. This may remind readers of the Johari window demonstrated in Chapter 2. However, what were the types of techniques to get to this information and help implement the changes reported? This chapter details some of the main consultancy techniques that can be employed on a project, the origin of these techniques and how they may be used in practice.

Method Driven Versus Laissez-Faire Consultancy

In the last chapter, different types of consultancies were observed from specialists through to generalists. Size was also commented upon in that larger firms may have distinct advantages (Gerstner, 2002; Saint-Martin, 2000). Another difference could be seen as method driven consultancy versus laissez-faire consultancy.

Laissez-faire consultancy is when a new method of conducting the work is created from scratch for each new assignment. Every project is bespoke. This approach can be directly contrasted with method driven consultancy, whereby each project uses the same methodology and procedures. Consultancies differ in terms of how much flexibility they allow and this can be seen on a continuum as shown in Figure 4.1. The more use of established methods and procedures (typically with younger less experienced consultants) by a consultancy the more they go towards the method driven consultancy.

Sturdy *et al.* (2009) described how humour was often used at the expense of third parties, typically competing consultancies. The term 'Andersen's androids' is one such remark that is discussed against the company by competitors and also the media (e.g., Economist, 1996; 2000). One publication stated that, 'Andersen is

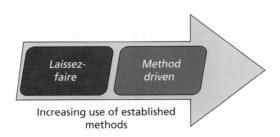

Figure 4.1

The laissez-faire and method driven continuum

the McDonald's of the consultancy business' (Economist, 1996; p. 72) in that everything is standardized and the same. The article also suggested that although the methods used are quite likely key to Andersen's (now Accenture) success. These mechanical methods systematically carried out make their operations too robotic, which is why the android name grew. In this regard, Accenture back in the late twentieth century may have leant more towards the method driven consultancy than the laissez-faire approach. However, as demonstrated in Thought Provoking point 4.1, the fact that Accenture consultancy are still a formidable company suggests that they are not as method driven as others would like us to believe.

Another way of examining this laissez-faire versus method driven consultancy is to apply it in circumstances of organizational change. Obolensky (1994) described a model for change dynamics as shown in Figure 4.2. This suggested that as an assignment or change project starts off with an unknown objective and unknown methodology, it must start off with a 'flexible' approach whilst the objective becomes clarified. This suggested using the laissez-faire approach to begin a project, and indeed most projects as revealed in Chapter 8, start with a period of uncertainty during the start-up and initiation period where the objectives of the project and the methods then become defined.

Change dynamics, according to Obolensky (1994), involved moving from flexibility where there is much unknown through to where the client takes over and has known procedures and objectives (see Figure 4.2). Consultancies may operate in any part of the change dynamics matrix that Obolensky (1994) described. Some may be better at the start of the project whereas others towards the end where they put into place clearly defined procedures and methods. This suggests that a consultancy assignment can be put on a scale as shown in Figure 4.2. In reality, most project assignments use a variety of different techniques (Biswas and Twitchell, 2001). So usually, whilst they are not typically made up from scratch as in the laissez-faire approach, they are unique, combining different methods and techniques for the benefit of the client.

Figure 4.2

The dynamics of organizational change (adapted from Obolensky, 1994)

Thought Provoking point 4.1

Problems with method driven consultancy

The danger with method driven consultancy is twofold :

1. If the methodology does not develop then it may become obsolete as was seen in the 1930s when the consultancies that did not progress beyond scientific management principles went out of business.

2. The methodology may be poached by others and then offered at a cheaper rate, which invariably means that, to compete, rates must decline.

Different disciplines in management consultancy

Consultancies employ many different experts in fields such as human resource management to engineers. Indeed, one particular consultancy listed a staggering 459 unique services and skills. Table 4.1 demonstrates some of the occupations that can be derived from their a–z list of services.

Diverse disciplines will invariably have different techniques they can use for the consultancy assignment. For instance, a business or occupational psychologist will have a number of methods (assessment centres, psychometric tests, etc) to use in the recruitment of high performing individuals. Individual disciplines, such as strategy management will also have unique methods studied at degree or postgraduate level to employ for assignments won. Moreover, a combination of different experts for a project, as observed in the last chapter, can give consultancies clear advantages as they can combine different methodologies.

Table 4.1   A selection of occupations within a multidisciplinary consultancy

Acoustics experts	Acquisition specialists	Archaeologists	Architects	Auditors	Biodiversity experts
Bridge engineers	CDM co-ordinator	Chemical risk experts	Civil engineers	Climate change consultancy experts	Communications and IT network and infrastructure experts
Counter terrorism consultants	Data capture and management experts	Decommissioning experts	Drainage and infrastructure experts	Due diligence and regulation experts	Environmental consultants
Ergonomists	Explosive experts	Expert witnesses	Geotechnical engineers	GIS system designers	Health and safety experts
Landscape and urban design architects	Mechanical engineers	Occupational psychologists	Odour analysts	Project managers	Programme directors
Rail experts	Safety engineers	Training consultants	Vibration and acoustic analysts	Water specialists	Wind experts

It would be almost impossible for any text to list absolutely every technique available to industry experts (Obolensky, 2001). However, in reviewing the literature there are techniques that arise time after time. Thus, a review of these techniques shown in the remainder of this chapter will be a useful introduction to some of the advanced methods used in management consultancy.

Consultancy Techniques and Models

The varying techniques of consultancy one might imagine is a closely guarded secret, as the application of these techniques in a commercial setting are what generate revenue for the management consultancy. Nevertheless, absolutely the opposite is true. In Chapter 1, it was noted that the consultancy that hired Hammer and Champy almost doubled their profits the following year (Saint-Martin, 2000). Even smaller consultancies, advertise what they do via the printed text. For example, Assessment and Development Consultants Ltd and Human Assets Ltd provide texts detailing their commercial assessment centre and development centre techniques (Ballantyne and Povah, 2004; Woodruffe, 2007). The techniques that consultancies use that are examined here are based on a number of good reviews on these methods (Biswas and Twitchell, 2001; Markham, 2004; Obolensky, 2001).

Obolensky (2001) defines three broad types of strategy formulation models consisting of:

1. Matrix based formulations models
2. Mnemonic letter based models
3. Issues and themes models.

Matrix based formulations models

The most famous of all matrix based models is Bruce Hendersen's (1970) Boston Consulting Group Growth-Share Matrix shown in Figure 4.3. This is a matrix based model where industry growth rate is contrasted to relative market share (Biswas and Twitchell, 2001) a company that wants to be successful must ideally

Figure 4.3

The Boston Consulting Group Growth-Share Matrix (adapted from Henderson, 1970)

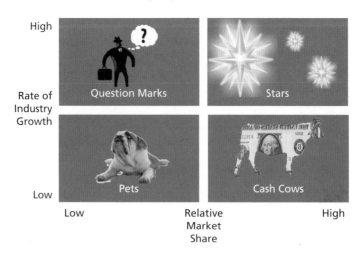

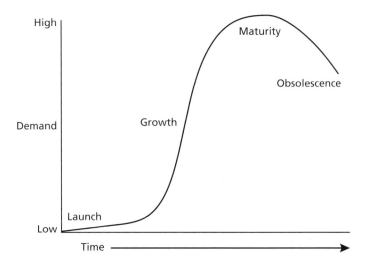

Figure 4.4

The product life-cycle (adapted from Biswas and Twitchell, 2001)

have a portfolio of products with different growth rates and different market shares (Hendersen, 1970).

Companies that have low rates of industry growth and low market penetration are 'pets' as although they may make profit this needs to be reinvested to maintain the market share so they are generally worthless (Hendersen, 1970). Indeed, many of the reinterpreted models often describe this quadrant as 'dogs' (e.g., Biswas and Twitchell, 2001) or even in the industry as 'dead dogs'.

Products that have a high market share but slow growth are cash cows (Henderson, 1970). These products generate large amounts of money in excess of the reinvestment to maintain market share. Products with low market share but with a high level of industry growth are question marks. Typically, these need a lot of investment over and above the returns they make. Stars are products that have high growth and high share. It is likely to show profits but as the need for reinvestment diminishes it will become a cash cow, especially if it retains its leadership (Henderson, 1970). Using this matrix it can be seen that if a company has a good portfolio of stars, cash cows and question marks that can be converted into stars then it should be able to capitalize on its growth opportunities. If a firm is losing market share and its portfolio of offerings are slowing in terms of growth then this could be an indication of trouble ahead. Indeed, Figure 4.4 demonstrates the product life-cycle which eventually ends up in obsolescence. Thus organizations must have a range of products and be constantly updating their portfolio.

Mnemonic letter based models

Mnemonic letter based models are the second category of strategy based models that Obolensky (2001) described. Ohmae (1982) put forward the 3 Cs model as shown in Figure 4.5. Ohmae (1982) argued that a firm's relative competitive advantage (RCA) is the degree to which it has unique properties that enable it to outperform the competition. The 3 Cs framework examines the interaction between the company with its unique advantages, the competitors with their distinctiveness and the customers who cast the final vote. Analysing an organization using the 3 Cs model enables it to assess its relative competitive advantage and to take action to build upon this using appropriate marketing strategies.

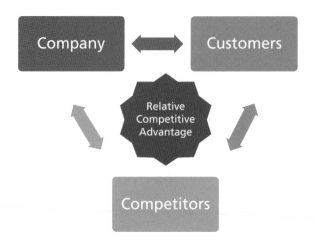

The 4 Ps model described by Biswas and Twitchell (2001) contains four elements consisting of product, price, place and promotion (see Figure 4.6). Although other authors have suggested that 'people' also needs to be added to this model making it a 5 Ps model (Obolensky, 2001).

Product is the attractiveness of the product, via its properties, to the customer
Price must be related to the customer perceptions but also to the product's characteristics
Place is the channel of sale which determines how the product will make contact with the customer
Promotion is the raising of customer awareness to the product

Adding people to this model then provides a checklist of considerations that need to be taken into account when assessing the customer need, the organization with its unique offerings (through its product and people) and the external environment in which the product is placed (Obolensky, 2001).

Biswas and Twitchell (2001) and Obolensky (2001) also describe McKinsey's 7 S model, which belongs to the mnemonic letter category of models. Figure 4.7

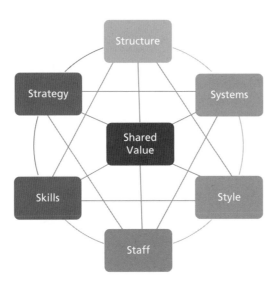

Figure 4.7

The McKinsey 7 S
framework (adapted
from Obolensky,
2001)

demonstrates this model. This approach is an internal orientated approach in that it is based around the idea that the internal dynamics of the organization need to be the primary consideration when formulating strategy (Obolensky, 2001). The seven aspects (structure, strategy, systems, skills, staff, style and shared value) need to be evaluated as though they are interdependent. The aspects must work in synergy to produce an effective organization (Biswas and Twitchell, 2001).

One of the most famous of all mnemonic models must be the SWOT analysis. SWOT stands for strengths, weaknesses, opportunities and threats. It is used by organizations to work out their internal strengths and weaknesses but also encourages individuals to look outside the company and evaluate opportunities that may exist as well as threats to the business. Figure 4.8 illustrates how a SWOT analysis

Figure 4.8

SWOT analysis
(adapted from
Biswas and Twitchell,
2001)

Table 4.2	Strengths	Weaknesses
A SWOT analysis of KPMG	Consistent revenue growth Strong market position Strong clientele	Lack of transparency Tax shelter fraud
	Opportunities	Threats
	Emerging markets Growth in private equity deals Solvency II framework	Increasing competition Consolidation in banking Sarbanes-Oxley Act 2002 Slowdown in the US and European economies

Source: Datamonitor plc, (2007). KPMG International Company Profile. Reproduced with permission from www.datamonitor.com.

works with the strengths of the organization pulling in the opposite direct to its weaknesses and conversely the opportunities of the organization opposing the threats. Many of the large consultancies have this analysis completed on them and they are readily downloadable for a fee (see www.datamonitor.com for details). An example of a SWOT analysis completed on the firm of KPMG is given in Table 4.2.

Issues and themes models

The final category of models listed by Obolensky (2001) are based on the idea that there are a number of issues that need to be accounted for in a model of strategic dynamics. Ansoff in 1965 is generally regarded as the first author to have created a practical model of strategy within an organization (Obolensky, 2001). Basically, Ansoff's approach was to perform a gap analysis to:

1. define the objectives
2. analyse where you are in terms of the objective
3. assess where you want to be and the gap between this and where you are at present
4. decide on the best course of action to close the gap

Porter's five force model examined the dynamics of competitive rivalry in an industry (Biswas and Twitchell, 2001). Porter's model is portrayed in Figure 4.9. These five forces determine an industry's level of profitability through their interaction (Porter, 1980):

1. Industry competitors – with companies competing for market share winning customers
2. Suppliers – who may have bargaining power and be able to reduce profits of the firm by increasing their own costs
3. Potential entrants – may threaten to steal existing market share by offering different and individual benefits to the customer
4. Buyers – may also be able to bargain for lower prices through negotiation
5. Substitutes – may replace products of the firm

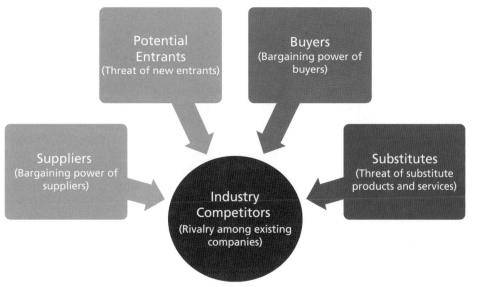

Figure 4.9

Porter's five forces
(adapted from
Obolensky, 2001)

Value chain analysis

Biswas and Twitchell (2001) describe a further model being the value chain model. This is often used by consultancies to make companies aware of where they are in the chain. In this analysis, a descriptive framework is generated to describe a sequence of operational or functional events. Value chains assume that all the links are not in competition with each other, which may be criticized from the view that Porter (1980) gives diagrammatically portrayed above in Figure 4.9.

In value chain analysis the end suppliers and the buyers work in harmony to create value for the customer. Each link in the chain may represent a company or department. Each of these subsequently adds value to the end product. An example of this is given in Figure 4.10 from my experience in the Birmingham UK rubber manufacturing trade. This is where the first company, retrieves the raw rubber pulp from a milky colloidal suspension of the rubber tree plant. This raw material is then treated (vulcanized) by the first manufacturer in the chain who creates rubber sheeting from the material. This rubber sheeting then goes to manufacturer 2, who adds textile material to the rubber and then cuts this into the form

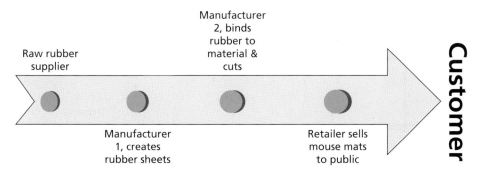

Figure 4.10

Value chain analysis
example of creating
mouse mats

of mouse mats. Manufacturer 2 then sells these items to the retailer who sells the product onto the customer.

Supply and demand

Value chain analysis serves as a useful way of assessing how interrelated departments or companies operate. Such analysis is great to use in conjunction with the economics principle of supply and demand, as within the value chain there are suppliers and buyers who demand goods from the suppliers. Figure 4.11 demonstrates this basic economic model. For a good or service there is a demand and supply, where the supply of a service equals the demand then the price of P* is reached. In economics this is considered to be the equilibrium point. Yet, should demand for a service fall, then there is a producer surplus and this leads to a fall in price. Conversely if supply does not equal the demand, then the price will increase. This type of analysis is useful to do as it can illustrate the net effects of organizational change in an economic framework (Biswas and Twitchell, 2001).

Financial orientated models

Financial orientated approaches evaluate any strategic decision on the basis of financial gain for the company (Obolensky, 2001). For new business ventures the key may be to operate without losing money. Breakeven analysis determines the minimum amount of profit that is required to ensure that a business does not produce a profit or a loss. The equation for this is given in Figure 4.12.

A cost-benefit analysis is conducted to determine whether the benefits of a project or business venture justify its initial investment. Figure 4.13 demonstrates the cost-benefit model. It is simple yet powerful especially for projects that involve

Figure 4.11

Supply and demand model (adapted from Biswas and Twitchell, 2001)

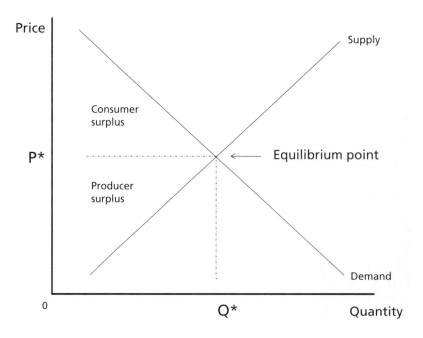

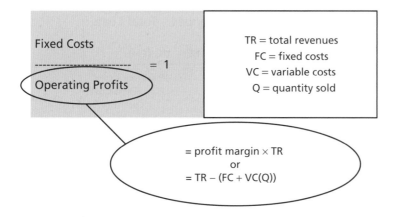

Figure 4.12

Breakeven equation (adapted from Biswas and Twitchell, 2001)

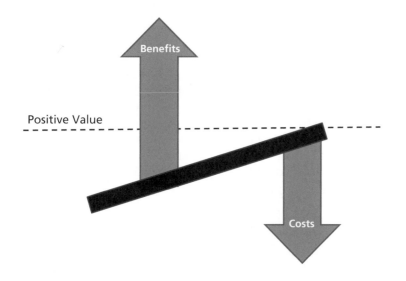

Figure 4.13

Cost-benefit (adapted from Biswas and Twitchell, 2001)

Figure 4.14

The popular BBC programme *Dragons' Den* examines potential business start-ups using a cost-benefit approach

Figure 4.15

Profit equation

Profits = Total Revenues − Total Costs
or
$$\pi = (P \times Q) - (FC + VC(Q))$$

π = **Profits**	**P = Price**
TR = Total Revenues	**FC = Fixed Costs**
VC = Variable Costs	**Q = Quantity Sold**

capital expenditure (Biswas and Twitchell, 2001). The costs of a project are assessed versus its benefits. If the benefits outweigh the costs then the project should proceed. In management accounting, net present value (NPV) is a more sophisticated method of calculating costs versus benefits (Biswas and Twitchell, 2001). NPV demonstrates the return on a capital investment project over a period of time as compared with a lower risk assessment (Collis and Hussey, 2007).

Central to the cost-benefit analysis is the idea that a service or product will create a profit. The equation for calculating profit is given in Figure 4.15, whereby total revenues less total costs equal profit. Obviously, if a service or product is new and the demand for it can be stimulated and is high, then more benefits will arise from investing into that service or product.

One of the most important methods of examining financial concerns is by using ratio analysis (Biswas and Twitchell, 2001; Obolensky, 2001). This is often used to test the mettle of potential consultants within case study interviews during selection (Asher and Chung, 2005). Ratio analysis is a key feature of management accounting and simplifies financial information so it can be understood easier than raw figures themselves. Collis and Hussey (2007) demonstrated the main types of ratio consisting of: profitability ratios; liquidity and efficiency ratios; gearing ratios and investment ratios (as shown in Figure 4.16). Biswas and Twitchell (2001) stated that at a case study interview, often used for recruiting new talent by consultancies, some of this ratio analysis may be expected to be displayed. Indeed, they link ratio analysis directly with assessing profitability and growth, as shown in Figure 4.17.

Ratio analysis is a useful technique to master and introductory textbooks in accounting like Collis and Hussey (2007) would give the potential consultant a keen insight into the art of management accountancy.

Figure 4.16

Ratio analysis
(adapted from Collis
and Hussey, 2007)

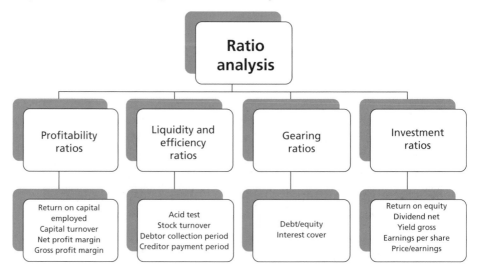

Figure 4.17

The components of profitability and growth (adapted from Biswas and Twitchell, 2001)

A further technique described by Obolensky (2001) involves the shareholder value approach. Obolensky (1994) described this approach in full whereby the shareholders want to ascertain their value in a business where they have invested money. Obolensky (1994) describes four ways that investors see value:

1. Asset based valuation: gives the break up value of an organization
2. Market based valuation: this is the share price multiplied by the shares outstanding that gives a good indication of what people are prepared to pay for the company
3. Cash flow based value: this is the NPV of future cash flows plus any residuals
4. Negotiation based value: an organization may have an increased advantage to another so this may lead to an increase in its price

Shareholder value approaches involve the cash flow based value and calculating this figure. The true value of any investment is the future cash generated by those assets. This in turn is discounted back to the present day by the cost of the capital to take into account the time value of money. In essence, the shareholder value approach is similar to NPV but for shareholders in that it is essentially an advanced form of cost-benefit analysis spread over time (Obolensky, 2001).

Chapter Summary

- Laissez-faire consultancy is when a new method of conducting the work is created from scratch for each new assignment
- Method driven consultancy is when each project uses the same methodology and procedures
- Most projects and sometimes consultancies sit on a continuum between laissez-faire and method driven consultancy
- Diverse disciplines invariably have different techniques
- A combination of different experts for a project give consultancies clear advantages as they combine different disciplines

- Consultancy techniques are often published as it leads to increased revenue for the firm as shown by Saint-Martin (2000)
- There are many different models used in consultancy. Obolensky (2001) listed these as:

  - Matrix based formulations models
  - Mnemonic letter based models
  - Issues and themes models

- Other models include value chain analysis, supply and demand analysis and financial models

Review Questions

1. What is a laissez-faire consultancy?
2. Would it be costly to have every project bespoke?
3. What are the advantages of method driven consultancy?
4. What are the disadvantages of method driven consultancy?
5. Are the varying techniques of consultancy a closely guarded secret?
6. What are the two axes in the BCG growth share matrix?
7. What do the letters SWOT stand for?
8. What are the five forces that Porter (1980) defined?
9. What are the two elements important in economics?

Assignment Questions

1. Critically describe whether the distinction between method driven versus laissez-faire consultancy is a real phenomenon.
2. Critically discuss the advantages and disadvantages of whether consultants should be like 'androids' utilizing the same methods, time and time again.
3. Describe and contrast two mnemonic models useful in management consultancy.
4. What is value chain analysis and is it as Fincham (1995) may describe a simplistic view of management reality?

Case Study 4.1

A consultant's comeuppance

By Robert Buday

It was cold in the luxury box at Shea Stadium, but otherwise the autumn Saturday was clear, sparkling, and perfect. The Mets were ahead 5 to 4 in the bottom of the eighth, and Edgardo Alfonso had just nailed a line drive with bases loaded. Life was good. Jeff Patterson and Bill Holland jumped from their seats and yelled their approval as each of the Mets crossed home plate.

▶

Aside from being Mets fans, Jeff and Bill were old friends. The annual ball game had been a feature of their relationship for the past ten years – ever since Jeff's firm, Flynn Fuller Consulting, had worked on its first project for Bill's company, the financial services giant GloBank. An afternoon at the ballpark always provided an excellent opportunity for the consultant and his favourite client to catch up on personal news and talk shop in a low-key way.

'Thanks again for writing that recommendation letter for Jessica', Bill told Jeff. 'My poor daughter has never been able to make up her mind. Now she can't decide between Harvard and Stanford, but I'm sure it will help her get into one or the other.' In Jeff's mind, Jessica had deserved his praise. She'd proved herself more than competent during her summer research internship at Flynn Fuller, where Jeff headed the firm's financial services practice. And, of course, the favour to Bill and Jessica was trivial when compared with the consulting work GloBank had given Flynn Fuller, whose fees had totalled more than $80 million in the past decade. In fact, Bill, who headed GloBank's retail banking unit, had more good news on that front.

'The strategic analysis your team just did was excellent', Bill remarked. 'It really sharpened our thinking about which retail services we should keep investing in and which we should consider pulling out of. We could really use that kind of analysis on the next piece of the puzzle. We need to develop an acquisition strategy and assessments of potential insurance company acquisitions, and we could use some help. I'm guessing it would be about a $1.5 million project for you – assuming, of course, it gets the go-ahead from the new CEO. Safe to assume you'd be interested in the work?'

Jeff, grateful that he hadn't had to bring up the topic of follow-on work, said 'Absolutely, Bill. I'll keep the team intact and ready to go whenever you say.' Despite this show of confidence, Jeff had misgivings; no one really knew yet where the new CEO would steer GloBank, whose business, like everyone else's, had faltered during the past two years. The new CEO was still a cipher, even to Bill. According to press and industry reports, H. Frank Maloney III had a reputation as an efficient manager, strong on both vision and execution, who had done a good job of pulling another large financial-services firm out of a difficult post merger slump. Bill had also said that Maloney had spent his first two months hunkered down, familiarizing himself with GloBank's business and 'spending a lot of time behind closed doors with the CFO'. Bill himself had not gotten much of a read on his new boss yet. 'Businesslike', was about the best that he could offer Jeff. 'He's the kind of person who expects you to be totally prepared with answers at all times'.

Privately, Jeff knew that 'keeping the team intact' wouldn't be a big challenge. With no major new projects in the pipeline, those consultants would probably 'hit the beach' for a while anyway. Business at Flynn Fuller, whose revenues had topped $500 million last year, was down substantially. Like the rest of the management consulting industry, it had been pulled down by the powerful undertow of the recession and the terrorist attacks of September 11. The firm's $50 million banking practice had already shrivelled by about 20 per cent this year. And there were few signs of relief. Flynn Fuller – and Jeff's team – needed the work.

Marshaling Maloney

Eating lunch the following Monday at his desk on the 35th floor of Flynn Fuller's headquarters, Jeff gazed at several skyscrapers whose occupants he had come to know well in 25 years of consulting work. These were his clients. His practice had helped them navigate the rapids in the financial services industry – dealing with the threat of brokerage firms siphoning off bank depositors; the forays of industrial giants like GE, GM, and Ford into the lucrative auto loan business; and the attempts by Sears and others at one-stop financial services shops.

Maybe we got a little exuberant with the whole dot-com thing, Jeff thought to himself. His firm had advised financial institutions to spin off their Internet businesses and take them public during the heyday of 1999. Good thing none of them did; in hindsight, the advice was off base. Retail banks need a 'clicks-and-bricks' capability, a separate Internet unit would have made that more difficult. Recently, Flynn Fuller had stopped placing its publication advocating spin-offs near the reception desk.

But that misstep was an exception to Flynn Fuller's overall strong track record with financial institutions. It hardly seemed fair that, after so many years of receiving sound advice, those companies were now forsaking him. The late-1990s consulting boom felt like it had happened a century ago. Thank God, Jeff thought, for Bill and GloBank. If it hadn't been for them, and the promise of new work, the outlook would be even bleaker. Jeff finished his tuna on wheat and then crumpled the wrapper and tossed it in the wastebasket. He swung around to check his e-mail. The first message in his in box, flagged with an 'Importance: High' exclamation mark, was from Bill:

> Jeff: I need to alert you to something. This morning we got word from the CFO that substantial cost reductions are required. Every division head has to come up with proposed cuts on the order of 10 per cent to 15 per cent. I don't know what it means yet for the project I mentioned. Hopefully, nothing. But we may need to rethink the scope, chop it up into phases, or something. In any event, the order is coming from the top. Will keep you posted.
> Best,
> Bill.

Jeff didn't have to ask what 'from the top' meant. It was clear the directive had come from Maloney. He tapped out a reply.

> Hmm. Thanks, Bill. Let me know what you hear as soon as you can. – Jeff.

Jeff leaned back in his chair and took a deep breath. He tried putting the news into its best light. Perhaps Maloney's business review and cost-cutting directive meant that GloBank would outsource more work to consultants and seek the advice and help that Flynn Fuller had provided for many years – especially to its retail business unit, which had done better than any other unit in that time. Later, as Jeff was about to leave for the day, his assistant Pam let him know that Bill Holland was on the phone. 'Jeff, I know I practically gave you the green light on that second project', Bill said in an apologetic voice. 'But the light just turned red. It's on hold'. His words felt like a punch to Jeff's stomach.

That afternoon, Bill explained, Maloney had called him and seven other divisional presidents into the boardroom. The CFO was there as well. Maloney and the CFO circulated a 'state of the bank' report, and the news wasn't good. It looked like the bank would lose money for the second straight year. Most divisions were losing market share, and costs were spiralling out of control. The reason the firm's stock price was at a 15-year low, Maloney said, was that GloBank's commercial lending business was out hundreds of millions of dollars from bad loans after a decade of decentralized lending authority. And Wall Street knew that there were more bad loans on the books.

Each president was given 15 minutes to talk about his or her division, explain the reasons for its performance, and discuss plans to improve it. Toward the end of the meeting, the CFO mentioned in passing that GloBank was spending $14 million on consultants this year. Maloney jumped on the topic and asked, 'Can anyone tell me why we're using so many consultants here?'

After getting no immediate responses from his division leaders, Maloney issued an edict: Each division president would have to justify every major consulting project – that is, those costing more than $100,000 per year. 'Have your consultants prove to me why we need them or else get rid of them'. The consultancies' meetings with Maloney would begin next week.

It wasn't clear, Bill told Jeff, whether that demand came from any particular concern with consultants or just the heat of the moment. And certainly, Flynn Fuller wasn't being singled out. Maloney was calling on the carpet every consulting firm doing work at GloBank. 'Jeff, there are at least six other consulting firms doing work in other divisions, and I'm sure you guys have a better story to tell than most of them.'

In a state of semi shock that his relationship with an annuity client could evaporate in a single week, leaving ten consultants without assignments, Jeff flailed. 'Do you have any idea what kind of story that should be?' he asked. 'I mean, what kind of information is he looking for?'

'I don't know, Jeff', Bill said. 'The only thing he told us was, "I'll give them each an hour to justify their existence here".'

For the first time since they met ten years ago, Jeff heard fear in Bill's voice. It dawned on him that this confident and competent banker might also be worried about his own position. What Bill said next confirmed it: 'All I know is, you guys can't embarrass me. You gotta make me look like Einstein for bringing you in all these years.'

The War Room

Warm with the aroma of freshly brewed coffee and Danish, the conference room at Flynn Fuller was like a second home to Jeff; he'd spent many long days and nights diagramming client strategies and outlining deliverables on its white boards. Now he was here with five colleagues: two senior project managers from the GloBank account, the head of business development in the retail bank practice, a consulting service development director, and the practice marketing manager. 'We're here this morning because our GloBank account may be in trouble', Jeff announced from the head of the oval table. 'And I need your help to save it.'

Though the team had been apprized of the corporate management change at GloBank, Jeff spent a few minutes going over everything he knew about Frank Maloney's reputation and prior work. He relayed the message from Bill Holland that each consulting firm would have an hour to make its case. Their session was scheduled for 10 am the following Thursday. Including today, the team had nine days to prepare. 'I'm not exactly sure how to use that time', Jeff confessed to his group. Truth be told, this was the first time in his career that he'd been asked to 'justify his existence', as Bill had said. It wasn't exactly the kind of beauty contest that Flynn Fuller was usually involved in when competing to work for a new client. And it certainly wasn't just a progress report. Jeff understood the right of any new CEO to do cost justification, especially given the current challenges in the banking industry. But it seemed like Maloney was looking for some more general understanding of what value consultants bring.

'Why don't we start by just going around the room and briefly outlining what we think should be in the presentation', he continued. All heads nodded. Glancing at the head nodding the hardest, he said, 'Alex, why don't we start with you'.

Alexandra Manning was a principal consultant at Flynn Fuller, one level below partner. She had been working on GloBank projects as Jeff's day-to-day 'person at the client' for the past four years. 'We can't go wrong if we use the time to bring him up to speed on all our past successes with GloBank', Manning began. Maloney, she noted, would most likely have heard about some of the work in which Flynn Fuller had been involved. 'The funny thing is that some of the projects that get talked up the most around there aren't ones we regard as big successes. Our counsel just rubber-stamped what someone wanted to prove – even though we didn't know that in advance.' In fact, she reminded the group, some of the work they were most proud of yielded advice that GloBank ultimately chose to ignore –for example, the questioning of an acquisition target and the counsel to make an unpopular divestiture.

'Even though I know we were right, those projects won't be viewed as successful because not having listened to us will put some people in a bad light', Manning said. 'So, unfortunately, we won't be able to bring up those projects. But we can still point to a lot of good decisions that were made on the basis of our analysis that Maloney might not know to give us credit for.'

Mark Tannenbaum, the other project manager, took another tack. 'I don't know how strongly we want to associate ourselves with GloBank's recent performance', he said. 'After all, Maloney isn't giving it much credit at all. He's looking to the future'. Tannenbaum pointed out that Maloney had been in financial services for 40 years, so Flynn Fuller needed to demonstrate its industry expertise. 'He's probably seen a lot of consulting firms that are an inch deep in real knowledge about how the industry works, even if they have dedicated financial-service consultants', he explained. 'That we have 150 consultants in this practice, many with at least 10 years of bank experience, is impressive'.

Perhaps, Tannenbaum suggested, the team should spend the next week pulling together a 'future vision for the financial services industry' – a highly informed look at three to five compelling scenarios based on trend lines from the past 30 years. This, he urged the group, would show that Flynn Fuller offered some critical insights that Maloney lacked – and needed – to chart a new direction.

'Okay. Two conflicting views', Jeff said. 'But, great. This is exactly the discussion we need. John?'

John Castle, the head of business development in Flynn Fuller's retail banking practice, noted that every consulting sale is a relationship sale. 'A client at this level isn't comfortable bringing in a certain firm unless the right chemistry with the key members of the consulting team is there. Jeff, look at your relationship with Bill Holland. You guys are pretty tight. You know what sports he likes, what whiskey he drinks, what magazines he reads, where his kids go to school.'

'We need to know what this Maloney guy is all about far better than we do right now', Castle continued. 'Where'd he go to business school? Maybe the same place you did? Or maybe he is close friends or golf buddies with another of our banking clients. All I know is, if we don't appeal to this guy in some way on a personal level, we're not going to connect with him. What I'm saying is we need a whole personality profile on him.'

'It's true enough', said Jeff. 'I'd have a much higher comfort level about this if I knew more about him. What do you think, Jane?'

Jane McCreary was the practice's director of service development, a weighty position that involved identifying best-practice methods developed in individual client engagements and embedding the most promising of them into companywide methodology and training programmes. 'I believe one of the things we're missing here is showing Maloney how we do our work', McCreary said. 'This is what clients pay us to do. How can he make a decision about whether to keep us unless he understands how we're different from the other consulting firms? I would focus most of your presentation, Jeff, on our approaches.'

The final person to speak was Jim Whalen, the practice's marketing director. 'I feel I need to take the role of the sceptical client', he said. 'GloBank has spent – what did you say, $80 million? – on us over the past ten years. If I were the CEO, I'd like to know what the ROI was. I know it's very hard to pin a dollar sign on a lot of our consulting work, but I think we have to try to sum it all up . . . .'

'Maybe', Jeff said, cutting off Whalen. 'But how could we possibly come up with that number? I've seldom had to make a hard financial case with a client on the value of our work with them. If they don't fundamentally trust that Flynn Fuller is doing them some good – more than what we earn in our fees – then they're not going to be our clients for the long term.'

By the time the group had finished hearing out each other's ideas, it was already noon. Jeff told them to assemble the data that they believed would make a compelling 'deck'. The following Monday morning, they would lay all of their information on the table and develop the presentation to save the GloBank account.

Presentation D Day

At 9 am on Monday of the following week, the team convened to spend the whole day 'storyboarding' the presentation. Jeff, John Castle, Alexandra Manning, Jane McCreary, Mark Tannenbaum, and Jim Whalen sat at the same places around the table, stacks of paper and rough presentations in hand. A graphic artist who specialized in overhead presentations joined the group so the team's work could quickly be put into production.

'Welcome back, everyone', Jeff began. 'I'm eager to hear how we can make this a great presentation that will knock Maloney cold.'

How should Flynn Fuller resell its value to GloBank?

Further Reading

Biswas, S. and Twitchell, D. (2001), *Management Consulting: A Complete Guide to the Industry, 2nd Edition.* New York: John Wiley & Sons

Markham, C. (2004), *The Top Consultant: Developing Your Skills for Greater Effectiveness.* London: Kogan Page Ltd

Obolensky, N. (1994), *Practical Business Re-engineering: Tools and Techniques for Achieving Effective Change.* London: Kogan Page Ltd

Obolensky, N. (2001), Strategy formulation models. In, Sadler, P. (Ed) *Management Consultancy: A Handbook of Best Practice.* London: Kogan Page Ltd

Sturdy, A., Handley, K., Clark, T. and Fincham, R. (2009), *Management Consultancy Boundaries and Knowledge in Action.* Oxford: Oxford University Press

CHAPTER 5

The client–consultant relationship

Learning Objectives

At the end of this chapter students will be able to:

- Know what the client–consultant relationship is

- Critically understand the three models of the client–consultant relationship

- Understand the key elements in the client–consultant relationship

- Have knowledge of the steps in forming a relationship with a client

- Understand some of the criticisms stated about the client–consultant relationship

Mini Case Study 5.1

Deloitte aids Winnipeg to become one of Canada's most efficient municipalities

The City of Winnipeg was developing an Enterprise Resource Planning (ERP) system to streamline and integrate more than 100 diverse systems scattered across the city's various departments. It was a challenging path, but the results have been remarkable. 'Winnipeg went from being the last major Canadian city without ERP to being seen as the leader with world-class software and full integration', said Rodger Guinn, project director for the City of Winnipeg.

The city's original systems were developed at a time when department accountability was the primary focus. But over the years, incompatible and disconnected applications led to a whole host of operational inefficiencies. The new ERP system had two major components. The Human Resources component included four modules: payroll, benefits, time and labour. The Finance component included five modules: general ledger, accounts payable, purchasing, project accounting and inventory control.

The city's HR issues were particularly critical given that half its workforce is eligible to retire by 2010. Departments needed tools to identify and coordinate their extensive hiring activities. They also needed to capture the knowledge of their most experienced employees whilst those people were still around, making it imperative to complete the new system as quickly as possible.

The City of Winnipeg was looking for an integration partner that would take ownership of the project, share the risks and commit to meeting the city's business objectives. 'We wanted one partner who would lead and oversee the project and who could commit to an "online, on-budget, on-time" approach', said Bob Gannon, CFO for the City of Winnipeg. 'We also wanted a self-sustaining solution where our employees were trained to run the system afterwards.'

Deloitte assembled a team of more than 50 consultants from across Canada, including specialists in finance, technology, human resources and municipal government – providing a 360-degree view that helped the city tackle problems from every angle. By capitalizing on Deloitte's experience and tools, the City of Winnipeg was able to implement all five financial modules – along with the first phase of the HR component – in less than 10 months. 'The city reaped the benefits of Deloitte's excellent working arrangement ... and implemented at a rate unheard of in the industry', said the City of Winnipeg's Rodger Guinn. The speedy deployment also gave the team more time to train city employees – an important benefit for a municipality wanting a self-sustaining system.

'Deloitte overcame challenges and approached the project with a good understanding of our environment and with a working style characterized by lots of open communications, respect for our organizational culture, risk-sharing and ongoing negotiations,' said Guinn. 'In fact our teams meshed so well you wouldn't know who was the consultant and who was the city employee if you walked into our offices. Working with Deloitte was a refreshing departure from the traditional consultant-client relationship.'

Source: © Deloitte & Touche LLP 2003. http://www.deloitte.com/view/en_CA/ca/services/consulting/case-study/7cfa01f0ed5fb110VgnVCM100000ba42f00aRCRD.htm. Reproduced with permission.

Client–Consultant Relationship

What is the client–consultant relationship?

The opening Mini Case Study demonstrates the importance of the client–consultant relationship. In this case, the consultancy Deloitte worked with the City of Winnipeg in a close relationship that rapidly implemented an Enterprise Resource Planning system. An alternative case study that contrasts with the opening case study may be taken from the UK's National Health Service (NHS). In 2002, the NHS established the National Programme for IT (NPfIT) which was designed as a single database for all patients, health professionals and hospitals in the UK. Described as one of the biggest and the most expensive IT project in world history (Brennan, 2005), Richard Granger the former Director General of IT for the NHS (and a former consultant at Accenture when it was Andersen Consulting) was quoted that he wanted to run the project so as to hold consultants'

'feet to the fire until the smell of burning flesh is overpowering' when negotiating the contracts. Then, that he would manage his suppliers like a 'team of huskies' shooting the lame ones and feeding them to the other dogs.

Quoted from http://www.consulting-times.com/June2008/10.aspx

This approach does not bear well for the client–consultant relationship. Indeed, many of the consultant firms engaged on the multi-billion project have since left escalating the original estimated cost of the project (Fleming, 2004; James, 2008) and making it fall four years behind schedule (King, 2009).

Since the exchange between the client and consultant is an ongoing social practice, it is essential to identify and analyse this relationship (Nikolova, Reihlen and Schlapfner, 2008). This chapter details this essential aspect of consulting and what is involved with the client–consultant relationship.

Who is the client?

Before detailing the complex nature of the client–consultant relationship it is important to detail who the client is, which is not always straightforward (Mulligan and Barber, 2001). The client could be a number of different individuals including:

- Initial contacts of the client organization who first approached the consultancy
- Sponsors financing the consultancy work
- Individuals who benefit from the consultancy work
- Individuals who have a vested interest in the consultancy work
- The superiors/subordinates of those who have a vested interest in the consultancy work

The client is therefore not a simple matter of just who pays or who benefits from the consultancy work. Indeed, effective business development managers selling consultancy services often think about the client's client and use this whilst constructing a bid for work.

Mulligan and Barber (2001) describe looking at the client from different angles. They suggest that an effective consultant needs to listen to three groups of individuals. These are:

- those who know;
- those who care; and
- those that can.

Those who know are those that are aware of the problems faced. Those that care are those that suffer from the issues in the organization and those that can are the sponsors of the project that have the authority to give the work the go ahead. All three groups are vital to engage. Indeed, the reason for many failed prospective projects was that often those who know and those that care were engaged but those that can were not. For example, a HR management team may well know the problems faced with an organization in not adopting a competency based framework for their management development needs. However, if the HR management team have no budget to implement the competency framework then even though they want the consultancy to go ahead, it cannot as no funding of the project is available.

Client–consultant relationship – A definition

The client–consultant relationship can be defined simply as the association between consultant and client, the interaction of which is essential for the long-term survival of consulting companies (Nikolova *et al.*, 2008). Appelbaum (2004) stated that the following success factors were important for an ideal client–consultant relationship. These were consultant focused suggesting that the consultant should be:

- competent and skilled at what they offer
- have an emphasis on client results
- have clear outcomes and expectations
- have visible executive support from a senior member of the consultancy firm
- adapt readily to the client's needs
- invest in learning about the client's environment
- include themselves in the implementation of any solutions

Appelbaum (2004) made this suggestion based on material gathered through anecdotal evidence and previous conceptual theories. Nevertheless, later these factors were confirmed in a quantitative survey of 102 middle and lower level managers that worked frequently with consultants in North American Telecommunications company.

The relationship may not be as straightforward as it may seem, as the consultants themselves may have subcontractors and the client may also have outsourced elements that need to be taken into account. However, Mulligan and Barber (2001) defined separately the client side and the consultant side of the relationship (see Figure 5.1). The client specifically needs support or expertise from an external source, which is not available from internal sources to the client. The consultant or consultancy then provides the assistance or the relevant skills and expertise that the client requires. This is by far the simplest model of the relationship but has been criticized as such (Clark and Fincham, 2002; Clark and Salaman, 1996; Devinney and Nikolova, 2004). This leads us to think about the models put forward for the client–consultant relationship, which will be examined in the next section.

Models on the client–consultant relationship

Engwall and Kipping (2002) claim that the relationship between client and consultant is poorly understood, which to a large degree is reflected in the literature. In recent times, four models have been put forward to try to explain the complex relations that occur between clients and consultants (Devinney and Nikolova, 2004). These models

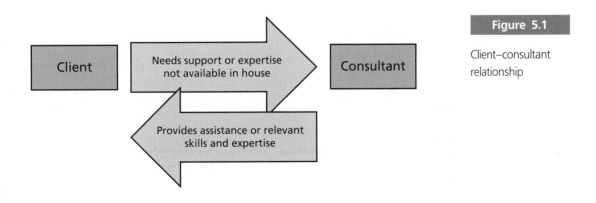

Figure 5.1

Client–consultant relationship

centre on the main role of the consultant but take into account the role the client has to play, so effectively they explain the relationship between the two parties.

The first model is the expert model where the consultant acts as the expert. In this model, the client typically has a problem that needs to be solved. The client delivers information about the problem to the consultancy or the consultancy engages with the client to generate information about any issues. The consultancy then generates solutions on the basis of their expertise and gives this back to the client in the form of a report or other product such as a presentation, workshops, etc. The client then implements the solution that the consultancy has generated (Devinney and Nikolova, 2004).

This approach is similar to the one put forward by Mulligan and Barber (2001). Any solutions generated are then given to the client, who should then implement. Problems with this approach may arise when the expert advice given gets rejected. Typically, this may happen as the expert has been solely focused on their area of expertise without considering the wider context of their advice (Mulligan and Barber, 2001). In assessment centres, it may not necessarily be the candidate with the highest scores that secures employment. It may well be the second, third or even fourth candidate due to their performance matching the client organization's needs as Thought Provoking point 5.1 demonstrates.

Thought Provoking point 5.1

Can you think of a time when someone rejected your advice, even though you knew you were right? This can happen in consultancy, where a candidate who is the top performer of an assessment centre is not recruited as the fourth highest performer out of seven candidates had previously worked with the organization as a contractor. In this situation, the consultancy can merely advise to recruit the top performer but the client can ignore this advice even if they have spent tens of thousands of pounds on a properly designed assessment centre.

The second model is the critical model (Clark and Fincham, 2002). In this model, rather than transferring knowledge as in the expert model, the aim is to provide support for the manager, director or chief executive officer of an organization so that they feel comfortable in their role. In my experience, managing directors and leaders often state that individuals below them can ask them for advice and support but who ultimately support them in the top job.

The critical model largely states that consultants as hired hands can fulfil this function. Clark and Salaman (1996) suggest that it is the consultant's role to convince their client of their knowledge and that 'they have something special to offer' (Clark and Salaman, 1996, p. 174). Consultants often join forces with clients and state that the client problems are the consultants' problems and as such share the responsibility of subsequent decisions made. Clark and Salaman (1996; 1998b) are quite critical of this process stating that impression management rather than actual transfer of knowledge is more important. Other authors have also been quite critical of the roles that management consultants have in the industry as shown in Chapter 2 (Clark, 1995; Craig, 2005; Craig, 2006).

Nevertheless, if all there was in the client–consultant relationship was impression management how is it that companies spend huge sums invested in consultants (Fincham, 2002)? To explain these issues, two further models were developed by Devinney and Nikolova (2004).

The third model is the reflective practitioner model. This was distilled from the literature by Devinney and Nikolova (2004) utilizing the work of Schön (1983, 1987) who states there are two types of consulting expertise being:

- knowing in action, which refers to utilizing tried and tested expertise
- reflection in action, which refers to utilizing reflection principles to understand situations not encountered before

The client–consultant relationship under the reflective practitioner model is complex. In essence, both the client and the consultant will have things to learn but each will bring to the table their own preconceived ideas, notions and methodology. In most situations, the client won't have much experience about the problem or situation. However, the client has the knowledge to deal with the situation that has to be extracted by the consultant.

On the consultant's side, some situations they would have seen before and therefore they can use tried and tested methodologies to deal with this. This is the knowing in action part of the reflective practitioner model. Nevertheless, there will be novel situations or issues for the consultant and as such the consultant will need to reflect on these afresh with the client. The client–consultant relationship becomes more balanced compared to other models, where either the consultant is the expert or the consultant is the impression manager. In the reflective practitioner model, both parties contribute in different ways to the situation or problem at hand.

The fourth model of consultancy is the interpretive model suggested by Devinney and Nikolova (2004) from the reflector practitioner model. The main difference between the two is that the consultant is still the reflective practitioner. However, they also interpret things around them in a meaningful sense. In this regard, the knowledge of an organization is dispersed between different individuals in that no one person will know the totality of all that is occurring. Individuals construct their own understanding based on their interpretive positions. The consultant's main role is to understand these interpretations, understand the client's language and as such be able to translate the interpretations. This model has had some academic support as Fincham (1999) found that the balance of power between consultant and client was fairly equal and that the relations between them mutually beneficial in an organizational development setting.

Figure 5.2 demonstrates how this interpretive model may work in practice. Consultants and clients meet and get to know each other's language and then discuss an issue in a familiar way. This then leads to reflection from both parties which creates a boundary around the issue or problem. This would typically be the project specification or terms of reference that the consultancy would draw up. This would help both parties to frame the problem and then by doing so creates further knowledge around the issue providing an eventual solution by reflecting on the framed issues. Out of all the models of consultancy this is perhaps the most relevant to the majority of management consultancy practices. For niche consultancies that specialize in say risk management, assessment centres, the expert model may be more apt. However, most consultancy work is complex and the interpretive model bears this in mind as both client and consultant have much to add to any consultancy work that commences.

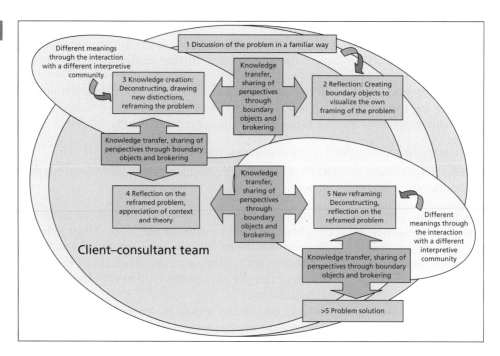

Functional relationships between consultant and client

The different models of the client–consultant relationship are complex as the last section demonstrated. Although the interpretive model is a good indication of how most management consultancies work in practice, Mulligan and Barber (2001) suggest that another way of examining the relationship is to look at the functional relationships involved. This is an excellent way of examining the relationship between the two parties as often there are differences between what is say, a contractual obligation versus the ethical or realistic obligation. Mulligan and Barber (2001) state that there are three types of functional relationship:

● The contractual relationship, which is the relationship defined in any offer of consultancy services. It should have firm boundaries and list the obligations under the agreed contract

● The idealized relationship, which is where both parties act as they think they are supposed to act. As such consultants become the undisputed experts of knowledge and clients the purchasers of this knowledge which they can either accept or reject

● The authentic relationship, which is where both parties are open and honest with each other and share their issues and threats that they perceive to themselves, the consultancy work, etc

This is certainly an interesting stance on the client–consultant relationship especially as many consultants will rely solely on the contractual relationship. Nevertheless, adopting an authentic relationship can solve many issues and lead to improved client and consultant relations. Industry snapshot 5.1 demonstrates this, whereby in the shadowy world of industrial espionage, problems can be dealt with by adopting an honest and open stance.

Firm to lead spy group

KPMG has confirmed that it has been asked by MI5 to lead a group to monitor cases of industrial espionage and coordinate information between large companies. The Big Four firm, which already works closely with the GCHQ listening station, has set up a 'risk management information exchange', which allows those who have responsibility for IT, security or risk management to share information and experiences 'in a trusted environment'. Last month the director-general of MI5,

Jonathan Evans, sent letters to 300 chief executives at major companies warning about the threat of electronic espionage from Chinese state organizations. Martin Jordan, principal adviser to KPMG on IT security and head of the new group, said: 'The intention is to give an early warning when threats appear'.

Source: Hanney, B. (2008). *Accountancy*; 141, 1373, p. 6. Reproduced with permission from *Accountancy Magazine*.

Phases of the Client–Consultant Relationship

So far the different models of the client–consultant relationship and the function aspects have been considered. Nevertheless, it is interesting to see how the client–consultant relationship is formed in the first place so as to explore the phenomenon in more depth before concluding this chapter.

Preparing for contact

Mulligan and Barber (2001) stated that the first stage in the formation of a client–consultant relationship is the actual preparation for contact. This initial preparation is vital in many professions including psychotherapy whereby the psychotherapist needs to prepare for meeting with their client for the first time even though they may have little information to prepare upon (Miller, 1999). In the world of management consultancy, fortunately services like the internet have made the preparation of knowledge about an organization much easier. Browsing through a client's website can give you a greater understanding of their organization, their culture, their management and their customers. In addition, if the interpretive model is to be applied any shared values or objectives should be identified as this will allow the consultant and the client to share experiences. Indeed, bringing along examples of other consultancy work of a similar nature to what the client is looking for may also help in the initial meeting with the client.

Other sources of research on an organization are available. One of the best sources is what the client has given to the consultancy for information, was it that they called up the consultancy looking for advice or was it the consultancy which made the first cold call selling services. In most cases it is likely to be the former so it is essential that any information the client gives is recorded. In addition, any information in the details given before expression of interest or tender can be used effectively in understanding the client's needs.

A customer relationship management (CRM) system is a great tool for this information. Essentially a CRM system is just a database in which any contact or information gleaned out of the client can be recorded. Nonetheless, it is a successful tool for generating sales and has a number of benefits including:

- increased sales to new and existing customers through better timing, identifying needs more effectively and cross-selling of other products
- effective marketing communications, through a more personal approach and the development of new and improved products or services
- enhanced customer satisfaction and retention
- increased value from your existing customers – and reduced cost to serve

Quoted from Business Link http://www.businesslink.gov.uk/bdotg/action

CRM systems can work extremely effectively especially if the consultant has a mobile copy in a personal organizer or PDA system. This allows knowledge of a client to be very accessible and enables the consultant on the road to respond to demands for services very quickly and effectively. Especially, if the client has had work completed for them in the past, which would be recorded on the CRM system.

Sobel (2006) stated that it is increasingly hard to establish new client relationships due to the increased use of competitive bidding and procurement processes for selecting appropriate firms. The advantage to this practice is that opportunities

---

Industry snapshot 5.2

Use of CRM databases in industry – some headlines

- The average expenditure on databases was £424 000 per year, with 48 per cent of companies expecting their database budget to rise by up to 20 per cent over the next two years.

- 68 per cent of marketing databases were built using customer accounts, 46 per cent deriving data from enquiries, 27 per cent from direct mail and 27 per cent from the internet.

- The average length of time that companies have held a database is seven years. 43 per cent have built one in the last five years and 9 per cent in the last 6 to 10 years.

- The mean size of the databases was 2 157 000, with 35 per cent holding 400 000 records and 36 per cent with under 50 000.

- The largest databases were found in the travel sector (10 million on average), FMCG (9.7 million), and financial services (6 million). On average consumer databases held 4.4 million records and business databases held 247 000, reflecting the narrower customer base of business to business markets.

- The most commonly held information on databases are customer contact details (90 per cent) and customer account detail is held on 59 per cent of databases.

- Amongst companies with departmental level databases, only 4 per cent say they are fully integrated with others in the company, although 43 per cent are partially integrated. Crucially, 49 per cent are not integrated at all.

Source: based on a quantitative survey of 100 firms by Direct Mail Information Service.

are more transparent. The downside is that you are competing with other firms for most work opportunities. Nevertheless, Sobel (2006) makes the point that if the focus is on what is valuable to the client then that is by far the most important first step in establishing a client–consultant relationship (see Thought Provoking point 5.2).

> ### Thought Provoking point 5.2
>
> Consultants need to do a better job of focusing on what's truly valuable to their clients. People talk a lot about adding value and value in relationships, but much of it is just talk. The very first step when you're discussing a potential project is to answer this question: what really is the value that the client is seeking and that we're going to create in this process?
>
> *Quote taken from an interview with Sobel (2006)*

Mulligan and Barber (2001) also stated that ensuring that the right individuals are at the initial meeting is also important. Earlier on it was revealed that the client can consist of those who know, those who care and those that can. If the initial meeting is just with those who know or those who care but not with those that can, then it may be difficult to lead to an eventual sale. Many consultants will, therefore, try and influence the initial meeting and invite the budgetary holders to maximize the amount of impact they have on the first visit. Sometimes though this is not possible and it is just part of consultancy life that sometimes those that can are not engaged with and therefore the work doesn't go ahead.

Orientation

Orientation is when the client and consultant meet for the first time in the spring of their relationship (Mulligan and Barber, 2001). In some management consultancy circles this phase is often given the rather uncouth title of a 'sniffing exercise' where the process is likened to two dogs sniffing each other out. However, it is an apt description as both the client and consultant do not know each other well and as such the early initial meeting is just really about both parties sounding each other out. Building rapport and sharing experiences is vital in this orientation phase (Devinney and Nikolova, 2004; Mulligan and Barber, 2001).

The preparation for the orientation phase would be a thorough understanding of what the client's needs are and what they are hoping to accomplish. However, no amount of literature or research on its own would give you this information so this is really the objective of the orientation meeting. However, as Mulligan and Barber (2001) suggested this initial phase is more of a sounding out process and according to the interpretive model of client–consultant relationships; it is about adopting a shared language between the different parties.

Initial impressions are also essential; dress should be suitable and appropriate. A professional stance should also be taken (see Thought Provoking point 5.3). But beyond this, Mulligan and Barber (2001) cite the well-known humanist work of

Rogers (1951) in forming successful relationships. In this regard, it is essential that there is congruence and positive regard between both parties. The relationships should be open, honest and authentic. So in this initial orientation it is best that both parties reveal something of themselves. As orientation meetings are often between specific people it is often beneficial if the personal objectives of completing the work are revealed. The client may feel strange about letting a stranger in, but if they feel included in the relationship, these worries are likely to fade over time. The consultant themselves will also have fears about access to the client and knowledge sources within the organization, so revealing these worries puts the client at ease as well as serves to show that it is ok to have fears, but in working together these can be resolved. (For more details see Chapter 13, especially Gary Copeland's work in Figure 13.4.)

Thought Provoking point 5.3

Meeting a client for the first time

When meeting with a client, dress appropriately to the situation. Find out what the clients environment is like and dress slightly better than that. Dressing for working in a merchant bank in the City of London is different to dressing for working in a rural setting. Do whatever to make you feel good about your appearance. If you are a man get your hair cut. If you are a woman then consider what make-up suits you best. Studies have shown that attractive people have more credibility. This then, rightly or wrongly, translates to success. Dressing well is not just for the client but if you will feel more confident if you look great.

Identification

If orientation is the spring in the client–consultant relationship, then identification is the summer when trust between the two parties is developed (Mulligan and Barber, 2001). During the identification phase both parties work together in identifying the issues at hand. As Fincham (1999) points out, the clients are not just passive receivers of wisdom, but they serve to point out the failings or shortcomings of their organization. Indeed, the client knows what the issues are in the organization and the consultant needs to relate to their experience to identify what issues need to be addressed.

At this stage, core questions need to be raised about any potential project that may arise from the preparation of a bid for work, which is typically the end of this phase. Underlying assumptions of both client and consultant need to be explicitly addressed by asking questions such as:

- What are the business benefits of the consultancy?
- How does the cost of the consultancy compare with the actual benefits realized?
- How will the consultancy be carried out?
- How will both parties participate in the consultancy agreement?

- What are the limitations of the project?
- What will the project not do, and where is there further work that may need to be completed?

These guidelines rely quite heavily on the expert type approach to the client–consultant relationship. Nevertheless, by stating what the objectives are in a rather loose fashion, i.e., a report will be generated from the results of the managerial interviews, this allows the consultants quite a bit of freedom to explore issues in the client's organization without deviating from the consultants brief too much. Nevertheless, as detailed in Chapter 6, this can give way to project creep, which is where the project scope expands and expands. Thus, by detailing the limitations of the project this situation can be avoided. And if the client wants work that is beyond the original brief then that is fine, but new contracts need to be raised.

Moorhouse Consulting (2008) produced a rather interesting guide on using consultants. They state that the relationship at the heart of consulting is paradoxical in that a client wants the consultant to be collaborative and almost intimate. Indeed, Sturdy, Schwarz and Spicer (2006) found that in their case study the Chief Executive Officer of the client firm invited the consultants and senior managers of the project to his home for dinner. Explaining that, 'it would be good to get together in a more informal way … to get to know each other better.' (Sturdy *et al.*, 2006, p. 939).

On the other hand consultants need to be scientific, objective and distant (Moorhouse Consulting, 2008). This is the type of ground rules for working collaboratively together that are formed in the identification phase. Typically, this stage is concluded by some sort of documentation such as a tender or bid, which the client and consultant agree with and then move forward.

Explorations

Once the contract or scope of work has been agreed, the exploration phase is the actual work commencing. Nevertheless, this is still a time to build the client–consultant relationship. Mulligan and Barber (2001) stated that during this phase, the strengths and weaknesses of all involved in the project are accommodated. Any conflict between individual parties should also be resolved. When there is a genuine relationship then that's when things can be resolved in times of difficulty. Mini Case Study 5.2 from Atos Consulting demonstrates this very factor where three organizations worked together for the good of the Royal Navy. This type of 'Alliancing' can work very effectively in practice.

Mini Case Study 5.2

Productively managing critical relationships

The Ministry of Defence (MoD) Nuclear Propulsion Integrated Project Team (NP IPT) is charged with delivering a safe and available nuclear propulsion plant to the Royal Navy's flotilla of nuclear powered submarines. The NP IPT is the principal customer of Rolls-Royce Submarines, placing 90 per cent of its business with the company. Rolls-Royce Submarines' business accounts for around 18 per cent of Rolls-Royce Marine Division turnover, amounting to some £1.4 billion a year.

▶

Business challenges

The contracting strategy between Rolls-Royce Submarines and the NP IPT had been in place since the late 1990s. The strategy included devolving project cost risk management to Rolls-Royce submarines to the detriment of timely performance and reduced costs to the MoD. The interpretation of MoD governance requirements led to too much time being spent by Rolls-Royce Submarines project managers on risk contingencies rather than quality of performance and timeliness of delivery. As a result, frustration and mistrust were starting to undermine an important relationship.

To their mutual credit, both the NP IPT and Rolls-Royce Submarines acknowledged the problem, and rightly identified that both the contracting strategy and their relationship needed to change. They agreed to embark upon a programme that would deliver a new joint approach to managing their relationship, based on a contracting strategy that satisfied their respective objectives in the most cost-effective way.

Solutions

The solution was made up of several linked components, each of which was essential in its own right and also formed part of a long-term programme designed to deliver productive, sustainable and trust-based change. The overall purpose was to align the individual business objectives of Rolls-Royce Submarines and the NP IPT, ratified in a new contracting strategy, and delivered via a joint partnering framework, new ways of working and a commitment to continuous improvement.

To this end, a co-located Joint Project Team was established, made up of Rolls-Royce Submarines and NP IPT resources, and set about articulating a vision that could be translated into a shared strategy and values. The Joint Project Team provided a simplified decision-making structure, without any duplication of roles, capable of delivering two core functions: Continuous improvement in performance and cost line with the strategy and values; Integrated programme planning and delivery.

Benefits

The partnering approach combined with target measurables has created confidence and trust as the basis for high quality management of the joint enterprise. Effort, targets and the routes to meeting targets are now mutually agreed and written into contracts, with the result that Rolls-Royce Submarines and the NP IPT are pulling in the same direction towards a common aim. Our input has helped to deliver:

- High quality management through co-ordinated and complementary efforts of NP IPT and Rolls-Royce submarines.
- Continuous performance improvement through joint planning, delivering focused change projects and initiatives.
- Tangible benefits in quality, value and service.

The core achievement has, therefore, been the delivery of genuinely mutual benefits. As the customer, the MoD has a commitment from Rolls-Royce Submarines to improve availability at a reduced cost within a long-term sustainable enterprise. As the supplier, Rolls-Royce Submarines has the opportunity to generate greater profitability through innovation and efficiency and a long-term commitment in this strategic business. For both parties, Atos Consulting has become a trusted consultant and facilitator and continues to support business improvement delivery.

Commodore Tony Johns, Director, Nuclear Propulsion, Royal Navy said:

'We now have a contracting strategy that delivers long-term benefits which can be measured, adapted and sustained through a fair and productive partnership in terms of price, profit, performance, quality and delivery timescales'.

Source: Atos Consulting, Ministry of Defence and Rolls-Royce, http://www.uk.atosconsulting.com/NR/rdonlyres/AB85BC09-2E81-4816-8A79-4F0263D50B50/0/RollsRoyce_MODSubs.pdf. Reproduced with permission.

Resolution

Resolution is the winter stage of the relationship (Mulligan and Barber, 2001). This is because the contract has now been completed and delivered successfully. Both parties take account of where the work has taken them and prepare for closure of the project. Dependent on the contract, there may be a report written or a service delivered in this phase that concludes the project.

Mulligan and Barber (2001) stated that although the project may be ended the client–consultant relationship may not necessarily be finished. Good consultants will always follow up work that has commenced in the past. Primarily as this ensures quality and service delivery to the client, but also because it can generate more leads even if the client is considered 'dead' or not prepared to take on other work. Some of the criticism levied at consultancy states that management consultants aim to get the client to rely on them as a service.

Clegg, Kornberger and Rhodes (2004) stated that management consultancies can turn a new client into 'a fertile soil' where further work could be harvested. Craig (2005) also stated that 'Poor management, management that is at war with itself or management that is out of its depth do buy consultancy – and lots of it.' (Craig, 2005; p. 179). From both of these perspectives, the management consultancy industry is parasitic, feeding off the goodwill of an organization. And as with most parasites, once they are within the host organism or in this case the host organization they don't let go. Craig and Brooks (2006) further comment that £70 billion is being plundered from taxpayer's money in the public sector.

However, Sturdy, Clark, Fincham and Handley (2004) criticized this stance stating that it is conservative and organizationally centric. During change, disruption is bound to happen and as a result management consultancies serve to transform organizations not just tinker and experiment with them. Management consultancies are also in the business of not just parasitically feeding off organizations but transforming them for the good of both the organization and the people within it (O'Shea and Madigan, 1997). In this regard, the resolution phase is important as the management consultant leaves the client organization and allows the client to be fully versed in whatever solutions have been given to them.

Chapter Summary

- The client–consultant relationship is not as simple as it might appear to be
- Identifying the client is a key aspect of forming a client–consultant relationship
- The client–consultant relationship can be defined simply as the association between the two parties; however, models demonstrate it is a complex phenomenon that has attracted some academic attention
- Four models examine the relationship consisting of the expert, critical, reflective practitioner and interpretive models
- Functional characteristics of the relationship are also important to consider in terms of the contractual obligations, the idealized relationship and the actual relationship
- The phases of forming the relationship are: preparing for contact, orientation, identification, explorations and resolution

Review Questions

1. Who is the client in the client–consultant relationship?
2. Who are those who know, those who care and those that can according to Mulligan and Barber (2001)?
3. What are the success factors in an ideal client–consultant relationship?
4. List the four models of the client–consultant relationship.
5. How does the interpretive model of consultancy differ from the expert model?

Assignment Questions

1. Why is it that clients should work collaboratively with consultants and not hold their 'feet to the fire until the smell of burning flesh is overpowering' as some clients have suggested is the way to deal with consultants (James, 2008).
2. Using an appropriate case study, critically discuss the idea of 'the client' detailing all the different parties involved.
3. Why is it important that a consultant addresses the client from different angles?
4. Do you agree with Engwall and Kipping (2002) that the client–consultant relationship is a poorly understood concept?
5. What are the phases in forming the client–consultant relationship and is the resolution phase a key element of this process?

Case Study 5.1

The client–consultant relationship and the consultancy process

By Roger Gill

This assignment was carried out for a government-owned oil company, Ownoil, in the Gulf region. The lead consultant (Robert), based in the UK, was assisted and supported by a locally-based consultant (John), who was director of consultancy for the Management Consultancy Centre (MCC), which provided management consultancy services in the same country. John, an Irish citizen, who until a few months previously had lived in Australia for 35 years, was to be the manager and coordinator of the assignment. MCC had won a tender for this assignment and several other associated assignments but felt it lacked the necessary expertise for this one.

Robert was approached through a third-party recommendation. The initial briefing of him by MCC by telephone and e-mail stated that the assignment was to be the development and delivery of a leadership development programme for up to 150 managers in Ownoil. A needs analysis had already been carried out by John and a British lecturer at a local college, Stephen, involving interviews with a few key executives, and this was provided to Robert. The key findings were as follows:

- Lack of clarity of responsibilities and goals;
- A 'silo mentality';
- Reluctance of managers to take decisions, deferring to senior managers or doing nothing;
- Lack of accountability across all departments;

- Lack of leadership and supervisory skills;
- Poor teamwork;
- Poor communication skills;
- A culture of blame in some departments.

Ownoil decided to address accountability – aiming to 'foster a climate of accountability within the organization' with a two-day workshop to be developed and 'pre-piloted' within a month, a 'pilot workshop' run within two months and then full roll-out with two workshops per month over the next 8–10 months. Ownoil envisaged a format including case examples, movie clips and a 'toolkit' – a managers' manual supplementing the workshop material and presentations. It was agreed that accountability was to be linked to leadership as much as possible within the time constraints.

Robert agreed, after negotiations with MCC by telephone and e-mail, to take on the assignment on this basis and travelled to the Gulf five days later for a two-day meeting with John and his colleagues (including Stephen) at MCC to plan and start the development phase. The pre-pilot workshop with senior managers was scheduled for five weeks later.

Another MCC consultant, Abdul, a local national, sourced culturally useful material for the workshop on leadership and accountability. However, shortly afterwards he was transferred by MCC to another pressing assignment. And at the same time, whilst Stephen was scheduled to shadow Robert and support John as a facilitator in the leadership workshops, he was dropped, at the request of Ownoil, because he was regarded as 'too didactic'.

The key contact in Ownoil was Chandra, Senior Training and Development Manager, who had been liaising with John. He suggested using lessons from Shackleton's expedition to the Antarctic in 1915. John and Robert acquired some books about Shackleton as an effective leader. Chandra also suggested some useful books relating to accountability. As a result of the planning session, Robert drew up a brief on who was going to provide what, decisions and actions needing to be taken and by whom, and a basic structure, content and methodology for the workshop.

Chandra continued to contribute ideas and suggestions but he was starting to express some impatience and strong preferences, even directives. A great deal of potential material was located and reviewed. Under pressure to produce the toolkit, Robert and John informed Chandra that it could not be produced until the content of the workshop was finalized. This phase produced material for the pre-pilot workshop comprising presentation slides, a performance and accountability culture assessment questionnaire and scoring system, case studies, group exercises, and an action planning process.

In the pre-pilot workshop, however, several cases and exercises were not carried out as intended but instead were discussed by the participants and workshop leaders for their suitability. Attendance was much smaller than expected, which was a common phenomenon in the company according to Chandra. Feedback from the pre-pilot workshop participants was reviewed and Robert and John made improvements for the pilot workshop planned for the following month.

By this time John and Robert were feeling that the emphasis for the workshop was shifting exclusively to accountability. Meanwhile a script (from a local corporate movie producer) for a proposed Ownoil company movie was reviewed and John and Robert made some minor suggestions. The movie was altered after feedback from Ownoil to the movie producer. However, at the last minute the film was pulled on the instruction of the CEO, who was unhappy with it and asked for it to be re-made. Two role-play exercises were developed, together with (pre-existing) related filmed behaviour models made by Robert, for agreeing accountabilities and performance expectations and for confronting performance problems. Chandra requested material for review as quickly as possible.

Chandra made several more suggestions by e-mail that Robert and John felt were unsuitable, including one for a new workshop outline. However, one suggestion, the use of RAMs (responsibility assignment matrices – borrowed from project management methodology), was included.

A few days before the pilot workshop Chandra requested the use of non-standard, localized clip-art and a new PowerPoint template, all of which Robert and John had to incorporate hurriedly. At about the same time, Chandra's manager, Bader, Head of Education, Training and Development, e-mailed him, John and Robert to express unhappiness about progress and instructing them to 'kindly expedite the outstanding issues'. John and Robert now sought approval or suggestions from Chandra concerning the programme content, tools and techniques (including the role-play exercises) and duly incorporated these following his approval. The pilot workshop was held as planned but, as for the pre-pilot, attendance was much smaller than expected.

Immediately after the pilot workshop, John and Robert carried out a review and planned what needed to be done. Chandra e-mailed to say that 'some progress' had been made but 'we have not yet developed the full confidence to go ahead with the first [roll-out] workshop' and that the workshop so far was 'entirely based on telling rather than facilitating'. He also requested a 'more professional' DVD to be sourced and used.

Development work continued, taking Chandra's input into account, but now proceeded more slowly owing to Robert's prior work commitments in the UK. Then suddenly, on a Thursday, Chandra e-mailed Robert in the UK asking for the workshop outline, timetable and materials to meet a request by the CEO for a briefing by himself and Bader three days later – on the following Sunday. Neither Robert nor John could comply in the time available.

Work now started on producing the toolkit and a draft was submitted. Chandra edited it, with both resulting errors and an adverse impact on its presentation. Chandra informed John and Robert that the CEO had decided to abandon using the company movie and that he would introduce the workshops in person.

Robert had received no feedback from Ownoil by nine days before the scheduled date of the first roll-out workshop so he requested it from John. He received this the next day, with full approval of the toolkit and workshop material and methodology. However, just before the workshop Chandra e-mailed John, with copies to Robert and his (Chandra's) manager, Bader, saying: 'Gentle reminder. Since the coming workshop will be attended by some senior managers in [the company], let us ensure that the agreements from the pre-pilot are applied with care. The attached notes [from Robert and John to Chandra] may serve as a good reminder for all of us to take care.' A further e-mail from Chandra said: 'We also need to remind Robert that lecture sessions should not be more than 20 per cent of the workshop ...'. Chandra requested that no copies of the PowerPoint presentation slides – only the (draft) toolkit – be distributed to participants.

Development work and cost were now well beyond what had been anticipated. Robert suggested to John that savings could be made by having a local consultant carry out the training workshops that were to be rolled out. In fact he was not relishing the prospect of the roll-out led by himself. MCC shelved this idea at this point.

The first two roll-out workshops were then held. The CEO did not attend either workshop owing to 'unavailability'; instead, Bader introduced them. In the first workshop Robert showed only one filmed behaviour model (demonstrating how to confront performance problems), which was to be used as a prelude to the role-play exercise but which on the day was abandoned. In the second workshop the toolkit was distributed and the second filmed behaviour model was replaced by a live role play performed by John and Robert. This was well received by the participants.

Ratings by participants in the first roll-out workshop on a 1 (low) to 5 (high) scale were all in the 4.0–4.8 range, with facilitation and support averaging 4.4 and quality and level of interaction, 4.5. The second roll-out workshop was also a success despite the now customary low turnout. Full roll-out now appeared appropriate and planning for this now started. It was interesting to observe that participants generally much preferred discussion of issues and ideas to skill practice and coaching. A month after the second roll-out workshop it was agreed that Robert would not continue to lead the workshops, which would be conducted by a local consultant yet to be sourced.

Outlines for the pre-pilot workshop and the second roll-out workshop are shown at the Appendix to show how the programme developed as a result of the pilot workshops, consultation process and development work.

Questions

1. Comment on the quality and use of the diagnostic phase in the consultancy process.

2. What consultancy style was used? How effective was it, and why? How might any other consulting style or process have been more effective, and why?

3. Comment on the client–consultant relationship. In what way(s) could it have been better, and why?

4. What lessons for effective management consultancy in multi-cultural and cross-cultural settings can be drawn from this case?

Appendix

Pre-Pilot Workshop Programme

Purpose of the workshop

To enhance overall leadership effectiveness and accountability in Ownoil by addressing:

- What is 'performance excellence'?
- Management versus leadership: what are they?
- The challenges and responsibilities of participants' management and leadership roles.
- Ownoil's core values: reality or aspiration?
- Communication, cooperation and collaboration across the organization.
- The meaning and realities of accountability.
- Empowerment as managers and leaders.

- Leadership and learning from mistakes and failure.
- Performance excellence through accountability and leadership.

Objectives

At the end of the workshop, participants will:

- Understand and accept their roles and responsibilities as managers and leaders.
- Have the knowledge and motivation – even inspiration – to develop themselves in these roles.
- Understand and embrace the ways in which they are accountable.
- Understand how failure and mistakes in a learning culture free of blame can lead to success.
- Be willing and able to operate as team players and serve the interests of the organization as a whole.
- Share the values that inform the vision, direction and purpose of the organization.
- Have the ability and desire to develop, empower and inspire their staff.

Methodology

- Interactive presentations.
- Case studies, examples and incidents (oil-industry related as far as possible).
- Small-group work in groups of 5 or 6.
- Small-group exercises/discussions and reports.
- Movie clips of role models and scenarios.
- Practical toolkit (prescriptions, guides on questions to ask and areas to consider, 'dos and don'ts', checklists, etc.) to be developed after the pre-pilot workshop based on feedback.

Timetable

Day One

07:00	* Introduction: what is 'performance excellence'?
	* Workshop objectives
	* DVD presentation and commentary: leadership lessons from Shackleton
	* Small group exercise and reports on a performance excellence scenario
08:30	Break
09:00	* Presentation on management versus leadership
10:30	Break
11:00	* Presentation on corporate culture and Ownoil's values: reality or aspiration?
	* Small group exercise, reports and review
	* Examples of dilemmas and challenges in Ownoil
12:30	Prayer break
13:00	* Communicating and working together: small group exercise, reports and review on encouraging communication, cooperation and collaboration across the organization
14:30	Lunch and end of Day 1

Day Two

07:00	* Presentation on the meaning and realities of accountability
	* Small group exercise, reports and review on a mini-case
08:30	Break
09:00	* Presentation on empowerment, risk and trust
	* Small group exercise, reports and review: empowering people
10:30	Break
11:00	* Presentation on leadership and values (learning from failure)
	* Individual exercise on achieving performance excellence: leadership and accountability
12:30	Prayer break
13:00	* Small group exercise and reports on individual exercise on achieving performance excellence and plenary session review
	* Workshop review, conclusion and evaluation
14:30	End of session and lunch

Second Roll-Out Workshop Programme

Purpose of the Workshop

To enhance accountability, leadership and performance in Ownoil.

Objectives

At the end of the workshop, you will:

- Understand the expectations of you as an Ownoil leader with regard to responsibility and accountability.
- Understand the defining attributes of effective company leaders and aspire to them.
- Be able to recognize and measure accountable behaviour and performance.
- Be able to confront and resolve performance problems.
- Be able to resolve complex issues of accountability and a blame culture at work.
- Be able to reinforce a new culture of performance, learning and accountability in teams.
- Be able to implement effective leadership at work.

Methodology

- Interactive presentations.
- Individual and group exercises, case discussions, group reports and plenary discussions.
- Movie/filmed illustrations.
- The Ownoil workshop toolkit.

Timetable

Day One

07:00	Registration and Coffee
07:30	Introduction to the Workshop
	* Welcome and address by the CEO: The Ownoil company vision
	* Introduction and expectations of staff and participants
	* What is 'performance excellence'?
	* The Ownoil workshop purpose, objectives and methodology
	* The Ownoil workshop toolkit
	* Assessment exercise: performance and accountability in Ownoil
09:00	Tea break

09:30   The Meaning and Realities of Accountability

* Assessment exercise: analysis and conclusions

* Movie presentation: 'Accountability that works'

* The nature of accountability

* Group exercise: accountability cases

* Group reports and plenary discussion

11:00   Break

11:15   Shackleton's Expedition to the Antarctic: Lessons in Leadership and Accountability

* The Shackleton story

* Group exercise: Shackleton's leadership and accountability

* Group reports and plenary discussion

* Lessons on leadership and accountability from Shackleton

12:30   Prayer break

13:00   The Accountable Leader

* Leadership as an accountability

* Five key themes of effective leadership and lessons for accountability

* Group exercise: leadership and the Ownoil vision

* Group reports and plenary discussion

14:30   Lunch and end of Day 1

Day Two

07:30   Agreeing Accountabilities and Performance Expectations

* Review of Day One

* Key elements of accountability

* Assigning responsibility and accountability: The RASCI tool [a form of RAM]

* Agreeing accountabilities and performance expectations: discussion steps

08:30   Tea break

09:00   Leadership, Accountability and Learning from Mistakes and Failure

* Empowerment and opportunity

* How mistakes and failure can lead to success

* Creating a learning culture

* Group exercise: learning from mistakes and failure

* Group reports and plenary discussion

10:30   Break

11:00   Confronting Performance Problems and Recognizing Progress and Achievement

* Progress reviews and feedback

* Ownoil policy on corrective guidance

* Coaching and counselling in confronting performance problems

* Documenting progress and feedback

* Key interpersonal skills in confronting performance problems

* Active listening

* Discussion steps in confronting performance problems

* Filmed behaviour model: confronting performance problems

* Group exercise: behaviour model analysis

* Group reports and plenary discussion

* Recognizing and reinforcing progress and achievement

12:30   Prayer break

13:00   Action Planning: Achieving Performance Excellence through Accountability and Leadership

* Attributes of an effective Ownoil leader

* Action planning: individual and group exercises

* Group reports and plenary discussion

* Workshop review

14:30   End of workshop and lunch

References

Fincham, R. (1999), The consultant-client relationship: Critical perspectives on the management of organisational change, *Journal of Management Studies*, 36(3), 335–351.

Hofstede, G. (1991), *Culture and Organizations: Software of the Mind*. Basingstoke: McGraw-Hill.

Kellen, V. (1997), *Managing the Client–Consultant Relationship*. www.kellen.net/Client ConsultantRelationship.htm.

Kubr, M., Editor (2002), *Management Consulting: A Guide to the Profession*, Fourth Edition, Geneva: International Labour Office. Re-published by permission in 2005 by Bookwell, New Delhi, India.

Lindblom, C.E. (1959), The science of muddling through, *Public Administration Review*, 19, 79–88.

Lippitt, G. And Lippitt, R. (1979), *The Consulting Approach in Action*. La Jolla, CA: University Associates, p. 31.

Nikolova, N. et al. (2008), Client and consultant interaction: Capturing social practices of professional service production, *Academy of Management Meeting Proceedings*, Anaheim, CA: 1–6.

Schaffer, R.H. (2002), *High-Impact Consulting: How Clients and Consultants Can Work Together to Achieve Extraordinary Results*. San Francisco: CA: Jossey-Bass.

Schein, E.H. (1987), *Process Consultation, Vol.II*. Reading, MA: Addison-Wesley.

Sturdy, A., Handley, K., Clark, T. and Fincham, R. (2009), *Management Consultancy: Boundaries and Knowledge in Action*. Oxford: Oxford University Press.

Wickham, P. and Wickham, L. (2008), *Management Consulting: Delivering an Effective Project*, Third Edition. Harlow: Pearson Education.

Further Reading

Clark, T. and Salaman, G. (1996), Telling tales: Management consultancy as the art of story-telling. In Grant. D. and Oswick, C. (Eds), *Metaphor and Organizations*. London: Sage, 167–184

Clegg, S.R., Kornberger, M. and Rhodes, C. (2004), Noise, parasites and translation, *Management Learning*, 35(1), 31–44

Devinney, T. and Nikolova, N. (2004), The client–consultant interaction in professional business service firms: Outline of the interpretive model and implications for consulting. Unpublished report Retrieved from http://www2.agsm.edu.au/agsm/web.nsf/AttachmentsByTitle/Egos+paper/$FILE/EGOS+paper.pdf

Fincham, R. (2002), Charisma versus technique: Differentiating the expertise of management gurus and management consultants. In Clark, T. and Fincham, R. Eds *Critical Consulting: New Perspectives on the Management Advice Industry*. Oxford: UK Blackwell Publishers Ltd.

Mulligan, J. and Barber, P. (2001) The client–consultant relationship. In, Sadler, P. (Ed) *Management Consultancy: A Handbook of Best Practice*. London: Kogan Page Ltd.

Sobel, A. (2006) Meet the masterminds: Andrew Sobel on the state of client relationships. *Management Consulting News*, accessed from http://www.managementconsultingnews.com/interviews/mckenna_interview.php

CHAPTER 6

Client engagement

Learning Objectives

At the end of this chapter students will be able to:

- Understand what client engagement is
- Understand how the sales pipeline works
- Initiate, plan and work with a client in order to set their expectations
- Recognize the importance of establishing client goals and expectations
- Recognize the importance of being honest with a client and not selling what cannot be delivered
- Recognize a contract and avoid project creep
- Recognize the essential importance of a contract

Mini Case Study 6.1

Financial services company: Employee and customer engagement

One of the largest diversified financial services companies in the United States set a vision and strategy to satisfy customers' financial needs whilst becoming the number-one financial services provider in the company's key market areas. Company leaders knew that achieving this mission and vision would require a strong base of engaged, committed employees who were willing to develop their talents.

The company hired The Gallup Organization to implement an integrated process to:

- manage employee engagement using the Gallup Q 12 process;

- implement manager-level training and action-planning programmes.

After two years, Gallup Business Impact Analysis revealed clear linkages between engaged employees and top-line revenue growth.

Between the first and second administrations of the Q 12, the client experienced a 24 per cent increase in the number of engaged employees (those most committed to their work) and a 19 per cent decrease in the number of actively disengaged employees (those fundamentally disconnected from their work).

Business units in the top quartile of employee engagement scores achieved substantially higher sales than did business units in the bottom quartile. Units that increased their employee engagement achieved 225 more sales per unit per year than did units that decreased in employee engagement. This equated to an additional $6.3 million in annualized profit for units that increased their employee engagement scores.

Business units in the bottom quartile of employee engagement scores had much higher turnover (231 per cent more) amongst a key class of full-time customer-facing employees.

To build on these successes, the client and Gallup then embarked on a programme to measure customer engagement and examine its linkages to employee engagement. The company and Gallup surveyed more than 4000 customers using Gallup's CE 11 metric to gauge customer engagement levels. The results indicated that 'optimized' business units – those that scored above the 50th percentile on both the CE 11 and Q 12 metrics – significantly outperformed non-optimized units – those scoring at or below the median on both CE 11 and Q 12.

Source: http://www.gallup.com/consulting/103/Financial-Services-Company-Employee-Customer-Engagement.aspx. CE11® and Q12® are trademarks of Gallup, Inc. Reproduced with permission.

Client Engagement

Why is client engagement important?

The opening case study demonstrates why client engagement is important. In Mini Case Study 6.1, Gallup was contracted to do work on encouraging employee commitment. Gallup worked with the client ensuring success through their two fold approach, which centred around engaging with the client. Client engagement is thus an essential topic in management consultancy. As without clients, consultants are unemployed. This chapter is concerned with the initial and continual engagement with the client building from the last chapter where the text concentrated on the formation and development of the client–consultant relationship.

> **Thought Provoking point 6.1**
>
> Can you think of a time when you wanted to speak to someone important, either a professor or more probably a potential romantic partner. How did you feel about that initial engagement? Do you think that the initial engagement went well? And if it didn't how do you think the relationship may have turned out like?

Client engagement: A definition

Client engagement is a concept difficult to define. Many training firms complete courses in client engagement as shown in Industry snapshot 6.1 below. Nevertheless, many of these training schemes are behavioural and skill based rather than concentrating on what exactly is client engagement. In examining Industry snapshot 6.1, it is in essence a personal development course, which is covered separately in this book in Chapters 13 and 14. So what exactly is client engagement?

Industry snapshot 6.1

Client Engagement Course

Overview
A two-day course covering the practical skills needed to successfully initiate and handle client engagements.

Who should complete the course?
The course is suitable for those who wish to increase their level of client engagements. It promotes the confidence of initially engaging with the client and the capability of offering client focused solutions.

What will you achieve?
Client engagement especially at the initial phases of contact is an essential area for professionals to master if they are to be successful. Winning and retaining clients not only depends on providing client focused solutions but on the successful engagement of the client which can be built upon to form longer lasting relationships. The course covers the theoretical underpinnings of client engagement. It also promotes the practical side of engaging with clients through practice, exercises and simulations.

What is the course programme?
Personal effectiveness: Impression management; Effective listening; Successful communication; Networking and social skills; Successfully managing meetings; Influencing strategies.

Project management: Project management concepts; Initiating a project; Using a project to build a client relationship; Managing client expectations; Handling organizational and client politics; Creating sales opportunities within the project environment.

Dealing with the challenges of client engagement: What factors go wrong in client engagement; Dealing with stress and uncertainty; Successful negotiation skills.

Course length: 2 days

Interestingly, the management consultancy literature has tended to avoid defining client engagement. Instead, the initial phases of client engagement in terms of negotiating entry and contracting are often cited in literature (Neumann, 1997; Hussey, 2001a). Whilst these stages are important and will be detailed in this chapter, a definition of client engagement in the management consultancy literature remains elusive.

Nevertheless, client engagement is explored thoroughly in the social services literature. Engagement similarly to the management consultancy literature typically refers the front end or early stages of the helping process with a client (Yatchmenoff, 2005). Client participation is also used as a measure of engagement, although arguably a client could participate but reticently, being not actively engaged in the work. In this regard, Yatchmenoff (2005) defines the importance of the five dimensions in client engagement. These dimensions can also be applied (with very little adjustment) to management consultancy clients as follows:

- Receptivity: openness to receiving help, characterized by recognition of problems or circumstances that resulted in agency intervention and by a perceived need for help
- Expectancy: the perception of benefit; a sense of being helped or the expectation of receiving help through involvement of others; a feeling that things are changing (or will change) for the better
- Investment: commitment to the helping process, characterized by active participation in planning or services, goal ownership, and initiative in seeking and using help
- Working relationship: interpersonal relationship with worker characterized by a sense of reciprocity or mutuality and good communication
- Mistrust: the belief that the consultancy is manipulative, malicious, or capricious, with intent to harm the client

Adapted from Yatchmenoff (2005); p. 87

Although there are obvious differences between engaging a susceptible individual and individuals within an organization or the organization itself, there are certainly commonalities. Thus, the five dimensions here can be included in a measure of client engagement. Given this, client engagement may be defined in a management consultancy context as follows:

Client engagement is the involvement with the client that has contractual and social boundaries set at the beginning of an assignment or evolves through the renegotiation of work.

Several issues therefore are important when examining client engagement. Initially, there is the initial setting up of the contractual and social boundaries. However, there may also be a renegotiation of duties on both the consultant and client side. This needs to be handled carefully to avoid 'project creep' which is where the project goes above and beyond what it was originally supposed to do.

The Entry Phase

Several authors have detailed the importance of the entry phase in consultancy (Hussey, 2001a; Neumann, 1997; Stroh and Johnson, 2006). This is because the success or failure of a consultancy project depends on client engagement. Without this, the assignment is invariably compromised. Client engagement therefore needs to be determined way before any contracts are signed in the entry phase (Stroh and Johnson, 2006).

The entry phase is very much a matching exercise between what the client wants and what the consultant can provide (Karantinou and Hogg, 2001). Indeed, the way that a management consultancy carries out an assignment will greatly affect whether the outcome is successful or not (David and Strang, 2006). Typically, the entry phase is defined as the period between the invitation to discuss a potential piece of work and the award of the contract (Hussey, 2001a). This starts with the sales pipeline and finishes with the final agreement and award of the consultancy project.

The sales pipeline

One of the most important factors that influence the entry phase is the sales pipeline. The sales pipeline is the number of leads that have the potential of becoming actual projects at any one time. The sales pipeline is a crucial part of business development that requires close monitoring and represents the life blood of a consultancy (Beam, 2006; Hrehocik, 2007). It has an impact on the entry phase as if there are not many leads going into the start of the pipeline then this puts additional pressure on the consultancy, to make the few leads that it has acquired into actual assignments. Within the consultancy field, there is a rule of thumb or heuristic that suggests that for every one project won there must be a minimum of about five potential leads at the start of the sales pipeline. However, for a healthier consultancy there may be less leads needed if they have a good conversion rate of leads into projects (Beam, 2006).

Beam (2006) explained the sales pipeline in a management consultancy context. In essence, the important part of a management consultancy is to develop new opportunities and projects. Beam (2006) suggested that consultants should review the pipeline at least once on a weekly basis if not more frequently. Nevertheless, if a consultant is working for a client this is often quite difficult. However, as Beam (2006) suggested it is an important aspect of management consultancy not to ignore. Otherwise consultancies can get into 'feast and famine' type situations, whereby when the consultants are working, they are busy on that particular contract and then do not market themselves for other work. This is known as the 'feast' stage as there is plenty of work available. However, when the project that they are working on comes to an end, as the consultants haven't been actively marketing themselves they are suddenly without work in the 'famine' stage.

Careful managing of the sales pipeline is essential to avoid the 'feast and famine' of consultancy. It is not the case of having lots of leads in the pipeline, but of careful management of the prospects available (Beam, 2006). Figure 6.1 demonstrates how the pipeline works. In this case, sales strategy determines what type of prospects are explored. A prospect in this instance is any potential client or even project that may be of interest to the consultancy. Prospects are gained in a number of ways from reading the business section of papers such as the financial times to understand what is going on in the market place through to more specialist resources such as specific trade journals or websites. A consultancy should have a number of prospects that in common with all organizations need to be reviewed on a regular basis (Buttle, Ang and Iriana, 2006). Beam (2006) suggests there should be a large number of leads in any consultancy business.

From the regular review of prospects comes the qualifying phase. This varies from industry to industry but in essence means identifying the requirements and being able to meet these criteria of the sales opportunity (Kibarian, 1966). The business literature is littered by sales gurus giving advice to qualify sales from being friendly to your client (Gitomer, 2006) through to just getting down to the basic needs of your client (Verzone, 2006). Techniques differ from person to person but qualities such as integrity, openness and honesty are important in qualifying sales

Figure 6.1

The sales pipeline

opportunities. Again, Beam (2006) suggested that in a consultancy this process should happen quickly whereby 90 per cent of all potential leads may be rejected as it is better to be firm with organizations that are not particularly serious about employing consultants.

Thought Provoking point 6.2

The first sale I ever made was where a solicitor described to me the problems his company had with their IT systems. On the basis of what he said, I described what the IT firm that employed me did in terms of going into an organization, investigating what hardware and software was needed, training up the individuals to use the equipment and then installing everything over a weekend so that the client literally went home on the Friday and then came back on the Monday to find new kit and new software, that they had been trained on, available. On this basis, I qualified the prospective client in an open and honest way stating what my firm did and made the sale. This was an unusual first sale as the qualification stage was completed in the sauna of my local gym!

Once the sales opportunities have been qualified this then leads onto managing opportunities. In a consultancy it is essential that the people are available to do the work proposed from the sales opportunity. Once these have been identified as available, a proposal for work is issued and on the basis of this the contract for the work goes ahead (Beam, 2006). Through effective client consultant relationships there should be a high ratio of proposals that become actual projects (Beam, 2006; Werr and Styhre, 2003). This in effect is the entry phase where entry is negotiated with the client on the basis of sound client consultant relations.

Negotiating entry

Negotiating entry with a client is an important phase of the client–consultant relationship (Werr and Styhre, 2003). Hussey (2001a) stated that negotiating entry has very specific purposes from both the client and the consultant perspective. The consultancy can think about what the client needs and wants and whether they are able to deliver products or services on the basis of these needs and wants. A client, on the other hand, must think about what benefits may be gained from the utilization of consultancy services (Hussey, 2001a). Table 6.1 demonstrates the purposes of the entry phase as suggested by Hussey (2001a).

Both the client and consultant have an economic necessity to go towards the successful signing of a contract (Heusinkveld and Benders, 2005; Hussey, 2001a). Hussey (2001a) argued that there are three objectives in the entry phase which are: understanding, relationship building and contractual.

Understanding the client's issues or problems is an essential aspect of matching the client needs with the most appropriate consultant (Heusinkveld and Visscher, 2006). However, assignments can be very complicated as the client may not know all the information around certain issues or may lack the insight into their own problems (Hussey, 2001a). The consultant's role is to understand the issues that the client faces, or have a good enough understanding of the issues that they can put forwards a methodology to investigate the issues further specifying what the project can and cannot do in terms of business benefits and limitations.

Relationship building is also an essential part of negotiating entry. In the last chapter, the client–consultant relationship was detailed in depth but throughout the whole of the entry stage the consultant should be actively building a relationship with the client. Relationships are formed on the basis of mutual understanding and respect so high pressured sales typically do not work in this environment

Clients purpose of entry	Consultants purpose of entry
Gain economic benefits from the project	Gain economic benefits from conducting and managing the project
Match the consultancy's understanding of the client issues with their own	Understand the issues facing the client
Understand the capabilities and limitations of the consultancy firm	Ensure that the resources are available to work with the client and that the consultancy has the desired competence
Trusts in the credibility of the consultancy	Satisfies the client of the firms credibility
Trusts that the firm are cost effective	Satisfies the client of the cost-benefit of the project
Issues a contract that will realize the business benefits proposed	Signs the contract that will agree the deliverables on a project and the fee rates chargeable
Reinforces the decision made on the most appropriate firm	Enhances the reputation of the consultancy

Table 6.1

Purposes of entering into a contract from the consultant and client perspectives (adapted from Hussey, 2001a)

(Hussey, 2001a). Indeed, it is likely that other consultancies will be involved in the negotiation of the contract so it is important to convince the client of the consultancy's competence but at the same time don't over sell the ability to do the job.

The contract in essence represents the commodification of knowledge in that the deliverables to the client in terms of the knowledge that they gain is translated into a document that specifies the business benefits available to them (Heusinkveld and Benders, 2005; McKenna, 2006a). A contract doesn't necessarily have to be in writing but it is an agreement between the client and consultant (Holtz and Zahn, 2004). Some contracts may be negotiated in person and then formalized in an informal manner, such as the following:

> Dear David,
>
> In principle, we can agree the 4 days @ £2500 + vat. I will take the lead on the project and then either Julie or I will do the interviews with the 7 senior managers. What we will then produce out of the interviews is a distinct report stating what we did, what we found and the training needs recommendations on the basis of what we found.
>
> Best regards,
> David

For simple projects, this type of communication may be fine especially if there is a good working relationship between all parties. However, project creep is potentially a problem. Project creep is where the contract is vague and as such the client can add more services to the project. For example, in the email above, the level of training needs analysis was not stated. In this manner, were the training needs for the whole group of seven managers discussed together or was it each manager having an in-depth profile written up. The email doesn't actually specify and the level of training needs analysis is important as individual profiles would take at least a further day over and above the four days agreed. In this regard, sometimes the contract can be more prescriptive as in the example in Figure 6.2. Nevertheless, there are still assumptions made in this contract, e.g., that the Scandinavian client will have trained assessors who have used assessment centre materials before. This was verbally agreed with the client but wasn't written in the contract and therefore was an actual problem when the work went ahead.

The process of negotiating entry

In examining the initial stages of client engagement, it is useful to examine the process of negotiating entry. This does depend on the work undertaken but even for the most simplest of jobs there is still a process that needs to be followed to negotiate entry. Hussey (2001a) stated there were four stages in negotiating entry as follows:

1. Agreeing the brief and the score of the work
2. Planning the project
3. Preparing the proposal
4. Presenting the proposal

Agreeing the brief and the scope of the work

Agreeing the scope of the work can be done over the telephone if the client is already well known. However, more typically agreeing a brief is done in the initial

This Assignment Sheet is, except where specifically stated below, subject to the terms and conditions contained in the **Contractor's Contract (Sole trading and Limited Company)** entered into between the Contractor and AMX Worldwide Limited.

Anticipated Start and End Date	7th August 2009, 08.00 to 19.00
Overtime Agreement	No overtime
Standard Hourly/Daily/Weekly or per Candidate Rate	£1200.00 (excluding reasonable travel and subsistence expenses)
Frequency of submission of Invoices	Once, at the end of the assignment
Purchase Order Number	26545 (please quote this on your invoice)
Notice Period	One week for both parties
Assignment Sheet to be returned to Company before	26/07/2009

SPECIAL CONDITIONS:

The Services
- to lead the Group Discussion assessment
- brief assessors on the day prior to exercise
- read out candidate instructions at the start of each group discussion (note: 5 candidates per group discussion)
- observe two of the candidates in the group discussion (there will be 3 other assessors observing one candidate each)
- score the two candidates
- lead a brief wash-up at the end of the group discussion scoring with the other assessors to ensure consistency in scoring
- after both group discussions have been completed to pass materials and scores to external consultant leading on this project

Please arrive for 08.00.
We anticipate that the day will finish around 19.00

Location
Holiday Inn
Amager Boulevard 70
Copenhagen, 2300
Denmark

Client Details
Urban Development Company

Roles
Administrative Officer

Figure 6.2

Example contract for a day's consultancy work

face to face meeting with the client (Holtz and Zahn, 2004). This is typically because the client has a specific need that needs to be listened to carefully. The client may not necessarily reveal this need in a formalized document such as a contract, so it is vital that this information is gained from the client (Holtz and Zahn, 2004). In addition, miscellaneous reasons for awarding or not awarding the contract as shown in Industry snapshot 6.2 can be avoided in a face to face situation.

Industry snapshot 6.2

Draynor Borough Council – Statement about pin-ups losing the contract

Draynor Borough Council were interested in an organizational development project which specifically meant the redesign of their competency framework and this being fed into additional services, such as training and recruitment. The need for such services was advertised and went through two phases. The first phase was the expression of interest phase and the second was the tender stage. These are both common practices in negotiating entry into work with a client. The consultancy was successful in getting through the expression of interest phase.

The consultancy would have also been, the client subsequently reported, successful in getting through the tender stage. Nevertheless, as part of the tender, the consultancy had to submit its employee handbook. This would of course not be a problem. However, the consultancy had also just taken over a small service company that were involved in landscape design and gardening for another local authority. Under the Transfer of Undertakings (Protection of Employment) Regulations 2006 (TUPE), when a company is bought, the employees terms and conditions are preserved.

During the merger, the consultancy had to address the previous company's statement about the explicit use of 'pin-up' posters of semi-naked individuals in garden and maintenance sheds. The consultancy did this but under TUPE could not go against the right of employees of putting up this type of poster although advised against it. Draynor Borough Council thought that this regulation applied to the consultancy offices and were concerned that an employee could, under this regulation, stick up a 'pin-up' poster of a naked fireman or page 3 model. As this was the only sticking point of the contract not being signed, the consultants preparing for the bid engaged the time of the company lawyers and got them to write a letter stating that the use of 'pin-ups' was prohibited in the offices. Nevertheless, the lawyer's letter basically stated that whilst individuals had the right to put up a 'pin-up' in an office environment this would be deemed to be unacceptable and therefore disciplinary action would result. Therefore no posters of inappropriate material would be displayed. The client was not convinced and subsequently the contract was not awarded.

Preparation before any meeting is vital (Holtz and Zahn, 2004; Hussey, 2001a). And as shown in the previous chapter Customer Relationship Management (CRM) systems can aid this process but whether it can be truly automated is open to academic debate (Buttle, Ang and Iriana, 2006). What is certain is that homework on a potential client truly pays off, as in the initial meeting the consultant will have already had a flavour of the client. CRM systems can help this process, by letting the field operative know about previous contact with the company, etc (see Chapter 5 for further details).

The meeting should then be used to engage the client and find out as much as possible (Holtz and Zahn, 2004). The consultant should try to make a positive impression and ensure that the right chemistry exists between them (Stroh and Johnson, 2006). However, this is taking a purely functionalist perspective (Werr and Styhre, 2003). As others have suggested that the initial meeting can be the start of a deceptive relationship whereby the management consultant uses impression management to win over the client (Clark, 1995; Werr and Styhre, 2003).

Hussey (2001a) suggested that consultants at the first meeting should find out as a minimum the following:

1. What is the issue for the client?
2. Why are the issues important to the client?
3. What has the client done previously to address the issues?
4. What is the scale of the potential project?
5. What resources would be available to the consultancy?
6. Why is the company looking for a consultancy to investigate the issues?

7. How many other competing consultancies are there for the work?
8. What process of selection will the client use to select the most appropriate consultancy?

These are all important but also key is finding out the budget a client has and who has the authority for the budget to be spent on the project (Holtz and Zahn, 2004). Nevertheless, many clients will refrain from giving these details.

Planning the project

Detailed planning will probably occur once the project has been won (Hussey, 2001a). However, it is essential that given what the client has stated, the project is conceptualized and thought out in adequate detail. In essence, the consultant must make sure that the client's requirements will be satisfied through the adequate placing of resources. The consultant must broadly speaking work out how much time particular tasks will take. Often a spreadsheet is used for this type of operation as shown in Figure 6.3. In the example in Figure 6.3 the total number of days work is 30. This is split between four stages consisting of the Operations Department service requirement phase by the IT consultant, the skills review phase where the bulk of the project is completed, the presentation phase and then some additional time for quality assurance. In Chapter 8, the time, cost and quality triangle will be discussed and the same principle applies here that the more time a project has the more flexible a project manager can be ensuring that the client's requirements are fulfilled.

Costs of the project should also be calculated at this stage. Figure 6.4 demonstrates how costs are typically calculated in a consultancy firm, although for simplicity expenses haven't been added to this model. Nevertheless, this represents the main method of calculating costs for most consultancies. In Figure 6.4, the first line represents the staff on the project and the total number of days that they are on the project. The next line is the individuals total salary cost (tsc). This figure represents how much the consultancy firm pays the individual per hour. The total tsc in this project is £12 708.

Nevertheless, office space, costs of running the consultancy business, etc. all need to be covered through consultancy work so the total salary cost is oncosted. The oncost value depends on the consultancy but as a minimum it is usually at least twice the tsc figure. In this particular consultancy, the oncost figure is 2.5 times tsc. This gives the actual oncosted tsc that should be covered by the project

STAFFING	Total	Director	Manager	HR Consultant	IT Consultant	Junior Consultant
Operations Department service requirement	3				5	
Skills review phase	21		9	9		3
Presentation (prep and attendance)	3		3			
Quality assurance and final sign off	1	1				
Total days	**30**	**1**	**12**	**9**	**5**	**3**

Figure 6.3

Brief plan for a small consultancy project

STAFFING	Total	Director	Manager	HR consultant	IT consultant	Junior consultant
Total days	**30**	**1**	**12**	**9**	**5**	**3**
tsc £/hour		106.00	61.52	50.89	60.09	30.56
Total tsc	12708	795	5537	3435	2253	688
Oncosted tsc (2.50)	31770	1988	13842	8588	5633	1719
Oncosted day rate		1988	1154	954	1127	573
Day rate agreed		2000	1500	1500	1200	1200
Fees	**43100**	**2000**	**18000**	**13500**	**6000**	**3600**
Day rate uplift		1.01	1.30	1.57	1.07	2.09

at £31 770. So if the project was given at cost, in other words it just covered the consultant's salaries and upkeep of the consultancy offices, etc. then the project would cost £31 770. Nevertheless, the consultants will have a market value and this will be the day rate agreed. This will be what the client is shown. Quoting this figure and using the days that the consultants work increases the price of the project to £43 100. And the following line represents the uplift value per consultant, which shows that for the director of the project not much additional income is received which is not the case for the junior consultant who earns the project a much healthier return. Overall, the fees charged at £43 100 means that the profit margin of the project will be £11 330, which is quite healthy but if the project was under-estimated in terms of time, would quickly be used up (see Thought Provoking point 6.3 for details). Also impacting this figure and not shown in Figure 6.4, are expenses. The rechargeable expenses in this project such as travel, hotels, etc. are charged at cost to the client. These don't influence the profit margin although Craig (2005) claims that many consultancies may get travel rebates or other 'scams' that invariably mean that additional profits are made. The non-chargeable expenses such as commissions paid to third parties who found the work, etc. need to be accounted for but can't be charged to the client so need to come off the profit margin.

Thought Provoking point 6.3

Underestimating the project costs

As a consultant, I once teamed up with a well-known university that was part of the Russell Group in submitting a bid for a high profile project that involved the production of a test that used clips of various hazards. The bid came in at just over £250K. However, we lost the work as a rival company wanted the project due to its high media profile and as such proposed the project could be completed at about £80K. The rival won the project, but delivered the project a year late. This rival firm had obviously reduced down the costs of the project, could not risk reducing quality so in the time, cost, quality triangle (see Chapter 8) sacrificed time, thus delivering the project late.

Preparing the proposal

The proposal is a key factor in obtaining the work. Stroh and Johnson (2006) describe it as:

> Proposals outline (or propose) how the consultant or consulting agency will perform the work the client desires. They usually include the various tasks to be completed, timelines, fees, consultant's qualifications, and whatever other information the client has requested.
>
> *(Stroh and Johnson, 2006)*

Typically the proposal is in a written format that varies from an email through to a lengthy formal document. Sometimes the proposal can be a verbal agreement. Nevertheless, as mentioned before 'project creep' can be a real problem with any verbal agreement as it is difficult to know what has been agreed. Indeed, project creep typically happens very slowly in that a client may ask for a further breakdown of figures, which then leads to something else interesting so is it possible that this is explored further, etc., etc. The advantage of a written proposal is that a consultant can always say, well I can do the additional analysis but it is over and above the originally planned work so I need to charge this for it. A client will then either agree or not to the additional work.

The proposal also needs to be a persuasive selling document (Hussey, 2001a). In essence, it is the key document that forms part of the contract between client and consultant. Typical headings within a formal proposal may be:

1. Introduction
2. Objectives and scope
3. Methodology
4. Timetable
5. Staffing
6. Costings
7. Annexes

The introduction will comprise of the background to the project. This will state why the client wants the project to go ahead and the key benefits that will come out of the project if it should go ahead. The consultancy's approach is also detailed here but typically with a caveat such as:

> Our approach is fully laid out in this offer and we will of course be happy to refine aspects of it in consultation with yourselves.

In the proposal, it is essential that the consultancy states what they think the client wants them to do and then their general approach; however, flexibility is also important. The introduction would also typically state something about the consultancy firm, e.g., 'We are one of the country's leading integrated planning, management and engineering consultancies. Through our experience and expertise in risk management, psychological research and survey work we believe that we are well placed to accomplish this project.' In addition, previous work with the client and similar types of projects that have been conducted would also be stated in the introduction.

The objectives and scope of the project would reiterate what the client wanted from the project and then how the project would fulfil these objectives. This section is usually quite precise and demonstrates to the client that the consultancy has understood their requirements. Often if the consultancy is not sure about the budget amount available as in Case Study 6.1 below, it is likely that they may offer a basic service and a more thorough process. This can be seen in the Industry snapshot 6.3 below as the consultancy quoted prices for 300 and 500 interviews as it was not sure of the client's budget.

Industry snapshot 6.3

Example objectives and scope

The following objectives and scope are taken from a project that Atkins Management Consultants won with the Health and Safety Executive (HSE), the results of which were published in a HSE book (Biggs and Crumbie, 2000). This original expression for interest by the HSE was published in the British Psycological Society Appointments memorandum.

Objectives

The objectives of this study are to:

- Identify groups with common characteristics who may require different information strategies and messages on chemical risks and control;
- Target future risk information campaigns more effectively;
- Understand how information is transferred between and within organizations.

Three project stages are proposed to achieve these objectives. These are:

- Development and pilot of a programme of semi-structured interviews.
- Fieldwork: data collection from organizations using chemicals.
- Analysis and report writing.

Scope

A semi-structured interview questionnaire will be developed and agreed with HSE. A frame of companies that use chemicals will be agreed with HSE, and random sampling will then be used with the selected frame.

Specific characteristics of individuals working with chemicals and the organization in which those individuals work in will then be identified in the interview programme. Costing for samples of 300 and 500 respondents have been given. The data will be analysed to derive profiles of chemical users and lead to recommendations in marketing risk prevention literature.

Ways of working will be as described in the Terms of Reference for the study, including:

- HSE will be updated on the progress of the project on a regular basis. This will include regular telephone contact, an interim progress report and at least three meetings.
- Both draft and final reports will be produced. The latter will incorporate client comments and amendments.

The next section that any proposal should detail is the methodology to be used in the study. This typically will start with an overview of the methodological challenges within the project followed by how these will be approached (see Figure 6.5). Nevertheless, a proposal should state that the consultancy can be flexible in

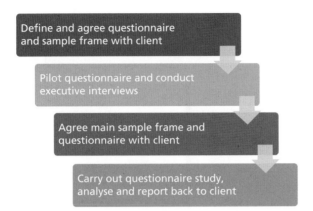

Figure 6.5

Typical methodology
that may be
proposed to a client

their approach and refine aspects after a detailed discussion on methodology at the inception of the project. The analyses conducted and also the results that are expected to come out of the project are then typically given in the methodology section, although Hussey (2001a) suggested that a results section from the approach taken may be better received by the client. Aspects of quality assurance should also form part of the methodology section ensuring that the client is aware of the professional and ethical handling of data, participants, etc.

The timetable for the work should also be given in the proposal. This can be as simple as just stating time and dates or can be rather more complicated breaking work up into stages. If the project is complicated, typically a Gantt chart would be used to demonstrate to the client the ability of the consultancy to adequately plan the work. An example Gantt chart is given in Figure 6.6.

Staffing is the next section in the proposal and this will demonstrate the skills and qualifications of the consultants put forward. Consultants will develop their own 'pen portraits' but orientated towards the particular work that is being proposed. An example pen portrait for say a research contract may be as follows:

Dr David Biggs is a Chartered Occupational Psychologist with experience in research and consultancy. He has conducted research on the UK labour force primarily using government surveys such as the Labour Force Survey. He has also conducted qualitative analysis of particular groups such as in the emergency services and within consultancies. David has recently been involved with assessing senior management development needs for a rapidly growing supplier in Gloucestershire. David also has experience in training, recruitment, occupational health and psychometric assessment.

Costings of the project are then covered in the proposal. Typically, this will give the total cost first and then break this down into staffing costs giving day rates and days spent on the project, etc. Expenses are also given in this section. However, non-recoverable expenses are not typically shown to the client, neither are the actual costs of the consultant such as total salary costs nor the oncost rates given. Indeed, the only figures given to the client from the example shown in Figure 6.4, would be the actual days spent on the project, the day rate agreed and then the fees chargeable. In large projects, the consultancy may also produce a payment schedule for the client. This has the advantage of spreading the payment out for the client and alleviating cash flow problems for the consultant (Holtz and Zahn, 2004). In addition, a basic and a more advanced approach may be costed out to the

Figure 6.6

GANTT chart
demonstrating the
timetabling of events
to a client

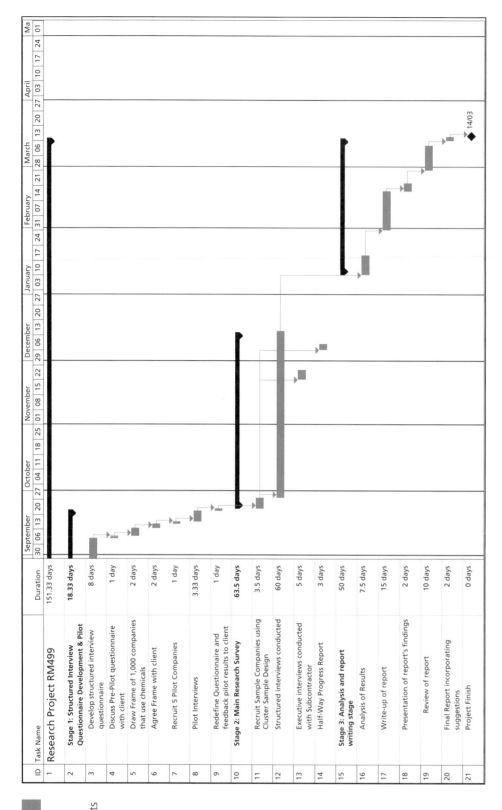

ID	Task Name	Duration
1	**Research Project RM499**	151.33 days
2	**Stage 1: Structured Interview Questionnaire Development & Pilot**	**18.33 days**
3	Develop structured interview questionnaire	8 days
4	Discuss Pre-Pilot questionnaire with client	1 day
5	Draw Frame of 1,000 companies that use chemicals	2 days
6	Agree Frame with client	2 days
7	Recruit 5 Pilot Companies	1 day
8	Pilot Interviews	3.33 days
9	Redefine Questionnaire and feedback pilot results to client	1 day
10	**Stage 2: Main Research Survey**	**63.5 days**
11	Recruit Sample Companies using Cluster Sample Design	3.5 days
12	Structured interviews conducted	60 days
13	Executive interviews conducted with Subcontractor	5 days
14	Half-Way Progress Report	3 days
15	**Stage 3: Analysis and report writing stage**	**50 days**
16	Analysis of Results	7.5 days
17	Write-up of report	15 days
18	Presentation of report's findings	2 days
19	Review of report	10 days
20	Final Report incorporating suggestions	2 days
21	Project Finish	0 days

client especially if there is no indication on the amount of budget the client has to spend.

The last section of the proposal is the appendices or annexes section. This is a vital part of the proposal as requirements from the client are given here. This may include: experience that the consultancy has in delivering similar work to the project proposed; curriculum vitae of consultants on the project; insurance details; professional indemnity details; quality assurance practices; health and safety policy; company title and registered office; technical and administrative contacts.

The structure outlined above is typical of a proposal. Nevertheless, as Hussey (2001a) warned, some public sector contracts may require a proposal written to their specific requirements in order that they can compare consultancy offerings. Indeed, the Ministry of Defence once required the following sections to be placed in a tender:

Section 1. – Completed DEFFORM 47 and Examples of Prices

Section 2. – A brief executive summary of the proposals

Section 3. – Responses to Mandatory Requirements

Section 4. – Statement of any interpretations, qualifications or assumptions made by the tenderer concerning the Statement of Requirements and/or conditions of Contract, along with a statement of any major difficulties and problem areas together with a potential or recommended approaches for their resolution

Section 5. – Any other information the tenderer wishes to provide that is not covered by the other responses

Presenting the proposal

A client may well receive a proposal for work but may still require the consultancy to make a presentation of their proposal. This is often called a 'beauty contest' in the management consultancy industry as consultants demonstrate how they are the partner of choice (Hussey, 2001a). However it can be a good opportunity for the consultancy to discuss any assumptions they have made in their proposal. Indeed, Stroh and Johnson (2006) advise that consultants may meet with the client in person to discuss the proposal and to ensure that the client agrees with the terms and conditions laid out.

Decisions on which consultancy is best may not necessarily be on the basis of price. Indeed, Hussey (1988) describes a case study whereby seven firms were in the running for a particular project and the assignment did not go to the cheapest offering. Some consultancies may miss core requirements of the client's need especially if these are not made explicit. Again as detailed later in Chapter 13, listening to what the client is saying or not saying is vital.

At the presentation stage there may be a renegotiation of the work. The key decision-makers of the project should be available from the consultancy side in order to be able to agree to any amendments that the client insists upon. This may involve upscaling the project in that it does more than what was originally proposed or the client negotiation may go the other way and state the project is too costly. This is often why consultancies will put forward both a basic offering of services and a more advanced offering to cater for the client's budget.

Chapter Summary

- Client engagement is important albeit difficult to define
- Client engagement has five key dimensions: receptivity, expectancy, investment, working relationship and mistrust that can be equally applied to a management consultancy setting
- Client engagement can be defined as the involvement with the client that has contractual and social boundaries set at the beginning of an assignment or evolves through the renegotiation of work
- Negotiation of entry with a client is crucial to client engagement
- The entry phase is very much a matching exercise between what the client wants and what the consultancy can provide (Karantinou and Hogg, 2001)
- The sales pipeline is the number of prospects that have the potential of becoming actual projects at any one time
- Careful managing of the sales pipeline is essential to avoid the 'feast and famine' of consultancy
- Both client and consultant strive towards the successful negotiation of the contract due to economic pressures
- The contract represents the commodification of knowledge in that knowledge that may be gained is specified
- There are four stages in negotiating entry:

    1. Agreeing the brief and the scope of the work
    2. Planning the project
    3. Preparing the proposal
    4. Presenting the proposal

Review Questions

1. What is client engagement?
2. What are the five dimensions of client engagement proposed by Yatchmenoff (2005) and can they be applied to a management consultancy perspective?
3. What is the entry phase?
4. What is the sales pipeline?
5. Is the sales pipeline important in client engagement?
6. Why should the sales pipeline be actively managed as Beam (2006) suggests?
7. What is the feast and famine situation?
8. How does a consultancy price out its work? Describe using the concepts of total salary costs, oncosts and day rates.
9. Does the client and consultant have an economic necessity to sign a contract?

Assignment Questions

1. Why is client engagement important in management consultancy? Could a project operate without the involvement of the client?

2. Is client engagement an easy concept to define? Critically discuss from a management consultancy perspective.

3. How does the sales pipeline operate in a management consultancy context?

4. Describe in detail the purpose and processes involved in the entry phase that culminates in the eventual signing of the contract between client and consultant.

5. How is a proposal for consultancy work structured and what are the key features that make it as selling document as Hussey (2001a) suggests?

Case Study 6.1

Exeter Group, Inc.

By Robert G. Eccles, Das Narayandas and Kerry Herman

Jonathan Kutchins and Mark Cullen both set their menus aside. It was November 2008 and the two were gathered at Morton's Steak House in Boston for a late dinner. Kutchins had founded Exeter Group (Exeter), a Cambridge, Massachusetts-based information technology (IT) consulting firm in 1984; Cullen joined a few years later. As the firm's two managing partners, Kutchins and Cullen managed 160-plus consultants across Exeter's Cambridge, MA, Bangalore, India and San Juan,

Senior Lecturer Robert G. Eccles, Professor Das Narayandas and Assistant Director Kerry Herman, Global Research Group, prepared this case. The authors are grateful to Global Research Group Research Associates Virginia Fuller, Natalie Kindred and Sarah Morton for their contributions. HBS cases are developed solely as the basis for class discussion. Cases are not intended to serve as endorsements, sources of primary data, or illustrations of effective or ineffective management.

Puerto Rico offices. For several years, the firm had been running smoothly at $15 to $25 million in annual revenues with projects spanning several sectors, although the firm had a focus on higher education, health care and government.

The firm ran about 10 to 12 large projects at any one time, typically across complex organizations with multiple information system needs. Decisions about new projects and clients were made jointly by Kutchins and Cullen. Today, four new projects were on the docket for consideration: three of them were potential engagements with existing customers in the higher education sector; one was a possible new client in a sector new to the firm. Whilst they knew what they wanted to eat and drink, their long-term vision for the firm was less clear. Exeter's five-year plan projected the firm to triple its growth by 2013 and Kutchins and Cullen wanted to be sure their portfolio optimized the firm's opportunities.

One of the current projects under consideration – for long-term client Tulane University – was a fixed-price proposal. The second client – a large Boston-based university – was requesting that Exeter merely provide a senior project manager to the client's existing team, a staff-augmentation request that went counter to Exeter's project-based business model. The third project – with a large Cambridge-based private university – was similar in form. After successfully executing several earlier projects over the course of more than ten years, the client now asked Exeter to assign a known project manager to manage an in-house team for a new implementation. The fourth project was a new prospect – a Boston-based strategy consulting firm. Although the proposed project was small in scope, Kutchins and Cullen wondered if it might lead to a broader relationship and additional opportunities for Exeter. Staffing considerations were a particular concern with these projects and for Exeter overall.

In addition to the financial and strategic considerations, Kutchins and Cullen had several tradeoffs to weigh. One issue was capacity constraint. Exeter was in good shape to take on all four projects for now, although the Boston-based university's request for a specific senior manager presented a challenge. 'This is someone that could support $25 million worth of work for us over the period of that engagement,' Kutchins said, 'so it's really tough to think about committing him fulltime to one project that might only run $2 million–$5 million.' Exeter's senior consultants – or engagement managers, of which the firm had seven to eight at any one time – provided most of the firm's professional development for its junior consultants. 'Having this manager tied up unleveraged on one project could have a significant, cascading impact on our overall firm,' Cullen added. Another important consideration for Kutchins and Cullen was which projects best represented opportunities to leverage Exeter's India organization that supported its consulting delivery capability by providing customized systems development for Exeter's US clients.

Exeter Group

Kutchins attended MIT's Sloan School of Management in 1979 and 1980, and during his second year decided to found an IT consulting company. The company developed from a project he executed for a Sloan faculty member. Soon thereafter, MIT's procurement office hired Kutchins to develop a system to comply with mandatory federal guidelines. By 1984, the 28-year-old decided to found Exeter Group. Early on, profits came primarily from application development and implementation, which Kutchins considered a 'natural extension' of strategy and planning.

'The initial questions I asked for each engagement were: 'Where can we be successful? Where can we add value down the road?" Kutchins recalled. 'Being small, strategy and consulting capabilities were scarce resources for us. Our goal from the outset was not to be a low-cost but a high-quality solution provider.' Early on, a relationship with a local large strategy consulting firm enabled Kutchins to pitch work to several large firms. This relationship soon led to an offer to buy Exeter Group. Although he turned it down, Kutchins recalled, 'It confirmed we were doing the right thing, and it was very flattering.'

By 1990, the firm had five employees, and Kutchins had brought Mark Cullen on board. Cullen, a Williams College graduate and elite-level rower, co-founded and managed Exeter Education Management Systems (EEMS), a separate entity which designed, developed, and sold administrative software products to higher education clients. The next year, Kutchins and Cullen launched Exeter Systems India (ESI) in Bangalore, which provided development capacity for EEMS. 'We wanted to explore the opportunities international development might provide to us in building product, and we wanted to keep that capability in house,' noted Kutchins.

Building the administrative products exclusively in India forced the teams to be 'exceptionally good communicators and very efficient across all dimensions of product and project management – both interpersonally and in our technical documentation and methodology,' Cullen said. Kutchins added, 'We went from a small start-up of really smart people to a platform that could grow and expand. At that time not many people realized we were doing our product development in India. We had matured very quickly into a relatively unknown business model, and were competing against companies like Oracle, PeopleSoft, and SAP.' The firm soon had about 15 people on the product side in the U.S. and about 80 in India.

A key advantage to the model was the Exeter Framework™, a document and systems-based methodology that set forth policies, procedures, deliverable and coding standards, and quality controls. Exeter invested heavily in the framework, and it evolved with the growth of the business, taking the successes and lessons learned from each project and codifying them to allow future projects and younger consultants to gain the benefits of others' experiences. It allowed the firm to grow quickly and to standardize quality across its various consulting teams and projects. The framework was a key piece of Exeter's selling and delivery strategy, and was designed to be particularly helpful for strategy and implementation projects at large, complex organizations.

By 1999 Exeter Group had expanded and developed a strong reputation for providing strategic IT consulting services, strategic planning (or road-mapping),[1] assessment planning and implementation services across a number of sectors. EEMS had grown as well, and served over 100 worldwide customers. In 1999 EEMS, along with ESI, were sold to Sallie Mae, a large US student loan provider looking to expand into higher education administrative systems and Cullen moved over to Sallie Mae Solutions as executive vice president (EVP) and COO.[2] (Cullen returned to Exeter in 2002). Sallie Mae offered to purchase Exeter Group consulting as well, but Kutchins insisted on excluding it from the sale.

In 2002, Exeter, together with Tom Green, a former Sallie Mae executive, established Exeter Government Services (EGS) in Rockville, Maryland. EGS was created to focus on federal government projects in response to the Bush administration's intention to earmark $52 billion in its 2003 budget proposal for IT, mainly focused on combating cyber-terrorism.[3] EGS provided consulting services in IT strategy and planning, custom application development, and systems integration.[4] Kutchins and Cullen also launched a new Exeter organization in Bangalore in 2002, Exeter Software India (ESI). 'We were starting to see we had developed some niche strengths and know-how in our first Indian company, and that there were opportunities we could take better advantage of with offshore development capabilities,' Kutchins said. Through blended teams – a mix of developers based in Bangalore and US-based Exeter consultants – ESI provided software development support to Exeter. Although there were increasing opportunities for ESI to be involved in EGS's federal government software development projects, Cullen noted, 'We've been averse to offshoring any of our federal government work. We prefer to keep our international resources in reserve for our private sector projects, and to staff our federal government work with domestic resources.'

As the firm continued to grow, Kutchins and Cullen looked to develop opportunities in sectors where the company was making new forays, including financial services. They hired two seasoned veterans from SAP: an engagement manager (Exeter's senior consultant role) and a vice president of sales, Eric Stine – they called him an 'opportunity champion'. Cullen noted, 'We were concerned about being too dependent on the chemistry between the two of us as we worked to achieve scale. Eric strengthened our growth

---

[1]Firms typically used road-mapping to determine their strategy, to develop and manage their project portfolio, and to enable technological strategy development and technology assessment across the firm.

[2]Sallie Mae Solutions was a subsidiary of Sallie Mae, a leading US provider of student loans, which purchased mainly federally-guaranteed student loans and repackaged them into securities for sale to investors. 'Sallie Mae Buys Education Management Software Firm,' *Reuters News*, October 19, 1999, via Factiva, accessed August 20, 2008.

[3]Enacted in October 2001, the Patriot Act mandated that colleges and universities keep detailed records of activities in laboratories housing certain chemicals. 'Exeter Joins Forces with Kroll to Help Universities Achieve Compliance with New Security and Environmental Regulations,' Exeter Group, Inc. press release (Cambridge, Massachusetts , February 11, 2002).

[4]Colin C. Haley, 'Exeter Hones Federal Focus,' *Boston.internet.com*, June 5, 2002, http://boston.internet.com/news/article.php/1268931, accessed June 3, 2008.

							CAGR %
Region	*2006*	*2007*	*2008*	*2009*	*2010*	*2011*	*2006–2011*
Americas	11 001	11 597	12 200	12 766	13 438	14 122	5.1
Africa, Europe, Middle East	10 520	11 226	11 927	12 657	13 433	14 269	6.3
Asia-Pacific	4 091	4 354	4 618	4 925	5 277	5 675	6.8
Total	25 612	27 178	28 745	30 348	32 148	34 065	5.9

Exhibit 6.1

Worldwide IT Consulting Spending, by Region (2006–2011) ($ millions)

Source: Dylan Cathers, 'Computers: Commercial Services,' May 1, 2008, Standard and Poor's Industry Surveys via NetAdvantage, accessed August 2008.
Note: CAGR: compound annual growth rate.

capabilities for SAP related work as well as for Finance and HR systems in general. He also brought an important dimension to our sales approach. Aside from being a strong sales executive, he followed through each of the engagements in which he was involved as a customer advocate.' They also hired Louis Gutierrez as a consultant in the health care sector in 2002. Gutierrez had served as chief information officer (CIO) for the Executive Office of Health and Human Services and as CIO of the Commonwealth of Massachusetts, first in Massachusetts Governor William Weld's and subsequently in Governor Mitt Romney's administration. Gutierrez brought deep capability and a reputation for leadership from the public and private health sectors.

Industry background

In 2007, the value of the global IT consulting and services industry was reported at $478.3 billion, with North and South America constituting 53 per cent of the global market (see Exhibit 6.1 for worldwide IT consulting spending by region).[5] Most firms had in-house IT capabilities, and turned to IT consultants for support or specific expertise and project work that went beyond the scope and expertise of their own in-house groups. IT consulting and services firms provided custom programming, data networking, design and delivery of integrated computer systems, hardware and software sales, outsourcing of technical support services and other business processes, production of computer system design specifications, testing and upkeep of computer systems, and strategic consulting and project management.[6] Many IT consultants relied on offshore capabilities, especially for business process services, call centre services or large programming projects. Product development – or customized systems and application development – and integration services were the industry's most profitable segments in 2007, generating $237 billion in sales.[7] (See Appendix A for details on the global IT market.)

Top software development companies included Adobe ($2.9 billion in revenues in 2008), Computer Associates ($4.1 billion), IBM ($20 billion in software revenue),[8] Microsoft ($46.1 billion), Oracle ($17.1

[5]'Global IT Consulting and Other Services,' data provided by OneSource Business Browser, an online business information product of OneSource Information Service, Inc. ('OneSource'), accessed August 2008.

[6]'Consulting Services,' via Hoovers, Inc., www.hoovers.com, accessed August 2008.

[7]'Global IT Consulting and Other Services,' data provided by OneSource Business Browser, an online business information product of OneSource Information Service, Inc. ('OneSource'), accessed August 2008.

[8]'Intnl Bus. Mach – IBM Reports 2008 Fourth-Quarter and Full-Year Results,' *Business Wire*, January 21, 2009, via Factiva, accessed February 2, 2009.

Exhibit 6.2

Region	2006	2007	2008	2009	2010	2011	CAGR % 2006–2011
Americas	121 363	132 084	143 382	155 544	168 120	181 085	8.3
Africa, Europe, Middle East	76 299	82 299	88 649	95 355	102 284	109 322	7.5
Asia-Pacific	32 759	35 698	38 718	41 883	45 135	48 731	8.3
Total	230 421	250 081	270 750	292 782	315 540	339 138	8.0

Worldwide Packaged Software Revenue Forecast, by Region (2006–2011) ($ millions)

Source: Zaineb Bokhari, 'Computers: Software,' April 17, 2008, Standard and Poor's Industry Surveys via NetAdvantage, accessed August 2008.

billion), SAP ($10.1 billion) and Symantec ($5.4 billion).[9] Software companies earned revenues from product licensing, and also from long-term service and maintenance contracts; the latter provided dependable revenue streams even in periods of slow economic growth (Exhibit 6.2 provides worldwide packaged software revenue forecasts, by region). Vendors ranged from large firms offering multiple software products, to small firms touting a single line of highly-specialized ('point-solution') software. Enterprise software companies sold large, complex systems into virtually every medium to large company across the globe. Cullen explained:

Those systems needed to be implemented and integrated, often at a cost of two to 30 times (or more) the cost of the software. IT services firms like Exeter specialize in this and compete with other firms through differentiation of approach, vertical niche focus, results, and brand. Because of the skewed revenues favouring implementation, software vendors themselves also got into the implementation game, creating simultaneously cooperative and competitive relationship between software vendors and implementation firms.

Firms worked hard to differentiate their product and to help keep their services from becoming a commodity, since, as Cullen added, 'increased price pressure made it difficult to attract and retain the calibre of consultant required to be successful.'

The computer software and IT services industries overlapped extensively, and both industries shared high rates of consolidation and offshoring.[10] Whilst firms in both industries relied on each other, and often provided complementary services to clients, they also engaged in intense competition for contracts. System implementation was a particularly coveted business over where both industries competed; implementation frequently led to lucrative relationships for long-term service and maintenance contracts. Mature players in both industries managed lucrative service contracts.[11]

Exeter Group 2008

By 2008 the firm had continued to refine its powerful Framework™ Methodology to deliver strategic and technological solutions to clients in four primary sectors: education, financial services, government, and health care. Exeter's services included assessment, planning, and strategy; custom application development; system integration; and business intelligence and data warehousing. In 2008, Exeter employed over 80 US based consultants, and served mainly US customers, although it had served clients in India, the Middle East, and the UK as well; close to another 80 developers worked for ESI.[12]

[9] Zaineb Bokhari, 'Computers: Software,' April 17, 2008, Standard and Poor's Industry Surveys via NetAdvantage, accessed August 2008.

[10] Bokhari (2008).

[11] Bokhari (2008).

[12] Exeter Group, Inc., 'Leadership Team: Jonathan Kutchins,' www.exeter.com, accessed August 20, 2008.

		Services Revenues ($ millions)	Total Revenues ($ millions)	Services % of Total Revenues ($ millions)	Number of Employees
Exhibit 6.3	Company				
Leading Worldwide IT Services Providers (2006) (ranked by services revenues)	IBM	49 278	91 424	53.9	355 766
	Electronic Data Systems	19 947	21 311	93.6	131 000
	Accenture	16 679	19 417	85.9	146 000
	Hewlett-Packard	16 230	93 273	17.4	162 000
	Fujitsu	14 500	43 283	33.5	162 122
	Computer Sciences	12 450	14 682	84.8	77 000
	Lockheed Martin	8 875	39 620	22.4	140 000
	Capgemeni	8 704	9 671	90.0	67 889
	Northrop Grumman	7 560	30 239	25.0	122 200
	Hitachi	7 600	86 369	8.8	385 072
	Total	161 744	449 288	36.0	1 749 049

Source: Dylan Cathers, 'Computers: Commercial Services,' May 1, 2008, Standard and Poor's Industry Surveys via NetAdvantage, accessed August 2008.

Exeter Group Puerto Rico, with nine consultants, provided on-site services to a large Puerto Rican client. EGS fielded another 75-80 consultants, but operated as an autonomous entity. Consultants typically billed 40-50 hours per week, travel time excluded. About 10 per cent of the firm's consultants billed significantly more than this average. Exeter planned its strategy and approach by industry, and Exeter's senior engagement managers tended to have vertical focus and industry expertise. However, the firm's consultants generally worked across all the vertical markets. This enabled the firm to provide its consultants with interesting and varied work, and the opportunity to develop a career path.

In 2008, Kutchins and Cullen contemplated future expansion in India through ESI. According to Kutchins, 10 per cent to 20 per cent of project work could usually be completed off-site through ESI (including custom development work, data conversion, integration, and reporting); however some aspects of face-to-face client interaction would remain essential.

Relationship with the software industry

The computer software and IT services industries overlapped extensively, and both industries shared high rates of consolidation and offshoring.[13] Whilst firms in both industries relied on each other, and often provided complementary services to clients, they also engaged in intense competition for contracts. System implementation was a particularly coveted business where both industries competed; implementation frequently led to productive relationships for long-term service and maintenance contracts. Mature players in both industries managed lucrative service contracts.[14] One industry insider noted 'A software vendor can charge up to 20 per cent in additional fees over time for maintenance on any customization they may do to their product, even if it is the same customization across a series of clients.' (See Exhibit 6.3 for revenues of leading IT service providers.)

Exeter frequently collaborated with software companies, and counted IBM, Oracle, SAP, Sun-Gard, and others as partners,[15] but these firms were also key competitors (refer to Appendix B). 'Most clients assume software companies by

[13]Seth Shafer, 'Computer Software,' via Hoovers, Inc., www. hoovers.com, accessed August 2008.

[14]Bokhari (2008).

[15]Exeter Group, Inc., 'Out Partners,' www.exeter.com, accessed August 20, 2008.

definition have the best consultants,' another insider noted. 'That's just not the case,' Kutchins explained. 'It is often difficult to retain star consultants, and product companies are typically not well positioned to retain them. Their incentives are often not well aligned with their customers' interests because software vendors sometimes can tend to under bid the service portion of a proposal in order to sell their product. That can make for a tough environment for their consultants to be successful and meet customers' expectations.'

Exeter chose not to resell vendor software, an unusual stance in the industry, in order to provide independent advice and guidance to their clients. Partnering with software companies enabled Exeter to gain better and more specific knowledge to be able to implement each company's products, as Cullen explained, 'It enabled us to provide impartial guidance to our clients. The majority of firms we compete against are much bigger than we are and many have ties to specific software vendors, so we compete on the basis of trust. Our customers know we don't resell and mark-up the products we evaluate, which helps us establish an inherent sense of credibility.'

In 2008, Kutchins and Cullen contemplated future expansion in India through ESI. According to Kutchins, 10 per cent to 20 per cent of project work could usually be completed off-site through ESI (including custom development work, data conversion, integration, and reporting); however some aspects of face-to-face client interaction would remain essential. The firm used a blended team approach that relied on at least one US and one Indian consultant managing the project at the client site, supported by a team in India. Cullen explained, 'This project structure promoted significant customer interaction and provided a controlled communication infrastructure from the client to the technical developers. The model improved deliverable quality and gave Exeter flexibility across clients and projects.'

Exeter's service offerings

Exeter's IT solutions typically fell into three categories:

1. strategic assessments and planning, including software and system evaluation and selection;

2. packaged software implementation and custom application development; and

3. business intelligence/reporting solutions (i.e. data warehousing)(see Exhibit 6.4).

For its type 1 strategy and selection projects, Exeter focused on providing systems decisions guidance for its clients. Kutchins explained, 'All our clients have limited resources, be they managerial, financial, or strategic. We help our clients understand the costs, benefits and implications of different opportunities and decisions given their resource levels and capabilities.' A natural extension of strategic analysis was planning. 'Once a client decides on a strategic direction,' Cullen said, 'we help them synthesize and evaluate options, and develop a solution that is consistent with their time, budget, and business constraints.' Strategy and planning phases then transition to the implementation of the defined solution, using Exeter's type 2 and 3 service offerings. 'Strategy and planning projects are interesting work and are typically conducted at the highest levels of an organization, but they tend to be small, focused projects,' explained Cullen. 'We use them to establish credibility and a familiarity with a client's business, but ultimately we grow through implementation projects, which are often significantly larger than the corresponding strategy piece.'

Kutchins and Cullen had recruited and developed a team of consultants who were able to work comfortably across all three service categories, with the exception of the offshore engineers in India who were typically best suited to supporting implementation and data warehouse projects. 'Our implementation experience lends credibility to any strategic advice we provide, and the resulting trust from a strategy project allows us to be successful in winning follow-on implementation work,' noted Kutchins. 'For our consultants and the firm to be successful, we need to maintain a balance across strategy, planning, and implementation.'

For packaged software solutions, many clients opted to use the software vendor for implementation services as well. 'Many clients like to have one point of contact, or as the saying goes "one throat to choke" on such large and complex decisions,'

Exhibit 6.4 Exeter Group Services	**Assessment, Planning, and Strategy** – Prior to synthesizing a strategy, Exeter completed a thorough assessment of a client's business opportunities in the existing environment. Exeter then worked closely with the client to deliver either a customized solution or packaged software. **Custom Application Development** – Exeter was skilled in building custom applications in situations where off-the-shelf solutions did not meet a client's need. Through its 'proprietary methodology', Exeter provided clients with improved business processes whilst increasing both customer and employee satisfaction. **System Integration** – From selecting and configuring appropriate software, to designing and building a usable interface, Exeter helped clients integrate new technological systems into their work environments. **Business Intelligence and Data Warehousing** – IDEA (Informed Decisions Enabling Architecture) was an enterprise solution that allowed client company managers to analyze data for informed decision-making by gathering disparate data into one source. IDEA addressed many of the challenges organizations faced by providing Data Integration Framework, Information Dissemination Structure, Data Analysis, and Workflow Foundation. **Supply Chain Solutions** – Exeter's supply chain solutions incorporated supply chain strategies into product development and design lifecycles by connecting the Internet's capabilities with business processes.

Source: Company documents.

Cullen explained. Clients often assumed that software companies also had the best consultants, and tended to believe that software vendors were best positioned to customize their own packaged software to the client's individual needs. 'We help clients understand the implications of their decisions,' Cullen said, 'and to represent their interests with the software vendor.' He explained:

> If a client is contemplating purchasing a new version of an established product, we can help them understand the leverage they have in getting new features into that product release. Because each software customization requires ongoing support as future product versions are released, each feature negotiated into the base product can save a customer substantial money. This same kind of advice can present a conflict if the implementer and software vendor are the same.

In fact, several of Exeter's client engagements had resulted from failed vendor implementation engagements, where the client then asked Exeter to come in to rescue the implementation.

Exeter Group's markets

Exeter's experience developing and adapting solutions for a spectrum of clients lent flexibility and creativity to its work across all sectors:

Financial services – Exeter worked with financial services firms — primarily investment management organizations and hedge funds — to provide strategic assessment, system road mapping, custom application development, and implementation services.

Government – Exeter sought to be part of the growing federal information technology market by helping the government provide online services to the public and manage large volumes of sensitive data. EGS, highly independent from the firm's other groups, targeted large, federal projects (with smaller margins than in Exeter's other industry foci).

Healthcare – Exeter provided strategic guidance and built enterprise solutions and Internet self-service options for providers, payers, members, and brokers. Exeter enabled health care organizations to streamline costs and improve efficiencies and customer service.

Higher education – Exeter's higher education practice group worked with over 100 colleges and universities to provide strategic direction and IT planning, software and system evaluation, implementation and integration services, and custom application development across the four major enterprise systems areas in the university environment: finance, human resources, student administration, and research. Exeter had worked with many of the world's largest and most prestigious universities, including Harvard, Caltech, the University of Chicago, Kuwait University, MIT, Pepperdine University, and the University of California.

See Exhibit 6.5 for US spending by vertical market

Client selection and management

Exeter's projects came from a variety of sources. Some clients approached the firm on the basis of its reputation and expertise in a particular sector. Other projects came to the firm through relationships clients had with Kutchins, Cullen, or other Exeter team members. Satisfied clients often referred new customers to the firm as well; Tulane's CIO, for example, had recommended Exeter to several peers. Repeat clients provided the bulk of Exeter's business, roughly 70 per cent – –80 per cent. Exeter typically proposed solutions in the same way and applied similar rate structures across all of its business sectors. The profitability of each sector had been reasonably consistent over time, although in 2008, with the financial markets in turmoil, the financial services sector had begun to see its profits squeezed. New clients often came on board through an initial small engagement – an assessment or evaluation project – which then could lead to larger projects. Whilst Kutchins, Cullen and a number of Exeter's senior managers might meet a potential client on their own, Kutchins and Cullen jointly approved all engagements.

Resources and staffing allocation were discussed very early in the process. 'We won't make allocations early on, but we have to decide whether we have the personnel to take on a new project,' Kutchins explained. Additionally, Kutchins and Cullen tried to rotate their teams across various projects. Team members might request to shift from strategy to technical work, or vice versa. 'When you overlay your internal professional development requests with the requests we get from clients for specific individuals,' Cullen noted, 'it's challenging. We want to maintain a good balance of projects that fit into the firm's growth strategy whilst providing interesting work for our consultants.'

Picking projects to grow the firm

Exeter's early projects had organized the firm 'to execute medium-sized projects', Kutchins said, 'and that was somewhat unplanned'. He would ask himself: 'Does the client have the ability to provide interesting work where we can add significant value, and does it look like there will be an opportunity to continue to provide additional services in the future?' Since many new clients were won by word of mouth, 'You make your own reputation here', Kutchins said, 'and build your portfolio through experience, successes and failures – all of these help you get a clear vision of who you are and how you can deliver great results to clients.' For strategy or planning engagements, good client relationships and successful past projects often defined future clients and projects. In contrast, 'with implementation projects, the client often believes that resources are interchangeable and commoditized, and ask that we deploy our managers and our methodology to manage either third party consultants or the client's in-house team performing the work, and,' Kutchins explained, 'that's not typically a strategy we've found to be very successful.'

Increasingly, Exeter looked to grow its portfolio with larger projects that created more profitable follow-up work and better leveraged Exeter's blended team approach to project management. 'Client selectivity is important to us now', Kutchins said, 'and will only become more so as we move forward.' He continued, 'I never thought we could grow large enough through small projects. Without careful attention, they can easily be distractions which divert key resources and personnel away from our strategic goals.' Small engagements also lacked the cost efficiency of larger ones: the managerial overhead for a $50 000 project could sometimes exceed that of a $2 million project.

Once Kutchins and Cullen determined a project was a good fit, they turned to pricing considerations. The lead business development and engagement managers put together the project delivery and proposal strategy, along with an effort and cost estimate. Kutchins and Cullen provided

Exhibit 6.5

US Spending by Vertical Market (in millions of dollars)

	2006	2007	2008	2009	2010	2011	CAGR % 2006–11
Business	219 982	236 166	253 526	272 143	291 481	311 784	7.2
Banking	25 980	27 982	29 993	32 052	34 116	36 222	6.9
Communications & media	28 511	31 325	34 385	37 709	41 200	44 875	9.5
Construction	1 662	1 725	1 789	1 855	1 921	1 987	3.6
Consumer & recreational services	4 090	4 294	4 532	4 801	5 094	5 423	5.8
Discrete manufacturing	36 018	39 258	42 540	45 919	49 292	52 717	7.9
Healthcare	12 393	13 291	14 280	15 347	16 459	17 620	7.3
Insurance	12 928	13 490	14 177	14 981	15 883	16 897	5.5
Process manufacturing	22 038	23 773	25 523	27 311	29 084	30 869	7.0
Professional services	14 237	15 027	15 944	16 984	18 127	19 388	6.4
Resource industries	3 633	3 820	4 035	4 273	4 527	4 807	5.8
Retail	13 710	14 961	16 240	17 561	18 884	20 225	8.1
Securities & investment services	13 873	14 626	15 492	16 449	17 464	18 531	6.0
Transportation	9 388	9 777	10 248	10 791	11 381	12 030	5.1
Utilities	14 983	15 894	17 030	18 384	19 920	21 659	7.6
Wholesale	6 540	6 922	7 319	7 726	8 131	8 533	5.5
Government	4 671	4 837	5 022	5 225	5 440	5 662	3.9
Education	46 930	50 074	53 286	56 527	59 728	62 836	6.0
Home business & consumer	1 356	1 414	1 468	1 520	1 573	1 623	3.7
Total US IT spending	**272 939**	**292 491**	**313 303**	**335 415**	**358 222**	**381 905**	**6.9**

Source: IDC's November 2007 forecast report.
Note: Totals may not add due to rounding. CAGR: compound annual growth rate.

input on every proposal, along with the head of Exeter's HR department and head of business development. Kutchins and Cullen undertook a final review of every proposal before it was delivered to the potential client.

'Our pricing strategy is not designed to win every project, but to identify customers and situations on which we think we can deliver great results and be successful', explained Cullen. During the proposal process, competing firms often lowered their bid prices by cutting margins intended to serve as risk buffers and accommodate potential overages – low priced fixed-price contracts could present significant risk for Exeter. From Kutchins's and Cullen's perspective, meeting or surpassing a client's expectations required accurate cost estimates. 'Rather than try to win a project with a low price, we focus on convincing clients that if they give us this project, we can make them successful,' he said.

Managing projects

Staffing capabilities and talent development also informed project selection. 'It's not just about identifying the person in the firm with the most experience and best skill-set for a given opportunity', Cullen explained. 'Developing consultants is our biggest challenge. We can't rely solely on hiring mid-career consultants to meet our growth needs – it's expensive and not particularly reliable. So, on some projects, whilst our customers may prefer fewer, highly experienced people doing all the work, we'll propose a mix of veteran and less experienced consultants. Staffing them alongside an experienced manager provides the client with great work at a significantly lower cost, and it allows us to provide our younger folks with valuable experience, learning from our senior staff and our customers, and developing them into future project managers.' Further, important experience and systems expertise could only be gained by solving real problems. 'Our junior consultants are great contributors, but they learn the most from doing,' Cullen continued, 'and our engagement managers have to manage the career development of each team member across the five to eight projects they may oversee at any one time.'

Exeter's model relied on fielding a multidisciplinary team (sometimes up to 20 or 30 employees) to a project site. Kutchins and Cullen believed in committing blended teams of Exeter consultants, rather than managing third-party consultants. 'We structure our projects with definable objectives that we can be held accountable to,' Cullen elaborated. 'Once that's in place, we prefer to deploy a team of our own consultants to achieve those objectives. If a client requests that we use an untested resource – a third-party team of consultants, for example – it can introduce significant risk into the equation.'

The four client projects

Kutchins and Cullen reviewed each of the four possible projects under consideration. Each one carried certain risks and opportunity costs, and represented potential for lucrative long-term relationships. Going forward on any one of the four meant making staffing decisions immediately.

Tulane University

Tulane initially became familiar with Exeter when another vendor brought the firm in as a subcontractor for a large software implementation. Exeter was in the midst of this implementation when Hurricane Katrina hit in August 2005, resulting in a suspension of the implementation. In early 2007 Exeter successfully completed a gap analysis to determine if Tulane should restart the prior implementation or choose a different software. Tulane then hired Exeter to review a set of business processes, resulting in modest project fees. Kutchins noted, 'They are a demanding client because their organization is very capable, and we've worked well together.' As a result, trust had developed between Kutchins and Paul Barron, Tulane's vice president for Information Technology and CIO since 2006.[16]

In spring 2007, Tulane again hired Exeter to evaluate new software the university was acquir-

---

[16]Barron was also Class of 1937 Professor of Law at Tulane Law School, where he specialized in Commercial Law and Negotiation and Mediation Advocacy.

ing from a large vendor. Tulane asked Exeter to consider managing the implementation when they were unable to negotiate successful implementation terms with the vendor. Exeter had no experience with this particular product; Kutchins explained some of the risks:

> We'd never led an implementation of this software before, so the question for us was (a) was it something we wanted to do and (b) could we be successful at it? The question for Tulane was: they knew us and liked our people and our approach to system implementation, but did they want to risk having us implement a product we weren't familiar with? They had to choose between us and the vendor's internal consulting organization, and we had to decide whether we wanted to take on the risk of a complex product that would take some ramp-up time, with a demanding client.

However, once the negotiations with Exeter got underway, Tulane's team decided that the vendor should implement the software after all. Tulane sent an implementation services contract to the software vendor to begin negotiations. As Barron recalled, 'I wanted to work off a performance-based document, and their contract was not that.' The software vendor declined to negotiate off the Tulane contract, and would only work off its own contract. For Barron this was a significant barrier to hiring the vendor; he called Kutchins to ask if Exeter would negotiate off Tulane's contract. 'I said that I would', Kutchins recalled, 'and we're now considering entering into a fixed-price contract with them, for about $5 million, all performance and deliverable-based, over two years.' (Exeter's prior engagements with Tulane had been smaller in size.) Additionally, Tulane requested a specific engagement manager who was already working on a project for another large client. 'If we reallocated this manager to Tulane, we'd have to make sure that another large client ended up with an equally good resource,' Cullen explained.

Kutchins elaborated on some of the finer points of this engagement. The software vendor was one of Exeter's most frequent competitors in the higher education sector and Exeter's team was very familiar with their work, although Exeter had never executed an implementation of the software in question. The company's products met the needs of small schools well, and they had established a strong reputation in that sector. Increasingly they were competing for larger universities where other products were the primary competitors. Some larger universities felt that the software company was weak in their project management capabilities, and Exeter had talked to several universities who struggled with their implementations. 'We knew what we were getting into with Tulane in some respects. We knew the vendor would be unhappy and resist losing the implementation business,' Cullen said. 'But we knew that if we were to succeed, we would have a great reference for other potential clients.' Kutchins added, 'If we fail, our reputation will take a hit. It's a pretty small world in the end.'

An additional factor was that the Tulane project would exhaust some of Exeter's remaining very specialized functional capacity in two areas for the next six months, leaving them unable to adapt should any of their other projects need more resources. The pair started to look over Kutchins's projections for the engagement, and to discuss staffing for the approximately $5 million project. Given the project was a fixed-price proposal with a less than perfectly defined scope of work (partly because Exeter had no specific experience with this product), Cullen was concerned about the opportunity costs of the project vis-à-vis other opportunities it might preclude them from pursuing.

A large university client

In early 2008 a large Boston-based university contacted Exeter because they had been implementing a new student systems[17] project and 'said it was not going well', Cullen recalled. Cullen had managed the relationship from the outset; Kutchins had no dealings with the university. Exeter had completed a small project for the university in

---

[17] A system to manage new/entering student data as students enrolled at the university.

November–December 2007; now the client approached Exeter about providing project management services – one or two project managers, for a year or two – as they implemented the new software. The software in question was the same product Exeter was negotiating to work on for Tulane. Cullen was concerned that the project was much broader in scope than the client recognized, and Exeter had responded with a broader proposal for assessment, project management services and implementation. 'The implementation, undertaken by the vendor, was failing, confirming many of the same concerns already articulated by Tulane,' he said.

The client proposed keeping pieces of the vendor's implementation approach and resources, but wanted Exeter to work up a new project plan and approach based on its methodology and manage the vendor's team. Cullen explained, 'If we assumed responsibility for results and were given clearly defined objectives and control over achieving those objectives, we could have a significant positive impact on the implementation.' This meant proposing a team of 20–21 consultants for an engagement priced at $10 million, rather than the one or two senior project managers the client was proposing. 'Providing one or two project managers in a high-end staff augmentation model would put our folks in charge of mostly client in-house and third-party consulting staff,' Cullen noted. 'We would not have the ability to help those project managers if the project got into trouble – they would be isolated – and they would likely spend much of their time managing people they had no authority over and fending off the other consultancies on the project.'

The negotiations involved a long conversation with the client's CIO. 'It was exceptionally hard to convince him,' Cullen recalled. 'He felt they had the people, staff and expertise, but just lacked project management skills.' From Exeter's perspective, the situation looked a bit different. Cullen explained:

They were essentially saying, 'We know Exeter has a great project management methodology and track record, but we think we can gain all of that advantage by just hiring a senior

manager and using the methodology. We'll do the rest.' But that's not likely to lead to success, and it's not the way we constructed our business model. And, whilst our methodology is an important part of our approach, it's just a tool, and useful only in the hands of a team that understands how to apply it to a fluid situation. That's the strength our team would bring.

Kutchins and Cullen felt the opportunity could lead to more and bigger projects, and, if done in parallel with the Tulane project, could strengthen both Exeter's understanding of this particular software and their position against this competitor. But both also knew that if they agreed to the client's project staffing requirements, the software vendor could use Exeter's expertise to improve their own capabilities. 'They're moving up-market, and have the potential to be very strong,' Cullen said. 'If we were to just provide a project manager and all our implementation blueprints, that's essentially setting up a training ground for our competitor's consultants.'

A large private university

Exeter had completed many projects for a large, prestigious Cambridge-based private university over the years. The first project was an identity card system, and subsequent engagements had been with the client's human resources department. The firm had also worked on an electronic requisitioning system for the one of the university's larger schools. In 2006, the client approached Exeter about help with the roll-out of its alumni development system,[18] a project in excess of $2 million for Exeter. The university's decentralized organization, with each school and most initiatives funded autonomously and independently, made for a challenging environment.

Exeter proposed a project based on their business model, and the client came back indicating they did not need a full Exeter team, but instead wanted to hire one particular project manager

---

[18]This system would enable the university to combine several legacy systems used by the development offices.

who had successfully led an earlier engagement for them. Additionally, the client's CIO personally appealed to Exeter to accept the project. Cullen noted, 'We said, "That's not a model we've traditionally been successful with or that fits our overall business model."' The Exeter team knew the project was likely to require a 20 person team, but agreed to consider a three- to four-person team instead. Cullen explained:

> They were a long-standing client, and we wanted to continue working with them. We felt a team of three to four people would be enough to make a significant impact on the overall success of the project, and provide our project manager with some dedicated resources he could lean on should things get difficult. And, because the proposed additional resources would all be in-house we felt more confident that we wouldn't be managing a third-party consulting firm, reducing the risk of vendor squabbling and allowing our team to focus exclusively on the client. We also knew the client had a dedicated, talented team and we had confidence in them.

Kutchins and Cullen had reservations about the engagement, however: 'They wanted very senior people', Kutchins noted, 'at, quite frankly, a discounted rate.' Particularly, the client wanted one of Exeter's most senior project managers to move over to the client as a dedicated resource for the duration of the project (about two years). 'This was one of our best project managers', Cullen recalled, 'and they wanted him, unleveraged, for two years.'

Nevertheless, an agreement was reached and the client agreed to a team of four Exeter consultants. 'The project itself was a big success', Cullen said. 'It came in on time and under budget. But we did it in a compromised situation. We had one of our best guys tied up for this lengthy period, at a time when some of our other teams could have used his expertise and mentorship.' Not long after, the client hired Exeter to upgrade their HR system, a smaller project of just over $1 million. Again they requested the same senior project manager, unleveraged; Exeter decided to go ahead with the project and the client's specific request.

In July 2008 another opportunity surfaced: a multi-phased budget project involving assessment and selection of software. Although the client again requested only project management help, Cullen and Kutchins indicated they would be willing to provide two people for the selection phase, in anticipation of fielding a larger, better leveraged team for future phases. 'We wanted to have the leverage discussion early on, given our experience in previous engagements', Cullen noted. Kutchins and Cullen provided the client with several resumes for the initial phase, including a mid-level project manager who would act as lead, along with a second, younger consultant. Kutchins elaborated, 'We knew the younger guy was probably stronger over the long run, and it turned out that they fell in love with him. We knew that was going to be the case. He is a rising star and a solid manager.'

As the assessment phase wound down, the Exeter team helped the client put the request for proposal (RFP) together for the next stage. 'We wanted to be in a position to bid for follow-on implementation work, so to avoid a conflict of interest, we limited the engagement to requirements gathering and evaluation framework, which meant the client would perform the selection on their own.' Exeter's follow-on bid called for assigning a manager and seven consultants to manage the implementation phase.

The client wanted only the young manager from the previous project to manage independent contractors and consultants from other firms. 'As the evaluation process stretched into months, we've had to assign him to another high-profile project,' Cullen explained. 'We told the client some time ago that this was a possibility, and that he might no longer available for follow-on work. Now we think the client is trying to hire him, despite his non-compete agreement with us guaranteeing he won't work independently for this client.' Kutchins and Cullen knew that projects such as this one could lead to much larger, university-wide projects, so they worried about saying no to this request. 'We've been here before with them', Cullen said. 'We've explained that our model calls for working with blended teams.' Was it time to drop this client? Could they afford to close the door on such a large and local customer?

A management consulting firm

Earlier that morning Cullen had spent some time at the offices of a large Boston-based strategy consulting firm. Exeter's COO had a prior working relationship with one of the firm's IT executives, and he and Cullen met with the firm's CIO and his senior manager to discuss a possible collaboration. The consulting firm's internal IT team was growing, and had started a group in Delhi, India, which currently had a staff of nine consultants. Cullen knew the company worked regularly with another technical firm, with whom they had a good relationship. The company's IT group wanted Exeter to build a system to capture information to be shared with their internal customers in business units across the company's worldwide offices.

The project was small and, according to Cullen, well-defined and straightforward, and Exeter's blended team approach could be an excellent fit. The morning's discussions about the potential engagement also touched on project delivery philosophy. 'As we discussed working together on their project', Cullen said, 'we talked a lot about our different approaches. They told me outright "We are not a good customer. We're cheap and very demanding". But they seem to want us to try each other out.'

Cullen and Kutchins knew the pitfalls of working for another consulting firm. 'Because they are a leading management consulting firm, they have their own methodology and approach to problem solving', Cullen said. 'So my concern was two-fold: either we get forced to use their approach, which would move our managers out of their element and introduce project risk; or we use our methodology and risk being evaluated mid-project on criteria and milestones not consistent with our approach.' At the morning's meeting Cullen had voiced these concerns to the consulting firm's team:

We have an exceptionally strong methodology. We use it with great results. But I can promise you, our approach will not exactly match yours and your people may not like the way we approach each phase of the engagement. We'll work with you, try to communicate our way through those differences, but we're not you. It's not going to be the easiest thing to deal with.

'I wanted to make sure we set ourselves up to be judged on results, rather than approach', Cullen explained. That evening, as Kutchins and Cullen discussed the project, both were already thinking of possible team members to assign and trying to determine if they even had the resources to staff the opportunity. A young, promising and capable manager was just finishing a project. 'He's been on a Chicago-based project for two or three years – but he's based in Boston,' Kutchins said. 'This guy's our best India liaison. He's managed the Bangalore team phenomenally from stateside. But he's been a bit isolated on this Chicago project for a few years and that can get old. We want to keep him and see his career grow. It'd be nice to throw him this great bone so he can stay put for a bit.'

Time to decide

Kutchins and Cullen turned to the desert menu. As they considered the four possible engagements, they returned to their ongoing discussions about long-range planning for the firm. Both believed that achieving the firm's growth goals required adhering to a large-client approach and a blended-teams project model, and offshoring services would play an important role in this growth. 'The path to $100 million seems pretty clear', explained Kutchins. 'Beyond that, we'll have to broaden our scope.' Cullen acknowledged, 'One worry I have is that once we cross the $100 million dollar threshold, we will be competing against a much different set of firms.' An ever-present challenge was to continue to deliver better results and value than the competition, as Kutchins concurred, 'I think our attitude is to be afraid of all of them, because you never know.'

Appendix A: The global IT market

The IT industry was frequently reshaped by acquisitions, whereby firms added technical capabilities and product offerings, entered new sectors, expanded geographically, and obtained skilled workers. The industry's largest players, which included Accenture, Electronic Data Systems, and IBM Global Services, consulted and provided services to governments and multinational companies. In contrast, smaller players included industry- and service-specialized local and regional companies, which usually targeted small businesses. Software vendors, such as Microsoft, Oracle, and SAP offered certification programs, enabling consultants to gain familiarity with their products, and regularly partnered with IT consulting firms, encouraging them to resell their products. Exeter partnered, and certified consultants with Microsoft, SAP, Oracle, IBM, Cognos, and a variety of other software product vendors, depending on specific customer requirements.

Profitability depended on a firm's size and expertise and was influenced by economic trends, albeit disparately: economic slumps could increase or decrease IT spending, depending on service type and market segment. Rising demand in some industries (e.g., in manufacturing or financial services) was often followed by increased IT spending by firms who sought to increase their capacity, add new capabilities and boost operating efficiencies. When the economy slowed, customers were less likely to contract with IT companies for long-term projects. In other industries IT consulting could be considered a discretionary expenditure, vulnerable to economic slowdowns. Government IT expenditures typically remained steady, as did demand for outsourcing. In 2008, analysts predicted that corporate demand for IT services would continue to increase, and that the best-positioned companies were those with diversified revenue streams and significant offshore capacities

IT consulting and services firms typically worked on a project basis, ranging from one-off engagements (sometimes followed by supplementary work) to long-term service contracts covering a series of projects. In response to clients' requests for proposals (RFPs), IT firms responded with proposals detailing their approach to the client's request, including estimated timeframes and costs. An early consideration in any proposal was pricing

structure: whether to bid on a fixed-price basis, or on a time and materials basis. The amount of the proposed services could also vary greatly depending on the assigned consultants' seniority. Because repeat business provided the bulk of IT firms' work, reputations and relationships were particularly important. In addition to relying on repeat business and referrals, some firms employed sales teams or business development managers specifically charged with pursuing new business.

Offshoring[a]

Throughout the 1990s and 2000s, IT companies increasingly utilized offshore capabilities to reduce costs, improve customer service, expand expertise, and allow customers to focus on core capacities. Typical offshore services included business process outsourcing, technical support call services, consulting, and software development. India's educated, English-speaking, inexpensive labour pool, favourable tax laws, and comparatively secure intellectual property (IP) protection made it the primary offshoring destination for IT services companies. Economic slowdowns minimally affected customers' spending on IT outsourcing, as firms were often inclined to either seek cost-saving mechanisms or continue to rely on providers of critical business functions. Some analysts predicted that rising process costs and wages in India, as well as the rupee's appreciation against the dollar, would encourage firms to diversify to additional locations such as Brazil, China, Eastern Europe, Malaysia, and the Philippines.

Source: Dylan Cathers, 'Computers: Commercial Services,' *Standard and Poor's Industry Surveys*, May 1, 2008, via NetAdvantage, accessed August 2008; David Hamerly, 'Information Technology Services,' via Hoovers, Inc., www.hoovers.com, accessed August 2008; 'Consulting Services,' via Hoovers, Inc., www.hoovers.com, accessed August 2008; 'Consulting Services,' via Hoovers, Inc., www.hoovers.com, accessed August 2008.

---

[a]Offshoring referred to the practice of moving a firm's business process to the same company or a different company located in a different geographic region; outsourcing, in contrast, referred to the practice of moving a firm's business process to a different company, either locally or overseas.

Appendix B : Selected Exeter competitors

Accenture – Accenture was the world's largest multidisciplinary consulting firm in 2007, with revenues approaching $21.5 billion – the majority of which came from outside the US During the 1990s, Accenture – then known as Andersen Consulting – established IT prowess when it advised financial service, government, and manufacturing clients' transitions into personal computers, and formed alliances[a] with emerging heavyweights such as Hewlett Packard, Microsoft, and Sun Microsystems. Renamed Accenture after spinning off from its parent in 1999, the company went public in 2001. Amongst the industries served by Accenture were: government (the firm acquired a $10 billion contract to develop an immigrant tracking system for the US Department of Homeland Security in 2004); health care; insurance; and many others. In 2007, Accenture was focusing on growing its systems integration and outsourcing consulting staff – particularly in Brazil, China, and India.

IBM Global Services – Though the 2002 acquisition of PwC Consulting, IBM integrated its IT consulting, hardware, and software arms to create IBM Global Services, which remained the company's most profitable division in 2007. With 2007 revenues approaching $54 billion – more than double the revenues of the industry's second largest player – IBM was the worldwide leader in systems integration and IT consulting, operating in 170 countries and serving both business and government clients. Like other large IT services firms, IBM Global Services sought growth through various acquisitions, including three data-storage and data-transfer companies obtained in 2007 and 2008.

Oracle – Oracle specialized in database management software in the areas of finance, graphics and human resources. In the mid-1990s the company established itself as the top database software maker with sales exceeding $2 billion.

Beginning in 1999 and extending through the late 2000s, Oracle introduced business application software for website management, supply chain and warehouse management, customer relationship management, and service packs for small businesses. In December 2004, the company acquired PeopleSoft, another software management developer, for $10.3 billion. The PeopleSoft deal was the start of a succession of mergers Oracle completed between 2004 and 2007. In all, the company spent $25 billion on acquisitions during this period, acquiring ten companies.

SAP – SAP provided companies with enterprise resource planning (ERP) software that streamlined distribution, manufacturing, accounting, and human resources functions. The software was used by 47 500 companies across the world. In addition to back-office operations, the company also offered web-based solutions and software that supported online transactions and other web-based services. In 2007, the company achieved over $14 billion in sales and recorded a 13.5 per cent 1-year net income growth. With a strong focus on end-to-business processes, SAP systems appealed to companies of all sizes (small, midsize and large enterprises) as well as across several sectors (finance, public services, manufacturing, and service industries).

SunGard Data Systems – Whilst SunGard offered administrative products for higher education and public sector customers, the company was best known for its financial services support systems – comprising over 50 software brands – on which the majority of financial services firms (including banks, insurance companies, mutual funds, and stock exchanges) relied for a spectrum of financial management and transaction functions. In 2006, SunGard derived $4.3 billion in sales from its over 25 000 customers located in 50 countries. Like many IT services companies, SunGard undertook numerous acquisitions in the mid-2000s, with more than 20 in 2006 and 2007 alone.

Tata Consultancy Services Ltd – Mumbai-based Tata Consulting Services Ltd. (TCS) provided outsourcing and consulting services to finance,

---

[a] In 2000, Andersen Venture Consulting (AVC), formed in 1999, forged joint e-commerce venture-funding partnerships with players such as Microsoft and Sun Microsystems.

manufacturing, retail, telecommunications, and other customers in more than 40 countries, though it conducted more than 60 per cent of its business in the Americas and 25 per cent in Europe. TCS specialized in customized business software development and maintenance, but also offered business process outsourcing; enterprise systems installation, infrastructure and engineering, and systems integration; as well as strategic consulting and project management. In 2007, TCS's sales reached $4.1 billion; though it faced increasing administrative expenses, the firm enjoyed steady income from IT and consultancy services, as well as software licensing.

Source: 'Accenture Ltd.,' via Hoovers, Inc., www.hoovers.com, accessed August 2008; 'IBM Global Services,' via Hoovers, Inc., www.hoovers.com, accessed August 2008; 'SunGard Data Systems, Inc.,' via Hoovers, Inc., www.hoovers.com, accessed August 2008; 'Oracle Corporation,' via Hoovers, Inc., www.hoovers.com, accessed January 27, 2009; 'SAP Aktiengesellschaft,' via Hoovers, Inc., www.hoovers.com, accessed January 27, 2009; Tata Consulting Services Limited,' via Hoovers, Inc., www.hoovers.com, accessed August 2008; OneSource Business Browser, an online business information product of OneSource Information Services, Inc. ('OneSource'), accessed August 2008.

Further Reading

Beam, C. (2006), How to assess your sales pipeline, *Consulting to Management*, 17(2), 18–21

Heusinkveld, S. and Benders, J. (2005) Contested commodification: Consultancies and their struggle with new concept development, *Human Relations*, 58(3), 283–310

Hussey, D. (2001a) The entry phase. In, Sadler, P. (Ed) *Management Consultancy: A Handbook of Best Practice*. London: Kogan Page Ltd

Neumann, J.E. (1997) Negotiating entry and contracting. In, Neumann, J.E., Kellner, K., and Dawson-Shepherd, A. (Eds). *Developing Organisational Consultancy*. London: Routledge

Werr, A. and Styhre, A. (2003) Management consultants: Friend or foe? *International Studies of Management & Organization*, 32(4), 43–66

Yatchmenoff, D.K. (2005) Measuring client engagement from the client's perspective in nonvoluntary child protective services, *Research on Social Work Practice* 15, 84–96

CHAPTER 7

Consulting in the internal and external environment

Learning Objectives

At the end of this chapter students will be able to:

- Understand the differences between being an external and internal consultant

- Understand the need that organizations have for an internal consulting team

- Recognize the advantages and limitations of both external and internal consultants

- Be introduced to some of the organizational features encountered in being a consultant

- Develop an understanding of the professional skills required to be an internal consultant

Mini Case Study 7.1

Skandia using internal consultants to revamp its IT department

Skandia UK's aim of adopting an SOA approach to revamp its legacy systems has led to the reorganization of its IT department, and outsourcing application development, maintenance and support to HCL Technologies.

The organization, which provides long-term savings products such as investments and pensions, is owned by the Sweden-based Skandia Group, which was itself acquired by London-based life assurer Old Mutual in 2005. Skandia UK started operating in 1979 and since then has run the business using IBM iSeries machines – formerly known as AS/400s.

Tim Mann, Skandia UK's customer services and technology director, says he noticed a level of entropy creeping in three or four years ago, which manifested itself in projects taking longer to get done at a higher cost. 'We were starting to suffer from over-complexity of system architecture and design and there was also a weakness in overall architecture governance,' he says. As a result, he introduced the Darwin Project in early 2006, which centred on how to overcome what could become a legacy problem and re-apply the applications architecture to move forward for the next 20 years. The initiative involved reorganizing the IT team to create an architectural design and implementation group. Members now undertake specialist functions, such as coding, testing or project management, rather than being technology generalists.

'IT people like to do a bit of everything, but it is not always great value for the company,' says Mann. 'It was not universally well received at first, but it gave the organization the ability to oversee resourcing more effectively and means that we have started to create centres of excellence.' One of these centres of excellence revolves around Tibco Software's offerings, which have been chosen as the glue of choice for all of the firm's future integration efforts. And one of the first projects in this area involves linking multi-fund systems handling investments such as unit trusts, offered by Skandia Mutual Funds and sister company Selestica, which are being merged. The integrated system is due to go live in July, with a second functional release planned for early 2008.

The half-dozen competency centre staff will provide internal consultancy services and become experts and champions to act as a reference point for information, both amongst IT and business colleagues. The ultimate goal is to ensure that new SOA-based methods of working become institutionalized rather than just a one-off. Mann felt it would not be possible to hire or train new skills quickly enough to match the company's growth ambitions or to cut internal costs in line with Old Mutual's expectations, so he decided to hire Indian services provider HCL.

The move will result in the IT organization reducing in size from 300 personnel to 45. About 250 roles will move to HCL under TUPE arrangements in February, and an assessment will be made as to whether these workers are suitable for offshoring by June. Such an assessment will lead to either staff redeployment or redundancy.

'With Darwin, I made the case that if we didn't do it, we'd have problems, but it is also about creating opportunities,' says Mann. 'If we can create something that is SOA-based, the opportunity to bring products and services to market quickly is hugely increased. It is not a magic bullet and it will have to be done in stages over five or six years, but it is strategic to the company's future.'

Source: Incisive Media http://www.computing.co.uk/computing/analysis/2189484/case-study-skandia-uk. Reproduced with permission.

Introduction

More than any other subject in the management consultancy literature being an internal or external consultant has attracted the most attention (Bellman, 1973; Pinto and Noah, 1980; Robinson and Younglove, 1984; Schaffer, 1976; Scharf, 1987; Weiss, 2006; Wright, 2008). The opening case study may demonstrate why. Organizations take on internal consultants as change agents or in this case to offshore a department to India, whilst retaining the valuable knowledge and expertise that the staff base may have for the company.

Internal and external consultants have many similarities and this book is applicable to both groups. However, there are also distinct differences. In a nutshell, internal consultants are employed by the firm that they consult for, whereas external consultants are employed by a consultancy or professional service firm and consult for third party organizations (Weiss, 2006). The skills and methodology that both use are the same. Nevertheless, there are quite a few differences between being an internal and external consultant, which will be addressed in this chapter. This chapter will then progress to ascertain how an internal consultant can be effective in their role.

Differences Between Being an Internal and External Consultant

Introduction

To examine the differences between being an internal and external consultant it is beneficial to go back to basics and look at the definition of what it means to be a consultant. A consultant has previously been defined as someone who provides a service or expertise for a client for a particular concern or issue. This definition includes both internal and external consultants. However, there are key differences being: remuneration, living with the legacy of success or failure, the political framework, organizational hierarchy, employment status, organizational blinders and organizational insight.

Remuneration

An external and an internal consultant both provide this service or expertise for remuneration (Weiss, 2006). For an external consultant, this is likely to be continued employment with the professional service firm as long as they continue working with external clients on behalf of the consultancy. External consultants have to be actively employed or be actively searching for contracts to win to keep them employed. It is also likely that the external consultant will be rewarded either through commission or other similar incentive package such as bonuses. In this regard, external consultants typically do earn more than internal consultants. In Sweden, Andersson and Andersson (2008) found that career development and acknowledgement were also used to incentivize external consultants. In the other countries, these factors are also important but in the author's experience of UK management consultancy, keeping your job has also been used as a motivator, especially in times of economic crisis. This is unlikely to be a key incentive though in the long term. Indeed, in any firm that uses job insecurity for its own advantage staff turnover may be high, which is costly for any business.

Interestingly, for the internal consultant the continuation of a job with their direct employer is considered to be a key motivator (Weiss, 2006). The internal consultant probably needs to still win work internally. This may be in competition with external consultants or even internal resources. Nevertheless, once the internal consultancy environment is set up, internal consultants are likely to have a continued existence within the client firm. One of the advantages of this is that all of their effort can go towards being successful in the consultancy process rather than the continued persistence of applying for new contracts and projects as with external consultancy.

Living with the legacy of success or failure

One of the key advantages that the author personally found in working as an internal consultant, which he missed when he became an external consultant for a number of years, was living with the legacy of the consultancy work. The internal consultant can see the positive benefits of their consultancy as they will still remain in the client organization long after the consultancy project is finished. Thus, if an improvement was made in say recruitment techniques, the internal consultant would be employed on this project, implement changes and then proceed to other in-house projects. Nonetheless, whilst involved with other projects the consultant would see the eventual impact of the improved recruitment in their organization such as a lowering of staff turnover, better quality customer service, etc. Thus, the internal consultant would see the success of projects that they worked on within their employer (Andriole, 2007). This is also likely to promote confidence in the internal consultant by the employer (Bellman, 1972).

Nevertheless, Andriole (2007) pointed out that the reverse is also true for the internal consultant. In this regard, if the consultancy project is a failure or does not live up to expectations then the internal consultant must live with this legacy. This may mean that they either get fired or they embark on another project to correct the failure as shown in Mini Case Study 7.2 below.

Mini Case Study 7.2

Failure of one project corrected by implementation of another

A multinational pharmaceutical giant needed a database system to keep track of its supply details across the world. The original solution that the internal consultants inherited was a series of MS Excel spreadsheets that contained the information about supplies from across the world. However, the organization found this system was cumbersome and slow. Indeed, although MS Excel can be used for databases, it has a limited functionality.

The pharmaceutical company decided to recruit an internal consultancy team that it attracted from its own members of staff and recruited from an external consultancy that had done previous work with the client. This six-person team then set about running the three month long project to convert the MS Excel databases into MS Access databases.

There were a lot of difficulties in implementing the project and problems arose with the use of MS Access for a commercial database system for the organization. In essence, it was originally thought that the three regions of the world being USA, Europe and the Far East would operate separately due to their different timelines. However, this was not the case and problems arose with the designed database due to the different regions changing the amounts of supplies simultaneously. The system designed could not cope with this and after it had been designed was then scrapped for another database system that used Oracle.

The internal consultancy sold the new project with the Oracle database as the optimal solution. However, it was left with egg on its face as the previous database collapsed under real world pressure. Nonetheless, the internal consultancy stated that many of the lessons learnt from the old system would be incorporated into the new system. Thus, rather than being a failed project it was promoted as a 'we learnt that lesson so let's move on' affair. The new project did go ahead; however, the original project manager was asked to leave as this was a foreseeable issue that should have been avoided.

The political framework

The politics of an organization are complex and difficult to learn (Krell and Dobson, 1999). However, clear differences emerge between internal and external consultants in terms of how they are affected by the political framework (Block, 2000). The internal consultant is directly inside the organization so is enmeshed within the clients political system (Massarik and Pei-Carpenter, 2002). The consultant is part of this political network as an individual and as part of their professional role. This gives the internal consultant clear insights into what will work and what will not within the organization as they are immersed within the political framework of the organization but should try to avoid getting drawn into power games or political struggle (Beagrie, 2008).

Thought Provoking point 7.1

I was once employed by a furniture retailer as an internal consultant for a year in my first role after leaving university. Two jobs later, I returned to that organization but as an external consultant rather than an internal consultant. Interestingly, as I was considered to be an old employee of the organization, I was given a very detailed insight into the politics of the organization, in terms of my previous manager being fired due to claiming many of the team efforts as her own. If I was just purely an external consultant, I would not have had this level of insight into the organization's politics.

The external consultant; however, is outside of the organization. Although as demonstrated in the last two chapters, consultants try to form an alliance and relationships with the client (Fincham, 1999), they are external to the client's political framework but connected with it at least for the duration of the consultancy assignment. In this way, the consultant is directly affected by politics within the client organization. They are also affected by the politics within their own consultancy, which may or may not be in conflict with the client's political considerations (Heusinkveld and Benders, 2005).

For instance, in Chapter 5, Thought Provoking point 5.1, a candidate who was the top performer of an assessment centre was not recruited but the fourth highest performer out of seven was selected. This was because it was politically wise to make this decision: the selected candidate had previously worked with the organization so was aware of their organizational structure and political framework. A good external consultant should recognize the political structure of the client organization.

Organizational hierarchy

Allied to the political structure of the organization is the organizational structure or hierarchy. The internal consultant in this regard is part of the client organization and located within its hierarchy. They will have accounting and reporting responsibility within this hierarchy and report to a manager or director within the client company (Massarik and Pei-Carpenter, 2002). This may make the client organization more comfortable with internal consultants as opposed to external ones as they have a greater remit of control as if they do a bad job they can be fired from the organization (as in Thought Provoking point 7.1 above).

The external consultant is external to the organizational structure within the client firm. However they are accountable to it in terms of the work that they produce. They are also separate from the client but are accountable to their own consultancy organization. Most consultancy projects will also have a hierarchy imposed upon them through project management techniques (Lock, 2003). Typically, this will be a project director and a project manager at the very least (see Chapter 8 for more details).

Employment status

The employment status of both internal and external consultants is typically permanent. For external consultants they are directly employed by the consultancy firm on a fixed salary or one that be fixed but then have commission and bonuses on top. The exception to this is the sole trader or the self-employed consultant who goes from one contract to another. Nevertheless, from the client's perspective the external consultant is a fixed term contractor. In other words, they are paid to do a specific finite piece of work that will last for a finite period of time (Massarik and Pei-Carpenter, 2002).

The internal consultant is a permanent worker in terms of continuing employment that lasts indefinitely. However, Massarik and Pei-Carpenter (2002) argue that this idea of permanence may be illusory. In other words, just like an external consultant lasts for as long as there is work, why should these rules not apply to the internal consultant? In this regard, although the internal consultant is employed on a permanent basis this may last as long as the contract lasts unless they can bid for further work within the organization.

Organizational blinders

Massarik and Pei-Carpenter (2002) define organizational blinders as the influence that the political and the organizational structure has on the consultant. An internal consultant is enmeshed into the organizational hierarchy, its structure and political system. These features have a conscious and unconscious effect on the internal consultant. The internal consultant may therefore not wish to 'rock the boat' within the client firm. They may find it impossible to speak out aloud due to the political pressures within the organization. They are also unlikely to behave in a way that may jeopardize their own position (see Thought Provoking point 7.2).

Thought Provoking point 7.2

In Mini Case Study 7.1, the IT company reduced its personnel down from 300 to 45 by sending many of the roles 'offshore'. If you were chosen as an internal consultant on the basis of your knowledge and expertise but knew that the company were making others like you redundant, how would you feel about telling the organization that offshoring the bulk of the work was a bad decision?

External consultants are also not immune to the risks associated with the political and organizational hierarchy (Massarik and Pei-Carpenter, 2002). Their actions may be influenced by unconscious responses to the political system within the client firm. Their actions may also be defined by organizational blinders within the consultancy firm. Thus, if a client decides that a project shouldn't go ahead, the consultant may argue the case for the project as it is in their interest for the consultancy work to go ahead due to the pressures upon them to get work from the consultancy firm.

Nonetheless, being an external consultant does give you the option of being able to state what you found without fear of reprisals or losing your job within the client firm. More than once or twice in my own career, I have had to deliver some really important messages that certainly rocked the politics of the organization I was working for. Yet, my consultancy supported me in giving the client the truth of the matter. The clients also appreciated the frank and open finding so supported the ongoing client–consultant relationship.

Organizational insight

One of the key differences between being an internal and external consultant already touched upon is organizational insight (Massarik and Pei-Carpenter, 2002). The internal consultant is a permanent employee of the client firm and as such will have considerable amounts of data and knowledge at their fingertips (Wright, 2008). This is a key advantage but is hampered by the fact they are enmeshed within the political climate and organizational structure of the firm.

The external consultant, as an outsider, may not have the quality of knowledge and insight afforded to the internal consultant (Block, 2000). Massarik and Pei-Carpenter (2002) argued that this may mean that the advice given by the external consultant is more artificial or superficial in nature. However, the reverse of this is that the advice given is more precisely related to the issues at hand. Thus, the external consultant may give a higher level of diagnostic insight (as shown in Industry snapshot 7.1).

Industry snapshot 7.1

Calculating performance in a credit card call centre environment

I was contracted to examine the performance ratings of eight call centres within one organization that wanted to examine metrics between all eight different departments that dealt with payments, lost and stolen, fraud, investor relations, etc. Up to about 100 measures were taken of the call centre environment that were varied within the eight departments. Nonetheless, one metric out of all the different measures was shown to have a high correlation with performance within all eight departments. This measure was average holding time, which is the amount of time a customer is on the phone for until their call is answered. This measure correlated highly with the amount of lost calls, customer dissatisfaction and whole range of other measures.

The research conducted found there was an optimal amount of time for calls to be answered within. Calls answered too soon, that is within five seconds, tended to lead to incorrect phone calls, wrong number dialled, etc. The organization didn't want these, but between 5 and 30 seconds was the optimum amount of time to answer a call. After 30 seconds, callers would hang up leading to lost opportunities for the credit card company or issues that weren't resolved.

By using the average holding time as an inter-departmental measure. The different departments could be rated against one another in a fair manner. Nevertheless, the politics regarding implementing this system were strong. At least one department rejected the idea that average holding time was the only important measure and insisted that other metrics were equally as important. Whilst this was certainly the case for that department, many of the other departments did not take the same measurements so could not be compared. However, being external to the organization (as I was paid by a third party for the contract) the changes in reporting metrics could be implemented on the basis of sound statistical rationale as opposed to inter-departmental political wrangling based on the balance of power in organizational relationships.

Being an Internal Consultant

There are key differences between the external consultant and the internal consultant as shown above. Like an external consultant, an internal one must also advise senior managers in full consideration of the key strategic issues facing the organization (Wright, 2008).

Involuntary or voluntary internal consultant

Meislin (1997) argued that individuals become internal consultants on an involuntary or voluntary basis. This distinction has cropped up in the temporary worker literature where Ellingson, Gruys and Sackett (1998) put together the questions shown in Industry snapshot 7.2 to determine whether someone was employed on

---

Industry snapshot 7.2

Questions relating to the involuntary/voluntary nature of the job

Please rate the degree, by CIRCLING the correct response, to which the following reasons played a part in your decision to work in your current role.

1. Sense of freedom.

1	2	3
No Role	Minor Role	Major Role

2. Flexible hours.

1	2	3
No Role	Minor Role	Major Role

3. Variety.

1	2	3
No Role	Minor Role	Major Role

4. Potential to work for a shorter length of time.

1	2	3
No Role	Minor Role	Major Role

5. Job loss.

1	2	3
No Role	Minor Role	Major Role

6. Difficulty in finding permanent work.

1	2	3
No Role	Minor Role	Major Role

7. Laid off.

1	2	3
No Role	Minor Role	Major Role

8. Tight labour market.

1	2	3
No Role	Minor Role	Major Role

Reproduced with permission from Ellingson, Gruys and Sackett (1998)

an involuntary or voluntary basis. Meislin (1997) argued that an individual may have the role of internal consultant foisted upon them as their management have decided that their job will change. In this case, the organization changes the person from a specialist in human resources, finances, etc. into an internal consultant. Indeed, in the Mini Case Study 7.1, it is likely that these individuals were made internal consultants on an involuntary basis as the other alternative to them would presumably be losing their jobs. Individuals answering the Industry snapshot 7.2 questions low for the first four questions and high for the remaining questions are likely to be employed more on an involuntary basis.

Nevertheless, not all internal consultants are employed on an involuntary basis but may have elected to take up this role and have a legitimate role within the organization (Wright, 2008). Meislin (1997) argued that for reasons such as wanting to have a greater challenge, wishing to have a greater impact on the business, and adopting an entrepreneurial flair and charisma that may steer the organization onto greater heights, some individuals go for the internal consultancy role first before venturing to become external consultants. Indeed, external consultancy is a natural and sought after position for many professionals especially in human resources (Robinson and Younglove, 1984).

Recruitment of internal consultants

Many organizations may wish to set up their own internal consultancies typically by hiring internal staff to the role or poaching management consultants from

---

Industry snapshot 7.3

Growing an internal consultancy firm within the Polish State Railways from expertise delivered externally

Successful implementation of new technology is more efficient if there are experienced people available to answer questions. The first time an organization uses a new technology it makes sense to employ external specialists to provide guidance. To get maximum advantage from investment in external consultants, an organization should only have to ask them each question once.

Rather than continual reliance on external experts, Project Clinics can be used as a mechanism for gathering the answers to questions and communicating those answers throughout the organization. The Polish State Railways used project clinics to progressively gather knowledge from external consultants, and build a knowledge base along with a team of internal consultants.

The project clinic was introduced as an alternative to advanced training. Instead of taking additional courses, the project clinic provides on the job training. The aim of a project clinic is to keep a project healthy. Fourteen developers (at least one from each of the nine locations) agreed to do the

training to become internal consultants. The training takes the form of: attendance at all of the project clinics, special technical sessions, sessions on how to do technology transfer. By the end of the year the aim is for each internal consultant to be able to run his or her own project clinics.

The internal consultants were then able to guide project groups in the application of core object-oriented skills like: data modelling, context modelling, event partitioning, process, data and state correlation, allocation modelling, component reuse and viewpoint modelling. The involvement of external consultants was limited to answering questions that the internal consultants needed help with. External consultants should be used as a way of introducing new techniques and tools to the organization. Internal consultants, project clinics and clinic modules provide a means of learning by and reusing this experience.

Source: Extracted from 'Experiences in Growing Internal Consultants with Object-oriented Skills' by Suzanne Robertson, The Atlantic Systems Guild. http://www.systemsguild.com/GuildSite/SQR/internal_Consultants.html. Reproduced with permission.

external consultancy firms (see Industry snapshot 7.3). Internal consulting groups are often formed around a practice area such as human resource management, information technology, or organizational development. This can be quite attractive to individuals early on in their career who want to get experience in their particular profession.

Know thyself

Neal and Lloyd (2001) stated that an internal consultant should 'be clear on their capabilities, preferences and values and the way in which they feel it is possible or appropriate to contribute to the organization' (Neal and Lloyd, 2001; p. 467). Both internal and external consultants need to know themselves and in this book this is explored in detail in Chapters 13 and 14. Indeed, the exercises in Chapter 14 can help illuminate behavioural and skills both developed and underdeveloped.

Most professions insist that the practitioner does not consult in areas they are not familiar with. This is important as the internal consultant does not want to lose credibility by consulting in an area they know little about (Anonymous, 2004). However, in addition to this the consultant does not need to replicate all the skills of the team that they are working with. It would be ludicrous to think that any project manager could do all the jobs of those subordinate to him or her and this is also the case with the internal consultant (Neal and Lloyd, 2001).

Neal and Lloyd (2001) argued that internal consultants need to be resilient in the face of adversity and be able to deal with issues that have gone wrong much more than other employees. Weiss (2006) also shares this sentiment and further argues that five important behaviours are essential for the internal consultant, these being:

1. Perseverance: the willingness and resiliency to rebound from setbacks and difficulties staying on course even in the face of criticism and scepticism
2. High self-esteem: the ability to not take rejection personally and to disassociate one's worth from negative feedback
3. Well-developed sense of humour/perspective: keep the perspective of any work completed as although it may be essential for the organization, what will its importance be in 100 years time?
4. Willingness to take risks: internal consultants shouldn't want to protect the status quo and should seek new opportunities and fresh ideas for their employer
5. Creativity and innovation: the real value of internal consultancy is that it improves standards and raises performance levels

Adapted from Weiss (2006); p. 479

Weiss (2006) further stated that three factors influence the internal consultant: the market need, competence and passion for the job. In this regard, the market need is the need within the organization for the services and value that the internal consultant can provide. The internal consultant must demonstrate or develop this need within the client firm. In addition, the internal consultant must have the skills and competence to deliver the work. Last but not least the consultant must be passionate about the role that they are undertaking and be enthusiastic and optimistic that their work will bring real world business benefits.

Earning trust

Weiss (2006) suggested that one of the key factors that an internal consultant needs to do is to earn trust within the organization. Interestingly, he argues that it is not departments or teams that earn trust but individual consultants. Beagrie (2008) also supported this view that internal consultants must demonstrate their expertise to enhance their professional standing and to make a valuable contribution to the organization.

Weiss (2006) suggested the following to earn trust internally:

1. Learn the key issues and organizational realities of the business objectives
2. Don't approach issues with a strict methodological approach but be open and listen to what is needed
3. Be proactive in communication and letting people know what the internal consultants are doing or working on at any one time
4. Don't rely heavily on email or voice messages but instead communicate on a one to one and personal basis
5. Be proactive and not reactive in making improvement suggestions
6. Get rid of the jargon so not to alienate anyone
7. Use only well-known and established tools and methodologies
8. Concentrate on the actual work that needs to be completed
9. Implement performance measures or deadlines to demonstrate the effectiveness of the work
10. Share and take credit for success and don't be afraid of advertising triumphs

Adapted from Weiss (2006); p. 471

Adopt a project management approach to work

Beagrie (2008) suggested that any internal consultant must adopt a project management type role within the client. The need for projects that will deliver business benefits must be identified. Internal projects, in a similar manner to external projects, must identify what the issues are and the business benefits in running the project. The project should have a solid business case and demonstrate how it will affect the organization. Time scales, budgets and resources should also be set out. This project approach should then be championed within the organization and agreed.

Once the project plan has been agreed, the resources and the team can be allocated in a similar manner to an external project (see Chapter 8 for more details). A good project proposal will generate credibility, trust and build firm relationships within the organization, which is essential for internal consultancy (Weiss, 2006). It will also help with issues of an ambiguous nature as project planning will tend to pin down issues and problems and so help in dealing with ambiguity, which has been shown to be important in internal consultancy (Neal and Lloyd, 2001).

Chapter Summary

- Internal and external consultants have key differences between them
- External consultants go from project to project in different firms whereas internal consultants stay with the same company
- External consultants tend to be more likely to receive commission for business development and generating sales through selling consultancy
- Internal consultants may be more motivated with the continuation of their job within the client firm
- Weiss (2006) argued that internal consultants are likely to last for as long as the consultant work lasts and are thus similar to external consultants
- Internal consultants are more likely to have deal with the fallout from any failure of a project but similarly they can share in the success of their work
- The political framework is extremely important for both internal and external consultants but the former may be influenced more as they are enmeshed into the political structure
- The organizational hierarchy is likely to influence the internal consultant who will be responsible to an individual or set of individuals located in the organizational hierarchy
- External consultants may be seen by the client firm as having an employment status similar to a fixed term contractor, going from job to job. Nonetheless, the external consultant is likely to see themselves as a permanent employee of the professional service firm
- Internal consultants are permanent members of staff of the client organization
- Organizational blinders and organizational insight are likely to be different between internal and external consultants
- Internal consultants may be recruited on a voluntary or involuntary basis
- Recruitment of internal consultants varies but internal staff may be attracted to the post with the view of becoming external consultants in the future
- Professional skills such as tenacity, self-esteem, perspective, risk taking and creativity are vital for the internal consultant
- Earning trust and adopting a systematic approach within the client firm is essential for the internal consultant

Review Questions

1. What is an internal consultant?
2. Are the skills that internal and external consultants use similar?
3. What type of rewards can be given to internal and external consultants alike?
4. Weiss (2006) suggested that internal consultants may wish to keep the status quo. What was the fundamental reason for this?
5. How can the external consultant's politics within the professional service firm be in conflict with the client organization's as Heusinkveld and Benders (2005) suggest?

6. Does the employment status between internal and external consultant vary?

7. How do organizational blinders affect the internal and external consultant?

8. Why might an internal consultant be employed on an involuntary basis?

9. What are the five competencies that Weiss (2006) suggested that internal consultants should have?

10. List the ways in which an internal consultant may invoke trust in the organization they work for.

11. Why is project management important in internal consultancy assignments?

Assignment Questions

1. Describe the consultancy skills that an external and internal consultant use and discuss whether they are similar in nature.

2. Critically discuss explaining why the internal consultant may have greater problems with credibility than the external consultant. What can the internal consultant do to sell themselves into the client organization.

3. Andriole (2007) suggested that internal consultants have to deal with their successes and failures within the client organization. Describe how this may be the case and why internal consultants may differ or be similar to external consultants in this regard.

4. Massarik and Pei-Carpenter (2002) argued that the internal consultant is enmeshed within the client's political system and organizational hierarchy. What advantages and disadvantages does this bring?

Case Study 7.1

*Pay Zone Consulting: A global virtual organization**

Columbus reported to his king and queen that the world was round, and he went down in history as the man who first made that discovery. I shared my discovery only with my wife: 'Honey', I confided, 'I think the world is flat'.

Thomas Friedman, author of *The World is Flat*

'We have five principals, eight consulting contractors and five software developers but no offices – only a mailing address for legal purposes. We have

no administrative people either, yet we consult globally for some of the biggest oil and gas companies in the world'. Owen Dart, a geoscientist, was explaining the unique organization and virtual teamwork of Pay Zone Consulting (Pay Zone). The Pay Zone partners provided information management consulting and software solutions to the exploration and production (E&P) segment of the global oil and gas industry. With the goal of becoming recognized as 'the world's best at what we do', Pay Zone had attracted clients such as BP, Shell, Phillips Petroleum, Halliburton, Chevron and IBM, to name only a few. In less than a decade, the five geoscientist founders had taken the company from a startup position to a highly respected specialty consulting firm.

'We conceived Pay Zone as a virtual organization from the outset', said Dart from his office in his country home 25 kilometers northwest of Calgary, Canada. Dart enjoyed a spectacular view of the Rocky Mountains and rolling Alberta foothills, with cattle grazing just beyond his property. Whilst Dart preferred rural Canada, his partners all lived in the United Kingdom, each pursuing his own lifestyle. One settled in a country village so his children could attend a top school and he could spend abundant time with his young family. Another partner enjoyed travel and flights to different parts of the world. A third partner preferred remote locations for his consulting assignments – a North Sea drilling platform or somewhere in Kazakhstan, the more exciting or exotic the better. Yet another principal wanted to live in a major city. The firm's software developers and contractors worked from their homes in various locations in Europe and North America. Pay Zone's flexible business model and the effective way it employed collaboration technologies, automation and the internet enabled everyone working for the company to pursue their own personal lifestyle objectives. This was a core value of Pay Zone.

Dart and his partners met for a few days annually in either the United Kingdom or one of the scenic executive retreats not far from Dart's home. While such meetings were necessary only to fulfill a legal requirement of the United Kingdom, the partners invested several days engaging in what Dart described as 'high bandwidth brainstorming'. At their most recent meeting, a range of issues had come into view. Firstly, the partners were conscious of the fact that in spite of their success, they had still worked with only 10 per cent of their potential clients. With no substantive direct competitors and plenty of current and future work, Pay Zone could simply carry on and expand their clientele as the opportunity for additional work arose. But if they wished to grow the company more rapidly, then increasing their consulting capacity by expanding the partnership was an option to be considered. Another issue concerned the long-term continu-

ation of the company: the Pay Zone principals would be starting to think about retirement within the next decade or so, but there were no younger partners in place to continue the firm. Thirdly, they recognized that successful boutique consulting operators like Pay Zone were attractive take-over targets for much larger companies with the resources to really go after the market. They also recognized that other companies might develop applications to compete with their own software products, thereby undercutting a major generator of consulting revenue for Pay Zone. Selling their major software products as a pre-emptive move, or even selling the entire company outright, were interesting alternatives for monetizing their assets. But each of these options had associated problems. Throughout their wide-ranging discussions, the partners remained acutely conscious of the lifestyles made possible through their virtual teamwork. What they really sought was a strategy that would grow the company and increase their revenue but still enable them to enjoy the lifestyle and professional growth that the Pay Zone virtual business model had provided to date.

Background

Before joining Pay Zone, Owen Dart had accumulated 25 years E&P experience including 12 years with a major global technology company for which he had worldwide responsibility for E&P information management. Dart was a registered professional geophysicist with a B.Sc. in applied geology and a M.Sc. in geophysics. He met his future business partners in the mid-1990s while working for the company on a project involving close to 120 people based mainly in Houston, London and Stavanger. Though many of the sub-project groups functioned as virtual teams part of the time, face to face meetings were still frequent, requiring a lot of people spending a lot of time on airplanes. Dart recalled it was not uncommon for him to fly to the United Kingdom for a one-hour meeting, with the whole matter taking three days – one day to fly there, one day for the one-hour meeting, and a third day to fly home. Jet lag and the time spent travelling were frequent conversation topics.

Everyone agreed that the process was costly and inefficient but seemingly unavoidable as the company undertook projects all over the globe. One benefit however was that as the project teams met, people got to know each other and over time became well acquainted.

Even though the project entailed a lot of travel, many of the project team members had enjoyed considerable flexibility with regard to working at home versus in the office. For his part, Dart had engaged in virtual teamwork for about five years. He recalled a situation that occurred in Toronto as the company moved into new quarters. For some months, there was insufficient space for 30 to 40 employees, so the company conducted an early experiment with telecommuting. Staff were provided with laptops, appropriate software, and the freedom to work at home. Productivity went up, and so did customer satisfaction as those involved in marketing were spending more time with their clients and less time travelling. Everyone won. The telecommuting experiment was instructive to Dart and his colleagues.

In 1998, a precipitating event occurred. The company decided to sell the entire project, and as part of the deal all project employees would be transferred to the new owners. Dart and his acquaintances began serious discussions about forming their own company. None of them really wanted to work for the new company, especially as it might mean returning to a less flexible, traditional office-based work environment.

The group took stock of their assets. In terms of professional expertise, they were an impressive lot. Educationally, the group had bachelors and masters degrees in geology, geophysics, computer science, and mechanical and electrical engineering. Their work experience ranged from 12 to 20 years in the industry, and they combined knowledge in a broad range of oil industry processes including seismic processing, reservoir simulation applications, petroleum engineering, information architecture, knowledge management, user requirements definition, and technical information management strategies along with many other topics relevant to exploration and production management. Through their work to date, all had gained some experience with virtual teamwork, exposure to the technology of the time, security issues, and so on. Furthermore, one of them had been developing collaboration software for their current company and knew quite a bit about it. They all agreed there were ways to improve the virtual teamwork process.

But education, relevant experience and technical skills were only part of the package. To become a member of the Pay Zone team, a certain mindset was essential: clear agreement with the rest of the group on both business and personal goals. For example, the group discussed whether or not their goal should be to grow the company very rapidly and make a lot of money in a short time or make adequate money while pursuing a particular lifestyle. They decided on the latter. This decision in turn made necessary a commitment to employ virtual teamwork at the heart of their business model. The group felt it would be difficult to retrofit a virtual model to an existing business, which meant they had to build the new company as a virtual organization through and through, right from the start. The group therefore needed individuals who were motivated, adaptable, and technically literate. In short, to participate in the Pay Zone business, principals needed the right combination of education, experience, shared vision and personality objectives. As Dart remarked, 'this company is all about both what we like to do and where we like to do it'. Dart noted that for a startup company oriented around virtual teamwork, you 'almost needed the stars aligned to have it all come together successfully. You couldn't afford to include people who didn't buy in fully at the beginning'.

Largely because of their virtual business model, there were no startup capital costs and very little operating cost either. No land, buildings, or office space were required. As for equipment, little more was needed at the beginning than a high-end laptop and internet access for each partner. Minimal investment was required from the new shareholders and no line of credit from the banks. Each of the founders was a well-established professional with the financial resources to survive for at least six months without income from the new company. An especially valuable and unique asset of the group was that as a result of their many years working within the oil industry, collectively they had contacts in most of the major E&P companies, and many of the minor ones. This engendered a feeling of confidence about their future. As Dart explained it, 'you had the sense that you were working with a safety net'. Indicative of their confidence, Dart stated they never developed a revenue projection spreadsheet to determine whether or not they could survive financially! In short, there were no financing issues at all – one of the several virtues of this new virtual company.

Industry drivers

A critical question they faced at the start was whether or not there was actually a market for their services. Dart and his partners identified four main business drivers in the energy industry. Firstly, worldwide competition for increasingly scarce commodities – oil and natural gas – was becoming considerably more challenging. New discoveries were occurring at a rate less than that of global consumption. Annual estimated reserves worldwide were decreasing and the need to locate new sources of oil and gas was increasing. Secondly, industry employment patterns were changing significantly. In many oil companies, a shift was under way from hiring and keeping long-term employees, to the use of project-focused contract staff. This often meant that many companies no longer had highly qualified in-house expertise needed to extract information easily from the company's information systems, a skill in which the Pay Zone team had particular depth. Thirdly, the global economy itself was changing dramatically. Businesses were becoming increasingly interconnected; global supply chains were speedily expediting the transfer of goods and services throughout the world. Firms in the oil and gas industry, long accustomed to managing risk through joint ventures, were active participants. Fourthly, given the often distant and remote sites for oil and gas exploration and production, newly developed information and communication technologies were becoming increasingly employed throughout the industry.

Considering these industry drivers, Dart and his business partners reasoned that information and knowledge were the key resources for competitive advantage in the oil and gas industry. The only sustainable competitive advantage in the industry was the ability to learn faster and apply knowledge more effectively throughout the business than one's competitors were doing. The Pay Zone founders decided to promote the concept that improved business performance, i.e., effectiveness and efficiency, was best achieved through the optimized use of information. They offered what they described as 'advanced information management thinking' as a means of creating a competitive advantage for their clients. In 1998 the group formed Pay Zone Consulting, the term 'pay zone' referring to the target of any drilling operation, a reservoir holding hydrocarbons that can be recovered in enough quantity to 'pay' an income.

Pay Zone startup and growth

The first task of the Pay Zone partners at startup was to build Pay Zone's virtual infrastructure and establish their credibility by showing that they were competent people who brought real value to their work. In their ambitious strategic plan, the partners identified a group of 'key target clients' to pursue in the next five years. These included BP, Shell, Phillips Petroleum, Chevron, Petro-Canada, IBM, Halliburton, Baker-Hughes, Anadarko, Talisman, Nexen, Canadian Association of Petroleum Producers, and several others, In time, each of these targeted companies was added to the list of Pay Zone clients (see Exhibit 7.1).

The strength of the Pay Zone partnership proved to be its specialization. Larger consultancies offered broadly similar services for business strategy, change management, and the like, but not for the oil and gas industry specifically. Since the Pay Zone principals were oil and gas professionals, they provided a level of business understanding that was not typically available from the big consulting companies. There were several small oil- and gas-specific consultancies, but these tended to specialize in areas of the business other than information management and process design, which Pay Zone addressed.

Exhibit 7.1	**Oil and Gas Companies**	**Service Companies**

Exhibit 7.1

Pay Zone Clients

Oil and Gas Companies

Alberta Energy Company International (AECI)
Anadarko
British Gas (BG) Group
BP (Norway)
Centrica
Danske Oil and Natural Gas (DONG)
Dynegy
Encana Corporation
ENI UK
Gaz de France
KIO – Karachaganak Project Development
    (Texaco, Agip, BG and Lukoil)
LASMO plc
Nexen Inc
Nimir Petroleum Limited
OMV
PanCanadian UK
Petro-Canada
Phillips Petroleum
Premier Oil
Scottish and Southern Energy
Shell International E&P
Shell Expro
Statoil
Talisman Energy

Service Companies

Baker Atlas Geoscience
Landmark Graphics
IBM
PetroData (Norway)
Petroleum Geo-Services
Silicon Graphics (SGI)
Wood Group
Wood Mackenzie (Deutsche Bank)
Industry Organisations
Canadian Association of Petroleum
    Producers (CAPP)
Common Data Access (CDA)
    (UKOOA subsidiary)
POSC
PPDM
IQPC

Research Projects
Henley Management College
University of Calgary
University of York
Government Agencies and Organisations
Norwegian Petroleum Directorate (NPD)

Other Energy Companies
Alliance Pipeline
Enbridge

Dart explained that the company started out as purely a consulting group but 'organically' moved into software development as a byproduct of their consulting. For instance, information requirements analysis, a common Pay Zone assignment, involved the consultant building a 'prototype system' and preparing PowerPoint slides to explain the new system to the users. The consultant would then meet with the user group to verify and refine the company's information needs. Dart described an early project in which a Pay Zone consultant spent a full month on a North Sea drilling platform working with the users and technicians. The gas company, impressed with their very intensive approach, invited Pay Zone to write the functional specifications and oversee the subsequent software devel-opment. This in turn led to Pay Zone being per-suaded to develop the software itself, as a way of adding value. In effect, Pay Zone got into software development by happenstance. The result was a highly-effective solution that was developed for significantly less than the projected budget and a client that consequently was very pleased with the outcome. The long-term outcome was a perman-ent relationship in which this company dealt only with Pay Zone on such problems.

The North Sea project also left Pay Zone with a new software product and a software team to support it. This experience in turn generated ideas for other software packages and Pay Zone eventu-ally developed a number of different products. These included an information management and knowledge integration package; a process control and knowledge capture tool; a production and reserves reporting application suite; and an activity and role-based training management system. The latter tracked the activities of staff working in complex environments, coped with shift days on site, shift patterns, holidays and other activities. It also managed training requirements based on the job description and the roles of an individual. Further expanding their offerings, Pay Zone developed training and education programmes, conducted remote demonstrations, and provided virtual client presentations employing teleconferencing and video conferencing.

Indicative of the importance of software development to Pay Zone was that while in the early years consulting itself generated other consulting jobs and accounted for all of Pay Zone revenue, more recently software sales had come to account for fully 50 per cent of the revenue, with the remaining 50 per cent coming from consulting. Furthermore, 90 per cent of this consulting revenue was in turn a spin off from extra work generated from installing software packages sold. In effect, a consulting project often resulted in a software sale that in turn generated additional consulting work.

The quality and integrity that the Pay Zone principals insisted upon in their work, as exemplified by the North Sea case, resulted in a high proportion of follow-on business. Approximately 80 per cent of their new business emerged from prior relationships. Clients often requested additional work on a project already under way, and were usually receptive to suggestions on the part of Pay Zone consultants for further work. As a consequence, Pay Zone did no direct advertising or marketing. Pay Zone principals presented papers at conferences and promoted their firm informally as they worked with clients, but the company was sufficiently well established that a satisfactory flow of business came to their doorstep without further effort. Overall, Pay Zone was a prospering operation with a steady cash flow, no administrative payroll to meet because of automated administrative systems, and software developers added to or removed from the payroll as required.

Working virtually

Pay Zone was an 'unstructured organization', a true contradiction in terms. The founding partners were all shareholders and served as their own board of directors. No one had a job title. Dart enjoyed saying that anyone could be 'CFO for the day' meaning that any one of the partners might assume any C-level position 'for the day' if a particular problem or issue arose, depending on which partner happened to be available. Thus, while certain responsibilities gravitated over time to particular individuals depending on their skills, in general roles were flexible.

Work typically came in by telephone or e-mail directly from clients. Dart explained that engagements often started small with a simple question from a client and led to a larger engagement later on. By way of example, in a recent situation, Dart held an initial brief meeting with a client, after which he was asked to put on a two-hour workshop to discuss the client's problem in greater detail. Dart held the workshop and was then invited to present a formal proposal for the work. Dart secured assistance in developing the PowerPoint proposal presentation from a Pay Zone consultant who was working at the time in Borneo. The consultant worked on the presentation during the evening and passed the result back to Dart over the internet. Dart then conducted the presentation, which resulted in Pay Zone securing a contract. In the meantime, another piece of work, from a different client, was also secured by Dart. With the first client's agreement, Dart communicated the details of the first project to another Pay Zone consultant in the United Kingdom using electronic mail, and effectively handed off the first project to him, even as Dart himself remained the principal contact with the client. A third piece of work was also secured at about the same time, and Dart handed it off to a Pay Zone contractor who was at the time working on a project in Texas. In general, as a job was received, it would be assigned to one or other of the principals depending on the nature of the problem.

In addition to offering its wide range of expertise in information management, Pay Zone was prepared to take on jobs that might last only a few weeks, full-time or part-time, through to projects lasting years. Most companies asked for an estimate on a project, including time and materials, and only occasionally asked for a fixed price contract.

Pay Zone employed a variety of hardware and software to create the infrastructure through which the company conducted its business. The hardware included high-end laptops and international cell phones along with multiple 'mirrored' servers employing auto-replication and 128-bit encryption to guarantee reliability and integrity, and to prevent against possible data loss. Dart noted that since all business-related data was replicated across all Pay Zone servers and all five principals' laptops, in theory they could lose all their servers and all but one laptop and still completely reconstruct the entire business.

Software products included Lotus Notes, Lotus Sametime (an instant messaging and Web conferencing system), NetMeeting for multi-point video-conferencing using VoIP,[1] and an electronic white board facility and PC Anywhere enabling remote desktop control, the latter two being essential tools for software developers working from home.

The Pay Zone administrative software included applications to handle contracts, expense reports, accounts receivables, invoices, receipts, meetings, to-do lists, and calendars. An in-house application called Pay Zone Time-Writing was capable of handling multiple projects and contracts along with multiple consultants per project. Pay Zone Expense could handle multiple currencies and had an automatic exchange rate update. The Pay Zone Invoicing System provided links to contracts, expenses, timesheets, and also employed automatic currency conversion. All applications were interlinked and freely passed data from one to the other as required. Pay Zone's virtual administrative system was accessible anytime, anywhere worldwide via the internet or off-line via laptop replication.

---

[1]VoIP stands for 'voice over internet protocol' (a way in which the internet and personal computers can be used to enable a two-way or multi-way telephone-like conversation with or without video. If video is also being used, the communication mode is referred to as 'desktop videoconferencing').

Pay Zone's administrative software was based on the Lotus Domino platform and was written, maintained and upgraded by Pay Zone's own salaried programming team. Pay Zone had to develop its own administrative software because nothing was available commercially that offered a web-enabled finance, contacts management, and contract tracking system that could handle multiple currencies, changing exchange rates and automatic invoicing. Domino also provided sophisticated security (it was the engine of many banking and brokerage systems) and allowed automatic mirroring on multiple servers for backup and redundancy. The web-enabled aspect was important because of the virtual nature of the business: any Pay Zone person needed to be able to interact with the systems from any location at any time.

Members of the Pay Zone team had a variety of media tools for communicating with each other and with clients, including e-mail, telephone, audio conferencing, videoconferencing, and electronic whiteboards, but instant messaging (IM) came to be used most frequently. IM provided them with capabilities in between e-mail and telephone or VoIP communications. For example, Dart compared instant messaging with Skype, the internet-based telephone service, noting that Skype involved 'conversation' whereas IM provided a little time to think and respond carefully. But in contrast to e-mail, IM was more 'conversation-like'. Furthermore, instant messaging dialogues could be archived automatically, whereas using Skype or a telephone required note taking if a record of the call was needed. The Pay Zone partners also liked the fact that IM told them immediately whether the person was there (unlike e-mail) and therefore whether the sender could expect to receive a response very quickly. The discipline necessitated by instant messaging meant that all of the Pay Zone principals had to learn to write succinctly. Dart also pointed out that since the Pay Zone partners knew each other very well, there was no particular need to employ videoconferencing (a feature of Skype). Generally speaking, videoconferencing, which might have seemed a boon to a virtual organization, proved of limited value for the Pay Zone partners.

He acknowledged that visual contact might be useful in situations in which a consultant was talking to a new client. Electronic whiteboards also came into occasional use but mostly for discussions between consultants working on programming projects.

The Pay Zone principals also often conducted remote presentations. For such meetings, Pay Zone would e-mail the PowerPoint presentation file to the client, and then have the client group follow along as the Pay Zone consultant, located remotely from the client site, worked through the slides. Speakerphones were used at the meeting site. This was a much less complicated option than one that involved the Pay Zone consultant controlling the slides remotely. Aside from avoiding costly time and travel for the consultant, a remote presentation provided timing flexibility for the client who could, for example, ask for a meeting to be postponed for a half hour or so if circumstances required it.

Dart could think of no substantive disadvantage of working virtually. Any single significant decision was reviewed by the team (by e-mail) and a consensus was reached '95 per cent of the time'. When a consensus could not be reached by e-mail, the partners used instant messaging and the occasional teleconference to bring about a resolution. Face to face meetings were almost never required to address specific questions. In fact, the 'virtual experience' seemed to have a positive impact on the rare occasions when the principals did meet in person. Conscious of the use of time in these very infrequent face-to-face meetings, the principals adopted the practice of dispensing with as many of the administrative matters as possible by e-mail prior to the meeting. Precious meeting time was reserved only for topics that required in-person exchanges. The bulk of the Pay Zone face-to-face meetings were used for brain storming, not detailed administration.

Pay Zone also provided a '24/7 Help Desk'. There was no helpdesk in the conventional sense. However, any of the Pay Zone partners, contractors or software developers, whoever happened to be online and had the appropriate expertise, would deal with a problem that came into the 'help desk'.

All employees and contract consultants worked virtually, many of them out of their homes, but consultants were often in clients' offices. While an immediate response at any given hour of the day was not always possible, the widespread geographical location of various Pay Zone people at any moment provided considerable time zone coverage and meant a reply would usually be forthcoming in a few hours at most.

Dart provided a few examples of Pay Zone's virtual teamwork in action. In one case, after receiving new data from his client, a Pay Zone consultant on a North Sea platform sent an urgent request to the Pay Zone 'shared task' data base. Consultants in both the United States and the United Kingdom received the request, which was to modify a critical document. Within 12 hours of the request, the changes were approved, completed, and workflow software notified the client by e-mail and made the changes available. As an example of collaborating across different time zones, Dart described a case involving consultants on three different continents – Asia, Europe, and North America. Pay Zone consultants working in London and at a Kazakhstan field base were developing a requirements document. With the help of the Pay Zone Virtual Administrative System, the client's team completed the work in a timely fashion, everyone having had access to the project documents via the web 24 hours a day, seven days a week, from both Kazakhstan and London. A consultant in Canada collaborated on the final project report.

The Pay Zone administrative system also enabled clients to access information about ongoing progress. At the start of an engagement, the lead consultant would set up a new project 'book'. The project book was used by consultants to manage all the project documents. Clients could access selected entries to review status, reports, and presentations. The entire process was tracked and published via Pay Zone's process management tool. This tool allowed a business process to be constructed as a series of steps, each with information inputs, outputs and process descriptions. It tracked and compared project steps against a predefined schedule to track progress and identify departures from the planned schedule. In summary,

Pay Zone's systems enabled collaboration at the same time or at different times, and the sharing of information and knowledge amongst Pay Zone staff as well as externally.

Dart observed they could not have set this business up much earlier since some of the technologies they required to facilitate collaboration hadn't existed. The invention of the World Wide Web (www) in 1991, followed soon after by the advent of Mosaic and Netscape, the first web browsers, triggered a dramatic investment in fiber-optic systems worldwide. The growth of the internet and the www enabled the rapid transmission of large volumes of data – a critical development for a virtual organization trading large data files with their clients. At about the same time Windows 95, equipped with built-in internet support, appeared; it served to standardize internet-based personal computing, and made communication between individuals and companies easier and more reliable. Improved collaboration software was also coming onto the market just as Pay Zone was founded. The software industry continually created new tools and systems enabling better and faster communication between the great variety of hardware and software in use throughout the world.[2]

While the Pay Zone infrastructure and approach to business had worked well so far, Dart was uncertain as to how scalable the virtual organizational model might be. He was uncertain whether Pay Zone could operate using the same structure with 500 people or with even 50 people.

Strategic options

The Pay Zone partners had evolved a business model that was not only lucrative but largely met both their professional and personal goals. Still, having done business with only 10 per cent of their potential clients, they knew they could earn significant additional income if they had the capacity to do so. One possibility was that Pay Zone could borrow capital to expand its number of programmers and ramp up software development. After all, the

sale of software products and associated consulting spinoffs were its main revenue generators. However, identifying and designing new software products were something the principals did, and they were all already fully engaged with work. Another option was that Pay Zone should acquire some new consultants, if consulting capacity was limiting corporate growth. Unfortunately, this was a significant challenge since the work was very specialized and attracting people with the right skills and background might be difficult. Dart commented that there were not more than 10 such people currently available in the industry and Pay Zone knew them all. They were all highly qualified and skilled people, and would expect to be paid a lot of money. Attracting professionals of this calibre might even necessitate making them partners in Pay Zone. But if a new consultant was brought on board as an equity shareholder, the existing partners would want to be compensated somehow for the 10 year investment they had made in the company to build it into a valuable asset, and this was likely a significant barrier for a new prospect.

If attracting new full partners proved too problematic, Pay Zone could attempt to employ additional consultants on a contract basis. However doing so would provide less stability for long-term growth, and a lower likelihood of finding someone who would be a good fit with the Pay Zone culture. Also, the annual salary cost for a contract consultant would probably exceed that of an equally qualified permanent person.

While none of the options was perfect, at the same time the partners were sensitive to the fact that with their demographic profile – several of the principals were aging – Pay Zone needed to bring in some new blood, perhaps new professionals with technical talents the existing partners didn't have, if the company was to remain invigorated and growing.

The partners also considered the possibility that a major software developer might enter the marketplace with products competing directly with the Pay Zone line. A large firm with deep pockets could market their wares aggressively and perhaps cut substantially into Pay Zone's profit. As specialized as Pay Zone software was, a firm with sufficient

---

[2]For an extensive discussion of the emergence of communication technologies, see *The World Is Flat* by Thomas L. Friedman, Farrar Straus and Giroux, New York , 2006.

resources might develop competing solutions, perhaps even superior ones, and threaten Pay Zone's dominance. A pre-emptive strike for Pay Zone might be to sell off the Pay Zone software line as a means of monetizing these assets, i.e., extracting their full value while Pay Zone software was still unique and before competitors appeared.

Dart also observed that Pay Zone software products held significant additional value, beyond the immediate return the products produced for the firm, because work associated with the software provided the lead-in for a substantial portion of Pay Zone's consulting revenue. Pay Zone software was not 'shrink wrapped' – that is, the software wasn't a standalone product. Any client acquiring a Pay Zone software application invariably needed to contract with Pay Zone consultants for assistance in installing, tailoring and learning how to use the software. This meant that a company buying their software line would also obtain an engine for generating consulting revenue. In that sense, the software had a great deal more value to a somewhat larger company than it did to Pay Zone since such a company would have the resources to more fully market the software and exploit the consulting spinoffs. Dart saw this as an important argument for maximizing the price of their software business, should they choose to sell it.

Easily the most dramatic option was to sell the entire company outright – the Pay Zone name, Pay Zone software products and even the services of the Pay Zone consultants until the new owners became sufficiently well established. Dart noted that the fact that the Pay Zone partners had contacts in nearly all of the significant E&P companies, and could exploit these to quickly establish the presence of the new buyer, comprised an asset of considerable value. If other options to grow the company proved too challenging, an outright sale might be an effective mechanism for the partners to extract the maximum value from the firm.

It was clear that the current conditions presented a major opportunity for the partners to increase their income significantly. However, none of the alternatives available was without flaws. While keen to increase their earnings, the partners were equally keen to ensure that whatever direction they chose, they would preserve and perhaps even improve the quality of life currently provided by the Pay Zone virtual business model. Their next step had to be considered with utmost care.

The Richard Ivey School of Business gratefully acknowledges Malcolm Munro at the Haskayne School of Business, University of Calgary and Sid Huff at the School of Information Management, Victoria University of Wellington in the development of this learning material.

Further Reading

Andersson, A. and Andersson, S. (2008), Directing consultants' effort – A study of four staffing companies. *University of Gothenburg Dissertation thesis* accessed at http://hdl.handle.net/2077/10238

Andriole, S. (2007), Consultants in the Hen House. Online article accessed from www.bitaplanet.com/alignment/article.php/3710151

Anonymous (2004), How to become an 'internal consultant', *Payroll Manager's Report*; 4(7), p. 8–9

Beagrie, S. (2008), How to become an internal consultant, *Personnel Today* p. 29. Accessed from http://www.personneltoday.com/articles/2008/02/04/44196/become-an-internal-consultant.html

Bellman, G.M. (1972), What does an internal consultant actually do? *Management Review,* 61(11), 26–30

Block, P. (2000), *Flawless Consulting: A Guide to Getting Your Expertise Used.* ; 2nd Edition

Brunning, H. and Huffington, C. (1994), *Internal Consultancy in the Public Sector: Case Studies (Systemic Thinking & Practice)* London: Karnac Books

Ellingson, J.E., Gruys, M.L., and Sackett, P.R. (1998), Factors related to the satisfaction and performance of temporary employees, *Journal of Applied Psychology,* 83(6), 913–921

Fincham, R. (1999), The consultant-client relationship: Critical perspectives on the management of organisational change, *Journal of Management Studies,* 36(3), 335–351

Heusinkveld, S. and Benders, J. (2005), Contested commodification: Consultancies and their struggle with new concept development, *Human Relations*; 58(3), 283–310

Karantinou, K.M. and Hogg, M.K. (2001), Exploring relationship management in professional services: A study of management consultancy, *Journal of Marketing Management,* 17, 263–286

Krell, T.C. and Dobson, J.J. (1999), The use of magic in teaching organizational behavior, *Journal of Management Education,* 23(1), 44–52

Lock, D. (2003), *Project Management.* Farnham: Gower Publishing Ltd

Massarik, F. and Pei-Carpenter, M. (2002), *Organizational Development and Consulting.* San Francisco: Jossey-Bass

McKenna, C.D. (2006), *The World's Newest Profession: Management Consultancy in the Twentieth Century.* New York: Cambridge University Press

Meislin, M. (1997), *The Internal Consultant: Drawing on Inside Expertise,* USA Thomson Crisp Learning.

Neal, M. and Lloyd, C. (2001), The role of the internal consultant. In Sadler, P. (Ed) *Management Consultancy: A Handbook of Best Practice.* London: Kogan Page Ltd

Neumann, J.E., Kellner, K., and Dawson-Shepherd, A. (1997). *Developing Organisational Consultancy.* London: Routledge

Robinson, D.G, and Younglove, B. (1984), To leap or slide: Transition from internal to external consultant, *Training & Development Journal,* 38(5), 40–47

Stroh, L.K. and Johnson, H.H. (2006), *The Basic Principles of Effective Consulting.* New Jersey: Lawrence Erlbaum Associates, Inc

Weiss, A. (2006), What constitutes an effective internal consultant. In, Gallos, J.V. (Ed) *Organizational Development A Jossey-Bass Reader.* San Francisco: Jossey Bass

Wright, C. (2008), Reinventing human resource management: Business partners, internal consultants and the limits to professionalization, *Human Relations,* 61(8), 1063–1086

Performance and management

The third part of this book explores the essential aspects of performance and management. Chapter 8 investigates project management, crucial in managing consultancy projects and monitoring performance. It illustrates the importance of project management concepts such as time, cost and quality. It also details the project management system, PRINCE2 to critically illustrate the need for products such as the business case and plans.

Chapter 9 extends this further, investigating programme management where a number of projects operate to deliver major business benefits. A system of programme management is introduced and then critically appraised with the latest research.

Chapter 10 then concludes the performance and management section by investigating the types of consultancy projects that are performed. This ranges from fact based to action based consultancy assignments. This chapter also details a wealth of case studies from industry demonstrating real projects that have occurred recently and illustrating the scope of consultancy work.

CHAPTER 8

Project management

Learning Objectives

At the end of this chapter students will be able to:

- Recognize why project management is essential in consultancy
- Understand major concepts, components and processes within project management
- Be able to initiate, plan, monitor and close a project
- Recognize the professional skills of project management

Mini Case Study 8.1

Bodged repairs due to incorrect plans

Repairs to the Pitsea Flyover Bridge in Essex began in 2004 much to the inconvenience of road users of this major route (Offord, 2009). The project was controlled and run by Essex County Council, with their consultant partner being Mouchel and Tarmac being the contractor onsite on the original project (Basidon District Council, 2004). The repairs had involved about £12m in total; replacing the crash barriers, resurfacing the road and replacing street lights (BBC, 2007).

Nonetheless, Austin (2006) stated that the bridge was still leaking just as badly as when the repairs had not been carried out. Later the BBC (2007) revealed the reason for this 'bodged job'. Apparently, the engineers at the site were not working from the most up-to-date versions of the plans. This had subsequently led to the problems involving the water drainage system not functioning properly. Estimates for correcting the error were estimated to be in the region of £200k (BBC, 2007). Offord (2009) further commented that MP (http://www.echo-news.co.uk/search/?search=Angela+Smith) Angela Smith has called for a public inquiry into why a further £2m needs to be spent on engineering work on the ill fated bridge in 2009. Congestion on the bridge is predicted to be heavy during the further repairs to the bridge starting in late October 2009 and continuing for a further 43 weeks (Offord, 2009).

References

Austin, J. (2006), £8m spent, so why is Pitsea flyover still leaking? Retrieved 3rd November from http://www.echo-news.co.uk/news/local_news/966799.__8m_spent__so_why_is_Pitsea_flyover_still_leaking_/

Basildon District Council (2004) The Bulletin ISSUE NO. 2004/29, retrieved 3rd November 2009 from http://www2.basildon.gov.uk/Website2/members/wdlmemlist.nsf/A4279C452323140980256ED200561629/$file/BULLETIN150704 Wk29.pdf

BBC (2007) Bridge work failed to fix problem Retrieved 3rd November from from http://news.bbc.co.uk/1/hi/england/essex/6995241.stm

Offord, P. (2009) Why has work to repair Pitsea flyover taken so long? Retrieved 3rd November from http://www.echo-news.co.uk/news/4662549.Why_has_work_to_repair_Pitsea_flyover_taken_so_long_/.

Project Management Fundamentals

Why use project management?

Failures in projects are all too common and can be costly as in the opening case study. Projects fail for a number of reasons. These include failure to meet with the client's expectations, overrun timeframes, overrun costs, or a simple mistake early on in the process like in our opening case study.

Project management does often centre on avoiding problems; however, it is typically thought of as a methodology of preparation, forecast and control. A more precise definition is given below from the British Standards Institute:

> Project management is the planning, monitoring and control of all aspects of the project and the motivation of all those involved in it to achieve the project objectives on time and to the specified cost, quality and performance.
>
> *Cited from BS6079-1, 2000: p. 5*

This definition demonstrates that both processes and people are essential in project management. So project management does go well beyond planning, it involves motivating people and allowing for contingencies as well. Project management may be simply put as just planning and management combined (Reiss, 2007).

Thought Provoking point 8.1

Can you think of an assignment that you needed to hand in and weren't able to or that you produced something not at your 'usual' standard. What were the major stumbling points of failing to get the assignment in on time? Could you avoid them next time?

Project management originated from the construction and engineering industries, which is why today many consultancies such as Arup and Atkins promote their background in these disciplines. Henry Gantt who was a mechanical engineer and management professional is considered to be one of the founding fathers of project management and his GANTT charts first used in the early twentieth century aided huge projects such as the Hoover Dam (Alexander, 2008).

What is a project?

Before proceeding on with how projects may be managed, it is important to define what a project is. Many authors have put forward their own definitions of a project. Saynisch (2005) for instance, reviewed the future of project management techniques and defined a project in three ways:

1. A project is an undertaking that is in principle characterized by its uniqueness of conditions, for example, as objectives, clear time, cost, and quality and other conditions, differentiation to other endeavours, project specific organization

2. A project is an endeavour in which human, material, and financial resources are organized in a novel way, to undertake a unique scope of work, of given specification, within constrains of cost and time, following a standard life cycle, so as to achieve beneficial change defined by quantitative and qualitative objectives

3. A project is a unique set of co-ordinated activities, with defined starting and finishing points, undertaken by an individual or organization to meet specific objectives within a defined schedule, cost and performance parameters

From Saynisch (2005); p. 556

All of these definitions are relevant to what a project is, although Saynisch (2005) argued that other aspects such as trust within a project should also be considered in a definition. Simplifying all of these definitions into one, we can adapt the definition from the project management methodology PRINCE2 (PRojects IN Controlled Environments) to define a project as:

A temporary organisation that is created for the purpose of delivering one or more business products according to an agreed Business Case.

Cited from OGC, 2009; p. 3

PRINCE was the original project management system that was originally designed for IT Projects only due to the limited successes that many IT projects had when they were run without a project management system. Nonetheless, PRINCE2 was developed as an all encompassing project management system (OGC, 2009). PRINCE2 can be used for large projects and small student projects and will be highlighted in this chapter.

Projects can either be large or small, be a group task at university or a multi-million pound road renewal scheme. All of these different projects will share similar characteristics but will be on different scales and require different issues to be resolved.

These characteristics may be listed as:

- A project is a finite non-repetitive undertaking
- A project typically creates something (product or service) that is new or updated
- A project brings together a team that require clearly defined roles and organization
- Projects are often complex and have many interrelated tasks
- The three project constraints are time, costs and quality

Atkins Management Consultants worked with a London Borough examining parking offences in the area. Two distinct methods of research were carried out; firstly, an observer would monitor and record a notorious area for parking offences; secondly the research involved a 'beat' technique whereby a researcher would walk along a prescribed route noting car park offences along the way.

The data for both pieces of research were then analysed by the consultancy who wrote up a report for the client. This project was commissioned again six months later and then several times subsequently. Due to the initial effective design of the project, the subsequent times that the project was run went very smoothly. This therefore generated revenue for the consultancy giving the client their requested data over a period of years. Practices such as these demonstrate that well-designed projects will have advantages such as repeated business as in this case.

Time, cost and quality

Most clients want the highest quality, at the cheapest rate and in the fastest time. Time, cost and quality are the three fundamental constraints in project management (Lock, 2003; Saynisch, 2005). All project management systems such as PRINCE2 and Project Management Body of Knowledge (PMBOK) published by the Project Management Institute (PMI) will incorporate these three factors. They can thus be regarded almost as the three primary colours of project management defined as:

- **Time**, the hours, days, months, years of linear time
- **Cost**, typically measured in terms of the money spent; however, other costs may also be considered such as environmental costs
- **Quality (or scope)**, are all the characteristics of the project, product or service that will satisfy the clients stated and implied needs

Many systems may just use these three factors (Lock, 2003). Other more advanced project management techniques, such as PRINCE2, will include other factors such as performance. Yet factors such as these tend to be a mixture of the fundamental factors with performance, for instance, being a mix of quality and time (Ward, 1994).

There are many different project management systems available to consultants and one of the most popular is PRINCE2. This system is used within both the private and public sector. It is free to use and has been employed in many of the most recent UK government large-scale projects (OGC, 2009). In describing the features within the PRINCE2 project management system the author can describe accurately how project management systems work in action.

Project Management Concepts

Many different project management systems have key features or concepts. In detailing the concepts in one particular type of the PRINCE2 project management system, this section will highlight important concepts in project management.

The key concepts in PRINCE2 are as follows:

- Business need and user demand
- Flexible and scalable
- Management v technical expertise
- Customer/supplier
- Stages
- Quality

Business need and user demand

One of the most important aspects of project management is that the business need and the eventual users are considered in full. Many times the two groups are in conflict or at the very least the users do not understand the inherent business needs (Lindahl and Ryd, 2007). Users will typically want the best available no matter what the costs. However, the business may not need the best available and more cost effective solutions can be created. Dialogue is needed between the two parties to create the optimum solution that satisfies the business need for the project. Indeed, many projects arguably fail as the stakeholders in the project are not consulted (McManus, 2004).

Most project management systems create something to address this issue, although some would argue a more participative approach is perhaps needed than just a formal document (McManus, 2004). In PRINCE2, the product or document known as the business case performs this function. The business case has the following attributes:

- Reason/justification for project
- How does the project support business strategy?
- Costs
- Benefits
- Time taken for benefits to emerge
- Investment appraisal

Often different departments will compete and state that there projects are more important than the projects of others (LePrevost and Mazur, 2005). This is the remit of programme management to prioritize projects and will be examined in the next chapter.

Flexible and scalable

As mentioned previously, projects vary in size and can involve a single person completing a few hours work through to many thousands of individuals putting in long hours (Saynisch, 2005). It is important that a project management technique is fit for purpose and can be flexible to deal with the precise needs of the project. The project management technique needs to be scalable dealing with large and small projects.

Management v technical competence

Most project management systems draw clear distinctions between managerial and technical expertise. Projects may be managed by non-technical staff trained in project management techniques who then manage technical employees. As long as the managers understand the essence of the project, they do not necessarily have to know the full technical details of the project to run it effectively. Similarly, technical staff need to be deployed where necessary on a project by the project management team but don't necessarily need to know the fine details of the project. Nevertheless, Lam (1996) argued that in an engineering context, where there were managers who were not engineers, e.g., had the management abilities but not the technical abilities, then in this instance the engineers were underutilized. Lam (1996) subsequently suggested that in terms of management that project managers should have a good understanding of the technical problems and issues that a technical project team may face.

> **Thought Provoking point 8.2**
>
> A good manager needs to know what makes for motivated staff but not necessarily what they do in terms of the technical details. By knowing what makes the IT wiz inspired, a manager can motivate that individual to produce work of exceptional quality, contributing to overall profitability.

Customer/supplier

In any project, there will be at least a customer and a supplier (Artto, Wikström, Hellström and Kujala, 2008). Customers may be defined as the person/group that commissioned the work and will be the main recipients of the benefit of the results. Suppliers are those that provide the project's products. Often a project may involve a number of suppliers that need to be managed effectively for successful completion of the work (Artto *et al.*, 2008).

Stages

Breaking a problem down into manageable stages is important to conquer the challenge of a project (OGC, 2009). Many project management systems do exactly this and break down a project into easily manageable stages. These have the advantages of being more easily controlled by top management and also will lead to several successes within the life-cycle of a project when the stage has been completed.

Quality

As previously defined, quality in project management terms represents the totality of the customer's needs. It is often a tick list of customer needs that should be satisfied if it is achieved (LePrevost and Mazur, 2005). These needs are predefined as quality. Quality comprises of functional, physical and symbolic product characteristics that must be achieved for the customer to be satisfied (Thomson, Austin, Devine-Wright and Mills, 2003).

Aspects of Project Management

Above, we examined the project management concepts that are the principal features inherent in any system. Components are different as these support the actual processes of project management. Figure 8.1 shows the main components in PRINCE2.

Organization

One of the key features of any project management system is that it defines a clear organizational structure for the project management team (OGC, 2009). The organization of a project refers to the roles and responsibilities of those carrying out the project. Typically, this is very hierarchical and is used by many consultancies as a method of progression through the organization, whereby a new consultant will progress becoming a project manager and then project director (Kuizinienė, 2008).

A project director has the overall responsibility for the project delivering its business benefits. Nevertheless, the project director is not typically involved in the detail or day to day running of the project. Indeed, if the upper management exert too much control typically there is a drop in overall project performance (Bonner, Ruekert and Walker, 2002).

So the day to day management of a project is typically the job of the project manager who actively manages all aspects of the project and leads individual experts and cross-functional teams (Leban, 2003). Indeed, the leadership style and the emotional intelligence of the project manager increases the probability of successfully completing a project enhancing the performance of individuals within the project (Leban, 2003; Limsila and Ogunlana, 2008). In large-scale projects, a Project Manager may also have team leaders or sub-Project Managers to aid their work.

PRINCE2 also follows a similar hierarchical approach to the organization of a project (See Figure 8.2). PRINCE2 is scalable so projects can be run with just the project director with overall responsibility and project manager with the daily running of the project. Figure 8.2 demonstrates the most complex project organization defined in PRINCE2. The Agency/Programme Management have overall charge of the project. In the next chapter we will be examining programme management and how multiple projects can be run concurrently in a programme. Below the

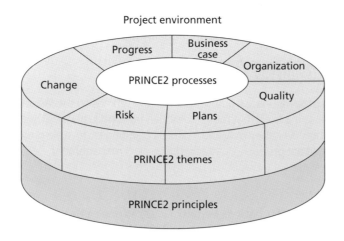

Project environment

Figure 8.1

Prince 2 project management components. Source: Managing Succesful Projetcs with PRINCE2. © Crown copyright 2009. All rights reserved. Material is reproduced with permission of the Office of Governmental Commerce under delegated authority from the Controller of HMSO.

Figure 8.2

The Organisation of a project. Source: Managing Succesful Projetcs with PRINCE2. © Crown copyright 2009. Material is reproduced with permission from OGC

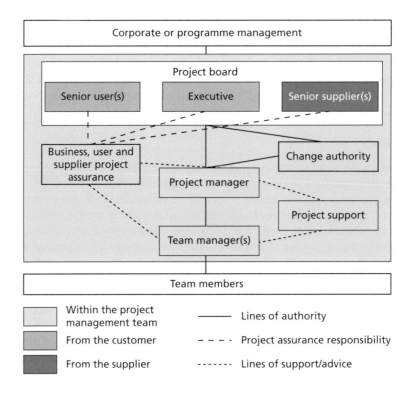

programme management level is the traditional project director role (OGC, 2009). In PRINCE2, this is the project board, represented by three individuals:

- Executive or Project Director
- Senior user, who is/are representatives of the eventual customers of the project
- Senior supplier, who is/are representatives of the provider of services/product

Just like in the project director role mentioned previously, the project board assumes the overall responsibility for the project delivering its business benefits. Reporting to the project board is the project manager who manages the day to day work of the project. On very large multimillion pound project it is not uncommon to have an assistant project manager; however, it is fairly rare to have two or more project managers. Again on very large projects, the project manager may delegate some of his/her responsibility to team managers. Project assurance and project support are also separate parts of the project and look after quality and administration respectively.

Thought Provoking point 8.3

Can you think of someone who never plans, leaves things to the last minute but yet does deliver? If so it is likely that these individuals perform just as well as their planning counterparts; however, they may find it difficult planning large-scale projects involving lots of others and are probably unattached to project management.

Plans

Planning was listed as far back as Bedaux (1917) as one of the eight principles of industrial efficiency according to Ferguson (2002). Planning refers to the defining of activities in a project and typically the time, cost and quality of these activities. A plan therefore tends to describe how, when and by whom a set of targets needs to be achieved (OGC, 2009).

Planning is a fundamental part of project management. Software packages (MS Project, Artemis and Primavera) aid the planning process immensely. The best way in which to learn about planning is to step through a project planning process. Planning can also be completed top-down or bottom-up. Top-down planning involves the planner looking at the wider objectives and then drilling down to the details. Bottom-up on the other hand, which is usually the more common in management consultancy involves working out what is needed and then planning what to do as in our example below.

Earlier we noted that if a complex task is broken down into stages it is easier to complete. Plans typically will break down projects into distinct stages that have review and decision points. The end of the stage is often marked by a milestone, which is a success point of completion within the project (Poettcker, 2009).

Example planning process

There are many ways in which to plan activities in a project. The following represents a tried and tested way and students should be able to use this in planning out a consultancy project.

Step 1: One of the most effective is to use a team in detailing all the activities that may need to take place (see also Chapter 12 – Working and problem solving in a team). In project planning often a flipchart (or for those more IT literate, MS Project) can be used to brainstorm and generate all the activities needed in a project.

Step 2: Once all these activities have been decided upon, they can then be put in order with erroneous activities being removed. One of the easiest ways of completing this is via Project Evaluation and Review Technique (PERT). Indeed, PERT charts can be easily created in MS Project (as shown in Figure 8.3). This links together all of the tasks needed for completing a project.

Step 3: PERT charts are brilliant for working out the process of a project. Nonetheless, often the timing of a project is lost in such a chart. Thus, planners will typically use a GANTT chart, which are automatically generated from a PERT chart in MS Project[1] (see Figure 6.6 for an example chart). GANTT charts have the advantage of showing time as a finite resource and are shaded on the diagram.

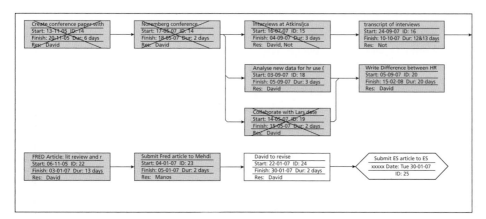

Figure 8.3

A PERT chart (extract from Microsoft Project)

---

[1]In the latest version of MS Project, PERT charts are now called Network Diagrams and can be easily accessed from the VIEW menu.

Step 4: Costs and resources may now be added into the project. Additional features within the software also mean that costs and resources can be added. This is a very useful function as the project manager can play with different models to see which gives the best outcome.

Business case

The business case and its creation is an essential aspect of PRINCE2 (OGC, 2009). Essentially, the business case determines what business benefits are to be released through the project and when. Often in smaller companies relating projects to their business case, in terms of what the project will do for the business, is a good way of prioritizing projects. Concentrating on the business case may furthermore encourage reluctant directors to address the business need as opposed to running their own pet projects.

Controls

Controls are essential for projects as they aid the decision-making process at the project and sometimes at the programme level. Controls ensure that the project management team can:

- Monitor progress
- Compare the actual delivery of objective against plans
- Review and update plans
- Authorize additional work

In PRINCE2, controls are typically specific documents that keep the project in check. Often in controls there is some leeway for which the project management team to operate within. In PRINCE2 this is called tolerance. As long as a project remains within the tolerated boundaries then it can progress. A project director doesn't need to know whether a project is slightly over or under project within the tolerance set. However, if the project is going to be twice as expensive as originally estimated then something needs to be done at the managerial level, such as cancelling or revising the project (Bonner *et al.*, 2002).

Management of risk

As we saw from the opening case study to this chapter, managing risks in projects is vital for project success. PRINCE2 defines a risk as:

> An uncertain event or set of events that, should it occur, will have an effect on the achievement of objectives. (PRINCE2, 2009, p.77)

There are two parts in the risk management process, risk analysis and risk management (Artto *et al.*, 2008). Risk analysis involves three activities:

- Identification – risks are determined by examining the assumptions made in a project
- Estimation – this is when each risk is assessed on two scales: likelihood of risk happening and the consequences of the risk
- Evaluation – this is where the level of risk is considered acceptable or not and what actions can be performed to lessen the risk

Once the risks have been analysed they need to be managed (Artto *et al.*, 2008; Kallman, 2007). Whole textbooks have been written on risk management; however, there in principle four main activities involved with risk management:

- Risk planning – deals with working out what countermeasures can be instigated to counteract the risk if it happens
- Resourcing – identifies what resources are available to carry out risk avoidance or damage limitation
- Monitoring – this involves ensuring that a risk is not manifesting and overall checking of progress
- Controlling – if the risk does occur then the actions in the risk plan are carried out to ensure that the risk is successfully counteracted even if this means the closure of the project

Quality in a project management environment

As we saw earlier, quality in a project environment represents the totality of characteristics needed for the customer to be satisfied. Projects cannot be run on implied needs due to uncertainty thus all the characteristics in a project should be explicit (LePrevost and Mazur, 2005; Thomson *et al.*, 2003). Thus, the scope or quality of a project needs to be defined well in advanced (OGC, 2009).

Industry snapshot 8.2

A well known consultancy developed a risk analysis and management system for a UK government department. The system received a great accolade as it was excellent in getting over the problems of Project Manager pride. It was found within the government department that project managers often felt a personal responsibility for project success. In this regard, when a project manager was asked about the foreseeable risks, the project managers often denied any risk at all fearing that the project might be discontinued.

The consultancy changed the language used and talked about assumptions of the project rather than risk. Assumptions were recorded rather than risks. This was considered to be more appropriate to the organizational culture within the government department.

An assumption, such as, Fred Bloggs will deliver the white boards to the training room on time, were turned into risks, e.g., there is a risk that Fred Bloggs won't deliver the white boards to the training room on time.

A graphical risk management system was then developed using the dimensions of likelihood and consequences of the risks plotted on a time-line. This was essentially the risk analysis stage of risk management.

Bubbles were used on this system plotted along a time-line, whereby the likelihood of the risk happening predicted the size of the bubble (the bigger the bubble the more likelihood it would happen) and consequences predicted the colour (green being classed as an inconvenience where as red was classed as a show stopper that would halt the project altogether).

The major criticism of a system such as this developed for the particular department, revolved around whether the system was truly bespoke. It cost the department millions to develop; nevertheless, with the exception of the graphical interface was the system so much more unique than other risk management systems available?

Configuration management

Configuration management (CM) is concerned with ensuring that the contents of products or documents are known, that any changes to products are legitimate and authorized, and that the documentation accurately describes the product (Burgess, Byrne and Kidd, 2003). Configuration management is thus essentially the system adopted to control products in a project environment. In a large-scale project there may be many different updates to a particular document, which is controlled via CM (Burgess *et al.*, 2003).

An example configuration management system is using versions. Thus, the first draft of this chapter may start as version 0.1. A few more changes may be made and then it becomes version 0.2, and so on. In practice, small projects will have fewer versions in their documents than larger projects. For one multi-million pound organizational change project, one document went up to version 0.22 before it was released to the client. Obviously, showing the client you have had 22 re-iterations of a document is probably not a good idea. Thus, when an event, such as sending the document off to the client happens, the version number changes to version 1.0. In this way, changes to a specific document can be charted in time (Burgess *et al.*, 2003).

> **Thought Provoking point 8.4**
>
> Cast your eye back to the Mini Case Study 8.1 that began this chapter. Do you think the proper use of configuration control would have saved the project money?

Change control

The world is constantly changing and projects are brought into this changing environment. Changes are expected as part of a project and managed in a formal and systematic manner within the project framework. Many clients may add to an initial brief of work, which has been examined in context. When this happens in a project environment it may trigger change control processes such as reviewing the project. Within a project, change control is typically managed through a product such as a change request form (Khan, 2004). This will then be considered with other products that also may request change in the original project brief (OGC, 2009).

Processes in Project Management

The processes involved in project management are often referred to as the project cycle. Biggs and Smith (2003) defined the project cycle as consisting of:

> a number of progressive phases that, broadly speaking, lead from identification of needs and objectives, through planning and implementation of activities to address these needs and objectives, to assessment of the outcomes
>
> *From Biggs and Smith (2003); p. 1743*

We will look at the process side of projects again using the PRINCE2 system. PRINCE2 is a product driven project management system, which has a number of

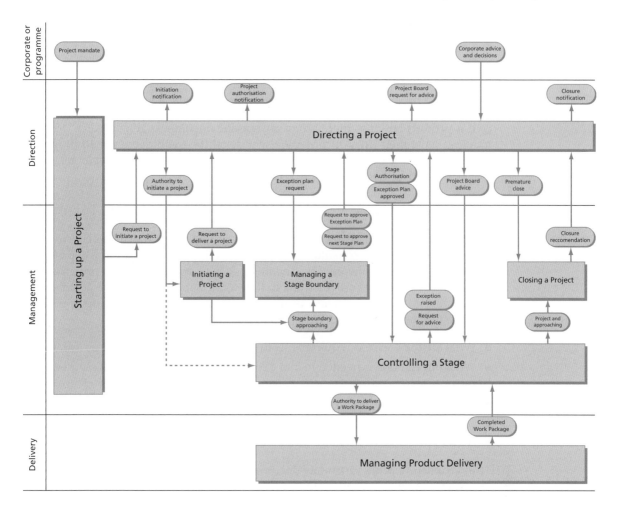

Notes:

Note 1: at the end of the initiation stage, the Initiating a Project process is used to request Project Board approval to initiate the project (with the submission of the Project Initiation Documentation) and in parallel the Managing a Stage Boundary process is used to request Project Board approval of the Stage Plan for the second management stage.

Note 2: the closure activities are planned and approved as part of the stage approval for the final stage; therefore the Closing a Project process takes place in the final stage.

Figure 8.4

Processes within PRINCE2. Source: Managing Succesful Projetcs with PRINCE2 © Crown copyright 2009. Material is reproduced with permission from OGC

different processes as shown in Figure 8.4 (OGC, 2009). It is a complex system but is more readily understood once all the processes have been detailed.

The PRINCE2 system can be summarized into six key processes:

- Starting up a project, where the facts and resources are gathered
- Initiating a project; this is when the project is agreed and then commences

- Project delivery, where the project is divided into stages and then controlled
- Planning, where plans are created, monitored and maintained
- Directing a project – the overall leadership of the project above and beyond the project manager
- Closing a project, where the project has achieved what it set out to complete

It is product based as there are many specific documents generated in the system that have their own purpose. We will detail the main documents produced; however, for a more detailed insight please read through available texts on PRINCE2 such as the guide produced by the OGC, 2009.

Starting up a project

The first process in any project management system is the start-up phase or pre-project phase. In many consultancy assignments this can represent the expression of interest for a piece of work (See Chapter 6 – Client engagement). In project management, the principles are the same in that work is done prior to the actual commencement of a more detailed proposal or tender stage. Starting up a project details a number of issues, such as:

- What are the business requirements that call for the project?
- What information is needed to make sound decisions on the commissioning of the project?
- Who will be the project team?
- A plan of how to initiate the project if it goes to the next stage.
- A list of possible risks that can occur in the project.

In PRINCE2 a project mandate document triggers off the start of this stage. This can be as simple as an email request from a manager or as complicated as a well drawn out planned document that forms part of a wider programme. At the end of this stage, a commitment by the commissioners of the project will be given to allocate resources to the initiation stage. Again, this is similar to what was noted in Chapter 6 – Client engagement, that a client will give some commitment to a consultancy (you are one of three firms, etc) so that the consultancy will invest money in writing a tender for an assignment. Industry snapshot 8.3 demonstrates an exercise that may be used in a commercial setting to encourage individuals to think about the issues.

Initiating a project

This stage of the process is a thorough investigation of the project in terms of whether it is feasible or not. The objectives of this stage are to ascertain whether there is a justification of the project creating a business case. It identifies who will be responsible for project deliverables. The stage also ensures that there is enough investment of time and effort by those taking part.

In PRINCE2, several documents are created in this stage the most important being the Project Initiation Document (PID). The PID plans the project and also defines how it will be done, why it is to be completed, by whom and when

New house exercise (project start-up)

This exercise can be used for students to fully explore the project start-up process. It is useful to complete as it will be the same process that is completed in project management.

Background

Imagine that you have just bought an old house that is in dire need of improvements. You have set aside $20 000 for improvements and would really like the following completed: 1. Guttering replaced, 2. Removal of electric storage heating, 3. Landscaped garden, 4. Painted outside of the house. The objective, as well as to create a more pleasant place to live, is to increase the value of the property. You have estimated from an investigation of local house prices that these repairs may add £35 000 to the value of your house.

Exercise

1. Given the above description sketch out a Project Brief by answering **briefly** the questions – WHAT, WHY, WHO, HOW, WHEN.

2. Are there any risks to the project? Detail these.

3. Are there alternative approaches to the project and if so are these less or more optimal than your original solution?

(Office of Government Commerce, 2005). Many projects, especially those involved with IT, fail due to the rush to get through the project initiation stage (Chua, 2009).

Project delivery

Once the project has been authorized and clearly defined, project delivery commences. This is the actual running of the project. Many people often want to go straight for running the project, but without thoroughly understanding the business case for the project, the why, how, when, what and who of the project, project delivery often fails (Chua, 2009).

In PRINCE2, the PID starts off the project delivery process which is then divided into three processes:

- Managing stage boundaries
- Controlling a stage
- Managing product delivery

Managing stage boundaries

Managing stage boundaries is important in project delivery as it gives the opportunity for a project board or project director for decision-making (OGC, 2009). This decision-making decides the fate of the project. At the end of each stage, a decision is made to continue with the project, delay the project or cancel the project altogether. Dividing a project into stages is an ideal way of ascertaining where the risk of project failure may occur (Chua, 2009). In Mini Case Study 8.2 below, the project was put on hold after it was found there was not enough resource time to successfully complete the project. Managing stage boundaries in PRINCE2 allows the project board to make such decisions.

Mini Case Study 8.2

Project delays

Qualitative data was gathered from a very exclusive client involved in co-ordinating police officers in emergency situations. The data was gathered off the back of a validation study of a psychometric instrument so was not planned for in any sense.

However, the project went ahead as it only involved at this stage the interviewing of staff. There was little budget to pay for transcription so the project was delayed although the client received a small consultancy report for their provision of participants.

Six months after the data gathering stage, another researcher was interested in our consultancy report and decided (for free) to perform a similar study for her MSc dissertation thesis. She did exactly this a year after the original interviews. Longitudinal data for the project was now available.

A small amount of budget was diverted from a successful consultancy project to pay for a tran-

scription service, which went ahead. However, there was little resource time in which to start the lengthy analysis of the project. Below is the original plan for the project, which had to be scrapped. The project is now waiting to be completed pending resource time and has been put on hold rather than cancelled as the data is so rich.

Research case study questions

1. Should the initial interviewing have gone ahead?

2. How would the creation of a project plan aid the completion of work?

3. Should additional resources be employed for the project to make it viable again – what would influence your decision?

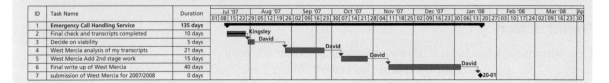

ID	Task Name	Duration
1	Emergency Call Handling Service	135 days
2	Final check and transcripts completed	10 days
3	Decide on viability	5 days
4	West Mercia analysis of my transcripts	21 days
5	West Mercia Add 2nd stage work	15 days
6	Final write up of West Mercia	40 days
7	submission of West Mercia for 2007/2008	0 days

Controlling a stage

The project manager has the overall charge of monitoring and controlling the work of the project (OGC, 2009). Project managers are expected to complete a number of different tasks in the day-to-day running of the project. This includes authorizing work to be completed, monitoring progress, watching out for risks and taking corrective action when necessary.

Managing product delivery

This stage involves the commission of others to perform tasks, or work packages, for the overall project. Thus, if a project is commissioning another organization to complete some work, this is the process involved with this action. Many large management consultancies may use specialist consultants for specific pieces of work, such as performing an assessment centre in an overall organizational change project or Niche consultancies may also use specialist companies that they do not have the internal resource to cope with themselves.

Planning

Above it was noted how important planning is to project management. Planning occurs during the entirety of the project and contributes to many of the processes listed above. Plans will need constant updating, which is one of the main reasons that planning software such as MS Project is important.

Directing a project

Directing a project is an important aspect of project management as the supervision of people is a major challenge to those directing projects (Bonner *et al.*, 2002; Kuruppuarachchi, 2001). PRINCE2 defined the directing of a project as a continuous process that is subject to the progress of the project (OGC, 2009). The project board, led by the project director, monitor progress made through reports and documents generated through the predefined system set up by the project board.

The project board authorize four main areas involved with the project and these are:

- Project initiation, ensuring that the project and its business case are realistic and feasible
- Stage boundaries are also monitored, so the project board can decide on the continuing viability of the project
- Ad-hoc direction, when needed
- Project closure; the project board or project director have the overall responsibility for the project – thus, when the project has met all its success criteria the board formally close the project down

The project board also manage by exception. What this means is that if anything goes wrong in the project outside of previously agreed tolerances, then the project board may take remedial action to ensure the project's success (Bonner *et al.*, 2002). Interestingly, project managers do have the tendency to stick with the project even when perhaps they should admit that it is going wrong (as shown in Industry snapshot 8.2). Nevertheless, other research also demonstrates that experienced project managers are likely to take in contextual information about a project and manage it within acceptable tolerances unlike say students who are less experienced in project management techniques (Chang and Ho, 2004).

Closing a project

Closure of a project is a vital stage that in management consultancies is often celebrated but not so in other organizations (see Industry snapshot 8.4). This process

Industry snapshot 8.4

A well-known university won a major grant from the ESRC and were promised that 'if they did a good job, there would be more money to come'. The lead researcher on the project, Fred, worked his proverbial socks off with the research team to ensure the successful delivery of the project. The project was successful and fred expected the project to be celebrated for its finish. However, the management at the university seemed not to close the project as there was more work to be done to win further work. This was the opposite of what Fred had observed in his previous employment, whereby after a mission everyone celebrated the successful conclusion of the operation even if it was just a pint in the pub. The result of this experience left Fred demotivated, uninspired and he left the establishment within a few months.

involves the closure of the project and the dissolution of the project team. The customer's needs should be shown to have been met in this stage. Any lessons learnt from the project should also be gathered. These will form vital learning for future projects. In some cases, there may be issues left unresolved that were uncovered during the project and these become 'follow-up' actions.

Chapter Summary

- A project may be defined as *a temporary managed environment that is created for the purpose of delivering one or more business benefits according to a specific brief*
- Projects are constrained by time, cost and quality
- Projects are a finite, non-repetitive undertaking
- Business need and user demand is frequently different and needs to be addressed
- Projects should be flexible and scaled down for small undertakings
- Managers may not necessarily be competent technically, although some authors argue that they should be
- Customers may be defined as the person/group that commissioned the work and will be the main recipients of the benefit of the results
- Suppliers are those that provide the project's products
- Quality is the scope of the project being the totality of the customer's needs
- A project will bring together a mixed team requiring a temporary organization
- Planning refers to the defining of activities
- Risk analysis and risk management form part of the risk management process
- Changes are expected and managed in a formal and systematic manner in a project
- Six processes make up the PRINCE2 system and these are:

  - Starting up a project
  - Initiating a project
  - Project delivery
  - Planning
  - Directing a project
  - Closing a project

Review Questions

1. List the key concepts in the PRINCE2 project management system.
2. How are concepts and components in project management different?
3. Do managers need to be technical experts?
4. Have you ever wished that you could get to an earlier version of a document; how would PRINCE2 aid this process?
5. Which PRINCE2 component facilitates the ability to go back to an earlier document?

6. Why is project management needed in consultancy?

7. Clearly define what a project is.

8. Is there a difference between a project and the creation of a product?

9. Can projects be repeated or are they likely to be different each time?

10. If a project is limited on time and cost, how do you think the quality of the project might be affected?

11. What is a 'product' in PRINCE2 and how do they help the running of the project?

12. Why is it important not to just start working on a project and to sit down and rationally work out what to do and the project's business case?

13. How should management be informed on the progress of a project?

14. Is the closure of a project an important process, and why?

Assignment Questions

1. Project management may seem to be a laborious process to some, but an absolutely essential one to others. What do you think the reasons are for this difference? Explain using examples of how project management can be effectively used and scaled to meet the needs of the project.

2. With a group of 4–6 people in your class, create a project that will achieve a particular goal. Go through the processes prescribed by PRINCE2 and record how you feel about going through this system.

3. Why is it important to assess risks in a project as they may never happen?

Case Study 8.1

Beijing Eaps Consulting Inc.

It was November 2007, and Mr. Zheng, the chief executive officer (CEO) of Beijing EAPs Consulting Inc. (BEC), was sitting in his office, thinking about the conversation he has just heard between two of his employees, Mr. Yang and Ms. Song. The two colleagues often collaborated on various projects, and the conversation that Mr. Zheng overheard took place at an internal training programme. The purpose of the training was to discuss problems and improve communication among employees. During the self-reflection part of the training, Mr. Yang, who managed the training department, commented:

> I notice that, recently, Ms. Song does not communicate with me as frequently as she used to. I guess the reason is that sometimes I get upset due to work pressure. My voice grows louder,

▶

and my tone is not always pleasant when Ms. Song passes tasks on to my department. Ms. Song, I apologize for that. You know, I have to work on 10 projects at the same time.'

Ms. Song, who was one of the two project managers, replied: 'I am not blaming you for that. I respect you very much, and I understand you are very busy, but your behaviour does make me feel afraid of communicating with you. Sometimes, I would rather stay late in the company to work on the tasks that are meant to be passed to you.'

The conversation reminded the CEO, Mr. Zheng, that recently Ms. Song had been asking him to pass training-related tasks to Mr. Yang and his subordinates even though, as a project manager, Ms. Song had the authority to assign tasks to other department managers, including Mr. Yang.

Mr. Zheng was not worried about the personal relationship between Ms. Song and Mr. Yang, which had always been positive. However, Mr. Zheng was concerned that there seemed to be some confusion over managerial responsibilities in BEC's current structure. He had heard employees complaining about receiving tasks from both their department managers *and* from project managers, a situation that often created conflicts in their task deadlines. As a result, employees were not sure how to prioritize these tasks. Another problem arose from the fact they were confused about who their direct supervisor was: was it the department manager or the project manager? Project and department managers were located on the same level of the BEC hierarchy, and they worked together on planning and conducting each project. This work relationship between the two kinds of managers confused the employees: Who had the power to make a final decision when there is disagreement? On the other side of that same coin, the project managers felt that they did not have enough authority to give direction to the departmental employees.

Since the project management structure had recently been adopted by BEC, neither the employees not the managers were familiar with its procedures. Even so, Mr. Zheng strongly believed that project management was the right approach for BEC. Since its adoption, he had seen an increase of BEC's busi-ness and profit. But he also wondered what he could do to improve the present structure and procedures in order to clarify work relationships and responsibilities for his managers and employees.

Company background of BEC

Founded in 2001, BEC was the first consulting company to provide employee assistance services in mainland China. Between 2001 and 2006, there were only six employees in BEC; this number increased to 20 by the end of 2007.

Employee assistant programs (EAPs) are employee benefit programmes offered by many employers, typically in conjunction with a health insurance plan. EAPs are intended to help employees deal with personal problems that might adversely affect their work performance, health and well-being[1]. EAPs are widely used in North America, but their use is rare in China.

BEC's customers and service

Most employees in BEC had a bachelor's degree or a master's degree in psychology, which made BEC the leader in providing professional EAPs services in China. BEC's market share was also the highest in mainland China. The company provided EAPs to many customers, including multinational organizations operating in China, such as Siemens, Samsung and IBM, and Chinese organizations such as Lenovo, the China Development Bank and Guangdong Mobile. These customers came to BEC with a common purpose: to provide their employees with psychological assistance to reduce stress and increase job satisfaction.

A typical project at BEC included the following procedures:

1. *Conducting interviews to collect information.* At the beginning of each project, BEC would interview employees in the customer company to collect information on employee stress, such as the sources of stress

---

[1] http://en.wikipedia.org/wiki/Employee_assistance_programs, accessed January 29, 2009.

and the behaviours that employees exhibit under stress.

2. *Delivering brochures.* BEC provided information brochures to its clients' employees. These brochures included some basic knowledge on stress management, an introduction to the employee assistant program, details of the EAP process at their own company, and instructions on how to seek help from BEC.

3. *Setting up a toll-free helpline:* BEC set up a toll-free helpline for their customers' employees who could then use it to access one-on-one psychological consulting. BEC guaranteed that these phone conversations were confidential, which allowed the employees to openly discuss their problems with counsellors. Over 40 counsellors worked at BEC, mostly as part-time employees, and made up of undergraduate and graduate students who were majoring in psychology. Others were school counsellors or hospital psychologists.

4. *Providing on-site training sessions:* BEC also provided on-site training to its customers. Attendees at these on-site training sessions ranged from front-line employees to senior managers. The training also provided managers with stress management skills.

BEC's strategy change

In BEC's early years, its founders lacked business experience, so they sought out BEC's opportunities to conduct practical research into stress management practices. Therefore, in the first few years, the founders did not put much effort into increasing their customer numbers. By the end of 2006, however, when its business had rapidly increased, BEC began to change its strategy and structure. Mr. Zheng decided to shift the company's focus away from research to focus more on business practices and to tap into the market's potential profit sources.

This shift in company focus was influenced by BEC's successful business with Guangdong Mobile, a subsidiary of China Mobile (see Exhibit 8.1). In

April 2006, BEC began to provide EAP services to Guangdong Mobile's branch in Guangzhou, which had more than 50 million customers across Guangdong Province, China, and more than 7000 customer service employees.[2] On average, each call centre employee answered a customer inquiry every two minutes, covering questions about a wide range of Guangdong Mobile's products, such as phone rates, fees, policies and so forth. To provide high quality service to their customers, call centre employees had to memorize a wealth of information about Guangdong Mobile's products and services. In addition, dealing with customer complaints and with difficult customers was an ongoing part of customer service. Guangzhou Mobile faced high turnover rates and low employee satisfaction in its customer service department, and this situation eventually lead the company to contact BEC.

In 2006, Guangzhou Mobile signed a contract with BEC to provide its employees with psychological assistance, representing BEC's largest contract since the company had been founded. To provide faster and more direct service to Guangzhou Mobile, BEC set up an office in Guangzhou, the capital city of Guangdong Province, and regularly sent employees to the Guangzhou office. Guangzhou Mobile was very satisfied with BEC's service.

In January 2007, China Mobile, Guangzhou Mobile's parent company, sent a policy statement to its 31 subsidiaries across China, stating that each office must provide its employees with psychological assistance, and encouraging the provincial subsidiaries to pay more attention to their employees' psychological health. Immediately after that announcement, Beijing Mobile, another subsidiary of China Mobile, also came to BEC for EAPs service.

With its accumulated experience and increased business opportunities, BEC decided to put all of its limited resources into the company's current and potential customers in the mobile phone industry, a move that put a lot of pressure on the company's

---

[2] Source: http://campus.chinahr.com/2008/pages/gmcc/index. asp, accessed January 29, 2009.

Exhibit 8.1	*China Mobile:* Officially established on April 20, 2000, China Mobile Communications Corporation ('China Mobile' for short) has a registered capital of RMB51.8 billion assets of more than RMB400 billion. It wholly owns subsidiaries in 31 provinces across China. The total number of customers had exceeded 240 million by the end of 2005.[1]
China: Location of Beijing and Guangdong Provinces	

Map of China and the Location of Beijing and Guangdong Provinces[2]

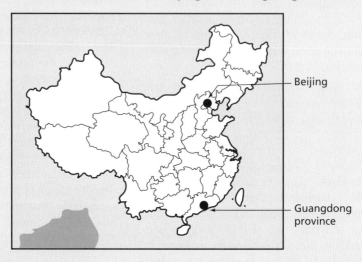

[1] http://www.chinamobile.com/en/mainland/about/profile.html, accessed January 29, 2009.

[2] http://commons.wikimedia.org/wiki/File:China_blank_map.svg, accessed January 29, 2009.

existing employees. Since all of BEC's employees were working on client projects, it was difficult to maintain the research stream that BEC had been working on. Due to the intense competition from the market at this stage, BEC had to focus on its business. BEC also had to face the realities of the labour market: the company needed employees with degrees in psychology, but only a few universities in Beijing provided such degrees. The difficulty of finding qualified employees restricted BEC's growth and forced BEC's current employees to become team players and multi-taskers.

EAP was an emerging industry in China, which meant there was great opportunity accompanied by great competition. To take advantage of such an opportunity, BEC was going to have to make some changes.

BEC's structural change

Faced with an increase in business volume and the resulting workload, Mr. Zheng felt that his company would need more people and a different structure in order to maximize the efficiency of BEC's human resources

BEC's structure before 2006

Before 2006, there was no clear structure at BEC. Six full-time employees, including the two co-founders as managers, worked in a single office in Beijing. One of the co-founders of BEC was a professor of psychology at a university in Beijing, and most of the employees at BEC were recent graduates of that same university. BEC also hired many graduate and undergraduate students from the psychology department as part-time counsellors, whose main responsibilities were to provide psychological assistance through the company's toll-free helpline.

Before 2006, there were no clearly identified departments in BEC, and the full-time employees' job responsibilities were not clearly designated.

Exhibit 8.2

BEC's Organizational
Structure in March
2007[1]

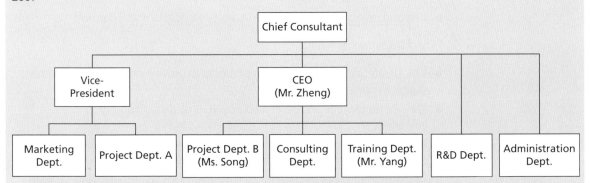

[1] Internal documents from Beijing EAPs

Whenever there was a project, all BEC employees got involved. Usually, the managers would assign tasks based on each employee's skills and schedules. All employees worked on two or more tasks, including designing the project plans, interviewing customer employees, providing telephone and face-to-face consulting, designing promotional brochures, and so on. Employees treated these projects as more than just a job; they looked on each one as a learning opportunity. Throughout their work on a given project, BEC employees discussed the difficulties they had experienced and provided each other with suggestions for improvement

At this stage, the informal structure worked quite well at BEC. The work process was mainly project-based, and all six members worked as a team on every project. Each employee's role and responsibilities were flexible and mainly depended on the employee's personal interests and schedule. This structure also allowed all employees access to all the stages of an EAP project, which helped them to learn new technology and understand each other's work. The small size and flexible structure of the company made BEC able to tailor its services to adapt to a variety of customer requirements. After each project, BEC would hold an internal workshop where employees would have an open discussion about the project: what they did well, what they needed to improve, what they had learned, and what they could expect from each other in the future. This flexible structure made BEC a learning-oriented organization with an open culture.

BEC's employees and structure since 2006

In October 2006, faced with an increase in business from China Mobile subsidiaries and from other companies, BEC started to recruit more employees and set up new departments as a way of specializing its employees' responsibilities. The new structure included a marketing department, a consulting department, a training department, a research and development (R&D) department, an administration department and two project departments. Having two project departments would reduce the number of projects for each of the project departments so that the project managers would not face too many scheduling conflicts. The functions of the two project departments were very similar. See Exhibits 8.2 and 8.3 for BEC's organizational chart and a list of departmental responsibilities.

Exhibit 8.3	1. Marketing Department:

Departmental
Responsibilities[1]

1. Marketing Department:

- Sell BEC's products and service to target markets
- Establish BEC's leading image in the market
- Promote BEC's brand name
- Manage relationships with media, industry associations and partners

2. Project Departments A & B:

- Co-operate with the marketing department to provide proposals to customers during the initial contacts
- Allocate employees and other resources to provide high quality service to customers
- Provide project documents to the R&D department; share the knowledge and technology created during each project with other departments
- Research information related to the customer companies to develop a better understanding of the customers
- Write advertizing articles and co-ordinate with the marketing department

3. Consulting Department:

- Develop and conduct a quality management system for consulting
- Based on the requirements of the company, organize consulting teams through internal promotion and external contact
- Provide consulting services to the customers based on the project department's design

4. Training Department:

- Design and develop training courses on psychological assistance for clients' employees
- Customize training sessions for various customers
- Initiate employee assistant programmes within customer organizations.
- Develop books and other publications on EAP

5. Research and Development Department:

- Develop and conduct BEC's research strategy; ensure BEC's leadership in technology, products and services
- Co-ordinate with other departments to develop new products
- Collaborate with external resources (such as universities) on R&D issues
- Design a project management process; design a research plan, data analysis process and report templates; provide training to relevant employees
- Manage project documents

---

[1] Internal documents from Beijing EAPs

- Co-operate with project departments to write the research plan, analyze data and write research reports

6. Administrative Department:

- Conduct financial functions
- Develop a human resources plan; develop reward and compensation systems; recruit new employees
- Conduct daily administration functions

The top management team included a chief consultant, CEO Mr. Zheng, and a vice-president (who joined BEC in 2006). They each managed different departments, according to their own areas of expertise. The chief consultant led the R&D department because he was a university professor and because he had the most knowledge in EAPs research. CEO Mr. Zheng led the consulting and training departments since he was very familiar with these tasks. The vice-president brought a wealth of experience to his role as the leader of the marketing department. Since the two project departments had similar responsibilities, the vice-president and the CEO lead project departments A and B respectively, which gave both of them sufficient time to manage the projects.

Ms. Song managed project department B, and Mr. Yang managed the training department; both of them reported to Mr. Zheng. Ms. Song had a master's degree in psychology and had been a licensed psychological counselor in a local hospital before she joined BEC in 2004. Since 2006, when BEC started its new project management structure, Ms. Song had led many projects. Mr. Yang had worked as a professional manager in training industry for over a decade before he joined BEC in 2005.

In 2006, BEC decided to adopt a project management approach. For each project, a project manager would lead a project team. Teams would be composed of employees from marketing, consulting, training, and R&D. Together, project managers and other department managers would work out a plan for each project and would then co-conduct the plan. Project managers could assign tasks to other department managers and their employees, and department managers were free to ask project managers to adjust work procedures, based on the actual processes of each department. This new structure allowed employees to focus on their specialized fields and to grow more familiar with certain work procedures. For example, employees in the training department could spend more time on designing and delivering training sessions and less time on discussing contract content. Once the new structure was established, it saved a lot of time with respect to work assignments and preparation.

Mr. Zheng felt that BEC was much more efficient after the structural change. By March 2007, the number of employees had increased to 20, and Mr. Zheng was planning to hire even more.

Specific problems

After the restructuring, Mr. Zheng felt that the company was more efficient and more market-oriented. He could see BEC growing rapidly, both in size and in profit in the near future. However, as BEC and its profits were growing, some problems began to surface. Since there were many projects going on at the same time, employees had to work on multiple tasks and face various demands from each project as well as meeting the day-to-day requirements of their own departments. Some employees were working on more than 10 tasks at the same time, many of which had strict deadlines. Employees had to carefully plan their schedules and work extra hours to meet all the deadlines. Moreover, sometimes tasks were urgent. For example, a customer would ask for an extra report or analysis, and BEC would try to meet this request, which meant that BEC employees would often have to fit a new task into their already tight timetable. It was very common for staff to work nights and weekends at BEC, just like the employees in many other organizations in Beijing.

Another problem at BEC stemmed from the project management system itself. The role of the project managers did not seem to be well accepted among the departmental staff. With two project management departments and five other functional departments, employees working on a project would receive directions from their department manager and from the project managers as well. When there was conflict between two managers' assignments, employees tended to use their own judgement to decide the priority of tasks and would then adjust their schedules according to their decision. On the other side of the fence, project managers felt frustrated by their relationships with managers and employees in the functional departments. Sometimes the project managers would feel uncomfortable assigning tasks to functional managers who were at the same level in the organizational hierarchy. According to the new structure, project managers and department managers were peers, so it was difficult to apply any direct influence on each other. And when the project managers did assign tasks directly to employees in these functional departments, they might find that the employees were already working on tasks assigned by their department manger and would therefore find it hard to make time for the project manager's task.

In general, BEC continued to experience problems with its rapid growth; the increase in business has certainly yielded an increase in profits, but these have been accompanied by several new challenges for management. Mr. Zheng planned to recruit more employees in the near future, but first he had to make sure that BEC's organizational structure and management processes were efficient and effective. He was not sure how he could continue to expand the company and solve the growing management problems at the same time.

Further Reading

Kwak, Y.H. and Anbari, F.T. (2009), Analyzing project management research: Perspectives from top management journals, *International Journal of Project Management* 27(5), 435–446

Lock, D. (2003), *Project Management*. Farnham: Gower Publishing Ltd

Nokes, S., Major, I., Greenwood, A. and Goodman, M. (2003), *The Definitive Guide to Project Management: The Fast Track to Getting the Job Done on Time and on Budget*. Financial Times/Prentice Hall; Ill edition

Office of Government Commerce (2009), *Managing Successful Projects with PRINCE2*. Stationery Office Books

Reiss, G. (2007), *Project Management Demystified*. London: Taylor & Francis Ltd

Saynisch, M. (2005), Beyond frontiers of traditional project management: The concept of 'project management second order (Pm-2)' as an approach of evolutionary management, *World Futures: The Journal of General Evolution*, 61(8), 555–590

CHAPTER 9

Programme management, power and politics

Learning Objectives

At the end of this chapter students will be able to:

- Understand what programme management is

- Distinguish between programme management and project management

- Understand how programme management can contribute towards organizational change

- Understand the processes involved with programme management

- Be knowledgeable about how power works in organizations

- Recognize the power that consultants have in organizations

- Understand the key aspects of organization politics in the workplace

- Recognize that different parties within an organization may have their own particular political game plan

Mini Case Study 9.1

UKAEA programme management at Winfrith

Project background

Winfrith is situated approximately halfway between Wareham and Dorchester in Dorset. UKAEA acquired the site in 1957 for research in support of the UK nuclear programme. Over the following 40 years it gained a worldwide reputation for scientific excellence – particularly in reactor safety. In the 1990s, when the UK Government ended research into nuclear fission, a decommissioning programme was started with the aim of restoring Winfrith's environment and releasing the land for other uses. Since 2005, UKAEA has managed this work under contract to the Nuclear Decommissioning Authority (NDA).

Key challenges

The main challenge was to safely manage the environmental restoration programme on the 343-acre site, including decommissioning redundant nuclear facilities, managing radioactive wastes from past work and remediating any contaminated land. Winfrith lies in a 250-hectare area of rare heath land, designated as a Site of Special Scientific Interest (SSSI), so careful management of this area was also essential.

As Winfrith was a key local employment site, UKAEA also sought to minimise the impact of decommissioning on the economy by regenerating the land for sustainable future use.

Finally, UKAEA aimed to reduce the time and cost of decommissioning – delivering a programme that brought value for money to the taxpayer and achieved restoration as quickly as possible.

The approach

UKAEA have planned and implemented a clear programme for progressive removal of the nuclear facilities at Winfrith. So far, they have decommissioned seven of the nine experimental reactors.

More than 400,000 square feet of other buildings and research facilities have been removed from site. Nearly ten acres of site were de-licensed and made available for new use in 2002 – the largest area at a UK nuclear site to date.

In addition, innovative programme planning has enabled them to develop a plan to cut the time needed for decommissioning by 35 years and save almost £300 million on original estimates.

In parallel with the clean-up programme, they fostered the regeneration of the site as a thriving science and technology centre. UKAEA worked with local agencies to create new commercial premises and attract a diverse range of tenants.

They also adopted a Heath land Management Plan in agreement with English Nature, and established close links with conservation bodies in order to preserve the heath land habitat and the wildlife it supports.

The results

UKAEA are continuing to deliver safe, cost-effective and environmentally friendly solutions whilst seeking to further refine and accelerate their plans for the full restoration of the Winfrith site.

The Winfrith Technology Centre (now owned and operated by English Partnerships) is a well-established location for business and now houses around 40 companies, employing over 1,000 people.

Source: http://www.ukaea.co.uk/casestudies/programme_management/winfrith_environmental_restoration/. Reproduced with permission.

Programme Management

What is programme management?

In the last chapter, the importance of project management was introduced. Project management is essential to deliver specific business benefits; however, several projects may be occurring concurrently or separately in an organization at any one time (Bonner *et al.*, 2002). These different projects form part of a programme. Management of these different projects is called programme management (Russell, 1998; Vereecke, Pandelaere, Deschoolmeester and Stevens, 2003).

Programme management is in essence the management of several projects to typically bring about organizational change (Vereecke *et al.*, 2003). Where there is a major change projects may have many interdependencies and links that the individual project managers and directors may not be wholly aware of, thus, there is a need for a programme level management structure (OGC, 2007).

The Office of Government Commerce (OGC) that publishes several guides on project and programme management defines programme management as:

> Programme management is the co-ordinated management of a portfolio of projects that change organisations to achieve benefits of strategic importance.
>
> *Cited from OGC (2007); p. 2*

Programme management is therefore the layer above project management and takes responsibility for the risks involved in multiple projects. This can equate to huge sums of money being invested. The Qatar–Bahrain crossing programme has been estimated to cost $2 billion and has had bids from at least two consultancy firms to carry out programme management services for the Qatar–Bahrain Causeway Foundation (Foreman, 2008). Other programmes may cost more, for instance, the rebuilding of the World Trade Center will involve 26 projects and need an estimated $16–18 billion (Anonymous, 2008).

Figure 9.1 demonstrates programme management diagrammatically. In this programme, five projects make up the entire KNAQ programme. Project 1 has a direct link to project 3, so project 3 cannot go ahead until project 1 is complete. The same goes for project 4 that is reliant on project 2 completing on-time. Nevertheless, if project 1 runs over, there is no impact on project 4, or project 5. Programme management thus interfaces with project management (OGC, 2007). In this regard, if projects run over time, budget, resources or scope then this may have an effect on the overall programme.

Programme management manages the interdependencies of different projects as shown in Figure 9.1. It enables a strategic overview to be maintained over a set of projects co-ordinating them within an organized plan. Programme management thus supports:

1. Links between the top level strategic direction of an organization and the management activities required to achieve these objectives

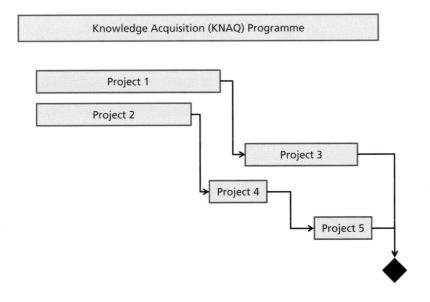

Figure 9.1

An example of programme management

2. The objectives of the programme in lieu of any environmental changes
3. The people that need to plan and organize activities, setting priorities and allocating resources appropriately
4. That risks are identified and carefully managed
5. The informing of stakeholders in that their interests are considered
6. The successful realization of business benefits through the projects being run within the project framework

When to use programme management

Programme management can be used where the organization has a number of shared objectives across a variety of projects (OGC, 2007). Programme management should thus be used when there is a need to co-ordinate initiatives involving one or more business functions. It should also be used to put forward a set of carefully planned projects that support an overall strategy or organizational change. Overall, all the projects should form part of a common programme goal to deliver some business benefit (Pellegrinellia *et al*. 2007). A programme differs from a project in many ways, in that it tends to define the vision of where it will be at the end of the programme; however, it does not necessarily have a clearly defined path to get there unlike in a project (OGC, 2007).

Programme management may also be used when there is more than one organization in the delivery of the overall business benefit (OGC, 2007). This is often the case on complicated issues that involve a number of different organizations to work effectively together. This can sometimes be difficult as Lycett *et al*. (2004) found in their study and as highlighted in Industry snapshot 9.1 below.

Industry snapshot 9.1

Resolving emotions and conflict between engineers, road builders and archaeologists

In a joint bid, four organizations won a £124 million programme to widen a motorway. This involved extensive renovating of existing structures and the building of both new roads and bridges in an archaeologically rich site. The programme involved archaeologists to excavate the site, geotechnical engineers to ensure the suitability of the ground, bridge engineers to renovate and build new bridges and road engineers to construct the actual road.

Individuals with these different areas of expertise tended to be located in different organizations and emotions could easily fly if individuals, teams or organizations came into conflict. This tended not to be a problem if the emotions could be sorted out in terms of open communication. However, if communication broke down often this would result in litigious claims especially when two or more organizations were involved.

Thus, the prevention and reduction of any hostilities and pent-up emotions was foremost in the mind of the programme manager before the programme started. The programme manager therefore commissioned a Development Centre that ran as a behavioural modification programme. These meant individuals would complete an exercise and then get feedback on the basis of how they performed. Exercises were constructed around the competencies of teamwork and communication.

Feedback was received on the DC process from the client who said that it had been a success. The DC process had started the multi-million pound project on a firm footing encouraging communication and teamwork.

The benefits of programme management

There are a number of benefits to programme management and these are typically realized at different stages of the programme. Delivery of organizational change is probably the key benefit of programme management (Bonner *et al.*, 2002; OGC, 2007). Changes can be planned in an integrated way ensuring that current business operations are not adversely affected. Strategy can be decided upon from an overview perspective and then this is fed down to the separate projects that are running (Lycett, Rassau and Danson, 2004; Pellegrinellia *et al.*, 2007).

Programme management provides management support to ensure activities are focused on the business case (Ferns, 1991; Pellegrinellia *et al.*, 2007). Resources are also more easily managed and projects can be given prioritization. Thus, if a project is going to be delayed, if this project affects other projects and will adversely affect the overall programme then the programme manager may decide to allocate extra resources to that project to get it back on track. However, Lycett *et al.* (2004) argued that often there are considerable tensions between the organizational level strategy and the project managers requesting resources on the ground. Thus a successful project manager may see their resources being taken away from them as another project is failing. This can obviously cause tension within the organization and needs to be carefully managed (Pelligrinelli *et al.* 2007).

The identification of project interdependencies can improve a number of issues (Lycett *et al.*, 2004). Identifying project interdependencies may reduce the incidence of work backlogs and delays due to improved co-ordination. In addition the amount of re-engineering due to inadequate dependency management is likely to decrease in well-designed programmes (Lycett *et al.*, 2004). On the skills side of project management, transfer of knowledge from one project to another can be facilitated through programme management, whereby experience gained in one particular circumstance can be translated to others aiding the project management process.

Further benefits may include reducing overall costs and enabling the more efficient usage of shared resources (OGC, 2007). In this regard, the grouping of projects is likely to produce cost savings by avoiding duplication of effort and recruiting appropriate personnel that can be employed from one project to another. The use of resources from a common pool such as from a business support office can also increase the utilization of shared resources between projects and within a programme.

Different types of programme

Programme management can bring a number of benefits to the organization. However, each programme is likely to be unique and bring its own politics and issues to be considered. Examples of programmes include:

- A strategic programme where an organization is striving towards a pre-determined set of objectives
- A business cycle programme where projects are co-ordinated within cyclic, financial or resource constraints
- An infrastructure programme where separate projects release investment or activities that move the organizations goals forward

- A research and development curriculum where independent projects are assessed and refocused according to the organizations needs
- A multiple partnership programme where different organizations collaborate together towards some unified business objective or goal

Adapted from OGC (2007); p. 7

Programme management environment and processes

Programme management should like project management be run in a controlled environment although Pellegrinelli *et al.* (2007) disagreed that programmes were always run like this in practice. Nonetheless, a key element in programme management is formulating a clear model of improved business operation (OGC, 2007). The processes involved with this are as follows:

1. Identifying a programme, based on the strategic initiatives of the sponsoring organization/organizations.
2. Defining a programme, developing and costing it out in terms of finances.
3. Establishing a programme, setting up the organization of the programme.
4. Managing the portfolio, overseeing the projects associated with the programme.
5. Delivering benefits, managing the realization of benefits through the separate projects.
6. Closing the programme, formally ending the programme confirming its objectives have been attained.

Just like in PRINCE2, there are associated products or documents generated through going through this process. The two key ones in programme management are the vision statement and the blueprint. The vision statement defines the end goals of the programme to all those that have a direct interest in these goals. The vision statement then forms part of the 'blueprint' of operations which defines the composition and structure of the organization that has changed through going through the programme (OGC, 2007).

Programme management organization

The guidelines for organizing a programme are very similar to organizing a project. In this regard, there should be a programme director who has the ultimate responsibility for the programme and is likely to be a senior executive within the organization (OGC, 2007). Just as in project management, there is then a person responsible for the daily running of the programme who is the programme manager. The programme manager sets up and runs the programme and co-ordinates the projects within it. Supporting the programme manager is a business change manager (OGC, 2007). The business change manager is responsible for ensuring that the organization is ready to take on the benefits realized through the various projects that are running. An example of how this may run in practice is given in Industry snapshot 9.2.

Industry snapshot 9.2

London Borough of Lambeth Corporate Programme

In 2006, the London Borough of Lambeth received a less than satisfactory rating on its services by the Audit Commission. The council therefore put forward a programme to revitalize its services to the general public and businesses in the area. Pushing this agenda forward, the Lambeth Corporate Programme Office was created as in Figure 9.2.

This demonstrates a programme organization that has all the key elements identified by the Office of Government Commerce (2007), in that there is a programme director, a (Senior) programme manager who has other managers reporting to him/her. There is also a Change Communications Officer who takes on the role of the business change manager.

Source: http://www.idea.gov.uk/idk/aio/5829709 Reproduced with permission.

Organizational Structure

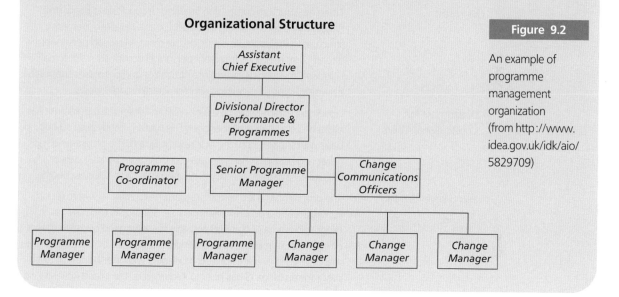

Figure 9.2

An example of programme management organization (from http://www.idea.gov.uk/idk/aio/5829709)

The Office of Government Commerce (2007) presented a standard way in which to run programmes. Nevertheless, Pellegrinelli *et al.* (2007) found that in six programmes run under this system they each deviated from the standard programme management guidelines. Some of these deviations were subtle such as in Industry Snapshot 9.2 renaming the business change manager. However, in other programmes the organizational structure contradicted the guidance given by the OGC (2007). Table 9.1 summarizes their research and demonstrates, for example, that in one programme there was no allocated programme manager, which is fundamental in programme management.

Pelligrinelli *et al.* (2007) stated that one of the most important aspects that need to be understood when going through a programme is knowledge of the dynamic cultural, political and business environments. This is an important aspect of programme management as well as within consultancy and will be addressed in the remainder of this chapter.

Table 9.1	Organization	Organization and leadership
Examples of programme management organization. Source: Pellegrinelli, et al. (2007). International Journal of Project Management. Reproduced with permission from Elsevier.	Daimler Chrysler UK	Each Board Director has a programme account manager to work with. Programme account managers plan and monitor projects through their cycle from identification through approval to delivery. The Board approves the annual project portfolio.
	AstraZeneca	Programme Sponsorship resides with the Vice President, Quality Compliance and Information Management, and a Steering Group of 18 senior managers from across AstraZeneca comprising the IS Quality and Compliance Leadership Team and additional key players. The members of the Steering Group are influential in promoting acceptance of the programme's validation related deliverables and reassurance that they are fit for purpose.
	Microsoft	Three tier structure comprising Steering Group, Project Board and Project Manager's Meetings. Microsoft has a parallel governance structure to the structure set up by the client. Microsoft personnel attend client meetings but client personnel do not attend 'internal' Microsoft meetings. Governance structures and processes supported by weekly cycle of meetings, conference calls and reviews.
	Department for Constitutional Affairs	Governance framework based on MSP. However the programme has never had a programme manager. The role is fulfilled on an ad-hoc basis with support from the programme board. The programme has never had business change managers (to ensure benefits delivery). SRO roles have been filled by IT people rather than business people.
	Inland Revenue	The programme is led by the programme director to whom report strategists and a programme manager. Strategists each own a programme area and are responsible for setting the overall business direction for that area. Project delivery is managed by the programme manager who oversees project managers with the support of the programme office. IS has been outsourced by the Inland Revenue, so IT changes are delivered by the outsource contractor. Each project has an Inland Revenue PM responsible for overall project deliver and a contractor PM responsible for delivering the IT components. The Inland Revenue programme manager also has a counterpart within the contractor responsible for programme-level IT issues, such as architectural decisions.
	Surrey Police	Programme management is overseen by a Programme Board whose members include Chief Officers, Divisional Commanders, Surrey Police Authority, Police Federation and Unison, and Senior Management Team. The programme management team consists of a programme manager, a deputy programme manager, and four project managers. The programme manager reports directly to the Deputy Chief Constable who is the programme director and, in turn, reports to the Chief Constable of Surrey Police.

Source: Pellegrinelli *et al.* (2007). Reproduced from International Journal of Project Management with permission from Elsevier.

Power and Politics

Introduction

Power and politics are important aspects of every organization (Ocasio and Pozner, 2005). Individuals responsible for managing aspects of an organization or those that comment on its functioning cannot be effective without understanding organizational power (Pfeffer, 1992). In a similar way, organizational politics are also crucial to understand as organizations and especially large ones are like governments political entities (Pfeffer, 1992). In Chapter 7, the power and politics between being an internal and external consultant was touched upon explaining the difference between being enmeshed into an organization as an internal consultant and being a commentator on the outside as an external consultant (Massarik and Pei-Carpenter, 2002). The remainder of this chapter details the fascinating study of power and politics from an exploratory and consultancy perspective.

Power

Power in organizations is still a controversial subject and is examined by organizational theorists, business psychologists and industrial sociologists alike (Ocasio and Pozner, 2005). Nevertheless, power can be defined as the ability or force at one's disposal to influence the behaviour and outcomes of another (McKenna, 2006b; Ocasio and Pozner, 2005). Power and leadership are therefore closely allied with each other (Pfeffer, 1992; McKenna, 2006b). Organizational hierarchy is important in examining the concept of power in organizations, but is not the only factor involved.

Dependency can play a crucial role, so an IT department in an organization may have a lot of power due to the fact that there is a strong dependency on the department to fix IT hardware and software issues. Indeed, the more dependent a person is on another within an organization the greater the amount of power that can be used on that dependent (McKenna, 2006b).

French and Raven (1959) described five different types of power important to note:

1. Reward power, is the ability to control extrinsic rewards such as pay and promotion and intrinsic rewards such as recognition and acceptance

2. Coercive power, if reward power is seen as the carrot then coercive power is the stick. Colloquialisms aside, coercive power is the use or threat of penalties against an employee such as unattractive assignments, denial of pay increases, verbal abuse, etc

3. Referent power, is when a person is seen as having desirable features, such as being charismatic, etc, and is able to use this charisma to influence others

4. Legitimate power, is when a person is seen as having the right to issue orders due to their place in the organizational hierarchy. It is similar to a military set-up, whereby a Vice-President or Managing Director of a company, may issue commands to Directors, and Directors to Managers. Nevertheless, in more organic organizations the lines of legitimate power are not clearly identifiable (McKenna, 2006b).

5. Expert power, is when the person exerting the power is seen as having superior knowledge and expertise

For consultants, all of these different sources of power are important. Indeed, consultants can use a combination of expert power, referent power and even a trace of coercive power and reward power.

Expert power is fundamental in the consultancy–client relationship with the consultant being seen as the relevant expert on the issues being addressed (Fincham, 1999). Expert power is seen as having the knowledge and expertise over and above those who are being influenced. The use of this power depends on the consultant's credibility. Credibility cannot be maintained by pretending to know about a subject a consultant is ignorant of and thus this serves as support against the criticisms of management consultancy that it has no basis in real organizational benefits and changes (Fincham 2002a).

Critics of the management consultancy industry would have us believe that all the power that consultants have is impression management and charisma (Clark and Salaman, 1996; Clark, 1995; Craig, 2005; Craig, 2006). Nonetheless, to deny that charisma isn't a part of what a management consultant does is taking a very functionalist approach to the subject matter. Management consultants have to often make presentations to gain assignments in, as Hussey (2001a) describes them, so called beauty contests. Consultants also have to use their charisma to engage in research gaining access to a client. After the project is completed the consultant is also likely to present their eventual findings in a convincing manner so it is likely that referent power is deployed in these situations.

Coercive power may be a surprising source of power for the consultant, but it is used albeit in a different manner to which a manager or leader may use coercive power. A manager is likely to use sanctions, a ban on overtime or lack of promotional opportunities. For the consultant these are not an option. However, stating what is likely to happen to an organization is a form of coercive power, in that if the organization doesn't remedy the issues it has it may have unfavourable consequences due to the lack of action. Indeed, many are afraid of using this type of power but it is a fundamental aspect of organizational life (Pfeffer, 1992).

Reward power may also be used by the consultant. When we examined project and programme management, both typically have a vision that at the end of the project or programme the organization will look like this. In this regard, the reward of a particular assignment may be a better future, leaner managerial structure, less costly finance system, better recruitment practices, better human resource policies, etc. This can be a powerful influence that the consultant can use in their work.

Markham (2007) also suggested there are two other types of power that the consultant may use. This consists of connection power, which is based on the connections with influential individuals inside and outside of the organization. It also consists of information power, which is the possession of, or access to valuable information.

Politics

The terms power and politics are often used interchangeably in the literature but are different (Eisenhardt and Bourgeois, 1988). Politics is the observable but typically covert mechanisms that individuals use to enhance their power to influence (Eisenhardt and Bourgeois, 1988). Political behaviour are therefore the actions that individuals or a group may take to obtain outcomes they desire especially when there is uncertainty or disagreement (Pfeffer, 1992). These behaviours may be functional or dysfunctional to the organization where individuals are perceived to put their needs above the organizations (Parker, Dipboye and Jackson, 1995).

Perceptions of politics may be more important than the actual reality (Parker *et al.*, 1995). Interestingly, studies differ on who perceives the organization as political. Gandz and Murray (1980) suggested that it was those at the top that experienced most politics in an organization. However, a more recent study suggested that it tended to be middle management that thought about the politics in an organization (Parker *et al.* 1995). Indeed, that would make sense as those at the top of the tree have legitimate ways in which to exert power and therefore may not engage in as much political scheming as those in middle management positions who may want to usurp the top management. Indeed, as Murray and Gandz (1980) eloquently put it:

> There is no question that there are devious, scheming, cynical people in organizations who really do plot to gain purely selfish ends with no thought of the success of the organization or the harm done to their opponents.
>
> *Cited from Murray and Gandz (1980); p. 21*

Antecedents of politics

A number of factors are said to contribute towards political behaviour that have been observed in business psychology (McKenna, 2006b). These are worth mentioning before political tactics are discussed. The antecedents to political behaviour can be largely separated out into organizational and individual factors.

Organizational factors include:

1. Organizational change: whereby change may lead individuals or groups to act in a political manner
2. Ambiguous goals: where the goals of a particular change strategy or programme are not clear so individuals or groups may again act in a political way
3. Organizational structure: if there is no room to move in the organizational hierarchy this may lead to political behaviour with individuals jostling their position to get promoted
4. Shortage of resources: when resources are scarce certain people may engage in political behaviour to get the resources they need
5. Technology and the environment: similar to organizational change the arrival of new technology or a change in the environment is likely to mean that individuals behave in a political manner to get what they want for their own aims (Murray and Gandz, 1980)
6. Non-programmed decisions: where decisions are made that are not clearly defined or the outcome is unsure
7. Low trust: negative political behaviour is likely to thrive in an organization that has a lack of trust

8. Role ambiguity: where the job role of a person is unclear they may be more likely to engage in political behaviour as the specification of their role is ambiguous
9. Unclear performance evaluation: appraisals can be quite subjective so individuals may engage in political behaviour to improve their evaluation
10. Organizational culture

Individual factors include:

1. Personality traits: those who are sensitive to what is going on around them may be more likely to engage in political behaviour
2. Locus of control: those who try to control their environment may also be likely to use tactics for political gains
3. Status within the organization: those with a high degree of status, power and autonomy may engage in political behaviours to a higher degree

For the consultant it is important to recognize not only the political environment in the clients firm but also the politics in the consultancy that the consultant is employed by. In other words, as mentioned in Chapter 7, the effective consultant needs to recognize the pressure put upon them by their own consultancy firm in order to give independent and impartial advice. Case Study 9.1 at the end of this chapter illustrates why this is essential to achieve.

Political tactics

The use of political tactics has been given considerable attention by academics and empirical studies (McKenna, 2006b). In summarizing the literature, McKenna (2006b) suggested that there were eight political tactics used:

1. Controlling information: whereby information is kept back and individuals are denied access to that information
2. Controlling lines of communication: this is where a person, commonly known as a gatekeeper, controls communication access to another person
3. Using outside experts: a manager may achieve their objectives by bringing in external consultants and misrepresenting information in that the consultant formulates advice biased towards what the manager wants
4. Controlling the agenda: controversial issues may be removed from an agenda at a meeting or may be placed at the end where the committee are fatigued so that the issue gets accepted without any resistance
5. Game playing: this is where managers operate within the rules of the organization but use timing or inaction for their own advantage
6. Image building: in social psychology it is well known that attractive people earn more money than unattractive people (Hamermesh and Biddle, 1994). In this regard, individuals may cultivate an outward appearance to impress influential people within the organization
7. Building coalitions: befriending people in higher positions within the organization may also be a political tactic

8. Controlling decision parameters: this is when a manager may reframe an issue in a manner by limiting information or by emphasizing less important information in order to get a favourable decision

These tactics could be further described as being: legitimate in terms of forming coalitions; illegitimate being morally difficult to defend; devious such as backstabbing when a person is pleasant towards another but at the same time is planning their demise; and lastly costly mistakes such as saying no to top management or violating the chain of command (McKenna, 2006b).

The consultant needs to be aware of these political tactics in order that their advice or services remain professional and impartial. By adopting a methodical approach to assignments and by being quite cautious in not accepting information at its face value and always ensuring that information comes from at least two different sources the consultant can hopefully avoid being manipulated by devious tactics. Furthermore, the consultant may also recognize their own political actions, whereby tactics such as image building may be vital.

Sex and politics

The use of sex and of sexualized connotations can also be common in organizations and linked to organizational politics (DuBrin, 1986). In some organizations sex can be used by both males and females to building coalitions in the workplace. Indeed, in Industry Snapshot 15.2 in Chapter 15, the individual secured her consultant position within the organization by having sex with her employing manager. In a similar situation, the Chief Executive Officer of Boeing was ousted after knowledge of his affair with a female executive came to light (Scheffler, 2005). Indeed, in an office based sex survey, 66 per cent of individuals said there was a lot of flirting in their office and 7 per cent said that they had been caught in the act although most were just embarrassed about it (Lever, Zellman and Hirschfield, 2006).

Sexualized terms are often used in consultancy such as, 'We want to get into bed with x client' and this language is found in other organizations (DuBrin, 1986). Indeed, at one interview in a reasonably reputable firm, the interviewer stated that consultants are just like whores who deliver whatever service the client wants for financial gain. Although such statements may be distasteful in polite company, sexualized statements may be acceptable in some organizational cultures (DuBrin, 1986) and in consultancy as humour is sometimes used for a number of reasons (Sturdy *et al.*, 2009). In Chapter 15, we examine sex in the workplace further in examining professionalism and ethics.

Industry snapshot 9.3

Limited sexual relations at work — a HR policy

An example of what an organization may do to discourage sexual relations at work was given by (Lever *et al.*, 2006) as follows:

The Company is committed to fostering a professional work environment where all employees are treated fairly and impartially by their managers.

Intimate personal relationships between supervisors and subordinates may result in workplace problems, such as a lack of objectivity in supervising and evaluating employees, the perception of favouritism by other employees (whether justified or not), and the potential for sexual harassment claims if a relationship ends. Therefore, supervisors are strongly discouraged from dating, engaging in amorous relationships with, or participating in sexual relations with employees who report to them, either directly or indirectly. Any supervisor who engages in such a relationship must immediately disclose the existence of that relationship to his or her immediate supervisor or Vice President of Human Resources. Upon receiving that information, the Company will make a decision as to whether it will continue to permit a direct reporting relationship or whether one or both of the employees in question must be transferred or required to seek employment elsewhere.

Source: Lever, et al. (2006). Reproduced with permission from The Conference Board Inc.

Chapter Summary

- Programme management is the co-ordinated management of multiple projects in order to achieve benefits of strategic importance
- Programme management acts as the layer above project management and supplements good project management (as explored in the last chapter)
- Programme management ensures that activities across multiple projects are focused on the business case
- Reallocation of resources from one project to another needs to be handled with tact in order not to reduce conflict between project managers competing for limited resources
- The process behind programme management is its identification, definition, establishment management, delivery of benefits and closure
- Power can be defined as the ability or force at one's disposal to influence the behaviour and outcomes of another
- Politics is the observable but typically covert mechanisms that individuals use to enhance their power to influence
- There are clear organizational and individual characteristics that may lead to political behaviour manifesting in organizations

Review Questions

1. What is a programme?
2. What are the differences between a programme and a project?
3. How should the organization be informed on the progress of a programme?
4. Is the closure of a programme an important process, and why?
5. What is the definition of power in organizations?
6. What are the five types of power according to French and Raven (1959)?
7. What is the definition of politics in organizations?
8. How do the terms power and politics differ?

9. What are the organizational factors that may lead to political behaviour?

10. What are the individual factors that may lead to political behaviour?

11. List the eight political tactics described by McKenna (2006b).

Assignment Questions

1. Programme management may seem to be a less exact process compared with project management. Critically discuss this, stating the reasons why programme management may be much harder to define in terms of the processes involved.

2. Why is setting a vision for the future and a blueprint for success important in programme management?

3. Discuss how a programme may be managed and the necessity of the different roles within the organization of a programme.

4. Describe how the concept of power may operate within an organization.

5. Is political behaviour necessarily a bad thing? Critically discuss within the context of organizational behaviour.

6. Describe the antecedents to political behaviour in organizations and how consultants can watch out for these precursors.

7. Describe how a client may use a consultancy for their own political gains using the concept of political tactics.

Case Study 9.1

'An example of complex inter-relationships and their effects in consultancy'

By Scott Harvey

The story starts in early 2008 when as a specialist change consultant, I was approached by an agency to consider some work for a well known organization. The project was to be a very long term one with considerable complexity and significant soft change issues (e.g. culture change, people change, TUPE etc).

The supplier situation was also complex with a consortium of three contractor organizations (which I will call A, B and C), company A was the lead. The end client had expressed some concern about the lead contractor not having the skills needed to achieve all of the project and they had been encouraged to seek partners that could round out the offering (e.g. in change management). This lead to the three party arrangement (which prior to the client agreeing the contract was an informal one with each company proceeding 'at risk'). One of the junior partner contractors (B) was responsible for change management and the scale and duration of the project had meant they had sought experienced people from across the UK market (including hiring through agencies). This resulted in a change team lead by a company B employee, but largely consisting of independent agency staff under contracts between their agency and company B.

I, along with many of my colleagues, was working through an agency. The diagram shows the

For obvious reasons the names of the various organizations involved in this case study have been removed. However they are all large UK and International businesses.

length and complexity of the links which, had I thought about them earlier, would have suggested a more careful approach than I took at the time.

Although this sounds like an involved arrangement, it could have worked had all the partners operated well together, but unfortunately it didn't.

The opening situation was that the consortium did win the contract (in competition with another group) but almost immediately, the lead (A) put pressure on sub-contractors (B and C) to reduce prices whilst increasing both the number and complexity of deliverables, some of which they had agreed between themselves and the client without any reference to the delivery teams and many of which had not appeared in the pre-contract agreements between the companies. For example, I was expected to produce a significant change deliverable within the first week of being on the contract, a deliverable that had been scheduled for month three of the project. Under any reasonable arrangement, the first week would be used largely to gain an understanding of the client and set up management systems so any attempt to produce a meaningful document would have been unsound at that stage of the project. The situation on delivery got progressively worse as tasks well beyond what had been in the pre-contract agreements were levied on the team (sometimes with delivery periods measured in hours rather than days) but despite this the inputs were produced.

Those of a suspicious mind might suggest the prime contractor (A) had simply entered into the relationship to gain the contract and then chosen to follow another route but there may be other explanations for some of this behaviour eg errors in initial cost estimates that later meant costs had to be cut and tasks re-assigned? A further complexity was that many of the client entry points were themselves third party contractors employed directly by the client to give specialist support, so instead of dealing directly with the end user and addressing their interests, we were engaging with individuals who may have had different agendas from the end client, or at least did not have the depth of knowledge of the client environment we needed. Although they were try-

A view of the various links from consultant to the organization

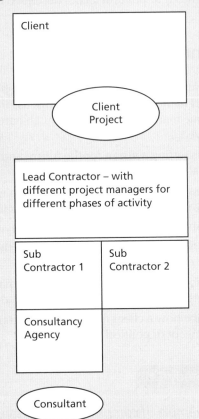

ing to deliver the project, they also had their own contract to defend and we saw some interesting behaviour.

This went on for three months and the situation for all the change consultants got progressively more frustrating. There was a perception that a pecking order had been set up in the consortium so staff in the lead contractor got priority in support, equipment, IT access etc. Obviously this contributed adversely to performance from companies B and C and our ability to communicate within and around the team (both the bigger project team and within the change team).

The eventual outcome was that various parts of the delivery arena (including the change team) were criticized for not delivering and an 'inquest' was held at which every product we had produced was identified. Despite proving we had produced everything asked of us, it was clear that the relationship between company A and company B had broken down and a delivery phase contract was not going to be signed. This left us with meaningless contracts as they were predicated on the delivery contract existing. The long and short of it is that almost all of the sub-contractor staff providing change services were notified we were no longer required and the prime contractor took over the change role (with mainly their own staff but they also kept four of the agency team but under new direct contracts). This didn't last for long and by six months they had largely been required to go.

The way this was done was that many of us were notified by phone with immediate effect having not had any prior notification of concerns with our performance or the individual opportunity to discuss it. The notice period was just five working days (whilst the notice period in the other direction was one month).

In case the foregoing has a flavour of defending our situation, let's assume that company A had a legitimate concern about performance. Under any test of reasonableness, individuals within that situation would normally be made aware of the issue and invited to correct the errors. This did not happen in this case and although there was some discussion, it did not take place at individual level. The absence of any attempt to correct those perceived deficiencies made the dismissals, in my view, unfair in its employment law sense.

Many of us had seen the contract duration as one to two years and therefore had made no attempt to find further work (and had no work 'in the bank').

There is much more that could be said about the detail of this situation (and almost everything about it was unusual) but the foregoing hopefully gives you an idea of both the complexity and also the 'odd' way things were being done.

The major learning points for me are:

- Be very clear who you are working for and that they will employ you fairly and in ac-

cordance with UK employment law. If in any doubt it's probably not worth doing!

- Avoid long complicated employment routes and ensure the contracts between main and subordinate contractors protect your rights and are in place before signing up (or place conditions on your acceptance).

- Check who you will be working with and if it's the client or a representative of the client (if so, who).

- Avoid full time working unless you have a cast-iron contract with reasonable notice periods that would allow you to find other work.

- Ensure performance criteria and reporting criteria are contained within any contracts and that performance concerns are handled reasonably in a process identified in the contract. It's also worth making sure you get a say in these.

- Ensure you know what the notice periods are and be prepared for them.

- If an agency worker, stay in touch with your agency and make sure they are working on your behalf and protecting your interests.

- Always have work you can move on to (e.g. maintain contact with the work market) and/or work part time on other tasks so you have some income to fall back on.

- The eventual outcome was that the client did not have the quality of change effort available from the events I outlined above until well after the project had begun (and only after further changes of staff did significant work begin) – around six months later. No doubt this has increased the frustration and expense to the client and had a significant impact on the progress of the project and the load on their staff.

Further Reading

Eisenhardt, K.M. and Kahwajy, L. (1997), How management teams can have a good fight, *Harvard Business Review,* 75(4), 77–85

Gray, R.J. (1997), Alternative approaches to programme management, *International Journal of Project Management,* 15(1), 5–9

Lycett, M., Rassau, A. and Danson J. (2004) Programme management: A critical review, *International Journal of Project Management,* 22(4), 289–299

Office of Government Commerce (2007), *Managing Successful Programmes.* London: The Stationery Office

Pfeffer, J. (1992), *Managing with Power: Politics and Influence in Organizations.* Boston: Harvard Business School Press

Vereecke, A., Pandelaere, E., Deschoolmeester, D. and Stevens, M. (2003), A classification of development programmes and its consequences for programme management, *International Journal of Operations & Production Management,* 23(10), 1279–1290

CHAPTER 10

Types of consultancy project

Learning Objectives

At the end of this chapter students will be able to:

- Recognize the broad categories of consultancy projects

- Understand both fact based assignments and action based assignments can be used together for their different advantages

- Determine the different areas of consultancy activity

Mini Case Study 10.1

Advert for management consultants

Management Consultancy in Atkins helps clients achieve genuine benefits from their investment and change programmes.

Part of Europe's largest multidisciplinary consulting firm, we are a leading provider of business, technology and project/programme consultancy to clients in the public and private sectors.

We advise at senior levels on complex business problems, but we also take a hands-on role, to ensure the solutions aren't just conceived, they are actually delivered.

Our ethos is to stand side-by-side with our clients until the real-world benefits of investment and change programmes are realized.

Source: Atkins http://www.atkinsglobal.com/areas_of_business/management_consultancy/. Reproduced with permission.

Introduction

Mini Case Study 10.1 was chosen from Atkins Management Consultancy to show the wide range of consultancy projects carried out in the industry. Words such as multidisciplinary, project/programme consultancy, public/private sectors describe the wide range of impact that a consultancy has and this is explored in this chapter. Furthermore, projects can involve a number of different factors including those challenging us to change the way we all live, which is essential for survival in the twenty-first century and beyond.

This chapter investigates the broad categories of consultancy projects and then concentrates on the different fields of consultancy activity defined by types of organizations as other authors (e.g., Czerniawska, 1999) have done in the past.

Broad Categories of Consultancy Projects

Facts versus action

Czerniawska (1999) critically appraised the consultancy industry in her influential book and broadly categorized the types of consultancy projects into fact based assignments and process based assignments. Fact based assignments are where a consultancy team is engaged by a client to investigate a particular issue. The investigation of this issue is mainly through gathering relevant data in 'relative isolation from the client' (Czerniawska, 1999, p. 111). It can only be effectively used when gathering data that can provide a factual answer to the issue or will form part of the wider problem solving process. It is useful in examining issues that are:

1. Discrete, where data can be gathered to understand the issues involved
2. Statistical or logistical, where data can be used to ascertain the environment
3. Finite – the issue is limited and in being so an analytical approach can provide a snapshot of that issue

The Mini Case Study 10.2 demonstrates a classic example of a fact based consultancy assignment. Although, the consultancy team worked on the project closely with the client, the bulk of the work was performed away from the client and all but the executive interviews were conducted by a sub-contractor of the consultancy firm that specializes in large scale surveys and interviews. Nevertheless, by revealing the facts to the client the client subsequently reviewed their policy on informing business users about chemicals in their organization.

Mini Case Study 10.2

Characteristics of people working with chemical products in small firms

The Health and Safety Executive is keen to increase its understanding of the characteristics of people working with chemical products in small firms, to assist in developing better targeted communications. It commissioned this survey research across five sectors – ladies hairdressers, dry cleaners, electroplaters, woodyards and garages, and a total of 521 face to face interviews were conducted.

The 305 firms represented were typically of four or fewer employees, relatively stable employers, and non unionized. Health and safety arrangements were frequently very basic and 40 per cent of managers did not cite any arrangements. Issues were usually communicated verbally to staff.

Overall about two-thirds of users thought the chemical products they worked with posed little or no risk, though all products had well-documented detrimental health effects. Knowledge of the potential harmful effects of products was low for short-term effects, and poor for long-term effects.

Knowledge of appropriate protection varied appreciably by sector. Importantly, managers were not notably better informed than employees on the above issues. Suppliers and sales representatives were clearly the preferred source for further information on chemical products. Two-thirds of all respondents had heard of Safety Data Sheets, but there was little evidence that they were often consulted.

Understanding of chemical symbols and terms used for risks and hazards was low, and associated with reading age – which itself revealed nearly two-thirds of respondents had a reading age of under 12 years 4 months. Several pointers for health and safety communications on chemical products in small firms emerged. These include: that com-

munications should assume a very low level of reading ability in small firms and recognize that a 'verbal' rather than 'written' culture predominates; that communications should not assume the manager is highly knowledgeable; that container labels appear to be a major source of information; and that a high proportion of those having experience of an accident involving chemical products claim that it has made them more safety conscious.

This report is one of a number of projects that form part of an HSE programme to improve the impact and effectiveness of health and safety messages. The communication of messages on chemicals risks and controls is a particular focus for this work and HSE will consider the implications of results from this and other studies on how risk information is communicated in a review in Autumn 2000.

Source: Executive summary reprinted from Biggs and Crumbie (2000). Reproduced with permission from Serco.

The reliance on data and facts varies from company to company (Czerniawska, 1999). However, it is similar to the medical analogy put forward by Gilbert (1998) who stated that like a medical practitioner where a patient goes to visit if they have a medical problem, the medical practitioner listens to all the facts, sees the evidence (if applicable) and then take biopsies for the lab (if applicable), etc. In a similar manner the consultant listens to the client takes down the facts, ascertains the evidence and then presents it back to the client typically in the form of report. Higdon (1969) commented that the medical model worked well for describing the professional nature of consultancy, although arguably since the 1960s management consultancy has moved on considerably.

Thought Provoking point 10.1

Must hit the desk with a thud

Allegedly, in the early 1990s there were a few management consultants who stated that if the report produced for a client didn't land with a thud it was not worth the clients attention. Fortunately modern day consultancy doesn't have such 'measures' of performance!

The disadvantage of fact based assignments, according to Czerniawska (1999), related to their very analytical approach. The issue with this is that if the research techniques used for gathering the data required to solve the client's issue are not suitable for purpose or in simply gathering data the client's issues are not resolved, then clearly fact based assignments will be disadvantaged in this predicament.

Fact based assignments were predominant in the early years of consultancy, which seemed to be the case in most countries such as the UK and Holland (Arnoldus and Dankers, 2005; Ferguson, 2002). Some firms reportedly still only offer this brand of consultancy; however, many have moved on to process based consultancy which is the second category of consultancy projects listed by Czerniawska (1999).

Czerniawska (1999) stated that the reaction of consultancies to the problems of fact based assignment was the move towards more process or action based consulting. The emphasis of process based consulting is on the implementation of the work rather than just uncovering the facts. In this type of consultancy, it is very much a shared partnership between the consultant and the client such as proposed by Mulligan and Barber (2001). Their work is detailed in greater depth in Chapter 5 and illustrated further in Mini Case Study 5.3 where Atos Consulting, the Ministry of Defence and Rolls-Royce worked together in a collaborative partnership.

Critically speaking, action based consulting is a wise move by any consultancy to adopt. After they have researched the 'facts' and uncovered what needs to be done then why not volunteer to be involved in further implementation. Industry snapshot 10.1 demonstrates this from a consultancy assignment that the author carried out recently. This initially examined the development needs of the senior management but then moved on to how the development needs were to be addressed in this highly successful company. In this assignment, the consultant could partner with the organization to ascertain how development needs will be met. This may involve delivering training on conflict management or aiding the company to develop their own personal planning development system. However, unlike with fact based consulting there is not an over-reliance on the report as a mechanism to do the consultancy work.

Industry snapshot 10.1

Data quality

Making data fit for purpose

"Data denial – a failure to recognise the true state of data quality – is the principal cause of unreliable and unpredictable data."

Data only exists to support business applications. Whether for billing, customer management, financial reporting or any other purpose, each system will require views and attributes that may well be very different – such as a legal entity for the chart of accounts compared to the product divisional view for performance management; single product views for supply chain management or single customer views for CRM. Data quality can only be defined in the light of the purpose it is designed to satisfy. All data profiling, data cleansing and data matching activity needs to be driven by the ultimate purpose of the data.

This concept of fitness for purpose means that to understand data quality, you must understand not just what data you have but what you intend to do with it. For most businesses, data collected for one purpose, often ends up being used in many different ways. Consequently, data quality is a complicated and constantly evolving business problem.

Source: © Deloitte & Touche LLP 2007, http://www.deloitte.com/view/en_GB/uk/services/enterprise-risk-services/data/article/b97aa1b5171fb110VgnVCM100000ba42f00aRCRD.htm. Reproduced with permission.

Furthermore, Czerniawska (1999) argued that action based consultancy is ideal in dealing with the complexities of modern businesses that are continually changing, developing and growing. Rather than accepting issues at face-value the consultant develops a key understanding of the underlying causes rather than the symptoms and provides an approach that deals with the longer more complex issues. This type of action consulting has been invaluable over the last 30 years or so (see Mini Case Study 10.3). Nonetheless, it does have disadvantages and Czerniawska (1999) listed these as follows:

- Process based consultancy can be subjective, as rather than relying on empirical data gathered at a certain time, it is a much more fluid phenomenological approach
- Issues may arise from the client interview which the consultant cannot deal with such as personal problems, etc
- Consultants may over indulge a client with privileged information; thus, rather than allowing the staff to discuss with management issues and problems in a suitable forum, the cat is let out of the bag so to speak and then the consultants position is rather redundant

Mini Case Study 10.3

Serco in the nuclear industry

Serco has had an integral role in the UK civil and defence nuclear industries for the past 50 years.

Serco's Technical and Assurance Services business provides specialist technical support to the UK nuclear industry. It provides expert safety, environmental, risk and asset management advice and operational solutions to many of the UK's civil nuclear sites. For nearly half a century, it has been providing independent specialist nuclear safety advice to the Royal Navy in support of their nuclear submarine fleet.

Since 2000, Serco has been entrusted with the management of the UK Atomic Weapons Establishment (AWE), which provides the warheads for the UK's independent nuclear deterrent. We do this as part of AWE Management Limited (AWEML), a 25-year joint venture with Lockheed Martin UK and Jacobs Engineering.

AWE is a complex nuclear facility on a 750 acre site at Aldermaston and an adjacent 225 acres site at Burghfield in Berkshire, and employs nearly 4500 people including scientists, engineers and skilled craftspeople.

Our primary role through AWEML is to provide advice and governance to the management of AWE plc and bring the experience and expertise of the parent companies to bear on AWE's development.

We have worked together to create a new nuclear programme and project management academy for AWE staff, which is now up and running, with almost a quarter of the staff being trained in the first year.

One of the projects involves a multi-disciplinary team of project managers, commercial experts, scientists, engineers and construction specialists delivering a state-of-the-art laser facility to enable scientists to replicate conditions at the heart of a nuclear reaction. The facility will also be used by civil scientists studying events such as the beginning of the universe.

Source: http://www.serco.com/markets/nuclear/index.asp Reproduced with permission.

Nevertheless, all of these disadvantages in turn can be criticized. The subjective nature of process based consulting is inherent in adopting an approach that doesn't simply ignore the complex nature of the social reality we all live in which is often the case with more analytical approaches (Bishop, Cassell and Hoel, 2009). In part, this over-reliance on phenomenological material can be counteracted by providing the client with objective data at critical key points. Thus, with setting up a project, key stages can be identified where objective data can be gathered either by questionnaire or other research based instruments. In effect combining the advantages of the fact based consulting with the action based consulting (Czerniawska, 1999).

In terms of 'personal' issues that may arise from the client interviews, these are often vital to uncover, especially if there are personal conflicts (see Thought Provoking point 10.2). In these situations, hopefully the analytical information gathered supports the personal view provided, e.g., in succession planning – the survey of staff, interviews with managers all corresponded with the managing director's personal view that at that time his son shouldn't be the replacement managing director. The latter disadvantage is all too easy to fall into; however, the consultant must ensure that analysis that is not ready to be revealed to the client isn't exposed and must maintain this level of discipline. (This can be especially hard if the client is buying drinks for the consultants for a job nearly finished and asks probing questions.)

Thought Provoking point 10.2

What! You want a coffee.

After joining an Applications Development (AD) division of a consultancy organization, a colleague described in detail that due to their previous systems design consultancy experience they were interested in exploring opportunities with the Systems Design (SD) division. Nevertheless, after several attempts to contact key members of SD they were met with disapproval even though one of the managers of AD said there shouldn't be a problem. In asking to go out for a coffee with SD they were asked to give a list of reasons for why representatives of SD should meet for a coffee in a rather abrupt manner. Later it was revealed that there was a historical animosity between AD and SD from 5 years previously. Once this was discovered and the conflict addressed, my colleague eventually ended up working on several projects within SD.

The Range of Consultancy Activity

Introduction

Recently the Institute of Business Consulting defined the range of the management consultant's work into topics as shown in Industry snapshot 10.2. Whilst an individual reading this book may already be versed in their own discipline e.g., business strategy, marketing, etc., and each of these topics could have their own textbook, it is still useful to examine the specific areas of business that a consultant may typically work in, which we will do for the remainder of this chapter.

Industry snapshot 10.2

What is the range of a management consultant's work?

Management consultants by their very nature are specialists because of the wide variety of management activities. The specialisms have been divided by the Institute of Business Consulting into the following areas of consulting activity:

Business strategy
This involves long-range planning, the reorganization of a company's structure, rationalization of services and products and a general business appraisal of the company.

Manufacturing and business services
Involving a review of the layout of a production department, production control arrangements, productivity and incentive schemes, or quality control problems.

Marketing
Market research and business forecasting, sales force training and the organization of retail and wholesale outlets.

Financial and management controls
The installation of budgetary control systems, profit planning or capital and revenue budgeting, office reorganization and administrative arrangements.

Human resources
Advising on personnel policy, manpower planning, job enrichment, job evaluation and industrial relations.

Information technology
Defining information needs, the provision of software, systems analysis and design, computer feasibility studies, implementing computer applications and making computer hardware evaluations.

Environmental management
This includes urban and regional development planning, international economic research, cost benefit and social analysis studies and physical, economic, ecological and sociological studies for the encouragement of quality of lifestyle.

Quality management
Setting of policy and strategy, customer satisfaction, performance measurement, people management and processes.

Source: The Inside Careers Guide to Management Consultancy (2009/10). Published in partnership with the IBC and MCA. Available online at www.insidecareers.co.uk. Reproduced with permission.

Business strategy

Strategy may be defined as the policies and procedures in an organization that give it a sustained competitive advantage (Lawler, 2006; Legge, 2005). Consultancy projects in strategic management range from small projects examining succession planning through to large-scale reorganizations of a company's structure. Business strategy as can be seen in Mini Case Study 10.4 involves more than just specifying an organization's mission, vision and objectives but also aiding the company through projects or programmes of growth. Strategy needs to take into account the key stakeholders of the business which are typically the customers, employees, suppliers and owners or shareholders (Obolensky, 1994).

These projects/programmes involve business strategy coordinating and integrating the activities of the various functional areas within the organization in order that it can identify and achieve its long-term objectives. Indeed, organizations that do not have an effective business strategy will lose their competitive edge (Lawler, 2006). Techniques such as those illustrated in Chapter 4 can aid consultants in dealing with business strategy.

Mini Case Study 10.4

Ernst & Young with Sony Professional Solutions Europe (winner of the 2008 MCA prize for business strategy)

Sometimes, being successful is just not enough. Sony's European business-to-business operation, Professional Solutions Europe (PSE), is its most profitable electronics division in Europe – but Sony HQ wants more. PSE must supercharge its revenues from €875m in the 2007 financial year to €2bn by 2010. PSE supplies Sony's electronic and audio-visual products and services to a range of sectors, from broadcasting, media and cinema to retail, healthcare and transport.

So how, pondered PSE's senior managers, could it reach such an aggressive revenue target whilst navigating the uncertain waters of digitization and the migration to high-definition (HD) technology? Initially, PSE thought the answer would lie entirely in acquisitions – until Ernst & Young's corporate M&A team advised that snapping up other companies represented just one piece of the jigsaw. PSE's senior management were introduced to Ernst & Young's business advisory team to help them formulate a sustainable growth strategy to achieve its target.

This strategy highlighted PSE's need to evolve from a product-led organization to a service-orientated one. Ernst & Young and PSE agreed four goals: PSE would become a top-three brand in all market areas where it has a presence – and if already in the top three, it should move up a place;

the organization would deliver 10 per cent to 15 per cent of its revenues from services; seek out fresh opportunities within its existing product portfolio, including HD; and expand aggressively into digital networking and broadcast managed services.

First, the consultants carried out a top-down assessment of the opportunities in PSE's existing and new market segments, along with a bottom-up analysis of how the product portfolio was positioned, and how it should change, to achieve the targeted revenues. The team began changing PSE's prevailing factory-led, product-centric mindset to a focus on market segments. Four new business segments were prioritized, but the consultants also identified areas for closure. Ernst & Young painted a clear picture of what a successful PSE organization would look like, designing the roadmap and organizational changes. This part of the project included creating ideas and sketching scenarios around completely new business models, such as digital signage, where revenue might be shared with ad agencies and public-space advertisers.

Meanwhile, two senior members of Ernst & Young's M&A team analyzed 60 potential acquisition targets, developing a set of scenarios and recommendations. In the second rubber-hits-road phase, the team helped PSE change its business, addressing fundamental issues such as organizational design, supply chain, merger integration, and learning and development.

A growth programme staffed by 67 people, including two Ernst & Young consultants from the original team, is in full swing, and a number of acquisitions are in train. Ernst & Young estimates that the new strategy will take PSE to the €2bn turnover mark by the sixth month of its 2010

financial year. Significantly, PSE now also has confidence that it will hit its target. 'Throughout the programme, Ernst & Young have demonstrated integrity', says Naomi Climer, Sony PSE's vice-president, 'and I genuinely believe they have the best interests of Sony at heart'.

Source: http://www.mca.org.uk/sites/default/files/ 2008%20Management%20Winners.pdf. Reproduced with permission from MCA.

Manufacturing and business services

Manufacturing is the use of machines, tools and people to create objects for use (by other manufacturers) or for sale either directly or via a retailer. It typically involves large-scale industrial production whereby raw materials are manufactured into finished goods. Consultancies work can work in this area examining issues such as production, quality control, use of human resources, etc. Indeed, Mini Case Study 10.5 and Mini Case Study 12.1 demonstrate specific projects in this area.

Mini Case Study 10.5

Proudfoot Consulting – Electrical manufacturer accomplishes two years of change in four months

A world leader in electricity and automation management, this organization provides its customers with comprehensive solutions that combine software, communication and services whilst meeting demanding targets in terms of safety, reliability and energy savings. This client had recently adopted a 'shared services' model for its purchasing and HO functions but needed help from Proudfoot to deliver the benefits of the reorganization. Shared services means centralizing the management of certain functions, often support functions, for multiple users.

What we found

A business review identified opportunities for efficiency gains: In the purchasing function, buyers were spending up to 50 per cent on non value added activities as a consequence of disconnected processes. Poor clarity in roles and responsibilities and lack of KPIs meant individuals were not clear

on where best to focus their efforts. The lack of KPIs also made it difficult to manage accountability. A lack of resource planning tools made it near impossible to evaluate the true requirements of customers. Within the new shared service organization, the HO function lacked clarity on how to define contract terms and didn't know how to present these to their internal customers. There was duplication of work between centralized and local departments and the centralized department was delivering less value than its potential.

What we did

Proudfoot reviewed a number of key processes team including performance management, supplier management, negotiation and tendering. It formalized and enhanced processes and procedures and clarified key roles and responsibilities. It developed a number of purchasing tools and

▶

implemented a management operation system based on active management and KPIs. Centralization of support functions meant managers needed to be trained in how to manage and coach individuals who were physically remote. They were also trained in negotiation skills. A management operating system enabled a major breakthrough in how the organization operated with weekly reviews between managers and purchasers based on individual objectives and action plan follow ups.

Tangible, sustainable results

At the outset the client was looking to increase the percentage of contracts it renegotiated each year from 14 per cent to 25 per cent. At the end of the project it was achieving 28 per cent repetitive re-negotiation. The process improvement work identified significant savings in resources and man hours. At the end of the project the client said that 'the cultural change is already visible and people talk about it between themselves positively . . . it has enabled us to accomplish in four months what would have taken two years.'

Source: http://www.proudfootconsulting. com/displayfile.asp ?id=97296 Reproduced with permission from Alexander Proudfoot.

Marketing

The American Marketing Association defines the activity of marketing as:

> Marketing is the activity, set of institutions, and processes for creating, communicating, delivering, and exchanging offerings that have value for customers, clients, partners, and society at large.
>
> *(Retrieved from http://www.marketingpower.com/AboutAMA/Pages/ DefinitionofMarketing.aspx)*

Additionally, they further define market research as:

> Marketing research is the function that links the consumer, customer, and public to the marketer through information – information used to identify and define marketing opportunities and problems; generate, refine, and evaluate marketing actions; monitor marketing performance; and improve understanding of marketing as a process. Marketing research specifies the information required to address these issues, designs the method for collecting information, manages and implements the data collection process, analyzes the results, and communicates the findings and their implications.
>
> *(Retrieved from http://www.marketingpower.com/AboutAMA/Pages/ DefinitionofMarketing.aspx)*

Management consultancy in this area may examine marketing as a function. This may involve reviewing and enhancing current levels of sales activity by, for instance, improving the customer service of the sales force. Market research may also be included in this area involving everything from surveying large geographical regions (examining water usage – for instance) through to employing mystery shoppers to determine the effectiveness of sales staff in a retail environment.

Financial and management controls

Financial planning and control are essential for any business (Collis and Hussey, 2007; Kind, 2001). Consultancy projects in this field may range from implementing

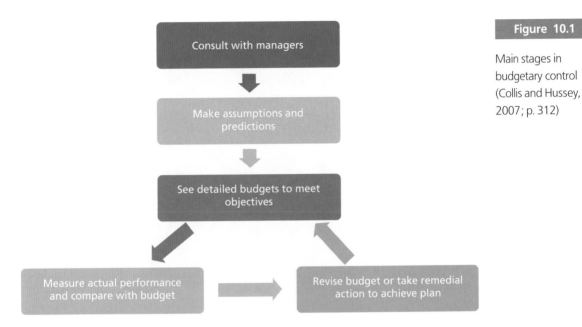

Figure 10.1

Main stages in
budgetary control
(Collis and Hussey,
2007; p. 312)

budgetary control the main process of which is shown in Figure 10.1. In this type
of project, managers of the organizations are consulted, leading to the formation
of assumptions and predictions about income and expenditure. This then leads to
the creation of detailed budgets designed to comply with the managers' predictions of income and expenditure. This is then measured and revised accordingly
ensuring business success (Collis and Hussey, 2007).

When an organization has a budgetary control system it is advantaged by
having all the various functions of the business coordinated, provides information
on the utilization of resources, motivates managers who stay within their preset
budgets and devolves the responsibility of the business down to managers (Collis
and Hussey, 2007). Nevertheless, there are disadvantages to such as it may
constrain managers from making sensible decisions on spending in areas when
this is needed (e.g., for marketing purposes, etc). It may also be a time consuming process as managers spend their time deliberating over budgets. Budgets
may also be unrealistic if the initial assumptions and predictions are not met
(Collis and Hussey, 2007).

Thought Provoking point 10.3

'Let's fix the roads as we need to spend the budget!'

In some organizations, budget is linked to previous spending. Thus, rather than being
praised and rewarded for keeping within a budget. The opposite becomes evident
and just before the year end, spending may be increased just to make sure that the
manager has the same financial resources in the following year!

Figure 10.2

The building of GCHQ which was underestimated by £268 million. Source: © Adrian Sherratt / Alamy Image no. A187T5

Typically, software is used to aid financial planning and control although there is no single model of a perfect budgetary control system (Collis and Hussey, 2007). Implementing software systems, such as SAP ERP, determines the coordination of resources, information, and activities required to complete business functions such as invoicing, billing, salary payments, etc.

Other projects in this area may be in terms of calculating large investments in capital such as new premises and buildings or indeed the rationalization of business operations that release large amounts of capital. Nevertheless, this is an area fraught with difficulties. An example of this is GCHQ which had a huge increase in the predicted cost (£40 million) versus the actual cost (£308 million) for the technical transition between the old sites to the new site. Nevertheless, a variety of reasons was given for this overspend such as the millennium bug (for further details see http://www.nao.org.uk/publications/0203/government_communications_head.aspx).

Human resources

The roots of human resources can be traced back to the 1950s but really developed in the 1960s where individuals in the behavioural science movement such as Maslow, Hertzberg and Argyris emphasized the value of human resources (Badhwar and Aryee, 2008). This moved on till throughout the 1970s researchers such as Hackman and Oldham (1975) found that business performance could be improved by adopting humanistic policies and procedures.

Managing human resources is the role of the discipline of human resource management (HRM) which may be defined as the strategic and consistent approach

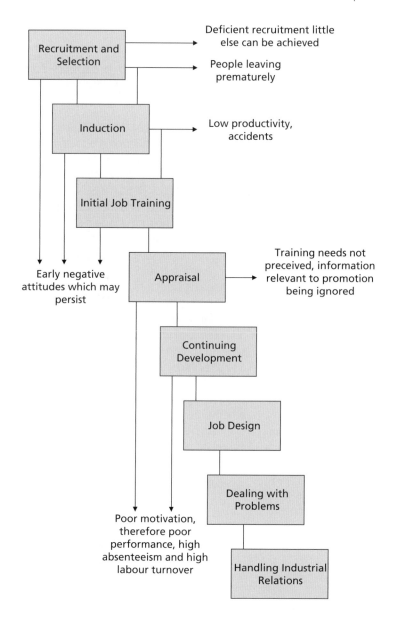

Figure 10.3

Stages in the human
resources process

to the management of individuals within that organization. Indeed, through the management of what are arguably the organization's most valued assets, great business benefits can be released (Hackman and Oldham, 1975). HRM represents a major investment in terms of what has been spent on individuals not only to recruit them but also to train and develop them into an effective employee. Management consultants deal with HRM issues on this basis. Other issues such as low levels of motivation or job enrichment programmes are also in the remit of the management consultant. Indeed, Figure 10.3 demonstrates the different stages in the human resources process and consultancy can help at all these different stages.

Hay Group devised a training course that has already improved prospects for ethnic-minority NHS staff (winner of the 2006 MCA prize for human resources in the public sector)

Trevor Phillips, chair of the Commission for Racial Equality, once likened the NHS to a snow-capped mountain where the boss is almost always white. Close to 35 per cent of doctors, 16 per cent of nurses and 11 per cent of non-medical staff are from ethnic minorities. Yet at the top, only 1 per cent of chief executives are from minority backgrounds. The NHS is Europe's biggest employer, so in 2002, health secretary John Reid laid out a 10-point action plan to address under-representation.

The 'Breaking Through' programme was established to develop and equip employees from black and ethnic-minority backgrounds with the skills and behaviours to progress. But simply doing a good job is not enough, and Hay Group's 'Aspiring Directors' plan has been an important part of the NHS programme, targeting staff whose self-belief has taken a hit or those who lack understanding about how to operate in a more political environment.

The 12-day course is broken down into four three-day modules. The first helps participants gain an in-depth understanding of themselves and others. Using a picture-story exercise that measures motives, participants learn what drives their behaviour and that of others. The second module uses a diagnostic tool that measures the most effective ways of influencing strategy and people within an organization. It also helps participants to a greater understanding of the norms, procedures, cultures and values of the NHS.

The next stage analyses different leadership styles, but also helps managers see leadership as a journey. Finally, participants are given the chance through simulations to 'step up' to the board, role-playing with real NHS CEOs and directors. Offering the Aspiring Directors course was a challenge in itself – some line managers felt threatened when their staff attended the course. But high-level endorsement of the programme from NHS CEO Sir Nigel Crisp and other directors ensured that managers fell into line.

Nearly nine out of ten participants have achieved some career development. Since the scheme began in 2003, the percentage of directors from black or ethnic-minority backgrounds has improved from 2 per cent to more than 7 per cent.

Source: http://www.mca.org.uk/sites/default/files/MT_MCA.Awards06.pdf. Reproduced with permission from MCA.

Information technology

Projects and programmes in information technology (IT) — or more often named Information Computer Technology (ICT) — can range in size like projects in other areas. The smallest project may be simply investigating why users are not using a particular programme in terms of human machine interaction (e.g., Biggs and Marshall, 1999). These projects need to examine the basic assumptions being made. Other projects, may be vast such as NPfIT, a computer system being developed for the NHS that records patient details and provides this and much more to medical practitioners (Brennan, 2005). Technology offers the NHS alternative ways of delivering clinical care so is central to the NHS modernization programme (Brennan, 2005). Indeed, many organizations do change with different systems put in place and the field of IT is a huge contributor towards the overall market of the management consultancy industry. Industry snapshot 10.4 demonstrates how in many IT projects not only the IT has to be considered but the people, culture and business case as well.

Atkins Management Consultancy – Delivering best practice ICT Shared Services at Northern Ireland Civil Service (NICS)

NICS needed to deliver ICT shared services to support eleven major civil service departments over a staged period, starting with the Department of Finance and Personnel (DFP) and the Department of Regional Development (DRD) and their agencies. Other civil service departments would come on-stream over two years. The initial shared service centre would support some 9000 users rising to 18 000. NICS wanted to implement service management based on ITIL which provides a cohesive set of best practices, drawn from the public and private sectors internationally. It is supported by a comprehensive qualifications scheme, accredited training organizations, and implementation and assessment tools. The best practice processes promoted in ITIL are supported by ISO 20000 Standard.

In order to achieve this, Atkins', work covered:

- The review of an outline business case and tightening down of costs to ensure optimum value for money.

- A culture assessment of staff from DFP and DRD who would become part of SSC.

- An ITIL maturity assessment and development and integration of five new ITIL processes.

- The provision of a New Service Management tool OJEU procured, and tested for use by new Service Desk.

- Full training of staff on processes and tools.

Atkins helped deliver the programme in demanding timescales, in around nine months in total to meet the target date for opening the Shared Service Centre (SSC) in May 2007. The compressed schedule included a business case review, a competitive OJEU procurement of the service management tool, the development of five new ITIL processes and full training.

Source: Atkins http://www. atkinsglobal.com/Images/Flyer%20-%20Delivering% 20best%20practice%20ICT%20shared%20 services%20at%20NICS_tcm12-2801.pdf. Reproduced with permission.

Environmental management

Given the recent changes in our environment caused possibly by global warming, environmental management is a growing area for consultancy projects. Projects within this area may include urban and regional development planning. Many projects also run internationally and as such seek to improve the quality of lifestyle for poorer nations. Other studies, such as the example in Industry snapshot 10.5, demonstrate how physical, economic, ecological and sociological studies examine our environment for the good of all human kind. This topic will be further explored in Chapter 16.

Pathways to a low-carbon economy

Whilst leaders in many nations discuss ambitious targets for reducing emissions of greenhouse gases (GHGs), there is also an intense debate underway regarding the technical and economic feasibility of different target levels, what emission reduction opportunities should be pursued, and the costs of different options for meeting the targets.

To provide a quantitative basis for such discussions, McKinsey & Company, supported by ten leading global companies and organizations – The Carbon Trust, ClimateWorks, Enel, Entergy, Holcim, Honeywell, Shell, Vattenfall, Volvo, WWF – has assessed more than 200 GHG abatement opportunities across 10 major sectors and 21 world regions between now and 2030. The results comprise an in-depth evaluation of the potential, costs and investment required for each of those measures.

Our analysis finds that:

- The potential exists to reduce GHG emissions by just enough to stay on track until 2030 to contain global warming below 2 degrees Celsius.

- Opportunities can be grouped into three categories of technical measures: energy

efficiency, low-carbon energy supply, and terrestrial carbon.

- Capturing all the potential will be a major challenge: it will require change on a massive scale, strong global cross-sectoral action and commitment, and a strong policy framework.

- Whilst the costs and investments seem manageable at a global level, they are likely to be challenging for individual sectors.

- Delays in action of even 10 years would mean missing the 2 degrees Celsius target.

This report builds on our first global study published in January 2007 and subsequent national studies. It includes an updated assessment of the development of low-carbon technologies, of macro-economic trends and a more detailed understanding of abatement potential in different regions and industries. Furthermore it assesses investment and financing requirements and incorporates implementation scenarios for a more dynamic understanding of how abatement reductions could unfold.

Source: Reproduced with permission from McKinsey & Company. http://www.mckinsey.com/clientservice/ccsi/pathways_low_carbon_economy.asp.

Quality management

The last category of types of projects set out by the Institute of Business Consulting is quality management. These types of project range in scope from revising how a department views its customers and how they measure performance through to large-scale implementation of ISO (International Organization for Standardization) quality procedures. Typically, projects would examine the existing quality procedures of a company and then revise this setting out policy, performance measures and revised quality assurance. Other types of projects may involve satisfying the requirements of quality assurance bodies. (See Mini Case Study 10.5.) For instance, Investors in People (IIP) provide procedures and principles for delivering business improvement through people. Indeed, organizations that adopt an integrated range of HR practices proposed by systems such as IIP are likely to perform better on profit and sales growth no matter what the type or size of the organization (Tamkin, Cowling and Hunt, 2008).

Mini Case Study 10.6

Braintree District Council (Clark and Appleby, 1997)

Background

Braintree's chief executive (who left the authority in 1994) saw his role when appointed in 1984 as transforming the organization to turn it into one of which staff and elected members could be proud. It was said by a staff member that he managed to use 'the right amount of abrasion ... to make the change happen.' It was repeatedly reported that he sold changes and improvements in management systems and his core values religiously. This included customer awareness, learning to love complaints, and a focus on the internal customer.

Characteristics of the total quality programme

The Council's quality initiatives did not begin with the decision to pursue quality assurance through BS 5750 (now BS EN ISO 9000), although it is that element of quality management for which the Council is now nationally and internationally renowned. In fact, a variety of initiatives were introduced throughout the Council by the chief executive over many years, some concentrated on the establishment of systems, e.g. quality assurance; some were about managerial systems and staff training; others were about the appropriateness of current service provision. It was reported that at first there were lots of initiatives but, 'they didn't all come together.' For a period of time people could not see the links between the various initiatives and there was a sense of 'initiative overload'. The main initiatives which have been introduced include:

- core values;
- customer care;
- performance appraisal;
- staff training/Investors in People (IIP);
- corporate strategy;
- BS EN ISO 9000.

Implementation of the total quality programme

One of the chief executive's first tasks was to identify who would support him in promoting and managing change within the organization. Three directors 'retired' from the senior management team and the second-tier management group was identified by him as his vehicle for making change happen. According to staff, the senior management team 'wasn't up to it'. The second-tier officer group all work well together as a team. They are, according to chief officers interviewed, very cohesive and it is still this group that drives and supports change. Whilst the second-tier management team were the chief executive's main product champions, other members of staff were also identified throughout the organization. This second group was not dissimilar from the Japanese model of 'The Parallel Hybrid Organization' described by Lillrank and Kano (1989), and Shani and Rogberg (1993).

The role of elected members

As we know, the central point for a democratic and political organization is reaching some form of agreement. In Braintree, the Council had been 'hung' for more than a decade although is now a Labour Council. This could potentially have been disabling in terms of providing a clear vision for the authority. However, the authority managed to develop effective mechanisms for cross-party working.

Given local government's political nature, discussed in our earlier paper, the role of elected members in the quality initiative is of interest. In Braintree there were a very small number of key members – mainly the Chair of Policy involved on the member side.

According to one officer: 'Members see quality as peripheral but let officers get on with it ... members saw the benefit with Compulsory Competitive Tendering (CCT) and with reducing costs. But there are few, if any champions amongst the members.' A different officer was quoted as saying: 'Members never decided to implement quality. Officers introduced it and then sought permission afterwards.' That was possible within this particular authority because members trust the officers. According to the leader of the Council 'Members trust officers implicitly and totally. All of the group leaders can contact any of the first-tier or second-tier officers at home. They rarely do, but it's possible.'

Conclusions

The Council has taken an eclectic approach to developing its quality initiative and has not crudely followed any individual quality guru. Over time, it has developed an approach to quality which draws on the thinking of, and contains characteristics of, many modern management writers (BS 5750: Oakland; Training-focus: Peters; Customer-focus: Deming and Juran). The Council's quality initiative is based more on the Council's five core values and the varied interests of the chief officers who are driving the initiative than any quality guru.

The literature on the management of local government greatly stresses the role of elected members as one of local government's special characteristics, that which differentiates local government from the private sector. Of particular interest in this authority's approach to developing quality is the limited elected member involvement in the planning (i.e. setting the vision and values) and implementation of the plan. The extent to which this is a reflection of the hung nature of the Council (as it was then) or the high degree of confidence that members have in officers in this authority is not clear. This is an area where further research would be of value. Also of interest in this authority is the way in which, through effective leadership and staff involvement, the authority has been able to develop a corporate approach to quality despite differences in characteristics across departments. High levels of departmentalism are a well known characteristic of local government and are seen in the literature as an important potential barrier to the implementation of TQ in local government.

Labour have now taken control of the authority but the Council's strategy following these political changes still reflects the belief that quality should underpin all activity and contains a commitment to quality seamlessly becoming a part of the organizational culture.

Chapter Summary

- Czerniawska (1999) broadly categorized the types of consultancy projects into fact based assignments and process based assignments
- Fact based assignments investigate a particular issue through gathering relevant data
- Action based assignments focus on the implementation of the work rather than just uncovering the facts
- Action based assignments are ideal in dealing with continually changing, developing and growing businesses
- Management consultants by their very nature tend to be specialists having developed in a particular field
- Management consultancy encompasses a wide variety of management activities comprising of:
  - Business strategy
  - Manufacturing and business services

- Marketing
- Financial and management controls
- Human resources
- Information technology
- Environmental management
- Quality management

Review Questions

1. What is a fact based assignment?
2. What issues are more readily investigated in a fact based assignment?
3. List the disadvantages of a fact based assignment.
4. Does a fact based assignment ignore the complex nature of the social reality we inhabit?
5. What is an action based assignment?
6. What are the advantages of an action based approach?
7. List the areas of consultancy activity defined by the Institute of Business Consulting.

Assignment Questions

1. Critically discuss how Czerniawska (1999) broadly defined consultancy projects listing the advantages and disadvantages of each category.
2. What are the disadvantages of taking an action based approach to assignments and how might these be remedied?
3. Describe the broad nature of management consultancy projects.
4. McKinsey & Company published a global study specifically investigating climate change. What role can the management consultancy industry play in this essential area of concern?

Case Study 10.1

Monitor's opportunities in India (A)

By Juan Alcacer & Jan W. Rivkin

As Mark Fuller, chairman of the Monitor Group, left the company's headquarters in Cambridge, Massachusetts, on November 15, 2004, he felt that the day's brainstorming session had gone well. He and a few senior colleagues had spent the day debating the company's future in India. The group had generated a dozen options and had pinpointed a handful that deserved further consideration. Internal teams in India and Cambridge would soon flesh out and examine the leading options.

After a stint as an assistant professor at Harvard Business School, Fuller had co-founded Monitor in

1983. The company had grown from a boutique strategy consulting firm to a group of affiliated companies that advised clients on strategic and financial matters, managed capital, and developed executives. Monitor had taken on its first project in India in 1990 and had operated a consulting office in Mumbai since 1994. The Mumbai office, however, had seen frequent changes in leadership, and revenues had plateaued at low levels. Fuller, a frequent visitor to India since the 1980s, returned from a two-week 'fact-finding mission' to India in September 2004 with a strong conviction: Major opportunities awaited Monitor in India, and it was time for the company to tap them.

The actions in India that Fuller and his colleagues considered fell into two categories. A set of straightforward decisions concerned the Mumbai office: Leadership in the office would be solidified, reporting relationships would be clarified, and Monitor would try to shift the client mix from foreign multinationals that wanted to do business in India toward fast-growing Indian clients that aimed to expand within India and beyond. The office would also spawn a distinct unit that focused on social issues in India, issues that many of Monitor's Mumbai consultants felt passionate about.

Far more controversial was a sketchy proposal to make India a hub of business research conducted by Monitor for clients around the globe. Fuller and his team knew that India offered a vast, educated, ambitious workforce at relatively low wages. Advances in information technology and telecommunications made it conceivable that this workforce could tackle the research requests of managers anywhere in the world. The requestors of the research might be leaders of Monitor case teams, who might then need fewer case team members in Cambridge, London, Tokyo, New York, and Monitor's other 25 offices; managers within existing Monitor clients; or managers who had no prior relationship with Monitor.

Even as his team met, Fuller knew that others at Monitor, in the back-office operations of the Group, also had their eyes on India. Like most professional services firms, Monitor employed individuals to produce slide presentations, to develop and deploy information technology, to manage financial operations such as billing and reimbursement, and to serve as administrative assistants for Monitor executives. Currently, the activities of these individuals were centralized in the Cambridge headquarters or dispersed amongst Monitor's many offices. It was possible, however, that some of the activities might be done more effectively or efficiently out of a centre in India or another developing country. Fuller knew that the geographic array of the Group's activities – what it did where – might look very different in the future than it looked today.

Strategy consulting

Although Monitor had expanded into many professional services by 2004, the heart of the firm remained its strategy consulting practice, and any geographic shift would have to be based on a detailed understanding of strategy consulting. As an industry, strategy consulting was a small but lucrative slice of the management consulting sector, which booked revenue of more than $200 billion per year worldwide.[1] Major players in the industry included many of the most aggressive recruiters of MBA students at leading business schools: Bain, Booz Allen Hamilton, the Boston Consulting Group, and McKinsey, for example. The industry also included divisions of broader management consulting firms (e.g., the strategy and change practice area of IBM Global Services); midsized firms, many specialized by industry (Kurt Salomon in the retail sector) or geography (e.g., Roland Berger in Europe); and a host of small boutiques.

Buyers of strategy consulting services were typically chief executives, their direct reports, or general managers of divisions of multi-unit corporations. Senior consultants felt that different customers sought different things when engaging a consultant: strategic insight, information, advice, a fresh perspective, experience from other firms or industries, extra personnel in busy times, problem-solving techniques, credibility within the client, political protection inside a corporation, credibility with outsiders, connections to outside parties, a scape-

[1] Datamonitor, 'Global Management & Marketing Consultancy: Industry Profile', September 2007.

goat for unpleasant decisions, a coach, a friend, a referee for internal disagreements, the confidence to make tough choices, and so on.

The most relevant unit of a strategy consulting firm, in terms of operations and economics, was the client project team. Firms differed in their structures and approaches, but a typical team would consist of a partner – an experienced rainmaker who might spread his or her time across roughly three engagements; a project manager, most commonly an MBA graduate with three to seven years' experience; two associates with MBAs and one to four years' experience; and two undergraduate analysts. Firms varied in the prices they could command. At a leading firm, the project team described above would typically be billed out at $325 000 per month plus expenses. Exhibit 10.1 shows a rough estimate of the annual financial contribution of a typical project team.

Projects differed dramatically in their content and character. David Maister, a long-time observer of professional service firms, identified three generic types of projects (Exhibit 10.2).[2] 'Brains' projects addressed unique and extremely difficult problems (e.g., responding to an entrant with an effective, al-

together new way of doing business). Brains projects required the smartest and most creative personnel, were tailored to the client's circumstances, and offered little opportunity to leverage senior consultants with junior personnel. 'Grey Hair' projects involved problems that were familiar to experienced consultants even if they were new to the client (e.g., expanding to a new region for the first time). Whilst tailored to the client, such projects had predictable initial steps, some of which could be delegated to junior consultants. 'Procedure' projects involved familiar problems whose solutions could be programmed, with steps parsed out to junior staff (e.g., launching a new product in a mature market). A consulting firm, Maister argued, had to tailor its internal hierarchy, all of its human resource policies, and its expectations for profitability to the type of projects it pursued.

Primary activities

Though each project was different, strategy consultants undertook a common set of primary activities. The primary activities of a specific project team typically occurred at the client's site and in one or a few of a firm's offices, but firms were experimenting with new ways to array activities around the world.

Sales

Personal relationships played a central role in the selling process for a consulting engagement. Partners spent hours upon unbilled hours courting the executives of potential clients – getting to know the client company, understanding its business issues, and building rapport. Some projects were 'pushed', that is, pitched by a consultant who spotted a client need. Others were 'pulled' by an executive who wanted advice: The executive would reach out to consultants he or she knew, to consultants recommended by colleagues or friends, or to firms with strong, relevant reputations. This might lead to a 'beauty pageant', in which competing consulting firms made pitches for a project. Though success in beauty pageants was important for opening up relationships, repeat business from returning customers was far more lucrative.

Exhibit 10.1	Annual Contribution of a Typical Consulting Team	
Revenue per billed month		$325,000
Utilization rate		70%
Annual revenue		$2,730,000
Personnel costs		
One-third of a partner @ $750,000/yr		$250,000
One project manager @ $300,000/yr		$300,000
Two associates @ $180,000/yr		$360,000
Two analysts @ $85,000/yr		$170,000
Total		$1,080,000
Contribution		**$1,650,000**

Source: Casewriter estimates.
Note: Contribution should be interpreted as the revenue brought in by an incremental consulting team minus the direct costs incurred to add a team to an existing office of a firm.

[2] David H. Maister, *Managing the Professional Service Firm* (Free Press New York:, 1993).

Exhibit 10.2	Attributes of Types of Consulting Projects

Attribute	Brains Projects	Gray Hair Projects	Procedure Projects
Character of client problem	• Problem is at the forefront of professional knowledge	• General nature of problem is familiar to the experienced	• Detailed nature of problem is well-recognized
Sales pitch	• Expertise: "Hire us because we're smart"	• Experience: "Hire us because we have been through this before"	• Efficiency: "Hire us because we know how to do this effectively"
Possibility of programming steps	• Few procedures can be routinized	• Early tasks are known in advance, but later tasks are not	• Most steps are known in advance and can be programmed
Opportunity for leverage	• Limited opportunity for leverage from juniors	• Juniors can accomplish early tasks well	• Most steps can be delegated
Firm hierarchy	• Steep pyramid	• Intermediate pyramid	• Broad pyramid
Fees/employee	• High	• Intermediate	• Modest
Training	• Apprenticeship, up-or-out policy	• Formal classroom sessions	• Classroom sessions, manuals, tutorials
Marketing	• Books, speeches, activities to build reputations of individual partners	• Activities to build firm's reputation for experience in target problem areas	• Efforts to communicate low cost, speed, and reliability
Governance and structure	• Collegial partnership of peers	• Permanent associates, practice areas	• Disciplined management hierarchy
Client churn	• Shifting mix of clients with frontier problems	• Stable mix of relationship clients	• Core of high-volume repeat customers

Source: Adapted from David Maister, *Managing the Professional Service Firm* (New York: Free Press, 1993).

Project design

The design of a consulting project started during the sales process but ramped up after a client signed on. Sizing up a client's problem, imagining potential solutions, identifying analyses that might distinguish amongst solutions, breaking the analyses into discrete steps, assigning consultants and client personnel to steps – this required a combination of art and science, with Brains projects relying more on art and Procedure projects involving more science. The partner and project manager led the design effort, drawing on their years of experience. At the same time, they wrestled within the consulting firm to get great personnel assigned to their team. For complex efforts and longstanding clients, it was not unusual for a consulting firm to sell a client a separate 'design phase', during which a team figured out and proposed a structure for the main project.

Project execution

A vast diversity of activities might occur during the execution of a project. Common steps included customer interviews, market surveys, market-size estimations, macroeconomic analyses, analyses of industry structure, competitor analyses, internal interviews and surveys, relative cost analyses, marketing tests, product prototyping, supplier assessments, interviews with external experts, scenario analyses, financial modelling, brainstorming sessions, and so on. Associates and analysts, the junior members of the team, typically decided what raw information to obtain, collected the information, processed it, and began to interpret it.

At times in this step, teams would rely on outside vendors. A team member might pull competitor financial data from the Compustat database, for example; get data on the information technology industry from a Gartner report; or commission a firm such as Direct Opinions to execute a consumer survey that the team had designed. In large consulting firms, teams might also rely on internal specialists – for instance, a research librarian or an expert in survey design.

Advice delivery

After synthesizing the information they gathered, often jointly with clients, consultants delivered advice. This took place face-to-face with the client, publicly and privately. The public culmination of a project was often a presentation to senior client management, given by a project manager or partner who had been carefully briefed by the team, followed by a discussion. PowerPoint slides were the standard medium for these presentations, prepared either by dedicated personnel or by junior consultants who relied on templates.

Consultants sometimes compared these presentations to 'ancient Greek theatre', in which all the real action occurred offstage. Beforehand and privately, team members 'prewired' key managers – letting them know what would transpire at the meeting, anticipating resistance, and working to overcome concerns.

After-sales service

Few strategy consulting projects had a hard stop on a particular day. Clients continued to ask for input, and consultants took these opportunities to explore follow-on projects.

Support activities

A set of support activities made possible the primary activities of a strategy consulting firm. Some firms distributed their support activities across offices, whilst others centralized the activities in regional headquarters, global headquarters, or separate service centres.

Human resources

Consultants themselves were the critical input to the consulting process, and accordingly, strategy consulting firms invested deeply to attract, select, train, develop, and compensate effective consultants. Both MBA and undergraduate hires presented challenges. As fast-moving, ambitious individuals, they expected to advance rapidly. They selected consulting because they sought variety and were reluctant to repeat the same kind of study many times. Courted at school by private equity firms, hedge funds, and investment banks, many consultants expected high compensation.

Firms tackled these challenges in different ways. Small firms offered recruits personal attention and mentoring. Large firms set up extensive processes for feedback and professional development, diversified into other professional services in part so that personnel could experience variety without leaving the firm, and invested in training programs. Even in firms that emphasized training, however, most of the real training came on the job as consultants learned by doing.

Some firms maintained a strict up-or-out policy, requiring consultants to make junior partner within a set period of time (typically seven to nine years after their MBA training) or leave the firm. Such companies offered generous outplacement and cultivated alumni networks. Alums, after all, were potential future clients. At times, outplacement was necessary at lower levels of a firm; locally or globally, demand for a firm's services could shift suddenly, forcing a firm to layoff employees. Surges in demand, equally common, could leave a firm shorthanded, and it could be difficult to find talent quickly.

Knowledge creation and management

Developing and leveraging knowledge was crucial for strategy consulting firms. Firms often attracted clients by touting their superior knowledge of an issue or a problem-solving technique. This had become more challenging over time as clients had gained knowledge about business. (Between 1998 and 2003, for example, the portion of S&P-100 chief executives with MBA degrees rose from 26 per cent to 37 per cent.[3]) To stay ahead of clients, large firms invested in knowledge-development projects, encouraged consultants to publish in the popular business press, maintained ties with academia, and developed practice areas centered on industries, issues, or regions. Practice areas

---

[3] Justin Martin, 'The Global CEO', *Chief Executive*, January–February 2004, pp. 24–31.

allowed consultants with related experiences to share expertise and best practices. Clients, however, sometimes worried that practice areas within a consulting firm would be an avenue for competitors to learn about their latest advances.

Consulting firms had experimented over time with ways to capture and spread the hard data and soft knowledge generated in each project. The 1990s, for instance, had seen efforts to create extensive, searchable databases that collected knowledge after each engagement. These databases were largely ineffective as overstretched consultants moved onto their next project and did not contribute to the database. Moreover, it was unclear whether the truly valuable knowledge gained in a project could be codified and placed in a database. By the 2000s, some firms deployed individuals who swept in at the end of a project to spot and capture valuable knowledge. Most firms, however, coupled sparse databases of who-knows-what with cultural norms that obliged individuals to help one another when called upon.

Infrastructure

Behind the scenes at strategy consulting firms were individuals who collected receivables, processed expenses, and paid bills; produced PowerPoint slides; made travel arrangements for consultants on the go; and provided administrative assistance. A large and growing portion of infrastructure expense was dedicated to information technology. IT personnel maintained computers and networks, manned help desks, and developed software applications tailored to the firm.

The case study is continued at the end of Chapter 11.

Further Reading

Inside Careers (2008), *Management Consultancy – The Official Career Guide to the Profession*. London: Cambridge Market Intelligence Ltd

Kind, J. (2001), Finance and control issues. In, Sadler, P. (Ed) *Management Consultancy: A Handbook of Best Practice*. London: Kogan Page Ltd

Kirk, J. and Vasconcelos, A. (2003), Management consultancies and technology consultancies in a converging market: A knowledge management perspective. *Electronic Journal of Knowledge Management*. Available from http://www.ejkm.com/volume-1/volume1-issue1/issue1-art5.htm

Lawler, E.E. (2006), Business strategy: Creating the winning formula In Gallos. J.V. (Ed) *Organisational Development*. San Francisco: Wiley & Sons

Legge, K. (2005), Human resource management. In, Ackroyd, S., Batt, R., Thompson, P. and Tolbert, P.S. (Eds) *The Oxford Handbook of Work and Organization*. Oxford: Oxford University Press

McLarty, R. and Robinson, T. (1998), The practice of consultancy and a professional development strategy, *Leadership & Organization Development Journal*, 19(5), 256–263

Individual consultancy skills

The fourth part of the book concentrates on the individual consultant. This starts with a critical appraisal of research techniques in Chapter 11. The importance of knowing the philosophy behind research is detailed as many consultancy research projects cross the divide between quantitative and qualitative methodologies. Epistemological considerations and a general overview of critically using research techniques are given in this chapter to aid the would-be consultant become conversant with the different methodologies available.

Chapter 12 examines working in a team. This chapter investigates improving performance within a group and also different methods of team problem solving.

Chapter 13 then completes the individual consultancy skills section exploring how to communicate successfully orally and in writing consultancy reports. This chapter also examines personal effectiveness serving as an introduction to the next section detailing professional development.

CHAPTER 11

Research techniques

Learning Objectives

At the end of this chapter students will be able to:

- Understand why research is essential in consultancy

- Distinguish between the two main epistemological perspectives

- Be knowledgeable about quantitative research techniques

- Recognize the importance and limitations of using statistics to support a position

- Be knowledgeable about qualitative techniques of research and their limitations

Data quality

Making data fit for purpose

"Data denial – a failure to recognise the true state of data quality – is the principal cause of unreliable and unpredictable data."

Data only exists to support business applications. Whether for billing, customer management, financial reporting or any other purpose, each system will require views and attributes that may well be very different – such as a legal entity for the chart of accounts compared to the product divisional view for performance management; single product views for supply chain management or single customer views for CRM. Data quality can only be defined in the light of the purpose it is designed to satisfy. All data profiling, data cleansing and data matching activity needs to be driven by the ultimate purpose of the data.

This concept of fitness for purpose means that to understand data quality, you must understand not just what data you have but what you intend to do with it. For most businesses, data collected for one purpose, often ends up being used in many different ways. Consequently, data quality is a complicated and constantly evolving business problem.

Research Techniques

What are research techniques and why are they important

The opening Mini Case Study 11.1 demonstrates the importance of why research techniques are important in management consultancy. Organizations depend on reliable data and this not only drives the correct decisions being made but other aspects such as client satisfaction. Indeed, without the use of proper research methods, the data gathered is not reliable and thus incorrect decisions may be made. Thus, it is essential that consultants have an understanding of research techniques even if they do not carry out the research themselves.

Diagnosis and data collection

Stroh and Johnson (2006) argued that deciding on the form of the diagnosis and the data collection is the first step in using research methods in management consultancy. They advocate a Five Step model approach to diagnosis and data collection (see Table 11.1). Solving the clients' problems is the focus of the research method adopted rather than a debate on whether quantitative techniques are superior to qualitative techniques. In this manner, it is not uncommon for a consultancy project to adopt a mix methods design combining the best of the quantitative and qualitative techniques that are outlined below.

Epistemology

Epistemology is a branch of philosophy concerning itself with understanding knowledge and how it originates (Crotty, 1998). It informs the diagnostic and data collection process as by adopting a particular epistemological approach. The research is influenced by the approach taken, in how it comes to know and understand the concepts in the study. In essence there are two epistemological approaches consisting of the quantitative or empirical approach and the qualitative or phenomenological approach.

Table 11.1	
	Step 1. Identify the 'real' problem that the client wants to be solved.
Steps for diagnosis and data collection	Step 2. What data need to be collected to solve the problem above?
	Step 3. Where is the information that will solve the problem available?
	Step 4. What is the most appropriate manner to collect this information?
	Step 5. What conclusions will be able to be reached by the information collected?

Source: Adapted from Stroh and Johnson (2006)

Quantitative Approach

In the nineteenth century, Emile Durkheim wrote 'The Rules of Sociological Method', which presented the earliest empirical philosophical tradition in social research still popular today. This methodology borrowed heavily from research designs used in the natural sciences (Crotty, 1998). The fundamental basis of this was that information existed and could be considered as measurable things in a social world that followed law-like propositions, which could be revealed through appropriate scientific enquiry (Haralambos and Holborn, 2008). The principles of this approach were:

- Phenomena can be measured quantitatively as a concept
- Causal relationships between phenomena can be used to explain attitudes and behaviour
- Large samples are needed to obtain statistical generalization
- Knowledge can be generated by hypothesis testing on representative samples, testing pre-existing theory
- The researcher does not influence the people or objects being researched

This approach assumes that phenomena exist and can be measured quantifiably (Crotty, 1998). Knowledge is extracted through a process of hypothesis testing on existing or proposed theory. This information can then be generalized from a sample to a wider population as long as the sample is in some way representative. Research in this tradition generally seeks to quantify variables of interest with the quality of research assessed in terms of methodological rigour and statistical measures of reliability and validity (Field, 2009).

Quantitative methods used in consultancy

There are a number of different quantitative methods used in the social sciences. However, in management consultancy the following techniques are predominantly used: simulations, surveys, and quasi-experimental design.

Simulations

Business simulations are used in management consultancy for two purposes: modelling businesses and their operations; and enhancing human resources functions such as using simulations in training or for personnel selection.

Traditionally mathematical models were used in business modelling to find out the most appropriate solution to the problems set. With the advent of the computer, this type of simulation has increased in use (Harrison, Lin, Carroll and Carley, 2007). In essence, the computer uses algorithms and data based on real life events to simulate what could happen in reality. This can be applied to a variety of situations ranging from business processes as shown in Figure 11.1 through to simulating customers or pedestrians as in Mini Case Study 11.2.

In organizational studies and strategic management, computer simulations and models have been a major driver behind some of the most recent theories produced in this area (Davis, Eisenhardt and Bingham, 2007; Harrison *et al.*, 2007). Table 11.2 demonstrates how research questions can be answered through the use of simulations. Organizational outcomes, managerial behaviour and strategy can

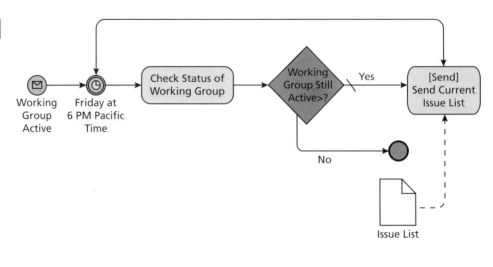

all be simulated with the modelling of the complex interaction simulated by the computer (Harrison *et al.*, 2007). Indeed, Davis *et al.* (2007) further concluded that simulations can offer a wealth of knowledge as the researcher can experiment with

---

Mini Case Study 11.2

Transport Strategies Research Group

Technical and management consultancy Babtie Group has joined forces with Transport for London (TfL) and the Department of Civil and Environmental Engineering at Imperial College, London, to research how a state-of-the-art transport simulation model can help pedestrian planning. Established by Paul Clifford FCIT FILT head of Babtie's Croydon-based transportation team, the three-way collaboration brings together a major transport authority, a renowned research department and an innovative consultancy.

A VISSIM highway model – for the major Stockwell Cross junction – has been supplied by TfL. The use of VISSIM micro-simulation to model pedestrian activity and progression delay will be assessed with research being undertaken by students of Imperial College, London, with advice being given by transport simulation experts from Babtie Group, Professor Michael Bell of Imperial College commented: 'We are delighted to be working with Babtie on this project, which covers the simulation of pedestrians and vehicles. We find this level of collaboration enriches the student experience and hope it also brings benefits to Babtie, We are increasingly introducing students to microscopic traffic simulation, as we see this is the only feasible way to analyze the complex interactions between the infrastructure and different road-user groups, particularly when the infrastructure itself is demand-responsive.

The introduction of pedestrians into microscopic traffic simulation – as has happened with VISSIM – was a significant advance, allowing the space simulated to be extended from roads into buildings.' Mike Tarrier of TfL Street Management said: 'One of the key objectives in the Mayor's transport strategy is to support local transport initiatives, including walking and cycling schemes. This project should enable us to understand better the interaction between pedestrians and traffic and their impact on each other,' (The Babtie Group has now merged with Jacobs Engineering Group Inc.)

Source: Courtesy of The Chartered Institute of Logistics & Transport (UK). Reproduced with permission.

Table 11.2   Steps for addressing research questions using simulation methods

Step	Activities	Rationale
1. Begin with a research question	• Determine a theoretically intriguing research question • Look for a basic tension like structure versus chaos, long versus short run	• Focuses efforts on a theoretically relevant issue for which simulation is especially effective
2. Identify simple theory	• Select simple theory that addresses the research question • Look for intertwined processes (e.g., competition and legitimation), nonlinearities, and longitudinal effects • Look for theory that requires data that are challenging to obtain	• Forms basis of computational representation by giving shape to theoretical logic, propositions, constructs, and assumptions • Focuses efforts on theoretical development for which simulation is especially effective
3. Choose a simulation approach	• Choose simulation approach that fits with research question, assumptions, and theoretical logic • If the research does not fit an approach or if the approach requires extensive modification, choose stochastic processes (that involve random variables)	• Ensures that the research uses an appropriate simulation approach given the research at hand
4. Create computational representation	• Operationalize theoretical constructs • Build computational algorithm that mirrors theoretical logic • Specify assumptions • Ensure that computational representation allows theoretically valuable experimentation	• Embodies theory in software • Provides construct validity • Improves internal validity by requiring precise constructs, logic, and assumptions • Sets the stage for theoretical contributions
5. Verify computational representation	• Replicate propositions of simple theory with simulation results • Conduct robustness checks of computational representation • If verification fails, correct theory and/or software coding	• Confirms accuracy and robustness of computational representation • Confirms internal validity of the theory
6. Experiment to build novel theory	• Create experimental design (e.g., vary construct values, unpack constructs, alter assumptions, add new features) based on likely theoretical contribution and realism	• Focuses experimentation on theory development • Builds new theory through exploration, elaboration, and extension of simple theory
7. Validate with empirical data	• Compare simulation results with empirical data	• Strengthens external validity of the theory

Source: Adapted from Davis *et al.,* (2007)

different and novel situations. Thus, the use of simulations can greatly improve our understanding of business and of business processes.

Simulations are also used in the human resources arena for recruitment and development purposes but are also useful as research techniques. For development, simulations can be used to inform individuals about business processes that they may never have considered in more conventional ways (see Industry snapshot 11.1). In recruitment, simulations constructed as assessment centre exercises are used to replicate the difficult aspects of the job that a person is applying for (Ballantyne and Povah, 2004; Woodruffe, 2007).

Assessment centre exercises can be divided into three categories that are dependent on the different ways that people work, i.e., in groups, in one to one situations and alone by themselves (see Figure 11.2). Innovative variations can also be developed from these exercises such as one participant negotiating with two role

Industry snapshot 11.1

'Learn or Burn'

Despite double-digit productivity gains and a 60 per cent decrease in costs generated by defective material, ABB Power Technologies wanted more. The Alamo, Tenn, power component manufacturer was keeping up with demands through lean manufacturing and Six Sigma programmes. The numbers were good, but ABB wanted to make sure its workforce was also good – able to know when, why and how to make changes on the factory floor that would benefit the company in the long run. After all, good numbers are only sustainable with a knowledgeable workforce.

ABB, along with its management consultancy, The Hayes Group, created 'Learn or Burn: Making The Right Business Decisions,' a one-day, workshop required of all employees. Working in teams of four, employees participate in a simulation in which they must run a manufacturing business for three years. They purchase materials, move products through production, pay for overhead, complete profit and loss statements and analyse financial ratios. The idea is that employees will be able to more clearly see the direct impact that their decisions have on an organization.

'It's everyone's responsibility to make decisions, not just management,' says Eduardo Miller, ABB manager and workshop co-instructor. 'If all of us are not learning to make the right decisions, we can burn the business.' The simulation is situated like a board game, with different sides representing the different components of manufacturing:

suppliers, production, finished goods and customers. Participants are able to watch the cash flow and the bottom line shift depending on their decisions. When they make mistakes, participants can go back and try different strategies or tactics.

Learn or Burn is based on Apples and Oranges, a business simulation solution developed by Swedish learning consultancy Celemi. Michael DiGiovanni, Celemi's US director, believes this type of business simulation is effective because it makes individual parts and pieces of an organization visible for employees who might otherwise only see the organization as a whole. He compares it to riding a bike. 'When you were a child learning how to ride a bike, no one explained or showed you the wheels, the chains or the handlebars,' he says. 'You got on the bike, and you fell, eventually truly learning through trial and error.' But with simulations like Learn or Burn, employees can zoom in on each component of the business and hopefully learn how to make the right decisions that will keep their organization successful for the long haul.

Miller says it is difficult to measure the effectiveness of participants' decisions after they have completed the workshop, but he believes the best proof of its success is increased employee morale, confidence and pride.

Source: Johnson, H. (2004) Learn or burn. *Training*; Vol. 41 Issue 4, p19–19. Nielsen Business Media, Inc. Reproduced with permission.

- Group
    - Non-assigned role group discussion
    - Assigned role group discussion

- 1 to 1
    - Internal (performance) interview
    - External (negotiation) interview
    - Fact find interview

- Alone
    - Analysis exercise
    - In basket
    - Scheduling exercise

Types of assessment
centre simulations

players in an interview simulation. Simulations can be used for research purposes by assessing the typical behaviours managers display when faced with a specific situation. Thus, they can be used to research managerial attitudes and behaviours, organizational culture, etc.

Surveys

By far the most common quantitative research method used in management consultancy is the survey. These can range greatly from examining employee job satisfaction through to examining poverty and the effects of international public policy (See Mini Case Study 11.3). The survey has an advantage over many other research techniques in that a lot of data can be generated in a relatively small amount of time. Nonetheless, it is essential to have an appropriately designed questionnaire to motivate participants to complete it (Oppenheim, 2000). Indeed, even if the research is asking many questions such as the questionnaire shown in Figure 11.3, breaking up the text, formatting the questionnaire appropriately all help to encourage individuals to complete the survey.

Thought Provoking point 11.1

A major difference between the management and specialist consultancies that I have worked for and students both at undergraduate and postgraduate level is that the consultancies spend a lot of time getting the look of a questionnaire right. This ranges from having the questionnaire shrunk down to A5 size through to having them printed on cards with the returned address on the reverse.

The first step in designing a survey is to ascertain what questions need to be asked. Oppenheim (2000) stated that 'too often' surveys are carried out with insufficient research design and in this regard you get the GIGO (garbage in, garbage out) effect, which is usually only apparent when the data collected in is analysed.

The aims of the survey must be specified along with the appropriate literature (Oppenheim, 2000). One advantage that students have over consultants without academic links is the ease of access to the appropriate literature. This is the reason why many consultants go back to complete their MBA, MSc and even (like myself over seven years whilst I was a consultant) their PhD.

Figure 11.3	

An example
questionnaire
(extract from Biggs,
2003)

WORKING LIFE QUESTIONNAIRE   **STRICTLY CONFIDENTIAL**

Please answer the following questions regarding your current permanent job or current temporary assignment

Please try to be as objective as you can in deciding how accurately each statement describes your job regardless of whether you like or dislike your job.

ALL REPLIES ARE STRICTLY
CONFIDENTIAL

1. Are you male or female? (Please cross relevant box)

    Male ☐   Female ☐

2. What is your presnet age?

    ☐ Years

3. How many hours on average do you work in a week?

    ☐ Hours

4. And is your job permanent or temporary?

    Permanent ☐   Temporary ☐

5. What is your current job title for the work you do?

    ☐

6. Which occupational level is this job (please cross relevant box)

    Semi-skilled ☐   Skilled ☐
    (e.g. lorry driver) (e.g. carpenter)

    Clerical ☐   Intermediate ☐
    (e.g. secretary) (e.g. teacher)

    Professional (e.g. architect) ☐

7. Which organisation are you currently working for? Or for which organisation Is your current temporary assignment based? (exclude employment agencies like Adecco)

    ☐

8. Is your job located in the South-East of England or In the Midiands?

    South-East ☐   Midiande ☐

9. What is your marital status?

    Sigle ☐   Married ☐
    Living with partner ☐
    Divorced / Widowed ☐

In the following questions a 7-point answer scale is used.

PLEASE CIRCLE THE MOST APPROPRIATE NUMBER

HOW ACCURATE ARE THE FOLLOWING STATEMENTS IN DESCRIBING YOUR JOB.
The numbers represent the following values.

1 Very inaccurate
2 Mostly inaccurate
3 Slightly inaccurate
4 Uncertain
5 Slightly accurate
6 Mostly accurate
7 Very accurate

10. The job requires a number of complex or high-level skills.

    1 2 3 4 5 6 7
    Very   Uncertain   Very
    inaccurate   accurate

11. The job requires a lot of co-operative work with other people.

    1 2 3 4 5 6 7
    Very   Uncertain   Very
    inaccurate   accurate

12. The job gives me considerable opportunity for independence and freedom in how I do the work.

    1 2 3 4 5 6 7
    Very   Uncertain   Very
    inaccurate   accurate

13. The job priovides me with the chance to completely finish the piece of work I begin.

    1 2 3 4 5 6 7
    Very   Uncertain   Very
    inaccurate   accurate

14. Just doing the work required by the job provides many chances to figure out how well I am doing.

    1 2 3 4 5 6 7
    Very   Uncertain   Very
    inaccurate   accurate

15. The job is one where a lot of people can be affected by how well the work is done.

    1 2 3 4 5 6 7
    Very   Uncertain   Very
    inaccurate   accurate

16. The job is quite simple and repetitive.

    1 2 3 4 5 6 7
    Very   Uncertain   Very
    inaccurate   accurate

17. The job can be done adequately by a person working alone- without talking or checking with other people.

    1 2 3 4 5 6 7
    Very   Uncertain   Very
    inaccurate   accurate

18. The job is arranged so that I do not have a chance to do and entire piece of work form beginning to end.

    1 2 3 4 5 6 7
    Very   Uncertain   Very
    inaccurate   accurate

19. The job itself is not very significant or important in the broader sense of things.

    1 2 3 4 5 6 7
    Very   Uncertain   Very
    inaccurate   accurate

20. The job denies me any chance to use my personal initiative or judgemnet in carrying out the work.

    1 2 3 4 5 6 7
    Very   Uncertain   Very
    inaccurate   accurate

21. The job itself provides very few clues about whether or not I am performing well.

    1 2 3 4 5 6 7
    Very   Uncertain   Very
    inaccurate   accurate

22. The organisation I work in supports employment agency workers in all job related and non-jop related matters.

    1 2 3 4 5 6 7
    Very   Uncertain   Very
    inaccurate   accurate

23. Some of the permanent staff are anti-employment agency workers.

    1 2 3 4 5 6 7
    Very   Uncertain   Very
    inaccurate   accurate

The following statements concern how satisfied you are with aspects of your job. Read each statement than circle the most appropriate answer depending on your level of satisfaction or dissatisfaction.

24. The amount of personal growth and development I get in this job.

    1 2 3 4 5 6 7
    Very   Uncertain   Very
    inaccurate   accurate

If the survey is still the most viable method of research, then the research questions must be clearly stated. The purists amongst researchers would argue that hypotheses need to be generated, but in an applied context that is not always practical. The population of individuals to be surveyed and any sampling then needs to be addressed. If any off-the-shelf questionnaires are to be used, then either carefully selected individual questions are used, or alternatively, if concepts such as job satisfaction or organizational citizenship behaviour are to be used then the reliability (the internal consistency of responses) and the validity (that the instrument measures what it says it is measuring) need to be checked for the measure (Field, 2009).

Wording of questions is also vital (Taylor-Powell, 1998). Use simple wording, not in a patronizing manner but in a manner that gets to what you are asking for quickly. In the same manner be specific using clear wording, e.g., don't say something like 'In which year was Kennedy shot?' Include all the information that you require comment on in the question. Avoid questions that are too long to answer or demanding on time. And above all reduce bias in questions, e.g., avoid questions such as 'How would you rate your car' with the responses superb, good or satisfactory. The lowest a person can rate their car is with the satisfactory statement, yet they may not like their car at all.

The survey is then adequately planned using project management skills (Oppenheim, 2000). Pilot studies are often useful even if they are just checking that people understand the instructions in the questionnaire. The field work then commences and then the data is collected. Once the data has been verified to ensure its quality, by ensuring features such as reliability and normality, the data can be analysed against the hypotheses previously generated. The results of this should then be presented in an understandable manner and inform the consultant's report. This is one of the attractions of using surveys as conclusions such as '86 per cent of staff felt supported by management' can be stated (Stroh and Johnson, 2006). However, there are obvious hidden dangers here, whereby statistics can just be presented with no explanation on how they were created. For instance,

Mini Case Study 11.3

ATOS Consulting with the Department for International Development (Winner of the 2008 MCA Prize for Best Public Sector Project)

Severe economic decline, poverty and social exclusion has been the lot of many Russian regions such as Leningrad Oblast, where, in 2002, 41 per cent of its population was classified as poor (the national average is 25 per cent). Leningrad Oblast covers an area larger than Scotland. Travelling to its far reaches can take up to five hours on poor roads in temperatures of $-45°C$. In its single-industry towns, pockets of even deeper poverty than in its agricultural areas existed. Not surprisingly, most young people have chosen to leave the Oblast. The UK Department for International Development (DFID) wanted to work with Leningrad Oblast to ensure that Russian economic growth translated into less poverty and a better quality of life for locals. Between 2003 and 2007, Atos Consulting led, on behalf of DFID, a consortium of 130 Russian and international consultants to deliver a £5m programme that would tackle Leningrad Oblast's complex and deep rooted problems.

The starting point was a comprehensive poverty tracking survey, the first of its kind in Russia. Those most at risk were found to be families with children

– not the elderly, as had previously been thought. Special policies were developed for the low-paid and families with children, and targeted at key areas of deprivation. Social-care services were rebuilt – thanks to new legislation on care standards – and a person-centred approach taken to care planning. The team created child-specific development plans for those suffering developmental problems. And to provide routes out of care, Atos consultants worked with institutions to develop systems for placing babies and children with their families or foster families.

Out in the private sector, the programme boosted local employment by fostering small and medium sized enterprises and improving their access to financing and support networks. Employment opportunities were increased amongst disadvantaged groups such as people with disabilities. In the voluntary sector, the programme encouraged innovation through a new grants scheme that funded 25 projects led by NGOs. The team helped Oblast and local government to strengthen its strategic planning, financial management, budgeting and performance

management. An unexpected upheaval in local administration increased the number of local-government units in the Oblast from 29 to 220. Atos responded to this urgent need for new skills with a range of measures, from one-to-one coaching to large-scale training events. The scheme has helped transform the lives of many socially excluded people living in institutions, enabling some to move into the community, and raising standards for the remainder. For example, at the Luga Baby Home, where infants taken into care stayed till they were 18, the team helped set up a system for new mothers that has halved the number of babies admitted. The private sector, voluntary bodies and local government work together to improve things for Oblast's disadvantaged. Now, more than 30 co-operatives provide financing to the poorest sections. Says Jim Butler, head of DFID Russia: 'This programme will not only help realize lasting benefits within Leningrad Oblast, but also be an excellent example for other regions.'

Source: http://www.mca.org.uk/sites/default/files/2008%20Management%20Winners.pdf. Reproduced with permission from MCA.

if it may only be 86 per cent of the staff that filled in the survey rather than 86 per cent of the total staff that felt supported by managers, in our previous example.

Quasi-experimental design

Quasi-experimental design is, in essence, an experiment but in an applied setting (Clark-Carter, 2004). In an experiment, the experimenter manipulates an aspect of a situation (the independent variable/s) and measures what are the assumed consequences of those manipulations (the dependent variables). Some authors state that it can be seen as a less rigorous method than an experiment; however, its advantage is that it has better ecological validity in that it is in an applied setting than a clinically based experiment (Clark-Carter, 2004).

An example of this may be seen in Mini Case Study 11.4 where a firm that produces pressure gauges wants to change the orientation of their business. Rather than changing the entirety of their business to produce quality gauges rather than quantity, the firm sets up a quasi-experimental design to assess the impact of going towards cellular manufacturing as opposed to a piece rate system for a small section of the workforce. In this manner, the client can ascertain whether or not cellular manufacturing works for their business. Indeed, the idea behind running a business based experiment is to ensure that it is accurate enough in terms of ecological validity to give meaningful results (Davenport, 2009).

Mini Case Study 11.4

Modifying behaviour in a Birmingham gauge manufacturer

The twenty-first century is a tough place for UK manufacturers. Faced with this challenge, a Birmingham gauge manufacturer used behaviour modification in combination with other techniques to motivate its staff to adopt a change in focus to a new quality orientated product range.

Previously, this company had concentrated on the lower end of the gauge manufacturing market where price was more critical than quality. Due to increasing foreign competition, the company decided to expand into more lucrative markets where the emphasis is on quality rather than price. I was contracted as an occupational psychologist along with engineering and management consultant colleagues to facilitate this change.

A small section of the 150 workforce was selected as a pilot group to produce the new product using past performance data and competency based interviews. The company had previously used piece rate payments to encourage productivity, but this had the expected effect of encouraging quantity rather than quality. In the pilot group, the piece rate system was replaced by team pay and quality incentives. The team focus was critical as teams, rather than individuals were involved in building the product from start to finish, and so the reward system emphasized team and task identity. Quality was weighted as being more important than quantity to ensure that products were right first time.

The potential for team conflict was a worry at the outset of this project given the switch from individually focused to team focused rewards with the potential for individuals to argue about perceived differences in performance and expected reward. However, such conflict did not manifest itself probably due to the detailed process of selecting team members.

The project was a success and the Managing Director, commenting that the project had been expensive to set up, saw the project as ensuring the longevity of the company by enabling it to exploit new quality and higher value markets. Today, the pilot group has been expanded to a further five project teams.

Reprinted from: Biggs D.M., (2004), Modifying behaviour in a Birmingham gauge manufacturer. *People and Organisations at Work*, Summer Edition, British Psychological Society, Leicester, ISSN 1746-4188

Qualitative Approach

The quantitative approach detailed above is problematic and has not been without criticism (Crotty, 1998). Alternative research approaches have thus been developed that basically reject the assumption that information is measurable and that data collected cannot be extracted and examined in isolation. The quantitative approach, through surveys for instance, takes a great effort in terms of the design used to explore the information available. Quantitative research also places a high value upon the objective, detached researcher, which is questionable. In response to these concerns, alternative philosophical approaches have been developed, which can be collectively termed 'phenomenological' to cover a number of viewpoints (Haralambos and Holborn, 2008).

> ### Thought Provoking point 11.2
>
> #### Student grades influenced by bias
>
> Experimenter bias or the observer-expectancy effect has dropped down many a grade for undergraduate and post-graduate degree students. For instance, one gifted student I supervised conducted an experiment between two communication methods and thought that one would be far superior to the other. Due to the findings showing the reverse, the student dismissed the results even though they uncovered some ground breaking issues. He therefore didn't put the effort into writing up a thorough discussion and thus through his own personal bias, his grade was reduced.

The qualitative or phenomenological approach states that research phenomena are rich in depth holding a construction of meanings specific to the investigation that is taking place and as such it cannot be explored just by pure quantitative analysis (Crotty, 1998). Consequently, knowledge gained from empirical research is flawed as it is detached from the rich explanations that individuals could give the data. Attitudes and behaviour are determined by their social setting and are 'socially constructed' and as such anyone investigating this should seek to understand and explain this in a localized manner (Biggs, 2003). In addition, sometimes the actual data that needs to be explored lends itself to conducting qualitative research, such as the example given in Thought Provoking point 11.3 below.

Nevertheless, many of the qualitative methods used by management consultants may actually span the quantitative–qualitative divide (Clark-Carter, 1998). Indeed, ground work, observation and interviews all have their quantitative equivalents. Nevertheless, the richness of context is often considered when using these techniques. Thus, they have been listed below whilst discussing more qualitative orientated research methods.

> ### Thought Provoking point 11.3
>
> #### Board room politics
>
> The Boards of many organizations work effectively driving the strategy and efficiency of the organization. When these Boards become uncooperative or dominated by clichés with their own separate agendas, these can be explored by using research techniques. However, given most Boards will consist of less than ten individuals, giving them a questionnaire may not be the most appropriate way of ascertaining sources of conflict within the Board. Indeed, qualitative interviews backed up with say observation and possibly psychometric measures of personality such as the MBTI, may be a far better way of exploring dysfunctional Boards.

Ground work

The first two steps for research put forward by Stroh and Johnson (2006) was the identification of the issues and then ascertaining what research needs to be carried out. Ground work is the process of exploring existing documents, reports, emails that the client may already have. It straddles the quantitative–qualitative divide as sometimes the methods used are quantitative as in content analysis, e.g., a consultant completing a review of the Zimbabwean perspective on AIDS may analyse newspaper reports the previous year revealing that there were 1020 articles that mentioned AIDS in Zimbabwe (Clark-Carter, 1998).

Alternatively, and more common in my experience, the ground work examines documentation, reports, etc and puts them in a context using the methods of narrative review or discourse analysis. Thus, in suggesting new ways in which to recruit people previous methods of selection and their reasoning may be highlighted as Industry snapshot 11.2 illustrates. However, often the consultancy report goes over and above what has gone on before and this also needs to be highlighted.

Industry snapshot 11.2

Extract from consultancy report

The following represents the typical illustration that ground work has been done in a report:

Much of the earlier work in recruiting for Residential Child Care Workers was concentrated on ensuring that inappropriate people were not employed following several national scandals. Whilst this is still an essential aspect of the recruitment process, it should not overpower selecting the best applicant for the role.

Most of the projects that have tackled the subject of recruiting for Residential Child Care Workers have thus far tended to opt for the Assessment Centre (AC) approach. This may be seen as the ultimate in recruitment techniques but has been seen as expensive due to the employment of assessors in the AC process.

The wider review that this report will be part of will examine carefully the studies of the past especially some of the international projects that have examined the area of recruitment. Nonetheless, these other studies do have their limitations in that the UK situation may be completely different to other areas of the world such as Australia.

Extract from: Biggs D.M. (2006) *Residential Child Care Workers: Job analysis, stakeholder analysis and selection techniques.* University of Gloucestershire

---

Observation

Observation is another technique that ranges between being quantitative in terms of structured observation through to qualitative in terms of participant observation or ethnography (McQueen and Knussen, 2006). Structured observation is when a checklist of events or behaviour that have taken place is devised and then used in a manner in which to quantify data. For instance, in working with a Birmingham based rubber manufacturer consultants may list how many machines broke down and the events that then followed in terms of getting the resident engineer to fix the machinery, etc.

Participant observation, or ethnography which is the qualitative side of observation, may actually be the initial basis of structured observation so as to generate a checklist of events (Clark-Carter, 1998). These events have to be recorded in an unstructured manner. Participant observation may be either overt or covert. Overt participant observation is when the client is told that consultants are coming in to observe working practices. This is by far the most common and ethical way in which to conduct observation studies. Industry snapshot 11.3 presents the abstract of a paper that in part used participant observation to engage with the masculine orientated culture of working as a bus driver. This is an interesting use of participant observation that really explored in depth why bus drivers underreported incidents of abuse and violence towards them by their customers.

Industry snapshot 11.3

Exploring the underreporting of customer anti-social behaviour (abstract)

This article explores bus drivers' underreporting of passengers' anti-social behaviour within the UK bus industry. Anti-social behaviour is a widespread phenomenon affecting a large proportion of the working population across many sectors and occupations. Although internal reporting systems can provide organizations with necessary information to tackle this problem, where employees regularly fail to report anti-social behaviour and where such underreporting is endemic, any effort to address the problem is likely to fail. Given this importance of reporting, an understanding of the factors affecting widespread underreporting is essential. Taking an interpretive, ethnographic approach, we explore bus drivers' accounts of the reasons for underreporting, as well as why bus drivers construct their interpretations in this way. In attempting to answer this question we found that underpinning participants' reasons for underreporting, was a dominant culture of masculinity. Introducing gender to the underreporting literature, we examine the construction of masculinity in the area of male dominated service work, a relatively under researched area. This article draws on data taken from multiple qualitative methods including semi-structured interviews, participant observation, observation and analysis of formal documentation.

Source: Bishop, Cassell & Hoel (2009) Human Relations. Reproduced with permission from SAGE.

Interviews

One of most popular methods of research in consultancy is the interview. (See Industry snapshot 11.4.) Interviews generally are set in two presentation modes either face-to-face or via the telephone. In all my years of research, face-to-face is a preferable medium of interviewing. Nevertheless, research wise there is often little difference between using the telephone versus face-to-face interviewing (Brummett, Maynard, Haney, Siegler and Barefoot, 2000).

The format of the interview sits on a bipolar scale between unstructured and structured as shown in Figure 11.4. In essence, structured interviews are like questionnaire items and have a series of limited responses. These are good to use when conducting large-scale interview studies (Clark-Carter, 1998). Nevertheless, often consultancy projects prefer to have some flexibility in deviating from questions. The greater the amount of freedom a set of interviews has, the more unstructured they become. Thus, with unstructured interviews a lot of information can be drawn out of them, but the consultant has to be careful not to deviate from the original research questions.

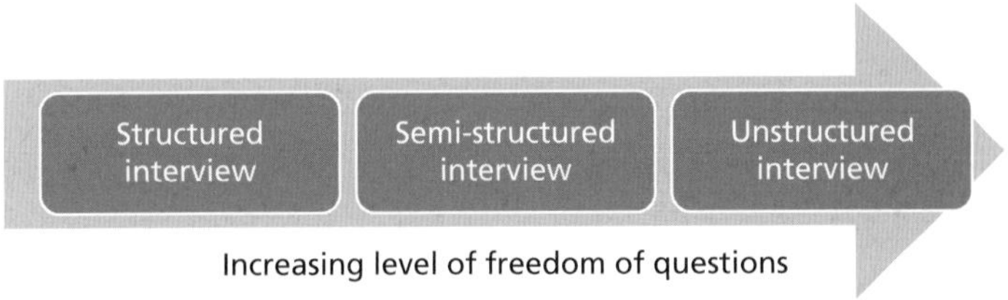

Figure 11.4

Format of the
interview

Industry snapshot 11.4

FSA sees shake-up in its crystal ball

The roles of advisers and life insurers are set for a shake-up, says a report for the FSA. KPMG management consultancy has published a report for the FSA on the future of UK retail distribution channels outlining 'plausible futures' for the retail scene from 2011 onwards.

The report, which was commissioned to help the FSA adapt to changes in the market, claims that the take-up of wrap has the potential to alter the financial services landscape and says it is likely there will be consolidation in the insurance sector.

The firm carried out its research between March and May, conducting interviews with over 40 intermediaries and product providers. Speaking at the FSA retail intermediaries' sector conference last week, FSA chief executive John Tiner stressed that the scenarios do not represent its predictions. He said: 'There is clearly greater scope for financial advice to reach consumers, particularly in a world where consumers continue to find financial products daunting, notwithstanding our work – and the work of others – to tackle financial capability.' 'This is increasingly pertinent in a world where the individual is increasingly being asked to take on more responsibility for their long term planning, including how to provide for their retirement, healthcare and dealing with debt.'

Source: J. Salmon (2006) © Money Marketing. Reproduced with permission.

Chapter Summary

- Consultants need to understand research techniques if they are to provide their client with reliable data and information

- Stroh and Johnson (2006) stated that there were five steps in the research process that identified: the issue, the data needed, where the data was, the most appropriate research technique and what conclusions would be reached

- Epistemology concerns itself with understanding knowledge and how it originates

- There are two epistemological approaches consisting of the quantitative and qualitative

- Consultants often used both epistemological approaches through mixed research methods on consultancy projects

- Business simulations are used to model data or to stimulate behaviours

- Surveys use carefully designed questionnaires and are useful in ascertaining data from large numbers of individuals

- Quasi-experimental design is arguably less rigorous than an experiment; however, it holds a higher level of ecological validity in that it can be more applied than an experiment
- Ground work is the process of exploring existing documents, minutes, reports, emails, etc.
- Observation ranges from being almost checklist driven through to much more qualitative as in the case of participant observation/ethnography
- Interviews are a popular method of research in consultancy and range from being structured to semi-structured to unstructured in nature

Review Questions

1. Why do organizations have to have reliable data about their operations?
2. What are the two primary philosophical stances in research?
3. What are the two main reasons that business modelling simulations are used in management consultancy?
4. What is quasi-experimental design and how does it differ from a standard experiment?

Assignment Questions

1. Discuss the notion that research in an applied context can either be quantitative or qualitative.
2. Describe two research methods and how each one of these research methods can be both qualitative and quantitative in nature.
3. Detail the advantages and disadvantages to a client of using quasi-experimental design.
4. Describe how the structure of an interview in a research context can alter the results obtained.

Case Study 11.1

Monitor's opportunities in India (B) continued from Chapter 10

By Juan Alcacer & Jan W. Rivkin

Business research

As developers of advice, strategy consultants conducted business research, but business research was also a separate industry. Monitor's Mark Fuller explained his interest in the industry:

Strategy consulting as it has been practiced in the past is a sunset industry. It has lots of structural problems. One problem is that it's nearly impos-

sible to grow revenue without a proportionate increase in costs. The economics of research are very different. You can create information one time and sell it again and again and again.

The continuous need of firms for accurate and timely information as input for decision-making fuelled the growth of the business research industry globally. Research firms, which collected and analyzed data for corporate clients, generated revenues of US$23.2 billion in 2004, an increase of 12 per cent from the previous year.[1] Over two-thirds of the revenues was generated in the five largest national markets: the United States, the United Kingdom, France, Germany, and Japan.

The wide range of informational needs of corporations – from traditional market data collection to specialized survey services – supported a diverse population of research firms. Firms differed along several dimensions. For example, some firms offered only 'primary research', collecting and analyzing original proprietary data; others focused on 'secondary research', analyzing data collected by others. With raw data widely available via the internet, some firms relied on knowing how to find and synthesize numerous data sources. Research firms also differed on whether they offered syndicated services, where a standard dataset or analysis was sold to numerous customers, or customized services, which were tailored to the specific informational needs of a particular client.

Syndicated research was provided under long-term contracts and often involved high upfront costs to set up information technology and to collect, analyze, and distribute data. Nielsen Media Research, for instance, deployed electronic meters and paper diaries in a sample of households in order to construct television ratings. For syndicated research, it was common to have one or two dominant players by data type. Under syndicated research agreements, clients received standard data and analysis periodically for an annual fee. This gave syndicated research firms a continuous and steady stream of income. The ability of a firm to sell its common product to more clients, by offering quality or uniqueness, was a key determinant of profitability for firms that offered syndicated research. The average margin amongst syndicated research firms was 15 per cent.[2]

Customized research involved lower upfront costs and was priced on a project-by-project basis, with price varying according to the need to collect primary data, the cost of specific secondary data, and the expected cost of labour involved in the project. As in consulting firms, the profitability of a given project was related to the firm's ability to predict the project's costs accurately. In most cases, clients asked research firms to bid for a project. Firms that offered customized research sought new clients or repeat projects within a client to provide a stable flow of income. The average margin amongst customized research firms was 9 per cent.[3]

A typical customized project started with identification of the data and analysis required by the client. With a clear idea of the scope of a project, the project manager assessed whether to use secondary data sources or to collect primary data, identified the analytical tools to be used, and estimated the amount of labour needed to complete the project. This information was used to set a price and a basic plan that served as a contract proposal. If the client accepted the proposal, the firm would perform the research, controlling the costs associated with the project as much as possible.

Besides deciding whether to use primary or secondary data and whether to offer syndicated or customized data, research firms could also specialize by focusing on specific industries (e.g., Gartner, Forrester Research, and IDC in information technology, and IMS Health in pharmaceuticals), a specific analysis technique (e.g., the Kantar Group in consumer polling and focus group analysis for brand management), or a specific region (e.g., Amadeus for financial research in Europe). In recent years, large global firms had acquired smaller, more specialized local research firms. As a result, firms such as Taylor Nelson Sofres (TNS) were able to provide services across industries, analysis techniques, and geographic markets.

Regardless of their size, research firms were labour intensive. In 2006, the average annual revenue per employee for American firms was $140 529.[4]

---

[1] ESOMAR World Research, 'Five Nations Lead Global Market Research Industry and a Strong Growth in Emerging Markets', September 17, 2007, http://www.esomar.org/index.php?mact=News,cntnt01,detail, 0&cntnt01articleid=110&cntnt01returnid=26.

[2] Theather and Greenwood, 'Taylor Nelson Sofres (TNS)', November 2005.

[3] Theather and Greenwood, 'Taylor Nelson Sofres (TNS)', November 2005.

[4] Bizminer, 'Marketing Research Profile for the Market Analysis, Business, and Economic Research Industry', July 2007.

Salaries, including benefits, represented approximately 45 per cent of total costs in the industry.[5] A typical research firm consisted of professional staff with various levels of analytical skills in charge of identifying data sources, defining measurements, and analyzing data; information technology personnel in charge of managing databases and secondary sources of information; and support personnel with technical and clerical skills. Some firms used specialized sales forces to cultivate clients. In the case of customized research, a project team might also adopt a sales role by identifying new information needs whilst working on an assignment. Sales forces might be geographically dispersed, close to clients, but overall, business research firms were more geographically centralized than strategy consulting firms.

The Monitor Group

From its roots in strategy consulting, Monitor had grown to become a family of professional service firms linked by ownership, personnel, personal relationships, and intellectual property. The Group organized itself around more than a dozen specialist business units with distinct management teams and missions (Exhibit 11.3). Some units, such as the Monitor Institute that advised non-profits, emerged from organic growth. Others, such as Monitor Global Business Network, which focused on scenario planning, were the result of acquisitions. Monitor's units fell into three categories:

- *Advisory services* included the core strategy consulting practice as well as a set of smaller units focused on marketing, pricing, planning, and economic development.
- *Capability-development units* trained executives, built clients' external networks, helped to design internal organizations, and developed custom software to support decision-making.
- *Capital services* advised clients on mergers, acquisitions, and corporate finance activities. An affiliated private equity fund, Monitor Clipper Partners, took direct stakes in companies.

Overall, the Monitor Group employed roughly 850 consultants in 29 offices around the world and booked revenue under half a billion dollars in 2004. A survey conducted by Vault, a publisher focused on career matters, listed Monitor as the fifth most prestigious consulting firm in the United States and the eighth most prestigious in Europe.[6] Monitor sought to distinguish itself from rivals by its unusual group structure, which it believed fostered entrepreneurship inside the firm; by its ties to business academia that dated back to a founding association with Harvard's Professor Michael Porter; and by its willingness to tailor career paths to individual interests. The firm prided itself on being a meritocracy. Compensation systems, for instance, were designed so that a first-year undergraduate consultant could earn more than an MBA hire if he or she contributed more client value than the MBA. Although Monitor served a wide range of clients, its portfolio was unusually strong in the life sciences, other areas of health care, and consumer goods. Historically, the firm had weighted its portfolio toward Brains projects and away from Procedure projects, though it had deployed tools such as Porter's Five Forces framework in efforts to standardize some parts of highly customized projects.

An Indian research company?

As Monitor and its clients emerged from the global economic slowdown of 2000–02, the firm's senior team turned its attention to growth. A June 2003 offsite on Cape Cod set a goal: to raise the Group's market capitalization to $1 billion. An ensuing Project Scale-up identified an array of opportunities for organic growth and acquisitions. A region of particular interest was India. Mark Fuller, Monitor's chairman, had long felt that there was a wide gap between the opportunities in India and Monitor's accomplishments there, and he took the lead to

[5] Bizminer, 'Industry Financial Analysis Profile for the Market Analysis, Business, and Economic Research Industry', July 2007.

[6] *Vault Guide to the Top 50 Management and Strategy Consulting Firms*, http://vault.com/nr/consulting_rankings/consulting_rankings-past.jsp?consulting2004=1&ch_id=252, and http://europe.vault.com/nr/consulting_rankings/euro-consulting-rankings.jsp?euroconsult2008=2&ch_id=252 accessed December 2007.

Exhibit 11.3   Business Units in the Monitor Group

Domain	Unit	Brief description
Advisory services	Monitor Action Company	Mainstream strategy consulting
	Monitor Global Business Network	Scenario planning
	Monitor Institute	Strategy development for non-profit, philanthropic, and social sector organizations
	Monitor M2C	Marketing strategies and marketing capability development
	Monitor Marketspace	Design and optimization of channel touchpoints, including digital marketing
Capability-building services	eMonitor	Workflow and learning tools for new capabilities
	Monitor Executive Development	Learning interventions
	Monitor Innovation Management Inc.	Innovation discipline and capabilities, focusing on technology and R&D strategy
	Monitor Lattice	Organization design and development
	Monitor Networks	Design and development of external business networks
	Monitor Software	Custom software development
Capital services	Monitor Clipper Partners	Affiliated private equity fund
	Monitor Ermgassen	Corporate development, mergers and acquisitions, and corporate finance
	Monitor MAST	Advisory services on strategic transactions such as alliances and acquisitions
	Monitor Ventures	Affiliated venture capital firm

Source: Company web site.

address the gap. A matter needing immediate attention was the existing consulting office in Mumbai. Fuller explained:

> We set up our first office in India in 1994. By 2003, it was a fine practice, but revenue was flat-lining at quite a modest level. Leadership changed constantly. In fact, one of our strongest Indian managers had left the office to found a fast-growing outsourcing company and a related investment firm. Lumped in with China and Southeast Asia in our organizational structure, Mumbai got little attention. Our highly talented Indian consultants deserved a better life.

In November 2003, Fuller enlisted Michael Wenban, an accomplished Monitor veteran based in Canada, to examine the situation in the Mumbai office and to report directly to Fuller.

To explore other opportunities in India, Fuller toured the country for two weeks in September 2004 with Harriett Edmonds, his chief of staff, and Neal Bhadkamkar, head of Monitor's venture capital affiliate. Speaking with local CEOs, government officials, and leaders of Indian business houses,[7] Fuller emerged from the tour struck by the vibrancy of the Indian economy and the wealth of skilled personnel available in the country. On November 15, 2004, Fuller convened in Cambridge with Wenban, Edmonds, Bhadkamkar, and Ralph Judah, then head of Monitor's innovation management business unit, to consider options. By this time, Fuller

[7] In India, a 'business house' is a diversified set of affiliated companies dominated by a family. The Tata Group, the Aditya Birla Group, and the Reliance Group are prominent examples of business houses.

had a strong hypothesis that Monitor should somehow tap into the opportunity to conduct business research in India: 'I want to couple Monitor's existing intellectual property with India's talent pool to produce research in a way that scales well.'

Options There were, however, many ways to tap this opportunity. One option was to outsource selected work to one of a handful of existing business research firms in India. OfficeTiger, for instance, had been founded in 2000 by Joseph Sigelman (HBS MBA 1997) and Randy Altschuler (HBS MBA 1998) to provide secretarial services to Wall Street firms, but it had quickly expanded to offer sophisticated financial analysis and other business research. Projects completed within an hour made up one-third of its assignments but a much smaller fraction of its total billed hours.[8] By early 2004, OfficeTiger employed 1200 individuals in Chennai, and its client list included at least one well-known strategy consulting firm. Revenues had reached $35 million in 2003 and were growing at 50–100 per cent per year.[9] By one estimate, nearly 200 similar firms had sprung up in India since 2000, but OfficeTiger was the largest.[10] Other prominent firms included Copal Partners, which specialized in research and financial analysis for Wall Street firms; Pipal Research, founded by former McKinsey consultants; and WNS, a 1996 spin-off from British Airways that had expanded from back-office operations for the travel industry and had recently begun to offer business research services.

An alternative approach was to found a Monitor business unit capable of conducting business research in India. This could be seeded by an acquisition or built from scratch. Whether acquired or grown, such a unit would face a key choice: Which customers would it target? The business unit might opt to serve Monitor case teams exclusively.

McKinsey, a key rival in strategy consulting, appeared to be taking this approach. Since 1998, the McKinsey Knowledge Center in Gurgaon had supported McKinsey case teams around the world. A Knowledge-on-Call service fulfilled information requests at short notice; a practice research group served specialty industry and functional practices; and an analytics group gave case teams access to sophisticated modelling techniques. In 2004, the staff of the McKinsey Knowledge Center numbered about 150.[11]

Alternatively, an Indian-based Monitor business unit might opt to serve external clients. These might be current clients of other Monitor business units or companies without a prior connection to Monitor. A host of other choices surrounded any Indian Research Center. What research products, customized or syndicated, would it offer, for instance, and how would it deliver its products?

The Indian context As Fuller and his team weighed options, they considered the attractions and challenges of doing business, and conducting research, in India. For many companies, the main draw of India was the presence of a large, educated, English-speaking workforce that commanded wages far below wages in the United States and Europe. (Exhibit 11.4 describes labour-market and other conditions in India and the United States.) The historical absence of a thriving and efficient labour market in India, some argued, made Indian employees willing to work longer and harder hours than their US or European counterparts. Amit Kumar, a Monitor consultant in Mumbai and a graduate of the prestigious Indian Institute of Technology, Delhi, explained:

> Each year, India produces approximately 100 000 MBAs. Roughly 10 000 of them have the business judgement to do high-end work. But the prestigious investment banks and consulting firms in the entire country hire only 800–1000 MBAs a year. I get 10 emails a week from classmates asking whether Monitor has a job opening. We get 80 applications for every offer we make.

[8] 'OfficeTiger: Tiger, Tiger, Burning Bright', *Business India Intelligence* (Economist Intelligence Unit), March 22, 2006.

[9] Joseph B. Lassiter, III and Johanna Blaxall, 'OfficeTiger', Harvard Business School case 804-109.

[10] Manjeet Kripalani, 'India's OfficeTiger: Hear It Roar', *Business-Week*, July 11, 2005.

[11] McKinsey and Company, http://www.mckinsey.com/locations/mckc/, accessed December 2007.

Exhibit 11.4   Conditions in India and the United States in 2004

	India	United States
Total gross national income ($ billions)	680	12 059
Gross national income per capita ($)	630	41 060
Number of new graduates per year		
Total undergraduates	2 500 000	1 417 000
Doctoral degrees conferred	18 000	49 000
Undergraduate engineers	365 000	65 000
Masters of Business Administration	100 000	81 000
Median annual wage, in dollars		
Undergraduate business researcher	6 000	65 000
Business researcher with a graduate degree	16 000	130 000
Computer programmer	6 600	63 000
Graphic designer	5 500	38 000
Accountant	4 000	51 000
Secretary	2 100	26 500
Nightshift premium	25-30% for designer or secretary; much higher for researchers	NA
Annual growth rate in wages in jobs listed above	10-20%	2-4%
Annual turnover amongst professional staff of business research firm	25-40%	Low
Period that a new hire is unproductive	1.5 months	NA
Headhunter fee for finding an employee	1-3 months of salary	NA
Rent per square foot		
Prime urban office space	$30	$50
Space in suburban office park	$8	$30

NOTE: Assumes exchange rate of 0.0217 dollars per rupee or 46 rupees per dollar.

Source: World Bank Development Indicators,' *The World Bank*, www.worldbank.org, accessed January 2008; National Center for Education Statistics, http://nces.ed.gov/fastfacts/display.asp?id=37, accessed January 2008; U.S. Bureau of Labor Statistics, www.bls.gov, accessed January 2008; Diana Farrell, Noshir Kaka, and Sascha Stürze, 'Ensuring India's offshoring future,' in *Offshoring: Understanding the Emerging Global Labor Market, McKinsey Global Institute*, ed. Diana Farrell (Boston, MA:Harvard Business School Press, 2006), 29, 33; Economist Intelligence Unit, *EIU Country Commerce: India*, November 2004, accessed January 2008; 'Annual Report 2006-2007,' *Department of Higher Education, Government of India*, http://www.education.nic.in/AR/AR0607-en.pdf, p. 101, accessed January 2008; Janaki Krishnan, 'BPO rush driving demand for 'built-to-suits' real estate,' *Business Standard*, September 12, 2004, p. 12, via Factiva, accessed January 2008; Peter Healy, 'Norwalk, Conn., has slightly higher office occupancy rate than Stamford,' *The Stamford Advocate*, November 9, 2004, via Factiva, accessed January 2008; Kevin Danehy, 'Midtown squeeze points to rebound for city's downtown office market,' *Real Estate Weekly*, November 17, 2004, Vol. 51, Issue 14, p. S1, via Factiva, accessed January 2008; 'Teaching the 'practitioner's art,' *Business Standard*, January 6, 2004; 'KPO salaries,' *Hindustan Times*, August 2, 2007, http://www.hindustantimes.com/StoryPage/Fullcoverage StoryPage.aspx?id=be02c05b-8100-45b3-90e9-6245ee2cd1ecCareerCall_Special&MatchID1=4660&TeamID1=5& TeamID2=2&MatchType1=2&SeriesID1=1172&PrimaryID=4660&Headline=KPO+salaries%3a+Some+case+studies+in+growth, accessed February 2008; 'All play, and yes, money,' *India Today*, January 4, 2008, http://indiatoday.digitaltoday.in/aspire/all-play-and-yes-money-3.html; Rayana Pandey, 'Company secys' pay skyrockets,' *Business Standard*, December 7, 2007, http://www.business-standard.com/search/storypage_new.php?leftnm=6&leftindx=6&subLeft=1&autono= 306801; casewriter estimates.

▶

Sceptics, on the other hand, argued that the attractions of India were outweighed by a number of factors: rising wages, high labour turnover, low labour productivity, high communication costs associated with time-zone and cultural differences, and a lack of business infrastructure. Reflecting on rising wages and labour turnover, Jaidev Murti, a recent MBA graduate from the Indian School of Business, commented:

> The top end of the job market is incredibly hot. People at the top of my class got four or five job offers each. Now, the best performers are getting headhunted. India is a country where everyone talks to everyone about everything, so people know how much others make and when others move. You almost ask yourself, 'I've been at one company for six months. Am I stagnating?' For a while, business process outsourcing – call centres and the like – were the hot thing. But now knowledge process outsourcing, where companies handle the knowledge needs of other firms, is growing quickly. Turnover there is between 25 per cent and 40 per cent a year. People sometimes leave a company because their annual salary increase is 'only' 20 per cent.

Sceptics also complained that, in the middle of the labour market, it was hard to find workers whose productivity and quality would meet Western standards. One Monitor manager with experience in India put it as follows:

> It's culturally different in India. There are dogs and trash in the streets, and in a typical office building, half the buttons in the elevator don't work. The infrastructure is improving, but traffic is an absolute disaster, and the power goes out often. In that kind of setting, it's hard to convince workers that German or American quality is crucial.

Another observer estimated that it might take four or five researchers in an Indian research firm to produce the output of three analysts or associates in a US or European consulting firm. It was unclear whether most Indian research firms conducted research carefully. Employees at a less careful firm might dig up an item via a quick internet search and present it as a validated fact.

Sceptics also argued that good business infrastructure was scarce in India. Rents in business districts like Mumbai's Nariman Point were approaching those in midtown Manhattan and the City of London, and many companies felt it necessary to maintain backup power sources to cope with short electrical outages that might hit several times a day.

Monitor's back-office

Whilst discussions about an Indian research company were underway, leaders of Monitor's back-office considered whether India might be an appropriate location for some of the functions that happened behind the scenes of a professional services firm.

Information resources Jim Pierce, Monitor's chief information officer, led the firm's Information Resources (IR) team. With 40 individuals dispersed in Cambridge, London, and Hong Kong, the IR team maintained the information technology infrastructure of the Group (personal computers, servers, and network), manned a help desk, and developed customized software applications such as a financial reporting system and a data warehouse. Pierce described his experience with India:

> Back in the early 1990s, before I joined Monitor, I worked for a company that made software for the back-offices of schools. We wanted to build a large team quickly, and we decided we could do that efficiently in Bangalore. The infrastructure was terrible back then, but we made it a success. It just takes a while to learn how to run offshore operations.

In 2003, Pierce realized that he lacked the programmer capacity to create all of the customized software applications that Monitor needed. To fill the gap, he turned to a company he had worked for many years earlier, an IT specialist with offices next door to Monitor's Cambridge headquarters. The IT specialist, in turn, used its programmers in India to develop the needed applications. Though this worked as a stopgap measure, Pierce said, 'we struggled with communication because they just didn't live in our world.' Moreover, Pierce knew that Monitor 'needed us to provide more capabilities whilst growing our expenses slower than the Group grew revenues.' He wondered if IR should set up its own operation in India for software development and other IT activities. Exhibit 11.5 shows some of the cost differences he might encounter between Cambridge and India.

Design Pierce also led Monitor's Design group, which prepared slides and other visual aids for consultants. The group consisted of 45 individuals: a central group in a Cambridge-based 'mother ship', plus one or two individuals in each of a subset of the other offices. Consultants and design personnel occasionally shifted work from one office to another to deal with local surges in demand and to take advantage of time-zone differences,

but in most cases, certain local resources became overworked whilst others sat idle because the shifts did not happen. In 2004, Pierce was reconsidering Design's arrangements.

Finance Similarly, Bob Samuelson, Monitor's chief financial officer, was assessing the company's financial operations. Currently, the operations included an accountant in each office and a significant group in Cambridge – altogether, 45–50 individuals. Office-level personnel fulfilled local reporting requirements, which differed from country to country. Cambridge-based personnel were divided across specific central functions: two people managed accounts receivable, a couple more handled the general ledger, a few others approved expense reimbursement requests, and so on.

Exhibit 11.5	Estimated Annual Expenses Associated with an Information Resources Facility		
		India	*United States*
Personnel expenses			
Salary, benefits, and taxes per IT professional			
Per senior IT professional (supervisory level)		$40 000	$150 000
Per junior computer programmer		$6 600	$63 000
Number of junior programmers per supervisor		5	10
Additional professionals needed to compensate for turnover and lower productivity		30%	NA
Expenses associated with security guard, office manager, and office boy		$15 000	NA
Rent			
Square feet per IT professional		80–120	120–150
Cost per square foot of suburban office space		$8	$30
Selected infrastructure costs			
Internet connection (T1 line for 10-50 people)		$18 000	$9 000
PCs, servers, and telephones per IT professional		$2 250	$1 500

NOTE: Assumes exchange rate of 0.0217 dollars per rupee or 46 rupees per dollar.

Source: Company and casewriter estimates.

Administrative assistance Spread across Monitor's offices were a set of roughly 120 administrative assistants who made travel arrangements, booked appointments, and so on. Some of these individuals had worked at Monitor for many years. With senior consultants persistently on the road and the average junior consultant staying at the firm for a little more than three years, administrative assistants were the human 'glue' of some offices.

Decisions

As Mark Fuller drove home on November 15, he reviewed the outcome of the brainstorming session. The group had reached a solid set of decisions about the Mumbai office, and Michael Wenban would follow up to implement them. Questions remained about if and how to tap India's research opportunities. Howie Rice, Monitor's chief operating officer, would follow up with an internal taskforce to weigh the options and return with a recommendation. The task force would tap the insight of internal constituencies and outside experts. Fuller had strong instincts about the options, but he wanted to hear from the task force before making a decision. Research was a core function in almost all of Monitor's business units. A change in where and how research was conducted would be taken seriously inside and outside the Group.

Further Reading

Crotty, M. (1998), *The Foundations of Social Research: Meaning and Perspective in the Research Process*. London: SAGE Publications Ltd

Davenport, T.H. (2009), How to design smart business experiments, *Harvard Business Review*, 87 (2), 68–76

Field, A. (2009), *Discovering Statistics Using SPSS*. London: SAGE Publications Ltd; Third edition

Jankowicz, D. (2004), *Business Research Projects*. London: Thomson Learning

Symon, G. and Cassell, C. (2004), *Essential Guide to Qualitative Methods in Organizational Research*. London: Sage Publications Ltd

CHAPTER 12

Working and problem solving in a team

Learning Objectives

At the end of this chapter students will be able to:

- Determine what a group is
- Understand the characteristics of a group
- Determine why people socially loaf
- Define what a team is and how it is different other groups
- Recognize and understand team conflict
- Be knowledgeable about functional and team roles
- Adopt problem solving techniques through team working

Poor employee relations and its effect on customer demand

Employee relations and worker conflicts are always problematic and the consequences difficult to predict (Fortado, 2001). Problematic relations can cause ill-feeling between colleagues, lowering job satisfaction (Biggs, Senior and Swailes, 2002) or causing stress and depression (Dormann and Zapf, 2002; Friedman, Tidd, Currall and Tsai, 2000). The case study below demonstrates how employee relations can impact service delivery and how this may be resolved.

This case study follows a Tool Manufacturer that was provided consultancy services as part of a large skills investment programme. In-depth organizational analysis was initially conducted comprising of qualitative interviews with senior management. From this consultation, process mapping was conducted to detail the main activities of the organization (see the figure below). The process mapping demonstrated how the customer and the organization interacted. The customer would initially approach the Tool Manufacturer through associated marketing or more typically on the basis of previous work completed. On the basis of customer requirements a preliminary drawing of the tool would be drafted and sent to the customer. The customer would then accept the draft drawing and then commission the creation of tool specified, which would then be manufactured accordingly.

Nevertheless, not all was well. Several projects had been delayed, resulting in a loss of revenue for the business. Worst of all, several tools had been manufactured to incorrect draft specifications, which then had to be scrapped and started again. All of these issues affected the bottom line so further qualitative research took place with both management and staff. This research revealed that individuals tended to see themselves working in a

vacuum or in a cliché as opposed to working within the wider organization. This had several consequences including worker conflict, interdepartmental conflict and poor employee relations.

An example of interdepartmental conflict can be demonstrated between the Drawing Department and the Machine Shop. Draft specification drawings rather than finalized drawings were given to the Machine Shop for them to produce the tool. This was done by the Drawing Department to give the Machine Shop notice that a particular tool had to be made. Nevertheless, the Machine Shop would spend time working on a drawing and would notice errors that would be sent back to the Drawing Department. In the meantime, the Drawing Department would send out a new draft of the drawing and as such typically ignore the work that the Machine Shop had completed. The Machine Shop did not always recognize that their work had been ignored and as such started work on an incorrect drawing. Furthermore, due to errors such as these the Machine Shop delayed

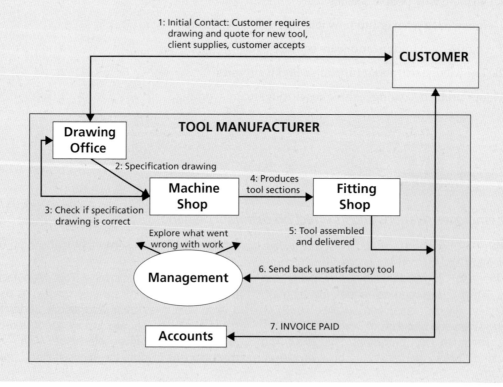

work on new drawings for as long as possible. However, in the Drawing Department this exacerbated the situation and as such they tended to produce earlier and earlier drafts to ensure that the Machine Shop was ready.

This conflict not only created internal problems reducing employee motivation and job satisfaction. The conflict had a wider implication that jeopardized the business as a whole. Customer orders were being delayed, orders were not being produced to the correct specification and some orders were of such inferior quality (due to their frequent reworking) that they broke down within weeks of being installed at the customer site. This led to a deterioration of the client's reputation of being a world-class tool manufacturer.

The solution

Recognizing the issues of poor employee relations and worker conflict was the first step in aiding the organization identifying what issues were involved in not meeting customer demand. Several solutions for resolving this were then put forward and adopted including: improving communication by adopting appropriate forums; training senior management to recognize and deal with conflict situations effectively; and teambuilding events to improve overall relations. The result of this action was very positive, with the organization:

- Retaining its competitive advantage by meeting customer deadlines and demands.
- Reducing the number of tools that had to be reworked or scrapped.
- Resolving many of the employee conflicts that had previously taken place.
- Improving management skills to resolve employee relations and hostility.

Source: http://www.top-consultant.com/articles/ Poor%20employee%20relations.pdf January 2009 Reproduced with permission.

Working and Problem Solving

The opening Mini Case Study, 12.1, demonstrates what may happen to a firm if individuals cannot work effectively and problem solve in a team. In this opening case study individuals were so busy either in conflict situations or trying to trip each other up that the business nearly collapsed as a result of this in-fighting. Indeed, my career as a management consultant and psychologist has revealed that this type of situation is all too common in organizations (see Figure 12.1).

This chapter examines the development of a team, working in a team environment, resolving any conflict within the team environment and then using the team to solve difficult issues. It should be read in conjunction with Chapter 14 that demonstrates that working successfully in a team is only one of eight essential competencies to master. However, like personal effectiveness in the next chapter, working in teams is essential for success and has a wealth of literature behind it so will be explored separately in this chapter.

Groups

Before proceeding with a definition of what a team is, it is useful to examine what comprises of a group. It is difficult to define what a group is but in essence when a number of individuals subscribe to agreed values, beliefs and objectives and there

Team work can prevent you falling flat on the ground (Image taken from a team building event with the technical staff of FCH, University of Gloucestershire)

is cohesiveness between these individuals then this can be described as a group (McKenna, 2006b). Johnson and Johnson (2009) define a group as follow:

> A group may be defined as a collection of individuals whose interactions are structured by a set of roles and norms. According to this definition, the individuals are not a group unless role definitions and norms structure their interactions.
>
> *(Johnson and Johnson, 2009; p. 7)*

Groups can be formal, where objectives are set by the members, or they can be informal such as a book club or other groups organized within a framework as the Thought Provoking point 12.1 demonstrates. McKenna (2006b) detailed the research in this area and defined the characteristics of a group as follows:

- Norms; these are common beliefs and social customs that guide and regulate the behaviour of individuals, e.g., promptness, courtesy, reciprocity, etc (Johnson and Johnson, 2009)
- Cohesiveness, is the level of agreement amongst individuals with regard to values, beliefs and objectives (McKenna, 2006b)
- Communication and interaction; groups need to effectively portray; ideas, accomplish task and support the social fabric of the group (Friga, 2009; Hargie, 2006)
- Structural factors; this includes how the group is structured and also the roles, status, composition, size and management of the group (McKenna, 2006b)

- Group dynamics; how the workings of the group have an emotional impact on the individuals' consideration of conformity, loyalty and feeling of belonging. Group dynamics is important to understanding how individuals behave in a collective manner *(Blanchard, Carew and Parisi-Carew, 1996)*

Thought Provoking point 12.1

Within the small town of Cheltenham, England, the University of the Third Age organizes a total of 88 separate groups that retired people can join. Thus, demonstrating the power of joining a group.

See http://www.cheltenhamu3a.org.uk/grouptab.htm for further details

Interestingly, not all researchers on groups agree with one another and two clear camps of thought emerge in the literature (Hogg and Vaughan, 2008). These are the individualists who claim that people in groups behave pretty much the same as they do on their own. The other perspective is the collectivist view that claims that a collection of individuals within a group will have their behaviour affected by the social dynamics within that environment (Hogg and Vaughan, 2008). This chapter concentrates on the collectivist perspective but does also consider the fact that in many groups and teams individuals do often work to their own agenda.

Groups and performance

Psychologists have been interested in groups and how they perform together from the earliest of studies. Triplett (1898) observed that cyclists peddled faster in a group than when they were on their own. He then repeated this using an experiment with children, whereby children reeled in a line slower than when competing in pairs. Allport (1920) termed the phrase social facilitation which was revived by Zajonc (1965) who looked at the performance of students. Zajonc (1965) concluded that a student should study alone, but take examinations in the presence of other students to achieve the best results. This drive theory determines what facilitates or inhibits performance (Hogg and Vaughan, 2008). In some regards, such as revision or individual based tasks, performance is better without a group present, whereas with other tasks, such as performing in exams, performance is better in a group (see Figure 12.2).

Later research discussed issues impacting upon social facilitation. For instance, in the presence of others, an individual may start to exhibit mediating behaviour, the outcome of which is social facilitation (Geen, 1991). Further research went beyond drive theory and detailed how individuals learn to co-operate (Hogg and Vaughan, 2008). The reverse of this is also true in that if individuals do not co-operate they learn about the social rewards and punishments.

Other theories important to mention in examining performance in groups include the social loafing effect. Social loafing is the reduction in individual effort when working with others compared with working alone (Hogg and Vaughan, 2008). In essence the individual exerts less effort when working with others (Lin

Figure 12.2

Zajonc's drive theory
of social facilitation
(adapted from Hogg
and Vaughan, 2008)

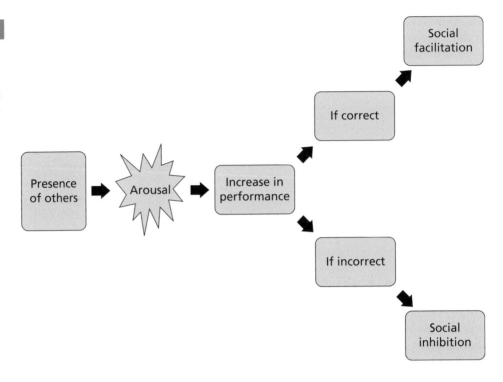

Zajonc's drive theory of social facilitation (adapted from Hogg and Vaughan, 2008)

and Huang, 2009). Social loafing can obviously hamper performance in a group. Geen (1991) suggested three reasons for social loafing and these are:

1. Output equity; individuals adjust their output to what they perceive to be the output of others
2. Evaluation apprehension; individuals adjust their performance if the task is seen as dull or uninteresting and can 'hide in the crowd' protecting their anonymity
3. Matching to standard; individual's loaf as they have no clear performance targets

Nevertheless, social loafing is not inevitable and can be reduced. Lin and Huang (2009) found that in a knowledge contribution setting social loafing can be reduced by increasing trust within the group and improving justice in terms of treating individuals comparably. Other studies show that individuals with personal involvement in the task, personal identifiability, competition with other groups and an expectation of poor performance with co-workers all lead to reductions in social loafing (Hogg and Vaughan, 2008).

Groups versus teams

Groups and teams are terms often used interchangeably in the literature and some maintain that it is difficult to know the difference between the two (Guzzo and Dickson, 1996). Nevertheless, although a team has the features described above for a group, it can also be described as a small number of individuals who have a developed sense of commitment, a common purpose, common performance goals and are accountable within the group (Adair, 1986; Guzzo and Dickson, 1996; McKenna, 2006b).

A team differs from the group as they have a common task and complementary contributions (Adair, 1986). Other differences between the team and the group are evident as shown in Table 12.1. Belbin (2000) argued that the word 'team' is taken from the sports analogy. Just as a cricket team work together with the captain as one unit then a 'team' in management operates the same way with all members of the team equally contributing to the overall success. Just like when England beat India at Cricket in 2007.

The appeal of teams over groups is fairly evident when examining Table 12.1. Fundamentally though, the belief is that a team will typically outperform individuals especially when the work involved requires multiple skills, judgement and experience (McKenna, 2006b). Belbin (2000) stated that teams are not brought together merely to engage in social relationships, teams are formed to perform work. The process of forming and enhancing the team is called team-building (McKenna, 2006b).

Teams	Groups	**Table 12.1**
Members recognize their interdependence and know that personal and team goals are successfully accomplished with mutual support	Members are individuals working independently grouped together for administration purposes	Differences between teams and groups
Little conflict in struggling for territory or personal gain at the expense of others	Conflict arises as individuals sometimes work at cross purposes with others	
Conflict recognized as a source of opportunity for new ideas and is quickly resolved	Conflict often left unresolved unless the supervisor recognizes it and intervenes	
Members feel ownership for their jobs and team because they are committed to the goals that they established	Members tend to focus on themselves and are not consulted in the establishment of the group's goals	
Members contribute by applying their unique talent to team objectives	Members are told what to do rather than asked for suggestions	
Members work in a climate of trust and freely express opinions and feelings	Members distrust others as they don't understand their role and personal goals	
Members work in an open and honest communicative environment	Members are cautious about what they say and may believe others are involved with game playing	
Personal development is encouraged as is the application of learning to the job	Members have limited opportunities in applying training directed only by the supervisor	
Members participate fully in decision-making concentrating on positive results rather than conformity	Members may or may not participate in decisions concentrating on conformity rather than positive results	

Source: Adapted from Maddux (1994); pp. 10–12

Teambuilding

Both individuals and organizations need to be concerned about the effective operations of a team. Teambuilding is concerned with this area and can be defined as the enhancement of the effectiveness of a team (McKenna, 2006b). The main concepts in teambuilding in terms of models of team development, team climate, high performance teams, management team development and team roles will be examined before leading on to solving problems in a team environment.

Models of team development

Tuckman (1965) was probably the first researcher to examine how teams develop. The model (see Figure 12.3) initially had four stages of development that were applicable to permanent teams; however, the fifth stage was added later applicable to temporary teams and is especially relevant to project teams (Tuckman and Jensen, 1977). The five stages of team development were as follows:

1. **Forming**: this is the foundation of the team's priorities, tasks and norms where the team is initially created and then sets out an agenda for action. Individuals then typically work on tasks set out for them, only reporting back to the team or being led by a supervisor.
2. **Storming**: this is where the team evaluates all the ideas generated and address the issues that the team is there to solve. The team works out any conflicts of interest in an open environment, although sometimes team members leave the team at this point. This stage is necessary for the team development in order that individual team members can put aside their conflict or personal agendas and work for the good of the whole team.
3. **Norming**: this is where individuals work with each other in a civilized manner by agreeing on acceptable behaviours, standards, outputs, etc.

Figure 12.3

Formation of a team (Tuckman and Jensen, 1977)

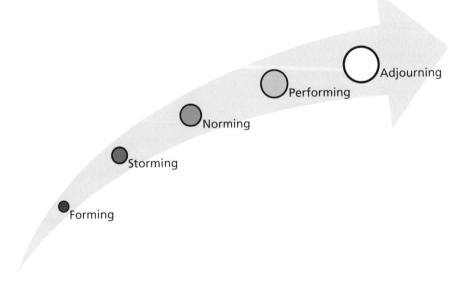

4. **Performing**: this is the stage where the team is competent and autonomous and is able to function well as a group getting the tasks complete with little conflict or need for supervision.

5. **Adjourning**: this was the last stage added to the team development stages whereby the team after completing what they have set out to complete, disband and celebrate a job well done.

Tuckman's model of team development is well cited in the literature; however, there are other models. Romanelli and Tushman (1994) examined team development in circumstances of organizational change, whereby after teams are formed there is much revolutionary action followed by periods of inertia where organizational demands tend to lead individuals back into roles they previously completed primarily due to resistance to change. Thus for teams to become effective periods of inertia need to be eradicated to stimulate fundamental organizational change (Romanelli and Tushman, 1994).

Indeed, Belbin (2000) stated that additional work may be required of a job-holder consisting of: grey work, which are activities that expand the core work of a job-holder and are considered useful; white work, which are new activities outside the range of work that are not expected by the manager; and finally pink work, which is work considered to be valueless 'but from which there is no escape' (Belbin, 2000, p. 114). Many teams as Romanelli and Tushman (1994) discussed fail to develop into high performing groups due to constraints put upon team members and additional 'pink' work that they have to complete.

Thought Provoking point 12.2

In a small specialist consultancy of no more than 12 consultants and about 7 support staff, they had approximately 22 projects ranging from revamping the IT systems through to developing on-line electronic versions of their products. All of the projects had started but none were really running primarily due to billable work taking precedence. By reducing the number of projects using a business case model, as proposed by PRINCE2, the projects most critical to the success of the business were identified. Autonomous project teams were then assigned to deliver the projects within agreed realistic timeframes. The project teams worked well on the projects assigned and when other paid work appeared the autonomy afforded them meant they could prioritize as necessary. As a result at least four projects were completed successfully within six months, that had for years just been considerations. This shows the importance of giving teams objectives and roles.

Team climate

Not surprisingly teams tend to flourish in an organizational context that is supportive of cooperatively functioning groups (Anderson and West, 1996; Beech and Crane, 1999; Ouwens, Hulscher, Akkermans, Hermens, Grol and Wollersheim, 2008). Parker (2006) suggests that for teams to be effective they need to have an informal working climate where the team members enjoy working. Michael West who has completed much research into organizational and team climate along with Neil Anderson stated that there were four aspects important in a team climate as follows:

1. Participative safety; how participative and psychologically safe team members feel in proposing ideas and solution
2. Support for innovation, relates to the actual support for novel ideas and innovation as opposed to the rhetoric of its support by senior management
3. Vision, is the degree to how clearly defined, shared and attainable is the team's objectives
4. Task orientation, is the commitment of the team to perform to the best of its ability

(Adapted from Anderson and West, 1996; p. 59)

Organizations that support these aspects within their own climate are much more likely to have high performing teams. In this regard, the adoption of human resource policies that concentrate on the development of individuals and their team participation should improve individual and organizational performance (Beech and Crane, 1999).

High performance teams

In the early to mid 1990s there was an emphasis on examining high performance teams such as the impressive Red Arrows (see Figure 12.4). McKenna (2006b) summarizes this research stating that higher performing teams have the following characteristics:

1. Abilities, skills and technical competence
2. Commitment to the teams goals

Figure 12.4

Formation flying of the Red Arrows
© Richard Cooke/ Alamy. AY1T53 Licenced

3. Team spirit or potency
4. Group based rewards
5. Group size not exceeding about 12 members
6. High mutual trust
7. Familiarity
8. Capacity to utilize external sources for the benefit of the team

Nevertheless, whether research into high performance teams can be related to normal working practice is debateable (Wilson, Burke, Priest, and Salas, 2005). Indeed, some authors (Robbins and Finley, 1998) have concentrated on why teams don't work as a way of tackling the obstacles that prevent teams from reaching their potential. A summary of these reasons is given in Table 12.2.

Problem	Symptom	Solution	Table 12.2
Allocating tasks and rewards on an individual basis	The team acts as a set of individuals as this is how they are rewarded	Focus on the combined effort of the team in allocating tasks and rewards and not on individuals	Why teams don't work
Failure to strike the right balance between using authority and democracy	Management can either be too dictatorial or not directive enough	Give the team its objectives and then leave the team to decide the most appropriate ways of managing	
Organizational structure doesn't allow teams	Organization left unchanged (apart from management rhetoric)	Critically appraise the organizational structure and change to one that allows 'teams'	
Lack of support for teams	Teams are left unsupported, not given the right resources or are given tasks that take them away from working on the teams objectives	Provide teams with adequate resources, training and rewards	
Individuals want to work as individuals not as team members	Individualist culture prevails	Provide training in team working and encourage people to work in teams	
Personality conflicts	Some team members may be in conflict	Learn what each party expects and use a forum to openly discuss difficulties	
Insufficient feedback	Performance is not measured or is measured only on an individual basis	Create performance measures providing the team with useful and valid measures	

Source: Adapted from McKenna (2006b) and Robbins and Finley (1998)

> **Thought Provoking point 12.3**
>
> Although for most the RAF Red Arrows consist of nine pilots, approximately 100 other people support the team consisting of managers, engineering technicians and other support staff.
> For more details on the Red Arrows go to http://www.raf.mod.uk/reds/

Team conflict

Conflict between workers within a team can be a huge issue for organizations and a difficult issue to manage. Indeed, conflict at work may even put employees in physical and psychological danger. Many books have been written on team conflict and how to resolve this phenomenon, which is beyond the scope of this book. Nevertheless, it is worth detailing one of the most useful models in conflict consisting of the Thomas-Kilmann Conflict Mode Instrument (TKI) which is reportedly the number one best selling instrument for conflict resolution. The TKI has five conflict-handling modes:

- Collaborating: finding a win-win solution
- Competing: where an individual wins with no regard to the gains of others
- Avoiding: procrastinate and delay
- Compromising: finding the middle ground where no-one really wins and no-one really loses
- Accommodating: where an individual loses but in order that other people gain

Conflict within a team should be on a collaborating basis, whereby the entire team seeks to have both parties 'win' in order that both have satisfactory outcomes. Confronting the issues that are creating the conflict in a controlled environment is by far the most successful way of dealing with conflict as the opening case study demonstrated. The TKI can help identify the ways in which individual team members handle conflict. Further training can also bring order to the team's conflict handling style towards collaboration.

Management team development

Teams have been promoted throughout the 1990s and well into the twenty-first century. Management team development has also been encouraged as an attempt by organizations to promote teams within their management. McKenna (2006b) asked that businesses who employ such a programme of change should ask:

- why is the development necessary
- can a suitable programme be devised
- who will the programme include
- should an external consultancy run the programme

In response to these questions, this chapter has shown why management team development is necessary as without some sort of intervention, people will act as individuals even though they may be called a 'team' through management rhetoric. A suitable programme can be devised either by using an in-house internal consultancy or by using an external consultancy like the one detailed in Mini Case Study 12.2.

Ballantyne and Povah (2004) argued that assessment centres used for recruitment can be used for management development centres (MDC). Nevertheless, Woodruffe (2007) suggested, the MDC can be divided into at least two different types as shown in Figure 12.5. One type is more diagnostic with an assessment programme first followed by developmental training that is then typically followed by assessment centre feedback. The alternative to this is that the MDC is geared towards behavioural change. In this instance, an assessment is carried out with the team, the team receive feedback on this exercise and then on the basis of this feedback carry on with further exercises that get progressively harder stimulating the behaviours that the development centre was designed to encourage within the management populations. These exercises can be intertwined with psychometric tests or specific training (e.g., conflict resolution, Belbin team roles, time management, etc).

Mini Case Study 12.2

Making an impact (SHL Group plc, 2004)

Working as a team can be difficult, especially when members of the team work in different locations and often on a part-time basis. Generating team spirit, trust and openness in these situations can be hard, but the dividends it pays are huge. Nikki Davey, who was working at the time as head of medicines management at Mid-Hampshire PCT, recognized this. Members of her team worked in different surgeries across the area and did not often have the chance meet up. The ten pharmacists in the team covered 11 GP surgeries, which at the time served 100,000 patients across the old PCT area. Working one or two days per week in any one surgery these pharmacists provided support to GPs in relation to prescription drugs. However, the part-time relationship with the GP surgery, combined with the dispersed nature of the team, meant that it was difficult for them to build effective networks and relationships within their work.

Nikki put team building very high on her priority list when she took up her post in early 2004. Having worked to create effective teams within other areas of the NHS, she was convinced of the benefits of investing in personal and team development.

'I'd worked with winning teams before, so I knew what was possible. My experience is that team development activities lead to much higher levels of confidence, more effective networking and information sharing which together lead to more effective performance from individuals and the team', Nikki commented.

She set about planning a three-day team-building event that would kick-start an ongoing development project. As an initial activity Nikki wanted to profile the members of the team and turned to SHL for the tools to do this. In the course of investigating possible products SHL's Team Impact Reports, based on the Occupational Personality Questionnaire (OPQ32), caught her eye. These easy-to-use reports are great for using with both individuals and teams.

'Most of my team had not had any personality profiling done before, so I was keen to introduce them to it as a way of providing a framework for the work that I was planning during the three days.' The OPQ can be taken online, which was perfect for the distributed team, all of whom were able to log-in and complete the assessment before the beginning of the three days. Individual and team profile reports were produced and Emma Engel, an HR professional and trained OPQ user, was asked to attend and provide feedback during the first part of this event.

▶

Emma facilitated this first stage and focused on getting the group to think about teams in general, covering some theory about how teams function. A practical ice-breaker was included to warm the team up: 'Slow Marble' challenged two teams to build a marble run using just paper and paper clips as well as giving Emma and Nikki the chance to observe the team in action.

Emma introduced The Team Impact Report with a discussion about the personality questionnaire and how the team had found completing it but then faced a choice:

'I had thought hard about how to structure this session. Should I give the individual reports out or discuss the group results first? In the end, I gave out the individual reports first, people were very keen to see these. This helped them to concentrate on the group results!'

On the whole, individuals could easily identify with the information presented in the reports and found it to be useful.

'People found the individual reports really easy to understand. The spider web diagrams and development tips were especially useful', commented Emma. Once people had a chance to absorb the information in their individual reports, Emma introduced the group report and facilitated a discussion around it. This included looking at the team's Tasks versus People focus and the team's overall strengths and development needs.

A team member led the next part of the session, encouraging people to share information about their individual team strengths and weaknesses. This was a significant step for a team that had previously had little interaction of this nature.

'One of the key benefits of the Team Impact Reports, was that they provided objective data that removed the emotions from often difficult conversations about individual strengths and weaknesses', Nikki commented. 'Many of the team members were not used to receiving personal feedback and so it was good to see them discussing these issues so honestly and openly.' Although no individual was obliged to share their own report, all the team members did so willingly. This in itself indicated progress on one of the areas identified as a weakness in the team – sharing information.

Other areas where the report helped identify development needs included exploring possibilities and networking. Whilst the team were creative and detail conscious within their usual terms of reference, they did not often go outside of these in search of solutions. Networking is a related issue. Many did not have close professional relationships with anyone in the surgery and felt that they must spend all of their time 'on task' and could not spend time talking to others in the surgery. Realizing that this was an essential part of becoming effective team players – and hearing that they were positively encouraged to chat over coffee with other staff, was an important outcome of the assessment.

The team then used all the insights gained from the reports to inform the other activities undertaken in the remaining days of the course. They have since requested that the next regular meeting be used to revisit some of the findings and themes from the Team Impact reports.

'I would like to find out a little more about the theory behind the Team Impact Reports and I would certainly use them again as they really added value to the session', said Emma. 'The information in the reports was great for stimulating discussion with the team. It also highlighted key areas for the team to focus on. Best of all, it gave people specific, structured action points to take away from the session.'

'Not only were the reports a very efficient way of gaining a snapshot of the individuals and the team as a whole, but they provided an important framework that I could use in the team development. The reports provided a level of data that removed the emotional element that can be very threatening in these situations. As such it has provided me with a stepping stone to further activities and a catalyst for change within the team,' concluded Nikki Davey.

Source: http://www.shl.com/SHL/en-int/Company/Clients/ Case_Studies/Case_Study_List/mid-hants- primary-care-trust. aspx. Reproduced with permission from SHL Group plc and Midhampshire Primary Care Trust.

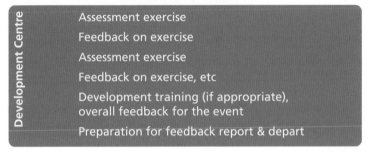

DIAGNOSTIC APPROACH

Assessment Centre	Development	Feedback
Assess behaviours against known competencies with assessment centre exercises	Provide development training to the delegates while their assessment is being completed	Give delegates feedback on their assessment centre results

COACH & DEVELOP

Development Centre

Assessment exercise

Feedback on exercise

Assessment exercise

Feedback on exercise, etc

Development training (if appropriate), overall feedback for the event

Preparation for feedback report & depart

Figure 12.5

The two types of development centre

Team roles

Alongside the encouragement that teams are the way forward for organizations surviving in the twenty-first century, the work of Meredith Belbin is frequently used by consultants exploring team roles at work. In essence, Belbin (2000) suggested that there were functional (tasks performed by individuals) and team roles. Belbin initially had eight team roles but then added a ninth role, 'the specialist' later on in his work. The nine team roles in terms of their characteristics are shown in Table 12.3. Teams that are likely to perform the best are the ones that have the right mix of both functional and team roles. The advantages of using Belbin's work are that there can be:

● Far less conflict and enhanced tolerance between team members

● Better appreciation and recognition between team members

● Greater contribution from individual team members

● Greatly reduced risk of mistakes being made

The team roles are a useful basis of defining team behaviour and useful for consultants to use when examining teams especially as the psychometric instrument used for assessing team type can be quickly completed and is available online (http://www.belbin.com). Nevertheless, the theory concentrates on individual team members and their assessment against the nine team roles. The team roles, whilst they do try to explore the interactions between team members and do give an indication of how the team dynamics may manifest, do not specifically examine team dynamics. This type of research is probably easier to investigate

| Table 12.3 | Belbin team roles |

Team role	Descriptors	Strengths	Allowed weaknesses
Completer-Finisher (CF)	Anxious, conscientious, introvert, self-controlled, self-disciplined, submissive and worrisome.	Painstaking, conscientious, searches out errors and omissions, delivers on time.	Inclined to worry unduly. Reluctant to delegate.
Implementer (IMP)	Conservative, controlled, disciplined, efficient, inflexible, methodical, sincere, stable and systematic.	Disciplined, reliable, conservative and efficient, turns ideas into practical actions.	Somewhat inflexible. Slow to respond to new possibilities.
Team Worker (TW)	Extrovert, likeable, loyal, stable, submissive, supportive, unassertive and uncompetitive.	Co-operative, mild, perceptive and diplomatic, listens, builds, averts friction, calms the waters.	Indecisive in crunch situations.
Specialist (SP)	Expert, defendant, not interested in others, serious, self-disciplined, efficient.	Single-minded, self-starting, dedicated; provides knowledge and skills in rare supply.	Contributes on a narrow front only. Dwells on technicalities.
Monitor Evaluator (ME)	Dependable, fair-minded, introvert, low drive, open to change, serious, stable and unambitious.	Sober, strategic and discerning, sees all options, judges accurately.	Lacks drive and ability to inspire others.
Co-ordinator (CO)	Dominant, trusting, extrovert, mature, positive, self-controlled, self-disciplined and stable.	Mature, confident, a good chairperson, clarifies goals, promotes decision-making, delegates well.	Can be seen as manipulative. Offloads personal work.
Plant (PL)	Dominant, imaginative, introvert, original, radical-minded, trustful and uninhibited.	Creative, unorthodox, solves difficult problems.	Too preoccupied to communicate effectively.
Shaper (SH)	Abrasive, anxious, arrogant, competitive, dominant, edgy, emotional, extrovert, impatient, impulsive, outgoing and self-confident.	Challenging, dynamic, thrives on pressure, has drive and courage to overcome obstacles.	Prone to provocation. Offends people's feelings.
Resource Investigator (RI)	Diplomatic, dominant, enthusiastic, extrovert, flexible, inquisitive, optimistic, persuasive, optimistic, persuasive, positive, relaxed, social and stable.	Extrovert, communicative, explores opportunities, develops contacts.	Over-optimistic. Loses interest after initial enthusiasm.

Source: The original source material was from Belbin (1993, p.22) and not from Aritzeta as in the book, this full reference is as follows: Belbin, M. (1993) A Reply to the Belbin Team-Role Self-Perception Inventory by Furnham, Steele and Pendleton. Journal of Occupational and Organizational Psychology 66, 259–60 cited by http://www.hull.ac.uk/hubs/downloads/memoranda/memorandum51.pdf. Reproduced with permission.

Figure 12.6

A poster showing the 6 thinking hats
Source : © Edward de Bono.
Reproduced with permission from the Book Six Thinking Hats first published in 1985.

using more phenomenological research due to the rich context of working relations (See Chapter 11 for more details). In addition, other research (e.g., Margerison and McCann, 1995) has specifically linked job functions with other team roles although less psychometrically valid data has been produced for other team role theories (McKenna, 2006b).

Problem solving in a team environment

This chapter has so far looked at the formation of teams and how they may be able to operate in a commercial setting. In Chapter 8, project teams were specially examined and project management is certainly one technique that teams can use to manage work. Nevertheless, there are other approaches to team problem solving that are worth a mention.

One of the earliest problem solving techniques was Edward De Bono's six thinking hats approach. This approach advocates looking at the problem from different perspectives visually represented by different hats, whereby white represents objective facts, red represents the emotional view, black represents a pessimistic outlook, yellow is optimistic, green is creative and blue is the overarching cool and controlling aspect of thinking (From the Book Six Thinking Hats by Edward de Bono, first published in 1985.).

Other problem solving strategies are more process driven such as the Productive Thinking Model (Hurson, 2007). The steps of which are:

● Step 1: Establish a context for the problems being addressed
● Step 2: Establish a vision for a future with the problem solved
● Step 3: Reframe the problem by turning it into a question
● Step 4: Brainstorm the questions producing many solutions
● Step 5: Choose the most appropriate solution by looking at it from different perspectives (similar to using De Bono's thinking hats)
● Step 6: Turn the solution into a project plan creating roles for different resources and implementing deadlines for action

Often these types of techniques are useful if there is a blockage in the problem solving process. So for instance, in organizational change situations, there are often a lot of emotions as people are likely to lose their jobs. Therefore by switching from the 'red' emotional hat to the 'white' objective hat may prove to be fruitful in generating solutions.

Another more recent team based problem solving technique was Friga (2009) who produced the TEAM-FOCUS model as shown in Figure 12.7. In essence, this model covers the interpersonal interactions of working in a team as follows:

● Talk: communicating clearly within and outside of the team
● Evaluate: assessment of the performance levels within the team
● Assist: individuals aid each other in pursuit of the team's goals
● Motivate: recognize contributions from the team and promote these driving the team forward

The model also examines the core analytical components of working in a team and defines these as follows:

● Frame: identify the key questions and issues for potential investigation
● Organize: teams arrange themselves around the key questions and split the work accordingly
● Collect: gather relevant data but avoiding collecting too much

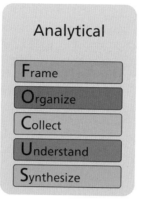

Figure 12.7

Friga's (2009) TEAM-FOCUS model

- Understand: as the data is gathered it should be examined in terms of its potential contribution in understanding the key issues under investigation
- Synthesize: this is when the data is put together in a narrative to give an account of what was found

Friga (2009) further suggested that teams that use the interpersonal interactions and the analytical components listed in this model are likely to be high performing. There are issues with the model that some of the more psychological based literature addresses such as what happens when someone does not pull their weight and are socially loafing (as detailed above). Nonetheless, the TEAM-FOCUS model serves as a good representation of how teams may effectively work together and solve issues. Mini Case Study 12.3 demonstrates how project teams were successfully utilized to improve the business using problem solving teams.

Mini Case Study 12.3

Training department generates ideas for survival

Rhapsody Computing (name changed) had created a training division from its primary service offering of ICT support and services on the basis of a business development grant. Nevertheless, the division was only funded for a period of two years. When this funding was over, the Managing Director (MD) was going to disband it. The training department was anxious that this closure was not going to happen and thus commissioned a number of internal projects.

The first and possibly most important project was to expand the amount of training courses that were offered. It was noted that mixing ICT training with relevant non-ICT training brought in significant revenues. An example of this was mixing Microsoft Project training (which involved the

creation of plans, Gantt charts, PERT charts, etc) with project management training. The course went from being held fairly infrequently to being very popular running every week or so with the additional project management element added to it.

The training division got together as a team with the help of the newly appointed Marketing and Sales Director. She motivated the team in creating more ICT and non-ICT courses by helping them to visualise what courses could be developed. Visualisations were made by drawing out what was offered already and then brainstorming a further set of training courses. Some of the new courses suggested were not taken up such as creating a multimedia application to help individuals learn new languages. Nevertheless, the brain storming stage did help the training department pull together as a team and work on improving its service offering. This then generated a whole new list of courses that was then marketed to the existing clients of the company.

Another project involved motivating the team. Many were disheartened by the fact that training seemed to be the lesser division in the company. This was tackled head on by not only reinvigorating the marketing of courses but by addressing the training teams concerns directly. One aspect of this was that the good performers felt as though there was no reward for a job well done and wanted part of their remuneration to include a performance element or even commission. This was implemented by the department who then rewarded good performance rated by feedback evaluation forms from the training courses. Discussions with those who brought in new clients were also held although it was considered that promotion opportunities within the company were better than

implementing a commission based system so the idea was not taken up.

The final project that the company did was to perform a statistically rigorous training evaluation of all training that took place in a selected month. This was funded by the company and involved the use of a questionnaire based survey to clients. The survey was very positive and revealed the business benefits of the various training courses that were running. This was a great opportunity to go to the MD with serious research findings to promote the department as having real business benefit not only as part of his original ICT support and services company but in its own right.

All of these projects worked saving the training division despite financial pressure to disband it. Indeed today, the training division still exists. The division still does its historic ICT training. Nonetheless, its training offering has expanded significantly to include courses ranging from interpersonal skills workshops through to PRINCE 2 project management training.

Chapter Summary

- Johnson and Johnson (2009) describe a group as a collection of individuals whose interactions are structured by a set of roles and norms
- McKenna (2006b) details the research in this area and defines the characteristics of a group as having to have norms, cohesiveness, communication and interaction, structure and group dynamics
- Hogg and Vaughan (2008) argue there are two camps of researchers on groups being the individualists and the collectivist
- Social facilitation theory is drive based and predicts when being with others enhances or inhibits performance
- Social loafing is the reduction in individual effort when working with others compared with working alone
- A team differs from the group as they have a common task and complementary contributions
- Teambuilding is concerned with the enhancement of the effectiveness of a team
- Tuckman's influential model of team development is forming, storming, norming, performing and adjourning
- Team climate is the condition within an organization that is supportive of cooperatively functioning groups
- Anderson and West (1996) describe four important aspects of team climate consisting of participative safety, support for innovation, vision and task orientation

- Conflict is dealt with in five ways in terms of collaborating, competing, avoiding, compromising and accommodating according to the Thomas-Kilmann Conflict Mode Instrument
- De Bono (1985) suggested there were six ways to look at a problem all visually represented by different hats
- The Productive Thinking Model (Hurson, 2007) is a process driven method of solving problems within a team
- Friga (2009) examined the interpersonal interactions and analytical components of working in a team with the TEAM-FOCUS model

Review Questions

1. What is the definition of a group and how is it different to a team?
2. What are the two camps of group research according to Hogg and Vaughan (2008)?
3. What do cyclists do when they are in a group compared to when they are out on the road on their own according to Triplett (1898)?
4. Define the term 'social loafing' and why it matters in a team environment.
5. Describe how a team differs from a group.
6. What are the five stages of Tuckman's model of team development?
7. Define the term, 'Team climate'.
8. What are the nine Belbin team roles?
9. What are the Edward De Bono's six thinking hats?
10. What are the elements of Friga's (2009) TEAM-FOCUS model?

Assignment Questions

1. Critically discuss the idea that groups are considered to have been an evolutionary adaptation to dealing with complex social systems.
2. According to Hogg and Vaughan (2008) not all researchers on groups agree with one another. Describe the two clear camps of thought that emerge in the literature and how they have influenced theories of teams.
3. Describe the concept of social facilitation theory and how it has developed since the 1920s.
4. What is team climate and how can organizations promote the functioning of teams using this concept.
5. Why is it that conflict within a team is not necessarily a bad thing.
6. Is a management development centre on the same continuum as an assessment centre? Critically discuss.
7. Critically examine how techniques such as Edward De Bono's six thinking hats or Hurson's (2007) Productive Thinking Model can help team based problem solving.

Case Study 12.1

TI Automotive (B): Building a global team

Be careful what you wish for! After leading a successful culture change in the North American HVAC group of TI Automotive in Michigan, Kuppler was named vice president and general manager for global HVAC operations.

Corporate culture would undoubtedly be an issue at the global level, if for no other reason than TI's HVAC group maintained facilities in eleven countries around the world. The scattering of the workforce around a wide geographic area and the influence of diverging national cultures would make Kuppler's efforts to improve the effectiveness and cohesion of HVAC's global operations more critical and more challenging.

The idea would be to extend the success of the change process that was initially rolled out in North America but to improve it based on employee feedback. First stop would be Europe, where the HVAC group operated in Spain, Italy, Germany and the Czech Republic. But would the same approach that brought an enhanced work environment and impressive financial performance also prevail in a European setting?

First Denison survey in Europe: 2004

Once employees in North America had seen their Denison results, it confirmed what they already knew deep down. With the insight and steady hand of the leadership team, they reformulated the way they worked together and, without great fanfare, decided the future would be different from the past.

So, one of the first moves undertaken in Europe was the administration of the Denison survey to get the pulse of the organizational culture. Although he

was managing this culture change from Michigan, Kuppler sensed that the strength of the European staff members was in their disciplined approach, respect for authority and dedication to following through on tasks. However, employees seemed sceptical of new initiatives and, therefore, less willing to candidly share their feelings and ideas. This group needed convincing that real change would come, no matter what they did or how much they talked. Kuppler's job this time was made more complex by the fact that five operating languages were in use at the European facilities. He had his work cut out for him but he had the strong support of the global HVAC leadership team he created with representatives from around the division.

The results in Europe were both different and more alarming than the initial survey feedback in North America in 2003. (*Refer to Exhibit 12.1 for the 2004 Denison survey results of European HVAC operations.*) Consistency, which was not so much of a problem for North America, turned out to be the weakest trait for Europe. The agreement index, within the Consistency trait, came in with a score of 17. The next lowest scores were noted in Capability Development and Empowerment. In general, there were many 'white spaces' on the Denison graphic, which meant that there were many opportunities for improvement.

What happened next?

The survey results were available in June 2004 and the first involvement meetings were scheduled for that same month. Once again, the agenda for the meeting included the presentation of the group's results and votes on establishing priorities for action plans. A vision and strategy for the European unit was discussed and clarified. The next meeting was scheduled for November 2004.

As in North America, Kuppler worked with his leadership team representatives to set up business teams throughout Europe. In all, 30 were established across the global business group by the time he was finished. Standard metrics and regular

Research Associate Colleen Lief prepared this case under the supervision of Professor Daniel Denison as a basis for class discussion rather than to illustrate either effective or ineffective handling of a business situation.

▶

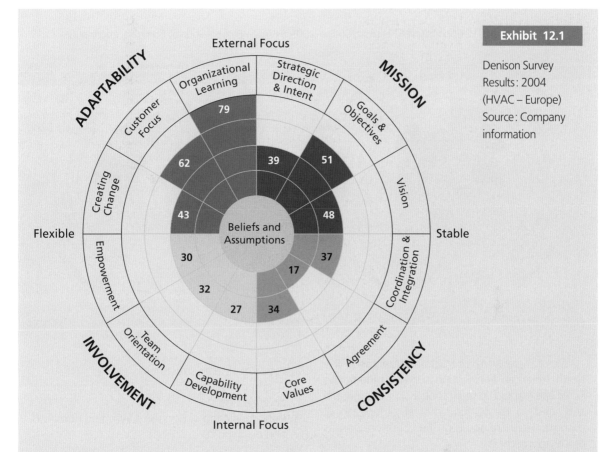

Exhibit 12.1

Denison Survey
Results: 2004
(HVAC – Europe)
Source: Company
information

progress reporting was required of the teams. Communication amongst teams was heightened through the use of the intranet. Kuppler noted:

> This was not a tightly planned effort from the start. It was more watching how things evolved over time and continuously obtaining employee feedback for improvement as we defined and updated our priorities. We learned what to emphasize as we went along. And we got a better appreciation for how culture touches everything.

Second Denison survey in Europe: 2005
After all the work on improving the work environment in HVAC Europe, everyone was curious to see the results from the next Denison survey in 2005. The changes were dramatic. (Refer to Exhibit 12.2 for a comparison of the 2004 to 2005 Denison survey results.) Much improvement was noted, with the results being better in every category. Whilst there was still much to be done, particularly in the three indices comprising Consistency – Core Values, Agreement, and Co-ordination & Integration, which were all in the second quartile – the leadership team had much to feel good about. As reflected in Exhibit 12.3, HVAC operations in Europe moved forward in a variety of ways. There were signs of progress in everything from financial performance against plan to new business wins to safety, quality and strategy advanced in the years since the first survey and the subsequent team building action agenda.

| **Exhibit 12.2** | Denison Survey Results: 2004 vs. 2005 (HVAC – Europe) Source: Company information |

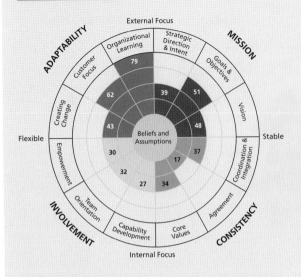 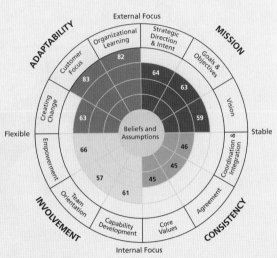

Whilst there were significant differences in the North American and European organizations, the European leadership team took a similar approach and tried to create fundamental organizational changes. Here are some of the common themes of the approach:

1. Initiation of team structures.
2. Alignment of vision, strategy, objectives, metrics and rewards.
3. Implementation of Denison survey and formal action planning.

Exhibit 12.3		*2002*	*2003–2006*
Improved Culture = Improved Results	Profit	● On plan	● 03–05: Beat profit plan
			● 06: NA restructuring
	Quality	● 37 PPM	● Single digit PPM
	New Business Wins	● 2 non-GM wins in prior 5 years	● Over 20 non-GM wins
	Globalization	● No Asia presence	● 4 programmes won in Asia
			● New plant established in China
	Global Leadership	● 8 leaders in 5 years	● 1 leader
	Global Coordination	● None	● Extensive global coordination

Source: Company information

| **Exhibit 12.4** | You are a Leader Global Leadership Training Programme Source: Company information |

Session 1

Common Sense Leadership

- Tim introduces the Ten Principles

The Denison Survey

- Principle 3: It's all about teams
- Principle 7: Never stop prioritizing
- Principle 9: Never stop learning

Personalysis

- Principle 8: Deal with your frustrations
- Principle 5: Maintain self-control & positive attitude
- Principle 10: Communicate & have fun

Communication

- Principle 4: Listen
- Principle 10: Communicate & have fun
- Principle 5: Maintain self-control & positive attitude

Session 3

Team Decisions

- Principle 2: Every member of our team is a leader
- Principle 3: It's all about teams
- Principle 6: Develop a shared vision: "We" instead of "I"
- Principle 9: Never stop learning

Session 2

Team Development

- Principle 2: Every member of our team is a leader
- Principle 3: It's all about teams
- Principle 6: Develop a shared vision: "We" instead of "I"

Conflict Resolution

- Principle 1: Honesty & integrity never compromised
- Principle 5: Maintain self-control & positive attitude
- Principle 4: Listen

Session 4

Roles

- Principle 2: Every member of our team is a leader
- Principle 6: Develop a shared vision: "We" instead of "I"

The Business

- Principle 1: Honesty & integrity never compromised
- Principle 2: Every member is a leader
- Principle 7: Never stop prioritizing
- Principle 9: Never stop learning

The Future!

The Group Project

"You are a Leader" Memory Map

4. Involvement meetings and business team meetings.
5. Establishment of extensive capability development processes.
6. Regular communication and team activities.

Some of the key components of this formula included:

- Extensive use of the Denison 360 degree performance appraisal instrument for senior managers.

- A commitment to regular development evaluations and training for all.
- Exchange programmes for employees of global HVAC work sites.
- Establishment of specific learning goals, behaviour changes and performance feedback at regular intervals.
- Institution of the 'You are a Leader' global leadership training programme, as illustrated in Exhibit 12.4.

Kuppler came to believe that the only way to survive as individuals and as a firm in the increasingly precarious auto industry was to strengthen the team. Rewarding success, developing individual capabilities, encouraging employee involvement, lining up behind one comprehensive and well-understood vision and regular follow-up and communication all led to substantial achievements and made TI a healthier, more enjoyable place to work.

What Comes Next?

After successes in culture change in North America and Europe, Kuppler went on to head the North America brake and fuel business and the North American HVAC group based in Michigan in 2007. He introduced his leadership and teamwork ideas to this work unit, as well. In mid-2008, following the ascension of a new CEO and implementation of a new global organizational structure, Kuppler left TI. But looking back on his efforts, he reflected:

> The most important factor in our success was the freedom given to me and our leadership team by my boss. He had confidence in me and my ideas. He trusted me to run the businesses the way I thought best. After reading literally hundreds of leadership and management books, I had ideas I wanted to try out. He gave me the opportunity to follow my instincts and knowledge. And, the results were satisfying – a more involved workforce and substantially improved performance when we initially managed the culture change.

Further Reading

Adair, J. (1986), *Effective Teambuilding*. Aldershot: Gower Publishing Ltd

Belbin, M. (2000), *Beyond the Team*. Oxford: Reed Elsevier plc

De Bono, E. (1985), *Six Thinking Hats*. USA: Key Porter Books Ltd

Friga, P.N. (2009), *The McKinsey Engagement: A Powerful Toolkit for More Efficient and Effective Team Problem Solving*. McGraw-Hill Professional

Johnson, D.W. and Johnson, F.P. (2009), *Joining Together: Group Theory and Group Skills*. London: Pearson Education EMA

CHAPTER 13

Personal effectiveness in consultancy

Learning Objectives

At the end of this chapter students will be able to:

- Recognize the importance of communication in consultancy
- Understand that communication exists at different levels
- Communicate effectively through speech, images and writing
- Recognize the professional skills of personal management

Mini Case Study 13.1

US investigates Taiwan arms error (BBC News, March 2008)

The US revealed that it had mistakenly sent four high-tech electrical fuses for the Minuteman intercontinental ballistic missile (ICBM) system to Taiwan instead of helicopter batteries due to a communications error discovered a year and a half after the erroneous shipment (Shanker, 2008). The Pentagon said that no nuclear materials were shipped and that the nose-cone fuses are commonly used for conventional munitions (Shanker, 2008). The fuses shipped trigger the nuclear warheads on Minuteman ICBM as they near their point of impact. Although the fuses themselves are not nuclear, the technology is a closely guarded secret in that the devices could be used to design or make nuclear arms and are thus carefully controlled (Shanker, 2008). The parts have now been returned to the US but the issue of arms sales by the US to Taiwan is sensitive as China still regards the island as a renegade province (BBC, 2008). Indeed, it has threatened to attack the island if they should declare independence (BBC, 2008). According to Shanker, (2008) Taiwan had pointed out the error but due to miscommunication the US remained unaware of the issue until almost two years later.

Source: BBC (2008) US investigates Taiwan arms error retrieved 3rd November 2009 from: http://news.bbc.co.uk/1/hi/world/americas/7313268.stmShanker, T (2008) U.S. Sent Missile Parts to Taiwan in Error. New York Times, retrieved 3rd November 2009 from http://www.nytimes.com/2008/03/26/world/asia/26military.html. Produced with permission.

Communication

Introduction

The case study that opens this chapter demonstrates how communication is essential and that mistakes that are made can result in international incidents. This chapter builds from the last two chapters in the Individual Consultancy Skills section and gives an indication of the skills needed by a consultant.

'Something we do everyday'

Each of us communicates everyday, whether by speech, in writing or even through art. Figure 13.1 demonstrates an artistic portrayal of a mermaid by John William Waterhouse. In this picture, what is the image trying to convey: is it simply a mermaid? Or has it wider representations of beauty? With art, the message is always in the perceptions of the viewer looking at the art.

In consultancy, the same perception applies especially in the art of communication (Mulligan and Barber, 2001). In essence, communication is via a medium either through speech, writing or art (see Figure 13.2). In Figure 13.2, the consultant needs to portray a message achieved by using a medium. This medium can be a single source, such as a project proposal, where the consultant communicates through the written text only. The medium may also involve a multitude of sources such as in face to face communication, where a number of sources are used to communicate, such as the vocabulary used, tonality, body language, regional accent, etc.

Figure 13.1

Mermaid by John William Waterhouse. Reproduced with permission from Royal Academy of Arts London.

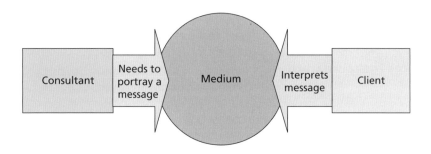

Figure 13.2

Communication in a consultancy context

Where there are multiple sources of information, they may not be given equal weight by the person receiving the communication. Thus, a distracting feature of a person's appearance may put off the person receiving the message that they are trying to convey. This may be a criticism about the industry in that it is all about impression management (Clark, 1995). Image also matters in effectively communicating a message across, thus a proposal should look good, as well as communicate the message across in an effective manner (Hargie, 2006).

Know thyself, know others

Personal knowledge is a great asset that enables one to communicate effectively. As part of a series launched by the Industrial Society, French (1993) argued that there were three steps in developing effective communication, these were:

● Have awareness of the way you communicate with others.
● Develop a broader repertoire of behavioural, communication, influencing and listening skills.
● Select the most appropriate response at the most appropriate time.

The fundamental start of this is self-knowledge. Everyone's personal characteristics, self-esteem, motives, emotions, disposition, etc, influence the way they communicate (Hargie, Saunders and Dickson, 1994). French (1993) argued that to be effective as a communicator, the first step was to take an objective and honest appraisal about the person wishing to improve their communication skills. From this, a person can then ascertain which are the distracting features of their communication. They can also ascertain which aspects can be changed developing a wider repertoire of skills. The Industry snapshot 13.1 is useful to undertake if students are interested in their communication style and understanding themselves. Understanding personality and emotions can also play a big part in developing effective communication.

Industry snapshot 13.1

Know thy communication style exercise

This exercise can be used for students to explore their communication style and provide them useful feedback. It is based on similar exercises used in 'Train the trainer' sessions, thus the advances made are quite spectacular with relatively little effort.

Apparatus

For this task, you will need a voice recording device such as a IPOD, MP3 player or a Dictaphone, which can record sound.

Exercise

1. Imagine that you want to introduce yourself to strangers in a room.

2. Spend say five minutes writing down the main points that you want to say.

3. Switch the recording device on and spend five minutes describing yourself using the points you previously wrote down.

4. After the recording, switch off the recording device and then just jot down your perceptions of how the recording went.

5. Listen to the recording, and take a note on how different the recording was to your perception.

6. Repeat this task, until you are happy that your communication has improved.

Further work

This exercise can be repeated by citing lecture notes, etc. The most salient point is to record your voice to give yourself feedback on your own communication style. Those with more advanced recording devices may even want to use a video camera to record themselves. This is good when analysing non-verbal behaviour as well as what is said. One way to really highlight distractions in communication style, and often completed in train the trainer sessions, is to speed up the camera footage, and distracting features such as scratching noses, etc, become more pronounced and as such provides useful feedback.

Emotional Intelligence

Aristotle was perhaps the first to mention the importance of emotions in human interaction. Aristotle stated that those who possess the skill, 'to be angry with the right person, to the right degree, at the right time, for the right purpose, and in the right way' would be at an advantage in life, (Langley, 2000). In 1927, Thorndike defined three different types of intelligence. The first type of intelligence was cognitive ability, understanding and manipulating verbal and mathematical concepts. The second type of intelligence was concrete intelligence, understanding and manipulating objects and shapes. The third type was social intelligence, which according to Thorndike is the ability to relate to people (Johnson and Indvik, 1999).

Social intelligence as defined by Thorndike in the 1920s is similar to the concept of emotional intelligence (EI). However, the actual term of EI was not defined until Salovey and Mayer (1989) who defined it as 'a set of skills hypothesized to contribute to the accurate appraisal and expression of emotion' (Salovey and Mayer, 1989; p. 185). Rapid expansion in the area can then be largely attributed to the work of Goleman and his book on EI published in 1996. He further defined EI as 'The capacity for recognizing our own feelings and those of others, for motivating ourselves, and for managing emotions well in ourselves and in our relationships' Goleman (1998, p. 317). EI can thus be considered to be an array of skills, capabilities and competencies that influence a person's ability to cope with the external world (Martinez-Prons, 1997).

The interest in the development of EI stems from the apparent lack of other measures such as IQ testing to successfully predict those who will succeed in life (Dulewicz and Higgs, 2000; Fineman, 2003). Indeed, Bahn (1979) identified that managers or executives with the highest IQ did not necessarily have the highest status within the company. This would identify that although IQ may be required to attain effective performance, it may not be the critical factor in predicting success (Dulewicz and Higgs, 2000). It is evident that the major driver of interest in EI has been the limitation of IQ testing and other conventional methods to account for sufficient variance in success criteria both in an educational and organizational context (Dulewicz and Higgs, 2000). The popularity of EI in the workplace has undoubtedly been due to the nature of the workplace environment and the constant search by organizations to find and sustain a competitive advantage through its workforce (Tischler, Biberman and McKeage, 2002).

Figure 13.3 demonstrates a popular model of EI. In essence, EI can be split between intrapersonal and interpersonal intelligence. Intrapersonal intelligence is being able to assess what is going on inside us and doing what we need to do about it (JCA, 2007). Interpersonal intelligence is being able to assess what is going on with other people and between people and doing what is needed. Both intrapersonal and interpersonal intelligence then have an awareness, management and self-regard aspect. With intrapersonal intelligence, these aspects manifest themselves as self-awareness and then self-management. Self-awareness is crucial in intrapersonal intelligence and those with little self-awareness may not necessarily know that they are not self-aware (JCA, 2007). With interpersonal intelligence, these aspects are awareness of others, managing the relationships with them and having a regard for others.

The most effective way in which to assess a person's emotional intelligence is to use instruments such as the Individual Effectiveness (IE) questionnaire devised by JCA Ltd (Maddocks and Sparrow, 2003). Nevertheless, being aware of your own feelings, managing your own feelings in an effective manner and also applying this to others can bring great benefits not only in communication but also in life in general (JCA, 2007).

Understanding the emotions of others is also important. French (1993) stated that there were seven key points in understanding others, being:

1. Avoid making your mind up about someone soon after meeting them.
2. Actively listen (covered in the section below) and show interest in what the person is saying.
3. Avoid stereotyping people based on their regional accent, race, age or sex.
4. Be aware that the situation people are in may make them behave differently than normal.

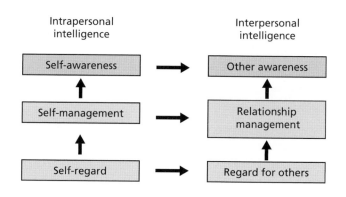

Figure 13.3

Emotional intelligence (reprinted courtesy of JCA Ltd, 2007)

5. Avoid looking favourably towards someone just because they come from the same hometown, school, college, university, etc.

6. Try to be equally influenced by the positive and negative things that people say.

7. Judge others after the conversation has finished taking in all of what they said rather than the first or last part of the communication.

Industry snapshot 13.2

Watching TV exercise

This exercise can be used to explore inherent stereotypes and judgements we make in everyday communication.

Apparatus

For this task, you will need just access to a television and a paper pad to write down your notes.

Exercise

1. Turn the sound off on your television set and turn to a channel you don't often watch.

2. Spend two minutes watching someone on that channel (e.g., soap star, a news reader, etc).

3. Note how you perceive the person on television and what are the distinguishing features you note.

4. Turn on the sound of the television and watch the same person.

5. Note if you notice any other distinguishing remarks, etc, with the sound on.

6. Note your perceptions of the person that you have viewed and think about any biases that have cropped up in your judgements.

Further work

This exercise can be repeated by watching people in the real world on a train, bus, or in a café, etc. It is interesting to observe your own judgements about other people and whether they are based on factual data or preconceived ideas and biases.

Listening

An essential ingredient for success in consultancy is listening (Holtz and Zahn, 2004). For communication to occur there must be both the sending and receiving of information through a medium which for listening is the spoken word (Hargie, 2006). There is a notable difference between hearing and listening. Hearing tends to be the physical process; however, listening can be defined as the 'learned human process of sensing, interpreting, evaluating storing and responding to oral messages' (Steil, 1991, p. 203). Listening is thus a cognitive activity rather than a physical one.

Thought Provoking point 13.1

When I was a new management consultant, my manager said to me that when discussing work with clients, I have two ears and one mouth. So I should listen twice as much as I talk.

	Level	Example
−1	Unaware	I do not notice you.
0	Avoiding	I am aware you want to tell me something but I do not want to listen.
1	"No, you are. . .	. . .wrong."
2	"You shouldn't feel that way. . .	You should not be upset."
3	"Let me tell you. . .	. . .how it really is."
4	"Tell me more.	Help me understand."
5	"What I hear you saying (and feeling) is. . .	. . .you are angry because I do not acknowledge your work."

Psychologists tend to distinguish between active and passive listening based on the amount of information that comes through to a person through communication at any one point (Hargie, 2006). In essence, human beings tend to be selective in what we hear. This is due not only to the wealth of information available to the individual at any one point, but also due to the fact that listening is a cognitive task requiring effort. Figure 13.4 demonstrates how individuals listen at different levels. (This model is used as part of a larger training approach, The Human Element, and for more information on this please visit www.bconnetwork.com.)

Levels 1 to 3 represent passive listening where the listener is not actively engaging in communication and is being talked at but not really responding in an effective manner. Level 4 represents the first stage of active listening where the person is engaging with the communicator asking for additional details. Level 5 is a further stage where the listener is not only actively engaged emotionally and cognitively but also responds back to the person talking clarifying what they are trying to say. This is really the level of communication that should be strived for when in dialogue with colleagues and clients alike. Many a potential consultancy project has been thwarted by not actively listening to what the person is trying to communicate.

Good listening therefore requires an ability to: concentrate on what the other person is saying; ascertain the actual message being conveyed; encourage open and honest expression; and understand and respond to the persons emotional state. French (1993) defined ten ways to improve listening skills, which are relevant here and comprise:

1. Maintain good eye contact.
2. Lean toward the speaker slightly when they talk.
3. Try and stay relaxed.
4. Try and keep an open mind about what is being said, especially if you disagree with the point of view being portrayed.
5. Don't interrupt unless it is to clarify your understanding of what is being said.
6. Offer verbal cues that you are actively listening, e.g., 'Mmm', 'I understand', 'yes', etc.
7. Try not to be distracted by other thoughts and feelings during the conversation.
8. Be patient with the speaker and give them time to talk.

9. Show the speaker that you want them to talk (don't start working on your computer or looking at your mobile phone whilst they are talking).

10. Demonstrate empathy with the speaker, putting yourself in their shoes.

Non-verbal communication

Non-verbal communication is essential to understand if a message is to be portrayed with honesty and sincerity. Face to face communication primarily consists of three elements: verbal (the words used), tonality (the way in which the words are spoken) and non-verbal communication (NVC) or body language (Mehrabian, 1971). Thomson (1996) illustrated the importance of NVC in a variety of managerial situations and especially during candidate interviews. When the words, voice and body language were all portraying the same message, the communication was that much more convincing. Thus, NVC is important to consider in terms of personal effectiveness.

Michael Argyle (1988) concluded that there are five main functions of NVC, which consist of:

- Expressing emotions
- Expressing interpersonal attitudes
- Accompanying speech in giving signals
- Self-presentation of one's personality
- Rituals (greetings).

Mehrabian (1971) is often cited in the literature as creating the 7 per cent–38 per cent–55 per cent rule. This rule suggests that in liking someone; 7 per cent comes from the words they use, 38 per cent from their tone of voice and 55 per cent from their NVC. It is obviously important to be liked in any effective communication. Nevertheless, many people do misquote the importance of NVC claiming that 80 per cent of communication is based around it, which is misleading as the words used are important (Hargie, 2006). What is certain is that when there is incongruence or a mismatch between the words that are being spoken and what the voice and body are portraying then this readily noticed by the receiver of the message. Thus, in any communication it is essential to look interested, believe in what you are saying and use the correct tonality and body language to support the message being said or received (Stroh and Johnson, 2006).

Industry snapshot 13.3

Pausing exercise

This is another exercise typical of those used in the industry that can be used to explore the importance of non-verbal communication in an applied setting.

Warning: This is particularly difficult for extraverts to perform, but excellent when you have mastery!

Exercise

Agree with a friend that you wish to explore the use of pausing in conversation. Then ask them to start a conversation about a topic you are interested in hearing about. During the conversation, ask them a question and pause your speech to try and illicit as much out of the person as possible. Ask your friend about how 'natural' it felt, and what the effect was of not speaking on them. Repeat the exercise but swap around roles so you can see the effect of the pause on yourself.

Further work

This exercise is most ideal in the real world with real conversations. It is interesting to observe how you may feel uncomfortable during silences in a conversation and how this effects the communication that is occurring. However, from this exercise you will note that the other person did not really notice the silence and took this part of the communication that occurred. More notable is that if you can master the pause, it is a very effective NVC to master that can really be effective in understanding what people are trying to communicate.

Communication in a Consultancy Context

So far we have looked at communication in a general sense and students who wish to examine this topic in more depth should read some of the more in-depth literature available (e.g., Hargie, 2006). Communication is also an important topic in a consultancy context. Indeed, Thought Provoking point 13.2 shows how essential communication is as noted by other authors (Thomson, 1996).

Thought Provoking point 13.2

In 2007, I attended the Consultancy Careers fair which was organized by Top-Consultant.com and had 50 management and IT consultancy firms looking for new graduate recruits. Having been a recruiter of graduate management consultants in the past, I wanted to confirm my own experiences specifically about employing occupational psychologists asking, 'What in your mind is the biggest barrier for graduates not getting jobs?' The majority of the consultancies I spoke to said that graduates tend to come in and talk about their discipline and what they want, rather than listen to what the interviewer is saying. This was very much the case with occupational psychologists, who would talk about what occupational psychology was rather than what the consultancy required from their graduates. So attending interviews with a specific mindset, not really listening to the questions being asked and not responding in an appropriate manner was the main barrier for not getting a management consultancy position for graduates.

Nevertheless, it is very easy to have a fixed mindset about a particular project or issue especially if the situation is similar to a previous experience. Many times have I heard consultants state, 'the client wants this', rather than actively listening to what the client's requirements are.

Rassam (2001a) gave a good account of communication stressing the importance of going back to basics when communicating in consultancy. In other words, it is essential to go back to the original brief when writing a report or to listen openly to what the client is saying in face-to-face communication. Pellegrin-Boucher (2006) noted that the consultant should always consider what they are there to do as the expert, the doer or facilitator of change. Indeed, consideration of the consultant's role is the first step in deciding the most appropriate communication. Once this has been decided, the scope of the project really needs to be considered. This is often where the difference between experienced and less experienced consultants lie, whereby experienced consultants will note how long they have on a project and avoid issues such as project creep covered in Chapter 6.

In management consultancy communication, Rassam (2001a) stated that the following questions need to be asked:

1. What is it that I want to achieve for the client?
2. What have been the main issues for the client?
3. Have there been any changes during the project that should be detailed?
4. Which issues are most critical for the client?
5. What is the timetable of action for the client?
6. What are the business benefits of action?

Adapted from Rassam (2001a), p. 145

Answering these questions can then either be done through the delivery of face-to-face presentations, reports and/or other deliverables such as training programmes (Holtz and Zahn, 2004).

Delivering face-to-face presentations

> McKinsey spends a lot of time training its consultants to structure their presentations . . . McKinsey consultants learn that a presentation must convey ideas to the audience in the clearest, most convincing way possible.
>
> *Rasiel and Friga (2002), p. 104*

Face-to-face delivery of presentations is a must for all consultants to master and some are better than others. Preparation is vital as is structure. The presentation must lead the audience down a clear logical path. If a presentation is well structured then it will lend itself to being clear to the audience. In addition, if the client wants a question answered that deviates from the prepared presentation this is possible only if the structure has been originally thought out and mapped out. The question raised can be given context if it is applicable or asked to put on hold if it isn't applicable to the presentation being performed.

Presentations do depend on a number of factors and these include:

1. **Size of the audience**: this is important as the more people there are the more tightly structured is the presentation. The fewer people there are the more the presentation can be informal.
2. **Length and content**: even the most riveting presenters can get dull after a while, so the length of the presentation has to be decided on in advance. If it is a particularly long presentation use more than one person to present.
3. **Visual aids**: visual aids can be used in presentations for most but the smallest of audiences. Most presentations can utilize IT packages such as Microsoft PowerPoint. The visual aid should support the presentation, not dominate it or provide annoying distractions. In using Microsoft PowerPoint there is the six

by six rule, whereby on each slide don't have more than six bullet points and then try to reduce each one of those bullet points to six words.

4. **Preparation**: is a vital ingredient with presenting. Practise the presentation by yourself and with others as applicable. But also performing the presentation with an audience can fine tune a presentation.

5. **Empathy**: the presentation will look different from the clients' perspective so putting yourself in their shoes as a final examination of the presentation aids the presentation to be focused and get the message across.

Writing reports

Writing reports in consultancy is not a simple task with most consultants having to learn their trade through years of experience (Markham, 2004). Reports come in all shapes and sizes from a three page summary of a situation through to a report the size of a book! Rassam (2001a) noted that a report may be generated at various stages of the consultancy process but essentially consists of three types:

1. Interim or progress reports.
2. Discussion reports.
3. End-of-assignment reports.

Adapted from Rassam (2001a), p. 148

The report and its format should be decided with the client before it is written. Often the client may also be used to confirm aspects of the report and provide a critical overview before the final report is produced (Rassam, 2001a). In this regard, configuration management is important (See Chapter 8) and most consultancies will have some sort of record within the project report stating which stage the report is at (see Figure 13.5). In Figure 13.5, it can be noted that the report went through three major development stages. The first stage of the report was the preliminary version. This was created by an originator, checked for consistency, reviewed and authorized by the Project Manager responsible for the day-to-day running of the project (see Chapter 8). This preliminary report would have then gone to the client for comments, which would have been incorporated in the report by the original author. The report would then be checked and reviewed by the Project Manager and then authorized by the Project Director who has overall responsibility for the project. This would normally be the final stage of producing a report. However, in the example given in Figure 13.5, the client had minor corrections to make on the report, which again were completed with the report being issued.

Structure is vital in a report (Markham, 2007; Rasiel and Friga, 2002; Rassam, 2001a). There are a number of ways to structure a report and each will depend on what you are trying to achieve (Rassam, 2001a). The following headings are fairly comprehensive and should be covered within the report structure:

1. **Executive summary**: represents the highlights from the report setting out objectives, methodology, findings and recommendations.
2. **Introduction**: this should outline the original terms of reference for the consultancy work and the rationale behind the work done.

Figure 13.5   Typical document review sheet used in management consultancies

Configuration control	Purpose description	DOCUMENT REF: Client report				
		Originated	Checked	Reviewed	Authorized	Date
V0.1	Preliminary version	Originator	Project Manager	Project Manager	Project Manager	02/04/09
V1.0	Draft final version, inclusive of client comments	Originator	Project Manager	Project Manager	Project Director	15/04/09
V2.0	Final version with minor corrections from client	Originator	Project Manager	Project Manager	Project Director	26/04/09

3. **Methodology**: in essence the way in which the data was gathered via interviews, questionnaires or multi-methods should be detailed here.

4. **Findings**: this should detail the results of what was gathered as part of the consultancy. A careful balance needs to be taken between being open to the client and the political nature of comments or findings made.

5. **Recommendations and Implications**: set out clear recommendations that come out of the consultancy work and what the implications of these may be. These can often be structured in terms of short, medium- and long-term recommendations.

6. **Conclusions**: at the end of the report summarize again what was the scope of the work, the methodology adopted and what was found.

7. **Appendices**: appendices can show data supporting the main report or provide further information to interested parties that does not necessarily form part of the report, e.g., McKinsey's wrote an excellent review of the recruitment agency industry in 2000 on the basis of their own research and additional data collected by Deloitte was included in their appendix (McKinsey & Company, 2000).

Reports using this structure should demonstrate a complete picture to the client. Nevertheless, as Markham (2004) suggested reports are difficult to write. They should be easy to understand but not too simplistic, explaining complicated phenomenon but able to be understood by the lay person. They should state how it is but show diplomacy and tact. They should also use diagrams, charts and graphs to get points across and also demonstrate the professional nature of the work completed. Gaining this balance is really as much of an art form as a science but mastery of report writing is an essential skill (Markham, 2004).

Other deliverables

Consultants tend to communicate primarily through the delivery of presentations and reports. Nonetheless, other deliverables such as an assessment centre, training programme or IT software solution may also be a way of communicating to the client (Holtz and Zahn, 2004).

However, the consultant's job does not stop there (Stroh and Johnson, 2006). Typically, there must be further information provided to the client. With a report for instance, it is no good if the report is left on the shelf gathering dust (Stroh and

Johnson, 2006). In this regard, there is at least for a short while a continuing dialogue with the client. Indeed, much of the work won in consultancy comes from repeat business as the client knows the consultant and engages them again.

Thought Provoking point 13.3

I once worked as an internal consultant for a furniture retail firm for a year followed by a similar position in a well-known financial institution. Both of these organizations then became clients of mine when I worked for another firm as an external consultant. Indeed, the well-known financial institution was built into a major client responsible for approximately 60 per cent of the turnover in the training division of my new employer. The retailer grew to about 10 per cent of the turnover of the division. This demonstrates the importance of keeping in touch and fostering relationships with previous clients as explored in Chapter 5.

Personal Effectiveness in Consultancy

Introduction

In the next chapter the behaviours associated with being effective as a consultant are listed down in our eight consultancy competency framework. Nonetheless, before finishing this chapter it is worth considering some of the literature that has detailed personal effectiveness as a consultant.

Time management

Personal effectiveness must combine efficiency and purpose (Scharf, 1987). In other words, personal effectiveness not only means doing the job or project assigned but in the most resource efficient manner achievable. Resources are an important aspect of personal effectiveness. Most individuals do not consider resources, such as time, finite and limited as detailed in Chapter 8. However, this is the fundamental aspect of personal effectiveness to realize the extent of oneself and that time is not unlimited.

Thus, most personal effectiveness training involves a substantial amount of time management training. This has the express purpose of providing a reorientation for individuals to realize that time is finite and that it can be used both as a managing and influencing tool as shown in Industry snapshot 13.4.

Industry snapshot 13.4

Time management training provided to the RAF by the University of Gloucestershire

Time management is important in all jobs but especially in time constrained organizations such as the military service. As part of a development programme provided to RAF personnel, time management training was provided. After the usual comments on the course such as 'I haven't got time for time management training' were dealt with, RAF personnel learned all the aspects of seeing time as a finite resource. This was especially important for middle ranking individuals who were often asked to complete certain projects with an already high work-load. Being a military service, it was difficult to refuse such requests.

Nevertheless, in working with the delegates, the trainer quickly demonstrated how seeing time as a finite resource could help influence the requests of the more senior officers. In effect, an officer who was requested to do some work with an already busy schedule, rather than just working harder to complete all aspects and becoming stressed over the workload (which was the case before the training), now had the ability to state, 'Ok I can do this piece of work, but it will mean that I won't be able to get X and Y done until N due to completing the work you have just requested.'

This meant that the Commanding Officer could see the effect of requesting additional work and either knew that other projects would be delayed or recognized the hard-working efforts of the officers completing the work.

The overriding principle of time management is that time is a resource and is finite. In time management, Scharf (1987) suggests time management is made up of three important components:

1. Know what you are supposed to achieve.
2. A small amount of time and effort produces most of your results (Pareto's law).
3. Do the most important things first.

Good time management encompasses these three components and is usually supported by a time management system. Systems for time management can range from producing to-do lists through to producing project logs (Wickham and Wickham, 2007). All aspects of project management principles can be used for time management. The main difference is that time management is typically on a smaller scale. Thus, understanding project management gives a thorough grounding of time management. For instance, when producing a to-do list, the list can be a simple list of tasks that need to be performed. However, if you apply project management principles the list can be more complicated and have a timeframe. IT packages such as MS Outlook help in time management for this very reason, as time can be allocated to tasks in a calendar type format that makes it easier to prioritize work. Figure 13.6 demonstrates a to-do list and to-do bar, which is a feature in MS Outlook 2007.

The seven habits of highly effective people

The biggest single source citied in the area of personal effectives must be Stephen Covey's 'The seven habits of highly effective people'. Covey (2004) argues that by adopting certain principles in one's life. A person can find their 'true north' and become highly effective. This principled approach differs from behavioural approaches (such as the eight consultancy competency framework in the next chapter) and relies on the formation of habits. The seven habits are defined as follows:

1. **Be proactive**: take responsibility for your life — initiative and action then follow. Will Schutz's (2005) the human element stated that you are responsible for everything in your life and adopting this rather than a reactive view, whereby

Figure 13.6   An example of a time management system – the Microsoft Outlook 2007 To-do list and To-do bar

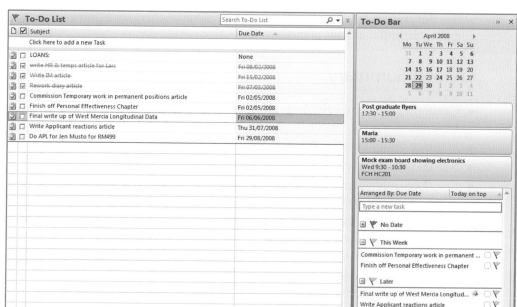

people and circumstances are typically blamed for problems, means a positive outlook on life.

2. **Begin with the end in mind**: visualize the completion of a task or long-term objective, in this way you concentrate on getting to the end as opposed to all the issues and problems that may prevent you getting to completion.

3. **Put first things first**: go for short-term goals and use delegation effectively focusing on results and benchmarks.

4. **Think win/win**: work towards mutually beneficial arrangements as opposed to winning due to someone else losing.

5. **Seek first to understand, then to be understood**: as discussed earlier on in the chapter you have two ears and one mouth so you should listen twice as much as speaking especially in early conversations where the emphasis should be on understanding the other person first.

6. **Synergize**: utilize effective teamwork in an open fashion whereby the team will be greater than the sum of its parts.

7. **Sharpen the saw**: the 1980s saw the phrase 'work hard and play hard' enter the cultural dictionary. Recreational activities that reenergize the physical, mental, emotional, social and spiritual well-being are important and essential for being highly effective.

The first three of these habits ensure that a person moves out of being dependent on others and situations towards a state of independence. Individuals who have these habits strive towards being independent and recognizing that they are masters of their own destiny. Habits 4–6 are then involved with realizing the independence with others. Thus, they are involved with teamwork and working with clients on a collaborative rather than a competitive basis. The final habit 7 involves the process of renewal, which is essential for re-energizing and keeping up with the stressful demands of modern life.

Chapter Summary

- Communication is always through a medium so there is often room for miscommunication
- Effective communication takes effort
- Self-knowledge is fundamental to communicating effectively
- Emotional intelligence is an important model to understand ourselves and others more effectively
- Tonality and body language should support the message being said, however, many authors put too much emphasis on non-verbal communication
- Preparation for presentations is vital to convey the correct messages
- Reports are often written in a consultancy context and their format should be client centred before delivery
- Time is a limited not an unlimited resource
- Moving towards a state of independence and then realizing this for others is essential for personal effectiveness

Review Questions

1. How is self-knowledge fundamental to communication?
2. How is self-regard important in emotional intelligence?
3. What are the seven key points in understanding others stated by French (1993)?
4. Why should you listen more than talk when meeting a client for the first time?
5. Is it important to 'go back to basics' when communicating in a management consultancy context?

Assignment Questions

1. What are the limitations of writing in terms of communication and how can these be addressed?
2. Is knowing thyself and receiving feedback on one's behavioural style an essential aspect of communication? Critically discuss using examples of where you have used feedback to adjust your communication to others.
3. Define the concept of emotional intelligence and discuss why it is important in communication.
4. Discuss how the seven habits of highly effective people impact upon working effectively in a management consultancy context.

Case Study 13.1

Dexter Nelson, summer analyst

By 6:30 p.m. on Wednesday, May 21, 2008, the rest of Dexter Nelson's team was en route to the airport, headed for the client site to conduct primary research. Dexter Nelson, a summer analyst at PPC Consulting in Toronto, was left to fend for himself. Nelson was overwhelmed by the events of his first two days on the project. He did not know what to expect in the days ahead and questioned whether he had made the right decision in accepting this supposedly perfect consulting job. His stomach churned as the blank Excel spreadsheet glared back at him. It was time to get started . . . but how?

PPC Consulting (PPC)

PPC Consulting (PPC) was a multibillion-dollar global consulting firm with offices located in Toronto, Canada. PPC focused on creating value at every level of the client organization and offered a full range of strategy and implementation services across three dimensions: pure strategy, technology

and human resources. PPC offered deep industry experience and strong functional expertise to help clients solve their most complex business problems. PPC served more than 50 per cent of the world's largest companies, primarily in the financial services, energy, life sciences, automotive and public sectors.

The corporate strategy practice

PPC's corporate strategy practice fell within the 'strategy umbrella'. 'The corporate strategy practice shaped and refined companies' strategic vision and objectives to drive superior shareholder returns. Typical projects included business strategy, customer and market strategy, sales effectiveness, mergers and acquisitions advisory and business information technology (IT) strategy (see Exhibit 13.1). The Toronto-based corporate strategy practice employed a staff of 125, of which 15 were summer students.

Dexter Nelson

Dexter Nelson was a certified Tennis Canada instructor and had enjoyed spending past summers outdoors, enhancing his tennis pupils' kinesthetic knowledge and personal development. He had spent two summers instructing children aged 3 to 14 at tennis camps offered by a prestigious athletic club in his hometown.

Prior to his studies at the Richard Ivey School of Business (Ivey), Nelson had worked as a research assistant. In this job, he had helped a professor identify potential areas of improvement for an introductory management course. His statistical analysis and in-class observations had led to recommendations that improved both the course attendance and student engagement.

Nelson had also worked for the wealth management arm of a large Canadian financial institution. His work involved developing promotional campaigns and increasing communications effectiveness through various marketing campaigns. Nelson had recently completed his first year of the HBA programme at the Richard Ivey School of Business in London, Ontario. Nelson had completed all the mandatory HBA1 courses, which included

Exhibit 13.1

PPC Consulting
Structure

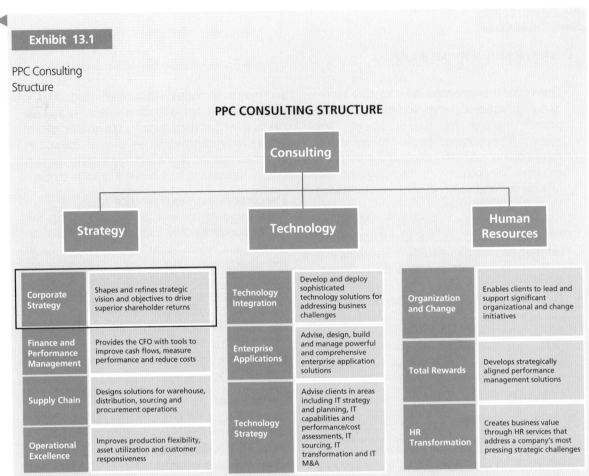

PPC CONSULTING STRUCTURE

Consulting

Strategy — Technology — Human Resources

Corporate Strategy	Shapes and refines strategic vision and objectives to drive superior shareholder returns
Finance and Performance Management	Provides the CFO with tools to improve cash flows, measure performance and reduce costs
Supply Chain	Designs solutions for warehouse, distribution, sourcing and procurement operations
Operational Excellence	Improves production flexibility, asset utilization and customer responsiveness

Technology Integration	Develop and deploy sophisticated technology solutions for addressing business challenges
Enterprise Applications	Advise, design, build and manage powerful and comprehensive enterprise application solutions
Technology Strategy	Advise clients in areas including IT strategy and planning, IT capabilities and performance/cost assessments, IT sourcing, IT transformation and IT M&A

Organization and Change	Enables clients to lead and support significant organizational and change initiatives
Total Rewards	Develops strategically aligned performance management solutions
HR Transformation	Creates business value through HR services that address a company's most pressing strategic challenges

Sources: Company records

finance and management science. He had been a strong student in both courses. Nelson had previously spent two years at another business school where he had completed a variety of courses, including four in accounting and finance and three in statistical and financial analysis and modelling.

Nelson was excited to take on the challenge of working in a high-performance organization. It had only been a few days since he had started his internship as a summer analyst at PPC in Toronto. He was keen to see what the organization had in store for him.

The interview process
When he had embarked on the interview process, Nelson had not yet decided between investment banking and management consulting. After interviewing with a few investment banks, he decided that his interest lay more in consulting. He was keenly interested in the strategy behind a business, as opposed to working with a firm's financials. He wanted a role that involved more than execution-based tasks; he wanted to challenge himself and his critical-thinking skills. At the same time, Nelson maintained a strong interest in finance.

When he interviewed with PPC, Nelson had expressed his eagerness to work in the area of mergers and acquisitions (M&A) strategy. Many of his interviewers had experience within that sphere (especially one manager who had plenty of past modelling experience and seemed to take a particular liking to him), and Nelson became excited at the prospect of what he could learn.

Furthermore, his interviewers explained that a large proportion of PPC's projects fell within the scope of the financial services industry. Although Nelson would not be guaranteed to have an opportunity to work within M&A, he would definitely gain experience by working on a financial services project.

After interviewing with several consulting firms, Nelson selected PPC. Working there would offer him insight into financial services because of the firm's expertise, strong presence and stellar reputation in the Canadian financial services market.

Training week

Training week was divided into two main modules: General Firm Training and Consulting Training (see Exhibit 13.2).

The first two days covered basic administrative training and included getting acquainted with the firm and the resources available. Laptops were distributed and all PPC policies and procedures were presented.

The final three days of training focused on the summer ahead. The training included the development of presentations, the logical structuring of ideas, an explanation of the analytical and research tools required to perform day-to-day tasks and a series of brief workshops that highlighted the skills required for success as a consultant. Each presenter provided a brief summary package of the materials used in the presentation.

The other objective of training was to provide the 15 summer students with the opportunity to familiarize, themselves with practitioners across the firm. PPC assigned two employees to each intern. A 'friend', would be available to help the new hire learn the ropes and to answer any informal questions. A 'mentor' was assigned to help establish goals and objectives and to track performance by soliciting feedback from team members working alongside the intern. Mentors were responsible for relaying this information to help improve performance. Additionally, because mentors were more experienced employees, they were able to provide guidance and support to assist the new hire with either general inquiries or specific issues.

Many 'meet and greet' sessions were scheduled to help interns both to meet others in the office and to learn more about the work they were doing. During the first week, the firm sponsored an after-hours networking event at a local restaurant where Nelson met both his friend and his mentor. His friend was charismatic and personable but did not spend much time with Nelson over the course of the evening. His mentor was much more subdued, but Nelson could sense he was very experienced and would be able to help him, should the need arise. His mentor had been with the firm for more than five years and showed a keen interest in Nelson by speaking with him for more than an hour about the keys to success at the firm and his own personal experiences at PPC.

Nelson also met Pam Hunter, the partner assigned to his project, and Ajit Sharma, the consultant to whom he would report for the duration of his first project. Nelson had the opportunity to meet Hunter only briefly before she had to step away to meet with other interns. Sharma arrived late to the event, and Nelson could sense that he was tense. Sharma implied that project work was keeping him busy and he told Nelson he was leaving for vacation in a few weeks. He was warm and welcoming and sought to understand the areas of work within the project that most interested Nelson. As a new member of the team, Nelson was keen to support his team. Because he saw this job as a great opportunity to gain insight into financial modelling, he asked to work on the project's financials. Sharma told Nelson he wanted to involve him in as many facets of the project as possible.

The project

The project team consisted of the partner, Pam Hunter; a manager, Tom Peterson; and two consultants, Ajit Sharma and Jack Smith. Nelson was added to provide support for the team, which had already been engaged on the project for some time. Nelson wanted to learn more about his team members. He found their profiles on the internal knowledge management database. Every member of the team was experienced, particularly in the area of payments, the focus of this project (see Exhibit 13.3).

▶

Exhibit 13.2

Training Week
Schedule (May
12-16, 2008)

TRAINING WEEK SCHEDULE (MAY 12–16, 2008)

Module 1 - General Firm Training

	Time	Session
Monday	9:00 - 10:00	Introduction to the Firm
	10:00 - 10:45	Facilities/Security
	10:45 - 11:00	Break
	11:00 - 12:00	Telecommunications
	12:00 - 1:00	Lunch
	1:00 - 2:00	Knowledge and Information Management
	2:00 - 2:15	Break
	2:15 - 3:45	HR Payroll and Benefits

Tuesday	8:30 - 9:15	Laptop Distribution and Technology Policy
	9:00 - 12:30	Technology Training
	12:30 - 1:00	Lunch
	1:00 - 1:30	Consulting Overview
	1:30 - 2:00	Human Resources
	2:00 - 2:30	Administration and Facilities
	2:30 - 3:00	Resource Management
	3:00 - 3:30	Learning and Growth
	3:30 - 4:00	Consulting - Knowledge Management

Module 2 - Consulting Training

	Time	Session
Wednesday	8:30 - 9:15	Welcome to Corporate Strategy
	9:15 - 9:30	Case Introduction
	9:30 - 9:45	Break
	9:45 - 11:15	Firm Tools - Knowledge Exchange, Research Sources, eRooms, Methods Library, Industry Print, Resume Tool
	11:15 - 12:00	Working Time with Firm Tools
	12:00 - 12:45	Lunch: Icebreaker
	12:45 - 1:45	Industry and Financial Analysis
	1:45 - 2:45	Working Time for Analysis
	2:45 - 3:30	Enterprise Value Map (EVM)
	3:30 - 4:15	Working Time for EVM

Thursday	8:30 - 12:30	Hypothesis Based Consulting, Logical Structuring, Story Boarding - Lecture and Exercises
	12:30 - 1:00	Lunch
	1:00 - 3:00	Conducting Executive Level Interviews - Working Session
	3:00 - 3:15	Break
	3:15 - 4:30	Financial Modelling and Business Case Development
	4:30 - 5:30	Team Working Time
	5:30 onwards	Social Event

Friday	8:30 - 10:30	Buidling Skillful Presentations
	10:30 - 12:00	Team Working Time
	12:00 - 1:30	Lunch: Friend & Mentor Lunch
	1:30 - 3:00	Present Case Findings & General Feedback
	3:00 - 3:30	Break
	3:30 - 4:00	How to be a Successful Consultant
	4:00 - 4:30	Straight Talk and Practitioner Panel

Sources : Company records

Exhibit 13.3	**Pam Hunter, BA (Economics), MA (Economics), CFA, Partner**

Project Team Profiles

Pam Hunter, BA (Economics), MA (Economics), CFA, Partner

Pam is a partner at PPC and leads both the Corporate Strategy consulting and Payments practices. She has over 20 years of experience working with wholesale and retail banks in Canada, the U S. Australia and Europe. She has significant payments experience which has been leveraged to assist leading financial institutions and card companies in developing new products and business strategies.

Pam's past experience includes over 100 engagements related to payment cards and extensive work with leading financial institutions on their payments strategies.

Tom Peterson, BSC (Pure Math and Physics), MSC (Physics), Manager

Tom is a manager within PPC and leads the 'Invoice to Payment' practice. He has over a decade of experience in the card and payments space with a focus in sales, new product development and launch, marketing, co-brand and alliances. Prior to joining PPC, Tom held national and global roles for a fortune 50 card provider leading its product marketing and strategy.

Along with a decade of experience, he also led national card marketing and sales for a global card provider. As part of this role, Tom led the company's alliances team helping to structure multiple new co-brand solutions and launch them in the market.

Ajit Sharma, BECON, MBA, Consultant

Ajit is a Consultant in the Strategy, Financial Services consulting practice. Ajit has completed several engagements within the payments industry. His project assignments include strategy development, market research, technology strategy assessment, and implementation roadmap development. Prior to joining PPC, Ajit worked for over four years in the financial services sector, with a large global bank in its credit cards division.

Jack Smith, BCOMM, MBA, Consultant

Jack has over six years of strategic marketing and customer analytics experience in the financial services industry – specifically payments.

Prior to PPC, Jack worked at Moneris Solutions where he managed the implementation of joint strategic sales and marketing programms with 12 bank channel partners.

Sources: Company records

The client had requested four specific items to be delivered upon completion of the project:

1. Identification of the value proposition to both the end customer and the client's prospective partner for this initiative.

2. Quantification of the financial opportunity.

3. Operational changes required to ensure profitability of the initiative.

4. Implementation road map and next steps.

During his final day of training on Friday, May 16, Nelson received an email from Sharma re-questing that he review a number of items prior to his first day on the project, on Tuesday, May 20, following the Victoria Day long weekend (see Exhibit 13.4). Nelson started to get anxious. He would need to jump in headfirst, after having only the weekend to become familiar with the materials. On Sunday morning, Nelson began to review the materials, which included four PowerPoint presentations (decks) that had been previously prepared. Some of the materials were intended to brief Nelson on the current state of this project, whereas other materials demonstrated the expectations of the 'look and feel' of final deliverables prepared at PPC. Nelson also scanned through a

Exhibit 13.4	**From:** Sharma, Ajit
	Sent: Friday, May 16, 2008 3:08 PM
Ajit Sharma's Email to	**To:** Nelson, Dexter
Dexter Nelson	**Cc:** Hunter, Pam; Peterson, Tom; Smith, Jack

Subject: Welcome

Hi Dexter,

Welcome to PPC. I'm sure you're enjoying the on-boarding training.

I just thought I'd reach out to you and let you know that you will be working with us on a very exciting strategy project at Client X.

Attached, please find the following:

1. The project proposal which includes all the materials that were used in selling this project to the client. This document also contains a general outline of the scope of the project and details the final deliverables we have promised to the client.
2. A draft of the project kickoff deck which includes the approach and project methodology, project timelines and budgets, a brief industry overview and our industry outlook and point of view. Finally, it includes the most recent status update explaining where we are to-date on this project.
3. Examples from prior projects so you get an idea of the style and format of final deliverables here at PPC, and some formatting pointers that should help to make things easier for you. These decks are from similar types of projects, so they may help you to gain a better understanding of the competitive dynamics of the industry.
4. A market research report which outlines the latest trends in the industry, key industry statistics, industry forecasts and competitor profiles.

Feel free to reach out anytime and I'd be more than happy to answer any questions you might have. You can reach me on my cell at 555-555-1234.

Look forward to working with you.

Thanks and regards,

Ajit

Attachments:

1. Project Proposal.ppt
2. Project Kickoff Deck.ppt
3. Past Engagement Example 1.ppt
4. Past Engagement Example 2.ppt
5. Market Research Report.pdf

large market research report and read the most relevant sections carefully.

By Monday of the holiday weekend, Nelson had learned a few key facts:

- The team was slightly behind on the project timeline and, therefore, was over budget. Nelson had been added to the team to help get the project back on track.

- The team's end goal was to evaluate the industry and to determine whether the client could develop a financially feasible product with a value proposition that was superior or at least competitive to other products in the industry.
- The industry in which the client operated was intensely competitive and mature. This new product, if designed properly, could help the client to remain competitive or even gain an advantage.

The first day

Nelson arrived at work early on Tuesday morning, ready to face the challenges ahead. When Sharma arrived, he introduced Nelson to the project manager, Tom Peterson. Peterson seemed eccentric to Nelson; he welcomed Nelson and poked fun at him. Nelson knew Peterson's behaviour was all in good fun, but also realized that he would very quickly have to prove that he could carry his weight, especially because the team was relying on him to help them bring the project back on schedule. The rest of the day was uneventful: Nelson provided logistical support for the team, sat in on a client status update call and performed some Internet research and analysis to learn more about the industry and provide some contextual information to his team. The team asked him to conduct some secondary research to better understand both the competitive landscape and, more specifically, the offerings of specific competitors. He was also assigned the task of formatting a deck that had been put together by other members of his team. Nelson worked diligently and left for the day

at around 8:00 p.m., feeling good about his accomplishments.

The second day

The next morning, the team was in a frantic rush. The client had requested meetings for the following day. The team needed to work quickly to complete certain interim deliverables in preparation for their interviews the next day. Nelson performed clerical tasks for his team members who were busy working to prepare for the next day's meetings. At 4:30 p.m., Sharma handed the financial model over to Nelson and agreed to provide him with directional advice. No one else on the team had any significant modelling experience. As the end of the day drew nearer, Nelson realized that he would not be receiving much additional guidance from his team before they headed off to the client site. Although everything seemed new and overwhelming, Nelson looked forward to the challenges ahead of him.

The team left the office at around 6:30 p.m., en route to the airport. Nelson wanted to get started on his first real assignment of the summer. Having recognized that this project was a new product launch, Nelson wanted to identify the key elements he should address in the financial model. He wanted to develop a sequence of actions to make a significant contribution both to his team and the client. He knew he had until Monday when the team would return from their out-of-town meetings with the client. He needed to identify the activities to tackle on Thursday, Friday and the weekend ahead.

Further Reading

Covey, S. (2004), *7 Habits of Highly Effective People.* London: Simon & Schuster Ltd (15th Anniversary Edition)

Fineman, S. (2003), *Understanding Emotion at Work.* London: Sage Publications

Hargie, O., (2006), *The Handbook of Communication Skills: 3rd Edition.* London: Routledge

Markham, C. (2004), *The Top Consultant: Developing Your Skills for Greater Effectiveness.* London: Kogan Page Ltd; 4 Rev Ed edition

Schutz, W. (2004), *The Human Element: 2nd Edition.* San Francisco: Business Consultants Network Inc

Professional development

The final part of the book represents a fascinating insight into the profession of management consultancy. Chapter 14 extends the previous section detailing the professional development of the individual consultant. It details a unique model of personal development, the eight consultancy competency framework. Exercises and techniques in evaluating an individual against the competency framework are given. These are then merged with another technique of evaluating skills introduced in an earlier chapter on consultancy techniques. Both methods are combined and can be used by students or those starting out in consultancy for their own professional development.

Chapter 15 takes a rather critical view of 'professionalism' not only in management consultancy but of organizations in general. This serves as a fascinating insight into some of the corporate scandals that have shaken the world such as Guinness, Enron, Chiquita and the World Bank. It also examines sex at work, nepotism and cronyism, and asks how consultants may deal with these issues. The chapter concludes by investigating the list of ethics suggested by the Management Consultancies Association and then examines this on an international level.

Chapter 16 concludes the book detailing the future of management consultancy. This chapter directly links in with the opening chapter detailing where the industry has grown and where it may prosper. Although a critical appraisal of the industry is given, an optimistic future is predicted. This illustrates how knowledge may be generated, packaged and sold. It also demonstrates how the environmental crisis may give rise to green technologies being created, fuelling a clean energy revolution and a boom to the economy.

CHAPTER 14

Mastering competencies and developing competence

Learning Objectives

At the end of this chapter students will be able to:

- Recognize why competencies and competence are important

- Plan and organize their continuing professional development (CPD) in a systematic manner

- Understand how to develop influencing, leading and other behaviours in consultancy

- Recognize skills necessary to deal with the darker side of the profession such as rejection from clients

Mini Case Study 14.1

Competency Based Consulting Skills Programme undertaken by Maxon Associates and Atkins Management Consultants for a major Metropolitan Council

Introduction

This paper describes a highly successful piece of work delivered in 2006 to a major local authority.

The purpose of the programme was to create an effective Internal Consultancy capacity within an HR function which would then be enabled to operate in a fully facilitative manner across the whole authority, providing a previously unavailable degree of professional support to colleagues in other areas. Whilst the work in this example was related to HR it could apply equally to any support function and indeed to virtually any kind of organization.

The central thrust of the programme comes in three sections, firstly a workshop element (five days in three modules) followed by individual coaching and then an evaluation (which includes the production by each attendee of a report detailing their understanding and application of their learning from the programme). Naturally, individual topics and the detail of each of the sections can be adjusted to specific business requirements and a tie-in to a competency framework, as in the example described, is optional.

A significant part of the success of this initiative is that, unlike many alternative offerings, it is a multifaceted programme stretching over six months and blending differing styles of input in order to cater effectively to the, inevitably, varied learning needs of participants. The opportunity to work in partnership with established and experienced consultants over a substantial period of time also allows participants to fully embed and gain confidence in their newly developing skills.

1. Summary of requirements

The brief given to Maxon Associates/Atkins Management Consultants was prepared by the Senior Leadership Team of the Council's HR function, and indicated that the main purpose of the proposal was to support a raft of change programmes being undertaken by the Council.

In order to offer optimum support to these programmes the HR function wished to move rapidly towards advocating and initiating approaches strongly focused on and aligned with business needs and clearly change oriented in their intent. To spearhead this functional refocus a 'change team' was established. This team, with aid from their other HR colleagues, was to be responsible for promoting and delivering the Council's HR Change Management/Service Improvement Offer.

The briefing document outlined that senior members of the HR team wished to acquire and develop the change agent skills of internal consultants, in effect to be business partners for change, through a competency based development programme so that they could provide a new and superior type of functional support to the Council.

The competency framework used for the development programme was to be designed specifically for the HR function of the Council and be based on best practice research, the Cabinet Office's paper 'Modernising People Management, HR Capability Framework' and primary research conducted by consultants in collaboration with members of the Council's Senior HR team.

2. Programme design

The programme had as its foundation the key components of research, learning, reflection, exchange and support.

- **Research**: to meet the particular needs of the Council's HR Change Management Team the whole programme was grounded in solid primary and secondary research.

- **Learning**: the essential learning targets were identified as confronting the challenges of change, organization development and the key requirements of the role of an internal consultant.

- **Reflection**: time was built-in for self-assessment; taking stock of personal and professional development.

- **Exchange**: during the programme and the coaching sessions, participants were encouraged to take the opportunity to have active debates and exchanges of thoughts and ideas not only amongst themselves but also with the session facilitators and the coaches.

- **Support**: throughout the programme, participants had on-going support from the Maxon/Atkins consultants responsible for delivery.

As the work with the HR team progressed, and the design of the programme itself began to take shape, it became clear that the participants would benefit from one-to-one coaching being an integral element of the development path.

Finally, it was agreed with the Senior Leadership Team from HR that, on completion, the participants would have their competence and internal consultancy skills assessed professionally.

3. Workshop overviews

Workshop One Topics: The Basic Consultancy Building Blocks plus MBTI & Strategy Development

Day 1
An exploration of skill levels regarding the Consulting Cycle.
Analysis of the Council's appetite for internal consultancy and the current perceptions of HR within the Council.

The Consulting Styles Continuum Collaborative Consulting.

Building a Relationship/Gaining Entry – phase one of the consulting cycle.

Contracting – phase two of the consulting cycle (the foundation of the whole consulting process).

Day 2

MBTI (Step II) including an overview of the MBTI and the role of MBTI in relation to Communicating, Making Decisions, Managing Change and Managing Conflict.

Strategy development including what strategy is, strategic drift, contextualizing strategy, strategy development, distortions and deceptions in strategic decisions, culture and strategy and stakeholder relationships.

Learning sets established.

Workshop Two Topics: Leadership, Managing Change & Problem Solving Tools and Techniques

Day 1

Principles of Leadership and Managing Change including Team Development.

Day 2

Problem solving and decision making tools and techniques. To aid understanding and skill development, the learning sets were each assigned a number of tools and techniques that they shared with the rest of the group during the consultant-facilitated workshop sessions.

Workshop Three Topics: Proposal Writing and Converting Theory into Practice

Final stages and some recap of earlier learning to equip the participants for their role as neophyte consultants.

4. Coaching

Coaching sessions

Following the series of Workshops, each programme participant was allocated two 90 minute coaching sessions, four weeks apart, with a consultant from either Maxon Associates or Atkins Management Consultants. The focus of the sessions was to reinforce the key messages and lessons learned from the Workshops and to coach or mentor individuals in their new consulting roles within the Council.

5. Evaluation

Written evaluation

Approximately six weeks after the final coaching sessions each participant was required to submit a report of between 2000 and 2500 words. They had to produce an analysis of the eight part coaching cycle covered during the three workshops together with a reflective description of a real case scenario where they had applied the competencies in work with clients. In addition they had to produce a description of their personal journey/distance travelled from the start of the programme.

Face to face evaluation

The reports were reviewed by the consultants engaged in the programme – Kathie Gilley, Alasdair Kelly and Jim Maxon. These consultants then acted as an interview panel. During a face-to-face meeting with the participants individually, the consultants asked a series of probing questions about the reports. The purpose being to establish how well individuals really understood the competencies and how to apply them successfully with clients.

6. Graduation

After the formal evaluation, during a brief graduation ceremony, each candidate who had completed the programme satisfactorily was given a certificate stating that they had successfully done so.

Source: Professor Jim Maxon, Alasdair Kelly and Kathie Gilley. Available from Atkins at http://www.atkinsmc.com/downloads/default.asp. Reproduced with permission.

Mastering Competencies and Developing Competence

Introduction

This chapter begins the last section of this text examining professional development. It builds from the previous section, highlighting some of the tougher skills needed by consultants. It uses a competency based approach, commonly used by occupational psychologists, investigating behaviours that need to be mastered for longevity in the industry. It also looks at skills needed in a competence based approach. The use of both approaches, will aid the student in mastering competencies and developing competence.

What is a competency?

A competency is a collection of behaviours associated with effective or superior performance (Ballantyne and Povah, 2004). Leadership, problem solving and strategic management are all examples of competencies. The competency itself should contain a number of different behaviours. Behaviour is typically the demonstration of skills, knowledge, attitudes or underlying motivations. Behaviours are not theoretical constructs and should therefore be observable through evidence. Behaviour in this context is what an individual 'says' or 'does' or 'does not say' or 'do' when something is expected of them.

A collection of behaviours is therefore grouped within a competence. Subsequently, a collection of competencies is called a competency framework. A competency framework should contain all of the behaviours necessary for effective performance in a particular job role (Bowler and Woehr, 2006). A competency framework can be designed for a client and can subsequently be used for assessment, strategic management and personal development purposes.

Nonetheless, a criticism that has been raised at a purely competency based approach is that it may miss key skills required of the job holder (Chapman and Lovell, 2006). So for instance, a firm may have an employee that scores well on all the competencies that have been shown as being effective for the job role. However, they may not necessarily know how to use PRINCE2. Supporters of a purely competency based approach, may argue that if the skills are not there in the person then they won't be able to demonstrate the behaviour. Nevertheless, in my experience and as shown by Chapman and Lovell, (2006). this is not necessarily the case. Thus, a hybrid approach is taken for this chapter, using the eight competency based approach and augmenting this with a competence approach through the SWOT analysis detailed below.

The eight consultancy competency framework

Competency frameworks are designed with a specific client or job role in mind. In this regard, the eight consultancy competency framework was designed as shown in Figure 14.1. In essence this was designed for students who wish to pursue a career in management consultancy. The framework uses unpublished job analyses performed in two different consultancies to define the competencies. It also borrows material from a meta-analysis of competencies completed by Woehr and Arthur (2003) in order to make it comprehensive, detailing all aspects of effective behaviours seen in the workplace.

Altogether eight competencies make up this framework. Some of the competencies can be combined, e.g., communicating and influencing others. However, these

Communication
The extent to which an individual conveys oral and written information and responds to questions and challenges

Influencing others
The extent to which an individual persuades others to do something or adopt a point of view in order to produce desired results and takes action in which the dominant influence is one's own convictions rather than the influence of others' opinions

Organizing and planning
The extent to which an individual systematically arranges his/her own work and resources as well as that of others for efficient task accomplishment; and the extent to which an individual anticipates and prepares for the future

Problem solving
The extent to which an individual gathers information; understands relevant technical and professional information; effectively analyses data and information; generates viable options, ideas, and solutions; selects supportable courses of action for problems and situations; uses available resources in new ways; and generates and recognizes imaginative solutions

Teamwork and consideration of others
The extent to which an individual considers the needs of others, participates as a member of a group and is aware of the impact and implications of decisions relevant to others

Leadership
The extent to which an individual takes on the responsibility for providing focus to a team and develops members of that team

Drive
The extent which an individual originates and maintains a high activity level, sets high performance standards and persists in their achievement, and expresses the desire to advance

Tolerance for stress/uncertainty
The extent to which an individual maintains effectiveness in diverse situations under varying degrees of pressure, opposition and disappointment

Figure 14.1

The eight consultancy competency framework

have been left as separate as in a consultancy context sometimes communication is used purely to inform and not necessarily to influence as noted in the last chapter.

Using the eight consultancy competency framework

The eight consultancy competency framework can be used by students and consultants alike to guide their professional development. Performance in competencies in assessment centres is often rated against the job that is being applied for (Bowler and Woehr, 2006). In this regard, students may consider an entry level position in a consultancy as a benchmark in which to compare performance. Competencies are given a 1 to 5 grading as follows:

5 Excellent performance

4 More than acceptable performance

3 Acceptable performance

2 Less than acceptable

1 Little evidence of the competency

The first step in the process is to try and evaluate what rating you are on each of the competencies in the framework. This is typically done in an assessment centre context (Garavan, 2007). Nevertheless, this text has developed three exercises that will assist personal development for students (see Industry snapshots 14.1 through to 14.3). The basis of these exercises can aid individuals throughout their entire careers. Individuals map out their recent activities in the achievement list and then rate these achievements in the evaluation against the competency model shown in Figure 14.1. These are then summarized in the final exercise that demonstrates how the person rates on each of the eight consultancy competencies.

Industry snapshot 14.1

Achievements list

This exercise is the first of three that is used to explore performance in industry. It does this initially by examining achievements completed over the last few years. It is rather time consuming but will provide students at the end of the three exercises with a comprehensive view of their behaviours and competencies directly associated with consultancy. It can thus be used to demonstrate where a student can add value to consultancy, at say the interview stage, but more importantly can provide a continual method of personal development for inexperienced and experienced consultants alike.

1. Generate a list of your major achievements over the last two years. Your Curriculum Vitae (CV) can be a useful memory jogger but don't be constrained by just the activities listed on your CV.

2. Describe each of the achievements in measurable terms where possible, such as time taken, income generated, result achieved, etc.
   For example, rather than state, 'I was happy with my result in Occupational Psychology', quantify the achievement in measurable terms and state, 'I was happy with my result in Occupational Psychology. It was a third year module and I achieved an 82 per cent score in an assignment that I did. Most pleasing of all was the feedback that I received which described my work as "an excellent summary of the job satisfaction literature" as rated by the lecturer. I was happy as it proved to me that the hard work and dedication that I put into this assignment paid off and showed me that I could achieve a distinction grade.'

3. Generate about 7–10 achievements preferably in an appropriate word processor (as you need to cut and paste these achievements in step 7 below).

4. Next generate a 2 × 4 table in a suitable word processor.

5. List in the first column on the table on a single page the following text: The achievement, Its influence, The situation, What actions did I do that contributed to the achievement e.g.,

The achievement	
Its influence	
The situation	
What actions did I do that contributed to the achievement	

NB: This table is available under support for Chapter 14, Achievements List form.

6. At the top of the table, make a note of the date of the achievement.

7. Each of your achievements should now be put in the table in the first row of the second empty column. A single page must be used for each achievements previously listed.

8. In the table, expand out the achievement identifying how the achievement influenced yourself or/and others; further detail what was the situation at the time, highlighting any constraints or difficulties you had to overcome; and lastly analyse the achievement in relation to what actions you did that contributed towards the overall achievement. In essence for each of the achievements listed you need to have about 200–300 words in total about that particular achievement. There should then be about 7–10 pages in total for all of your achievements. Save this document as your achievements list.

Achievement evaluation

This exercise is designed to use the achievements listed above and focus the student onto a behavioural based examination of performance as opposed to a task orientated view. This is important as students will then be able to see what behaviours were effective and which were not, or missing, in an overall context.

Exercise

1. Generate a suitable table with the titles as below.

2.

3. Reproduce this table eight times for each of the competencies. At the top of each page type in the competency and its definition.

4. From your achievements list generated before, choose a competency, e.g., communication. Go through each of your achievements and highlight where you used the behaviours listed in this competency. Complete the rows of the Competency Evaluation with this information. Feel free to add rows to the bottom of the table to add more evidence.

5. You should now have about a page completed per competency, so nine pages altogether. Now you have to evaluate your performance on the competency. So on each of the competencies look at what actions you did, consider the situation and the influence of the achievement and rate each achievement using a 1–5 scale as follows:

   5   Excellent performance

   4   Good performance

   3   Acceptable performance

   2   Needs improvement to get to an acceptable standard of performance

   1   Poor or no evidence of competency.

6. Write the score in per achievement in the evaluation column. Once you have finished rating all the evidence per competency, give yourself an overall score for that competency using the 1–5 rating scale.

Competency summary

This exercise is designed to summarize the competency ratings developed in the evaluation exercise. It is the last step of three but is essential as from this summary an individual can ascertain which competencies are missing from their repertoire of behaviours. It also points out areas that need to be worked on in terms of developmental needs.

1. Generate the following table in a suitable word processor.

Competency	Evaluation				
	1	2	3	4	5
Communication					
Influencing others					

Competency	Evaluation				
	1	2	3	4	5
Organizing and planning					
Problem solving					
Teamwork					
Consideration/ Awareness of others					
Leadership					
Drive					
Tolerance for stress/ uncertainty					

NB: This table is available under support for Chapter 14, Competency Summary form.

2. For each of the competencies, colour in the relevant boxes demonstrating the appropriate rating ascertained in the evaluation exercise. Below is an example of a completed Competency Summary Form:

Competency	Evaluation				
	1	2	3	4	5
Communication	▓	▓	▓		
Influencing others	▓	▓			
Organising and planning	▓	▓	▓	▓	
Problem solving	▓	▓			
Consideration of others	▓				
Leadership	▓	▓			
Drive	▓	▓	▓	▓	
Tolerance for stress/ uncertainty	▓	▓	▓		

3. The Competency Summary Form is now complete.

The advantages with exercises listed in Industry snapshots 14.1 to 14.3 is that they can aid a student build up a competency profile and show where there are deficits. It is especially useful when planning for future activities and goals which will be covered later in this chapter, when each competency in turn will be examined.

Developing competence/continuing professional development

So far in this chapter, competencies defined as a collection of behaviours and competence as a rating scale of 1–5 has been covered. Before moving on though it is worth considering the difference between competencies and competence and these are given in Table 14.1 below. In essence, competence is a rating of capability and a competency is a collection of behaviours.

Typically, competencies are assessed by external measures such as on an appraisal system or at an assessment centre (Millmore, Biggs and Morse, 2007). Competencies can also assessed by individuals (see Industry snapshots 14.1 to 14.3). This step of taking stock of where there are development needs is the beginning process of continuing professional development.

Continuing professional development (CPD) is an essential aspect of modern professional life. It can be described as 'the holistic commitment to structured skills enhancement and personal or professional competence' (DTI, 2002). It is essential that professionals have the knowledge and expertise to fulfil their role and responsibilities and CPD can ensure that this is kept up-to-date (Keats, 2008). Most professions demand that their members engage in CPD activities due to the lack of a job

Key differences	Competency	Competence
Focuses on	The behaviour of a person	The task
Summarizes	Characteristics of the person	The capability of completing the task
Typically assessed by	Behaviour on the job/job based simulations	Outputs from tasks
Typically used for	Ascertains how a person performs currently in terms of behaviours exhibited and leads to performance improvement on the basis of improving these behaviours	Establishing function and quality standards

Table 14.1

Competency versus competence

for life in conjunction with a rapidly changing globalized economy (Jackling, De Lange and On, 2007). Table 14.2 highlights further reasons why CPD is essential for professionals.

The key features of CPD are that it is:

- Continuous throughout working life
- The learner is generally in control of how CPD progresses
- CPD is a holistic process that can address all aspects of life and work/home balance but is principally professional/organization focused
- Aimed at developing knowledge, skills and personal qualities relevant to the profession
- Structured – systematic and regular, continuously reflecting on present skills and knowledge and planning future direction and development needs
- Works with or without employer support – although leads to better motivated staff where employer actively supports process
- Core requirement of many professional bodies

Many professional bodies have on-line versions of CPD. These serve to support the process in a systematic way but can also be used by the relevant professional body to ensure that all professionals registered or accredited conform to their CPD

From:	To:
Expectation of a 'job for life'	Reality 'no job is safe'
Develop a single specialist skill	Multiple skills required
Vertical promotion	Horizontal/lateral movement
'Keep your head down'	'Innovate and take risks'
Single employer (for entire career)	Multiple employers (portfolio of careers)
Careers planned	Plan your own career
Develop a skill during an initial training period	Continuous lifelong learning

Table 14.2

Recent business changes affecting the personal need to engage in CPD activities

Source: http://www.CPDuk.co.uk/intro2/intro2c.htm

requirements (Keats, 2008). Professional bodies may then have a number of sanctions against non-conforming professionals. This may include the removal of non-conforming individuals from their preferential status (Keats, 2008).

Steps in continuing professional development

In essence, there are four elements in the CPD process. The first element is taking stock of where you are now. The CPD certification service, for instance, suggested applying the SWOT analysis (detailed in Chapter 4) directly to 'where you are now' as shown in Table 14.3. Rather than relying solely on behavioural evidence, the SWOT analysis has the advantage of looking at core skills, skills to improve, opportunities and obstacles for moving forward. However, it does have the major disadvantage of exclusively relying on skills rather than behaviour based measures of performance.

Thought Provoking point 14.1

It is suggested that students wishing to use this book to guide their personal development use both competency based approach in Industry snapshots 14.1, 14.2 and 14.3, supplemented by a SWOT analysis concentrating on the skills required. Although this hybrid approach may evoke criticism, it does get the best out of the competency and competence approach to personal development.

Table 14.3		
SWOT analysis used for informing CPD activities (http:// www.cpduk.co.uk/ intro2/intro2a.htm)		*'Swot' Analysis*

Strengths
What are your core skills?
What do you do well?

- technical skills and knowledge?
- other transferable skills
- financial /commercial management
- information technology
- business management
- communication skills etc.

Weaknesses
Where are your skills/knowledge lacking?
What would you like to improve?

- from your own point of view?
- from the point of view of other people?
- colleagues
- clients

Opportunities
What are the opportunities facing you?
What are the interesting new trends?

- changes in markets and professional practice
- emerging new specialisms
- developments in technology
- moves towards quality assurance
- assuming a management role

Threats
What obstacles do you face?
Is your professional role changing?

- competition from other businesses
- merger with other bodies
- legislative changes
- different skills required when running a small business
- limited opportunities for progression
- threat of redundancy

The second step in CPD is to ascertain where a person is going. Typically, in a CPD process this may be completed within a year. Nonetheless, the term can be lengthened especially if a person wants to start a new career in management consultancy for instance. In this process, it is important to ascertain what career aspirations a person has and then to work out the reasons behind this. For instance, many students start our MSc Occupational Psychology with the very firm focus that they just want to be chartered as an occupational psychologists. However, a few students each year decide that they are interested only in specific aspects such as change management. Once they realize this, they change their focus to suit the career that they want. Essentially, in this element it is imperative to realize what is important to the person.

The third element is to ascertain the goals needed for a person to realize their career aspirations. Once a person's career aspirations are ascertained the steps to get there need to be worked out in a systematic manner. Looking at the barriers for entry into different careers is also fruitful as once these are identified steps can be taken to overcome any obstacles. For instance, many students find that a lack of work experience prevents them getting jobs within consultancy. In this regard, many volunteer to do placements, research projects and distinct elements of consultancy projects either for universities or for local consultancies willing to take on these individuals on a temporary basis. By working out where a person wants to go and what they need to do to get there then career aspirations can be realized.

Thought Provoking point 14.2

My early career was dominated by my need to gain chartered status as an occupational psychologist. This meant calculating where I needed to work and joining the relevant organization and department in order to fulfil the British Psychological Society's criteria.

The fourth element in CPD is defined by the CPD certification service as 'how will I know I have got there' (see http://www.cpduk.co.uk for further details). By the very nature of CPD a person is always developing, growing and learning. Nonetheless, it is important to have an evaluation of achievements that have been made. These can consist of records such as the curriculum vitae, list of publications, etc. Nevertheless, sometimes it is important just to have a summary of what have been important achievements.

Suggested Development Activities

Development within the eight consultancy competence framework

One of the most useful features of using a competency framework is that competencies that need development can be quickly ascertained and then steps taken to develop competence within that competency. In the remainder of the chapter, each of the eight competencies is examined in detail, suggesting further development activities for each one listed.

Communication

This competency relates to the delivery of oral and written information and the ability to actively listen. Whilst this competency was covered to a larger part in the previous chapter, there are additional development activities that can be performed to improve this further, which include the following:

- Before communicating, think about the message that needs to be said and ensure that this is firmly in your mind whilst communicating with others
- Listen to the main points being said during a conversation and if appropriate clarify the understanding of these points by repeating them back
- If the message has been conveyed don't add unnecessary conversation
- Feel free to question the appropriateness of the communication medium, e.g., is an email the best way to communicate the message effectively
- Watch lecturers in action and see how they effectively deliver complicated theories in an easily digestible format
- Listen to BBC Radio 4 for effective communication strategies by expert interviewers and interviewees
- Volunteer to give information during lectures, seminars and presentations

Influencing others

The majority of recruitment assessment in consultancy consists of work based tasks such as case studies. Indeed case studies are often used to see how the individual leads not only the problem solving and solution generation side but also how they lead and influence the selection panel in accepting their solution (Asher and Chung, 2005). Influencing others therefore concerns the persuasion of others to do something or adopt a point of view in order to produce desired results. Influencing is important in consultancy especially when emotions are high.

Suggested development activities improving influencing skills include the following:

- Engage in strategies to bring a win-win situation, whereby all parties benefit
- Get agreement on small steps and then if appropriate summarize all of these steps together convincing the other person of the desired course of action
- Think about your strategies you use for influencing and alternatives
- Try and evaluate any event where you could have been more influential
- Watch or listen to effective communicators in action and see which part of their argument has the greatest influence over the audience

Organizing and planning

Structure and organization is essential to many successful management consultancy projects (Rasiel and Friga, 2002). The organizing and planning competency relates to the degree to which an individual systematically arranges work for themselves and for additional resources. It also anticipates work that needs to be completed in the future. Planning was covered to a large degree in Chapter 8 on Project Management. Nevertheless, there are other development activities that an individual can do to improve their rating on this competence, as follows:

- Make a to-do list of activities that need to be done describing the date and time they need to be completed
- Prioritize activities in terms of importance and urgency
- Consider time as a finite and limited resource
- Plan a regular time to review activities according to the overall objectives that need to be achieved
- Use a diary to regularly monitor where time is spent
- Identify a student who appears to be very effective in planning and organizing and ask them to describe what they do to manage their time, activities and projects
- Use project management for all projects and in line with good project management practice monitor progress on a regular basis

Problem solving

There are three key components to problem solving. The first is to gather and analyse information. The second is to make effective judgements on what is relevant to the problem at hand. The third is deciding the most appropriate solution.

Many individuals fail to recognize the three components in problem solving and may get stuck at the initial stage where they try and find more and more data. Management consultants call this analysis paralysis. In this regard, it is important to know when you have gathered enough information so as not to in McKinsey's management consultancy speak 'boil the ocean' (Rasiel, 1999). There have been a number of different approaches to problem solving, such as those detailed in Chapter 11 looking at research techniques and De Bono's six thinking hats approach examined in Chapter 12.

Teamwork and consideration of others

John Donne (1572–1631) famously stated that 'no man is an island' and he is a testament to the importance of teamwork and consideration of others. Being inclined to work with others may be related to personality; however, in modern day business it is essential to participate fully within a group for the benefit of the whole. Consideration of others is also vital as it is important in any team situation that individuals work together and to alienate others will lose their contribution in group orientated tasks.

Nevertheless, working in teams may be quite alien to students who often work independently, and are encouraged to do so, on assignments, exams and in other forms of assessment. However, development opportunities do exist in improving teamwork as follows:

- Think about ways in which a group focus rather than an individual focus may be better
- Identify opportunities in which to demonstrate more interpersonal sensitivity, e.g., by encouraging the less confident individuals to state their opinions, etc
- If there is a complicated issue to research create small groups to look at individual parts and then bring this knowledge back to the whole group
- Examine individuals differences and ask whether this affects the way these individuals contribute towards team based tasks

- Organize a social event for a class involving as many people as possible in the decision-making process

Leadership

Most individuals probably think that leadership comes later in consultancy as the individual develops. However, most consultancies expect their junior members of staff to exhibit leadership behaviour providing focus to groups especially when they are client facing.

Setting project objectives or a mission statement for an organization is a vital aspect of leadership. Giving this type of focus is important in order to get others to concentrate on the deliverables of a particular task or project and is a vital leadership function. Another aspect of leadership is to understand the strengths and weaknesses of others. This information is then used to develop the individual and in return improve them for the organization. It also provides the individual with a focus for their energies to go towards a positive outcome. This may involve them recognizing their own strengths and weaknesses. After which they may evolve strategies to deal with or to improve their own particular limitation.

Development activities designed to improve this competency do not necessarily involving constantly taking on a leadership role but more often than not require the observation of leaders in terms of how they behave and what they do. Development strategies for encouraging leadership consist of the following:

- Think of a time where a group activity did not work out well and consider how effective was the leader in this activity
- Take on a leadership role for an assigned task or group exercise
- Make a list of inspiring leaders from the past or present and explore why you consider them inspirational
- Think about what it would be like to be a leader and how the role could be handled
- Make a list of students in your class. Are there some that have obvious development needs? If so think about how you would approach them about addressing these development needs

Drive

This competency is the extent to which someone is motivated and is prepared to get the job done. Someone demonstrating drive will show enthusiasm and determination. They are likely to maintain a high activity level and also set high performance standards. Individuals are likely to want to advance and to demand high performance from others. Drive is an essential quality in a business environment but not to the cost of other behaviours outlined in the eight consultancy competency framework.

Drive comes from within. The need to succeed and the need to perform are inherent qualities that are demonstrated through this competency. Drive can be demonstrated and developed as all of the other competencies. The following represent activities that will help develop drive:

- Ask yourself what would you do to achieve a difficult goal, e.g., a distinction in an assignment

Figure 14.2

Drive is essential for success for Sir Alan Sugar as he searches for 'The Apprentice' (retrieved from http://picasaweb. google.com/lh/ photo/t6MVjyT- 1bsMdGtaI1Vpng)

- Identify someone who seems to be a high achiever. How do they succeed in their achievements and keep up their levels of energy and enthusiasm
- Orientate your attitude on achieving results rather than concentrating on problems and issues
- If individuals are not focusing on a particular task or assignment feel free to use phrases such as, 'can we concentrate on the task at hand' to refocus the team
- Set challenging goals for yourself and review the progress that you make on these goals on a regular basis
- Regularly reward yourself for your successes

Tolerance for stress/uncertainty

In consultancy, this is by far one of the most important competencies to master above all else. Consultants that don't master a tolerance for stress and uncertainty tend to leave the industry after a year or so as consultancy by its very nature is a precarious industry. This competency represents the extent where under varying degrees of pressure, opposition, and disappointment the individual maintains their effectiveness.

> **Thought Provoking point 14.3**
>
> In our professional skills module at Masters level, one of the exercises used requires the students to prepare an expression of interest for winning a consultancy assignment. Before the students go on to prepare the full tender, a rejection letter is given to them. Although, it is rather mean to do this to students, it is a good learning point as quite a lot of debate typically follows about how students feel about this rejection.

There are plenty of studies that link feelings of uncertainty and job insecurity with negative outcomes such as low psychological well-being (De Cuyper and De Witte, 2007). One way that individuals deal with uncertainty is by looking at the fairness of any decisions made (Van den Bos and Lind, 2002). In this regard, one ideal way of looking at say rejection is to think whether or not the decision to reject was fair on behalf of whoever made that decision. In this regard, it is useful to evaluate whether anything could have been better in the light of the decision made and if it could to make this a learning point for next time.

Tenacity is key in this competency, and mastering the ability to pick oneself up after a defeat and carry on is vital to this capability. Other development activities that an individual could do to improve their tolerance of uncertainty and stress include:

- Don't beat yourself up about defeats but learn from them
- Reframe feelings of fairness evaluating constraints and issues at the time of uncertainty and whether these can be resolved next time
- Learn to deal with uncertainty concentrating on past and future successes
- Detail situations, people or activities that generate high levels of stress and look for any commonality between the causes of the stress
- Consider exercise and other coping mechanisms to deal with the stresses and strains of everyday life
- Identify the key drivers that affect thoughts and behaviour and be aware of how these may affect overall levels of stress
- Try to identify ways of creating more positive thinking patterns, e.g., such as affirming that only one in five expressions of interest are successful

Chapter Summary

- A competency is a collection of behaviours associated with effective performance
- Behaviour is what someone says or does or what they don't say and do
- Competencies are distinct but held together as a collective in a competency framework
- Competency frameworks are effective for assessment and development purposes
- The eight consultancy competency framework was designed specifically for identifying key behaviours in management consultants

- Continuing professional development (CPD) is essential for professionals and is continuous throughout working life
- CPD is often a requirement of professional bodies aimed at developing knowledge, skills and personal qualities relevant in that profession
- Competence relates to skills rather than behaviours
- Skills that a person needs can be identified using a SWOT analysis
- Individuals can identify and develop their own levels of effective behaviour by using the exercises in Industry snapshots 14.1, 14.2 and 14.3, in addition to the suggested development activities given on a competency by competency basis

Review Questions

1. What is a competency?
2. What is a competency framework?
3. What are the eight consultancy competencies?
4. Why should career aspirations be important in continuing professional development (CPD)?
5. Why are teamwork and the consideration of others important as a set of behaviours in consultancy?

Assignment Questions

1. Critically discuss whether a competency framework has to detail all the behaviours necessary for on the job success.
2. Using the eight consultancy competency framework critically discuss how this can be used to develop the individual.
3. Define the concept of continuing professional development (CPD) and discuss why it is important for professionals to engage with these activities.
4. Discuss the advantages and limitations of concentrating solely on behaviours as a way of continuing professional development. Suggest ways in which skills can also be used as part of the development process.

Case Study 14.1

The best advice I ever got

Hans-Paul Bürkner interviewed by Daisy Wademan

Good advice often comes in the form of deeds, not words. The best advice I ever got came not by listening, but by observing one of my colleagues – by watching his behaviour, coming to understand his philosophy, and then adapting it to my own style.

When I joined BCG as a consultant in 1981, Tom Lewis was a principal, and quickly became one of my role models, though he was only about five years my senior. On one of our earliest projects together, we worked for a high-technology client evaluating potential entry into new businesses.

Tom was responsible for a remarkably mixed team: We had one person who was strong on organizational issues but incredibly weak with numbers, another who was a computer on legs – superb with analytics, much less so with anything else – and so on. At that time, I assumed it was better (or certainly easier) to build a team from people with similar strengths that were ideally suited to the task, so I didn't envy Tom the job of leading such a disparate group, nor did I anticipate a positive outcome with the client.

But Tom, who's a very modest man, didn't have the same philosophy. He simply went about the task of turning that diverse set of individuals into a high-performing team – methodically, gradually, and quietly. Every week or so, he would engage us one-on-one to discuss how we perceived our performance, what we liked to do, what we thought would help the project go well, all in a non-threatening way. Rather than saying to the person weak at numbers, 'You want to do economic modelling? Are you kidding?' Tom helped steer him toward tasks he excelled at, letting him use and – more important – show off his abilities to the best advantage. As a result, team members developed a deep appreciation of each individual's skills, and that increased our investment in the group effort. The client implemented our recommendations, and that project became the basis of a very long relationship with BCG.

Tom never articulated this team-building philosophy directly, but I watched him act on it many times, and it is central to how I now think about leading individuals, teams, and this firm. When we're faced with what looks at first like an unsolvable problem, a team with what I call 'spikes' of different talents will come up with a better solution than a team whose members have similar strengths. One person makes an oddball suggestion, the next person misunderstands it but in a fruitful way, and together they end up devising a novel solution. The process can be slow and uncomfortable; spikiness often hurts. But it can yield spectacular results – as long as the firm or the project leader ensures that team members appreciate one another's talents.

Building teams is not about being nice. Tom is unusual; he's a natural diplomat, and people like to work with him. Yet however graceful and non-threatening, his talks went to the heart of a subject most people would rather avoid: what they're good at and what they're not. Whilst I've adopted Tom's philosophy, I apply it differently. Tom was subtle; I'm more direct. When putting together a team, I make sure it's spiky. And when people complain that their differences will cause problems, I'll bluntly disagree. I'll tell an unhappy manager, 'It doesn't matter that he's weak in finance. Find out what he's best at, and show his strength to the team.' Tom's subtlety was effective for him, but directness comes naturally to me. Acting on advice works best when you do it your way.

President and Chief Executive Officer, The Boston Consulting Group

Further Reading

Bowler, M.C. and Woehr, D.J. (2006), A meta-analytic evaluation of the impact of dimension and exercise factors on assessment center ratings, *Journal of Applied Psychology*, 91(5), 1114–1124

Garavan, T.N. (2007), Using assessment centre performance to predict subjective person-organisation (P-O) fit: A longitudinal study of graduates, *Journal of Managerial Psychology*, 22(2), 150–167

Hurson, T. (2007), *Think Better: An Innovator's Guide to Productive Thinking*. New York, New York: ?McGraw Hill

Jackling, B., De Lange, P. and On, J.R. (2007), Accounting graduate employment destinations and commitment to CPD: A study from two australian universities, *Accounting Education*16(4), 329–343

Keats, S. (2008), What's new in CPD, *Chartered Accountants Journal* 87(1), 25–26

Woehr, D.J. and Arthur Jr., W. (2003), The construct-related validity of assessment center ratings: A review and meta-analysis of the role of methodological factors, *Journal of Management*, 29(2), 231–258

CHAPTER 15

Professionalism and ethics

Learning Objectives

At the end of this chapter students will be able to:

- Define what is meant by professionalism

- Understand the history behind being a professional and why there are disparities in its use as a word in the English language

- Understand why professional behaviour should be guided by a set of principles

- Recognize why ethical codes of conduct are needed

- Have knowledge of ethical codes of conduct in the management consultancy industry

---

Mini Case Study 15.1

False advertising

False advertising is where goods or services are passed off as something that they are not (Astrachan Gunst Thomas, 2009).

Across the Globe, various organisations monitor the claims made by advertisers to prevent false advertising. In Europe, The European Advertising Standards Alliance (EASA) is an umbrella corporation that brings together several organisations that monitor the advertising industry in the respective European countries (ASA, 2009). In the US, the Federal Trade Commission takes on this role, protecting the public against false advertising (Astrachan Gunst Thomas, 2009).

False advertising also applies to individual professionals or professionals working in a firm. A professional may claim that they are an expert in a particular field in which they only have limited knowledge. They may also claim a particular level of membership or status to a Professional body to which they are not entitled. Individuals, who engage in false advertising do it typically to gain financial reward.

Regulation of professionals is predominantly carried out by the professional body that the individual is a member. It is essential that the professional body does everything it can to ensure that the claims being made against the individual are true and can be collaborated with evidence. Nevertheless, there are times when it is difficult to prove what an individual does or says is wrong.

Sanctions against the individual by professional organisations can range from a warning and removal of all false claims through to being struck off a register to practice. In extreme examples criminal or civil action may also result. This is why it is essential for professionals to have professional indemnity insurance in case they mislead their clients.

References

ASA (2009), *Advertising Regulation in Europe* retrieved from http://www.asa.org.uk/asa/about/europe/

Astrachan GunstThomas (2009), *What is False Advertising?* retrieved from http://www.aboutfalseadvertising.com/

Professionalism and Ethics

Introduction

Professionalism and ethics are important aspects of management consultancy (Hagenmeyer, 2007). In the opening case study, Jon Doe (name changed) was promoting himself and his skills in a deceptive manner. Professionalism and ethics encompasses issues such as these and will be reviewed in this chapter.

Thought Provoking point 15.1

I joined my first consultancy, The Alexander Consulting Group, in 1987 where I worked in the Pensions department. Claiming that I joined my first consultancy in 1987, taken out of context, might imply that I have over 22 years consultancy experience. This is not the case so would be deceptive and unethical to claim. Thus, I tend to be more specific about my consultancy experience, listing positions and roles.

Professionalism

Lynch (2001) asked the question what does professionalism mean especially in a management consultancy context. The word profession derives from a Latin combination of pro (forth) and fateri (confess), meaning to announce a belief (Roddenberry, 1953). In its early usage the word concerned binding yourself by vows of faith or purpose. It was primarily the monks and those from a religious order who used the word (Roddenberry, 1953). In Tudor times, people became relaxed about applying the word profession (Anonymous, 2007). It therefore became common language and used in a number of occupations. Indeed, we hear the word applied today in this context such as professional pickpocket or thief (Roddenberry, 1953).

Later in the nineteenth century the upper echelons of society used the word 'profession'.

These early professions were: Medicine, Law and Theology (Lynch, 2001). These professions were built around strict ethical and philosophical codes (Roddenberry, 1953).These codes typically promoted the understanding of the service provided to others (Lynch, 2001). Many professions exist today that take on-board this same philosophy (Roddenberry, 1953). Abraham Flexner in 1912 defined the modern meaning of 'profession' as any group governed by a code of ethics (Christensen, 1988). Accepting a code of ethics is certainly part of any profession, so professionalism is in essence abiding by these ethics.

Another essential part of professionalism is a prolonged period of study (Roddenberry, 1953). This prolonged period of intellectual study should be grounded in general principles that can be applied in professional practice. This professional practice is where the professional through disciplined judgement applies the correct principles relevant to the work at hand. Thus, professions are quite different to other occupations, even those that require a period of study, such as hairdressing, because general principles of practice and ethics are taught (Roddenberry, 1953).

Lynch (2001) goes further and argued that the meaning of professionalism should encompass the wider societal view. In other words, professionals should not only be aware of their own particular skills and code of conduct. They should also be aware of how they operate in a complex society (Kamath, 2007). In most countries, there is a preference for self-regulation of professional bodies and societies that regulate professionals (Kamath, 2007). Nevertheless, Lynch (2001) warned that if these professional bodies do not keep up with the changes in society then society itself may seek to regulate the professions.

There is a more critical view of being a professional. Restrictions are put on to entry into a profession such as a minimum amount of education, supplementary examination or evidence and the imposition of varying clauses and provisions (OECD, 2009). This restriction may translate itself into less supply of expertise, and with less supply comes a higher price especially if demand is high. So becoming a professional could be advantageous as your profession is restricted to a certain few, as a professional can charge more (Anonymous, 2007). Nevertheless, in defence of professionals everywhere, Roddenberry (1953) quoted Adam Smith justifying professional fees in that:

> We trust our health to the physician; our fortunes and sometimes our life and reputation to the lawyer and attorney. Such confidence could not be safely reposed in people of a very mean or low condition.
>
> *Cited from Adam Smith, 'The Wealth of Nations' by Roddenberry (1953); p. 122*

Indeed, the oldest profession was prostitution as coined in 1888 by Rudyard Kipling (Anonymous, 2007). The newest profession coined by McKenna (2006a) as a double entendre is management consultancy. This terminology demonstrates that the term profession is still not particularly well understood (Lynch, 2001). Perhaps then this is why professions themselves seek to generate a list of ethics, rules and regulations by which their members should abide (Kamath, 2007).

Professionalism in Occupations

Professions and professionalism may be difficult to define, but the notion of being professional exists in the real world. Thus, a fruitful line of enquiry might be to ascertain what professions are in terms of occupations. Indeed, Roddenberry (1953) stated that the profession as an occupational group practises with the following obligations:

1. to serve mankind generally rather than self, individuals, or groups
2. to prepare as fully as practicable for service before entering active practice
3. to work continually to improve skills by all means available and to freely communicate professional information gained
4. to employ full skill at all times regardless of considerations of personal gain, comfort, or safety, and to at all times assist fellow professionals upon demand
5. to regulate practice by the franchising of practitioners, setting the highest practicable intellectual and technical minimums; to accept and upgrade fellow professionals solely upon considerations of merit; to be constantly alert to protect society from fraudulent, substandard, or unethical practice through ready and swift disfranchisement
6. to zealously guard the honour of the profession by living exemplary lives publicly and privately, recognizing that injury to a group serving society, injures society
7. to give constant attention to the improvement of self-discipline, recognizing that the individual must be the master of himself to be the servant of others

This list of duties may define the minimum that a profession should strive for; however, before examining the professional rules of the management consultancy industry, it is wise to see why these rules may be important by examining the well-known scandal of Enron and other corporate scandals.

Enron

Lynch (2001) stated that some would criticize the words 'professionalism' and 'ethics' being applied to management consultancy. Indeed, the Enron crisis highlighted this strongly. Enron was one of the world's leading energy companies but started operations in other areas including as a financial institution (Fox, 2004). The company's revenues soared from $4.6 billion in 1990 to $101 billion in 2000 (Fox, 2004). Enron employed approximately 22 000 people before its collapse in 2001 (McLean and Elkind, 2004).

Newspaper articles openly criticized Enron in a series of accountancy revelations that bordered on fraud during the 1990s (McLean and Elkind, 2004). This involved the energy company itself and the accountancy firm Arthur Andersen. Arthur Andersen was at the time one of the 'Big Five' accounting firms providing auditing services to large corporations (see Chapter 1 for more details).

McLean and Elkind (2004) demonstrated how Enron plunged towards bankruptcy due to its financial irregularities. Indeed, much of its debt were not shown on its accounts making the company seem more profitable than what it was

Andersen guilty in Enron case

A jury in the United States has found accountancy firm Arthur Andersen guilty of obstructing justice by shredding documents relating to the failed energy giant Enron.

The verdict could be the death knell for the 89-year old company, once one of the world's top five accountants.

Andersen has already lost much of its business, and two-thirds of its once 28 000 strong US workforce. Following the conviction, multi-million dollar lawsuits brought by Enron investors and shareholders demanding compensation are likely to follow, and could bankrupt the firm. The company called Saturday's verdict 'wrong' and is contemplating an appeal, but at the same time did promise to stop auditing publicly traded companies – preempting an official ban that now is a near certainty.

Enron's collapse last December was partly blamed on questionable accounting that kept hundreds of millions of dollars in debt off its books. Andersen, which audited Enron's accounts, went on trial in Houston, Texas, after allegations that employees had illegally destroyed thousands of documents and computer records relating to its scandal-hit client, which was based there.

The 12-member jury had heard nearly five weeks of testimony and was in its 72nd hour of deliberation over 10 days when it finally reached the verdict. Andersen's defence lawyer, Rusty Hardin, said the firm was disappointed by the verdict. He said it would file an appeal but had to wait until after the sentencing date – 11 October – to do so. He added: 'This company did not commit a crime'. Andersen also faces a fine of up to $500 000.

The firm's lawyers had argued that the shredding of documents had been routine housekeeping, but the jury decided it was an attempt to thwart federal regulators investigating Enron. The trial heard how one Andersen executive said on a training video that if documents were shredded and then the investigators arrived, that would be good.

But Mr Hardin had argued that a number of important documents had survived the shredding, suggesting there was no conspiracy to cover up Andersen's work on Enron's books. The prosecution's star witness was former Andersen partner David Duncan, who was in charge of the Enron audit team. He admitted obstructing justice in April and told jurors that he had signed an agreement with Andersen to present a united front, claiming that neither had done anything wrong. He said that he had reneged on the agreement after much 'soul searching'.

The verdict came after US District Court Judge Melinda Harmon made what is believed to be a landmark legal decision to break a deadlock amongst the jury. She ruled that jurors could reach a verdict on the company as a whole, even though they failed to agree on the individual responsible for ordering the shredding. Judge Harmon agonized over the decision for more than a day as she sought to clarify a point of law that mystified even seasoned attorneys and other experts on American jurisprudence. 'I'm kind of in a position of a case of first impression, which is terrifying for a district judge', she said, aware that her ruling could set a precedent and be subject to future legal challenges.

Source: http://news.bbc.co.uk/1/hi/business/2047122.stm. Reproduced with permission.

(McLean and Elkind, 2004). Enron filed for bankruptcy in 2001, which affected its firm of auditors Arthur Andersen (see Industry snapshot 15.1).

Critics of the management consultancy industry often cite Enron as a case study that illustrated the need for regulation (McKenna, 2006a). The management consultancy fees gained from the energy giant were approximately $27 million and the auditing fees around $25 million for Andersen Consulting and Arthur Andersen (McKenna, 2006a). This highlighted conflicts of interest between the auditing and management consultancy functions of a professional service firm. Other consultancy practices were also implicated in the scandal as the CEO of Enron, Jeffery Skilling was ex-consultant at McKinsey & Company (McKenna, 2006a). Skilling is now serving up to 24 years in prison for his part in the Enron scandal (Yeung, 2006).

Thought Provoking point 15.2

Arthur Andersen was founded in 1913, and during the 1970s and 1980s it saw its management consultancy growing at a much faster rate than the accountancy business. Through the 1990s there was increasing tension between the two businesses: Andersen Consulting and Arthur Andersen. Andersen Consulting had to pay 15 per cent of its profits each year to Arthur Andersen, which led to much tension during the 1990s and the eventual split of the consultancy that became Accenture in 2001.

Other scandals have also come to light in the corporate world. The well-known examples are financial irregularities such as those at Enron. This is basically white-collar crime where large amounts of money are generated and then taken for the use of the corporation and its directors. Enron may seem like an extreme example but other financial irregularities have been revealed in other firms such as Guinness, WorldCom, HealthSouth, American International Group and Ahold (the world's third-biggest retailer, based in the Netherlands).

Other scandals – financing terrorists

Other cases of scandal can be found either in good newspapers or through some internet sources such as Wikipedia (http://en.wikipedia.org/wiki/Corporate_scandal). One of the most extreme examples of corporate scandal is when companies contribute towards terrorist activities. Examples of this include the infamous Chiquita case which was an American based company who paid $25 million in fines after pleading guilty to engaging with Colombian paramilitary groups (Aljazeera, 2007). These groups consisted of the right wing AUC (Autodefensas Unidas de Colombia) and other organizations which were responsible for numerous massacres, forced displacements and drug trafficking (Evans, 2007). Chiquita was accused of paying at least $825 000 after the AUC was designated a Foreign Terrorist Organization (FTO) by the US in 2001 (Evans, 2007). Several executives were also under investigation after allegedly supplying the AUC with 3400 AK-47 rifles and 4 million rounds of ammunition in 2001 (Evans, 2007). Nevertheless, as Evans (2007) pointed out the executives may have little to fear as supplying terrorist organizations may just be the cost of trading with Colombia.

Other scandals – sex, nepotism and cronyism

Other scandals are abound in corporate life and range from cases of using sex for political gain, through to cases of nepotism. An example of using sex for political gain is given in Industry snapshot 15.2. Here a consultant from an external consultancy is recruited into the organization and is promoted quickly through

Industry snapshot 15.2

Manager uses sex to secure her internal consultancy position

A team of consultants were called into a well-known retailer to examine issues involving the development of their store managers and recruitment of store based staff. The retailer took on-board the advice of the consultancy and implemented several changes embarking on a management development programme and redesign of the recruitment procedures.

During this time, one of the consultants Kate became very friendly with the project manager Stefan from the client. Both of these individuals were married to other people. The relationship grew and Kate joined the retailer full-time. At this point Kate claimed several professional qualifications such as being chartered by her professional body, which was untrue.

Nevertheless, Kate as an internal consultant embarked on a massive organizational change, which the retailer needed if it was to survive in the twenty-first century. The organizational change was implemented and the consultant built up a small internal consultancy team primarily from retail staff but also recruiting external individuals. Kate also became the manager of the internal consultancy.

Kate rapidly increased both her salary and her status within the organization. Suspicion about this and the extent of Kate's power within the organization grew. Several questions were asked not only of the power wielded by Kate but also of her professional standing. To resolve this, Kate shed some of her internal consultancy team saving money for the organization and applied for chartered status which after working two years within the retail organization she now qualified for.

Nevertheless, rumours of a more than friendly relationship between Kate and her boss Stefan would not go away. These rumours were not helped by the fact that the work completed by Kate was hotel based. Kate had pretty much transferred her work to others in her team but was frequently seen with her boss at the five-star hotels where the management development centres took place. Soon after, Stefan was fired from the organization. Kate was also asked to leave and took redundancy. The internal consultancy still remained although managed by a former store manager of the firm.

recommendations from her boss who is in fact was sleeping with the consultant at the time. In another example, the President of the World Bank was accused of giving his romantic partner a promotion and a number of large pay increases at the bank (Goldenberg, 2007). This type of 'affair' is probably not that uncommon but is unlikely to bring good press so very infrequently makes the headlines (see Industry snapshot 15.3).

Cases of nepotism may also be common in organizations. Nepotism is the preferment shown by individuals in authority to relatives in the bestowal of privileges or positions on the basis of their relationship rather than those of merit (for a detailed investigation of the origins of the word visit http://saints.sqpn.com/ncd05726.htm). Nepotism may abound in smaller organizations whereby the son of the managing director who formed the company may become the rightful successor. This may or may not be acceptable in organizations dependent on their organizational culture. It may also be frowned upon by outside concerns such as shown in Industry snapshot 15.4.

Cronyism is similar to nepotism but involves the preferential treatment of friends as opposed to blood relatives. In Chapter 5, the Thought Provoking point

Industry snapshot 15.3

It pays to be the boss's wife

The British government's tax fraud department didn't have to look too far afield to find an ethical lapse. David Partridge, the COO of the Revenue and Customs Prosecutions Office, was fired for gross misconduct after awarding his wife what a government report termed a 'lucrative' consultancy contract that paid her £100 000 (roughly $160 000). A report about the situation by the House of Commons Public Accounts Committee found shortcomings in internal controls which allowed the contract to be awarded, according to several British media accounts. Additionally, the report said the agency's director was 'thrown into the deep end' when appointed from outside the public sector, because he lacked the necessary support, training and experience to identify or mitigate any risks that occurred.

Source: *Journal of Accountancy*; Feb 2009, Vol. 207 Issue 2, p. 20. Reproduced with permission.

Industry snapshot 15.4

Rupert and the joys of nepotism by Bell (2003)

What could be more terrifying than Rupert Murdoch? Why, a 30-year-old Rupert Murdoch with a £12bn television company to play with.

There has been much whingeing amongst shareholders about the appointment of James Murdoch to the top job at BSkyB, the satellite television company 35 per cent controlled by his father, Rupert. But it has to be said that whilst for reasons of schadenfreude we may wish to see Mr Murdoch humiliated, it is a racing certainty he is rather better placed than a group of short-termist profiteers to know what is best for the company he built from scratch.

This is not a particularly fashionable way to describe shareholder activism, which in principle sounds like a very fine thing. But in practice the groups of shareholders we are talking about – institutions which look after our pensions – are interested primarily in their own dividends and short-term considerations of profit.

Mr Murdoch, on the other hand, is far more interested in what we would like to see from all our businesses – long-term investment, succession planning, strategic durability. And of course profitability too. One would have thought the pinstripes would have rejoiced at the fact that, short of finding the secret to eternal life, Rupert has done the next best thing and produced mini-me just in time to ensure the future of the dynasty. After an 'exhaustive' search for a shortlist of candidates who were subjected to the usual headhunter nonsense of psychometric tests – and one assumes a DNA test – young James won the day with dad's endorsement.

This figleaf of correct procedure cannot really be an appropriate way for one of Britain's largest companies to choose its chief executive, says the Association of British Insurers, former Murdoch editor and executive Andrew Neil, and the National Association of Pension Funds. On Newsnight, Mr Neil gave a moving account of how little his Sky shares had shifted. For competitors who have felt the rapacious breath of the Murdoch machine on their backs for three decades, nothing could be better fun than joining in the chorus of 'shame!' and hoping against hope that the mighty would be humiliated.

Hang on a minute, though. What exactly is the problem here? The objections ignore the way Rupert Murdoch has always run his businesses – with a ferocity, ingenuity and individual sense of purpose that has left the rest of the media by turn

▶

breathless, scared and outraged. The fact that every single chief executive of BSkyB to date has been recruited from an incredibly small corporate gene pool within Murdoch's News Corporation was never a problem before. Neither was the fact that when any of these executives, however cherished, showed signs of differing from chairman Rupert they were generously but swiftly dispatched.

We sometimes get confused between good corporate governance and the interests of shareholders, as if they were synonymous, whilst nothing could be further from the truth. Shareholders and particularly fund managers have little to say about shocking lapses of corporate governance when the share prices rise and the cash tills ring. Few City institutions in my memory have ever bailed out of a company because earnings were 'suspiciously high' or because the company's diversity policy was not up to scratch. We applaud the shareholder activism against 'fat cat' salaries, quite rightly so, but the redistributive altruism of fund managers begins and ends with their own performance charts. And our pensions.

And this is the £12bn question. Who would you rather look after the future of BSkyB – Murdoch and son, or a set of City institutions? It might be a case of devil, meet the deep blue sea, but at least Murdoch has a track record both of picking winners and ditching losers before they actually fall at the hurdles. What ought to perplex shareholders more is whether this is a sign Rupert is going soft in his old age. He was utterly reliable in the past in putting business before all else. His daughter Elisabeth had a relatively short tenure at BSkyB; many assumed she was being groomed for the top job, but it never came to pass.

Murdoch has also suggested that the natural heir to his businesses was, on the quaintly old-fashioned basis of primogeniture, eldest son Lachlan. Whilst Lachlan is still a player in the print firmament of the News Corp galaxy it would seem that James, who has at least held down a top job at the Asian Star TV network, is now the star son. James Murdoch will not be allowed to fail. This should be at least some comfort to grumpy shareholders. He might even turn out to be a chip off the old block. Which, for the rest of us, would be the worst possible news.

5.1 demonstrated an example of cronyism whereby the top performer of the assessment centre was not given the job they had applied for because the fourth highest performer was appointed as they were already known to the organization. Other examples of cronyism can also be found in the media. Goldenberg (2007) for instance described how the President of the World Bank was accused of cronyism by employees after he had appointed a number of former colleagues to important posts within the bank.

Professionalism – what should the consultant do about scandals

By examining some of the recent corporate scandals that have come to light, it can be noted that professionalism and ethics may not be the highest priority in some organizations. Dealing with these scandals as a consultant is fraught with difficulty. Hagenmayer (2007) suggested that as consulting is a form of situation specific assistance provided by an expert, if a scandal resulting from that assistance was to be uncovered then in the ideal situation both the organization and the consultancy firm would share the blame (see Figure 15.1).

However, in most cases of unethical practice the sharing of blame as Hagenmayer (2007) suggested may not be practical. Indeed, in the Industry snapshot 15.2, if you were appointed as a consultant within the internal consultancy and the relationship

Figure 15.1

The sharing of
corporate failings
(Hagenmayer, 2007)
Source:
U. Hagenmayer
(2007) Business
Ethics: A European
Review. Reproduced
with permission of
Wiley-Blackwell.

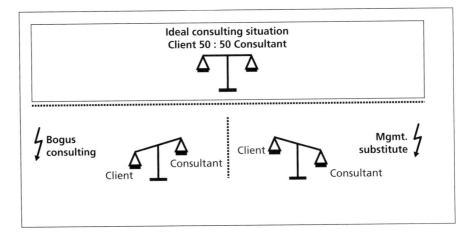

between your manager Kate and her boss Stefan was discovered, what would you do? This poses a difficult question, as if you reported Kate to perhaps her boss's boss, then the whole internal consultancy may be under threat. In this regard, would you lose your job? It is a difficult area to make judgements on and even more difficult if you are faced with the scandal yourself. Nevertheless, adopting the word professional puts a person under obligations that they should be guided as Roddenberry (1953) suggested by moral principles of behaviour and conduct.

Thought Provoking point 15.3

My first experience of corporate scandal was during my university years in the early 1990's where the father of a close friend was one of the Directors of Guinness. The Guinness share-trading fraud is a famous case of the 1980s where the former chief executive was sentenced for five years in prison, of which he served less than half the sentence. Others in the scandal were also jailed or were given heavy fines for their part in the affair.

(Lenzner, 1987; O'Shea & Madigan, 1997; Perry & Caminiti, 1987).

Professionalism is an important aspect of working in a consultancy. A consultant must abide by moral principles and standards for the good of not only the client but of society itself (Hagenmayer, 2007; Kamath, 2007; Lynch, 2001; O'Shea and Madigan, 1997). Management consultants must if they make a mistake disclose this at the earliest opportunity (Casella, 2008). They must also refuse to take work that seems to be bogus assignments or to act as a management substitute where their ethical business principles are contradicted (Hagenmayer, 2007).

Ethics

Introduction

Ethics is the aspect of the management consultancy profession that safeguards the public from either deception or dishonesty. It is not a list of commandments but the guiding principles which prescribe what to do given certain situations (Kamath, 2007). The International Council of Management Consulting Institute (ICMCI) is the global association of national management consulting professional bodies. Table 15.1 demonstrates the current professional bodies that are members of the ICMCI. Members of the ICMCI and its related professional bodies located in various countries take ethical codes of conduct very seriously (Kamath, 2007).

> ### Thought Provoking point 15.4
>
> Medicine has achieved recognition as a profession and consultants hunger for similar recognition. The picture of the skilled professional ministering to his worshiping patients apparently appeals to many consultants.
>
> Quoted from Higdon (1969); p. 46

In the UK, there are two professional bodies that safeguard the public, and these consist of the Management Consultancies Association (MCA) and the former Institute of Management Consultants who have become the Institute of Business Consulting (IBC).

MCA list of ethics

The following list of ethics is provided by the Management Consultancies Association, which is a professional body within the industry in the UK. The full set of rules is provided on 56 pages at the following web page (http://www.mca.org.uk/mca/pdf/bylawssep03.pdf). These rules are summarized by the MCA below:

2.1 A Code of Professional Conduct designed to cover all eventualities must necessarily be written in general terms expressing broad ethical principles. Almost every case of doubt as to the proper course of action required to conform to the Code of Professional Conduct arises from a conflict between Members' business or commercial interests and their duty to their client. In general, the principle adopted by the MCA is simple – in any conflict between the interests of the Members and the interest of the clients, the duty to the clients must prevail.

2.2 Each Member accepts that it is in the interests of all Members of the Association that each member maintains the highest possible professional and ethical standards so as to uphold the dignity and reputation of their profession. They shall exercise their professional skill and judgement to the best of their ability and discharge their professional responsibilities with independence of thought and action, objectivity and integrity. Members therefore undertake to abide by the Code of Professional Conduct, which provides that Members shall:

- in matters relating to a client's affairs act solely in the interests of the client;

- not enter into any arrangement which might detract from the objectivity and impartiality of advice given to the client;

Table 15.1	Australia	Institute of Management Consultants – Australia
	Austria	Fachverband Unternehmensberatung und Informationstechnologie
Members of the International Council of Management Consulting Institutes (ICMCI) 2008. Reproduced with permission from www.icmci.org.	Bangladesh	Institute of Management Consultants Bangladesh [IMCB]
	Bosnia-Herzegovina	Local Economic Service Providers Network (LESP-net)
	Brazil	Instituto Brasileiro dos Consultores de Organizacao
	Bulgaria	Bulgarian Association of Management Consulting Organizations
	Canada	Canadian Association of Management Consultants
	Caribbean	Caribbean Institute of Certified Management Consultants
	China	The Management Consulting Committee (MCC) of the China Enterprise Confederation (CEC)
	Chinese Taipei	Business Management Consultants Association (BMCA)
	Croatia	Association of Management Consultants – Croatia
	Cyprus	Cyprus Institute of Business Consultants
	Czech Republic	Association for Consulting to Business
	Denmark	Danish Management Board
	Finland	The Finnish Management Consultants
	Germany	Bundesverband Deutscher Unternehmensberater
	Greece	Hellenic Association of Management Consulting Firms
	Hong Kong	Institute of Management Consultants – Hong Kong
	Hungary	Association of Management Consultants in Hungary
	India	The Institute of Management Consultants of India
	Ireland	Institute of Management Consultants and Advisers – Ireland
	Italy	Associazione Professionale Italiana Dei Consulenti Di Direzione
	Japan	Zen Noh Ren
	Jordan	The Institute of Management Consultants of Jordan
	Kazakhstan	Kazakhstan association of Certified Management Consultants (KACMC)
	Korea, Republic of	Korea Management and Technology Consultant Association
	Latvia	Latvian Association of Business Consultants
	Macedonia	Management Consulting Association 2000
	Malaysia	Institute of Management Consultants – Malaysia
	Netherlands	Orde van organisatiekundigen en-adviseurs
	New Zealand	Institute of Management Consultants New Zealand Inc.
	Nigeria	Institute of Management Consultants – Nigeria
	Norway	Institute of Management Consultants Norway
	Poland	Stowarzyszenie Doradcow Gospodarczych Association of Economic Advisors
	Romania	Institute of Management Consultancy of Romania
	Russian Federation	National Institute of Certified Management Consultants (NICMC)
	Singapore	Institute of Management Consultants – Singapore
	South Africa	Institute of Management Consultants – South Africa
	Spain	Instituto de Consultores de Organizacion y Direccion
	Sweden	Swedish Association of Management Consultants
	Switzerland	Association of Management Consultants – Switzerland
	Thailand	The Institute of Management Consultants – Thailand
	Turkey	Yonetim Danismanlari Dernegi (YDD)
	United Kingdom	Institute of Business Consulting
	United States	Institute of Management Consultants – IMC USA

Source: http://www.icmci.org/MemberInstitutes/index.cfm. Reproduced with permission.

- disclose, at the earliest opportunity, any special relationships, circumstances or business interests which might influence or impair, or could be seen by the client or others to influence or impair, the Member's judgement or objectivity on a particular assignment;
- foster the highest possible standards of professional competence amongst those for whom they are responsible;
- comply with the letter and the spirit of:
  - the law of any country in which they practice
  - contractual obligations
  - any guidance which may from time to time be issued by the MCA;
- reject any business practice which might reasonably be deemed improper;
- keep confidential all confidential information regarding the client's business and staff;
- only accept work for which it is qualified and has capacity to undertake;
- agree terms of remuneration and the basis of calculation thereof with the client in advance or (see next point);
- define and agree terms of engagement, the nature of an assignment to be carried out, how the work will be performed, the desired outcomes of the assignment, how performance will be evaluated, the terms of remuneration, and the basis of calculation thereof, and the provision for termination, with the client in advance;
- where a Member is a subsidiary of a parent body, or enters into an alliance with a body, which is not in the public practice of management consultancy, ensure that all advice will be untied and independent of any influence of that parent body or alliance partner;
- at all times act so as to maintain or improve the status of Management Consultancy as a profession;
- act with fairness and integrity towards all persons with whom their work is connected and towards other Members.

2.3 Where any breach of the Code of Professional Conduct is brought to the attention of the Executive Director it shall be put before the General Policy Committee and the procedure in Section 210 followed. (See also C- Disciplinary Procedures).

2.4 Where, following the completion of the procedure set out in Section 210, a finding is made that there has been a breach of the Code of Professional Conduct, the General Policy Committee may recommend any of the following sanctions:

- reprimand published to the Members of the Association
- public reprimand
- conditions imposed on continued membership
- suspension from membership
- expulsion from membership, with a prohibition on re-entry for two years

- In all cases save reprimand within the Association, the action taken and the background to such action may be publicized by the Association in trade and/or national press and on the Association's website.

2.5 For the avoidance of doubt, conduct of a Member outside of the United Kingdom will constitute an infringement of this Code as if it were conduct in the United Kingdom where such conduct is or is likely to become known within the United Kingdom and where it presents a risk to the reputation of the Association, the Management Consultancy profession or the individual Member.

Quoted from the Management Consultancies Association at http://www.mca.org.uk/MCA/AboutUs/CodeOfConduct.aspx

Thought Provoking point 15.5

The Institute of Management Consultants USA have put forward a series of 16 questions dealing with ethical issues in a management consultancy context. Feel free having read this chapter to have a go at answering these questions located at the following website: http://imcusa.articulate-online.com/7924645535

International view of consultancy ethics

The ethical principles stated by the MCA have much in common with other countries codes of conduct. Kamath (2007) conducted a review of management consultancy ethics across the globe. Interestingly out of the 43 members of the ICMCI only 26 were included in the review. This was due to problems of translation with countries such as Germany, Korea and China not having English translations of their code of ethics.

This may limit the generalization of the study especially to non-English speaking nations. English speaking nations that contributed to the study included: Australia, Canada, Ireland, New Zealand, UK and USA. Nevertheless, many non-English countries were included in the review (i.e., Bangladesh, Bosnia-Herzegovina, Bulgaria, Croatia, Denmark, Finland, Greece, Hong Kong, Hungary, India, Japan, Jordan, Macedonia, Netherlands, Romania, Russian Federation, Singapore, South Africa, Spain and Sweden).

The review concluded that seven core values were important across the 26 countries consisting of:

1. **Confidentiality**, in that all the information that a management consultant receives from a client remains confidential and cannot be used without authorization
2. **Transparency**, where a consultancy has relationships with a third party that may result in a conflict of interest, the consultancy should declare such relationships
3. **Integrity**, where as the Danish code states a consultant should work loyally towards their client and profession

4. **Reliability**, is where the client trusts the consultant to comply with stated agreements and to keep any promises made

5. **Objectivity and independence**, in that a consultant must keep separate from the client and act as an impartial third party

6. **Expertise and competence**, where members will have the knowledge, experience, personal qualities and capacity for the assignment

7. **Professionalism**, is the overarching principle making sure all the requirements of the client are met and that the consultant acts in a professional manner in dealing with all aspects of the assignment

Adapted from Kamath (2007); p. 35–38

Enforcement of management consultancy ethics

Academics have recently questioned whether the ethical guidelines promoted by professional bodies can be enforced (Nitsch, Baetz and Hughes, 2005). Indeed, the ability to enforce an ethical code of conduct influences whether it is effective in shaping behaviour (Nitsch *et al.*, 2005). The enforcement of ethical standards relies on members reporting violations of the code (Nitsch *et al.*, 2005; Shawver and Clements, 2008). However research suggests that less than half of the individuals who witness code violations actually report them (Nitsch *et al.*, 2005).

Interestingly, Kamath (2007) in his review of international management consultancy ethics found a disparity between different professional bodies regarding the way in which they handled enforcement of ethical standards. Out of the 26 professional bodies surveyed, only 9 did anything at all about enforcing the ethical guidelines, violations or disciplinary. Out of these 9 professional bodies only 7 contained concrete disciplinary mechanisms. This meant that out of the 26 countries surveyed by the ICMCI, only 27 per cent had guidance to enforce the ethical code.

The findings by Kamath (2007) make for worrying reading in countries that have no mechanism to enforce the ethical codes of their professional body. As Lynch (2001) suggested, self-regulation should be enforced by the professional bodies that oversee the work of consultants and if this is not done then perhaps society will regulate the industry.

Chapter Summary

- Professionalism and ethics are important aspects of management consultancy
- Professionalism derives from the Latin combination meaning to profess or to announce a belief
- Abraham Flexner defined the modern meaning of a profession as any group governed by a code of ethics
- Adam Smith stated that those in a profession should not be of a very mean or low condition
- Corporate scandals such as Enron make the need for ethical principles all the more clear
- Sex used for personal gain, nepotism and cronyism may all be encountered by the consultant contracted to work in different organizations

- Dealing with scandals and issues of professional practice is difficult but should be guided by ethical principles
- Enforcement of ethical principles may be different dependent on the country that the consultant practices in

Review Questions

1. Define what professionalism is.
2. Is a professional pickpocket actually a professional?
3. How are professions different to other occupations?
4. Does professionalism have wider societal impacts?
5. What is the list of regulations a profession seeks to generate to which its members should abide by?
6. Define the term nepotism.
7. What is cronyism?
8. What do ethics safeguard?
9. Are ethics just a list of commandments?
10. What are the seven core values across the international management consultancy industry?
11. Are ethics enforced?

Arthur D. Little in China: A whole new ball game

By Marcus Schuetz

In 2006, Thomas Schiller, a managing director of Arthur D. Little (ADL), arrived in hazy Beijing with a crystal clear objective: to resurrect a consultant practice that lacked brand recognition in China. Despite its success and being world-renowned for its technology-focused consultancy business, ADL's first venture into the Chinese market in the early 2000s was hamstrung by its global restructuring. With ADL's uneasy downscaling in China at the hands of his predecessor in mind, Schiller knew that reinvigorating ADL's practice in China would require a fresh perspective and approach. Drawing from his experience with ADL's practice in Munich, Schiller was fully aware of what it took to create and sustain success for a consulting practice. However, he was equally aware that, as ample as the funding from headquarters might be to jump-start the practice in China, it was a drop in the ocean considering the vastness of the market. Was there a magic key to unlock the giant market that had eluded Schiller's predecessor? How could Schiller ensure success for ADL in China?

Ricky Lai prepared this case under the supervision of Dr Marcus Schuetz for class discussion. This case is not intended to show effective or ineffective handling of decision or business processes.

The consulting industry

Consulting had developed alongside the study of management. The first management consulting firm was ADL, founded in 1886 by Arthur Dehon Little and Roger Griffin.[1] It was followed by the Business Research Service, which was founded by Edwin G. Booz in 1914 and later became Booz Allen Hamilton.[2] Next came McKinsey & Company (McKinsey), which was founded by James O. McKinsey in 1926 after he left his accounting professorship at the University of Chicago.[3] One of his partners, Andrew T. Kearney, branched off and started his own practice, which since 1946 had been known as A.T. Kearney.[4]

After the second world war, more management consulting firms emerged, most notably the Boston Consulting Group, which was founded in 1963[5] and favoured a rigorous analytical approach to management and strategy. Throughout the 1960s and 1970s, it worked with Booz Allen Hamilton, McKinsey and the Harvard Business School to develop the tools and approaches that would reshape the emerging field of strategic management and establish the groundwork for the consulting industry.

One of the reasons behind the growth of management consulting in the US was the general belief that companies' management and boards fell short of all-round competence. External competency was brought in to make up for this shortfall and to achieve a higher level of corporate competence. It was only after the second world war, in the wake of international trade development led by the US, that management consulting emerged in Europe.

Owing to the flexible definition of consultancy, it was almost impossible to identify the exact size of the consulting market. One estimate suggested that the global management and strategy consulting market was worth US$300 billion in 2007, after two consecutive years of double-digit growth.[6]

Functions of a management consultant

Management consultants were hired to help client organizations improve performance 'by assessing the business structure and delivering a strategic plan for attaining goals'.[7] Other reasons for hiring management consultants included clients' wish to obtain third-party opinions and advice, to tap into the consultant's expertise,[8] or simply to solicit temporary help rather than hire permanent staff for one-off or short-term projects.

Due to their widespread exposure, relationships and connections, consultancies were deemed to be aware of industry best practices, although the transferability of such practices was long questioned.[9] Consultancies might also be involved in organizational change management, development of coaching skills, technological implementation, strategy development or performance-improvement services.[10]

General business model of management consultancy

Typically, management consultants were hired on a contractual basis. Depending on the nature of the client's demand, a consultant's contract could

[1] ADL (2008) 'About Us', http://www.adl.com/9.html (accessed 24 November 2008).

[2] Booz Allen Hamilton (2008) 'History of Booz Allen 1914–29', http://www.boozallen.com/about/history/history_2 (accessed 24 November 2008).

[3] McKinsey & Company (2008) 'A History of McKinsey – 1920s', http://www.mckinsey.com/aboutus/wherewestarted/1920s.asp (accessed 24 November 2008).

[4] A.T. Kearney (2008) 'History', http://www.atkearney.com/main.taf?p=1,1,1 (accessed 24 November 2008).

[5] Boston Consulting Group (2008) 'BCG History: 1963', http://www.bcg.com/about_bcg/history/1963.html?y=63 (accessed 24 November 2008).

[6] Newman, N. (August 2007) *Vault Guide to the Top 50 Consulting Firms (2008 Edition)*, Vault Inc: New York.

[7] Maslia, D.H. (January 2008) 'Execution Key to Hiring Management Consultant', *Atlanta Business Chronicle*.

[8] Institute of Management Consultants USA (2002) 'How to Hire a Management Consultant', p. 4, IMCUSA: Washington D.C.

[9] Lahti, R. and Beyerlein, M. (January–February 2000) 'Knowledge Transfer and Management Consulting: A Look at "The Firm",' *Business Horizons*.

[10] Altman, W. (July 2008) 'What's the Point of Management Consultants?', *E&T Magazine*, The 'Institution of Engineering and Technology.

| **Exhibit 15.1** | Typical Tasks of a Consultant |

Typical tasks, particularly for new graduate recruits, involved:

- Carrying out research and data collection.
- Conducting analysis.
- Interviewing the client's employees, management team and other stakeholders.
- Running focus groups and facilitating workshops.
- Preparing business proposals/presentations.
- Spending the majority of time at the client's site.

In addition to the above, tasks for more experienced and senior consultants involved:

- Identifying issues and forming hypotheses.
- Formulating and implementing recommendations/solutions.
- Ensuring that the client received the assistance needed to implement the recommendations/solutions.
- Managing jobs and programmes.
- Leading and managing those within the team, including analysts.
- Larger leadership role in the management of client relationships.

Graduate Prospects Ltd (2008) 'Management Consultant: Job Description and Activities', http://www.prospects.ac.uk/cms/ShowPage/ Home_page/Explore_types_of_jobs/Types_of_Job/p!eipaL?state=showocc&pageno=1&idno=391(accessed 27 August 2008).

be a one-off assignment or involve recurrent jobs. For bigger, more complex and therefore potentially more financially lucrative jobs, a bidding and selection process involving multiple consulting firms might be involved.

A consultant would be paid according to contracted terms and would profit by the difference between the client's payment and the expenditure on completing the job. The day-to-day activities of management consultants were often complex and varied. Consultancy was 'essentially entrepreneurial in nature' and could be 'based at one site or across several international borders' [see Exhibit 15.1 for typical tasks of a consultant].[11] Therefore, the management of a consulting firm would constantly have to balance the amount of resources invested in each job. Allocating insufficient resources would risk poor

support and response to clients, whilst deploying excessive resources would erode profitability.

A new market

As China's economy continued to climb [see Exhibit 15.2], urbanization and infrastructural development accelerated. In 1980, 190 million people comprising 20 per cent of the national population lived in urban areas. Between 1980 and 2000, the urban population increased by 270 million, reaching 36 per cent of the national population, and another 200 million were estimated to be added by 2015, when 60 per cent of the population would reside in urban areas.[12] When China reformed and opened its market in the late 1970s, the Chinese people were keen to learn the experiences, practices and theories of urban development and planning from developed countries. However, the relative lack of resources made it

[11] Graduate Prospects Ltd (2008) 'Management Consultant: Job Description and Activities', http://www.prospects.ac.uk/cms/ShowPage/Home_page/Explore_types_of_jobs/Types_of_Job/p!eipaL?state=showocc&pageno=1&idno=391 (accessed 27 August 2008).

[12] World Bank (2008) 'Urban Development in China', http://go.worldbank.org/B8M5U91MG0(accessed 23 April 2008).

Exhibit 15.2   Economic Growth of China (1999–2007)

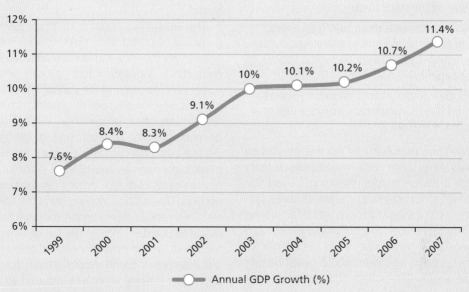

World Bank (April 2008) 'China Data and Statistics'.

very difficult to invite international experts or consultants to perform their work commercially in China. At the time, the projects were funded primarily by international funding agencies, such as the World Bank, Asia Development Bank and UN Development Programme, or by developed nations through mutual government agreements.[13]

After two decades of development, China had already achieved a certain degree of sophistication and diversification. Both businesses and consumers had come to expect higher standards in products and services. Therefore, despite limited revenue contribution from China in the past, many consulting firms began to target the Chinese market as the next platform for expansion. Not only was there a growing number of multinational companies operating in China, but also more companies of Chinese

origin were looking to consulting services for improvement in a wide range of areas.[14]

China's ownership transformation

China's recent development had ample precedents throughout the world, where 'in diverse circumstances, policy-makers have been critically re-examining the performance of publicly-owned economic assets, and in gathering numbers have turned to the improved performance that private ownership brings. The word *privatization*, almost unknown [until the late 1980s], is here to stay whether as the necessary first step on the long road toward a competitive market economy in former socialist countries, or as the key to unlocking private sector-led growth in Latin America, Asia and elsewhere.'[15] There were three main methods of privatizing state-owned enterprises (SOEs):

[13] Li, Y. (2001) 'The Urban Development Consulting Market in China', *Global Business and Economics Review*, 1(2), p. 5.

[14] Zhang, D. (14 June 2006) 'Chinese CEO Expected to Boost Profits', *China Daily*, North American edition, p. 10.

[15] Donaldson, D. and Wagle, D.M. (1995) *Privatization: Principles and Practice*, World Bank: Washington, DC, Preface.

- Share issue privatization: Repackaging SOE ownership into shares and selling them on the stock market.

- Asset sale privatization: Selling an entire firm or part(s) of a firm to a strategic investor, usually by auction or through a specialized agency.

- Voucher privatization: Distributing shares of an SOE to all citizens, usually for free or at a very low price.

Privatization's popularity by no means implied that it was easy. There were myriad political fears on which it could founder, including 'selling the family silver' to foreigners, company closures, layoffs, social asset losses and monopoly of economic power. The hearts and minds of management and employees of an enterprise could be difficult to win. Of course, privatization would never benefit all people equally. There were often losers, at least in the short run, particularly when redundancies or hiving off social assets were vital to improving efficiency and competitiveness. The short-term social and political costs of privatization were often clearer than the long-term economic benefits to countries, so many governments still hesitated to go down the privatization path. The political considerations involved in privatization decisions would usually require finding a way forward in which the legitimate interests of affected parties would be taken into account, which the International Finance Corporation (IFC) dubbed 'doing the doable'.[16]

In most countries, ownership transfer had been largely done by share issue privatization. 'An IFC-compiled database of larger, non-voucher-based transfers recorded about 2300 transactions in over 60 developing countries between 1988 and 1993, yielding US$96 billion in revenues. These figures excluded the rapidly growing number of new private entrants to infrastructure sectors, such as independent power producers'. The IFC also observed 'a symbiotic link between privatization and capital markets development: faster rates of privatization were associated with broadening and deepening the supply of domestic and international capital'.[17]

The economic benefits of privatization were generally accepted and could include: 'improving enterprise efficiency and performance; developing competitive industry which would serve consumers well; accessing the capital, know-how and markets which would permit growth; achieving effective corporate governance; broadening and deepening capital markets; and, of course, securing the best price possible for the sale'. However, privatization was always political in the sense that governments had aims other than the purely economical. These could involve, 'as in the former Soviet Union and Eastern Europe, the swift transfer of assets to private hands, in the full knowledge that the needs of the new owners for help in turning the enterprises round would remain for another day. Other political objectives included achieving a wide shareholder distribution, targeting certain classes of buyers (and excluding others, particularly foreigners), ensuring that enterprises did not close, reducing budget deficits/raising money, and maintaining employment and other social obligations. There were also political impediments to overcome, primarily the conservative or sometimes obstructive attitudes of existing managers and employees of state-owned businesses, who might be fearful of the challenges of the market place.'[18]

Problems with China's transition
In 1997, the Chinese government inaugurated a sweeping reform to transform the ownership of SOEs. Though officially termed 'common ownership', the reform was regarded as a coded reference to privatization. Given the size of China's economy, the scheme was the most ambitious privatization plan ever in the world. Because the Chinese economy had been based on the dominance of the state sector for over half a century, the

---

[16] Ibid.

[17] Ibid, Executive Summary, p. 1.

[18] Ibid.

reform was an immediate psychological shock, both domestically and internationally. To some, China's privatization foretold a crusade, sparking political debate at home and fuelling speculation abroad about the political involvement in enterprise in China.[19]

Unfortunately, attempts at large-scale privatization, which was meant to correct the mistakes of the past, were instead fostering new problems. From poorly trained management to uncompetitive products to a bloated labour force, many SOEs saw attempts to privatize them – the apparent panacea to their ills in general – as only aggravating the situation. That was because privatization only partly addressed their problems; it left companies half-reformed and therefore even more vulnerable to competitors.[20] Scores of SOEs witnessed managers stumbling despite getting everything right in theory. Insiders often realized too late that restructuring was the easy part; meeting the demands of the market was much harder.

With China joining the World Trade Organization (WTO) in late 2001, SOEs faced an increasingly grim outlook. Their woes were, by and large, the country's. Saddled with debt and excess workers, they still accounted for almost half of national output at the turn of the century and dominated crucial industries such as oil, steel, transportation and telecommunications. They formed the basis for a troubled banking system due to their heavy indebtedness and deadweight of about two-thirds of the country's credit. The vulnerability of SOEs were a main reason Beijing embarked on years of fiscal stimulus and a bank-recapitalization programme that, despite boosting profits at some SOEs, had loaded the government with record levels of debt.[21]

The frantic changes left many state enterprises in reform limbo. The central government had cultivated its biggest companies for stock listings, but had also faced stiff resistance in expanding privatization through the capital markets. Even those companies that had restructured in theory still struggled to shed the skin of old-style state enterprises, encumbered by aging workforces and unable to attract young talent. Compounding the SOEs' plight was the tax regime, in which Chinese companies were asked to pay over 30 per cent in profits tax whilst foreign ventures paid only 15 per cent, with tax exemptions for the first two years. The country also lacked a nationwide pension system, leaving SOEs to partially shoulder workers' retirements whilst competitors had no such responsibility.[22]

China's demand for consultancy

The consulting market in China

Business process outsourcing was seen as one of the growth drivers for the consulting industry as clients pursued bigger profits and lower costs. Multinationals taking advantage of a globalized market solicited the help of consultants to navigate foreign business environments, overhaul operations and redefine strategies. India had been the traditional outsourcing destination of choice. In 2006, Accenture expanded its staff in India by 400 per cent, IBM announced plans to add 100 000 positions in India by 2010 and Capgemini doubled the size of its Indian consulting practices. However, the outsourcing market in India was reaching a plateau and the rising labour costs began to push outsourcing clients to places like Singapore, Manila and Hong Kong. As China's university graduate population grew, the skills gap between China and other Asia-Pacific countries narrowed, generating an influx of outsourcing business. Market intelligence provider IDC Research estimated that the value of the outsourcing market in Asia-Pacific

[19] Kong, Q. (August 2003) 'Quest for Constitutional Justification: Privatization with Chinese Characteristics', *Journal of Contemporary China*, 12 (36), p. 537.

[20] Wonacott, P. (1 November 2001) 'China's Privatization Efforts Breed New Set of Problems – Frantic Policy Changes Leave Many Companies Only Partly Reformed', *The Wall Street Journal*, Eastern edition, p. A15.

[21] Ibid.

[22] Ibid.

would grow by over US$1 billion to US$8.3 billion by the end of 2007.[23]

Despite the teeming potential, by the mid-2000s, China's consulting market was still in its infancy.[24] It was not until the 1990s that China had begun developing a demand for sophisticated business models and corporate restructuring. Even so, in the absence of substantial expertise and experience, the local consulting market had trouble taking off. However, at the end of the 1990s, the combination of a mushrooming economy and repatriation of educated Chinese fuelled rapid development of the consulting market in China. The growth process was further accelerated by China's accession to the WTO, which opened up the vast market to international consultancies. Many were lured by the enormous growth potential exhibited by China's information technology consulting sector, which posted a 15.8 per cent quarterly growth at the end of 2006.[25]

State-owned enterprises

Despite the Chinese government's retention of state control over seven strategic industries as late as the end of 2006,[26] the majority of Chinese SOEs had been facing stiff competition ever since the launch of economic reform. A new crop of more-efficient private enterprises emerged as a result of a more market-oriented economy. Owing to their adherence to market demand and supply, private enterprises were better positioned to cater to the market and hence make more efficient use of resources. The resulting discrepancy in economic output between SOEs and private enterprises was apparent [see Exhibit 15.3]. Meanwhile, foreign

| **Exhibit 15.3** | Import and Export Trends of State-Owned and Private Enterprises |

Note that whilst import growth was roughly level for both SOEs and private enterprises, SOEs clearly lost out to private enterprises in terms of export growth, suggesting lacklustre output and productivity.

Enterprise type	Import	Year-on-year change (%)	Export	Year-on-year change (%)
State-owned	27.7	39.8	20.8	24.7
Foreign-funded	49.6	19.1	59.9	20.9
Other	12.9	41.7	29.0	43.0
Collective	2.4	41.1	4.5	29.2
Private	10.2	39.5	24.3	46.2

Source: Ministry of Commerce of the People's Republic of China (21 March 2008) 'Import by Type of Enterprises (2008/01)' and 'Export by Type of Enterprises (2008/01)'.

market entrants sprung up at an increasing rate, attracted initially by China's cheap labour and later by China's huge market potential. These foreign entrants had succeeded in market economies and were therefore much leaner and more efficient than the SOEs. This efficiency also helped them to overcome cultural differences and adjust quickly to the Chinese market.

The legacy of state ownership weighed down on the SOEs' survivability as revenue was no longer guaranteed. SOEs, infamous for inferior products and services, had to revolutionize their operations – including ownership structure through privatization – if they were to sustain customer demand and revenue. However, having blocked out the outside world until the reforms, neither the Chinese economy at large nor the SOEs themselves had adequate experience and knowledge to conduct business in closer alignment with the market.

Consultancy help to SOEs fell into two categories: improvement and privatization. Because SOEs lagged in productivity and efficiency and had little hope of fixing these problems on their own, consultants became their best hope for improvement and, in more extreme cases, survival. Without first improving internal operations to match inter-

---

[23] Newman, N. (August 2007) *Vault Guide to the Top 50 Consulting Firms (2008 Edition)*, Vault, Inc: New York.

[24] China Daily (21 August 2007) 'BCG Sees China as a Top Market in 5 Years'.

[25] Analysys International in China (February 2007) 'China IT Consultancy Market Quarterly Tracker Q4 2006'.

[26] The seven industries were: armaments, power, oil and petrochemicals, coal, telecommunications, civil aviation, and shipping. See: *South China Morning Post* (19 December 2006) 'State Control a Recipe for Weakness and Sloth'.

national practices, an SOE could not hope to achieve privatization. No investor would dare to put money on an enterprise that constantly under-performed and which lacked the transparency re-quired of openly traded enterprises. Consultants could help SOEs ramp up their operation, efficiency and transparency to more closely match inter-national standards for openly traded enterprises. Once this had been accomplished, consultants were also in demand to assist in privatizing SOEs because China had little experience in this type of corporate financial activity. SOEs needed to draw on the expertise of consultants to prevent state as-sets from being sold below proper value to private ownership. The reputation of international consult-ants also lent confidence to foreign investors about an SOE's health and the transfer of its ownership.

Entrepreneurial markets

Expansion When China first reformed its econ-omy, it did so by setting up zones within the econ-omy to undergo experimental transformation. These special economic zones (SEZs) were concen-trated in the coastal regions in the east of the country. Private enterprises, mostly with entrepre-neurial roots, sprang up in the SEZs but, due to the nation's economic structure at the time, were mostly confined to their SEZ of origin. As economic reform spread across the nation, these enterprises also began to push their agendas nationwide.

Hiring consultants allowed private enterprises to scout new markets with reasonable flexibility. Firstly, because consultancies were external organ-izations, they would not increase headcount or cause personnel issues for a private enterprise. Sec-ondly, projects involving external consultants would have a well-defined budget, unlike those conducted in-house. Clearly defined budgets were vital to keeping a proper and disciplined balance book, which in turn was essential to keeping au-thorities and investors happy. Thirdly, commission-

ing external consultants made it easier to quantify and evaluate progress.[27]

Mergers and acquisitions With the Chinese economy increasingly resembling market econ-omies in the West, the concept of mergers and ac-quisitions (M&A) was introduced along with private ownership. Because M&A was an import, Chinese enterprises would require a considerable level of advice to go through M&A processes, in addition to hiring investment banks to implement them. The complicated and ever-morphing legal landscape in China meant that rarely would enter-prises be fully prepared to handle an M&A process on their own.[28] Even foreign entrants that were used to M&A in the global markets had to rely on consultants to navigate China's legal system.[29] Likewise, cash-rich Chinese enterprises looking to acquire assets in the international market would also require consultancy assistance due to their in-experience with global M&A.

Innovation

When China first opened up its economy to foreign investment, its cheap labour and low cost of pro-duction attracted unprecedented amounts of cap-ital, transforming the once-pauper state into 'the world's factory'.[30] Years of breakneck growth in China had driven up inflation and, in turn, the cost of production. With cheap labour evaporating quickly, China could no longer count on low-tech manufacturing, which was shifting to cheaper neighbouring countries like Vietnam and Myan-

---

[27] Kibbe, B. and Setterberg, F. (1992) *Succeeding with Consult-ants*, The Foundation Center: New York.

[28] Berry, J. (June 2006) 'M&A – The Next Big Thing?', *Consulting to Management*, 17 (2), p. 30.

[29] Li, X. (5 September 2006) 'Chinese Firms "Not Ready" for Over-seas M&As', *China Daily*, North American edition, p. 11.

[30] Leggett, K. and Wonacott, P. (10 October 2002) 'The World's Factory: Surge in Exports from China Jolts Global Industry – From Cheap to Cutting-Edge, Deluge of Goods Rewrites Book on Business Strategy – Price Pressure on U.S. Griddles', *The Wall Street Journal*, Eastern edition, p. A1.

mar. Migrating up the value chain through innovation had therefore become a necessity.[31]

The situation was not unlike what the developed economies in the West had gone through. Chinese entrepreneurs and enterprises therefore recognized the value of consultants and the knowledge they had gained through the transformations of developed economies. Rather than developing their knowledge and innovation through costly experiments and trials, the Chinese, rich from their manufacturing exploits, could easily afford to buy it from the consultants instead. Studies also showed that 'if capital accumulation proceeds at the current pace, innovation capabilities will rapidly be built up in China'.[32]

Technological strategy

By the late twentieth century, the developed world had migrated from an industrial age to a technological age. Modern technology had transformed the characteristics of demand and supply, leading to the formation of a 'dynamic balance between the consumers and the suppliers'. The industrial capital of developed countries had already evolved into technological capital. By monopolizing new technological standards, patents and intellectual property, developed countries 'controlled industrial profit distribution and technological system'. Thus, enterprises competed not only on productivity and cost, but also on the ability to acquire technological assets and to increase the speed of product development. Intellectual property ownership became a new key standard in measuring an enterprise's achievements and sustainability of development.[33]

In an increasingly globalized market, Chinese enterprises found themselves lagging in transforming industrial capital to technological capital to compete effectively with the rest of the world. Likewise with innovation, Chinese enterprises found an easier solution to capital transformation in consultants from the West, whose know-how and experience garnered from their countries of origin met the needs of the Chinese. On the macro level, the Chinese Government and its agencies were also keen to accelerate China's development through the strategic use of technology.[34] By bringing in Western consultants, they hoped to uncover a shortcut to achieving the capital transformation process of the West.

ADL in China

ADL first set foot in China in 1986 with a practice in Hong Kong. Having built an international reputation for expertise in technology and a clientele in both private and public sectors,[35] ADL found its first Chinese clients in government agencies and companies interested in buying other companies. Influenced by the aggressive expansion of its practices worldwide, ADL also hastily expanded its practice in China, concerning itself with the size of its consultant roster rather than qualifications. In 2002, ADL found itself having to undergo a global ownership restructuring. When the ripple effect spread to Asia, ADL's practices in China also began to unravel. Competitors took advantage of the situation and lured significant numbers of consultants away from ADL.

The ADL way

Client service

ADL promoted its uniqueness in 'linking strategy, innovation and technology to master clients' business complexity to deliver sustainable solutions'. It placed heavy emphasis on staff quality to combine 'deep industry expertise and innovative thinking for a client-focused service offering'.[36] ADL therefore stated in its marketing material that it would not provide clients with 'armies of young consultants and generalists, but experienced experts who [could] blend

---

[31] He, S. (8 March 2008) 'China Pushes Industries Up the Value Chain', *The Bangkok Post*.

[32] Altenburg, T., Schmitz, H. and Stamm, A. (February 2008) 'Breakthrough. China's and India's Transition from Production to Innovation', *World Development*, 36(2), p. 325.

[33] Du, L., Hou, J. and Lu, J. (2007) 'Relationship between the Development of Chinese Non-State-Owned Enterprises and Its Cultivation of Scientific and Technological Competence; an Empirical Study', *Journal of Technology Management in China*, 2(3), p. 237.

[34] Lin, Y. (28 February 2007) 'Technology Innovation Needs Practical Strategy', *China Daily*, North American edition, p. 10.

[35] *Middle East Company News* (12 July 2008) 'Affinitiv Announces Strategic Integration with Arthur D. Little'.

[36] ADL (2008) 'About Us', http://www.adl.com/about-us.html (accessed 17 October 2008).

context, vision and detail, bridging the gap be-tween strategy, management and technology'.[37]

ADL channelled significant amounts of energy into maintaining its industrial expertise. Therefore, instead of dabbling in a wide spectrum of indus-tries as many of its competitors had done, it chose to stay extraordinarily focused on selected indus-tries [see Exhibit 15.4]. This approach led to the de-velopment of what ADL referred to as a global 'knowledge bank' that its consultancies worldwide could tap into in helping clients access innovation expertise and integrate strategy, innovation and technology.[38] Generally, ADL practices would pro-vide services to clients through local consultants backed by non-local colleagues with specific expertise as part of this knowledge bank.[39] In this way, client communication and consultancy expertise could be optimized to maximize client satisfaction.

Exhibit 15.4   ADL's Industry Focuses

The ten industries in which ADL extensively cultivated expertise:

Industry	Key Issues (Particularly in the West)
Automotive	Economies of scale, overcrowding of models, tight resources to tailor to individual markets and segments, legal and environmental demands, selecting the 'right' innovations, shortening development cycles, perpetuating discounts and price wars, and management having to fulfil the short-term expectations of the financial markets without harming the future base of competition.
Chemicals	An unrelenting focus on value creation driven by competition for capital and investors or the possibility of a private equity takeover, uncertainty over the impact of emerging markets, reappraisal of vertical integration, and the coming-of-age of sustainability.
Energy & Utilities	Private oil companies facing stiffer competition from national oil companies, reducing reserves, extremely high shareholder expectations, expectation to enhance refineries, pressure on retail margins, major utility companies facing emissions trading, stalled liberalization of electricity and gas markets in Europe, collapse of the energy merchant business model in the US, growing gas import requirements, and difficult permitting for new infrastructure.
Financial Services	Industry consolidation, increasing demands from the customer and decreasing loyalty, increased performance pressure leading to shrinking margins, changes in the regulatory environment and the fast pace of technological developments, and rapid evolution of the supply chain in financial services.
Healthcare	Increasing resource constraints, and steeper challenge to seek out the right investment opportunities to satisfy both societal and shareholder needs.
Manufacturing	Globalization, cost pressure, intensifying competition, cyclical nature or stagnation of the markets, and incorporation of innovation into business.
Private Equity	Oversupply of equity and debt capital, and scarce deal opportunities worldwide.
Public Services	Managing interdependencies, demands for more openness and transparency, performance and measurements, market-type mechanisms, unfamiliar technologies, and risk and security concerns.
Telecoms, Information, Media & Electronics	Changing business climate, disruptive technologies, new regulations, shifting ambitions and organizational upheaval.
Travel & Transportation	Change initiatives, management of sustainability, safety issues and rising costs.

---

[37] ADL (2008) 'Uniquely Different, Universally Rewarding', Com-pany brochure.

[38] ADL (2008) 'CEO Update', http://www.adl.com/11.html (ac-cessed 31 October 2008).

[39] Company interview with Dr Thomas Schiller on 15 October 2008.

In Schiller's experience, the critical team size for a consultant practice was around 20 people.[40] Having lower numbers would overstretch the practice and affect the quality of service. However, having too many consultants could result in unnecessary drags. ADL prided itself on its trademarked 'Side-by-Side' approach, whereby working together on-project and even off-project with clients ensured effective transfer of knowledge whilst respecting the insights, experience and culture of clients.[41] Having the right team size was crucial to the implementation of this 'Side-by-Side' approach.

Working life

According to a management consultancy recruitment survey, ADL insiders described their colleagues as laid-back and fun to work with, besides having the typical traits of management consultants (e.g., energetic, intelligent, ambitious and driven). As one manager said, 'The culture has a great combination of entrepreneurship and professionalism in a work hard, play hard environment'. ADL practices were also known to have office events and outings to let consultants get to know each other better, and many consultants regarded their professional colleagues as friends. Moreover, it was reported that ADL practices had a 'very open culture' and promoted a 'very positive and collaborative environment', where the atmosphere was 'very friendly' and 'very collegial' with 'virtually no hierarchy'. In this survey, ADL was ranked first in 'Diversity for Minorities', second in 'Relationships with Supervisors' and third in 'Overall Satisfaction'.[42]

Resurrecting a business

When Schiller first arrived in ADL's Beijing office, he was shocked by how differently the office functioned from the one in Munich. He found that even though the practice had been considerably down-sized, most consultants demonstrated little sense of teamwork or community, which were hallmarks of ADL's practices worldwide [see Exhibit 15.5]. He also saw a low level of industrial focus as reflected in the nature of jobs that the practice was pursuing, which also differed from the usual practice at ADL in building up expertise. What were the problems plaguing ADL's practice in China? How could Schiller turn things around to ensure success in China? What changes and strategies, if any, would he need to implement?

Ricky Lai prepared this case under the supervision of Dr Marcus Schvetz for class discussion. This case is not intended to show effective or ineffective handling of decision or business process.

Exhibit 15.5	ADL's Values, Mission and Ambition

Values

Clients first	Quality	Independence
Integrity	Sustainability	Teamwork
Leadership	Concern for staff	Pride

Mission

Be the top management consulting firm linking strategy, innovation and technology to master clients' business complexity to deliver sustainable results.

Ambition

- Become the consultant of choice for clients.
- Become the thought leader who makes the difference.
- Become the place to work.

ADL (2008) 'Arthur D Little', company presentation.

---

[40] Ibid.

[41] ADL (2008) 'Uniquely Different, Universally Rewarding', Company brochure.

[42] Vault.com (2008) 'Arthur D. Little Snapshot', http://www.vault.com/companies/company_main.jsp?co_page=2&product_id=318&ch_id=252&v=2&tabnum=2 (accessed 18 October 2008).

Assignment Questions

1. Describe what professionalism means in a management consultancy context.

2. Detail the societal impacts that the management consultancy profession may have.

3. Using the example of Chiquita Brands International, critically explore the role that a consultant could take if they made the discovery that paramilitary groups were being financed.

4. Describe the concept of ethics and professionalism specifically in a management consultancy context.

5. Discuss the concept of client confidentiality. Why is it important especially in a management consultancy context?

Further Reading

Casella, D. (2008), Practical ethics for new consultants. *Consulting Magazine* from http://www.paconsulting. com/news/by_pa/2008/Consulting_Magazine_article_on_ethics.htm

Hagenmeyer, U. (2007,) Integrity in management consulting: A contradiction in terms? *Business Ethics: A European Review*, 16(2), 107–113

McLean, B. and Elkind, P. (2004), *The Smartest Guys in the Room: The Amazing Rise and Scandalous Fall of Enron.* London: Penguin Books Ltd

O'Shea, J. and Madigan, C. (1997), *Dangerous Company: The Consulting Powerhouses and the Business They Save and Ruin.* London: Nicholas Brealey Publishing Ltd

Roddenberry, E.W. (1953), Achieving professionalism, *Journal of Criminal Law, Criminology & Police Science*, 44(1), 109–115

CHAPTER 16

The future of the industry

Learning Objectives

At the end of this chapter students will be able to:

- Understand that assessing the past can create an insight into the future

- Recognize the difficulties in predicting the future of any industry

- Recognize both the positive growth aspects and the negative decline based aspects of the industry

- Understand that by 2020 the management consultancy industry may be very different to what it is today

- Recognize that the exploitation of green technologies and the management know-how that comes with this may lead to advances in the industry

Mini Case Study 16.1

Department for International Development – St Helena Air Access

Introduction

St Helena (population 3900) is one of the world's most isolated inhabited islands. It lies in the South Atlantic 4000 miles from the UK and 1700 miles from Cape Town. It is off shipping lanes and is currently accessible only by sea from Africa or Ascension Island on the subsidized Royal Mail Ship, RMS St Helena, which is due to be retired in 2010.

Following extensive studies by Atkins, the Department for International Development (DFID), a part of Her Majesty's Government (HMG), agreed in March 2005 to provide air access.

The feasibility study and business case, headed by Atkins' Management Consultants team, relied heavily on technical and cost inputs drawn from experts across the Group.

It called upon Atkins' multidisciplinary skills in:

- Aviation
- Geotechnical, civil and environmental engineering
- Market research (demand for tourism, travel costs, sources of sea cargo supply)
- Social and institutional impact
- Financial/economic and probabilistic risk modelling
- Knowledge of procurement.

Close liaison with the airport operations regulator ensured a safety-led approach to the process.

Outputs we deliver to our clients

The recommendation to DFID and the St Helena Government (SHG) was for a design, build and operate (DBO) solution. Operating Boeing 737-800 aircraft, or similar, the airport will enjoy regular scheduled services by 2010. For the one viable site, Prosperous Bay Plain, Atkins produced an outline design for a 1950m runway – backed up by surveys and core sample extraction.

The business case relies on the take-up of tourism, so St Helena must prepare for change on a scale not yet seen in its history. Its challenge is to remove itself from subsidy, which the study showed, is achievable. The study provides the strategy – to be led by Atkins – for the procurement of a DBO consortium and an air service provider. Public competition will be used to identify suitable contenders and maximize value for money.

The study also identified institutional, legislative and regulatory arrangements needed to support air access and effect radical economic change through tourism development. It shaped DFID/SHG's approach to procurement of contractors and to development of the island's economy, including:

- Management arrangements
- Strategic planning
- Government reform
- Investor codes
- Social development.

It therefore enables forward planning in a comprehensive and highly practicable way.

Our approach

Co-ordination of the outputs of large multi-disciplined teams with the contributions of DFID and SHG demanded rigorous project management and effective client interaction, frequently on a daily basis and spanning large geographical distances. Principles of the PRINCE2 approach to project management were applied to the three phases of work.

Detailed project plans assigned resources and split tasks and activities into manageable work streams. Every piece of work submitted was reviewed by the Project Manager to ensure quality of output. Risk and issues lists were maintained throughout, addressing client project perspective and Atkins' commercial requirements.

A website was developed to facilitate the international public procurement process, the main channel for which was the Official Journal of the European Union (OJEU). The principal plank of innovation in this exciting project, which will have a very real impact on the lives of island's inhabitants – and on world tourism – was the combination, under one consulting roof, of the engineering capability and the commercial analysis.

The chosen airport location represents a difficult site for conversion to a long level platform for a runway. Teams of surveyors and geotechnical engineers were therefore dispatched to study the site prior to the start of the engineering and design process.

The commercial view was established by researching the scope for tourism and by comparing how similar islands had been developed as a result of air access. The impact on the life of St Helena was studied by a further visiting team.

All of the consulting outputs fed into a complex financial/economic model, which was subjected to Monte Carlo risk simulation, producing confidence envelopes for revenue and spend profiles.

Outcomes we deliver to our clients

The quantifiable outcomes were generated by modelling the economy for the three access options. The results showed that UK Government financial support for the island could reach zero by 2025 under the 1950m runway option (mean risked date); by 2045 using only business jets on a shorter runway; and would never be achieved if it was decided to replace the retiring mail ship.

Intangible benefits for the islanders include:

- Lifting of morale
- Dramatic improvements to family and community life

- Opportunities for employment and income generation
- Institutional and infrastructure improvements.

Source: http://www.atkinsglobal.com/Images/Department%20 for%20International%20Development%20-%20St%20 Helena%20Air%20Access_tcm12-1843.pdf. Reproduced with permission.

Introduction

The opening case study is a great example of how a management consultancy such as Atkins can have a major effect on not only a business but an entire island. In this chapter, leading views of practitioners, industry experts and academics will be brought together, along with a future orientation going further ahead knowledge transfer from consultancies into industries and the exploitation of green technologies.

The Industry's Future

It is always difficult to predict what lies in store for any industry (Czerniawska, 2008). Nevertheless, it is interesting to investigate what leading experts such as McKenna, Czerniawska and Ringland have said on the subject before moving on to criticism of the industry.

McKenna (2006) is a business historian based at Oxford University's Saïd Business School. Chapter 1 detailed his work illustrating how the management consultancy arose. Some of the more recent movements in the management consultancy industry also relate to its past. The identification of corporate culture was a leading area for investigation in the 1990s and indeed the early twenty-first century has seen much written about this subject in terms of organizational culture and climate (Patterson, West, Shackleton, Dawson, Lawthom, Maitlis, Robinson and Wallace, 2005) and then the commodification of professional practice (Fincham, 1995). In addition, firms would also use advice from management consultancies to protect them from law suits in a push to reduce their professional liability as shown in the Thought Provoking point 16.1 below. McKenna (2006) suggested that this type of activity as well as the regulatory impact that government policies may bring could be very profitable for consultancy (see Industry snapshot 16.1).

Thought Provoking point 16.1

Employers use of stress surveys

The study of stress has been a fascination ever since Professor Tom Cox's lectures at the University of Nottingham illustrated the subject area. Many of the early projects that I did as a consultant occupational psychologist in stress, one involving two deaths in part due to stress at work, were probably assigned due to impending law suits. Employers by utilizing consultants could state that they were doing something about the problem in a court of law.

Industry snapshot 16.1

McKenna on the future of the industry

McLaughlin: As you look toward the future, do you foresee any disruptors or enablers that will impact the growth of the industry?

McKenna: Yes. My thoughts return first to government regulations, which we've discussed. Once you create regulation, its subsequent dismantling can be equally disruptive. If regulation provides new business, deregulation may also either take away from that business or provide other opportunities. So, if you believe that some new deregulatory movement is in the works – which wouldn't surprise me – then you should consider serving industries which will be subject to the new regulatory environment.

The other potential disruptor is professional liability. If you view the history of the industry as cycles, you see a pattern: mounting cycles of liability, followed by regulatory efforts to diminish or resolve the problem. The same kind of crisis of liability that happened in the late 1980s and culminated in the Enron scandal of 2000 may be in process again. And I think it could disrupt the industry enormously.

McLaughlin: What's your sense of how that trend will play out for professional service firms?

McKenna: What we're seeing right now is exactly the same process that happened in the late 1980s and early 1990s. At that time, decisions in a set of court cases resulted in more liability for corporations, which they tried to avoid in new and innovative ways, mostly by hiring consulting firms to perform management audits to offset their liability.

That liability, in turn, shifted to the professional firms, which had to find ways to offset it themselves. Well, the same thing is happening now. We're noticing that the accounting firms are screaming about their increasing liability and saying that Sarbanes-Oxley has put them in a real bind by demanding a certain level of accountability.

Their accounting work is very profitable, but at the same time, their potential liability, should a lawsuit hit them, is enormous. The firms are pushing regulators, theorists, and others to reduce that liability.

If that happens, of course, the business environment will become less risky for firms, encouraging further expansion of their businesses. Such expansion can lead to lowering of professional standards of care and, if that happens, the result would be increased liability.

And then I would expect to see more service failures and more litigation.

McLaughlin: Do you believe consultants will also be subject to increased litigation in the future?

McKenna: I think consultants will face more lawsuits. Consultants claim to be experts and verify that clients are pursuing the right strategy, or have strong managerial controls, or have the right organizational structure, or have good governance. Simultaneously, they argue that this is merely advice, not actionable information, a stance that is impossible in other professions.

In other fields like law, accounting, and engineering, it's impossible to make those claims and not be held to standards of malpractice. Consultants have managed to avoid this and it's quite a remarkable feat. The question is to what extent consultants will be able to continue walking this tightrope, which I see as a very dangerous one. I think it's almost impossible for them to do it for very much longer.

If I were in a strategy consulting firm, I'd be buying as much insurance as I could. In terms of liability, I think the day is coming when consultants will be seen as equivalent to lawyers, investment bankers, engineers, and accountants. I don't think consultants can continue to claim that they provide valuable professional advice and yet cannot be held accountable for it.

Source: http://www.managementconsultingnews.com/interviews/mckenna_interview.php. Reproduced with permission.

Dr Fiona Czerniawska has written much on the future of the consultancy industry both in her own publications (e.g., Czerniawska, 1999; Czerniawska, 2002) and the publications of industry attracting eager MBA and other graduates (Czerniawska, 2008). Czerniawska is a director of the UK Management Consultancies Association's (MCA) Think Tank and after a successful practitioner career spanning some 15 years is the managing director of her own company Arkimeda, which specializes in researching and consulting on strategy for the consulting industry. Indeed, she is writing a new book entitled, 'Buying Professional Services' that again seeks to look at the future of the industry especially in light of the huge amount of money being spent on public sector consultancy that will be covered later on in this chapter.

Czerniawska (2008) stated that in the UK there was an increase of 26 per cent of fee earning consultants to 18 000 in 2006. Indeed, in 2007 the size of the industry was estimated to be about £8 billion (MCA, 2009). This growth has led to 'a war on talent' (Czerniawska, 2008; p. 16) whereby consultancies can only grow by recruiting the best analytical and bright graduates. This is an issue for consultancies whom via the various surveys conducted by the MCA stated that this was one of the main restrictors of growth. With a shortage of people and more demand, companies often inflate salaries to get the best talent. This may present the industry with future problems as large salaries tend to have to be paid for with larger billing, which may deter organizations from using consultancies. In addition, much of the new talent being recruited tends to be in very specialist areas, which is fine when the assignments are running but not so good when the work is no longer there (Czerniawska, 2008).

Czerniawska (2008) suggested that there are three traditions where consultancies can deal with the demand and supply of resources and lists these as:

1. Offshoring, when the consultancy uses a cheaper international alternative to using expensive western based services, e.g., telephone interview marketing, data entry, data analysis, etc.

2. Forming alliances with other consultancies, which is often done to ensure that the right mix of skills is available to the client, e.g., a large management consultancy may team up with a psychometric test publisher to offer a client a mixture of assessment services.

3. Increasing the use of associate consultants; associates can be given the appropriate work based on a fixed term contract agreement.

All of these techniques are being employed to add value to the clients that the consultancies aid (Czerniawska, 2008). It will certainly be interesting to see how this will be developed, especially with the generation Y or 'Millennials' coming into the workplace as technically savvy, multi-tasking but rather self-centred and egotistic (CBS News, 2007). Nevertheless, generation Y, speaking from a generation X perspective, has witnessed massive employment changes in the late 1980s and early 1990s. Indeed, their parents during their early childhood were either trying to keep their jobs or regaining employment when unemployment was rife. It was perhaps in this time where society became more of a risk society where individuals took their chance with precarious employment conditions (Forde and Slater, 2006).

At this time the 'protean career' became more common place where the lack of commitment offered by firms was reciprocated with individuals steering their own careers gaining necessary skills from one employer and then moving on to the next employer that would give them another set of skills (Hall, 1976). This practice is epitomized by associate work, so perhaps the future may lie in an increase in the use of associate consultants rather than the recruiting of individuals into permanent positions (Forde and Slater, 2006).

Ringland and Shaukat (2004) also comment on where the management consultancy industry may be in the future. They suggest that future growth within the industry is never certain and indeed, this point will be raised in the next section that concentrates on public sector consultancy but applies to all areas. Ringland and Shaukat (2004) developed three different scenarios of what the industry may look like in 2020, based on the results of involving 120 consultants and clients over three sessions examining the future of the industry. The scenarios of where the 2020 management consultancy industry would be were:

1. WW2004: this is where existing trends continue and there is a strong need for consultancies driven by client demands. In this model, the successful firms are likely to be big and small with niche firms depending on their in-depth industry knowledge and larger firms competing on a global level.

2. Smallies: this is the suggestion that Charles Handy first made in his concept of the Shamrock Organization whereby firms outsource everything apart from their core competencies. This has advantages of bringing together experts in a virtual firm, who may have more in-depth knowledge than general consultants and then disbanding them when the job is finished. The model of offshoring and outsourcing may represent this trend a few years after Ringland and Shaukat (2004) made this suggestion.

3. Watson World: this is the view that the top five firms will have 50 per cent of the consultancy market with the smaller firms and internal consultancies developed in-house taking on smaller assignments.

All of these different scenarios are interesting. The WW2004 scenario suggests that there may be about 15 top firms dominating half the industry and these firms may be from developing nations such as India. Certainly there is evidence of developing nations improving their consultancy offering with firms such as the Indian based Tata Consultancy Services becoming a more global concern.

The Smallies scenario would mean massive growth to the industry; however, just as some suggested that many people would be temporary workers by the early twenty-first century this phenomenon never actually happened and in fact reversed with temporary workers declining due to legislation and a more stable economy (Biggs, Burchell and Millmore, 2006).

The Watson World scenario sees the rationalization of the current large management consultancy firms who in bidding for talent become larger to attract staff. This scenario also predicts the rise of internal consultancies, whereby firms wanting to cut consultancy costs develop their own departments that do the work of external firms in the present day. All of these scenarios are all quite as likely as each other to occur or occur in a mixture of formats. However, there is another more negative scenario not put forward by Ringland and Shaukat (2004) which will be considered next.

Critics of the industry: Public sector consultancy

So far, the chapter has concentrated mainly on the positive outlook for the industry. Nonetheless, there is also a negative one, where the industry falls into disrepute and collapses. Although this view may be a little extreme, it is interesting to examine the case of public sector consultancy in the UK as an example of why the industry may decline.

The public sector is increasingly becoming more businesslike in its focus and as such consultancy can aid these government sponsored organizations (Roodhooft and Van Den Abbeele, 2006). Nevertheless, the most critical literature on management consultancy has investigated its use within the public sector. David Craig, for instance, condemns the management consultancy industry in his 2006 book, *Plundering the Public Sector: How New Labour is Letting Consultants Run Off With £70 Billion of Our Money*. Craig (2006) argued that the amount of money being spent on consultants by public sector organizations had increased dramatically. Using the period from 2003 to 2004 Craig (2006) states that spending on consultancy has risen by 460 per cent in local government, 340 per cent in the NHS, and 178 per cent in the Ministry of Defence.

Between 2005–06, approximately £2.8 billion was spent on consultants, with central government accounting for £1.8 billion (House of Commons Committee of Public Accounts, 2007). Nevertheless, with larger ICT projects currently being undertaken such as NPFIT for the NHS, the current bill may be much larger, but it is difficult to discern how much is currently being spent by the public sector (Craig, 2006).

Jarrett (2001) detailed the challenges for working in the public sector as a consultant. Some consultancies have specialized in this type of work but Jarrett (2001) claims there are three main challenges:

1. The consultant's task not only concerns the project being undertaken but should be seen as part of a wider political and organizational system

2. The consultant should avoid prejudging the situation and acting out of anxiety or confusion in terms of answering the client as the 'expert'

3. The consultant should develop a wide repertoire of consulting styles and form a deep understanding of the psyche of the public sector organization

Given the above, public sector consultancy can be difficult especially in terms of demonstrating the benefit received by the client. Nevertheless, all consultancy if carried out in an effective manner should explicitly state what the business, or in the case of the public sector, the organization's benefits are. However, given that governments are elected on the basis of public opinion it is doubtful whether successive governments would maintain a high level of spending on consultancies if this was contrary to public opinion. Industry snapshot 16.2 represents a interview transcript where it is clear that the House of Commons Committee of Public Accounts represented by Mr Khan is dismissive of the Office of Government Commerce the procurer of consultancy services in the UK represented by Mr Oughton.

Industry snapshot 16.2

The glory days of management consultancy in the public sector are over?

Discussion between Mr Khan and Mr Oughton

Mr Khan: Are the glory days for consultancies over as far as public sector contracts are concerned?

Mr Oughton: I do not know about 'glory days'. It has to be the case that after three spending reviews where there have been very significant investments in major capital projects and in a comprehensive spending review 2007 where capital will clearly be much tighter and, in a sense inevitably, because if we have invested in the capital stock and improved it why would we need to do so further, I would expect that there would be fewer opportunities.

Mr Khan: The graph is going to go down.

Mr Oughton: The graph for that sort of support probably will go down.

Mr Khan: It seems to me that you are saying that the reasons for the graph going down is not because of your fantastic work over the last three years, but because the amount of money the Government spend on these projects is going down. It seems a sad indictment of your work.

Mr Oughton: I hope it is a combination. I hope that we are tightening up on procedures and we will be able to do so further with greater powers. I also hope that the trend is moving for other reasons.

Mr Wright: May I just point out to the Committee that prior to 2003 I used to work for Deloittes, as a consultant.

Source: parliamentary material is reproduced with the permission of the Controller of HMSO on behalf of Parliament.

Some attention has been given to the procurement process in the public sector (Roodhooft and Van den Abbeele, 2006). Roodhooft and Van den Abbeele (2006) observed the differences between private and public sector procurement. Their findings suggested that the public sector may need to improve their procurement procedures improving their buying skills in market management, project specification, competitive process, negotiation regulation and monitoring. They even went on to suggest that a higher level of management involvement was needed when procuring services from consultancies. The House of Commons Committee

(2007) agreed with this finding from the academic literature. They listed several developments that needed to take place for the public sector procurement of consultancy services including:

1. using internal resources instead of consultants
2. improving the quality of information on the use of consultants
3. gaining a better understanding of the different suppliers of consultancy services
4. getting better deals by using different payment methods and making more use of competitive tendering
5. using the Office of Government Commerce publications on good practice and
6. assessing the Office of Government Commerce's own use of consultants

Nevertheless, many public sector organizations now outsource essential business functions such as recruitment to consultancies. Indeed, the public sector has been faced with many changes and consultancies can provide support on the strategic role of an organization as well as take on some of its functions, such as recruitment, training and organizational development (Jarrett,2001). In this regard, it is difficult to claim that the public sector does not benefit from management consultancy as Berry (2007) detailed earlier in Industry snapshot 3.4 and as demonstrated in Industry snapshot 16.3 where public sector agencies actively use consultancy.

Industry snapshot 16.3

Becoming a private sector company

Public sector organisations have used consultancy services for many years. Illustrating this, I can use my personal experience of the Army Personnel Research Establishment (APRE) where I worked during my placement year in 1991. This organisation was part of the UK Ministry of Defence (MOD) and had been formed in April 1965 to carry out research into soldiering (National Archives, 2009). The Establishment used many different disciplines and had the same paymasters as the rest of the UK forces, i.e., the MOD.

As part of my Diploma in Industrial Studies, I had to complete an organizational review of the Establishment. During this, I was curious to learn that other forces, such as the Royal Air Force and the Navy repeated many of the functions that the APRE was involved with for the British Army. The Senior Management after my time had also come to the same conclusion. The APRE was merged into the DRA (Defence Research Agency) initially and then in 1995 into DERA (Defence Evaluation and Research Agency). This was to rationalise some of its service offerings with other parts of the armed forces. In 2001, DERA was split into two organisations. The smaller organization, the Defence Science and Technology Laboratory (DSTL) was run on a business like basis but was funded by the UK taxpayer to give efficiency in defence that could only be done within government.

The larger of these two organisations, QinetiQ was floated on the stock exchange in 2006(QinetiQ, 2009). QinetiQ with its private investment backing has expanded further into the United States, European, Middle Eastern and Australian markets (QinetiQ, 2009). It is a large graduate employer hiring numbers of science and engineering based graduates each year. QinetiQ's clients are also numerous ranging from the MOD to US National Aeronautics and Space Administration (NASA)

Source: QinetiQ, (2009), Our history. Retrieved 3rd November 2009 from http://www.qinetiq.com/global/about_us/our_history.

html. The National Archives (2009) Reports of the Army Personnel Research Establishment, Series details WO 404. Retrieved 3rd November 2009 from http://nationalarchives.gov.uk/cata logue/displaycataloguedetails.asp?CATID=61658&CATLN=3 &FullDetails=True. Reproduced with permission.

An Optimistic View of the Future

Now that the text has detailed some of the main commentators of the industry and examined some of the more negative criticisms that the industry received, the last part of this chapter examines the industry in a more optimistic format detailing knowledge transfer followed by movements into the green economy.

Commodification/selling knowledge

In Chapter 1, we saw that the early management consultancy industry generally started with the selling of knowledge to organizations, with individual engineers and management gurus such as F.W. Taylor selling their knowledge to the highest bidder (McKenna, 2006). In looking at the future of the industry, the commodification or selling of knowledge is also a way forward for the industry to explore (Heusinkveld and Benders, 2005).

Heusinkveld and Benders (2005) suggested that theorists reporting on the management consultancy industry have done so in two waves. First, to examine the process of selling knowledge, the process of commodification itself. This demonstrated commodification as a linear set of practices starting with the generation of ideas and then resulting in the market launch of that product. Fincham (1995) for instance examined the process of business process reengineering (bpr) as an example of the commodification of management knowledge. In his article, Fincham (1995) does not dispute the claims of bpr but openly investigated why it was held in such high regard by managers, suggesting that it may be through the promotional activities of consultancies.

Later theorists examined the fashion aspect of commodification. Indeed, Fincham (1995) suggests that bpr unlike some of the management fads of the 1980s may have longer lasting impact. However, Fincham (1995) and others (Abrahamson, 1996; Clark and Salaman, 1996; 1998a; 1998b) also discuss the fashion aspects of the industry stating that management consultants promote the latest fads generated from business schools and business gurus, just as reported in the past (McKenna, 2006).

Nevertheless, as Chapter 1 demonstrated, the management consultancy industry has endeavoured to lose its fad based, fashion or even unprofessional image by creating professional bodies such as the AMCF in the US and the MCA in the UK. Heusinkveld and Benders (2005) further argued that based on their research with 40 consultants across 24 firms, both the linear process of selling knowledge and the promotion of managerial fashions did not seem to be the case in their sample. Purveyors of management knowledge found the process aspect of it, 'particularly problematic' (Heusinkveld and Benders, 2005; p. 304). Knowledge was packaged, branded and sold as it related to the client and not how it related to the latest management fashion encouraged by the latest business guru or from the business colleges (Heusinkveld and Benders, 2005).

Heusinkveld and Benders (2005) further conclude that the process of selling knowledge is not particularly clear although there is an emerging interest in the subject. Selling knowledge is certainly harder than selling a product, but in creating a knowledge product commodification is assured. Commodities created, whether a development service or guidance for management de-layering in a university setting, need to be worked out with the client.

As we saw in Chapter 3, consultancies that only adopt a particular stance, are doomed unless they change with the times. Commodification is therefore not only about creating a coherent product for the client, it is also about working closely with them in a trusting relationship (as noted in Chapters 5 and 13). More research is required to investigate what ideas have good currency with the client as Heusinkveld and Benders (2005) suggested. However, working with the client in an open, honest fashion as this text has revealed is bound to bring fruitful results.

Movement into the green economy

An expansion from the last section is examining what type of knowledge may be generated for clients. The early history of management consultancy was dominated by engineers and accountants and then later on from the 1950s by IT professionals. Given the rate of climate change the planet faces, perhaps a more environmental concern will be provided by the management consultancies. Indeed, examining websites of the major management consultancies this does seem to be the case.

McKinsey and Company, for instance, have a number of articles on environmental concerns published by the McKinsey Global Institute. Oppenheim, Beinhocker and Farrell (2008) commented that with a 'right mix of policies, investments, new technologies, and changes in behaviour, we can shift to a clean-energy economy whilst continuing to grow'. They suggest that investments made in a clean energy infrastructure and technology can boost the global economy and advocate that the time is now for a clean energy revolution.

Other consultancies have also adopted this green agenda. The Boston Consulting Group, for instance, on their front web page discuss a study that they conducted into the production and sales of electric cars that whilst likely to offset the carbon emission of the global economy may be unlikely to have a significant impact by 2020 (BCG, 2009). Another consultancy, Arup, has a Sustainability Director and remark that they are a 'pioneer of sustainability solutions' (ARUP, 2009). Atkins, whose case study started off this chapter have also invested significantly in carbon critical designs and are investigating newer technologies as presented in Mini Case Study 16.2.

Not all management consultancies however have adopted this strong environmental approach. Some of the well-known consultancies advertise very little on their websites about environmental concerns. Yet, just as management consultancy started with the second industrial revolution of scientific knowledge and received a boost with the information revolution (McKenna, 2006), it waits to be seen whether the industry will be instrumental in the clean-energy revolution. History does have a habit of repeating itself.

Mini Case Study 16.2

Anaconda wave energy converter in final concept testing – 6 May 2009

The Atkins inspired Anaconda wave energy device is delivering results in testing that suggest it could produce electricity at a cost that would easily rival any other renewable energy product.

Anaconda is a 200 metre long rubber tube that works on bulge wave theory – first documented by medical experts who looked at how blood was pumped around the human body. The blood pulses – with bulge waves rippling along every vein and artery. These pulses carry energy and it is the same basic idea behind Anaconda.

Each device would be anchored offshore in water around 50 metres deep, sitting just below the water surface, head to the waves. The action of the passing waves would cause bulges to pulse down the inside of the tube – transferring energy from the passing water to the device. This energy travels down the tube and via high and low pressure chambers it powers a generator. The resulting electricity would then be cabled ashore.

It is now in final proof of concept testing at a 270 metre long wave tank in Gosport, Hampshire where it is showing impressive results. This news is a real boost to Professor Rod Rainey from Atkins, who came up with the original idea.

Professor Rainey said: 'The testing is extremely important because Anaconda is so radical it wasn't entirely clear that it would actually work. However the results completely bear out the theory and scaling it up also shouldn't be a problem.'

Prof Rainey has been involved with the wave energy sector for ten years. He'd seen projects work well in testing but when it came to scaling up they often suffered because the harsh environment they'd be working in raised serious maintenance questions.

'I realized that making wave energy machines from rigid materials was always going to cause problems. The industry needed a much more radical solution to make the breakthrough to a commercial product. To me the obvious jump had to be to a rubber bodied device – the idea had been looked at before but not in the way I subsequently came up with'.

The device is being developed by double Queen's Award winners, the Checkmate Group, who is also being backed by the Carbon Trust.

Chairman, of Checkmate Seaenergy, Paul Auston, said: 'Subsidies for wave energy projects are getting very attractive – making more devices look commercially practical. However that is not our ambition – we want to get Anaconda to the stage where it makes economic sense with zero subsidy. So far in testing the results have been impressive – with energy output data suggesting Anaconda will produce electricity at a cost that will be excitingly low – and offer a serious and cost effective alternative in the delivery of clean energy. The first full-sized units should be in production within three years.'

It seems Anaconda's emergence in the world of wave energy is hitting a peak at exactly the right time. Only last week Minister for Sustainable Development, Lord Hunt, told an clean energy conference that English and Welsh coastal waters would be investigated for their marine renewable energy potential.

Lord Hunt told the conference: 'The marine energy sector has reached a pivotal stage with more and more devices ready to go into the water. The screening exercise in English and Welsh waters is a significant step forward in our plans to harness the power of our seas and secure a renewable and low carbon energy supply.'

Source: http://www.atkinsglobal.com/media_centre/press_releases/anaconda_wave_energy_converter_testing.aspx. Reproduced with permission.

Chapter Summary

- Management consultancies not only influence organizations but can bring about powerful change affecting the lives of thousands
- It is difficult to predict the future for any industry (Czerniawska, 2008)
- McKenna (2006) assessed the past to predict the future finding three issues being important
  - Understanding business culture
  - Commodification of professional practice
  - Reduce clients from their professional liability
- Czerniawska (2008) stated the limited source of talent may influence the industry in both the short-term in utilizing resources and the long-term in perhaps setting salary expectations too high
- Ringland and Shaukat (2004) suggested three scenarios for the management consultancy industry all of which suggested growth
- Some criticism of the industry has been raised by the amount of public sector spending on consultants
- The procurement of consultants by the public sector needs to be improved (Roodhooft and Van den Abbeele, 2006)
- Commodifying knowledge may be the way forward for consultancies
- Aiding organizations and even countries exploit green technologies is likely to be challenging for the industry but also likely to bring great reward

Review Questions

1. What are the three things that McKenna (2006) said may effect the future of the industry?
2. Should consultancies be buying more professional liability insurance according to McKenna (2006)?
3. What are the three traditions that consultancies can use to adequately resource assignments?
4. What is offshoring?
5. What is Hall's (1976) concept of the protean career as related to an individual consultant?
6. What are the three scenarios of the industry in 2020 according to Ringland & Shaukat (2004)?
7. What is commodification?
8. Has the clean energy revolution manifested yet?

Assignment Questions

1. Critically discuss how a management consultancy may have an impact on a remote island such as St Helena in the South Atlantic.

2. Does examining the past of management consultancy influence the prediction of its future?

3. What is the 'war on talent' termed by Czerniawska (2008) and how may this battle effect the future of the industry?

4. Critically evaluate the use of consultants by the public sector and how this may influence the future of the industry.

5. Discuss the green revolution and how consultancies may be able to profit from sustainable economic growth in this industry and the global economy.

Case Study 16.1

Honda's green technology strategy in the US auto market

'To be a company that society wants to exist. It's not just words; it's something that has always been at the core of our company.'[1]

Takeo Fukui, President, Honda Motor.

'Through self-innovation, we are challenging ourselves to make the power-train of today and tomorrow cleaner and more efficient in our automobiles, motorcycles and power products. In this way, we will continue to provide our customers with the fun and excitement they have enjoyed in the past, while creating a better future for the environment and society. This will give new meaning to the words 'powered by Honda a phrase so important to our past that, I believe, will have even more power in the future.'[2]

Hirojuki Yoshino, Director and Advisor, Honda Motor Company.

Introduction

In 2006, Tokyo, Japan based Honda Motor Company, was a leading global automobile manufacturer with revenue of $90 billion. Honda manufactured a variety of products like small general-purpose engines, cars, motorcycles, trucks, scooters, robots, jets and jet engines, all-terrain vehicle, water craft, electrical generators, marine engines, lawn and garden equipment, aeronautical and other mobile products. With more than 14 million internal combustion engines built each year, Honda was the largest engine-maker in the world. The company had manufacturing facilities in the US, Canada, Europe and Brazil. In Asia, Honda operated through joint ventures in India[3], China[4] and Pakistan[5].

Since 1999, Honda had been aggressively developing eco-friendly technologies and incorporating them in its automobiles. In the 2000s, the volatility in fuel prices and greater environmental awareness[6] forced many consumers to look for fuel efficient alternatives. It led to increased competition in the alternative fuel vehicle segment. Honda found its one fuel strategy risky and decided to focus on technologies like clean diesels, hybrids and fuel cells which gave it more flexibility. Honda took several initiatives to gain market share in the alternative fuel vehicle segment. Would it be successful?

---

[1]Jonathan Fahey and Tim Kelly, 'Engineers Rule,' www.forbes.com, 4th September, 2006.

[2]'Japan auto trends,' www.jama.org, March, 2000.

[3]Honda Siel Cars India Ltd.

[4]Dongfeng Honda Automobile Company.

[5]Honda Atlas Cars Pakistan.

[6]Depleting oil and fuel resources.

Background note

In 1938, Soichiro Honda, a mechanic developed his own piston ring designs and tried to sell it to Toyota which got rejected. For the next two years, Soichiro Honda further studied and refined the design and bagged a contract for Toyota. He set up a new piston manufacturing facility which was destroyed during World War II. In 1946, after the war, Soichiro Honda started a new company in Hamamatsu, Japan with what was left and named it Honda Research Institute Company Ltd. Japan was in a crisis and needed investments, fuel and basic transportation. So Honda used his manufacturing facility and created a new and cheap mode of transportation by attaching an engine to a bicycle. By 1947, a 50cc, 2-cycle engine product was started. The first on sale in the Japanese market was the A-Type. On 24 September 1948, Honda Motor Company (Honda) was officially founded. The company started manufacturing a range of lightweight scooters and motorcycles. In 1949, Honda launched its first full-fledged motorcycle with a 98cc engine called Dream D-Type. Between 1950 and 1960, Honda launched a number of highly popular scooters and motorcycles. In 1958, the American Honda Company was established and later Honda C100 Super Cub[7] was launched in the US. In the 1960s, the Japanese Government did not allow Honda to manufacture cars as it felt that there were too many car manufactures in the market.[8] In 1963, Honda produced a two door small car driven by a motorcycle chain and named it S-500. Later it also manufactured T360, a small pickup truck with four different body styles. Honda launched the 'You meet the nicest people on a Honda' advertising campaign. Between 1964 and 1965, Honda expanded its product line to include light trucks, compact cars, outboard motors, power generators. The company registered rapid growth in the export market by adding newer models of motorcycles, motorbikes and motor scooters. In 1965, Honda's Formula One race-car won the formula Mexican Grand Prix.

Even after participating in international motor racing, Honda was not able to sell automobiles in the US market. Imported cars like the N600 2-Door Sedan with a 600cc engine designed for the Japanese consumers, proved to be too small and unappealing for the American consumers. By the 1970s, Honda became the largest producer of motorcycles in the world. In 1970, the US faced an energy crisis and the government implemented new emission laws in the US, forcing American car makers to add expensive catalytic converters to exhaust systems which increased car prices. In 1972, the company launched Civic in two door and three door hatchback versions. It was slightly larger than Honda's earlier cars. It helped the company gain a foothold in the US market.

In 1975, the Civic series was expanded to include a line of cars with a new CVCC engine[9] which helped it pass the emission tests without a catalytic converter. In 1976, Honda launched the Accord which was larger than Civic and offered more value economy, and fun-to-drive nature. It became popular and gave Honda a niche market in the US. In 1981, an all new redesigned Civic 4-Door Sedan, powered by the 1500cc engine, was

---

©2009, IBS Research Center.

[7]Honda C100 also known as Honda cub was a 49 cc 4 stroke motorcycle.

[8]At the time, all of the Japanese automakers were associated with the former zaibatsu, or keiretsu – Japanese business conglomerates which had close connections with the government. These conglomerates absorbed the smaller car makers into large brands that could be marketed internationally. Honda operated as an independent manufacturer which was a new concept in the Japanese industry.

[9]The 1500cc Compound Vortex-Controlled Combustion (CVCC) engines used an advanced ratified charge design for low emissions, and were the first to meet federal Clean Air Act standards without the use of a catalytic converter.

launched. In 1982, Honda became the first Japanese company to set up a manufacturing plant in the US at Marysville, Ohio to produce the Accord[10]. In 1988, the larger fourth generation Civic models and new Accord Coupe were launched. In 1989, Honda launched VTEC[11] engines in its cars. The fourth generation Accord was launched in 1990. In 1995 Honda introduced Accord with a V6 engine[12] and entered the minivan segment with Odyssey which offered stylish looks and capacity to seat seven people. On July 17, 1995, Honda sold its 10-millionth car in the US. And in 1996 the company launched the sixth generation Civic.

Industry scenario

Before the industrial revolution discharges such as coal smoke were the main pollutants but later the increased use of automobiles led to auto emissions. Addition of thousands of cars every year led to increased use of fossil fuel and posed different problems. In the 1940s, citizens of Los Angeles faced yellow-brown haze in the air which they called smog.[13] In 1923, the use of tetraethyl lead as a gasoline additive added another toxic substance to automobile emissions. In 1947, California became the testing ground for several emission-control devices and some pioneering legislation.[14] In 1975, catalytic exhaust devices were developed to convert nitrogen oxides into harmless by-products. Catalytic converters were made mandatory on all cars sold in California in 1975. By the 1960s, smog became a national problem and it led to formation of federal laws like the Clean Air Act in 1963, the Motor Vehicle Pollution Act of 1965 which produced national standards comparable to California law for the 1968 model year and the Air Quality Act in 1967 to reduce lead emissions. In 1970, the Environmental Protection Agency (EPA) was formed to set emission standards for new automobiles and other motor vehicles. The Clean Air Amendments of 1990 set a new plan to classify cities according to the severity of their emission problems and their degree of attainment of earlier goals.[15] It set more stringent emission standards for automobiles and some trucks for model years 1996 to 2003.

In Europe, the acceptable limits of exhaust emissions were defined in a series of European Union directives which applied increasingly stringent standards in various stages. The stages were referred to as Euro 1, Euro 2, Euro 3, Euro 4 and Euro 5. Emission standards were set according to vehicle type.

As gas prices rose to above $3 a gallon, consumers began to focus on alternative fuel vehicles (AFV) which provided a solution to high gas prices. Many of these technologies continued to evolve as demand increased. Major Japanese automobile manufacturers like Toyota and Honda offered clean engine technologies in their products and also offered AFVs like hybrid and fuel cell vehicles.

---

[10]Honda had four plants located in Ohio: two in Marysville *(the Marysville Auto Plant and the Marysville Motorcycle Plant)*, Anna, and East Liberty, Lincoln, Alabama *(Honda Manufacturing of Alabama)* and Timmonsville, South Carolina and a new plant in Tallapoosa, Georgia. Honda also had an extensive after market parts operation located in Marysville, Ohio, and a Research and Development facility in Raymond, Ohio.

[11]Variable valve timing (VTEC) which enabled tuning of one engine to operate at two different 'settings' depending on load.

[12]V6 engines had six cylinders arranged in a V shape.

[13]The more recent version of smog, primarily from automobile emissions, is composed of a complex of carbon monoxide, hydrocarbons, sulphur oxides, nitrogen oxides, waste heat, and aerosols (liquid droplets, solid particles, and other various mixtures of liquids and solids suspended in air).

[14]In California new diesel cars had not been sold since tailpipe pollutant levels were tightened beyond the reach of available engine technology. In 2005, California developed a strategy to diversify its transportation fuel supply through increased use of alternative fuels in an effort to reduce oil dependency and air pollution. The State's Alternative Fuels Plan has set alternative fuels production goals for 2012, 2017 and 2022. It had also set a budget of $25 million for alternative fuels.

---

[15]The classification allowed different levels of action for each category. The categories were: marginal, moderate, serious, severe, and extreme. The EPA plans to implement new regulations to reduce pollution by 80 per cent. It would increase the cost of gasoline by 1 or 2 cents per gallon and add $100 or $200 to the price of a new vehicle. The cost of implementations for auto and gas industries would be $3.4 billion to $4.4 billion. The tailpipe emission standards for cars, light trucks and SUVs would result in a 77 per cent fall in car pollution and a 95 per cent reduction in pollution by the larger vehicles.

General Motors had focused on fuel cells,[16] Toyota on hybrids[17] and DaimlerChrysler on diesels. US auto manufacturers were slow in formulating strategies for AFVs.

The sales of AFVs were slow because the price of such vehicles was more than gas driven vehicles.[18]

In order to encourage the use of such vehicles the US Government offered tax credits[19] for alternative fuel vehicles which was available for original purchasers. In the US sales of hybrid vehicles increased from less than 10 000 units in 2000 to 200 000 in 2005.[20] (See Exhibit 16.1.)

Exhibit 16.1

Increase in sales of hybrids

Source: www. detnews.com

On a roll

Demand for hybrid vehicles is expected to continue to grow.

Unit sales of all models:

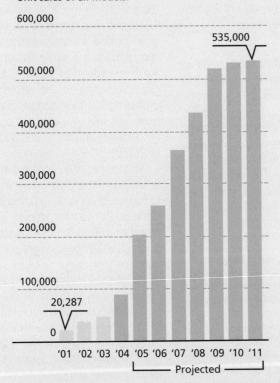

Source: J.D. Power and Associates

The Detroit News

[16]Fuel cell was an electrochemical device which converted energy into electricity.

[17]Hybrid vehicles run on two fuel sources like electricity and petrol for propulsion. It had an on board rechargeable energy storage system and a fuelled source.

[18]That premium varies but can go up to $7000.

[19]The Energy Policy Act of 2005 replaced the clean-fuel burning deduction with a tax credit. A tax credit was subtracted directly from the total amount of federal tax owed which reduced or even eliminating the taxpayer's tax obligation. Consumers who bought a hybrid in 2003 receive a $2000 tax credit. Under the current federal tax credits for hybrid cars the tax breaks start to phase out once a manufacturer reached a certain threshold of vehicles sold and would end by 2007.

[20]That was only about 1 per cent of the roughly 17 million cars and light trucks sold in the US.

Honda's strategy for diesel segment

In 2001, Honda was way behind in the diesel engines segment.[21] Hence the company decided to revamp its European model line-up, adding diesel-powered cars. In 2002, Honda launched Civic five door and three door diesel models using 1.7-litre turbo diesel engines. The company adopted the 1.7-litre diesel turbo engine made by Isuzu Motors Incorporated at its Polish plant[22] and started manufacturing the car in UK. The 1686 cc DOHC diesel engine was specially developed for the Civic and incorporated a common-rail, high-pressure fuel injection system which improved fuel economy.

In 2003, with the ever growing demand for diesel fuel economy, Honda developed a new all-aluminium 2.2 litre i-CTDi power unit[23] which was a part of Honda's intelligently-controlled i-series family of engines.[24] The project gave consumers a new alternative to gasoline engines. It also featured a turbocharger for extra power. The engine was high on performance, low in emission and complied with Euro 4 emission standards. The engine was used to power the new Accord which made its debut in the Frankfurt Motor Show in 2003. Whilst developing the new Accord diesel, Honda asked the question 'Could you ever love a diesel?'.

The car was launched in 2004, and was backed by an ad campaign which featured various components of the car being used to construct a beautifully complex domino effect.[25] The ad ended with a slogan 'Isn't it nice when things just work?' The new Honda Accord i-CTDi was up against some very serious competition from established players like the BMW, Mercedes, Ford Mondeo, Vauxhall Vectra, SAAB 9-3 and Rover 75. But the Accord proved a phenomenal success with fleet managers and private owners and sales increased. Sales of the Accord Diesel, reached 20 000 units, which helped increase total Accord sales in 2004 to 50 000 units, compared to 35 000 units in 2003.

In 2005, Honda introduced an improved CR-V with its 2.2 litre turbo diesel engine. The CR-V had consistently been one of the best selling petrol compact SUVs in Europe and by adding the diesel model to the line-up, CR-V became even more attractive. It featured sharper, more rugged styling, revised interiors, better driving comfort and additional safety features.[26] It delivered a significant performance advantage over its main rivals in a wide variety of driving conditions. It also delivered good fuel economy and low emissions that comfortably exceeded Euro IV requirements. In the same year, Honda introduced the i-CTDi engine in the FR-V six seater compact mini van (MPV)[27] in the European market. In 2005, Honda had achieved record automobile sales in Europe, reaching an all time high of 285 924 units during 2005 against an industry downturn of 0.7 per cent. The success of the company's CR-V and FR-V models contributed significantly to the sales increase. (See Exhibit 16.2.)

Honda's strategy for hybrid segment

In 1999, Honda first introduced American consumers to gas electric hybrid[28] technology with Insight – a two seat car at a price of $20 500. It was

---

[21]In Europe, where diesel-powered vehicles now account for 30 per cent of the market.

[22]In December 1999, Honda made an agreement with General Motors Corporation (GM) to supply GM with Honda's V6 ULEV engine and transmission, and Isuzu, a GM Group company, to provide Honda with diesel engines for Honda. Under the contract Isuzu had to provide approximately 5,000 engines to Honda through March of 2002 and another 15 000 engines annually commencing in April for Civics to be sold in the European market.

[23]i-CTDi engine had more advanced combustion control which reduced emissions sent to the catalytic converter.

[24]The I series engines also had the i-VTEC and i-DSI range of petrol engines.

[25]A giant game of cog nudging cog, walking windscreen wipers and rotating panes of glass.

---

[26]Honda's efforts to build one of the safest SUVs on the market was endorsed when the CR-V scored a four-star occupant safety and a three-star rating for pedestrian safety in the Euro NCAP Test – the only 4WD vehicle to date to have achieved such a result.

[27]The FR-V was launched in 2004 and was one of the best selling six seaters.

[28]A hybrid was a vehicle which used an on-board rechargeable energy storage system (RESS) and a fuelled power source for vehicle propulsion. The HV pollutes less and uses less fuel during its useful life.

Exhibit 16.2

Diesel car sales in
Europe
Source : www.
greencarcongress.
com

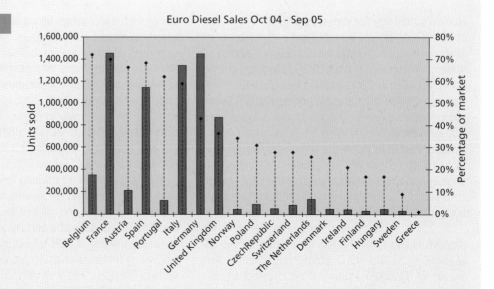

Euro Diesel Sales Oct 04 - Sep 05

the first fuel efficient mass produced hybrid sold in the US. The car was powered by the company's innovative Integrated Motor Assist (IMA) system,[29] which combined an efficient 1.0-liter, 3-cylinder gasoline engine with electric-motor assist. Insight gave an impressive mileage 57 to 60 mpg[30] in the city, and 56 to 66 mpg on highway, depending on the transmission choice which was the EPA's best ever mileage rating. The initial marketing strategy for the Honda Insight included a small budget for national television and internet advertising, most of which was spent on educational and promotional materials for dealers to present regionally to local media.

Meanwhile, Toyota also introduced its own hybrid vehicle called Prius. The Toyota Prius was a midsize hybrid car and had ample cargo space with comfortable seating for four adults. Honda's hybrid system differed from Toyota's. Honda used

a gasoline engine assisted by an electric motor to give extra power whereas Toyota's system was an electric motor assisted by a gasoline engine. Honda Insight hatchback and Toyota Prius sedan were smallish vehicles and offered eccentric designs and largely appealed to techies and early adopters who embraced their unique look and feel. Toyota also launched the Estima minivan hybrid with electric four wheel drive system. Though Honda and Toyota introduced hybrid-powered vehicles, the Prius and the Insight did not sell more units due to limited production.

In 2002, as a part of its strategy to bring hybrid technologies to the mainstream and attract a broader range of buyers, Honda introduced the Civic hybrid. The company took the lessons learned with the Insight and applied them to its popular Civic sedan. As a four-door sedan, the Civic Hybrid was capable of competing with any other small sedan and was priced between $19 900–$21 000. But consumer reviews showed that Toyota Prius was more popular than Honda Civic Hybrid because it was more comfortable and more fun to drive than the Civic which was found to be underpowered even with the assistance of the electric motor.

In 2003, Honda launched an upgraded version of Civic hybrid with a continuously variable

---

[29]The Honda IMA system relied on engine power, calling upon electric motor power assistance when required to provide powerful acceleration and low fuel consumption. This allowed for a significant reduction in complexity and weight, providing for both high power output and low fuel consumption in a wide range of situations from city to highway driving.

[30]Miles per gallon (MPG).

transmission and an Integrated Motor Assist hybrid system similar to that of the Insight, creating a fuel efficient hybrid sedan and the 'Hybrid' logo on the rear. The company projected that 10–15 per cent of Civic sales would come from hybrid versions. But Toyota sold more than 20 000 Prius subcompacts, beating Honda's Civic and Insight hybrid models in US sales. Toyota sold about 1500 to 2000 Prius each month.

In 2005, Honda introduced its first-ever V6-powered hybrid, the Accord Hybrid. Boasting of the highest fuel efficiency for a V-6-powered automobile, Accord Hybrid utilized the third generation of Honda's exclusive IMA hybrid system[31] featuring new Variable Cylinder Management (VCM)[32] technology. That improved fuel efficiency to an estimated 30 mpg city/37 highway which was better than virtually all four-cylinder mid-sized sedans and similar to that of the compact class Civic Sedan. Honda's strategy[33] with the Accord Hybrid Sedan was to show that a hybrid power train could be an important component in the mainstream of America's automotive landscape with exceptional fuel economy whilst still improving power, performance and comfort. But the Accord hybrid failed to attract consumers as they found the base price of $31 000, about $3700 above the price of a standard Accord, too high. The hybrid model's performance was emphasized over fuel efficiency, which dealers say hurt its sales. Honda's Insight sales had reduced and total of just under 13 500 Insights were sold in the US in 2005.

Meanwhile, Toyota launched its second-generation Prius in four door hatchback version which was larger, more stylish, more accommodating, and more powerful than its predecessor. It also featured some of Toyota's best new technologies like the new high-voltage/high-power Hybrid Synergy Drive power train[34] which increased fuel efficiency by 15 per cent and decreased emissions by nearly 30 per cent. Toyota also developed new technology to enable consumers to plug in their hybrid cars – potentially doubling the mileage of its already efficient hybrids. Prius became bigger, faster, more fuel efficient, fewer emissions, and much more fun to drive. This model became so popular during the early stages of rising gas prices that an unprecedented backlog of 24 000 orders piled up, causing Toyota to increase production from 36 000 cars to 47 000 for the US market. The car became a favourite of Hollywood celebrities who helped make it an environmental icon. In 2005, Toyota also launched the Highlander gas-electric hybrid at $33 595 for the base model and $34 995 for the AWD[35] model. Its sales in was 2869 units in 2005.

Other auto manufacturers also entered the hybrid vehicle segment. Ford Escape Hybrid which was the first American SUV hybrid. Manufacturers like General Motors, DaimlerChrysler and Ford also started focusing on diesel hybrids which gave 25 to 30 per cent. GM unveiled the Opel Astra Diesel Hybrid, a sedan concept vehicle; DaimlerChrysler produced 100 Dodge Ram hybrid electric vehicle diesel pickup trucks and Ford Motor Company with its Mercury Meta One, a crossover wagon.

In 2006, Honda decided to discontinue the production of Insight as it sold only 320 units[36] in the first four months of the year as compared to 30 357 for the competing Toyota Prius. The Insight had seen no major upgrades since 2002. Honda faced losses as all vehicles manufactured to date

[31]Integrated Motor Assist system improved the recovery of breaking energy by more then 10 per cent and improving the performance by 20 per cent.

[32]Variable Cylinder Management (VCM) system that allows for deactivation of three of the engine's six cylinders during cruising. The system also features an Active Control Engine Mount (ACM) an Active Noise Control (ANC) system to eliminate the potential effects of three-cylinder operation on cabin noise and engine vibration.

[33]Honda had packaged its hybrid technology in three different vehicles designed around different principles: the insight for extreme efficiency, the Civic hybrid for mass market appeal, the Accord hybrid for performance, luxury and efficiency.

[34]The full hybrid system was capable of operating in gas or electric modes, as well as a mode in which both the gas engine and electric motor are in operation.

[35]All wheel drive. Limited FWD started at $38 455; Limited AWD at $39 855.

[36]The Insight, sold just 666 vehicles in 2005. Since its launch in 1999 in the US, Honda sold a total of 13 484 Insight vehicles in total till May 1, 2006.

Exhibit 16.3

Decline in sales of
Honda Insight
Source: www.insight
central.net

Sales Statistics for: United States

		1999	2000	2001	2002
Monthly Sales:	January	–	51	294	237
	February	–	159	340	221
	March	–	187	424	232
	April	–	357	573	239
	May	–	380	903	190
	June	–	412	439	178
	July	–	354	323	133
	August	–	490	305	193
	September	–	446	300	148
	October	–	375	506	163
	November	–	291	242	142
	December	17	286	319	140
Annual Sales:		17	3,788	4,726	2,216
Total Insights to Date:			10,730		

were not sold yet. Due to decrease in demand most cars were sitting on lots and in transport. (See Exhibit 16.3.)

Honda also launched an upgraded model of the Accord. Priced at $ 30 990 with exclusive features, including exterior trim, alloy wheels, heated exterior mirrors with built-in turn signals, a dashboard display panel for the hybrid system, special lightweight hood and body components, and standard power moon roof. Honda also completely redesigned the Civic giving it a more athletic, curvier look. Additionally, the 2006 models acquired an Ultra Low Emission Vehicle (ULEV-2) rating and boasted of a more powerful 1.8 litre engine with good fuel economy.

Toyota launched an upgraded Prius in 2006. It was a full hybrid and had the capability to run solely on its batteries under certain conditions without the need for a recharge. The benefits proved useful in urban driving, shutting off its gasoline engine when stopped at a light. Priced at $21 725 the car had new styling, with spacious interiors. The company also launched an upgraded version of the Estima hybrid which featured the latest Toyota hybrid system (THS II). It helped in achieving better

environmental and driving performance based on the concept of Hybrid Synergy Drive,[37] which gave high fuel efficiency, low emission.

In 2006, Toyota sold its 50 000th Toyota Prius in Europe. The September sales of 2895 units was up 30 per cent compared to September 2005, and marked the best sales month of Prius in Europe. In the US Toyota had sold nearly 266 212 by 2006. (Exhibit 16.4)

Honda's strategy for fuel cell segment

In 1999, Honda introduced fuel cell prototype vehicles FCX-V1 which ran on hydrogen and FCX-V2 which ran on methanol. Subsequent models FCV X3 and FCV X4 were tested in 2000 and 2001. In 2002, Honda established a hydrogen infrastructure like hydrogen fuelling stations in collaboration with local governments. The city of Los Angeles started

---

[37] Hybrid Synergy Drive (HSD), was an alternative to a normal gear transmission with a electronic system. HSD replaced the gear box, alternator and starter motor with a pair of electrical motor-generators, a computerized shunt system to control them, a mechanical power splitter that acts as a second differential, and a battery pack that serves as an energy reservoir.

Sales of Main Toyota Hybrid Models

Exhibit 16.4

Prius		Estima Hybrid	Crown mild Hybrid	Harrier Hybrid (Rx400h)	Kluger Hybrid (Highlander)
Start of sales in Japan	Dec 1997	Jun 2001	Aug 2001	Mar 2005	Mar 2005
Japan	177,600	26,900	5,900	4,100	2,100
Overseas	249,200	–	–	20,600	14,000
Total	**426,800**	**26,900**	**5,900**	**24,700**	**16,100**

Sales of Toyota hybrid models
Source: www.greencarcongress.com

a leasing program with two Honda FCX vehicles, which was the world's first commercial application of a fuel cell vehicle. By 2003, Honda FCX became the first and only hydrogen-powered fuel cell vehicle to receive both EPA and CARB[38] certification for commercial use.

In 2003, Honda developed a fuel cell stake for its FC vehicles which operated at temperatures below freezing whilst improving fuel economy, range and performance with reduced complexity and potential for reduced cost. In the same year the city of Los Angeles took delivery of three more FCX vehicles for commercial use. Honda also developed the next generation EV PLUS platform[39] which served as a basis of further research.

In 2005, Honda's second-generation fuel cell vehicle (FCX) and the first to be powered by a Honda designed and manufactured fuel cell stack, was certified by both the United States Environmental Protection Agency (USEPA) and the California Air Resources Board (CARB) for commercial use. The 2005 model FCX achieved a nearly 20 per cent improvement in its EPA fuel economy rating and a 33 per cent gain in peak power. In the same year, Honda in collaboration with technology partner Plug Power Inc[40] introduced the Home Energy

Station, which provides heat and electricity for the home as well as fuel for a hydrogen-powered fuel cell vehicle. The Company had found through its initial sale of electric cars that consumers were pleased to refill at home. The home energy station also helped the company build limited refuelling infrastructure to gain consumer confidence and design of future products.

Looking ahead

In 2009, California and nine other states would mandate diesel emission rules that were stricter than those of the federal governments. In Europe, the European parliament adopted a legislative report for implementation of Euro 5 emission standards by 2009. The new standards would cut permitted emissions from new diesel vehicles by 80 per cent as compared to the Euro 4 standards. That would ban sales of vehicles which would not comply with these stipulations. For 2009, Honda was developing a new hybrid that would be smaller than the current Civic, priced below the current Civic Hybrid, would give 45 miles to a gallon and would be suitable for family use. Honda would be selling 100 000 of such new smaller hybrids in 2009 and that too with a much lesser price. Toyota had its Camry Hybrid and Lexus GS 450h hybrid sedan in the pipeline. Ford Fusion and Nissan Altima models were in the development stage and would be out by 2012.

Honda planned to solve all of fuel cell vehicles' technical problems by 2012 and to bring the cost of fuel cells down by year 2020. The company felt

---

[38]California air resource board.

[39]The EV PLUS was not an upgradation but a new platform on which Honda built the whole new product with new technology.

[40]Plug Power Inc was a provider of clean, reliable on-site energy products.

that by 2020 six fuels would split the market: gasoline, diesel, biofuels,[41] hydrogen, natural gas and electricity, perhaps working side by side in a single vehicle.[42] So it would be useful to have a multi fuel strategy which would act as an insurance against future rise in fuel prices. Meanwhile, GM's goal was to build a fuel cell prototype by 2010 that could be reasonably priced if mass-manufactured whilst Toyota did not make any public predictions about its hydrogen fuel cell efforts.

Honda planned to launch new products in the diesel category that would pass the stringent emission regulations of 50 states. Honda intended to introduce a new 4-cylinder V6 diesel engine that met the world's toughest emission standards. It would also bring the i-CTDi engines to the US by 2010. The engine would meet the demanding Tier II Bin 5 regulations applicable in California and the Northeast states in the US. With hybrid technology focused more on small cars, the company believed that diesel technology was the best fuel efficient technology for larger vehicles. In the large vehicle category Honda would offer a new four-cylinder diesel engine in its CRV and Element by 2010.

Honda was targeting a further reduction than the stipulated 10 per cent reduction in emissions by 2010 which would pit several new technologies against each other. Volkswagen was planning launch new clean diesel cars that could be sold in all states in 2008. It would start with a more powerful Jetta diesel which would give 40 mpg in town, 60 mpg on the highway. Mercedes-Benz would replace its E320 CDI diesel sedan with $52 325 E320 which would incorporate a Bluetec engine[43] with particulate filter and other exhaust features that cleaned the emissions. By 2008, Ford planned to add a 6.4-liter V-8 diesel engine which it claimed to be the cleanest and quietest engine to its Super Duty F-Series pickup. GM planned a 50-state-compliant V-8 turbo-diesel in big pickups that would use urea to lower emissions and meet stiffer 2010 emissions standards.

With growing stringent emission standards and increasing competition would Honda be a force to reckon with in the environment friendly vehicle segment? How would Honda measure up to the new scenario?

---

[41]Biofuels were derived from renewable sources of energy like biomass such as manure.

[42]Jonathan Fahey, Tim Kelly 'Engineers rule,' www.forbes.com, 4th September, 2006.

[43]In the Bluetec engine had a mechanical pump that fed each cylinder individually by a central fuel rail that supplied fuel at extremely high pressure. Combustion was achieved compressing air to raise its temperature and then injecting fuel. The fuel burns and expands, pushing the cylinder down.

Annexure I

Estimated Alternative-Fueled Vehicles in Use and Alternative Fuel Consumption, 1992–2000

Source: www.eia.deo.gov

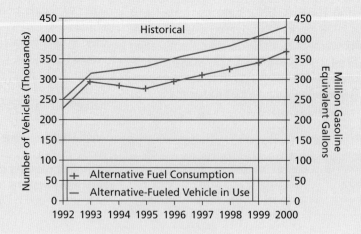

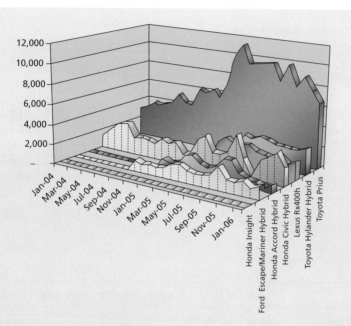

Annexure II

Monthly US hybrid
sales 2004–2006
Source : www.
greencarcongress.
com

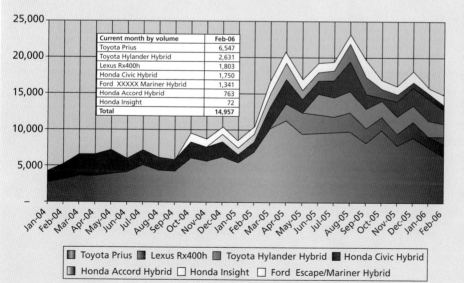

Current month by volume	Feb-06
Toyota Prius	6,547
Toyota Hylander Hybrid	2,631
Lexus Rx400h	1,803
Honda Civic Hybrid	1,750
Ford XXXXX Mariner Hybrid	1,341
Honda Accord Hybrid	763
Honda Insight	72
Total	**14,957**

Legend: ■ Toyota Prius ■ Lexus Rx400h ■ Toyota Hylander Hybrid ■ Honda Civic Hybrid
■ Honda Accord Hybrid □ Honda Insight □ Ford Escape/Mariner Hybrid

Annexure III

US hybrid sales
2004–2006
Source :
www.greencar
congress.com

Who's more fuel-efficient?

Foreign automakers have consistently produced more fuel-efficient fleets of cars and light trucks than Detroit's Big Three.
But the gap has narrowed for trucks as imports makers make bigger pickups and SUVs to better against U.S rivals.
Average feet fuel economy, In miles per galon:

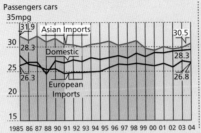

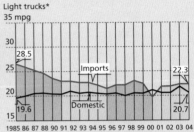

The Detroit News

Annexure V

US Federal emission
standards

The lower the bin number, the cleaner the vehicle.

Tier 2 bin 1	The cleanest Federal Tier 2 standard. A zero-emission vehicle (ZEV).
Tier 2 bins 4-2	Cleaner than the average standard.
Tier 2 bin 5	'Average' of new Tier 2 standards, roughly equivalent to a LEVII vehicle
Tier 2 bins 9-6	Not as clean as the average requirement for a Tier 2 vehicles
Tier 2 bin 10	Least-clean Tier 2 bin applicable to cars
Tier 1	The former Federal standard ; carried over to model year 2004 for those vehicles not yet subject to the phase-in.

Annexure VI

European emission
standards
Source : www.
answers.com

Standards applicable to heavy duty engines to be fitted in vehicles with a gross weight over 3.5 metric tonnes. The tiers are :

Euro 0 (1988–1992)	limits emissions to 12.3 g/kWh CO, 2.6 g/kWh HC, 15.8 g/kWh NOx
Euro I (1992–1995)	limits emissions to, 4.9 g/kWh CO, 1.23 g/kWh HC, 9.0 g/kWhNOx, 0.4 g/kWh particles
Euro II (1995–1999)	limits emissions to, 4.0 g/kWh CO, 1.1 g/kWh HC, 7.0 g/kWh NOx, 0.15 g/kWh particles
Euro III (1999–2005)	limits emissions to, 2.1 g/kWh CO, 0.66 g/kWh HC, 5.0 g/kWh NOx, 0.1 g/kWh particles
Euro IV (2005–2008)	limits emissions to, 1.5 g/kWh CO, 0.46 g/kWh HC, 3.5 g/kWh NOx, 0.02 g/kWh particles
Euro V (2008–2012)	limits emissions to, 1.5 g/kWh CO, 0.46 g/kWh HC, 2.0 g/kWh NOx, 0.02 g/kWh particles

A number of West Coast and Northeast states In the US have adopted California's more stringent LEV II standards, which place vehicles into four categories: zero emissions (ZEV), super ultra-low emissions (SULEV), ultra-low emissions (ULEV), and low emissions (LEV). The best category, ZEV, is roughly equivalent to the federal Bin 1, whilst LEV is equivalent to Bin 9.

Annexure VII

ULEV rating norms
Source: www.ucsusa

Annexure VIII

Production statistics
for hybrids
Source: http://en.
wikipedia.org

Year	1995	2000	2005	2007	2010 (projected)	2015 (projected)
Hybrid models in production	0	1	5	10	20	50
Best gas mileage of Hybrid Models in production	22	25	32	42	62	96
Percentage of cars on the road that are Hybrids	0	0	0.01	0.5	2	10
Percentage of car Models in production that are Hybrids	0	0	0	0.01	2	10

European Diesel Sales

Annexure IX

Sales of diesel
vehicles in Europe
Source: www.
greencarcongress.
com

Country	Diesel sales Oct 04–Sep 05	% Total market	% Change sales	Diesel fuel price vs. gasoline
Belgium	349,545	72%	3%	−19%
France	1,449,381	70%	6%	−12%
Spain	1,137,162	68%	9%	−7%
Austria	205,870	66%	−4%	−6%
Portugal	118,850	62%	11%	−17%
Italy	1,337,162	59%	2%	−8%
Germany	1,441,577	43%	6%	−12%
United Kingdom	873,121	36%	8%	5%
Norway	36,195	34%	29%	−5%
Poland	77,312	31%	−17%	−3%
Czech Republic	36,829	28%	−10%	−1%
Switzerland	73,414	28%	11%	9%
The Netherlands	125,279	26%	9%	−24%
Denmark	32,719	25%	21%	−11%
Ireland	36,917	21%	30%	1%
Finland	22,802	17%	2%	−17%
Hungary	35,229	17%	29%	3%
Sweden	21,635	9%	6%	−4%
Greece	4,039	1%	−56%	−3%
Total	**7,415,198**	**49%**	**7%**	**−8%**

Annexure X

Honda's fuel efficient vehicles
Source: Compiled by IRC Pune

Honda Accord hybrid Honda Civic hybrid

Honda FCX fuel cell   Honda Insight hybrid

Honda fuel cell concept car Honda CRV diesel

Honda Accord diesel

Years ended March 31	2002	2003	2004	2005	2006
			Yen (millions)		
Motorcycle Business:					
Net sales and other operating revenue (Unaffiliated customers)	¥947,900	¥978,095	¥996,290	¥1,097,754	¥1,225,812
Operating income	68,315	57,230	42,433	69,332	113,974
Operating income/Net sales	7.2%	5.9%	4.3%	6.3%	9.3%
Automobile Business:					
Net sales and other operating revenue (Unaffiliated customers)	5,929,742	6,440,094	6,592,024	6,963,635	8,004,694
Operating income	512,911	551,392	438,891	452,382	628,372
Operating income/Net sales	8.6%	8.6%	6.7%	6.5%	7.9%
Financial Services Business:					
Net sales and other operating revenue (Unaffiliated customers)	201,906	237,958	242,696	255,741	306,869
Operating income	76,365	107,813	108,438	89,901	90,585
Operating income/Net sales	37.8%	45.3%	44.7%	35.2%	29.5%
Power Product & Other Business:					
Net sales and other operating revenue (Unaffiliated customers)	282,890	315,352	331,590	332,975	370,621
Operating income	3,611	8,092	10,382	19,305	35,974
Operating income/Net sales	1.3%	2.6%	3.1%	5.8%	9.7%
Total:					
Net sales and other operating revenue (Unaffiliated customers)	¥7,362,438	¥7,971,499	¥8,162,600	¥8,650,105	¥9,907,996
Operating income	661,202	724,527	600,144	630,920	868,905
Operating income/Net sales	9.0%	9.1%	7.4%	7.3%	8.8%

Source: http://world.honda.com

Honda Motor Co., Ltd. and Subsidiaries
Years ended March 31, 2004, 2005 and 2006

	Yen (millions)			U.S. dollars (millions)(note 2)
	2004	2005	2006	2006
Cash flows from operating activities (note 12):				
Net income	¥464,338	¥486,197	¥597,033	$5,082
Adjustments to reconcile net income to net cash provided by operating activities:				
Depreciation	213,445	225,752	262,225	2,232
Deferred income taxes	113,422	115,519	(2,756)	(23)
Equity in income of affiliates	(75,151)	(96,057)	(99,605)	(847)
Dividends from affiliates	46,780	35,824	64,055	545
Provision for credit and lease residual losses on firance subsidiaries-receivables	45,937	50,638	36,153	308
Loss (gain) on derivative instruments, net	(84,783)	(60,432)	10,351	88
Gain on transfer of the substitutional portion of the Employees' Pension Funds (note 11)	—	—	(138,016)	(1,175)
Decrease (increase) in assets:				
Trade accounts and notes receivable	22,829	(70,145)	(113,259)	(964)
Inventories	(51,836)	(79,483)	(109,661)	(934)
Other current assets	(154,320)	(11,797)	(75,771)	(645)
Other assets	(33,376)	(52,198)	(61,482)	(523)
Increase (decrease) in liabilities:				
Trade accounts and notes payable	132,541	76,338	41,360	352
Accrued expenses	64,830	71,469	98,273	837
Income taxes payable	(31,068)	33,704	39,900	340
Other curret liabilities	13,763	19,973	6,126	52
Other liabilities	43,656	19,826	5,740	49
Other, net	(8,739)	17,320	15,891	134
Net cash provided by operating activities	722,268	782,448	576,557	4,908

Cash flows from investing activities:

Increase in investments and advances	(10,822)	(25,661)	(17,314)	(148)
Decrease in investments and advances	18,049	15,985	3,711	32
Payment for purchase of available-for-sale securities	(61)	(1,608)	(6,915)	(59)
Proceeds from sales of available-for-sale securities	10,082	13,140	5,666	48
Payment for purchase of held-to-maturity securities	(13,409)	(20,856)	(63,395)	(540)
Proceeds from redemption of held-to-maturity securities	—	—	55,990	477
Capital expenditures	(287,741)	(373,980)	(460,021)	(3,916)
Proceeds from sales of property, plant and equipment	19,157	14,216	39,951	340
Acquisitions of finance subsidiaries-receivables	(2,689,554)	(2,710,520)	(3,031,644)	(25,808)
Collections of finance subsidiaries-receivables	1,156,888	1,561,299	1,870,675	15,925
Proceeds from sales of finance subsidiaries-receivables	820,650	684,308	930,595	7,922
Net cash used in investing activities	(976,761)	(843,677)	(672,701)	(5,727)

Cash flows from financing activities:

Increase (decrease) in short-term debt	(7,910)	(20,244)	(124,941)	(1,064)
Proceeds from long-term debt	885,162	704,433	865,677	7,369
Repayment of long-term debt	(289,107)	(495,107)	(568,371)	(4,838)
Cash dividends paid (note 10)	(33,541)	(47,797)	(71,061)	(605)
Increase (decrease) in commercial paper classified as long-term debt	280	(131)	(234)	(2)
Payment for purchase of treasury stock, net	(95,312)	(84,147)	(77,064)	(656)
Net cash provided by financing activities	459,572	97,495	24,006	204
Effect of exchange rate changes on cash and cash equivalents	(28,062)	12,851	45,927	392
Net change in cash and cash equivalents	177,017	49,117	(26,211)	(223)
Cash and cash equivalents at beginning of year	547,404	724,421	773,538	6,585
Cash and cash equivalents at end of year	¥724,421	¥773,538	¥747,327	$6,362

Readings and References

1. Christine Tierney, 'Detroit carmakers push to be greener,' www.detnews.com, 6th January, 2007.

2. Ron Cogan, 'Hybrids on Main Street USA,' www.greencar.com, 2007.

3 Christine Tierney, 'Carmakers fight to be king of green,' www.detnews.com, 4th January, 2006.

4. David Kiley, 'Selling the love of diesel,' www.businessweek.com, 15th February, 2006.

5. Jacob Gordon, 'Will Honda produce the cheapest hybrid,' www.treehugger.com, 23rd February, 2006.

6. 'Hydrogencars on a road to viability,' http://fuelcellsworks.com, 17th March, 2006.

7. John W. Schoen, 'Hybrids alter economics for carmakers, owners,' www.msnbc.msn.com, 7th April, 2006.

8. 'New hybrid and clean diesel vehicles in US and Canada by 2010,' www.greencarcongress.com, 17th May, 2006.

9. Sholnn Freeman, 'Honda to expand production in US, unveil new hybrid,' www.stopglobalwqrming.org, 18th May, 2006.

10. James B. Treece, Lindsay Chappell, 'Honda kills the insight,' www.autoweek.com, 17th May, 2006.

11. Jonathan Fahey, Tim Kelly 'Engineers Rule,' www.forbes.com, 4th June, 2006.

12. 'Alternative fuel cars provide a solution to today's gas prices,' www.renewableenergystocks.com, 19th June, 2006.

13. Alan Ohnsman, 'Has smog met a match?: Honda patent plasma technology to clean diesel,' www.findarticles.com, 3rd July, 2006.

14. Matt Vella, 'New choices boosts hybrids into mainstream,' www.msnbc.msn.com, 1st August, 2006.

15. Mike Magda, 'Honda's environmental strategy includes diesels, affordable hybrids,' 24th August, 2006.

16. Chris Woodyard, 'What's under the hood?,' www.usatoday.com, 3rd October, 2006.

17. Lawrence Ulrich, 'The axis of diesel,' http://money.cnn.com, 10th October, 2006.

18. Kevin Cameron, 'A love-hate relationship bears a 50 state diesel,' www.nytimes.com, 15th October, 2006.

19. 'Honda outlines aggressive focus on diesel, FCV's, hybrids are just one approach,' www.biodieselnow.com, 9th August, 2006.

20. Ian Rowley, 'Honda revs up its green tecs,' www.businessweek.com, 25th September, 2006.

21. 'Honda shows off fuel cell, diesel, ethanol,' www.msnbc.msn.com, 25th September, 2006.

22. Mark Clayton, 'Race to make clean, fuel-sipping cars rev up,' www.csmonitor.com, 28th September, 2006.

23. 'Honda's green (Diesel) machine,' www.businessweek.com, 30th October, 2006.

24. Alan Ohnsman, 'Honda to Start US Leasing of Fuel-Cell Cars in California,' www.bloomberg.com, 15th November, 2006.

1. Sandra Duffy, 'Hybrids out in force at 100th LA auto show,' www.hybridcar.com, 23rd November, 2006.

2. 'Honda introduces city of Las Vegas as next fuel cell customer,' http://fuelcellsworks, 3rd February, 2005.

3. John Gartner, 'Diesel hybrids on the fast track,' www.wired.com, 21st March, 2005.

4. 'Honda's more powerful fuel cell concept with home hydrogen refueling,' www.greencarcongress.com, 19th October, 2005.

5. Ron Cogan, 'Is a hybrid in your future,' http://autos.yahoo.com, 22nd November, 2005.

6. 'History of hybrid cars,' www.whybuyhybrid.com.

7. John Gartner, '2004: Year of the green machine,' www.wired.com, 5th January, 2004.

8. Miguel Llanos, 'Fill'er up-at home and with hydrogen,' www.msnbc.msn.com, 6th December, 2004.

9. 'Honda reveals next generation fuel cell vehicle,' www.greenfleet.org.nz, 2004.

10. Martin V. Melosi, 'The automobile and the environment in American history,' www.autolife.umd.umich.edu, 2004.

11. Frank Bohanan, 'Honda bets on hybrid,' www.thecarconnection.com, 28th January, 2002.

12. 'Giving New Meaning to 'Powered by Honda,' www.jama.org, March, 2000.

13. Mary Joyce, 'Development in alternative fuel markets,' www.eia.doe.gov.

14. www.wikipedia.com.

15. www.google.com.

Further Reading

Czerniawska, F. (2008), The future of the industry. In Inside Careers (2008) *Management Consultancy – The Official Career Guide to the Profession.* London: Cambridge Market Intelligence Ltd

House of Commons Committee of Public Accounts (2007), *Central Government's Use of Consultants: Thirty-first Report of Session 2006–07* Retrieved from http://www.publications.parliament.uk/pa/cm200607/cmselect/cmpubacc/309/309.pdf at 30.3.09

McKenna, C.D. (2006), *The World's Newest Profession: Management Consulting in the Twentieth Century.* New York: Cambridge University Press

Oppenheim, J., Beinhocker, E. and Farrell, D. (2008), Not sky high. *Newsweek International* downloaded from http://www.mckinsey.com/mgi/mginews/skyhigh.asp

References

A

Abrahamson, E. (1996), Management fashion, *Academy of Management Review*, 21(1), 254–285

ACME (1964), *Numerical Data on the Present Dimensions, Growth, and Other Trends in Management Consulting in the United States.* New York: Association of Consulting Management Engineers

Adair, J. (1986), *Effective Teambuilding.* Hants: Gower Publishing Ltd

Ainamo, A. and Tienari, J. (2002), The Rise and Fall of a Local Version of Management Consulting: The Case of Finland. In Kipping, M. and L. Engwall Eds, *Management Consulting: An Emerging Knowledge Industry.* Oxford: Oxford University Press

Alexander, J. (2008), GlaxosmithKline: Improving global project management capability, *Chief Learning Officer*, 7(6), 58–59

Aljazeera (2007), Chiquita faces Colombia lawsuit. *Aljazeera report.* Retrieved from http://english.aljazeera.net/news/americas/2007/06/2008525121622267726.html

Allport, F.H. (1920), The influence of the group upon association and thought, *Journal of Experimental Psychology*, 3, 159–182

Anderson, N. and West, M.A. (1996), The Team Climate Inventory: Development of the TCI and its applications in teambuilding for innovativeness, *European Journal of Work & Organizational Psychology*, 5(1), 53–67

Andersson, A. and Andersson, S. (2008), Directing Consultants' Effort – A Study of Four Staffing Companies, *University of Gothenburg dissertation thesis.* Retrieved from http://hdl.handle.net/2077/10238

Andriole. S. (2007), *Consultants in the Hen House.* Retrieved from www.bitaplanet.com/alignment/article.php/3710151

Anonymous (2004), How to become an 'internal consultant', *Payroll Manager's Report*, 4(7), 8–9

Anonymous (2007), Words-worth: Profession. *Management Today*, Feb 2007, 17–17

Anonymous (2008), Delays, cost overruns prompt 90-Day review of WTC projects, *Bond Buyer*, 365(32910), 35

Appelbaum, S.H. (2004), Critical success factors in the client-consulting relationship, *Journal of American Academy of Business*, Cambridge, 4(1/2), 184–191

Argyle, M. (1988), *Bodily Communication* (2nd ed.). Madison: International Universities Press. ISBN 0-416-38140-5

Aritzeta, A., Swailes, S. and Senior, B. (2007), Belbin's Team Role Model: Development, validity and applications for team building, *Journal of Management Studies*, 44(1), 96–118

Arnoldus, D. and Dankers, J. (2005), Management consultancies in the Dutch banking sector, 1960s and 1970s, *Business History*, 47(4), 553–568

Artto, K., Wikström, K., Hellström, M. and Kujala, J. (2008), Impact of services on project business, *International Journal of Project Management*, 26(5), 497–508

ARUP (2009), *History and Culture.* Retrieved from http://www.arup.com/arup/historyandculture.cfm

ARUP (2009), *Partnership with Cambridge University Sustainable Cities Programme.* Retrieved from http://www.arup.com/arup/newsitem.cfm?pageid=12220

Asher, M. and Chung, E. (2005), *Vault Guide to the Case Interview: Launch Your Consulting Career With Winning Strategies for Your Case Interviews.* New York: Vault Inc

Atkins (2008), *WS Atkins Annual Report 2008.* Retrieved from http://ir.atkinsglobal.com/atkins/financials/annual08/annual_rep08_2.pdf

B

Bäcklund, J. and Werr, A. (2008), Constructing the legitimate buyer of management consulting services, *Journal of Organizational Change Management*, 21(6), 758–772

Badhwar, P. and Aryee, S. (2008), An Introduction to Strategic HRM. In, *Strategic Human Resource Management*. London: Chartered Institute of Personnel and Development

Bahn, C. (1979), Can intelligence tests predict executive competency? *Personnel*, 52–58

Bailey, G. and Biggs, D.M. (2005), Instant Messaging Mortgage Advisors: The Need, Job Analysis and Selection. *BPS Occupational Psychology Conference 2005* – Book of Proceedings and Compendium of Abstracts. 203–205.

Ballantyne, I. and Povah, N. (2004), *Assessment & Development Centres*. Hants: Gower Publishing Ltd

Barley, S.R. and Kunda, G. (2004), *Gurus, Hired Guns and Warm Bodies*. Princeton: Princeton University Press

Beagrie, S. (2008), How to become an internal consultant, *Personnel Today* p. 29. Retrieved from http://www.personneltoday.com/articles/2008/02/04/44196/become-an-internal-consultant.html

Beam, C. (2006), How to assess your sales pipeline. *Consulting to Management*, 17(2), 18–21

Bedaux, E. (1917), *The Bedaux Efficiency Course for Industrial Application*. Grand Rapids, Michigan: The Bedaux Industrial Institute

Beech, N. and Crane, O. (1999), High performance teams and a climate of community. *Team Performance Management*, 5(3), 87–102

Belbin, M. (2000), *Beyond the Team*. Oxford: Reed Elservier plc

Bell, E. (2003), Rupert and the joys of nepotism: Ignore the shareholders – Sky's the limit now the son has risen. *The Guardian*, 5 November. Retrieved from http://www.guardian.co.uk/media/2003/nov/05/broadcasting.rupertmurdoch

Bellman, G.M. (1971), Trains-consults-results: A packaged approach to organization change. *Training & Development Journal*, 25(9), 2–5

Bellman, G.M. (1972), What does an internal consultant actually do? *Management Review*, 619(11), 26–30

Bellman, G.M. (1973), Assorted thoughts of an internal consultant, *Industrial & Commercial Training*, 5(1), 26–27

Berry, M. (2007), Management consultants hit back at Commons Public Accounts Committee report which claims departments waste millions of pounds on their services, *Personnel Today*, 6/26/2007. Downloaded from http://www.personneltoday.com/articles/2007/06/26/41236/management-consultants-hits-back-at-commons-public-accounts-committee-report-which-claims-department.html

Bevilacqua, M., Ciarapica, F.E. and Giacchetta, G. (2009), Business process reengineering of a supply chain and a traceability system: A case study, *Journal of Food Engineering*, 93(1), 13–22

Biggs, D.M. (2003), Employment agency workers, their job satisfaction and their influence on permanent workers. Unpublished PhD thesis, University of Leicester. Available from http://hdl.handle.net/2381/4479

Biggs D.M. (2004), Modifying behaviour in a Birmingham gauge manufacturer, *People and Organisations at Work*, Summer Edn, British Psychological Society, Leicester

Biggs, D.M. (2005), Poor employee relations and its effect on customer demand, *Top Consultant Newsletter*, Jan 2005. Retrieved from http://www.top-consultant.com/articles/Poor%20employee%20relations.pdf

Biggs, D.M., Burchell, B and Millmore, M. (2006), The changing world of the temporary worker: The potential HR impact of legislation, *Personnel Review*, 35(2), 191–206

Biggs, D.M. and Crumbie, N.F. (2000), *Characteristics of People Working with Chemical Products in Small Firms*. HSE Books. ISBN 0-7176-1814-5

Biggs, D.M. and Toms, S. (In Prep), Are permanent jobs so permanent after all? Temporary aspects in permanent sales workers

Biggs, D.M. and Marshall, J. (1999), User interaction with the public registration system and suggestions for improvements. Client report, Atkins Management Consultants Ltd, Epsom

Biggs, D.M. and Sagheb-Tehrani, M. (2008), Providing developmental feedback to individuals from different ethnic minority groups using expert systems, *Expert Systems*, 28(2), 130–143

Biggs, D.M., Senior, B. and Swailes, S. (2002), Differences in job satisfaction between agency workers and permanent workers. *Proceedings of the HRM in a Changing World* Conference, ISBN 1-873640-36-6, Oxford Client Report, Atkins Management Consultants Ltd, Epsom

Biggs, S. and Smith, S. (2003), A paradox of learning in project cycle management and the role of organizational culture, *World Development*, 31(10), 1743–1757

Biggs, D.M. and Swailes S. (2006), Relations, commitment and satisfaction in agency workers and permanent workers, *Employee Relations*, 28(2), 130–143

Bishop T.J. and Hydoski, F.E. (2009), *Corporate Resiliency: Managing the Growing Risk of Fraud and Corruption*. New Jersey: John Wiley & Sons

Bishop, V., Cassell, C.M. and Hoel, H. (2009), Preserving masculinity in service work: An exploration of the underreporting of customer anti-social behaviour, *Human Relations*, 62(1), 5–25

Biswas, S. and Twitchell, D. (2001), *Management Consulting: A Complete Guide to the Industry,* 2nd Edn. New York: John Wiley & Sons

Blanchard, K., Carew, D. and Parisi-Carew, E. (1996), *The One Minute Manager Builds High Performing Teams.* London: Harper Collins

Block, P. (2000), *Flawless Consulting: A Guide to Getting Your Expertise Used.* Jossey Bass; 2nd Edn

Bonner, J.M., Ruekert, R.W. and Walker, O.C. (2002), Upper management control of new product development projects and project performance, *Journal of Product Innovation Management*, 19(3), 233–245

Boston Consulting Group (2009), *Electric Cars Are Unlikely to Help Carmakers Cut CO2 Emissions Significantly by 2020.* Retrieved from http://www.bcg.com/impact_expertise/publications/publication_view.jsp?pubID=2819&language=English

Bowler, M.C. and Woehr, D.J. (2006), A meta-analytic evaluation of the impact of dimension and exercise factors on assessment center ratings, *Journal of Applied Psychology*, 91(5), 1114–1124

Brennan, S. (2005), *The NHS IT Project.* Oxford: Radcliffe Publishing

British Standards Institute (2000), *BS 6079-1: 2000 Project Management: Part 1: Guide to Project Management.* BSI Standards

Brummett, B.H., Maynard, K.E., Haney, T.L., Siegler, I.C. and Barefoot, J.C. (2000), Reliability of interview-assessed hostility ratings across mode of assessment and time, *Journal of Personality Assessment*, 75(2), 225–236

Brunning, H. and Huffington, C. (1994) *Internal Consultancy in the Public Sector: Case Studies (Systemic Thinking & Practice).* London: Karnac Books

Burgess, T.F., Byrne, K. and Kidd, C. (2003), Making project status visible in complex aerospace projects, *International Journal of Project Management*, 21(4), 251–260

Buttle, F., Ang, L. and Iriana, R. (2006), Sales force automation: Review, critique, research agenda, *International Journal of Management Reviews*, 8(4), 213–231

C

Casella, D. (2008), Practical ethics for new consultants, *Consulting Magazine.* Retrieved from http://www.paconsulting.com/news/by_pa/2008/Consulting_Magazine_article_on_ethics.htm

CBS News (2007), retrieved from http://www.cbsnews.com/stories/2007/11/08/60minutes/main3475200.shtml

Chang, C.J. and Ho, J.L. (2004), Judgment and decision making in project continuation: A study of students as surrogates for experienced managers, *Abacus*, 40(1), 94–116

Chapman, J.A. and Lovell, G. (2006), The competency model of hospitality service: Why it doesn't deliver. *International Journal of Contemporary Hospitality Management*, 18(1), 78–88

Chen, R-S, Sun, C-M, Helms M.M. and Jih, W-J (2008), Role negotiation and interaction: An exploratory case study of the impact of management consultants on ERP system implementation in SMEs in Taiwan. *Information Systems Management*, 25(2), 159–173

Christensen, B.A. (1988), Strictly speaking, *Journal of the American Society of CLU & CHFC*, 42(3), 33–34

Chua, A.Y.K. (2009), Exhuming it projects from their graves: An analysis of eight failure cases and their risk factors, *Journal of Computer Information Systems*, 49(3), 31–39

Clark, A. and Appleby, A. (1997), Quality management in local government: Four case studies, *Leadership & Organization Development Journal*, 18(2), 74–85

Clark, T. (1995), *Managing Consultants: Consultancy as the Management of Impressions.* Milton Keynes, Open University Press

Clark, T. and Fincham, R. Eds (2002), *Critical Consulting: New Perspectives on the Management Advice Industry.* Oxford: Blackwell Publishers Ltd

Clark, T. and Salaman, G. (1996), Telling tales: Management consultancy as the art of story-telling. In (Grant. D. and Oswick, C. (Eds), *Metaphor and Organizations.* London: Sage, 167–184

Clark, T. and Salaman, G. (1998a), Creating the 'right' impression: Towards a dramaturgy of management consultancy, *Service Industries Journal*, 18(1), 18–38

Clark, T. and Salaman, G. (1998b), Telling tales: Management gurus' narratives and the construction of managerial identity, *Journal of Management Studies*, 35(2), 137–161

Clark-Carter, D. (1998), *Doing Quantitative Psychological Research.* Hove: Psychology Press

Clark-Carter, D. (2004), *Quantitative Psychological Research Textbook: A Student's Handbook.* Hove: Psychology Press

Clegg, S.R., Kornberger, M. and Rhodes, C. (2004), Noise, parasites and translation, *Management Learning*, 35(1), 31–44

Collis, J. and Hussey, R. (2007), *Business Accounting: An Introduction to Financial and Management Accounting.* Basingstoke: Palgrave Macmillan

Computergram (1996), Cap Gemini plans Groupe Bossard takeover. Retrieved from http://www.cbronline.com/news/cap_gemini_plans_groupe_bossard_takeover

Costas, J. and Fleming, P. (2009), Beyond dis-identification: A discursive approach to self-alienation in contemporary organizations, *Human Relations*, 62(3), 353–378

Covey, S. (2004), *7 Habits of Highly Effective People.* London: Simon & Schuster Ltd (15th Anniversary Edn)

Craig, D. (2005), *Rip-off!:The Scandalous Inside Story of the Management Consulting Money Machine.* London: The Original Book Company

Craig, D. (2006), *Plundering the Public Sector.* London: Constable

Craig, D. and Brooks, R. (2006), *Plundering the Public Sector.* London: Constable

Crotty, M. (1998), *The Foundations of Social Research: Meaning and Perspective in the Research Process.* London: SAGE Publications Ltd

Czerniawska, F. (1999), *Management Consultancy in the Twenty First Century.* London: Macmillan Press Ltd

Czerniawska, F. (2002), *Management Consultancy: What Next?: Growth and Future Directions.* Hampshire: Palgrave

Czerniawska, F. (2008), The Future of the Industry. In Inside Careers (2008) *Management Consultancy – The Official Career Guide to the Profession.* London: Cambridge Market Intelligence Ltd

D

Davenport, T.H. (2009), How to design smart business experiments, *Harvard Business Review*, 87(2), 68–76

David, R.J. and Strang, D. (2006), When fashion is fleeting: transitory collective beliefs and the dynamics of tqm consulting, *Academy of Management Journal*, 49(2), 215–233

Davis, J.P., Eisenhardt, K.M. and Bingham, C.B. (2007), Developing theory through simulation methods, *Academy of Management Review*, 32(2), 480–499

De Bono, E. (1985), *Six Thinking Hats.* USA: Key Porter Books Ltd

De Cuyper, N. and De Witte, H. (2007), Job insecurity in temporary versus permanent workers: Associations with attitudes, well-being, and behaviour, *Work & Stress*, 21(1), 65–84

Deloitte (2008), *From the Roots Up.* Retrieved from: http://www.deloitte.com/dtt/leadership/0,1045,sid%253D143880,00.html

Department of Trade and Industry (2002), *Accelerating Change, A Report by the Strategic Forum for Construction.* Retrieved from http://www.strategicforum.org.uk/pdf/report_sept02.pdf

Devinney, T. and Nikolova, N. (2004), The client-consultant interaction in professional business service firms: Outline of the interpretive model and implications for consulting. Unpublished report Retrieved from http://www2.agsm.edu.au/agsm/web.nsf/AttachmentsByTitle/Egos+paper/$FILE/EGOS+paper.pdf

Djelic, M.L. (2004), L'arbre banian de la mondialisation, *Actes de la recherche en sciences sociales*, 150, 107–113

Donne, J. (1624), *Devotions Upon Emergent Occasions – Meditation 17.* Retrieved from http://www.luminarium.org/sevenlit/donne/meditation17.php

Dormann, C. and Zapf, D. (2002), Social stressors at work, irritation, and depressive symptoms: Accounting for unmeasured third variables in a multi-wave study, *Journal of Occupational & Organizational Psychology*, 75(1), 33–58

Dubrin, A.J. (1986), Pillow talk in the executive suite, *Business & Society Review*, 58, 65–67

Dulewicz, V. and Higgs, M. (2000), Emotional intelligence: A review and evaluation study, *Journal of Managerial Psychology*, 15(4), 341–72

E

Economist (1996), Andersen's androids, *Economist*, 339(7964) 72

Economist (2000), Andersen's android wars, *Economist*, 356(8183) 64

Eisenhardt, K.M. and Bourgeois III, L.J. (1988), Politics of strategic decision making in high-velocity environments: Toward a midrange theory, *Academy of Management Journal*, 31(4), 737–770

Eisenhardt, K.M. and Kahwajy, L. (1997), How management teams can have a good fight, *Harvard Business Review*, 75(4), 77–85

Ellingson, J.E., Gruys, M.L. and Sackett, P.R. (1998), Factors related to the satisfaction and performance of temporary employees, *Journal of Applied Psychology*, 83(6), 913–921

Engwall, L., Furusten, S. and Wallerstedt, E. (2002), The changing relationship between management consulting and academia: Evidence from Sweden. In Kipping, M. and L. Engwall Eds, *Management Consulting: An Emerging Knowledge Industry.* Oxford: Oxford University Press

Engwall, L. and Kipping, M. (2002), Introduction: Management consulting as a Knowledge Industry. In M. Kipping, and L. Engwall (Eds) *Management Consulting Emergence and Dynamics of a Knowledge Industry*, 1–18, Oxford: Oxford University Press

Ernst & Young (2009), *Two Men One Vision*. Retrieved from http://www.ey.com/UK/en/About-us/Our-history

European Commission (2009), *The New SME Definition*. Retrieved from http://ec.europa.eu/enterprise/enterprise_policy/sme_definition/sme_user_guide.pdf. Retrieved on 24 March 2009

Evans, E.J. (2001), *The Forging of the Modern State: Early Industrial Britain, 1783–1870*. Harlow, England: Pearson Education

Evans, M. (2007), 'Para-politics' goes bananas, *The Nation* report. Retrieved from http://www.thenation.com/doc/20070416/evans

F

Ferguson, M. (2002), *The Rise of Management Consulting in Britain*. Aldershot: Ashgate

Ferns, D.C. (1991), Developments in programme management, *International Journal of Project Management*, 9(3), 148–156

Field, A. (2009), *Discovering Statistics Using SPSS*. London: SAGE Publications Ltd; 3rd edn

Fincham, R. (1995), Business process reengineering and the commodification of managerial knowledge, *Journal of Marketing Management*, 707–719

Fincham, R. (1999), The consultant-client relationship: Critical perspectives on the management of organisational change, *Journal of Management Studies*, 36(3), 335–351

Fincham, R. (2002a), Charisma versus technique: Differentiating the expertise of management gurus and management consultants. In Clark, T. And Fincham, R. Eds, *Critical Consulting: New Perspectives on the Management Advice Industry*. Blackwell Publishers Ltd, Oxford: UK

Fincham, R. (2002b), Narratives of success and failure in systems development, *British Journal of Management*, 2–14

Fincham, R. and Clark, T. (2003), Management consultancy: Issues, perspectives, and agendas, *International Studies of Management & Organization*, 32(4), 3–18

Fineman, S. (2003), *Understanding Emotion at Work*. London: Sage Publications

Fleming, N. (2004), Bill for hi-tech NHS soars to £20 billion. *Daily Telegraph* 12 Oct 2004. Retrieved from http://www.telegraph.co.uk/news/uknews/1473927/Bill-for-hi-tech-NHS-soars-to-andpound20-billion.html

Forde, C. and Slater, G. (2006), The nature and experience of agency working in Britain, *Personnel Review*, 35(2), 141–157

Foreman, C. (2008), Firms vie to manage causeway project, *Middle East Economic Digest*, 52(14), 18

Fortado, B. (2001), The metamorphosis of workplace conflict, *Human Relations*, 54(9), 1189–1221

Fox, L. (2004), *Enron: The Rise and Fall*. Hoboken, NJ: Wiley

Fox, R.C. (2005), Cultural competence and the culture of medicine, *New England Journal of Medicine*, 353(13), 1316–1319

Frankenhuis, J.P. (1977), How to get a good consultant, *Harvard Business Review*, 55(6), 133–139

French, A. (1993), *Interpersonal Skills*. London: The Industrial Society

French, J.R.P. and Raven, B. (1959), The basis of social power. In Cartwright, D. (Ed) *Studies in Social Power*, Michigan: Institute for Social Research

Friedman, R.A., Tidd, S.T., Currall, S.C. and Tsai, J.C. (2000), What goes around comes around: The impact of personal conflict style on work conflict and stress, *The International Journal of Conflict Management*, 11(1), 32–55

Friga, P.N. (2009), *The McKinsey Engagement: A Powerful Toolkit For More Efficient and Effective Team Problem Solving*. New York: McGraw-Hill Professional

G

Gandz, J. and Murray, V. (1980), The experience of workplace politics, *Academy of Management Journal*, 23(2), 237–251

Garavan, T.N. (2007), Using assessment centre performance to predict subjective person-organisation (P-O) fit: A longitudinal study of graduates, *Journal of Managerial Psychology*, 22(2), 150–167

Geen, R.G. (1991), Social motivation, *Annual Review of Psychology*, 42(1), 377–399

Gerstner, L.V. (2002), *Who Says Elephants Can't Dance?: Inside IBM's Historic Turnaround*. HarperBusiness

Gilbert, K. (1998), Consultancy fatigue: Epidemiology, symptoms and prevention, *Leadership & Organization Development Journal*, 19(6), 340–346

Gitomer, J. (2006), First make them feel comfortable, and then sell it, *Long Island Business News*, 53(39), 27A

Goldenberg, S. (2007), Wolfowitz under fire after partner receives promotion and pay rise, *The Guardian*. Retrieved from http://www.guardian.co.uk/business/2007/apr/07/usnews.imf

Goleman, D. (1996), *Emotional Intelligence – Why It Can Matter More Than IQ*. London: Bloomsbury Publishing

Goleman, D. (1998), *Working with Emotional Intelligence*. London: Bloomsbury Publishing

Gray, R.J. (1997), Alternative approaches to programme management, *International Journal of Project Management*, 15(1), 5–9

Griffiths, M. and Light, B. (2009), An investigation into resistance practices at an SME consultancy, *Journal of Enterprise Information Management*, 22(1/2), 119–136

Guzzo, R.A. and Dickson, M.W. (1996), Teams in organizations: Recent research on performance and effectiveness, *Annual Review of Psychology*, 47(1), 307–338

H

Hackman, J.R. and Oldham, G.R. (1975), Development of the Job Diagnostic Survey, *Journal of Applied Psychology*, 60(2), 159–170.

Hagenmeyer, U. (2007), Integrity in management consulting: A contradiction in terms? *Business Ethics: A European Review*, 16(2), 107–113

Hall, D.T. (1976), *Careers in Organizations*. Glenview: Scott Foresman & Company

Hall, J. (1999), Consulting internationally. In Sadler, P. (Ed) *Management Consultancy: A Handbook of Best Practice*. London: Kogan Page Ltd

Hamermesh, D. and Biddle, J. (1994), Beauty and the labor market, *American Economic Review* 84(5), 1174–1194

Hammer, M. and Champy, J. (1993), *Reengineering the Corporation: A Manifesto for Business*. New York: HarperBusiness

Hammer, M. and Champy, J. (2001), *Reengineering the Corporation: A Manifesto for Business*, 3rd Edn. New York: Nicholas Brealey Publishing

Haralambos, M. and Holborn, M. (2008), *Sociology Themes and Perspectives*. Collins Educational; 7th revised edition

Hargie, O. (2006), *The Handbook of Communication Skills:* 3rd Edn. London: Routledge

Hargie, O., Saunders, C. and Dickson, D. (1994), *Social Skills in Interpersonal Communication*, 3rd Edn. London: Routledge

Harris-Loxley, R. and Page, T. (2001), Small and medium-sized firms In, Sadler, P. (Ed) *Management Consultancy: A Handbook of Best Practice*. London: Kogan Page Ltd

Harrison, J.R., Lin, Z., Carroll, G.R. and Carley, K.M. (2007), Simulation modeling in organizational and management research, *Academy of Management Review*, 32(4), 1229–1245

Henderson, B.D. (1970), The product portfolio. In Stern, C.W. and Deimler, M.S. Eds (2006), *The Boston Consulting Group on Strategy: Classic Concepts and New Perspectives*. New Jersey: John Wiley & Sons Ltd

Henry, O. (2002), The acquisition of symbolic capital by consultants: The French case. In Kipping, M. and L. Engwall Eds, *Management Consulting: An Emerging Knowledge Industry*. Oxford:Oxford University Press

Heusinkveld, S. and Benders, J. (2005), Contested commodification: Consultancies and their struggle with new concept development, *Human Relations*, 58(3), 283–310

Heusinkveld, S. and Visscher, K. (2006), On the construction of problems and solutions in the client-consultant relationship, *Academy of Management Proceedings*, D1–D6

Higdon, H. (1969), *The Business Healers*. New York: Random House

Hogg, M.A. and Vaughan, G.M. (2008), *Social Psychology*. Harlow: Pearson Education Ltd

Holtz, H, and Zahn, D. (2004), *How to Succeed as an Independent Consultant*, 4th Edn. Chichester: John Wiley and Sons Ltd

House of Commons Committee of Public Accounts (2007), *Central Government's Use of Consultants: Thirty-First Report of Session 2006–07*. Retrieved from http://www.publications.parliament.uk/pa/cm200607/cmselect/cmpubacc/309/309.pdf

Hrehocik, M. (2007), Pipeline equals lifeline, *Sales & Marketing Management*, 159(9), 31–32

Hufton, N. and Elliott, J. (2000), Motivation to learn. The pedagogical nexus in the Russian school: some implications for transnational research and policy borrowing, *Educational Studies*, 26(1), 115–136

Hurren, B.L. (2006), The effects of principals' humor on teachers' job satisfaction, *Educational Studies*, 32(4), 373–385.

Hurson, T. (2007), *Think Better: An Innovator's Guide to Productive Thinking.* New York: McGraw Hill

Hussey, D. (1988), *Management Training and Corporate Strategy.* Oxford: Pergamon Press

Hussey, D. (2001a), The entry phase. In Sadler, P. (Ed) *Management Consultancy: A Handbook of Best Practice.* London: Kogan Page Ltd

Hussey, D. (2001b), Techniques, methods and models of consulting. In, Sadler, P. (Ed) *Management Consultancy: A Handbook of Best Practice.* London: Kogan Page Ltd

I

IBM (2009), *IBM Highlights 2000–2006.* Retrieved from http://www-03.ibm.com/ibm/history/documents/pdf/2000–2006.pdf

Igo, T. and Skitmore, M. (2006), Diagnosing the organizational culture of an Australian engineering consultancy using the competing values framework, *Construction Innovation,* 121–139

Inside Careers (2008), *Management Consultancy – The Official Career Guide to the Profession.* London: Cambridge Market Intelligence Ltd

J

Jackling, B., De Lange, P. and On, J.R. (2007), Accounting graduate employment destinations and commitment to CPD: A study from two Australian universities, *Accounting Education,* 16(4), 329–343

James, M. (2008), Why can't we get government IT right? *Consulting Times.* Retrieved from http://www.consulting-times.com/June2008/10.aspx

Jankowicz, D. (2004), *Business Research Projects.* London: Thomson Learning

Jarrett, M.G. (2001), Consulting in the public sector. In Sadler, P. (Ed) *Management Consultancy: A Handbook of Best Practice.* London: Kogan Page Ltd

JCA Ltd (2007), Updated model of emotional intelligence, *Unpublished report*

Jeans, M. and Page, T. (2001), Large corporations In, Sadler, P. (Ed) *Management Consultancy: A Handbook of Best Practice.* London: Kogan Page Ltd

Johnson, D.W. and Johnson, F.P. (2009), *Joining Together: Group Theory and Group Skills* London: Pearson Education EMA

Johnson, P.R. and Indvik, J. (1999), Organizational benefits of having emotionally intelligent managers and employees. *Journal of Workplace Learning,* 11(3), 84–88

K

Kallman, J. (2007), Measuring risk, *Risk Management,* 54(7), 48–49

Kamath, G. (2007), The state of ethics: Comparison of domestic codes, *ICMCI Report.* Retrieved from http://www.icmci.org/Documents/The%20State%20of%20Ethics%20report%20Gautam%20Kamath.pdf

Kanter, J. and Walsh, J.J. (2004), Toward more successful project management, *Information Systems Management,* 21(2), 16–21

Karantinou, K.M. and Hogg, M.K. (2001), Exploring relationship management in professional services: A study of management consultancy, *Journal of Marketing Management,* 17(3–4), 263–286

Karsten, L. and van Veen, K. (2002), Management consultancies in the Netherlands in the 1950s and 1960s. In Kipping, M. and L. Engwall Eds, *Management Consulting: An Emerging Knowledge Industry.* Oxford: Oxford University Press

Keats, S. (2008), What's new in CPD, *Chartered Accountants Journal,* 87(1), 25–26

Kelley, R.E. (1979), Should you have an internal consultant? *Harvard Business Review,* 57(6), 110–120

Khan, J.H. (2004), Project management approaches at techlogix. *Asian Case Research Journal,* 8(1), 1–35

Kibarian, B. (1966), Consumer selling: How to find your best prospects. *Management Review,* 55(2), 35–43

Kieser, A. (2002), Managers as marionettes? Using fashion theories to explain the success of consultancies. In Kipping, M. and L. Engwall Eds, *Management Consulting: An Emerging Knowledge Industry.* Oxford: Oxford University Press

Kind, J. (2001), Finance and control issues. In, Sadler, P. (Ed) *Management Consultancy: A Handbook of Best Practice.* London: Kogan Page Ltd

King, L. (2009), NHS underspends again on NPfIT after late care record rollouts: Tough payment on delivery structure to hurt suppliers, *Computer World UK* April 10, 2009: retrieved from http://www.computerworlduk.com/management/government-law/public-sector/news/index.cfm?newsid=14248

Kipping, M. (2002), Trapped in their wave: The evolution of management consultancies, In Clark, T. and Fincham, R. Eds, *Critical Consulting: New Perspectives on the Management Advice Industry.* Oxford: Blackwell Publishers Ltd

Kipping, M. and Saint-Martin, D. (2005), Between regulation, promotion and consumption: Government and management consultancy in Britain, *Business History*, 47(3), 449–465

Kirk, J. and Vasconcelos, A. (2003), Management consultancies and technology consultancies in a converging market: A knowledge management perspective. *Electronic Journal of Knowledge Management.* Retrieved from http://www.ejkm.com/volume-1/volume1-issue1/issue1-art5.htm

Krell, T.C. and Dobson, J.J. (1999), The use of magic in teaching organizational behavior, *Journal of Management Education*, 23(1), 44–52

Kuizinienė, I. (2008), The planning of project based activity and management in cultural organizations, *Acta Academiae Artium Vilnensis*, Issue 50, 205–224

Kuruppuarachchi, P.R. (2001), How IT project managers are leading change, *Management Services*, 45(12), 8–11

Kwak, Y.H. and Anbari, F.T. (2009), Analyzing project management research: Perspectives from top management journals, *International Journal of Project Management*, 27(5), 435–446

L

Lam, A. (1996), Engineers, management and work organization: A comparative analysis of engineers' work roles in British and Japanese electronics firms, *Journal of Management Studies*, 33(2), 183–212

Langley, A. (2000), Emotional intelligence – a new evaluation for management development, *Career Development International*, 5(3), 177–183

Laudicina, P.A. (2004), *World Out of Balance: Navigating Global Risks to Seize Competitive Advantage.* New York: McGraw-Hill

Lawler, E.E. (2006), Business strategy: Creating the winning formula. In Gallos. J.V. (Ed), *Organisational Development.* San Francisco: Wiley & Sons

Leban, W.V. (2003), The relationship between leader behavior and emotional intelligence of the project manager and the success of complex projects, *ProQuest Information & Learning. Dissertation Abstracts International Section A: Humanities and Social Sciences*, 64(5-A), 1749

Legge, K. (2005), Human resource management. In, Ackroyd, S., Batt, R., Thompson, P. and Tolbert, P.S. (Eds) *The Oxford Handbook of Work and Organization.* Oxford: Oxford University Press

Lenzner, R. (1987), Boston firm tries to separate itself from Guinness scandal, *The Boston Globe*, Jan 22, 1987

LePrevost, J. and Mazur, G. (2005), Quality infrastructure improvement: Using QFD to manage project priorities and project management resources, *International Journal of Quality & Reliability Management*, 22(1), 10–16

Lever, J., Zellman, G. and Hirschfeld, S.J. (2006), Office romance. Are the rules changing? *Across the Board*, 42(2), 32–41

Lillrank, P. and Kano, N. (1989), *Continuous Improvement.* Ann Arbor, MI: The University of Michigan

Limsila, K. and Ogunlana, S.O. (2008), Performance and leadership outcome correlates of leadership styles and subordinate commitment, *Engineering Construction & Architectural Management*, 15(2), 164–184

Lin, H., Fan, Y. and Newman, S.T. (2009), Manufacturing process analysis with support of workflow modelling and simulation. *International Journal of Production Research*, 47(7), 1773–1790

Lin, T.C. and Huang, C.C. (2009), Understanding social loafing in knowledge contribution from the perspectives of justice and trust, *Expert Systems with Applications*, 36(3), 6156–6163

Lindahl, G. and Ryd, N. (2007), Clients' goals and the construction project management process, *Facilities*, 25(3/4), 147–156

Lock, D. (2003), *Project Management.* Hants: Gower Publishing Ltd, 8 Rev Ed

Luft, J. and Ingram, H. (1955), The Johari Window: A graphic model of interpersonal awareness, *Proceeding of the Western Training Laboratory in Group Development.* Los Angeles: University of California Extension Office.

Lycett, M., Rassau, A. and Danson J. (2004), Programme management: a critical review, *International Journal of Project Management*, 22(4), 289–299

Lynch, P. (2001), Professionalism and ethics. In P. Sadler (Ed) *Management Consultancy: A handbook for Best Practice.* London: Kogan Page Ltd

M

Maddocks, J. and Sparrow, T. (2003), Individual effectiveness and team effectiveness – Training manual. *Unpublished Report*

Management Consultancies Association (2009), 3 out of 4 Management Consultants Educated in State Schools. Retrieved from http://www.mca.org.uk/news/3-out-4-management-consultants-educated-state-schools

Margerison, C. and McCann, D. (1995), *Team Management: Practical New Approaches.* Cirencester: Management Books 2000

Markham, C. (2004), *The Top Consultant: Developing Your Skills for Greater Effectiveness.* London: Kogan Page Ltd; 4 Rev Ed

Markham, C. (2007), *Practical Management Consultancy*, 5th Edition. Kingston Upon Thames: Croner CCH Group Ltd

Marsh, S. (2009), *The Feminine in Management Consulting: Power, Emotion and Values in Consulting Interactions.* Basingstoke: Palgrave Macmillan

Martinez-Pons, M. (1997), The relation of emotional intelligence with selected areas of personal functioning, *Imagination, Cognition and Personality*, 17(1), 3–13

Massarik, F. and Pei-Carpenter, M. (2002), *Organizational Development and Consulting.* San Francisco: Jossey-Bass

Matthewman, L., Rose, A. and Hetherington, A. (2009), *Work Psychology.* Oxford: Oxford University Press

McKenna, C.D. (1996), Agents of adhocracy: Management consultants and the reorganization of the executive branch 1947–1949, *Business and Economic History*, 25(1), 101–111

McKenna, C.D. (2006a), *The World's Newest Profession: Management Consulting in the Twentieth Century.* New York: Cambridge University Press

McKenna, E. (2006b), *Business Psychology and Organisational Behaviour: A Student's Handbook.* Hore: Psychology Press

McKinsey & Company (2000), *Orchestrating the Evolution of Private Employment Agencies Towards a Stronger Society.* Brussels: CIETT

McLarty, R. and Robinson, T. (1998), The practice of consultancy and a professional development strategy, *Leadership & Organization Development Journal*, 19(5), 256–263

McLean, B. and Elkind, P. (2004), *The Smartest Guys in the Room: The Amazing Rise and Scandalous Fall of Enron.* London: Penguin Books Ltd

McManus, J. (2004), A stakeholder perspective in software project management, *Management Services*, 48(5), 8–12

McQueen, R.A. and Knussen, C. (2006), *Introduction to Research Methods and Statistics in Psychology.* Harlow: Pearson Education Ltd

Mehrabian, A. (1971), *Silent Messages.* California: Wadsworth

Meislin, M. (1997), *The Internal Consultant: Drawing on Inside Expertise.* USA: Thomson Crisp Learning

Miller, R. (1999), The first session with a new client: Five stages. In Bor, R. & Watts, M. (Eds) *The Trainee Handbook: A Guide for Counselling and Psychotherapy Trainees*, 146–167. London: Sage Publications Ltd

Millmore, M., Biggs, D.M. and Morse, L. (2007), Gender differences within 360-degree managerial performance appraisals, *Women In Management Review*, 22(7), 536–551

Moorhouse Consulting (2008), *The Inside Track on Using Consultants.* Retrieved from http://www.moorhouseconsulting.com/site_assets/downloads/Inside_Track_on_Using_Consultants.pdf

Mughan, T., Lloyd-Reason, L. and Zimmerman, C. (2004), Management consulting and international business support for SMEs: Need and obstacles, *Education & Training*, 46(8-9), Special issue: Critical perspectives of VET in a small business context, 424–432

Mulligan, J. and Barber, P. (2001), The Client Consultant Relationship. In P. Sadler (Ed) *Management Consultancy: A Handbook for Best Practice.* London: Kogan Page Ltd

Murray, V. and Gandz, J. (1980), Games executives play: Politics at Work, *Business Horizons*, 23(6), 11–23

N

Neal, M. and Lloyd, C. (2001), The role of the internal consultant. In Sadler, P. (Ed) *Management Consultancy: A Handbook of Best Practice.* London: Kogan Page Ltd

Neumann, J.E. (1997), Negotiating entry and contracting. In, Neumann, J.E., Kellner, K. and Dawson-Shepherd, A. (Eds) *Developing Organisational Consultancy.* London: Routledge

Neumann, J.E., Kellner, K., and Dawson-Shepherd, A. (Eds), (1997), *Developing Organisational Consultancy.* London: Routledge

Nikolova, N., Reihlen, M. and Schlapfner, J.F. (2008), Client and consultant interaction: Capturing social practices of professional service production, *Academy of Management Proceedings*, 1–6

Nitsch, D., Baetz, M. and Hughes, J.C. (2005), Why code of conduct violations go unreported: A conceptual framework to guide intervention and future research, *Journal of Business Ethics*, 57(4), 327–341

Nokes, S., Major, I., Greenwood, A. and Goodman, M. (2003), *The Definitive Guide to Project Management: The Fast Track to Getting the Job Done on Time and on Budget.* Financial Times/ Prentice Hall; Ill edn

O

Obolensky, N. (1994), *Practical Business Re-engineering: Tools and Techniques for Achieving Effective Change.* London: Kogan Page Ltd

Obolensky, N. (2001), Strategy formulation models. In, Sadler, P. (Ed) *Management Consultancy: A Handbook of Best Practice.* London: Kogan Page Ltd

Ocasio, W. and Pozner, J. (2005), Beyond dependence: A political capital perspective on power in organizations. *American Sociological Association Conference, Annual Meeting*, Philadelphia, 1–40

OECD (2009), Strengthening competition to boost efficiency and employment, *OECD Economic Surveys: France*; 2009(5), 101–130

Office of Government Commerce (2005), *Managing Successful Projects with PRINCE2.* Stationery Office Books, 5 Rev Ed

Office of Government Commerce (2007), *Managing Successful Programmes.* London: The Stationery Office

Ohmae, K. (1982), *The Mind of a Strategist.* New York: McGraw-Hill

Oppenheim, A.M. (2000), *Questionnaire Design, Interviewing and Attitude Measurement.* London: Continuum

Oppenheim, J., Beinhocker, E. and Farrell, D. (2008), Not sky high. *Newsweek International.* Retrieved from http://www.mckinsey.com/mgi/mginews/skyhigh.asp

O'Shea, J. and Madigan, C. (1997), *Dangerous Company: Consulting Powerhouses and the Companies They Save and Ruin.* UK: Nicholas Brealey Publishing

Ouwens, M., Hulscher, M., Akkermans, R., Hermens, R., Grol, R. and Wollersheim, H. (2008), The Team Climate Inventory: Application in hospital teams and methodological considerations, *Quality & Safety in Health Care,* 17(4), 275–80

P

PA Consulting (2009), *PA in Norway: Our history.* Retrieved from http://www.paconsulting.com/locations/norway/in_norway/entry_pa_history.htm

Parker, C.P., Dipboye, R. and Jackson, S.L. (1995), Perceptions of organizational politics: An investigation of antecedents and consequences, *Journal of Management,* 21(5), 891–912

Parker, G.M. (2006), What makes a team effective or ineffective. In, Gallos. J.V. (Ed) *Organisational Development.* San Francisco: Wiley & Sons

Patterson, M.G., West, M.A., Shackleton, V J., Dawson, J F., Lawthom, R., Maitlis, S., Robinson, D L. and Wallace, A.M. (2005), Validating the organizational climate measure: Links to managerial practices, productivity and innovation, *Journal of Organizational Behavior,* 26(4), 379–408

Peiperl, M.A., Arthur, M.B., Goffee, B. and Morris, T. (2000), *Career Frontiers: New Conceptions of Working Lives.* Oxford: Oxford University Press

Pellegrin-Boucher, E. (2006), Symbolic functions of consultants, *Journal of General Management,* 32(2), 1–16

Pellegrinelli, S., Partington, D., Hemingway, C., Mohdzain, Z. and Shah, M. (2007), The importance of context in programme management: An empirical review of programme practices, *International Journal of Project Management*, 25(1), 41–55

Perry, N.J. and Caminiti, S. (1987), A consulting firm too hot to handle? Bain & Co. gets its hands 'deep in the trousers of client companies,' says an executive who knows it well. Maybe too deep, the Guinness scandal suggests. *Fortune:* 27 April, retrieved from: http://money.cnn.com/magazines/fortune/fortune_archive/1987/04/27/68952/index.htm

Pfeffer, J. (1992), Understanding power in organizations, *California Management Review,* 34(2), 29–50

Pinto, P. and Noah, S. (1980), Internal vs. external consultants: Background and behaviors, *Academy of Management Proceedings,* 75–79

Poettcker, B.A. (2009), SAP: An effective tool for managing multiple small projects, *Cost Engineering*; 51(3), 9–14

Porter, M. (1980), *Competitive Strategy: Techniques for Analysing Industries and Competitors.* Boston: Harvard Business School Press

R

Rasiel, E.M. (1999), *The McKinsey Way.* New York: McGraw-Hill

Rasiel, E.M. and Friga, P.N. (2002), *The McKinsey Mind.* New York: McGraw-Hill

Rassam, C. (2001a), Presenting advice and solutions. In P. Sadler (Ed) *Management Consultancy: A Handbook for Best Practice.* London: Kogan Page Ltd

Rassam, C. (2001b), Data collection and diagnosis. In P. Sadler (Ed) *Management Consultancy: A Handbook for Best Practice.* London: Kogan Page Ltd

Reiss, G. (2007), *Project Management Demystified*. New York: Taylor & Francis Ltd

Ringland, G. and Shaukat, A. (2004), An uncertain future for management consulting, *European Business Forum*, 19, 58–61

Riordan, W. (2009), A brief history of the management consulting profession, *Careers in Business*. Retrieved from http://www.careers-in-business.com/consulting/hist.htm

Robbins, H. and Finley, M. (1998), *Why Teams Don't Work, What Went Wrong and How to Make it Right*. London: Orion Publishing Ltd

Robinson, D.G. and Younglove, B. (1984), To leap or slide: Transition from internal to external consultant, *Training & Development Journal*, 38(5) 40–47

Roddenberry, E.W. (1953), Achieving professionalism, *Journal of Criminal Law, Criminology & Police Science*, 44(1), 109–115

Rogers, C. (1951), *Client-Centered Therapy: Its Current Practice, Implications and Theory*. London: Constable

Romanelli, E. and Tushman, M.L. (1994), Organizational transformation as punctuated equilibrium: An empirical test, *Academy of Management Journal*, 37(5), 1141–1666

Roodhooft, F. and Van den Abbeele, A. (2006), Public procurement of consulting services, *International Journal of Public Sector Management*, 19(5), 490–512

Russell, E. (1998), Programme guide, *Automotive Engineer*, 23(9), 68–70

S

Sadler (2001), *Management Consultancy* 2nd Edn. London: Kogan Page Ltd

Saint-Martin, D. (2000), *Building the New Managerialist State: Consultants and the Politics of Public Sector Reform in Comparative Perspective*. Oxford: Oxford University Press

Salmon, J. (2006), FSA sees shake-up in its crystal ball, *Money Marketing*, 22 June 2006, 16

Salovey, P. and Mayer, J.D. (1989), Emotional intelligence, *Imagination, Cognition and Personality*, 9(3), 185–211

Saynisch, M. (2005), Beyond frontiers of traditional project management: The concept of 'project management second order (Pm-2)' as an approach of evolutionary management, *World Futures: The Journal of General Evolution*, 61(8), 555–590

Schaffer, R.H. (1976), Advice to internal and external consultants: Expand your client's capacity to use your help, *Advanced Management Journal*, 41(4), 39–52

Scharf, A. (1987), Improving your personal effectiveness as a change agent, *Industrial Management*, 29(5), 17–22

Scheffler, M. (2005), Office romance, busted: It's déjà vu all over again, *Crain's Chicago Business*, 28(11), 39

Schön, D. (1983), *The Reflective Practitioner. How Professionals Think in Action*. New York: Basic Books

Schön, D. (1987), *Educating the Reflective Practitioner*. San Francisco: Jossey-Bass

Schutz, W. (2005), *The Human Element*: 2nd Edn. San Francisco: Business Consultants Network Inc

Shani, A.B. and Rogberg, M. (1993), Quality and quality improvement: Towards a practice driven theory, *EFI Research Paper No 6501*, Stockholm School of Economics, Sweden

Shawver, T. and Clements, L.H. (2008), Whistleblowing: Factors that contribute to management accountants reporting questionable dilemmas, *Management Accounting Quarterly*, 9(2), 26–38

Silbiger, S. (2005), *The 10-day MB*. London: Piatkus Books

Sobel, A. (2006), Meet the masterminds: andrew Sobel on the state of client relationships, *Management Consulting News*. Retrieved from http://www.managementconsultingnews.com/interviews/sobel_interview_2006.php

Steil, L. (1991), Listening training: The key to success in today's organisations. In D. Borisoff and M. Purdy (Eds) *Listening in Everyday Life*. Maryland: University of America Press

Stern, C.W. and Deimler, M.S. (2006), *The Boston Consulting Group on Strategy: Classic Concepts and New Perspectives*. New Jersey: John Wiley & Sons Ltd

Stroh, L.K. and Johnson, H.H. (2006), *The Basic Principles of Effective Consulting*. New Jersey: Lawrence Erlbaum Associates, Inc

Sturdy, A. (1998), Customer care in a consumer society: Smiling and sometimes meaning it? *Organization*, 5(1) 27–53

Sturdy, A., Clark, T., Fincham, R. and Handley, K. (2004), Silence, procrustes and colonization: A response to Clegg et al 'Noise, Parasites and Translation: Theory and Practice in Management Consulting', *Management Learning*, 35(3), 337–340

Sturdy, A., Handley, K., Clark, T. and Fincham, R. (2009), *Management Consultancy Boundaries and Knowledge in Action*. Oxford: Oxford University Press

Sturdy, A., Schwarz, M. and Spicer, A. (2006), Guess who's coming to dinner? Structures and uses of liminality in strategic management consultancy, *Human Relations*, 59(7), 929–957

Symon, G. and Cassell, C. (2004), *Essential Guide to Qualitative Methods in Organizational Research.* London: Sage Publications

T

Tamkin, P., Cowling, M. and Hunt, W. (2008), People and the bottom line, *Institute for Employment Studies.* Retrieved from http://www.investorsinpeople.co.uk/Documents/Final%20full%20report%20inc%20 appendices.pdf

Taylor-Powell, E. (1998), *Questionnaire Design: Asking Questions With a Purpose.* Madison: University of Wisconsin Extension Publications

Thomson, D., Austin, S., Devine-Wright, H. and Mills, G. (2003), Managing value and quality in design, *Building Research & Information*, 31(5), 334–345

Thomson, R. (1996), Actions speak louder than words. In Billsberry, Jon (Ed) *The Effective Manager: Perspectives and Illustrations*, 276–286. Buckingham: Open University Press

Tischler, L., Biberman, J. and McKeage, R. (2002), Linking emotional intelligence, spirituality and workplace performance, *Journal of Managerial Psychology*, 17(3), 203–218

Triplett, N. (1898), The dynamogenic factors in pacemaking and competition, *American Journal of Psychology*, 9, 507–533

Tuckman, B.W. (1965), Development sequence in small groups, *Psychological Bulletin*, 63, 384–399

Tuckman, B.W. and Jensen, M.A.C. (1977), Stages of small-group development revisited. *Group & Organization Studies*, 2(4), 419–427

V

Van den Bos, K. and Lind, E.A. (2002), Uncertainty management by means of fairness judgments. In M.P. Zanna (Ed), *Advances in Experimental Social Psychology.* San Diego: Academic Press

Vereecke, A., Pandelaere, E., Deschoolmeester, D. and Stevens, M. (2003), A classification of development programmes and its consequences for programme management, *International Journal of Operations & Production Management*, 23(10), 1279–1290

Vergidis, K., Turner, C.J. and Tiwari, A. (2008), Business process perspectives: Theoretical developments vs. real-world practice, *International Journal of Production Economics*, 114(1), 91–104

Verzone, R.D. (2006), Get back to basics, *Best's Review*, 106(9), 68

W

Ward, J.A. (1994), Productivity through project management: Controlling the project variables, *Information Systems Management*, 11(1), 16–21

Weiss, A. (2006), What constitutes an effective internal consultant. In, Gallos, J.V. (Ed) *Organizational Development: A Jossey-Bass Reader.* San Francisco: Jossey Bass

Werr, A. and Styhre, A. (2003), Management consultants: Friend or foe? *International Studies of Management & Organization*, 32(4), 43–66

Wickham, P.A. and Wickham, L. (2007), *Management Consulting: Delivering an Effective Project.* London: Financial Times/ Prentice Hall; 3rd edn

Wilson, K.A., Burke, C.S., Priest, H.A. and Salas, E. (2005), Promoting health care safety through training high reliability teams, *Quality and Safety in Health Care*, 14, 303–309

Woehr, D.J. and Arthur Jr., W. (2003), The construct-related validity of assessment center ratings: A review and meta-analysis of the role of methodological factors, *Journal of Management*, 29(2), 231–258

Woodruffe, C. (2007), *Development and Assessment Centres: Identifying and Developing Competence.* London: Human Assets Ltd

Wright, C. (2008), Reinventing human resource management: Business partners, internal consultants and the limits to professionalization, *Human Relations*, 161(8), 1063–1086

Wright, M., Clarysse, B., Lockett, A. and Knockaert, M. (2008), Mid-range universities' linkages with industry: Knowledge types and the role of intermediaries, *Research Policy*, 37(8), 1205–1223

Y

Yatchmenoff, D.K. (2005), Measuring client engagement from the client's perspective in nonvoluntary child protective services, *Research on Social Work Practice*, 15(2), 84–96

Yeung, R. (2006), Executive derailment, *Accountancy*, 138(1360), 63

Z

Zajonc, R.B. (1965), Social facilitation, *Science*, 149, 269–274

Index